Lecture Notes in Computer Science 9946

Commenced Publication in 1973
Founding and Former Series Editors:
Gerhard Goos, Juris Hartmanis, and Jan van Leeuwen

Paolo Milazzo · Dániel Varró
Manuel Wimmer (Eds.)

Software Technologies:
Applications and Foundations

STAF 2016 Collocated Workshops:
DataMod, GCM, HOFM, MELO, SEMS, VeryComp
Vienna, Austria, July 4–8, 2016
Revised Selected Papers

 Springer

Editors
Paolo Milazzo
Dipartimento di Informatica
Universita di Pisa
Pisa
Italy

Manuel Wimmer
Vienna University of Technology
Vienna
Austria

Dániel Varró
Budapest University of Technology and
  Economics
Budapest
Hungary

ISSN 0302-9743   ISSN 1611-3349 (electronic)
Lecture Notes in Computer Science
ISBN 978-3-319-50229-8   ISBN 978-3-319-50230-4 (eBook)
DOI 10.1007/978-3-319-50230-4

Library of Congress Control Number: 2016958996

LNCS Sublibrary: SL2 – Programming and Software Engineering

Printed on acid-free paper

This Springer imprint is published by Springer Nature
The registered company is Springer International Publishing AG
The registered company address is: Gewerbestrasse 11, 6330 Cham, Switzerland

Preface

This volume contains the technical papers presented in six of the eight workshops collocated with "Software Technologies: Applications and Foundations (STAF 2016)," a federation of leading conferences on software technologies. The workshops took place at TU Wien, Austria, during July 4–8, 2016.

STAF 2016 brought together researchers and practitioners from both academia and industry to advance the state of the art on all aspects of software technology. The satellite workshops provided a highly interactive and collaborative environment to discuss emerging areas of software technologies, model-driven engineering, and formal methods.

The six workshops whose papers are included in this volume are:

- DataMod 2016 – 5th International Symposium "From Data to Models and Back"
- GCM 2016 – 7th International Workshop on Graph Computation Models
- HOFM 2016 – Third International Workshop on Human-Oriented Formal Methods
- MELO 2016 – Second International Workshop on Model-Driven Engineering, Logic and Optimization
- SEMS 2016 – Third International Workshop on Software Engineering Methods in Spreadsheets
- VeryComp 2016 – First International Workshop on Formal to Practical Software Verification and Composition

Two more workshops were organized as satellite events of STAF 2016, but with separately published proceedings. They are the International Workshop on Formal Methods for the Quantitative Evaluation of Collective Adaptive Systems (FORECAST 2016) and the 4th International Workshop on Scalable Model-Driven Engineering (BigMDE 2016).

Messages from the organizers of STAF 2016 and of the six workshops listed above, as well as the abstracts of the keynote talks of the six workshops, follow this preface.

We are grateful to EasyChair for the support with the paper submission and reviewing process for all workshops, and with the preparation of this volume. For each of the workshops at STAF 2016, we thank the organizers for the interesting topics and resulting talks. We also thank the paper contributors to these workshops and those who attended them. We would like to extend our thanks to all keynote speakers for their excellent presentations, and also to the members of each workshop's Program Committee. Finally, we would like to thank the organizers of STAF 2016 and, in particular, the general chair, Gerti Kappel.

September 2016

Paolo Milazzo
Manuel Wimmer
Dániel Varró

STAF 2016 Organizers' Message

Software Technologies: Applications and Foundations (STAF) is a federation of leading conferences on software technologies. It provides a loose umbrella organization with a Steering Committee that ensures continuity. The STAF federated event takes place annually. The participating conferences may vary from year to year, but all focus on foundational and practical advances in software technology. The conferences address all aspects of software technology, from object-oriented design, testing, mathematical approaches to modeling and verification, transformation, model-driven engineering, aspect-oriented techniques, and tools.

STAF 2016 took place at TU Wien, Austria, during July 4–8, 2016, and hosted the five conferences ECMFA 2016, ICGT 2016, ICMT 2016, SEFM 2016, and TAP 2016, the transformation tool contest TTC 2016, eight workshops, a doctoral symposium, and a projects showcase event. STAF 2016 featured eight internationally renowned keynote speakers, and welcomed participants from around the world.

The STAF 2016 Organizing Committee thanks: (a) all participants for submitting to and attending the event; (b) the program chairs and Steering Committee members of the individual conferences and satellite events for their hard work; (c) the keynote speakers for their thoughtful, insightful, and inspiring talks; and (d) TU Wien, the city of Vienna, and all sponsors for their support. A special thank you goes to the members of the Business Informatics Group, coping with all the foreseen and unforeseen work (as usual ☺)!

July 2016   Gerti Kappel

DataMod 2016 Organizers' Message

The 5th International Symposium From Data to Models and Back (DataMod 2016), formerly known as MoKMaSD, was held in Vienna, Austria, on July 8, 2016.

The symposium aims at bringing together practitioners and researchers from academia, industry, government, and nongovernmental organizations to present research results and exchange experiences, ideas, and solutions for modelling and analyzing complex systems and using knowledge management strategies, technology, and systems in various domain areas such as ecology, biology, medicine, climate, governance, education, and social software engineering.

After a careful review process, the Program Committee accepted seven papers, five full and two short, for presentation at the symposium. The program of DataMod 2016 was also enriched by the keynote speeches of Mirco Musolesi entitled "Mining Big (and Small) Mobile Data for Social Good" and of Emanuela Merelli entitled "The Topological Field Theory of Data: A Program Towards a Novel Strategy for Data Mining Through Data Language."

Several people contributed to the success of DataMod 2016. We are grateful to the Steering Committee, and in particular to Antonio Cerone, Paolo Milazzo, and Anna Monreale, who assisted us in some organizational aspects of the event. We would like to thank the organizers of STAF 2016, and in particular the workshops chairs, Manuel Wimmer, Dániel Varró, and Paolo Milazzo. We would also like to thank the Program Committee and the additional reviewers for their work on reviewing the papers. The process of reviewing and selecting papers was significantly simplified through using EasyChair.

We thank all the symposium attendees and hope that this event facilitated a good exchange of ideas and generate new collaborations among attendees.

The organization of DataMod 2016 was supported by the Future and Emerging Technologies (FET) program within the Seventh Framework Programme (FP7) for Research of the European Commission, under the FP7 FET-Proactive Call 8 Dynamics Multi-level Complex Systems (DyMCS), Grant Agreement TOPDRIM, Number FP7-ICT-318121.

September 2016

Luca Tesei
Roberto Trasarti

DataMod 2016 Steering Committee

Antonio Cerone	IMT Institute for Advanced Studies Lucca, Italy
Jane Hillston	University of Edinburgh, UK
Marijn Janssen	Delft University of Technology, The Netherlands
Stan Matwin	University of Ottawa, Canada
Paolo Milazzo	University of Pisa, Italy
Anna Monreale	University of Pisa, Italy

DataMod 2016 Program Committee

Ezio Bartocci	Vienna University of Technology, Austria
Luca Bortolussi	University of Trieste, Italy
Giulio Caravagna	University of Edinburgh, UK
Paweł Dłotko	Inria, Saclay, France
Nadia Essoussi	University of Carthage, Tunisia
Alexeis Garcia-Perez	Coventry University, UK
Yiwei Gong	Wuhan University, China
Tias Guns	KU Leuven, Belgium
Joris Hulstijn	Delft University of Technology, The Netherlands
Krzysztof Krawiec	Poznan University of Technology, Poland
Donato Malerba	University of Bari, Italy
Emanuela Merelli	University of Camerino, Italy
Paolo Milazzo	University of Pisa, Italy
Patrick Mukala	Eindhoven University of Technology, The Netherlands
Nicola Paoletti	University of Oxford, UK
Giovanni Pardini	University of Pisa, Italy
Nikos Pelekis	University of Piraeus, Greece
Anna Philippou	University of Cyprus, Cyprus
Barbara Re	University of Camerino, Italy
Giulio Rossetti	ISTI-CNR and University of Pisa, Italy
Bruno Rossi	Masaryk University, Brno, Czech Republic
Luca Tesei	University of Camerino, Italy (Co-chair)
Manolis Terrovitis	IMIS, Athena Research Center, Greece
Roberto Trasarti	ISTI-CNR, Pisa, Italy (Co-chair)

GCM 2016 Organizers' Message

The 7th International Workshop on Graph Computation Models (GCM 2016) was held in Vienna, Austria, on July 4, 2016.

Graphs are common mathematical structures that are visual and intuitive. They constitute a natural and seamless way for system modeling in science, engineering, and beyond, including computer science, life sciences, business processes, etc. Graph computation models constitute a class of very high level models where graphs are first-class citizens. They generalize classical computation models based on strings or trees, such as Chomsky grammars or term rewrite systems. Their mathematical foundation, in addition to their visual nature, facilitates specification, validation, and analysis of complex systems. A variety of computation models have been developed using graphs and rule-based graph transformation. These models include features of programming languages and systems, paradigms for software development, concurrent calculi, local computations and distributed algorithms, and biological and chemical computations.

The aim of GCM 2016 was to bring together researchers interested in all aspects of computation models based on graphs and graph transformation techniques. The workshop promotes the cross-fertilizing exchange of ideas and experiences among researchers and students from the different communities interested in the foundations, applications, and implementations of graph computation models and related areas. Previous editions of the GCM series were held in Natal, Brazil (GCM 2006), in Leicester, UK (GCM 2008), in Enschede, The Netherlands (GCM 2010), in Bremen, Germany (GCM 2012), in York, UK (GCM 2014), and in L'Aquila, Italy (GCM 2015).

After a thorough review process, the Program Committee accepted five papers for publication in the proceedings and four additional papers for presentation and publication before the proceedings.

Several people contributed to the success of GCM 2016. I would like to thank the organizers of STAF 2016, and in particular the general chair, Gerti Kappel, and the workshops chairs, Manuel Wimmer, Dániel Varró, and Paolo Milazzo. I would also like to express my thanks to the Program Committee and the additional reviewers for their valuable help. The EasyChair system greatly facilitated the submission and program selection process.

I would furthermore like to thank all authors, speakers, and participants of the workshop.

September 2016

Barbara König

GCM 2016 Program Committee

Rachid Echahed	Laboratoire d'Informatique de Grenoble, France
Annegret Habel	Universität Oldenburg, Germany
Alexander Heußner	Universität Bamberg, Germany
Dirk Janssens	Universiteit Antwerpen, Belgium
Barbara König	Universität Duisburg-Essen, Germany (Chair)
Hans-Jörg Kreowski	Universität Bremen, Germany
Ian Mackie	University of Sussex, UK
Mohamed Mosbah	LaBRI, Université de Bordeaux, France
Detlef Plump	University of York, UK

HOFM 2016 Organizers' Message

The Third International Workshop on Human-Oriented Formal Methods (HOFM 2016) was held on July 4, 2016 in Vienna, Austria. This workshop was affiliated to the Software Technologies: Applications and Foundations (STAF 2016), a federation of leading conferences on software technologies.

The aim of the HOFM workshop series is to establish a community that will investigate the field of application of human factors to the analysis and to the optimization of formal methods. Formal methods (FMs) have been successfully applied in software engineering research for several decades. However, many software engineers largely reject FMs as "too hard to understand and use in practice" while admitting that they are powerful and precise. The reason for this rejection is the lack of usability features: If usability is compromised, methods cannot fit in a real software development process.

HOFM 2016 received submissions from 16 authors, affiliated with universities and industries from Australia, Austria, Czech Republic, Germany, Italy, Kazakhstan, The Netherlands, and Norway. Every submitted paper was carefully reviewed by the Program Committee members, and eight papers were accepted for presentation at HOFM 2016. All authors of the HOFM workshop were invited to submit extended versions of their peer-reviewed papers to the proceedings, taking into account feedback from the HOFM reviewers as well as the discussions during the workshop.

The program of HOFM 2016 was enriched by two keynote talks:

- Daniel Ratiu, Siemens AG, Germany: *"Enabling Software Verification for Practicing Engineers with Domain Specific Languages"*
- Michael Sedlmair, University of Vienna, Austria
  "Human-Centered Methods in Visualization Research"

We would like to thank all authors who contributed to HOFM 2016 as well as all the workshop attendees. We hope that the attendees found the program relevant to their interests and inspiring. We also thank the STAF Workshop chairs and local organizers for their help. We would like to express our gratitude to the Program Committee members for their support and considered reviews.

September 2016

Maria Spichkova
Heinz Schmidt

HOFM 2016 Program Committee

Luis Barbosa	University of Minho, Portugal
Daniel Berry	University of Waterloo, Canada
Jan Olaf Blech	RMIT University, Australia
Antonio Cerone	IMT Inst. for Advanced Studies Lucca, Italy
Eitan Farchi	IBM Haifa Research Lab, Israel
Pedro Isaias	Universidade Aberta, Portugal
Irit Hadar	University of Haifa, Israel
Peter Herrmann	NTNU Trondheim, Norway
Gerwin Klein	NICTA/Data61, UNSW, Australia
Jayprakash Lalchandani	IIIT Bangalore, India
James Noble	Victoria University of Wellington, New Zealand
Srini Ramaswamy	ABB, USA
Daniel Ratiu	Siemens AG, Germany
Guillermo Rodriguez-Navas	Maelardalen University, Sweden
Bernhard Rumpe	RWTH Aachen, Germany
Thomas Santen	Microsoft, Germany
Heinz Schmidt	RMIT University, Australia (Co-chair)
Maria Spichkova	RMIT University, Australia (Co-chair)
Richard Trefler	University of Waterloo, Canada
Andreas Vogelsang	TU Munich, Germany
Anna Zamansky	University of Haifa, Israel

MELO 2016 Organizers' Message

The Workshop on Model-Driven Engineering, Logic and Optimization (MELO 2016) was held in Vienna, Austria, on July 4, 2016.

The main goal of this workshop was to bring together three different communities: the model-driven engineering (MDE) community, the logic programming community, and the optimization community, to explore how each community can benefit from the techniques of the other. The workshop aimed at developing bridges and synergies between these communities, and at providing a forum for researchers to discuss new or ongoing projects and forge new collaborations. The widespread application of MDE in all kinds of domains (e.g., critical systems, software product lines, embedded systems, etc.) has triggered the need of new techniques to solve optimization, visualization, verification, and configuration problems at the model level. Instead of reinventing the wheel, most of these problems could be solved by reexpressing the modeling problem as a logic programming problem or as an optimization or search problem. As an example, verification (satisfiability) of large static models can be addressed by reexpressing the model as a constraint satisfaction problem to be solved by state-of-the-art constraint solvers.

Similarly, logic programming can benefit from the integration of MDE principles. As in any other domain, introduction of MDE would help to raise the abstraction level at which the problem is described (e.g., by providing domain-specific languages that allow non-technical users to specify the problem using a vocabulary closer to the domain), improve the separation of concerns by using different model-based views of the problem at different levels of detail, achieve tool independence (e.g., by following a typical platform-Independent model – platform-specific model separation where, for instance, at the platform-Independent model level we could define tool-independent logic programming metamodels), and increase reusability. In addition, optimization techniques can benefit from closer connections to MDE principles, e.g., to help develop generic solutions to optimization problems (e.g., standardized representations of optimization problems, benchmarks).

The workshop focused on presentation of ongoing work at the intersection of at least two of the aforementioned areas (e.g., MDE + logic programming, MDE + optimization). After a thorough review process, the Program Committee accepted five papers for publication in the LNCS proceedings.

September 2016

Jordi Cabot
Richard Paige
Alfonso Pierantonio

MELO 2016 Program Committee

Achim D. Brucker	The University of Sheffield, UK
Athanasios Zolotas	University of York, UK
Daniel Varro	University of Technology and Economics, Hungary
Esther Guerra	Universidad Autónoma de Madrid, Spain
Federico Ciccozzi	MDH, Sweden
Manuel Clavel	Universidad Complutense de Madrid, Spain
Marsha Chechik	University of Toronto, Canada
Raphael Chenouard	Ecole Centrale de Nantes, France
Robert Claris	Universitat Oberta de Catalunya, Spain
Rolf Drechsler	University of Bremen, Germany
Romin Eramo	University of L'Aquila, Italy
Shiva Nejati	University of Luxembourg, Luxembourg
Sophie Demassey	MINES ParisTech, France
Steffen Zschaler	King's College London, UK
Zinovy Diskin	McMaster University/University of Waterloo, Canada

SEMS 2016 Organizers' Message

The Third International Workshop on Software Engineering Methods in Spreadsheets (SEMS 2016) was held in Vienna, Austria, on July 4, 2016, as a satellite event of STAF 2016. The first edition of SEMS co-located with the annual conference of the EuSpRIG in 2014, in Delft, The Netherlands, was successful in bringing together the spreadsheet research community, and spreadsheet practitioners. The second edition, held as satellite event of ICSE 2015 in Florence, Italy, was aimed at bringing together the communities of software engineering research and spreadsheet research. In this third edition, a new direction was explored as SEMS became part of a federation of conferences oriented for modeling, transformations, formal methods, and testing.

Once more, the workshop was a success, with several submissions, including papers from members of the STAF community who had not yet participated in SEMS. In particular, we received nine submissions, all receiving three reviews. From these, eight were accepted for presentation at the workshop. The set of authors spans across eight countries: Austria, Canada, Germany, Poland, Portugal, Spain, The Netherlands, and Vietnam. The program was further enriched by the keynote speech of Sumit Gulwani, from Microsoft Research Redmond, entitled "Spreadsheet Programming Using Examples."

We would like to thank the Steering Committee for their guidance and support during the entire organizational process. We would also like to thank the Program Committee and reviewers, who did an excellent job reviewing and subsequently participating in the discussion for acceptance of the papers. Furthermore, we want to thank the organization of STAF 2016 for their impressive responsiveness and help, and in particular the workshop chairs, Manuel Wimmer, Dániel Varró, and Paolo Milazzo. We also extend our gratitude to EasyChair for its support in the entire organization process of SEMS 2016.

Finally, we express our heartfelt thanks to all the participants of SEMS 2016 who, as always, are key in making the workshop a success as a premier venue for discussing spreadsheet research.

September 2016

Jácome Cunha
Daniel Kulesz
Sohon Roy

SEMS 2016 Steering Committee

Felienne Hermans   Delft University of Technology, The Netherlands
Richard Paige   University of York, UK
Peter Sestoft   IT University of Copenhagen, Denmark

SEMS 2016 Program Committee

Martin Erwig   Oregon State University, USA
João P. Fernandes   Universidade da Beira Interior, Portugal
Felienne Hermans   Delft University of Technology, The Netherlands
Birgit Hofer   Graz University of Technology, Austria
Richard Paige   University of York, UK
João Saraiva   Universidade do Minho, Portugal
Peter Sestoft   IT University of Copenhagen, Denmark
Leif Singer   Automattic Inc., USA

SEMS 2016 Additional Reviewers

Bas Jansen   Delft University of Technology, The Netherlands
Jorge Mendes   Universidade do Minho, Portugal
Karl Smeltzer   Oregon State University, USA

VeryComp 2016 Organizers' Message

The First International Workshop on Formal to Practical Software Verification and Composition (VeryComp 2016) was held in Vienna, Austria, on July 4, 2016. The aim of the workshop is to counteract the specialization of traditional venues by bringing together researchers and practitioners from different areas concerning software verification and composition, to fill the gap between the requirements of modern applications and current verification and composition methods. In particular, VeryComp 2016 aimed at attracting contributions related to the subject at different levels, from modeling to verification and analysis, from componentization to composition. The workshop constituted a forum for scientists and engineers in academia and industry to present and discuss their latest ongoing research as well as radical new research directions that represent challenging innovations.

After a careful review process, the Program Committee accepted four papers. Several people contributed to the success of VeryComp 2016. We would like to thank the STAF 2016 Workshops organizers as well as the general chair. We would also like to thank the Program Committee for their work in reviewing the papers. The process of reviewing and selecting papers was significantly simplified through using EasyChair.

We thank all the workshop attendees and hope that this event facilitated a good exchange of ideas and new collaborations among attendees.

The organization of VeryComp 2016 was partially supported by the H2020 EU project CHOReVOLUTION[1].

September 2016

Marco Autili
Marcello Bersani
Davide Bresolin
Luca Ferrucci
Marisol Garcia-Valls
Manuel Mazzara
Massimo Tivoli

---

[1] http://www.chorevolution.eu/bin/view/Main/.

VeryComp 2016 Program Committee

Luciano Baresi	Politecnico di Milano, Italy
Carlo Bellettini	Università degli studi di Milano, Italy
Amel Bennaceur	The Open University, UK
Domenico Bianculli	University of Luxembourg, Luxembourg
Antonio Brogi	Università di Pisa, Italy
Antonio Bucchiarone	FBK-IRST, Italy
Radu Calinescu	University of York, UK
Mauro Caporuscio	Linnaeus University, Sweden
Vincenzo Ciancia	ISTI-CNR, Italy
Ivica Crnkovic	Malardalen University, Sweden
Guglielmo De Angelis	CNR-IASI/ISTI, Italy
Stéphane Demri	NewYork University and CNRS, France
Salvatore Distefano	Università di Messina, Italy
Schahram Dustdar	University of Technology Wien, Austria
Nikolaos Georgantas	Inria, France
Carlo Ghezzi	Politecnico di Milano, Italy
Silvio Ghilardi	Università degli studi di Milano, Italy
Paola Inverardi	University of L'Aquila, Italy
Patricia Lago	VU University Amsterdam, The Netherlands
Julio Medina	Universidad de Cantabria, Spain
Hernan Melgratti	Universidad de Buenos Aires, Argentina
David M.R. Pereira	Polytechnical School of Porto, Portugal
Saad Mubeen	Mälardalen University, Sweden
Pascal Poizat	Paris Ouest University and LIP6, France
Nafees Qamar	Vanderbilt University, USA
Victor Rivera	Innopolis University, Russia
Gwen Salaün	Inria, Grenoble-Rhone-Alpes, France
Cesar Sanchez	IMDEA Software Institute, Spain

Keynote Talks

The Topological Field Theory of Data: A Program Towards a Novel Strategy for Data Mining through Data Language

Emanuela Merelli

School of Science and Technology, University of Camerino, Camerino, Italy

Keynote Speaker of DataMod 2016

We aim to challenge the current thinking in IT for the Big Data question, proposing a program aiming to construct an innovative methodology to perform data analytics in a way that returns an automaton as a recognizer of the data language: a Field Theory of Data. We suggest to build, directly out of probing data space, a theoretical framework enabling us to extract the manifold hidden relations (patterns) that exist among data, as correlations depending on the semantics generated by the mining context. The program, that is grounded in the recent innovative ways of integrating data into a topological setting, proposes the realization of a Topological Field Theory of Data, transferring and generalizing to the space of data notions inspired by physical (topological) field theories and harnesses the theory of formal languages to define the potential semantics necessary to understand the emerging patterns.

Mining Big (and Small) Mobile Data for Social Good

Mirco Musolesi

Intelligent Social Systems Lab, University College London, London, UK

Keynote Speaker of DataMod 2016

An increasing amount of data describing peoples behaviour is collected by means of applications running on smartphones or directly by mobile operators through their cellular infrastructure. This information is extremely valuable for marketing applications, but it has also an incredible potential to be beneficial for society as a whole, thanks to applications in a variety of fields, from healthcare to transportation, from geodemographics to national security. In particular, mobile data can be extremely valuable for developing and evaluating quantitative models of human behaviour, which can be used as a basis for the development of intelligent mobile systems. In this talk I will analyze the challenges and opportunities in using big (and small) data for applications of high societal and commercial impact discussing the current work of my lab in the area of mobile data mining and anticipatory mobile computing. The scope of my talk will be broad, encompassing both modelling and systems-oriented issues.

Enabling Software Verification for Practicing Engineers with Domain Specific Languages

Daniel Ratiu

Siemens AG, Munich, Germany

Keynote Speaker of HOFM 2016

Despite the maturity of current verification techniques, formal verification tools have not found their way in the daily practice yet. The main reason for the low adoption is related to pragmatic aspects such as usability or the cost of applying formal verification (e.g. specifying properties, running the analyses, interpreting the results). For a large majority of developers, formal verification techniques are seen rather as expert tools and not as engineering tools that can be used on a daily basis. This is mostly the case in the context of main stream systems (e.g. automotive, medical, industrial automation) where pragmatics (e.g. personnel skills, cost structures, deadlines, existent processes) plays a major role. I will present our approach and experience to tackle some of these challenges with the help of domain specific languages in the mbeddr project (www.mbeddr.com) and its extensions at Siemens.

Human-Centered Methods in Visualization Research

Michael Sedlmair

University of Vienna, Vienna, Austria

Keynote Speaker of HOFM 2016

Visualization systems provide a unique way for people to interact, explore, and better understand their data. Visualization systems might, for instance, help medical doctors to base tricky medication decisions on historic patient data; journalists to get a quick overview over large sets of documents; or economists to better understand stock trends.

As visualization systems target human users, closely involving them into design and research processes is crucial. While this importance has been acknowledged many times, realizing such a human-centered focus in day-to-day research practices is challenging.

This talk will shed some light into existing human-centered methods that are used in visualization research, as well as the challenges that come with them. To illustrate these aspects, I will present case studies from several visualization research projects, such as my own 3.5-year collaboration with automotive engineers at BMW. The ultimate goal of the talk would be to help building a bridge between the human-centered challenges faced in visualization research and those in formal methods.

Spreadsheet Programming Using Examples

Sumit Gulwani

Microsoft Research, Redmond, USA

Keynote Speaker of SEMS 2016

99% of spreadsheet users do not know programming, and struggle with repetitive data wrangling tasks such as extracting tabular data from text files, string transformations, and table re-formatting. Programming by Examples (PBE) can revolutionize this landscape by enabling users to synthesize intended programs from example-based specifications.

A key technical challenge in PBE is to search for programs that are consistent with the examples provided by the user. Our efficient search methodology is based on two key ideas: (i) Restriction of the search space to an appropriate domain-specific language that offers balanced expressivity and readability (ii) A divide-and-conquer based deductive search paradigm that inductively reduces the problem of synthesizing a program of a certain kind that satisfies a given specification into sub-problems that refer to sub-programs or sub-specifications.

Another challenge in PBE is to resolve the ambiguity in the example based specification. We will discuss two complementary approaches: (a) machine learning based ranking techniques that can pick an intended program from among those that satisfy the specification, and (b) active-learning based user interaction models.

The above concepts will be illustrated using various PBE technologies including FlashFill, FlashExtract, and FlashRelate. These technologies have been released inside various Microsoft products including Excel. The Microsoft PROSE SDK allows easy construction of such technologies.

Contents

SEMS

VeryComp

DataMod

Separating Topological Noise from Features Using Persistent Entropy

Nieves Atienza[1]([✉]), Rocio Gonzalez-Diaz[1], and Matteo Rucco[2]

[1] Applied Math Department, School of Computer Engineering,
University of Seville, Seville, Spain
{natienza,rogodi}@us.es
[2] Computer Science Division, School of Science and Technology,
University of Camerino, Camerino, Italy
matteo.rucco@unicam.it

Abstract. Topology is the branch of mathematics that studies shapes and maps among them. From the algebraic definition of topology a new set of algorithms have been derived. These algorithms are identified with "computational topology" or often pointed out as Topological Data Analysis (TDA) and are used for investigating high-dimensional data in a quantitative manner. Persistent homology appears as a fundamental tool in Topological Data Analysis. It studies the evolution of $k-$dimensional holes along a sequence of simplicial complexes (i.e. a filtration). The set of intervals representing birth and death times of $k-$dimensional holes along such sequence is called the persistence barcode. $k-$dimensional holes with short lifetimes are informally considered to be topological noise, and those with a long lifetime are considered to be topological feature associated to the given data (i.e. the filtration). In this paper, we derive a simple method for separating topological noise from topological features using a novel measure for comparing persistence barcodes called *persistent entropy*.

Keywords: Persistent homology · Persistence barcodes · Shannon entropy · Topological noise · Topological features

1 Introduction

Persistent homology studies the evolution of $k-$dimensional holes along a sequence of simplicial complexes. Persistence barcode is the collection of intervals representing birth and death times of $k-$dimensional holes along such sequence. In persistence barcode, $k-$dimensional holes with short lifetimes are informally considered to be "topological noise", and those with a long lifetime are "topological features" of the given data.

In general, "very" long living intervals (long lifetime) are considered topological features since they are stable to "small" changes in the filtration. Nevertheless, the definition of what a "topological feature" is, depends on the application. This way, the technique presented in this paper should be considered as an option

© Springer International Publishing AG 2016
P. Milazzo et al. (Eds.): STAF 2016, LNCS 9946, pp. 3–12, 2016.
DOI: 10.1007/978-3-319-50230-4_1

that can be used for discriminating between topological features and topological noise. Moreover, we claim it is very easy (and fast) to compute, and easy to adapt depending on the application.

In [1] a methodology is presented for deriving confidence sets for persistence diagrams to separate topological noise from topological features. The authors focused on simple, synthetic examples as proof of concept. Their methods have a simple visualization: one only needs to add a band around the diagonal of the persistence diagram. Points in the band are consistent with being noise. The first three methods are based on the distance function to the data. They started with a sample from a distribution $\mathbb{P}$ supported on a topological space $\mathfrak{C}$. The bottleneck distance is used as a metric on the space of persistence diagrams. The last method uses density estimation. The advantage of the former is that it is more directly connected to the raw data. The advantage of the latter is that it is less fragile; that is, it is more robust to noise and outliers.

Persistent entropy (which is the Shannon entropy of the persistence barcode) is a tool formally defined in [2] and used to measure similarities between two persistence barcodes. A precursor of this definition was given in [3] to measure how different the intervals of a barcode are in length.

In this paper, we use the difference of persistent entropy to measure similarities between two persistent barcodes. More concretely, we derive a simple method for separating topological noise from topological features of a given persistence barcode obtained from a given filtration (ie., a sequence of simplicial complexes) using the mentioned persistent entropy measurement.

2   Related Work

Persistent homology based techniques are nowadays widely used for analyzing high dimensional dataset and they are good tool for shaping these dataset and for understanding the meaning of the shapes. There are several techinques for building a topological space from the data. The main approach is to complete the data to a collection of combinatorial objects, i.e. simplices. A nested collection of simplices forms a simplicial complex. Simplicial complexes can be obtained from graphs and point cloud data (PCD) [4,5]. For example, PCD can be completed to simplicial complexes by using the Vietoris-Rips approach. Vietoris-Rips filtration is a versatile tool in topological data analysis. It is a sequence of simplicial complexes built on a metric space to add topological structure to an otherwise disconnected set of points. It is widely used because it encodes useful information about the topology of the underlying metric space. The mathematical details of Vietoris-Rips filtration are given in Sect. 3.

Let's take a look at Fig. 1, it represents a collection of RNA secondary suboptimal structures within different bacteria. All the shapes are characterized by several circular substructures, each of them is obtained by linking different nucleotides. Each substructure encodes functional properties of the bacteria. Persistent homology properly identifies these substructures. For the love of preciseness, Mamuye et al. [6], used Vietoris-Rips complexes and persistent homology

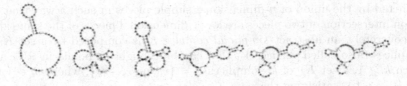

Fig. 1. From left to right: RNA secondary suboptimal structures within different bacteria.

for certifying that there are different species but characterized with the same RNA suboptimal secondary structure, thus these species are functionally equivalent.

In [7], the authors proposed a new methodology based on information theory and persistent homology for classifying real length noisy signals produced by small DC motors. They introduced an innovative approach based on "auto mutual information" and the "CAO's method" for providing the time delay embedding of signals. The time delay embedding transforms the signal into a point cloud data in $\mathbb{R}^d$, where d is the dimension of the new space. Vietoris-Rips complex is then computed and analyzed by persistent homology. The authors classified the signal in two classes, respectively "properly working" and "broken".

However, Vietoris-Rips based analysis suffers of the selection of the parameter ϵ. Generally speaking, for different ϵ, different topological features can be observed. In [7], ϵ was selected as the euclidean distance among the points in the new space. We remark that the parameter ϵ does not have a unique physical meaning and it depends on the problem under analysis. For example, in [8], several applications of Vietoris-Rips based analysis to biological problems have been reported and examples of different ϵ with different meaning were found. In order to select the best ϵ, some statistics have been provided what it is known as "persistence landscape" [9]. Landscape is a powerful tool for statistically assessing the global shape of the data over different ϵ. Technically speaking, a landscape is a piecewise linear function that basically maps a point within a persistent diagram (or barcode) to a point in which the $x-$coordinate is the average parameter value over which the feature exists, and the $y-$coordinate is the half-life of the feature. Landscape analysis allows to identify topological features and which are not. In Sect. 5 we propose an alternative approach to landscape. The main difference between landscape and our method is that the former uses the average of ϵ, while the latter works directly on a fixed ϵ.

3   Background

This section provides a short recapitulation of the basic concepts needed as a basis for the presented method for separating topological noise from features.

Informally, a topological space is a set of points each of them equipped with the notion of neighboring. A simplicial complex is a kind of topological space constructed by the union of n-dimensional simple pieces in such a way that the common intersection of two pieces are lower-dimensional pieces of the same kind. More concretely, an abstract *simplicial complex* K is composed by a set K_0 of 0–simplices (also called vertices V, that can be thought as points in $\mathbb{R}^n$); and, for each $k \geq 1$, a set K_k of k–simplices $\sigma = \{v_0, v_1, \ldots, v_k\}$, where $v_i \in V$ for all $i \in \{0, \ldots, k\}$, satisfying that:

- each k–simplex has $k + 1$ faces obtained removing one of its vertices;
- if a simplex σ is in K, then all faces of σ must be in K.

The underlying topological space of K is the union of the geometric realization of its simplices: points for 0-simplices, line segments for 1-simplices, filled triangles for 2-simplices, filled tetrahedra for 3-simplices and their n-dimensional counterparts for n-simplices. We only consider finite (abstract) simplicial complexes with finite dimension, i.e., there exists an integer n (called the dimension of K) such that for $k > n$, $K_k = \emptyset$ and for $0 \leq k \leq n$, K_k is a finite set. See [10,11] for an introduction to algebraic topology.

Two classical examples of abstract simplicial complexes are each complexes and Vietoris-Rips complexes (see [12, Chapter 3]). Let V be a finite set of points in $\mathbb{R}^n$. The *ech complex* of V and r denoted by $_r(V)$ is the abstract simplicial complex whose simplices are formed as follows. For each subset S of points in V, form a closed ball of radius $r/2$ around each point in S, and include S as a simplex of $_r(V)$ if there is a common point contained in all of the balls in S. This structure satisfies the definition of abstract simplicial complex. The *Vietoris-Rips complex* denoted as $VR_r(V)$ is essentially the same as the ech complex. Instead of checking if there is a common point contained in the intersection of the $(r/2)$–ball around v for all v in S, we may just check pairs adding S as a simplex of $_r(V)$ if all the balls have pairwise intersections. We have $_r(V) \subseteq VR_r(V) \subseteq _{\sqrt{2}r}(V)$. See Fig. 2.

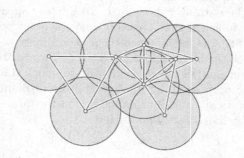

Fig. 2. [12, p. 72] Nine points with pairwise intersections among the disks indicated by straight edges connecting their centers, for a fixed time ϵ. The ech complex $_\epsilon(V)$ fills nine of the ten possible triangles as well as the two tetrahedra. The Vietoris-Rips complex $VR_\epsilon(V)$ fills the ten triangles and the two tetrahedra.

Homology is an algebraic machinery used for describing topological spaces. The $k-$Betti number β_k represents the rank of the $k-$dimensional homology group of a given simplicial complex K. Informally, β_0 is the number of connected components, β_1 counts the number of loops in $\mathbb{R}^2$ or tunnels in $\mathbb{R}^3$, β_2 can be thought as the number of voids and, in general, β_k can be thought as the number of k-dimensional holes.

Persistent homology is a method for computing $k-$dimensional holes of K at different spatial resolutions. The key idea is as follows: First, the space must be represented as a simplicial complex and a distance function must be defined on the space. Second, a filtration of the simplicial complex, that is a nested sequence of increasing subsets (referred above as different spatial resolutions), is computed. More concretely, a filtration of a simplicial complex K is a collection of simplicial complexes $\{K(t)|t \in \mathbb{R}\}$ of K such that $K(t) \subset K(s)$ for $t < s$ and there exists $t_{\max} \in \mathbb{R}$ such that $K_{t_{\max}} = K$. The filtration time (or filter value) of a simplex $\sigma \in K$ is the smallest t such that $\sigma \in K(t)$.

Then, persistent homology describes how the homology of a given simplicial complex K changes along filtration. If the same topological feature (i.e., $k-$dimensional hole) is detected along a large number of subsets in the filtration, then it is likely to represent a true feature of the underlying space, rather than artifacts of sampling, noise, or particular choice of parameters. More concretely, a $k-$dimensional Betti interval, with endpoints $[t_{start}, t_{end})$, corresponds to a $k-$dimensional hole that appears at filtration time t_{start} and remains until filtration time t_{end}. The set of intervals representing birth and death times of homology classes is called the *persistence barcode* associated to the corresponding filtration. For more details and a more formal description we refer to [12].

4   Persistent Entropy

In order to measure how much the construction of a filtered simplicial complex is ordered, a new entropy measure, the so-called *persistent entropy*, were defined in [2]. A precursor of this definition was given in [3] to measure how different the intervals of a barcode are in length. In [13], persistent entropy is used for addressing the comparison between discrete piece-wise linear functions.

Given a ech or Vietoris-Rips filtration $F = \{K(t)|t \leq T\}$ (in practice one will never construct the filtration up to the end and will stop at a certain time T), and the corresponding persistence barcode $B = \{[a_i, b_i) : 1 \leq i \leq n\}$, let $L = \{\ell_i = b_i - a_i : 1 \leq i \leq n\}$. The *persistent entropy* H of the filtration F is:

$$H_L = -\sum_{i=1}^{n} \frac{\ell_i}{S_L} log \frac{\ell_i}{S_L}, \qquad \text{being } S_L = \sum_{i \in I} \ell_i.$$

Note that the maximum persistent entropy would correspond to the situation in which all the intervals in the barcode are of equal length. Conversely, the value of the persistent entropy decreases as more intervals of different lengths are present. More concretely, if B has n intervals, the possible values of the persistent entropy H_L associated with the barcode B lie in the interval $[0, log(n)]$.

The following result supports the idea that persistent entropy can differentiate long from short intervals as we will see in the next section.

Theorem 1. *For a fixed integer i, $1 \leq i \leq n$, let $L_i = \{\ell_{i+1}, \ldots \ell_n\}$, $S_i = \sum_{j=i+1}^{n} \ell_j$ and let H_i be the persistent entropy associated to L_i. Let*

$$L'(i) = \{\ell'_1, \ldots, \ell'_i, \ell_{i+1}, \ldots, \ell_n\}, \quad where \ \ell'_j = S_i/e^{H_i}, \quad for \ 1 \leq j \leq i.$$

Then $H_L \leq H_{L'(i)}$.

Proof. Let us prove that $H_{L'}(i)$ is the maximum of all the possible persistent entropies associated to lists of intervals with n elements, such that the last $n - i$ elements of any of such lists is $\{\ell_{i+1}, \ldots, \ell_n\}$. Let $M = \{x_1, \ldots, x_i, \ell_{i+1}, \ldots, \ell_n\}$ (where $x_j > 0$ for $1 \leq j \leq i$) be any of such lists. Let $S_x = \sum_{j=1}^{i} x_j$. Then, the persistent entropy associated to M is:

$$H_M = \sum_{j=1}^{i} \frac{x_j}{S_x + S_i} \log\left(\frac{x_j}{S_x + S_i}\right) + \sum_{j=i+1}^{n} \frac{\ell_j}{S_x + S_i} \log\left(\frac{\ell_j}{S_x + S_i}\right).$$

In order to find out the maximum of H_M with respect to the unknown variables x_k, $1 \leq k \leq i$, we compute the partial derivative of H_M with respect to those variables:

$$\frac{\partial H_M}{\partial x_k} = \frac{1}{(S_x + S_i)^2} \left(-S_i H_i + S_i \log\left(\frac{S_i}{x_k}\right) + \sum_{j \neq k} x_j \log\left(\frac{x_j}{x_k}\right) \right).$$

Finally, $\{x_k = \frac{S_i}{e^{H_i}} : 1 \leq k \leq i\}$ is the solution of the system $\{\frac{\partial H_M}{\partial x_k} = 0 : 1 \leq k \leq i\}$.   □

5   Separating Topological Features from Topological Noise

Let us start with a sample V from a distribution $\mathbb{P}$ supported on a topological space $\mathfrak{C}$. Suppose the Vietoris-Rips filtration F is computed from V, and the persistence barcodes B is computed from F. The following are the steps of our proposed method, based on persistent entropy, to separate topological noise from topological features in the persistence barcode B, estimating, in this way, the topology of $\mathfrak{C}$.

1. Order the intervals in B by decreasing length. Then $L = \{\ell_i = b_i - a_i : 1 \leq i \leq n\}$ satisfies that $\ell_i \leq \ell_j$ for $i < j$;
2. Compute the persistent entropy H_L of B. Denote $H_{L'(0)} := H_L$.
3. From $i = 1$ to $i = n$,
   a. Compute the persistent entropy $H_{L'(i)}$ for $L'(i) = \{\ell'_1, \ldots, \ell'_i, \ell_{i+1}, \ldots, \ell_n\}$, being $\ell'_k = \frac{S_i}{e^{H_i}}$ for $1 \leq k \leq i$ as in Theorem 1.
   b. Compute $H_{rel(i)} = (H_{L'(i)} - H_{L'(i-1)})/(\log(n) - H_L)$.

c. If $H_{rel(i)} > \frac{i}{n}$, then the associated interval $[a_i, b_i)$ represents a topological feature. Otherwise, the interval $[a_i, b_i)$ represents noise.

Steps 1, 2 and 3.a can be considered as a general method for any kind of application. For $1 \leq i \leq n$, $H_{L'(i)}$ is the entropy of the barcode obtained by replacing the intervals $\ell_1, \ldots, \ell_i$ by i intervals that maximize the entropy. Observe that $H_{L'(0)} = H_L$, $H_{L'(i)} < H_{L'(j)}$ for $0 \leq i < j \leq n$ and $H_{L'(n)} = \log(n)$ by Theorem 1.

Step 3.b and 3.c are used to test a possible dissimilarity measure to differentiate topological features from noise. These two steps could be modified later depending on the application. In this paper, we use $H_{L'(i)} - H_{L'(i-1)}$ to measure the influence of the current interval ℓ_i in the initial persistent entropy H_L. It is in order to appreciate this influence, why we divide $H_{L'(i)} - H_{L'(i-1)}$ by the difference of the possible maximal entropy (which is $\log(n)$) and H_L. Then, we compare the resulting $H_{rel}(i)$ with $\frac{i}{n}$ since $H_{rel(i)}$ is affected by the total number of intervals and the number of intervals we are replacing.

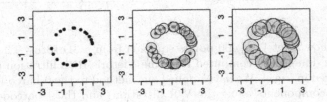

Fig. 3. Left: 30 data points sampled from a circle of radius 2. Middle: Balls of radius 0.5 centered at the sample points. Right: Balls of radius 0.8 centered at the sample points.

We have applied our methodology to two different scenarios. First, we take 30 data points sampled from a circle of radius 2 (see Fig. 3(Left)). This example has been taken from paper [1]. Vietoris-Rips complex for $t = 0.5$ can be deduced from the picture shown in Fig. 3(Middle) which consists of two connected components and zero loops. Looking at Vietoris-Rips complex for $t = 0.8$ (see Fig. 3(Right)), we assist at the birth and death of topological features: at $t = 0.8$, one of the connected components has died (was merged with the other one), and a loop appears; this loop will die at $t = 2$, when the union of the pink balls representing the distance function becomes simply connected.

In our method, an interval is considered to be a feature if $H_{rel(i)} > \frac{i}{n}$. In Table 1(Left), we have applied our method to the intervals that make up the barcode (without differentiating dimension). This way, only the intervals with length 2 (that corresponds to the connected component that survives until the end) and 1.2 (that correspond to the loop that appears at $t = 0.8$ and disappears at $t = 2$) are considered features. Later, in Table 1(Right) we have applied our method to the intervals that make up the 0-barcode (i.e., the lifetime of the connected components along the filtration). This way, the intervals with length

2 and 0.7 (that corresponds to the connected components that dies just before the loop is created) are considered features. This example highlight that we the results may be different depending on if we apply our method to the whole set of intervals of the barcode or if we do it dimension by dimension.

Table 1. Results of our method applied to the intervals that make up: (Left) the barcode (i.e., without differentiating dimension); and (Right) the 0-barcode; both associated to the Vietoris-Rips filtration obtained from 30 data points sampled from a circle of radius 2 (see Fig. 3(Left)).

ℓ_i	$\frac{H_i}{\log(n)}$	$H_{rel(i)}$	Feature
2.	0.967011	0.542391	yes
1.2	0.985761	0.260088	yes
0.7	0.991422	0.07853	no
0.45	0.992506	0.0150434	no
0.45	0.993746	0.0171948	no
...	...	...	...

l_i	$\frac{H_i}{\log(n)}$	$H_{rel(i)}$	Feature
2.	0.985109	0.77248	yes
0.7	0.991032	0.0905039	yes
0.45	0.992167	0.0173301	no
0.45	0.993463	0.0198057	no
0.4	0.994199	0.0112466	no
...	...	...	...

Consider now a set V of 400 points sampled from a 3D torus. The barcodes (separated by dimension) computed from the Vietoris-Rips filtration associated to V are showed in Fig. 4. We have applied our method to the 0-barcode (lifetime of connected components along the V-R filtration) and the 1-barcode (lifetime of loops along the V-R filtration). See Table 2(Left) and (Right), respectively. The interval of length 1.9 in the table on the left corresponds to the connected component that survives until the end. The intervals of length 1.531 in the table on the right corresponds to the two tunnels of the 3D torus. In Table 3 we show the results of our method applied to all the intervals of the barcode without separating by dimensions. We can see in this case that we obtain the same features as before plus the interval representing the void.

Table 2. Results of our method applied to the 0-barcode (table on the left) and the 1-barcode (table on the right) associated to the Vietoris-Rips filtration obtained from 400 points sampled from a 3D torus.

ℓ_i	$\frac{H_i}{\log(n)}$	$H_{rel(i)}$	Feature
1.9	0.996295	0.442767	yes
0.396	0.996325	0.00449624	no
0.387	0.996351	0.00386916	no
0.387	0.996376	0.00389884	no
0.387	0.996403	0.00392887	no
...	...	...	...

ℓ_i	$\frac{H_i}{\log(n)}$	$H_{rel(i)}$	Feature
1.531	0.918238	0.238936	yes
1.531	0.950752	0.302654	yes
0.27	0.952044	0.012028	no
0.261	0.953275	0.011451	no
0.234	0.954209	0.00869544	no
...	...	...	...

Table 3. Results of our method applied to the barcode (without differentiating dimension) associated to the Vietoris-Rips filtration obtained from 400 points sampled from a 3D torus.

ℓ_i	$\frac{\ell_i}{L}$	ℓ'_i	$\frac{\ell'_i}{L'(i)}$	$\frac{H_{L'(i)}}{\log(n)}$	$H_{rel(i)}$	Feature
1.9	0.0145219	0.268369	0.00207708	0.971259	0.0799069	yes
1.531	0.0117016	0.262812	0.00205432	0.972992	0.0554616	yes
1.531	0.0117016	0.257239	0.00203115	0.974775	0.0570812	yes
1.234	0.00943158	0.253276	0.00201566	0.975978	0.0385369	yes
0.396	0.00302667	0.252916	0.00201511	0.976021	0.00137745	no
...	...	...	...	...	...	...

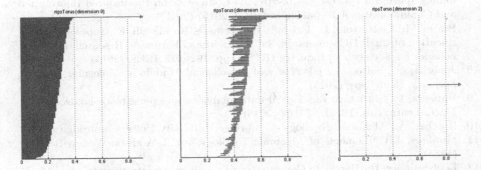

Fig. 4. Barcodes (separated by dimension) computed from the Vietoris-Rips filtration associated to a point cloud lying on a 3D torus. Left: lifetimes of connected components. Middle: lifetimes of tunnels. Right: lifetimes of voids.

6 Conclusions and Future Work

In this paper, we have derived a method for separating topological noise from topological features using the Shannon entropy of persistence barcode. We have proven that the method is consistent by proving that in step i of the method we replace i intervals by the same number of intervals but with the length that maximizes the entropy. This way we "neutralize" the effect of such i intervals and, by computing the difference of the entropies obtained in step $i-1$ and step i, we can deduce if the interval at position i is a topological feature or not.

We intend to adapt our method to study RNA data from healthy and unhealthy cells. We argue the method will let to highlight the topological features that are formed by the most relevant genes associated to pathologies.

Acknowledgments. Authors are partially supported by IMUS, University of Seville under grant VPPI-US and Spanish Government under grant MTM2015-67072-P (MINECO/FEDER, UE). We also thank the reviewers for their valuable and constructive comments.

References

1. Fasy, B.T., Lecci, F., Rinaldo, A., Wasserman, L., Balakrishnan, S., Singh, A.: Confidence sets for persistence diagrams. Ann. Stat. **6**, 2301–2339 (2014)
2. Rucco, M., Castiglione, F., Merelli, E., Pettini, M.: Characterisation of the idiotypic immune network through persistent entropy. In: Proceedings Complex (2015)
3. Chintakunta, H., Gentimis, T., Gonzalez-Diaz, R., Jimenez, M.J., Krim, H.: An entropy-based persistence barcode. Pattern Recogn. **48**(2), 391–401 (2015)
4. Binchi, J., Merelli, E., Rucco, M., Petri, G., Vaccarino, F.: jHoles: a tool for understanding biological complex networks via clique weight rank persistent homology. Electron. Notes Theoret. Comput. Sci. **306**, 5–18 (2014)
5. Adams, H., Tausz, A.: Javaplex tutorial (2011)
6. Mamuye, A., Merelli, E., Rucco, M.: Persistent homology analysis of the RNA folding space. In: Proceedings of 9th EAI Conference on Bio-inspired Information and Communications Technologies (BICT 2015) (2015)
7. Rucco, M., Concettoni, E., Cristalli, C., Ferrante, A., Merelli, E., Topological classification of small DC motors. In: 1st International Forum on Research and Technologies for Society and Industry (RTSI), pp. 192–197. IEEE (2015)
8. Jonoska, N., Saito, M.: Discrete and Topological Models in Molecular Biology. Springer, Heidelberg (2013)
9. Bubenik, P.: Statistical topological data analysis using persistence landscapes. J. Mach. Learn. Res. **16**(1), 77–102 (2015)
10. Hatcher, A.: Algebraic Topology. Cambridge University Press, Cambridge
11. Munkres, J.R.: Elements of Algebraic Topology, vol. 2. Addison-Wesley, Reading (1984)
12. Edelsbrunner, H., Harer, J.: Computational topology: an introduction. Am. Math. Soc. (2010)
13. Rucco, M., Gonzalez-Diaz, R., Jimenez, M.J., Atienza, N., Cristalli, C., Concettoni, E., Ferrante, A., Merelli, E.: A new topological entropy-based approach for measuring similarities among piecewise linear functions. CoRR abs/1512.07613

An Accelerated MapReduce-Based K-prototypes for Big Data

Mohamed Aymen Ben HajKacem[✉], Chiheb-Eddine Ben N'cir,
and Nadia Essoussi

LARODEC, Université de Tunis, Institut Supérieur de Gestion de Tunis,
41 Avenue de la Liberté, Cité Bouchoucha, 2000 Le Bardo, Tunisia
medaymen.hajkacem@gmail.com, {chiheb.benncir,nadia.essoussi}@isg.rnu.tn

Abstract. Big data are often characterized by a huge volume and a variety of attributes namely, numerical and categorical. To address this issue, this paper proposes an accelerated MapReduce-based k-prototypes method. The proposed method is based on pruning strategy to accelerate the clustering process by reducing the unnecessary distance computations between cluster centers and data points. Experiments performed on huge synthetic and real data sets show that the proposed method is scalable and improves the efficiency of the existing MapReduce-based k-prototypes method.

Keywords: K-prototypes · MapReduce · Big data · Mixed data

1 Introduction

Given the exponential growth and availability of data collected from different resources, analyzing these data has become an important challenge referred to as Big data analysis. Big data analysis usually refers to three mains characteristics also called the three Vs [7] which are respectively *Volume, Variety* and *Velocity*. Volume refers to the large scale data, Variety indicates the different data types and formats and Velocity refers to the streaming data [6]. One of the most important challenges in Big data analysis is how to explore the large amount of mixed data using machine learning techniques. Clustering is one of the machine learning techniques, which has been used to organize data into groups of similar data points called also clusters. Examples of clustering methods categories are hierarchical methods, density-based methods, grid-based methods, model-based methods and partitional methods [13]. However, traditional clustering methods are not suitable for processing large scale of mixed data. For example, k-prototypes clustering [18] which is one of the most popular method to cluster mixed data, it does not scale with huge volume of data [20].

To deal with this issue, Ben HajKacem et al. [3] have proposed a parallelization of k-prototypes method through MapReduce model. Although this method offers for users an efficient analysis of a huge amount of mixed data, it requires computing all distances between each of the cluster centers and the data points.

© Springer International Publishing AG 2016
P. Milazzo et al. (Eds.): STAF 2016, LNCS 9946, pp. 13–25, 2016.
DOI: 10.1007/978-3-319-50230-4_2

However, many of these distance computations are unnecessary, because data points usually stay in the same clusters after first few iterations. Therefore, we propose in this paper an **A**ccelerated **M**ap**R**educe-based **k-p**rototypes method called AMR k-prototypes. The proposed method is based on pruning strategy to accelerate the clustering process by reducing the unnecessary distance computations between cluster centers and data points. The experiments show that the proposed method is scalable and outperforms the efficiency of the existing MapReduce-based k-prototypes method [3].

The organization of this paper is as follows: Sect. 2 presents related works in the area of Big data clustering. Then, Sect. 3 describes the proposed AMR k-prototypes method while Sect. 4 presents experiments that we have performed to evaluate the efficiency of the proposed method. Finally, Sect. 5 presents conclusion and future work.

2   Related Works

Big data clustering has recently received a lot of attentions to build parallel clustering methods. In this context, several parallel clustering methods have been designed in the literature [2,4,9,14,16,17,19,23]. Most of these methods use the MapReduce [5], which is a programming model for processing large scale data by exploiting the parallelism among a cluster of machines. For example, Zaho et al. [23] have proposed a parallelization of k-means method using MapReduce model. Kim et al. [14] have introduced an implementation of DBSCAN method through MapReduce model. Recently, a parallel implementation of fuzzy c-means clustering algorithm using MapReduce model is presented in [17]. Indeed, Big data are often characterized by the variety of attributes, including numerical and categorical. Nevertheless, the existing parallel methods can not handle different types of data and are limited to only numerical attributes.

To deal with mixed data, a pre-processing step is usually required to transform data into a single type since most of proposed clustering methods deal with only numerical or categorical attributes. However, transformation strategies is often time consuming and produce information loss, leading to undesired clustering results [1]. Thus, several clustering methods for mixed data have been proposed in the litterateur [1,8,11,15]. For instance, Huang [11] have proposed k-prototypes method which combines k-means [18] and k-modes [12] methods for clustering mixed data. Li and Biswas [15] have proposed Similarity-Based Agglomerative Clustering called SBAC, which is a hierarchical agglomerative algorithm for mixed data. Among the later discussed methods, k-prototypes remains the most popular method to cluster mixed data, because of its simplicity and linear computational complexity [8].

In the following, we present an accelerated MapReduce-based k-prototypes method to deal with large scale of mixed data.

3   An Accelerated MapReduce-Based K-prototypes for Big Data

We propose in this section an accelerated MapReduce-based k-prototypes method. Before presenting the proposed method, we first introduce the k-prototypes method [11], then the MapReduce model [5].

3.1   K-prototypes Method

Given a data set $X=\{x_1 \ldots x_n\}$ containing n data points, described by m_r numerical attributes and m_t categorical attributes, the aim of k-prototypes [11] is to find k clusters where the following objective function is minimized:

$$J = \sum_{i=1}^{n} \sum_{j=1}^{k} p_{ij} d(x_i, c_j), \tag{1}$$

where $p_{il} \in \{0, 1\}$ is a binary variable indicating the membership of data point x_i in cluster c_j, c_j is the center of the cluster c_j and $d(x_i, c_j)$ is the dissimilarity measure which is defined as follows:

$$d(x_i, c_j) = \sum_{r=1}^{m_r} \sqrt{(x_{ir} - c_{jr})^2} + \gamma_j \sum_{t=1}^{m_t} \delta(x_{it}, c_{jt}), \tag{2}$$

where x_{ir} represents the value of numeric attribute r and x_{it} represents the value of categorical attribute t for data point x_i, c_{jr} is the mean of numeric attribute r and c_{jt} is the most common value (mode) for categorical attributes t for cluster c_j. For categorical attributes, $\delta(p,q)=0$ when $p = q$ and $\delta(p, q) = 1$ when $p \neq q$. γ_j is a weight for categorical attributes to cluster c_j. The optimization of the objective function J is performed using an alternating iterative process by looking for the optimal cluster centers. These two steps are alternated iteratively until convergence. The main algorithm of k-prototypes method is described in Algorithm 1.1.

Algorithm 1.1. Main algorithm of k-prototypes method

Input: X=$\{x_1 \ldots x_n\}$, k

Output: Centers=$\{c_1 \ldots c_k\}$

begin

> Choose k cluster centers randomly from X
>
> **repeat**
>
> > Compute distance between data points and clusters using Eq. 2
> > Update the cluster centers (Save the previous cluster centers as $Centers^\wedge$ to analyze the convergence)
>
> **until** $Centers^\wedge = Centers$;

end

3.2   MapReduce Model

MapReduce [5] is a parallel programming model designed to process large scale data sets among cluster nodes. The MapReduce model works as follows. The input and output of the computation is a set of $<key/value>$ pairs. The algorithm to be parallelized needs to be expressed by map and reduce functions. The map function is applied in parallel to each input $<key/value>$ pair and returns a set of intermediate $<key'/value'>$ pairs. Then, shuffle phase groups all intermediate values associated with the same intermediate key and passes them to the reduce function. The reduce function takes the intermediate key and set of values for this key. These values are merged together to produce a set of values. Figure 1 illustrates the flowchart of MapReduce model. The inputs and outputs are stored in an associated distributed file system that is accessible from any machine of the cluster nodes. The implementation of the MapReduce model is available in Hadoop[1]. Hadoop provides a distributed file system named Hadoop Distributed File System, (HDFS) that stores data on the nodes.

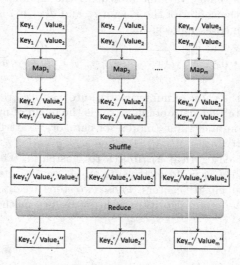

Fig. 1. MapReduce model flowchart

3.3   An Accelerated MapReduce-Based K-prototypes Method for Big Data (AMR K-prototypes)

To offer for users the possibility to build grouping from large scale of mixed type data, we propose the accelerated MapReduce-based k-prototypes method. The proposed method mainly consists of two functions: *map function* which performs the assignment of each data point to the nearest cluster, and *reduce function* which is devoted to update the new cluster centers. Then, we iterate

---

[1] http://hadoop.apache.org/.

calling the two functions several times until convergence. It is important to note that the initial cluster centers are chosen randomly.

3.3.1 Map Function:

During this function, we assign each data point to the nearest cluster by computing distance of Eq. 2 between data points and cluster centers. To reduce the number of distance computations, we propose a pruning strategy using triangle inequality. More precisely, the triangle inequality is used to prove that if cluster center c_1 is close to data point x, and some other cluster center c_2 is far away from another cluster center c_1, then c_1 must be closer than c_2 to x. The following theorem shows how to use the triangle inequality to reduce the distance computations and more details can be found in [10].

Theorem 1. *Let x a data point and let c_1 and c_2 cluster centers. If we know that $d(c_1,c_2) \geq 2 * d(x,c_1) \Rightarrow d(x,c_1) \leq d(x,c_2)$ without having to calculate $d(x,c_2)$.*

Proof. According to triangle inequality, we know that $d(c_1,c_2) \leq d(x,c_1) + d(x,c_1) \Rightarrow d(c_1,c_2) - d(x,c_1) \leq d(x,c_2)$. Consider the left-hand side $d(c_1,c_2) - d(x,c_1) \geq 2 * d(x,c_1) - d(x,c_1) = d(x,c_1) \Rightarrow d(x,c_1) \leq d(x,c_2)$.

After assigning each data point to nearest cluster, we update a local information about clusters. To do so, we first update the values of the numerical attributes of data points. Second, we update the frequencies of different values of categorical attributes of data points. Third, we update the number of data points assigned to clusters. Keeping these information is inexpensive and avoids the calculation over all data points for each iteration. Each time a data point changes cluster membership, the local information are updated. After few iterations, most data points remain in the same cluster for other iterations. Then, the map function outputs the local information about clusters to the reduce function.

Let $X=\{X^1 \ldots X^m\}$ the input data set where X^g the portion of input data set associated to map function g. Let $Centers=\{c_1 \ldots c_k\}$ the set of cluster centers. Let $SUM^g=\{sum_1^g \ldots sum_k^g\}$ the set of sum of data values of numerical attributes relative to different clusters. Let $FREQ^g=\{freq_1^g \ldots freq_k^g\}$ the set of frequencies of data values of categorical attributes relative to different clusters. Let $NUMBER^g=\{number_1^g \ldots number_k^g\}$ the set of number of data points relative to different clusters. Let *new* (resp. *old*) the cluster index of data point x_i in the current (resp. previous) iteration. Let $Cluster - Cluster$ a matrix which records the distances between each pair of cluster centers where $Cluster - Cluster_{ij}$ returns the distance between c_i and c_j. The main steps of map function is described in Algorithm 1.2.

3.3.2 Reduce Function

During this function, we merge the local information which are produced from all map functions in order to calculate the new cluster centers. So, for each cluster, we first sum the numeric values of data points. Second, we compute the total

Algorithm 1.2. Map function

Input: $< key : g/value : X^g >, Centers$

Output: $< key' : 1/value' : SUM^g, FREQ^g, NUMBER^g >$

begin

> $SUM^g \leftarrow \emptyset \quad FREQ^g \leftarrow \emptyset \quad NUMBER^g \leftarrow \emptyset$
>
> **for** $i \leftarrow 1 \ldots k$ **do**
>> **for** $j \leftarrow 1 \ldots k$ **do**
>>> $Cluster - Cluster_{ij} \leftarrow d(c_i, c_j)$
>
> **foreach** $x_i \in X^g$ **do**
>> **for** $j \leftarrow 1 \ldots k$ **do**
>>> **if** $p_{ij} = 1$ **then**
>>>> $old \leftarrow j$
>>
>> $minDistance \leftarrow d(s_i, c_{old})$
>>
>> **for** $j \leftarrow 1 \ldots k$ **do**
>>> **if** $minDistance \leq 2*Cluster - Cluster_{jold}$ **then**
>>>> $j \leftarrow j+1$
>>>
>>> **else**
>>>> % Distance computation
>>>>
>>>> $Distance \leftarrow d(x_i, c_j)$
>>>>
>>>> **if** $distance < minDistance$ **then**
>>>>> $minDistance \leftarrow distance$
>>>>>
>>>>> $new \leftarrow j$
>>
>> **if** $new \neq old$ **then**
>>> $sum^g_{new} \leftarrow sum^g_{new} + x_i$
>>>
>>> $sum^g_{old} \leftarrow sum^g_{old} - x_i$
>>>
>>> $freq^g_{new} \leftarrow freq^g_{new} + 1$
>>>
>>> $freq^g_{old} \leftarrow freq^g_{old} - 1$
>>>
>>> $number^g_{new} \leftarrow number^g_{new} + 1$
>>>
>>> $number^g_{old} \leftarrow number^g_{old} - 1$
>
> return $< 1/SUM^g, FREQ^g, NUMBER^g >$

end

frequencies of different values of categorical attributes relative to the data points. Third, we sum the number of total data points. Given the above information, we can compute both the mean and mode value of the new cluster centers. Once the new cluster centers are computed, the proposed method moves to the next iteration until convergence. The convergence is achieved when cluster centers become stable for two consecutive iterations. We notate that the new cluster centers are stored in HDFS to be ready for next iteration.

Let $NewCenters = \{newc_1 \ldots newc_k\}$ the set of new cluster centers. Let Highest-Freq($freq_j$) a function which returns the mode value of cluster j from $freq_j$. The main steps of reduce function is described in Algorithm 1.3.

Algorithm 1.3. Reduce function

Input: $< key : 1/value : SUM^1, FREQ^1, NUMBER^1, \ldots, SUM^m, FREQ^m,$
     $NUMBER^m >$

Output: $< key' : 1/value' : NewCenters >$

begin

    $NewCenters \leftarrow \emptyset$

    for $j \leftarrow 1 \ldots k$ **do**

        for $g \leftarrow 1 \ldots m$ **do**

            $sum_j \leftarrow sum_j + sum_j^g$

            $freq_j \leftarrow freq_j + freq_j^g$

            $number_j \leftarrow number_j + number_j^g$

    for $j \leftarrow 1 \ldots k$ **do**

        Calculation of mean value

        $newc_j \leftarrow sum_j / number_j$

        Calculation of mode value

        $newc_j \leftarrow Highest - Freq(freq_j)$

    return $< 1/NewCenters >$

end

4   Experiments and Results

In this section, we describe the experiments which are performed to evaluate the efficiency of the proposed AMR k-prototypes method. First, the execution environment, and the information of the data sets used are given. Then, the evaluation measures are presented, and the experimental results are provided and discussed.

4.1   Environment and Data Sets

The experiments are performed on Hadoop cluster running the latest stable version of Hadoop 2.7.1. The Hadoop cluster consists of 4 machines. Each machine has two Pentium(R) Core i5 (2.70 GHz) CPU E5400 and 1 GB of memory. The operating system of each machine is Ubuntu 14.10 server 64 bit. We conducted the experiments on the following data sets:

- Synthetic data set: four series of mixed data sets generated using the data generator developed in[2]. The data sets range from 1 million to 4 million data points. Each data point is described using 3 numeric and 3 categorical attributes. In order to simplify the names of the synthetic data sets, we used names with specific pattern based on the data size. For example: the Sy1M data set consists of 1 million data points.
- KDD Cup data set (KDD): This is a real data set which consists of data about TCP connections simulated in a military network environment. Each connection is described using 7 numeric and 3 categorical attributes. The clustering

---

[2] https://projets.pasteur.fr/projects/rap-r/wiki/SyntheticDataGeneration.

process for this data set detects type of attacks among all the connections. KDD data set was obtained from UCI machine learning repository[3].

- Cover Type data set (Cover): This is a real data set which represents cover type for 30×30 meter cells from US Fores. Each measurement is described using 5 numeric and 3 categorical attributes. The clustering process for this data set identifies types of trees. Cover data set was obtained from UCI machine learning repository[4]. Statistics of these data sets are summarized in Table 1.

Table 1. Summary of the data sets

Data set	Number of data points	Number of attributes	Domain
Sy1M	1.000.000	6 (3 Numeric, 3 Categorical)	Synthetic
Sy2M	2.000.000	6 (3 Numeric, 3 Categorical)	Synthetic
Sy3M	3.000.000	6 (3 Numeric, 3 Categorical)	Synthetic
Sy4M	4.000.000	6 (3 Numeric, 3 Categorical)	Synthetic
KDD	4.898.431	10 (7 Numeric, 3 Categorical)	Detection intrusion
Cover	581.012	8 (5 Numeric, 3 Categorical)	Agriculture

4.2   Evaluations Measures

In order to evaluate the quality of the obtained results, we use Sum Squared Error (SSE) [21] which is defined as follows.

- The Sum Squared Error [21] is one of the most common partitional clustering criteria and its general objective is to obtain a partition which minimizes the squared error. This criterion is defined as follows:

$$SSE = \sum_{i=1}^{n} \sum_{j=1}^{k} d(c_j, x_i). \tag{3}$$

We used in our experiments the Speedup and Scaleup [22] measures to evaluate the performance of AMR k-prototypes method, which are defined as follows.

- The Speedup [22] is measured by fixing the data set size while increasing the number of machines to evaluate the ability of parallel algorithm to scale with increasing the number of machines of the Hadoop cluster, which is calculated as follows:

$$Speedup = \frac{T_1}{T_h}, \tag{4}$$

where T_1 the running time of processing data on 1 machine and T_h the running time of processing data on h machines in the Hadoop cluster.

---

[3] https://archive.ics.uci.edu/ml/datasets/KDD+Cup+1999+Data.
[4] http://archive.ics.uci.edu/ml/datasets/Covertype.

- The Scaleup [22] is a measure of speedup that increases with increasing data set sizes to evaluate the ability of the parallel algorithm for utilizing the Hadoop cluster effectively, which is calculated as follows:

$$Scaleup = \frac{T_{n_1}}{T_{h*n_h}},$$ (5)

where T_{n_1} the running time of processing data with size of n on 1 machine and T_{h*n_h} the running time of processing data with size of $h*n$ on h machines of the Hadoop cluster.

4.3   Results

We first evaluate the performance of the pruning strategy to reduce the unnecessary distances computations. Tables 2 and 3 report the number of distance computations performed by AMR k-prototypes compared to existing MapReduce-based k-prototypes (MR k-prototypes) method [3] for synthetic and real data sets respectively using ten runs. A different initialization of cluster centers have been used over the ten runs, whereas within each run the same initialization of cluster centers has been used for the different methods. The number of iterations is fixed as 10 for each run. From Tables 2 and 3, we can observe that the proposed method can reduce a lot of distance computations over MR k-prototypes method on both synthetic and real data sets. More importantly, this reduction becomes more significant with the increase of k. For example, the number of distance computations is reduced by 46.12% when $k = 50$ and by 78.09% when $k = 100$ for Sy4M data set.

Table 4 presents results obtained with AMR k-prototypes versus MR k-prototypes in terms of SSE values for real data sets. From Table 4, we can observe that the proposed method produces the same SSE values compared to MR-KP method. Therefore, we can conclude that AMR-KP avoids unnecessary distance

Table 2. Comparison of the number of distance computations for the synthetic data sets (averaged over 10 runs)

Data set	Number of distance computations ($*10^8$)	
	MR k-prototypes	AMR k-prototypes
Sy1M (K = 50)	5.0000 (± 0.01)	4.6553 (± 0.17)
Sy2M (K = 50)	10.0000 (± 0.03)	9.3087 (± 0.28)
Sy3M (K = 50)	15.0000 (± 0.01)	10.3966 (± 0.22)
Sy4M (K = 50)	20.0000 (± 0.01)	10.8620 (± 0.18)
Sy1M (K = 100)	10.0000 (± 0.02)	2.2671 (± 0.15)
Sy2M (K = 100)	20.0000 (± 0.01)	4.4502 (± 0.31)
Sy3M (K = 100)	30.0000 (± 0.01)	6.8056 (± 0.25)
Sy4M (K = 100)	40.0000 (± 0.03)	9.0711 (± 0.33)

Table 3. Comparison of the number of distance computations for the real data sets (averaged over 10 runs)

Data set	Number of distance computations ($*10^8$)	
	MR k-prototypes	AMR k-prototypes
KDD (K = 50)	24.4921 (± 0.56)	3.8136 (± 0.26)
Cover (K = 50)	19.7198 (± 0.17)	2.1147 (± 0.54)
KDD (K = 100)	48.9843 (± 0.28)	6.2263 (± 0.44)
Cover (K = 100)	38.2515 (± 0.58)	1.6948 (± 0.23)

Table 4. Comparison of the SSE values for the real data set (averaged over 10 runs)

Data set	SSE ($*10^8$)	
	MR k-prototypes	AMR k-prototypes
KDD (K = 50)	8.8131 (± 0.17)	8.8131 (± 0.17)
Cover (K = 50)	6.5124 (± 0.33)	6.5124 (± 0.33)
KDD (K = 100)	7.6916 (± 0.25)	7.6916 (± 0.25)
Cover (K = 100)	5.2678 (± 0.19)	5.2678 (± 0.19)

computations while still always producing exactly the same quality result as MR-KP method.

Then, we evaluate the speedup of the proposed method when the data set grows. Figure 2 shows the speedup results on the synthetic data sets. As the size of the data set increases, the speedup of AMR k-prototypes becomes approximately linear, especially in the case of Sy3M and Sy4M data sets. In addition, Fig. 2 shows that when the data size is 1 million, the performance of 4 machines of the Hadoop cluster is not significantly improved compared to that of 2 machines. The reason is that the time of processing 1 million data points is not very bigger than the communication time among the machines and time occupied by fault tolerance. Therefore, we can conclude that the larger the data set, the better the speedup.

To study the scalability of the proposed method, we have evaluated scaleup measures when we increase the size of the data set in direct proportion to the number of machines of the Hadoop cluster. The Sy1M, Sy2M, Sy3M and Sy4M data sets are processed on 1, 2, 3, 4 machines respectively. Figure 3 illustrates the scaleup results on the synthetic data sets. The scaleup has almost a constant ratio and ranges between 1 and 1.06. For example, the scaleup for Sy1M is 1 while for Sy4M it is 1.06, which is a very small difference. Therefore, we can conclude that the proposed method is scalable.

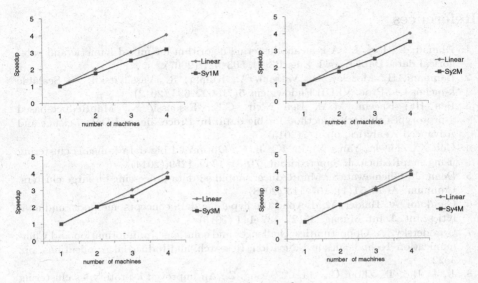

Fig. 2. Speedup results

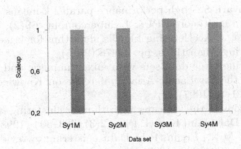

Fig. 3. Scaleup results

5   Conclusion

In this paper, we have proposed an accelerated MapReduce-based k-prototypes method to deal with large scale of mixed data. The proposed method is based on pruning strategy to reduce the unnecessary distance computations. The experiment results show that our method is scalable and can improves the efficiency of existing MapRedced-based k-prototypes method without decreasing the quality. A proper initialization of k-prototypes method is crucial for obtaining a good final solution. Thus, we plan to propose an efficient initialization of k-prototypes using MapReduce model in the future work.

References

1. Ahmad, A., Dey, L.: A k-mean clustering algorithm for mixed numeric and categorical data. Data Knowl. Eng. **63**(2), 503–527 (2007)
2. Bahmani, B., Moseley, B., Vattani, A., Kumar, R., Vassilvitskii, S.: Scalable k-means++. Proc. VLDB Endowment **5**(7), 622–633 (2012)
3. Ben Haj Kacem, M.A., Ben N'cir, C.E., Essoussi, N.: MapReduce-based k-prototypes clustering method for big data. In: Proceedings of Data Science and Advanced Analytics, pp. 1–7(2015)
4. Cui, X., Zhu, P., Yang, X., Li, K., Ji, C.: Optimized big data k-means clustering using mapReduce. J. Supercomput. **70**(3), 1249–1259 (2014)
5. Dean, J., Ghemawat, S.: MapReduce: simplified data processing on large clusters. Commun. ACM **51**(1), 107–113 (2008)
6. Gandomi, A., Haider, M.: Beyond the hype: big data concepts, methods, and analytics. Int. J. Inf. Manag. **35**(2), 137–144 (2015)
7. Gorodetsky, V.: Opportunities, challenges and solutions. In: Information and Communication Technologies in Education, Research, and Industrial Applications, pp. 3–22
8. Ji, J., Bai, T., Zhou, C., Ma, C., Wang, Z.: An improved k-prototypes clustering algorithm for mixed numeric and categorical data. Neurocomputing **120**, 590–596 (2013)
9. Hadian, A., Shahrivari, S.: High performance parallel k-means clustering for disk-resident datasets on multi-core CPUs. J. Supercomput. **69**(2), 845–863 (2014)
10. Hamerly, G., Drake, J. Accelerating Lloyd's algorithm for k-means clustering. In: Partitional Clustering Algorithms, pp. 41–78 (2015)
11. Huang, Z.: Clustering large data sets with mixed numeric and categorical values. In Proceedings of the 1st Pacific-Asia Conference on Knowledge Discovery and Data Mining, pp. 21–34(1997)
12. Huang, Z.: Extensions to the k-means algorithm for clustering large data sets with categorical values. Data Min. Knowl. Disc. **2**(3), 283–304 (1998)
13. Jain, A.K., Murty, M.N., Flynn, P.J.: Data clustering: a review. ACM Comput. Surv. (CSUR) **31**(3), 264–323 (1999)
14. Kim, Y., Shim, K., Kim, M.S., Lee, J.S.: DBCURE-MR: an efficient density-based clustering algorithm for large data using mapReduce. Inf. Syst. **42**, 15–35 (2014)
15. Li, C., Biswas, G.: Unsupervised learning with mixed numeric and nominal data. Knowl. Data Eng. **14**(4), 673–690 (2002)
16. Li, Q., Wang, P., Wang, W., Hu, H., Li, Z., Li, J.: An efficient k-means clustering algorithm on mapReduce. In: Proceedings of Database Systems for Advanced Applications, pp. 357–371 (2014)
17. Ludwig, S.A.: MapReduce-based fuzzy c-means clustering algorithm: implementation and scalability. Int. J. Mach. Learn. Cybern. **6**(6), 923–934 (2015)
18. MacQueen, J.: Some methods for classification and analysis of multivariate observations. In: Proceedings of the Fifth Berkeley Symposium on Mathematical Statistics and Probability, vol. 14, no. 1, pp. 281–297 (1967)
19. Shahrivari, S., Jalili, S.: Single-pass and linear-time k-means clustering based on mapReduce. Inf. Syst. **60**, 1–12 (2016)
20. Vattani, A.: K-means requires exponentially many iterations even in the plane. Discrete Comput. Geom. **45**(4), 596–616 (2011)
21. Xu, R., Wunsch, D.C.: Clustering algorithms in biomedical research: a review. Biomed. Eng. IEEE Rev. **3**, 120–154 (2010)

22. Xu, X., Jäger, J., Kriegel, H.P.: A fast parallel clustering algorithm for large spatial databases. In: High Performance Data Mining, pp. 263–290 (2002)
23. Zhao, W., Ma, H., He, Q. Parallel k-means clustering based on mapReduce. In: Proceedings of Cloud Computing, pp. 674–679 (2009)

Refinement Mining: Using Data to Sift Plausible Models

Antonio Cerone[(✉)]

Department of Computer Science, Nazarbayev University, Astana, Kazakhstan
antonio.cerone@nu.edu.kz

Abstract. Process mining techniques have been developed in the ambit of business process management to extract information from event logs consisting of activities and then produce a graphical representation of the process control flow, detect relations between components involved in the process and infer data dependencies between process activities. These process characterisations allow the analyst to *discover* an annotated visual representation of the conceptual model or the performance model of the process, *check conformance* with an *a priori* model to detect deviations and *extend* the *a priori* model with quantitative information such as frequencies and performance data. However, a process model yielded by process mining techniques is more similar to a representation of the process behaviour rather than an actual model of the process: it often consists of a huge number of states and interconnections between them, thus resulting in a spaghettilike net which is hard to interpret or even read.

In this paper we propose a novel technique, which we call *model mining*, to derive an abstract but concise and functionally structured model from event logs. Such a model is not a representation of the unfolded behaviour, but comprises, instead, a set of formal rules for generating the system behaviour. The set of rules is inferred by sifting a plausible *a priori* model using the event logs as a sieve until a reasonably concise model is achieved (*refinement mining*). We use rewriting logic as the formal framework in which to perform model mining and implement our framework using the MAUDE rewrite system. Once the final formal model is attained, it can be used, within the same rewriting logic framework, to predict future evolutions of the behaviour through simulation, to carry out further validation or to analyse properties through model checking. We illustrate our approach on a case study from the field of ecology.

Keywords: Formal methods · Model-driven approaches · Process mining · Application to ecosystem modelling

1 Introduction

The large amount of data available in online repositories have recently driven research towards the development of techniques and methodologies aiming at

© Springer International Publishing AG 2016
P. Milazzo et al. (Eds.): STAF 2016, LNCS 9946, pp. 26–41, 2016.
DOI: 10.1007/978-3-319-50230-4_3

extracting meaningful information from data and exploiting it to describe and understand the processes that have generated such data. Large online repositories exist in various areas, ranging from economy, learning, sociology and other social sciences to biology, medicine and ecology.

One of these data analysis techniques is *process mining*, which emerged in the field of business process management (BPM). It is used to extract information from event logs consisting of activities and then produce a graphical representation of the process control flow, detect relations between components/individuals involved in the process and infer data dependencies between process activities [17]. Process mining supports not only the *discovery* of an *a posteriori* process model and its representation as a process map, but also the *extension* of a pre-existing *a priori* model by enriching it with new aspects and perspectives and the comparison, by using a technique called *conformance analysis* [13], of the *a priori* model with the event logs.

These three approaches, i.e. discovery, extension and conformance analysis, are alternative ways of using process mining and, although it is possible to apply them all to the same case, their outcomes cannot be automatically integrated, but require the analyst to proceed manually with a comparison work [10].

Only recently the potentialities of process mining in disciplines other than BPM are starting to be understood and realised. Process mining and conformance analysis can be used in a number of contexts, in and across areas such as human-computer interaction (HCI) and learning [3]. Some of these ideas have already resulted in research outputs: process mining have been used to extract learning processes from open source software (OSS) project repositories and check conformance of learning models based on the literature [10,11].

Process mining aims at understanding the process and validating its efficiency. It is therefore appropriate for *descriptive* purposes but not for actual modelling. We want to take a step forward and exploit real data in a *constructive* rather than descriptive way by integrating techniques from the realm of process mining with modelling approaches. In particular, we are interested in formal approaches to modelling, which have the potential to make the modelling process automatic, by appropriately manipulating the information extracted from data logs, and produce a model that can be automatically verified. Although there are a number of works in the areas of synthesis of programs [7,14,15] and synthesis of biological and probabilistic systems from data [5,8,12], to our knowledge, the only attempt to integrate process mininig and formal verification is a work by van der Aalst, de Beer and van Dongen's, which aims at verifying whether an event log satisfies a property expressed in linear temporal logic (LTL) [16]. To accomplish our objective we use rewriting logic [9], and the Maude system [6], a tool based on rewriting logic that has a great expressive power and is equipped with an efficient model checker.

Section 2 introduces the notion of structured event used in our framework and shows how to instantiate it within various application fields, also providing motivations for our work. Section 3 introduces our Model Mining Formal Framework (MMFF) by defining the required data structure while Sect. 3.1 describes the model mining engine. Section 4 presents how to sift a plausible *a priori* model using event logs and illustrates the approach using a case study on the dynamics of a mosquito population. Section 5 describes the possible uses of the generated model and the advantages of the model mining approach to modelling. Finally, Sect. 6 illustrate further possible applications and future research challenges.

2   Event Structure and Instantiation

In order to be successfully processed with the purpose of extracting process control flow information, event logs have to meet a number of structural properties, namely to contain adequately organised and clustered data. Therefore, unstructured data contained in event logs stored in repositories have first to be semantically interpreted according to the purpose of the model we aim to devise, so that such interpretation can drive their structuring and clustering. Structural and semantical organisation can be attained by applying text mining techniques, in particular semantic indexing, in combination with an appropriate ontology from the given application domain. This approach is commonly used in process mining, which is thus applied to a set of *pre-processed* event logs.

For the purpose of model mining we assume to have already pre-processed events organised as a sequence of structured entities. In order to devise a general methodology to efficiently apply formal methods to drive the mining engine, we consider an essential structure of events, as a list of attributes that are general enough to be instantiated depending on the application domain and purpose. In particular, we aim to define a methodology that is partly independent of the precise semantics of the attribute.

We consider the reality to be modelled as an ecosystem of dynamic entities linked together through causality relationships and activity flows. These causality relationships and activity flows are what we need to discover in order to build the ecosystem model. The dynamic evolution of the ecosystem, namely of its entities, is visible through events.

An *event* is defined as a quadruple

$$[[t, d, s, v]]$$

where

- t is the *time* at which the event occurs;
- d is the *domain name*, the name of the domain to which entities belong;
- s is the *subdomain name*, namely a further categorisation of the entity within the domain;
- v is the *concrete value* that refers to domain and subdomain.

We consider two level of domains (domain and subdomain), but this could be generalised to n levels.

Moreover, we have entities which are the *target* of our modelling process and others that make up the *environment* in which our target entities evolve. Thus we identify two categories of events:

target event which describes the activities or actions to be modelled;
environmental event which modifies the conditions that enable activities and actions.

We denote an environmental event by $env[[t, d, s, v]]$ and a target event by $target[[t, d, s, v]]$. We describe below possible instantiations of target and environmental events in various application fields, as summerised in Table 1, in which a "Value" within the "Domain" quantifies or qualify the event, while "Weight" quantifies a relevant attribute of the "Value" within the environment.

In the field of ecology, if we wish to model the dynamic of a population, target events may describe the population size (hence its growth activity) or location (hence its movement or migration activity). In a typical target event, the domain is the population species, the subdomain is the maturation stage of the individual (e.g. larva, juvenile or adult) and the concrete value is the actual population size. Environmental events determine or modify all conditions that affect the life and maturation of the population (e.g. food availability, predation, human impact, temperature, humidity, etc.).

For more examples, we can consider the realm of social networks. In a review community (about resorts, hotels, restaurants, books, or specific products) activities are reviews, ratings, replies, recommendations, while possible environmental conditions are changes to or launch, closing/discontinue of services/products. In an online product support forum, activities are postings and replies while possible environmental conditions are release of upgrades and new products.

One of the most popular social networking website is Facebook. If we wish to analyse the friendship relationships (target domain) between community members, we need to characterise the level of friendship or the trustiness or reputation of the friend (value). Conditions that affect these values are intensity, richness/rate and valence (weight) of posts, "likes" and comments (value) on the friend's wall (environmental domain). Intensity comprises the frequency and size of the post/like/comment, richness refers to the contents (e.g. text, stickers, photos) and valence is the emotional impact (positive, neutral or negative).

A very articulated case of social network is an OSS community. Project contributors perform a large range of activities: post, reply to a post, send a message, review code and commit code. If we consider these activities as environmental domains, as in Table 1, with aspects of their contents as value, and their persistence (posts, replies and messages persist when they generate conversations/interactions) and impact (the impact of reviews and commits is their effectiveness in improving the code) as weights, these can be seen as conditions that affect the growth of individual community members in terms of knowledge, expertise and skills, the evolution of the entire community, as well as the project productivity and, to a greater extent, the quality of the produced software [2]. Table 1 shows how these environmental conditions affect domains in the ambit of collaborative learning: learning process and skill acquisition. The learning process can be described in terms of learning stages. Examples of learning stages of a project contributor are: "understanding", the initial stage wherein the contributor observe community activities, use the code, exchange emails and post messages with the purpose of understanding contents but does not produce new content; "practising", wherein the contributor proposes new contents and production activity starts as a trial and error process; and "developing", an advanced stage wherein the contributor already commits code [2]. Skill acquisition can be described in terms of the activities carried out by the contributor: coding, reviewing, etc.

Table 1. Example of event instantiations depending on the environment and target domains from a number of application fields.

Applic. Field	Environmental			Target		
	Domain	Value	Weight	Domain	Value	Activity
Ecology	Food	availability	duration	Population	location	migrate
	Temper.	level	duration		size	grow
	Predation	life impact	periodicity			intervent.
	Human Impact	habitat deterior.	extension severity			measures
Emerg. Manag.	Quake	intensity	frequency	Casualties	number	monitor
	Rain	amount	water persistence	Damage	amount	
		intensity	duration		severity	response
	Temper.	level	duration	Bushfires	extension	activities
Social Network (Facebook)	Wall	post	intensity	Friendship	level	increase
		like	richness/rate		trust	or
		comment	valence		reputation	decrease
Collab. Learning in OSS Commun.	Post	content aspects	persistence (conversation, interaction)	Learning Process	learning stage	achive maturation
	Reply					
	Message			or		
	Review		impact (effectiveness)	Skill Acquisition	contributor activity	acquire skill
	Commit					
HCI	Task	outcome	frequency	Interface	state	transition
Cognitive Science	Interface	experience	frequency	Mental Model	interface state	human action

In the field of HCI, state and transition of an interface depend on the tasks performed by the human in interacting with the interface, with the value representing the outcome of the task (successful outcome or failures) and a possible weight given by the frequency with which the task is performed. In the more general view of human behaviour considered in cognitive science, humans have the skill of exploiting their experiences to build mental models of the reality. In a way, we can say that humans realise a form of "model mining" when building models out of experiential data. Interacting with a specific interface produces this kind of experiencial data and allows the human to build a mental model of the way the interface works. We can describe this situation in our framework as shown in the last row of Table 1.

The last column of Table 1 shows the activities that refer to the target domains. Most of these activities are *descriptive*, namely they describe how the domain values change. For example, if we consider a population as a domain, a change in its location is a migration, while a change in its size is a growth. Activities shown in italic are instead *responsive*, namely they aim to modify or, at least, restrain the descriptive activity. For example, in ecology, intervention measures are carried out to favour or control the growth of a population.

3 Model Mining Formal Framework

In order to characterise the effect of events on their domain, we need to define the notion of domain state. Moreover, while events are concrete entities that accurately represent the reality, states rather refer to the model than to the reality. They are thus abstract entities, whose values are abstract values.

A *domain state* is defined as a quintuple

$$(|d, s, a, w, f|)$$

where

- d is the *domain name*;
- s is the *subdomain name*;
- a is the *abstract value* that refers to domain and subdomain;
- w is the *weight* of the value.
- f, called *weighting function*, is a function from abstract domains to weights.

We mentioned in Sect. 2 that the *weight* quantifies a relevant attribute of the value within the environment. Thus the *weight* quantifies a relevant attribute of the *abstract value*. Weight is initialised by f at each change of abstract value and normally varies as time progresses, independently of the occurrence of events. For example, in Table 1, we note that in Ecology, a relevant attribute of the value for "Food availability" is "duration", since it is the duration of food availability that modifies the state of the environment. Similarly, relevant attributes of the value for "Habitat deterioration" are "extension" and "severity" and, in the area of Collaborative Learning in OSS Communities, relevant attributes of a "Post content" are its "persistence" in conversations and interactions and its "impact" on the OSS product, in terms of effective contribution to its improvement.

We denote an *environmental state* by $env(|d, s, a, w|)$ and a *target state* by $target(|d, s, a, w, f|)$. The *global state* of the ecosystem we are modelling consists of a set of domain states.

Concrete and abstract values are linked by an *abstraction relation*

$$\{d, s \mid v_1, v_2 \rightarrow a\},$$

where v_1 and v_2 may be distinct only if domain d is totally ordered and in this case $v_1 \leq v_2$. This relation maps any value v of domain d and subdomain s such that $v_1 \leq v \leq v_2$ to abstract value a.

The occurrence of environmental event $env[|t, d, s, v|]$ changes environmental state $env(|d, s, a_0, w_0|)$ to $env(|d, s, a, w|)$ iff there exist an abstraction relation

$$\{d, s \mid v_1, v_2 \rightarrow a\} \text{ such that } v_1 \leq v \leq v_2,$$

such that

$$w = \begin{cases} f(a) & \text{if } a \neq a_0 \\ w_0 & \text{otherwise} \end{cases} \tag{1}$$

Therefore, the state weight is reset to $f(a)$ only if there is a change in the abstract state. In the examples in this paper, we will always have $f \equiv 0$ and represent state $(|d, s, a, w, f|)$ simply as a quadruple $(|d, s, a, w|)$. The state weight is regularly incremented by the passage of time.

We use rewriting logic to define the state transitions. Since one purpose of model mining is the application of model refinement to a plausible set of models, we need to consider sets of alternative plausible rules.

A *plausible rule* is defined as

$$\{i \mid pre_1, ..., pre_n \Rightarrow post\}$$

where

- i is the *identification number* of the plausible rule;
- $pre_i = [d_i, s_i, a_i, \tau_i] \triangleright$ are *preconditions*, with d_i and s_i environmental domain and subdmain, respectively, for $i = 1, \ldots, n$, and τ_i denoting a threshold $\mid \tau_i \mid$ for the effect of the precondition abstract value on the postcondition;
- $post = \ll d, s \mid a_0 \xrightarrow{\alpha} a \gg$ is a *postcondition*, with d and s target domain and subdomain, respectively.

The plausible rule is enabled on environmental state $(|d_0, s_0, a_0, w_0|)$ iff, for each precondition

$$pre_i = [d_i, s_i, a_i, \tau_i] \triangleright, \ i = 1, \ldots, n,$$

such that $d_i = d_0$, $s_i = s_0$ and $a_i = a_0$, the following conditions hold

1. $\tau_i - w_0 \geq 0$ if $\tau_i > 0$;
2. $\tau_i + w_0 \geq 0$ if $\tau_i \leq 0$.

The application of the rule causes a transition from state $(|d_0, s_0, a_0, w_0|)$ to state $(|d_0, s_0, a, w|)$, where w is defined as in Eq. (1) above.

A positive threshold $\tau_i > 0$ means that the precondition is satisfied only if the abstract value a_0 in the current state has been persisting for at most a time w_0 (Condition 1 above is satisfied). A non positive threshold $\tau_i \leq 0$ means that the precondition is satisfied only if the abstract value a_0 in the current state has been persisting for at least a time w_0 (Condition 2 above is satisfied).

In order to illustrate the definitions presented in this section, let us consider the following example. Let $env(|Temp, avg, med, 3|)$ be the temperature state at day 131. It denotes that astract value med, defined according to the abstraction relation given in Table 2, persisted for 3 days. Environmental event $env[|131, Temp, avg, 25|]$, which describes a concrete temperature value of 25° at day 131, changes such temperature state to $env(|Temp, avg, high, 0|)$.

Let us consider an application to ecology where the target domain is represented by a mosquito population of species *Aedes albopictus*, which rapidly increases in size when the temperature is high. Let us consider the abstraction relations in Table 2. Plausible rule

$$\{1 \mid [Temp, avg, high, -10] \triangleright \Rightarrow \ll Aedes, adult \mid med \stackrel{increase}{\longrightarrow} high \gg\}$$

has a single precondition and states that if a high temperature persists for at least 10 days, then the size of the adult population of *Aedes a.* increases from medium to high. If between day 131 and day 141 there are no events that change the temperature state, $env(|Temp, avg, high, 0|)$ at day 131 becomes $env(|Temp, avg, high, 10|)$ at day 141. The latter state satisfies Condition 2 above, thus, at day 141, a population state $env(|Aedes, adult, med, w|)$ would be changed by the plausible rule above to $env(|Aedes, adult, high, 0|)$.

3.1 The Model Mining Engine

We perform model mining using rewriting logic. A prototype of the model mining engine, implemented using the MAUDE rewrite system [6], and its application to the case study presented in Sect. 4.1 can be downloaded at

http://sysma.imtlucca.it/refinement-mining-datamod-2016/.

We consider discrete time with a granularity suitable to the specific application domain. For example, a daily time progress would, in many cases, suit the analysis of the dynamic of a population, while for a social network the granularity depends on the frequency of the activity relevant to the model we want to capture. The data structures defined in Sect. 3 are organised in a *configuration*, which is manipulated by the model mining engine using rewrite rules. To distinguish such rules from the plausible rules we call them *meta-rules*.

A configuration comprises:

abstraction a set of abstraction relations;
past events a list of events that have already been processed by the current step of the engine;
current events a list of events that are currently being processed by the current step of the engine;
future events a list of events that have not been processed yet by the current step of the engine;
option set a collection of plausible rules stuctured as described in Sect. 4;
current state the global state at the current time, which consists in a set of domain states;

control containing *static information* for reset purpose, i.e. initial domain state for the target domain, initial time, start and end time for simulation and model mining, and *dynamic information*, i.e. information to control the meta-rule selection and the current choice of plausible rules as well as incrementally built **constructed model** and **refinement**, and possibly a list of **rejected models**.

The engine makes use of the following meta-rules:

1. **Time Progress** to increase the *current time* and the weight of every domain state at the beginning of each step and move the events occurring at the next time from **future events** to **current events**;
2. **Init Simulation** to initialise **future events** as the list of all events and **control** with the initial and final times for the simulation;
3. **State Update via Events** to modify the current state using environmental events and abstraction relations as shown in Sect. 3, if there are any environmental events in **current events**;
4. **State Update via Model** to select a plausible rule with preconditions satisfying the **current state** and modify the current state as shown in Sect. 3;
5. **No State Update via Model** to skip the selection of a plausible rule with preconditions not satisfying the **current state**;
6. **Model Validation via Events** to compare the current state with the target events, if there are any target events in **current events**;
7. **Init Model Refinement** initialise **future events** as the list of all events and **control** with the initial and final times for the model refinement;
8. **Refinement Step** to sift the plausible model using the target events, if there are any target events in **current events**.

Meta-rules 2–6 perform the simulation and meta-rules 7 and 8 perform the model refinement. The architecture of our model mining engine is shown in Fig. 1. Each component consist of the evaluation and possibly application of the meta-rule with the same name, apart form component **State Update via Model** which comprises meta-rules 4 and 5.

4   Refinement Mining

Refinement mining is a data-driven model refinement that consists in sifting a plausible *a priori* model using the event logs as a sieve until a reasonably concise model is achieved. In order to carry out refinement mining, plausible rules must be structured into sets of alternatives called *option sets*. An *option set* is defined as

$$[i]\langle pRule_1, ..., pRule_n \rangle$$

where

- i is the *identification number* of the option set;
- $pRule_i$ are alternative plausible rules for $i = 1, \ldots, n$.

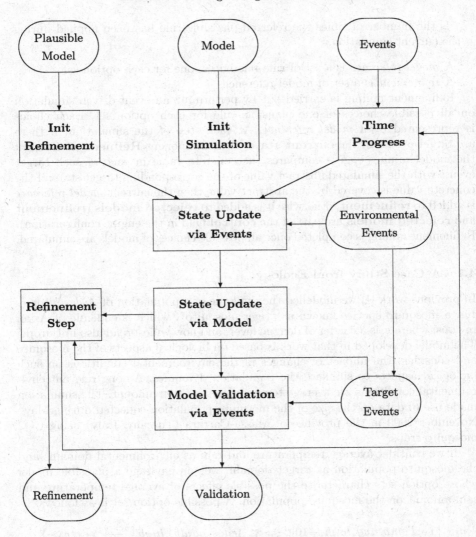

Fig. 1. Architecture of the model mining engine.

A *plausible model* is a set of option sets.

A *rule reference* is defined as

$$[n : i(j)]$$

where

- n is a reference to the option set whose identification number is n;
- i is a reference to the plausible rule whose identification number is i within the option set identified by n;

- j is the number of times the referred plausible rule has been applied during the current simulation.

A *model reference* is a set of rule references, one for each option set.

A *refinement* is a set of model references.

Refinement mining is carried out by performing an event-driven simulation on all possible choices of one plausible rule for each option set. Each choice is represented by a *model reference*. At each step of the simulation, if there are target events in the **current state**, then component **Refinement Step** of the model mining engine compares the concrete value in each of such target events with the simulated abstract value of the corresponding target state: if the concrete value is covered by the abstract value then the current *model reference* is added to **refinement**, otherwise it is added to **rejected models** (**refinement** and **rejected models** are part of the **control** field in the engine configuration). Refinement mining is completed once all possible choices of models are simulated.

4.1   A Case Study from Ecology

In previous work [1] we modelled the dynamic of a population of *Aedes albopictus*, a mosquito species known as "tiger mosquito", which is endemic of Asian regions, where it is a carrier of dengue fever, and now widespread also in Europe. The model developed in that work is based on biological aspects of the mosquito and considers the impact of changes in the environmental conditions on such biological aspects to simulate the population dynamics. Among relevant environmental conditions are average temperature and rain amount. The simulation made use of data on the size of the mosquito population collected during May–November 2009 in the province of Massa-Carrara (Tuscany, Italy) using CO_2 mosquito traps.

If we consider average temperature and rain as environmental domains and the mosquito population as target domain, we can envisage a plausible model whose option sets characterise the possible effects of average temperature and rain amount on the mosquito population. A possible option set is as follows.

$$[n] \, \langle \, \{1 \mid [Temp, avg, high, -10] \triangleright \; \Rightarrow \ll Aedes, adult \mid high \stackrel{increase}{\longrightarrow} extr \gg \}$$

$$\{2 \mid [Rain, amount, high, +5] \triangleright \; \Rightarrow \ll Aedes, adult \mid high \stackrel{increase}{\longrightarrow} extr \gg \}$$

$$\{3 \mid [Temp, avg, high, -1] \triangleright, [Rain, amount, high, +10] \triangleright$$

$$\Rightarrow \ll Aedes, adult \mid high \stackrel{increase}{\longrightarrow} extr \gg \}$$

$$\rangle$$

The three alternative plausible rules of option set n state that

1. if a high temperature persists for at least 10 days, then the size of the adult population of *Aedes a.* increases from high to extreme;
2. if a high rainfall occurred at most 5 days earlier, then the size of the adult population of *Aedes a.* increases from high to extreme;

3. if a high temperature persists for at least 1 day, and a high rainfall occurred at most 10 days before, then the size of the adult population of *Aedes a.* increases from high to extreme;

If we consider the sequence of events

$$env[|56, Temp, avg, 25|] \longrightarrow target[|56, Aedes, adult, 360|] \longrightarrow$$
$$env[|59, Temp, avg, 24|] \longrightarrow env[|59, Rain, amount, 72|] \longrightarrow$$
$$env[|60, Temp, avg, 23|] \longrightarrow env[|61, Temp, avg, 22|] \longrightarrow$$
$$env[|62, Temp, avg, 23|] \longrightarrow env[|64, Temp, avg, 24|] \longrightarrow$$
$$env[|66, Temp, avg, 25|] \longrightarrow env[|67, Temp, avg, 26|] \longrightarrow$$
$$target[|67, Aedes, adult, 561|]$$

which is a fragment of the data collected in 2009 in the province of Massa-Carrara and the abstraction relations defined in Table 2, we obtain the abstract values and weights shown in Table 3. We note that only plausible rule 3 is applicable at day 67 and thus validated by the sequence of events (i.e. by the data). In fact, plausible rule 1 is not applicable because the high temperature persisted for just 1 day rather than the minimum of 10 required by the rule precondition; plausible rule 2 is not applicable because the high rainfall occurred already 7 days earlier rather than the maximum of 5 required by the rule precondition. If we suppose that the plausible model consists of just the option set n above and the refinement mining is driven only by the dataset given in Table 3, then the final refinement would be set $\{[n : 3(1)]\}$, which consists of just the rule reference of 3 with 1 as the number of times rule 3 has been applied during the only possible simulation.

5 Model Usage and Model Mining Advantages

The purpose of our framework is not only to generate a model refinement but also to use it in three possible ways.

The most obvious usage is for *prediction*. Simulation can be run to predict the behaviour of the target domain.

Table 2. Abstraction relations for average temperature (*Temp, avg*), amount of daily rain (*Rain, amount*) and *Aedes a.* population size (*Aedes, adult*).

Abstract value	Concrete value for		
	Temp, avg	*Rain, amount*	*Aedes, adult*
low (low)	0–19	0–5	0–100
med (medium)	20–24	6–40	101–300
high (high)	25–35	41–200	301–500
extr (extreme)	36–50	201–500	501–800

Table 3. Abstract values (abs) and weight (weight) for real data average temperature ($Temp$, avg), amount of daily rain ($Rain$, $amount$) and $Aedes\ a.$ population size ($Aedes$, $adult$), collected in 2009 in the province of Massa-Carrara (the abstract values are added in accordance with the abstraction relations in Table 2).

Date	Day no.	Temp, avg			Rain, amount			Aedes, adult	
		val	abs	weight	val	abs	weight	val	abs
3 July	56	25	high	?	-	-	0	360	high
6 July	59	24	high	> 0	72	high	1	-	-
7 July	60	23	med	0	-	-	2	-	-
8 July	61	22	med	1	-	-	3	-	-
9 July	62	23	med	2	-	-	4	-	-
11 July	64	24	med	3	-	-	5	-	-
13 July	66	25	high	0	-	-	6	-	-
14 July	67	26	high	1	-	-	7	561	extr

Another important usage is *model validation*. Although the refinement process is based on validation against real data (target events), the resultant model may need further validation due to changes in environmental domains as well as in the target domain. This is a common situation both in biological/ecological contexts and in socio-economic contexts. In ecological contexts the environment changes due to natural degradation and human interventions while populations get adapted to new environments. In socio-economic contexts the continuous development of new technologies changes the environmental conditions while the users of such technologies, on the one hand, get adapted to them and, on the other hand, invent new ways to use them, often ways that the designer themselves could not predict. In these continuously evolving contexts, an important advantage of model mining is that the generated model can be revised through further validation and, if the model is invalidated by the data, then model mining may be run again on the initial plausible model or on a revision of it.

The last possible usage of the generated model refinement is *property checking*. This is possible by exploiting the model checking capabilities of the MAUDE rewrite system by which plausible models are manipulated.

6   Conclusion and Future Work

We defined a formal framework (MMFF), based on rewriting logic and implemented in the MAUDE rewrite system, for generating a data-validated model starting from a plausible model defined *a priori*. We illustrated MMFF on a case study from the field of ecology.

As our future work, we are planning to apply MMFF to the various fields mentioned in Sect. 2 and illustrated in Table 1, in particular to collaborative learning, HCI and cognitive science. These applications will build on our previous work and aim to investigate how refinement mining would scale to large datasets. The initial plausible model may either be based on theoretical hypotheses or be manually built through the observation of the dataset. In the former case refinement mining can be used to verify such hypotheses. In the latter case, however, the larger the dataset is the harder the definition of the plausible model is, which possibly makes it difficult to apply refinement mining to big data.

In our previous work on the application of rewriting logic (also using the MAUDE system) to HCI and cognitive science [4] we have characterised the behaviour of a user that exploits a pre-defined mental model and compared two interface designs with respect to the cognitive errors that may emerge during interaction. We plan to use model mining to extend such work, on the one hand by exploiting environmental events generated by the outcome of human tasks carried out on a set of different interfaces and target events generated by the interface states to identify the interfaces that support the successful completion of the task and, on the other end, by extracting the mental model from event logs produced by interactions between user and interface.

In our previous work on collaborative learning in OSS communities [11] we analysed participants interaction and knowledge exchange in emails repositories of OSS projects by retrieving data carrying information on the learning activities that occur in distinct phases of the learning process to produce pre-processed event logs. Such event logs were fed to a process mining tool to produce visual workflow nets that represent the traces of learning activities in OSS as well as their relevant flow of occurrence. However, such workflow nets consist of huge numbers of states and interconnections between them, which make them hard to interpret. To overcome this problem we plan to revisit our process mining work and transfer our mining approach to MMFF.

Finally, we must note that there are situations in which target domains do not directly correspond to observable events. This happens, for example, in social contexts, when social relationships either are characterised from an introspective point of view (e.g. friendship), which is not directly externalised through events (e.g. friendship level, trust and reputation are not directly observable in events), or evolve over a long time (e.g. learning process), with no events characterising the change of values (learning stages are not directly observable in events). With reference to Table 1 we can observe neither a target event of domain Friendship, whose value directly describes a change in level of friendship or trust, nor a target event of domain Learning Process, whose value directly describes a change of learning stage. Since in these situations there are no observable target events, refinement mining cannot be used.

Therefore, in our future work, we also plan to investigate the possibility of *directly constructing* the model from the event logs, rather than extracting it from a plausible model through refinement mining. We hope that this would allow model mining to both scale well with big data and deal with target domains that do not feature observable events.

References

1. Basuki, T.A., Cerone, A., Barbuti, R., Maggiolo-Schettini, A., Milazzo, P., Rossi, E.: Modelling the dynamics of an Aedes albopictus population. In: Proceedings of AMCA-POP 2010, Electronic Proceedings in Theoretical Computer Science, vol. 227, pp. 37–58 (2010)
2. Cerone, A.: Learning and activity patterns in OSS communities and their impact on software quality. In: Proceedings of OpenCert 2011, ECEASST, vol. 48 (2012)
3. Cerone, A.: Process mining as a modelling tool: beyond the domain of business process management. In: Bianculli, D., Calinescu, R., Rumpe, B. (eds.) SEFM 2015. LNCS, vol. 9509, pp. 139–144. Springer, Heidelberg (2015). doi:10.1007/978-3-662-49224-6_12
4. Cerone, A.: A cognitive framework based on rewriting logic for the analysis of interactive systems. In: De Nicola, R., Kühn, E. (eds.) SEFM 2016. LNCS, vol. 9763, pp. 287–303. Springer, Heidelberg (2016). doi:10.1007/978-3-319-41591-8_20
5. Češka, M., Dannenberg, F., Kwiatkowska, M., Paoletti, N.: Precise parameter synthesis for stochastic biochemical systems. In: Mendes, P., Dada, J.O., Smallbone, K. (eds.) CMSB 2014. LNCS, vol. 8859, pp. 86–98. Springer, Heidelberg (2014). doi:10.1007/978-3-319-12982-2_7
6. Clavel, M., Durán, F., Eker, S., Lincoln, P., Martí-Oliet, N., Meseguer, J., Talcott, C.: The Maude 2.0 system. In: Nieuwenhuis, R. (ed.) RTA 2003. LNCS, vol. 2706, pp. 76–87. Springer, Heidelberg (2003). doi:10.1007/3-540-44881-0_7
7. Gulwani, S.: Automating string processing in spreadsheets using input-output examples. In: Notices, A.S. (ed.) Proceedings of POPL 2011, vol. 46, pp. 317–330. ACM (2011)
8. Koksal, A.S., Pu, Y., Srivastava, S., Bodik, R., Fisher, J., Piterman, N.: Automating string processing in spreadsheets using input-output examples. In: Notices, A.S. (ed.) Proceedings of POPL 2013, vol. 48, pp. 469–482. ACM (2013)
9. Martí-Oliet, N., Meseguer, J.: Rewriting logic: roadmap and bibliography. Theor. Comput. Sci. 285(2), 121–154 (2002)
10. Mukala, P.: Process models for learning patterns in FLOSS repositories. Ph.D. thesis, Department of Computer Science. University of Pisa (2015)
11. Mukala, P., Cerone, A., Turini, F.: Mining learning processes from FLOSS mailing archives. In: Janssen, M., Mäntymäki, M., Hidders, J., Klievink, B., Lamersdorf, W., Loenen, B., Zuiderwijk, A. (eds.) I3E 2015. LNCS, vol. 9373, pp. 287–298. Springer, Heidelberg (2015). doi:10.1007/978-3-319-25013-7_23
12. Paoletti, N., Yordanov, B., Hamadi, Y., Wintersteiger, C.M., Kugler, H.: Analyzing and synthesizing genomic logic functions. In: Biere, A., Bloem, R. (eds.) CAV 2014. LNCS, vol. 8559, pp. 343–357. Springer, Heidelberg (2014). doi:10.1007/978-3-319-08867-9_23
13. Rozinat, A., van der Aalst, W.M.P.: Conformance checking of processes based on monitoring real behavior. Inf. Syst. 33(1), 64–95 (2008)
14. Solar-Lezama, A., Rabbah, R.M., Bodik, R., Ebcioglu, K.: Programming by sketching for bit-streaming programs. In: Proceedings of PLDI 2005, ACM SIGPLAN Notices, vol. 40, pp. 281–294. ACM (2005)

15. Srivastava, S., Gulwani, S., Foster, J.S.: From program verification to program synthesis. In: Notices, A.S. (ed.) Proceedings of POPL 2010, vol. 45, pp. 313–326. ACM (2010)
16. van der Aalst, W.M.P., de Beer, H.T., can Dongen, B.F.: Process mining, verification of properties: an approach based on temporal logic, Beta Working Paper Series WT, p. 136. Eindhoven University of Technology, Eindhoven (2005)
17. van der Aalst, W.M.P., Stahl, C., Processes, M.B.: A Petri Net-Oriented Approach. The MIT Press, Cambridge (2011)

Towards Platform Independent Database Modelling in Enterprise Systems

Martyn Ellison[✉], Radu Calinescu, and Richard F. Paige

Department of Computer Science, University of York, York, UK
{mhe504,radu.calinescu,richard.paige}@york.ac.uk

Abstract. Enterprise software systems are prevalent in many organisations, typically they are data-intensive and manage customer, sales, or other important data. When an enterprise system needs to be modernised or migrated (e.g. to the cloud) it is necessary to understand the structure of this data and how it is used. We have developed a tool-supported approach to model database structure, query patterns, and growth patterns. Compared to existing work, our tool offers increased system support and extensibility which is vital for use in industry. Standardisation and platform independence is ensured by producing models conforming to the Knowledge Discovery Metamodel and Software Metrics Metamodel.

1 Introduction

Model driven engineering has been shown to aid the modernisation and re-engineering of enterprise software systems [18]. Public clouds are a common target platform for these systems, as investigated in the ARTIST [9] project and CloudMIG [6]. However, this existing work gives minimal consideration to data (and the database layer) despite this being the most valuable and irreplaceable part of many systems [5]. Extensive work has been done on database modelling [2,12] and reverse engineering [4,16], although this is disconnected from the work on software modernisation and does not focus on the cloud.

In order to determine the costs of migrating and storing data in the cloud the workload of the enterprise system's database, i.e., query patterns and growth patterns, must be known. Furthermore, the database structure must be known to decide which tables or columns to migrate and whether any modernisation tasks should be performed during migration (e.g., table merging). In this paper we investigate how to model these properties in a platform independent way so that further analysis and migration simulation is possible.

We have developed a prototype model extraction tool, called DBLModeller, which transforms a schema dump and query log into a structure and a workload model. These conform to the Knowledge Discovery Metamodel (KDM) and the Structured Metrics Metamodel (SMM) respectively. Most existing model-driven modernisation and cloud migration approaches use these metamodels, and the range of existing tools mean they are an ideal choice for our work. Approaches for obtaining these two inputs are also proposed.

© Springer International Publishing AG 2016
P. Milazzo et al. (Eds.): STAF 2016, LNCS 9946, pp. 42–50, 2016.
DOI: 10.1007/978-3-319-50230-4_4

DBLModeller has been developed in partnership with Science Warehouse (www.sci-ware.com), a UK-based e-business company that specialises in enterprise procurement software. They have provided access to their core system to support the evaluation of DBLModeller. This is a large Java-based system that business customers use to order and compare products from multiple suppliers.

One key challenge when modelling databases is heterogeneity, as a variety of SQL dialects exist. This becomes an issue when developing a platform independent tool which supports a wide range of systems. We have overcome this in a number of ways: (1) our approach incorporates existing tools from database providers, (2) a single grammar has been developed to support multiple SQL dialects, and (3) a model-to-model transformation has been removed from the model extraction process required to produce KDM and SMM models. These changes increased the range of enterprise systems supported by DBLModeller and improved extensibility compared to the state-of-the-art Gra2MoL SQL-to-KDM tool [8].

The rest of the paper is structured as follows. Section 2 presents our DBLModeller approach. Section 3 describes our evaluation of DBLModeller. Section 4 concludes the paper with a brief summary and suggests future work directions.

2   DBLModeller Approach

Our approach for producing the structure (KDM) and workload (SMM) models is shown in Fig. 1. Step 1 (T1 & T2) is performed by existing external tools, such as Oracle SQL Developer [15] for the schema and P6Spy [1] for the SQL trace. Nearly all databases will have an accompanying management tool which can produce a SQL schema dump, this is preferable to using any existing SQL scripts in the organisation as these may be out of date. Similarly, several approaches exist to capture a SQL trace (i.e., the SQL queries being sent to the database) but we propose using a 'spying' library. These wrap the existing database driver used by the system and save all queries to a log file, therefore code changes to the system are not required.

DBLModeller can process the SQL traces produced by P6Spy into a sequence of load measurements (Step 1 T3), if the SQL trace is captured via another method then this must be done manually. The load measurements include: entity count, entity reads, entity writes, unused entities, and database size. An 'entity' is the primary data artefact the database is storing and is selected by the user; e.g. products in an e-commerce system or pages in a Wiki. Abstracting the measurements in this way greatly simplifies the workload model extraction, and makes the process more generic.

Steps 2 & 3 are fully automated and performed by DBLModeller. The text-to-model transformation (Step 2) consists of two separate transformations, one for each metamodel, as shown in Fig. 2. This uses grammar-to-model mapping (the approach from [7]), with SQL and Metrics grammars (G1 & G2) that are mapped to the KDM and SMM (MM1 & MM2) via a set of rules we developed.

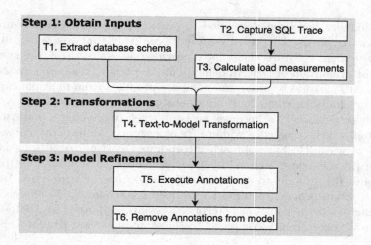

Fig. 1. Overview of the DBLModeller approach

Traditionally when using a grammar-to-model approach a publicly available grammar is reused, however for DBLModeller we developed our own multi-dialect SQL grammar. Given that the source grammar and mapping rules are tightly coupled, a new rule-set (i.e., R1 on Fig. 2) would be required for each grammar. This would not be a scalable approach if a large number of SQL dialects were to be supported. A multi-dialect grammar is feasible when the target metamodel (KDM) is at a far higher level of abstraction than the source language, e.g., the TEXT (in MySQL) and VARCHAR (in Oracle) types both map to the KDM type String. Furthermore, support for a new dialect can be achieved by adding the unsupported constructs to the grammar (many constructs will exist in both) and without modifying the mapping rules, improving extensibility.

If a model is highly abstract or significantly different from a source text, model extraction typically requires a model-to-model (M2M) transformation to be combined with a text-to-model (T2M) transformation [8,13]. This is undesirable when designing a model extraction tool to be extensible, because the M2M transformation is an additional code block to modify. In the case of KDM model extraction, the M2M transformation is only needed to perform simple tasks like moving elements or resolving references. We developed an annotation-based model-extraction approach to remove simple M2M transformations.

In our approach three annotation types exist: Add, Move, and Reference. These are inserted during the T2M transformation (Step 2) to produce an annotated model, which is processed by a model refinement engine (Step 3). The user will never see the annotated model and he/she will never have to consider which annotations to use unless DBLModeller is being extended to support a new SQL dialect or version. We have used annotations to support: ALTER statements, CREATE INDEX statements, and to resolve references. These three use cases require the model to be searched after the initial T2M transformation, e.g. an

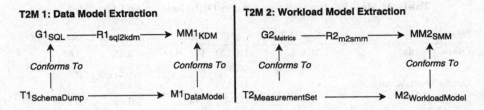

Fig. 2. Text-to-model transformations in DBLModeller

ALTER statement might add a primary key to a previously created table, this model element must be found and modified.

3   Evaluation

The evaluation of DBLModeller is based around the following research questions:

RQ1 To what extent are the models produced by DBLModeller complete and correct?

RQ2 How is the model extraction time impacted by the M2M transformation replacement?

RQ3 How does the set of SQL keywords supported by DBLModeller compare to those used in Oracle/MySQL dumps from real-world systems?

RQ4 What is the effect of a multi-dialect grammar and annotated T2M transformation on extensibility?

3.1   Model Extraction

This section evaluates the completeness and correctness of the extracted models (RQ1) and the performance of DBLModeller (RQ2). These research questions have been examined together as they impact on each other. DBLModeller has been compared to Gra2MoL's PLSQL2KDM example [3] as this had the highest level of SQL support at the time of writing. We extracted KDM models from the database schemas of four systems: Apache OFBiz, MediaWiki, Science Warehouse, and a student record system [8]. With OFBiz and MediaWiki we obtained Oracle and MySQL versions of the schema by installing them on both databases. Additionally, SMM models were extracted from Wikipedia (using 6 months data from [10,19]) and Science Warehouse.

Model completeness was assessed by comparing the number of model elements and input elements, while for correctness the properties of the model elements and input elements were compared. We developed a small model checking tool to automate this analysis. DBLModeller was able to extract models from the 6 schemas successfully, and from the output of our tool we concluded: that the input text and the output model had the same number of elements, all table, column, and sequence names were correct, and relationships between tables were

Table 1. Model extraction times using DBLModeller and Gra2MoL

Schema	Size (KLOC)	Tool	Mean (Secs.)	Std. Dev.	sec/KLOC
Oracle OFBiz	31.5	DBLM	174	2.35	6
	10.3	G2M	237	3.4	24
Oracle MediaWiki	2	DBLM	7	0.23	4
	0.8	G2M	14	0.68	18
Oracle Science Warehouse	1	DBLM	5	0.19	5
	0.4	G2M	14	0.62	35
Oracle UoM Student System	0.3	DBLM	5	0.21	17
	0.3	G2M	10	0.62	33
MySQL OFBiz	21.7	DBLM	104	2.13	5
	9.5	G2M	230	9.73	24
MySQL MediaWiki	1	DBLM	5	0.24	5
	0.4	G2M	13	0.53	33

correct. Furthermore, we confirmed the models conformed to KDM and SMM using the Eclipse Modelling Framework.

The performance of DBLModeller was assessed by extracting a KDM model for each schema and measuring the time taken. This process was repeated 20 times per schema. We expected that the removal of the M2M transformation from the model extraction process will have significant performance gains. A virtual machine on the Digital Ocean cloud platform with 4 GB of RAM and two Ivy Bridge based Intel Xeon cores was used to perform the experiment.

The performance results are presented in Table 1, which shows that DBLModeller can extract a KDM model in less time for every schema. As Gra2MoL supports fewer SQL statements than DBLModeller, in order to obtain results it was necessary to modify the schemas by removing unsupported content until they could be processed by Gra2MoL. We used the metric "sec/KLOC" to simplify comparison, based on this we conclude the model extraction time has been reduced by up to 86% for Oracle schemas and up to 84% for MySQL.

3.2   RQ3: SQL Keyword Usage Study

Fully supporting every SQL dialect was impractical due to the number that exist and the size of the language, therefore DBLModeller supports a subset of two dialects (Oracle and MySQL). Whilst it is straightforward to identify which dialects to support (many organisations report on the estimated market share), it is harder to select statements and keywords to support within these. We have re-used the 6 schemas from Sect. 3.1 and obtained 9 others, giving a sample size of 15 (listed in Table 2). The additional schemas were obtained using the same process, i.e., deploying an instance of the system then connecting to its database with MySQL Workbench or Oracle SQL Developer.

Figure 3 shows the 25 most used keywords in our schema set. None of the words which appear in the MySQL top 25 are unsupported, while only two in

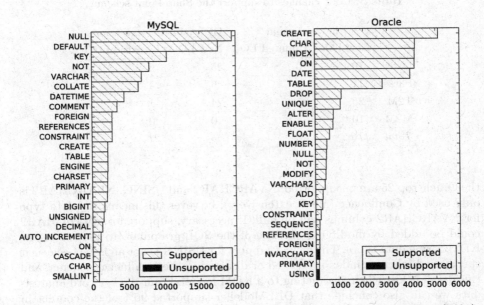

Fig. 3. Most frequent SQL keywords for the MySQL (left) and Oracle dialects (right)

Table 2. Database schemas used for keyword analysis

System	Type	Domain
Science Warehouse	Oracle	E-commerce
Record System [8]	Oracle	Record System
Apache OFBiz	Oracle & MySQL	Business Management & E-commerce
MediaWiki	Oracle & MySQL	Collaboration
Confluence	Oracle & MySQL	Collaboration
Joomla	MySQL	Website Management
Magneto	MySQL	E-commerce
SonarQube	MySQL	Software Engineering
Mantis	MySQL	Software Engineering
WordPress	MySQL	Website Management
Moodle	MySQL	Education
OrangeHRM	MySQL	Record System
SuiteCRM	MySQL	Business Management
RefBase	MySQL	Education
OpenMRS	MySQL	Record System

Table 3. Code changes to support the SharePoint schema

	G2M new grammar		DBL modeller extension	
	New LOC	Updated LOC	New LOC	Updated LOC
Lexer	70	0	25	6
Parser	11	0	6	14
T2M	25	85	24	1
M2M	10	5	0	0
Total	116	90	55	21

the Oracle top 25 are unsupported: NVARCHAR2 and USING. NVARCHAR2 is only used by Confluence (albeit extensively), however this means the data type for NVARCHAR2 columns will be null. If necessary, support for NVARCHAR2 could be added by modifying one line of the SQL grammar (to map it to the KDM:String data type). The lack of support for USING is not an issue because it specifies whether an index is enabled or disabled in the Confluence schema, and this detail is lost when abstracting to a KDM model. From the keyword analysis data we can also conclude that DBLModeller supported 96% of the content in the MySQL schemas and 99% of the content in the Oracle Schemas.

3.3   RQ4: Microsoft SQL Server Specialisation

Given the heterogeneity of schemas, databases, and SQL dialects, it is inevitable that DBLModeller may need to be extended. A case study has been performed where DBLModeller and the Gra2MoL SQL-to-KDM extraction tool [3,8] were extended to support a Microsoft SharePoint schema.

A schema dump was obtained from a Microsoft SQL Server database used by a Microsoft SharePoint 2013 instance. This instance was created specifically for the case study by installing SharePoint (the schema rather than the data is needed here, so the results are unaffected by the SharePoint instance not being live/in-use). As SharePoint uses 16 schemas the largest was selected; this contains 7 KLOC consisting of 136 tables, 5442 columns, and 61 indexes. The goal here was not to select a schema which is representative of all Microsoft SQL Server based databases, but rather to have a schema which is unsupported by both tools in equal measure.

The changes needed to DBLModeller to support the schema were determined by attempting to extract a model, then noting any errors produced. These were then fixed incrementally and the number of modified lines of code were counted. However, with Gra2MoL a new ANTLR grammar was developed to parse the schema dump. This makes it possible to compare the work required to extend a grammar against the work required to develop a new grammar.

Table 3 presents the results and shows that the extension of DBLModeller required fewer code changes. The use of our annotated T2M transformation meant that no M2M rule changes were needed. The use of a multi-dialect grammar meant it was unnecessary to write a new grammar for the Microsoft SQL dialect, instead we modified various rules in our existing grammar. However, when comparing the development time/effort in extending the two tools it is important to consider whether a new LOC represents the same effort in each. As identical technologies are used in the Gra2Mol PLSQL example and DBLModdler (ANTLR for the Lexer/Parser, and the G2M DSL for the T2M rules), the results should be comparable. Returning to RQ4, we conclude that the changes made in DBLModeller have had a positive effect on extensibility. Furthermore, the similarities between SQL dialects meant that extending the DBLModeller was a straightforward task.

4   Conclusions and Future Work

We introduced DBLModeller, a tool-supported approach for modelling the database layer of enterprise software systems. Using this we were able to extract a structure model conforming to the KDM [17] and a workload model conforming to the SMM [14]. These standardised metamodels ensured interoperability with exiting modelling and cloud migration tools [9,11]. Previous database modelling tools did not capture the properties which influence cloud migration costs, i.e., growth and query patterns. Furthermore, we decoupled the extraction of KDM and SMM based models from their use (e.g. SMM was used within CloudMIG [6] but the user is not able to access the model and other SMM models can not be used as input).

We evaluated DBLModeller using database schemas and log files from multiple real systems. Our experiments showed that DBLModeller can extract models from a wider range of systems and can be extended with less effort than the leading existing tool (Gra2MoL [8]). These key benefits were achieved by removing a model-to-model transformation from the model extraction process and by using a single multi-dialect grammar instead of using a grammar for each dialect.

In the future we plan to use DBLModeller to extract models from other live systems and to use these to simulate and optimise data migration from legacy systems into the cloud. Other potential areas of future research include analyses of the extracted models to identify design issues or anti-patterns, and to identify suitable database types for the system being modelled. Finally, we envisage that the use of annotations to avoid the need for multiple model transformations will have applications in other areas of model-driven software engineering.

Acknowledgements. This work was funded by the UK EPSRC grant EP/F501374/1. Science Warehouse Ltd granted access to their systems for evaluation purposes and provided feedback on the industrial application of DBLModeller.

References

1. P6Spy Framework. http://p6spy.github.io/p6spy
2. Alalfi, M.H., Cordy, J.R., Dean, T.R.: SQL2XMI: Reverse engineering of UML-ER diagrams from relational database schemas. In: Proceedings of the 15th Working Conference on Reverse Engineering, pp. 187–191 (2008)
3. Canovas, J.: Gra2Mol: PLSQL2ASTM example project. https://github.com/jlcanovas/gra2mol/tree/master/examples/Grammar2Model.examples.PLSQL2 ASTMModel
4. Davis, K.H., Alken, P.: Data reverse engineering: a historical survey. In: Seventh Working Conference on Reverse Engineering, pp. 70–78. IEEE (2000)
5. Díaz, O., Puente, G., Izquierdo, J.L.C., Molina, J.G.: Harvesting models from web 2.0 databases. Softw. Syst. Model. **12**(1), 15–34 (2013)
6. Frey, S., Hasselbring, W.: Model-based migration of legacy software systems into the cloud: the CloudMIG approach. Softwaretechnik-Trends **30**(2), 84–85 (2010)
7. Izquierdo, J.L.C., Molina, J.G.: A domain specific language for extracting models in software modernization. In: 5th European Conference on Model-driven Architecture Foundations and Applications (ECMDA-FA), pp. 82–97 (2009)
8. Izquierdo, J.L.C., Molina, J.G.: An architecture-driven modernization tool for calculating metrics. IEEE Softw. **27**(4), 37–43 (2010)
9. Menychtas, A., Konstanteli, K., Alonso, J., Orue-Echevarria, L., Gorroñogoitia, J., Kousiouris, G., Santzaridou, C., Bruneliere, H., Pellens, B., Stuer, P., Strauß, O., Senkova, T., Varvarigou, T.A.: Software modernization and cloudification using the ARTIST migration methodology and framework. Scalable Comput. Pract. Experience **15**(2), 131–152 (2014)
10. Mituzas, D.: Page view statistics for Wikimedia projects. http://dumps.wikimedia.org/other/pagecounts-raw
11. Mohagheghi, P., Sæther, T.: Software engineering challenges for migration to the service cloud paradigm: ongoing work in the REMICS project. In: IEEE World Congress on Services (SERVICES), pp. 507–514 (2011)
12. Mori, M., Noughi, N., Cleve, A.: Mining SQL execution traces for data manipulation behavior recovery. In: Joint Proceedings of the CAiSE 2014 Forum and CAiSE 2014 Doctoral Consortium Co-located with the 26th International Conference on Advanced Information Systems Engineering (CAiSE 2014), Thessaloniki, Greece, 18–20 June 2014, pp. 41–48 (2014)
13. Normantas, K., Vasilecas, O.: Extracting term units and fact units from existing databases using the knowledge discovery metamodel. J. Inf. Sci. **40**(4), 413–425 (2014)
14. Object Management Group: Structured Metrics Metamodel (1 2012)
15. Oracle: SQL Developer. http://www.oracle.com/technetwork/developer-tools
16. Pérez-Castillo, R., de Guzmán, I.G.R., Caivano, D., Piattini, M.: Database schema elicitation to modernize relational databases. In: 14th International Conference on Enterprise Information Systems (ICEIS 2012), pp. 126–132 (2012)
17. Pérez-Castillo, R., de Guzmán, I.G.R., Piattini, M.: Knowledge discovery Metamodel-ISO/IEC 19506: a standard to modernize legacy systems. Comput. Stan. Interfaces **33**(6), 519–532 (2011)
18. Sadovykh, A., Vigier, L., Hoffmann, A., Grossmann, J., Ritter, T., Gomez, E., Estekhin, O.: Architecture driven modernization in practice-study results. In: 14th IEEE International Conference on Engineering of Complex Computer Systems, pp. 50–57. IEEE (2009)
19. Wikimedia: Wikimedia dump index. http://dumps.wikimedia.org/backup-index.html

AUDIO ERGO SUM
A Personal Data Model for Musical Preferences

Riccardo Guidotti[1,2]($\boxtimes$), Giulio Rossetti[1,2], and Dino Pedreschi[1]

[1] KDDLab, University of Pisa, Largo B. Pontecorvo, 3, Pisa, Italy
{guidotti.riccardo,rossetti.giulio,pedreschi.dino}@di.unipi.it
[2] KDDLab, ISTI-CNR, Via G. Moruzzi, 1, Pisa, Italy
{guidotti.riccardo,rossetti.giulio}@isti.cnr.it

Abstract. Nobody can state "Rock is my favorite genre" or "David Bowie is my favorite artist". We defined a Personal Listening Data Model able to capture musical preferences through indicators and patterns, and we discovered that we are all characterized by a limited set of musical preferences, but not by a unique predilection. The empowered capacity of mobile devices and their growing adoption in our everyday life is generating an enormous increment in the production of personal data such as calls, positioning, online purchases and even music listening. Musical listening is a type of data that has started receiving more attention from the scientific community as consequence of the increasing availability of rich and punctual online data sources. Starting from the listening of 30k Last.Fm users, we show how the employment of the Personal Listening Data Models can provide higher levels of self-awareness. In addition, the proposed model will enable the development of a wide range of analysis and musical services both at personal and at collective level.

1 Introduction

The unstoppable rise of smartphones joint with their increasing ability of collecting individual information is creating a huge increment in the production of personal data. Personal information like visited locations, web-searches, purchases, phone calls and even music listening are collected and stored without any clear benefit for the user. Consequently, it is being defined the need for a personal model to manage and exploit these large amounts of data.

In the last years in the scientific community is taking place the idea of the *personal data store*. A personal data store is a personal, digital identity management service controlled by an individual where each user can choose at which level she wants to share her own data [3]. In our context, we would like that a personal data store could allow an individual not only the data storage and management, but also the automatic extraction of systematic behaviors and the providing of proactive suggestions on the basis of the user's profile [7].

Since music is a pervasive dimension of our life, and due to the abundance of online data sources like Spotify, iTunes and Last.Fm, we propose a *Personal*

© Springer International Publishing AG 2016
P. Milazzo et al. (Eds.): STAF 2016, LNCS 9946, pp. 51–66, 2016.
DOI: 10.1007/978-3-319-50230-4_5

Listening Data Model (*PLDM*) able to capture the characteristics and the systematic patterns which are present in our musical listening behavior. The PLDM is built on a set of personal listening represented by an abstract data type taken as input. A listening is formed by the song listened, the artist of the song, the album, the genre and the listening time-stamp.

A crucial component of the PLDM are the *indicators* extracted from the listening features. They summarize the listener and explain her level of repetitiveness in the listening. Moreover, in the PLDM we define some listening *patterns* coming from the listening *frequencies*. These patterns are the top listened genre, artist, album etc. and the most representative preferences. In addition, the PLDM contains the frequent listening *sequences*. Those are the typical repetitions followed by the user during a listening session. In short, the proposed data model is an instance of the personal data store specialized for listening data and equipped to provide an improved level of self-awareness.

We employed the PLDM to study Last.Fm users. Last.Fm is an online platform, where people can listen music, share their own musical tastes and discover new artists and genres on the bases of what they, or their friends, like. We retrieved the last 200 listening of about 30k users resident in the UK. We calculated the PLDM for each user given their listening. The obtained PLDMs allowed us to estimate how the Last.Fm audience is segmented in terms of repetitiveness in their listening. There are some well defined classes: listeners systematic with respect to the listening day or time hour, listeners which are predictable with respect to the artists or with respect to the genre, and also "random" listeners. Another finding is that the musical profile of each user is best outlined using a limited set of distinct musical preferences, but not by a unique liking. Furthermore, we explain how the PLDM can enable the development of a broad range of musical analysis and services both at personal and at collective level.

The paper is organized as follows. Section 2 surveys the works related to personal data model and Last.Fm. Section 3 describes our model for analyzing musical listening. In Sect. 4 are presented the analysis of the PLDM applied to Last.Fm users, while Sect. 5 provides an outline of different possible applications. Finally, Sect. 6 summarizes conclusion and future works.

2   Related Work

The need to handle individual data is leading to the development of personal models able to deal with and summarize human behavior. These data models can be generic or specific with respect to the type of data. In [3] is described *openPDS*, a personal metadata management framework that allows individuals to collect, store, and give fine grained access to their metadata to third parties. openPDS is oriented to the protection of the metadata shared and on the privacy of the data contained in the system. Similarly, in [9] the authors analyzed a new personal data ecosystem centered around the role of *Bank of Individuals Data*, i.e. a provider of personal data management services enabling people to exploit their personal data. In [16] the authors presented *My Data Store*, a tool allowing people to control and share their personal data. A test with a small set of real users showed improvement over the users' awareness of their personal data and the perceived usefulness of the tool. My Data Store has been integrated in [15] into a framework that permits the development of trusted and transparent services and apps whose behavior can be controlled by the user, allowing the growth of an eco-system of personal data-based services. Finally, the proposal described in [1] is that each user can select which applications have to be run on which data, facilitating in this way diversified services on a personal server. In such a way, the personal server would contain all the user's favorite applications and all the user's data that are currently distributed, fragmented, and isolated.

The majority of the works in the literature [1,3,9] focus their attention on the architecture of the personal data store and on how to treat data sharing and privacy issues. Hence, the main difference between the personal data model proposed and those present in the literature is that our focus is to obtain an added value from the personal data through the application of data mining techniques. Indeed, we aim to apply the methodological framework proposed in [7] for mobility data to analyze personal musical preferences. The authors proposed a framework for personal mobility data able to automatically perform individual data mining and to provide proactive suggestions for supporting decisions. An application of this approach in mobility data can be found in the *MyWay* system [14]. MyWay is a predictive system based on individual mobility profiles which exploits systematic behaviors models to predict human movements.

To the best of our knowledge this work is the first attempt to define a data model able to capture human listening behavior. We believe that the treatment of musical listening is becoming valuable because in the last decade the music world has started receiving more attention from the scientific community. Last.Fm offers a privileged playground to study different phenomena related to the online music consumption. Hence, by following the example of some recent works, we decided to test our personal data model on this dataset. In [11] the authors measured different dimensions of social prominence on a social graph built upon 70k Last.Fm users whose listening were observed for 2 years. By analyzing the *width*, the *depth*, and the *strength* of local diffusion trees, the authors were able to identify patterns related to individual music genres. In [10] the authors formally defined the effect of social influence providing new models and evaluation measures for real-time recommendations with very strong temporal aspects. The authors of [12] analyzed the cross-cultural gender differences in the adoption and usage of Last.Fm: *(i)* men listen to more pieces of music than women, *(ii)* women focus on fewer musical genres and fewer tracks than men. Finally, in [2] the authors studied the topology of the Last.Fm social graph asking for similarities in taste as well as on demographic attributes and local network structure. Their results suggest that users connect to "online" friends, but also indicate the presence of strong "real-life" friendship ties identifiable by the multiple co-attendance to the same concerts.

3   Personal Listening Data Model

In this section we formally describe the *Personal Listening Data Model*. By applying the following definitions and functions it is possible to build for each user a listening profile giving a picture of her habits in term of listening.

Definition 1 (Listening). *Given a user u, we define $L_u = \{\langle time\text{-}stamp, song,$ artist, album, genre$\rangle\}$ as the set of listening performed by u.*

Since a song can belong to more than a genre and can be played by more than an artist, each listening l (see Fig. 1) is an abstraction of a real listening. However, we can assume this abstraction without losing in generality.

Fig. 1. A listening $l = \{\langle time\text{-}stamp, song, artist, album, genre\rangle\}$ is a tuple formed by the *time-stamp* indicating when the listening occurred, the *song* listened, the *artist* which sings the song, the *album* the song belongs to, and the *genre* of the artist.

From the set of listening L_u, for each user we can extract the set of songs S_u, artists A_u, albums B_u and genres G_u. Their sizes ($|\cdot|$) are valuable *indicators*.

- $S_u = \{song | \langle \cdot, song, \cdot, \cdot, \cdot \rangle \in L_u\}$
- $A_u = \{artist | \langle \cdot, \cdot, artist, \cdot, \cdot \rangle \in L_u\}$
- $B_u = \{album | \langle \cdot, \cdot, \cdot, album, \cdot \rangle \in L_u\}$
- $G_u = \{genre | \langle \cdot, \cdot, \cdot, \cdot, genre \rangle \in L_u\}$

The user behavior can be summarized through frequency dictionaries indicating the support (i.e. relative number of occurrences) of the listening features.

Definition 2 (Support). *The support function returns the frequency dictionary as a set of couples (item, support) where the support of an item is obtained as the number of occurring items on the number of listening.*

$$sup(X, L) = \{(x, y) | y = |Y|/|L| \wedge x \in X \wedge Y \subseteq L s.t. \forall l \in Y, x \in l\} \qquad (1)$$

We define the following frequency dictionaries: $s_u = sup(S_u, L_u)$, $a_u = sup(A_u, L_u)$, $b_u = sup(B_u, L_u)$, $g_u = sup(G_u, L_u)$, $d_u = sup(D, L_u)$ and $t_u = sup(T, L_u)$ where $D = \{mon, tue, wed, thu, fri, sat, sun\}$ contains the days of weeks, and $T = \{(2-8], (8-12], (12-15], (15-18], (18-22], (22-2]\}$ contains the time slots of the day.

These dictionaries can be exploited to extract indicators and patterns.

Definition 3 (Entropy). *Given dictionary $X = \{(x_1, y_1), \ldots, (x_n, y_n)\}$, the entropy function returns the normalized entropy defined as*

$$entropy(X) = \frac{-\sum_{i=1}^{n} P(y_i) \log_2 P(y_i)}{\log_2 n} \quad \in [0, 1] \qquad (2)$$

Fig. 2. The raw listening of a user L_u can be turn into a Personal Listening Data Store P_u extracting the songs S_u, artists A_u, albums B_u and genres G_u and by applying to them the functions sup, top, $repr$, $entropy$, $getseq$ and $freqseq$.

The entropy tends to 0 when the user behavior is systematic, tends to 1 when the behavior is not predictable. These indicators are similar to those related with shopping behavior described in [5]. We define the entropy for songs, artists, albums, genres, days and time-slots as $e_{s_u} = entropy(s_u)$, $e_{a_u} = entropy(a_u)$, $e_{b_u} = entropy(b_u)$, $e_{g_u} = entropy(g_u)$, $e_{d_u} = entropy(d_u)$ and $e_{t_u} = entropy(t_u)$.

The simplest pattern we consider is the most listened song, artist, genre, etc.

Definition 4 (Top). *Given dictionary* $X = \{(x_1, y_1), \ldots, (x_n, y_n)\}$, *the* top *function returns the most supported item. It is defined as:*

$$top(X) = \underset{(x,y) \in X}{argmax}(y) \tag{3}$$

We define the most listened songs, artists, albums and genres as $\hat{s}_u = top(s_u)$, $\hat{a}_u = top(a_u)$, $\hat{b}_u = top(b_u)$ and $\hat{g}_u = top(g_u)$, respectively.

Moreover, we want to consider for each user the set of most representative, i.e. significantly most listened, subsets of artists, albums and genres.

Definition 5 (Repr). *Given dictionary* $X = \{(x_1, y_1), \ldots, (x_n, y_n)\}$, *the* repr *function returns the most representative supported items. It is defined as:*

$$repr(X) = \underset{(x,y) \in X}{knee}(y) = \underset{(x,y) \in X^*, y' \in X'}{argmax}(|y - y'|) \tag{4}$$

where X^* *is* X *sorted with respect to the supports* y, $X' = \{y' | y' = mx' + n\}$ *with* $m = (max(sup(X)) - min(sup(X)))/|X|$ *and* $n = min(sup(X))$.

The method $repr(X)$ returns a set of preferences with a support higher than the support of most of the other listening. For example if $g_u = \{(rock, 0.4), (pop, 0.3), (folk, 0.1), (classic, 0.1), (house, 0.1)\}$, $repr(g_u)$ returns $\{(rock, 0.4), (pop, 0.3)\}$.

This result is achieved by employing the *knee* method [13]. Given a dictionary X, the *knee* method sorts the pairs (x_i, y_i) according to the supports generating X^*. Then, it selects the point x_k^* on the support curve X^* which has the maximum distance $|y_k^* - y_k'|$ with the correspondent point x_k' in X', where X' is the straight line passing through the minimum and the maximum point of the curve described by X^*. In this way the *knee* x_k^* is different for each user because it is driven by personal data. Finally, the method returns the pairs with a support greater or equal than the support y_k of the knee x_k. We define the most representative songs, artists, albums and genres as $\tilde{s}_u = repr(s_u)$, $\tilde{a}_u = repr(a_u)$,

$\tilde{b}_u = repr(b_u)$ and $\tilde{g}_u = repr(g_u)$, respectively. Obviously we have $\hat{g}_u \subseteq \tilde{g}_u \subseteq g_u$ that holds also for songs, albums and artists.

Finally, we want to define the frequent sequences of listening to capture the typical sequences of the listeners. Given the set of listening L_u we can extract for each day a sequence with respect to a certain feature.

Definition 6 (Listening Sequence). *We define a* listening sequence *$seq = [i_1, \ldots, i_n]$ as a list built by concatenating the items of the listening L in a given time window τ, ordered by time-stamp and describing a feature of the listening.*

The function $getseq(X, L) = Seq_u = \{seq_1, \ldots, seq_m\}$ orders the listening by time-stamp, divide them in sequences and returns a set of ordered items describing a certain feature, i.e. songs, albums, genres, artists. We name them $Seq_u^S = getseq(S_u, L)$, $Seq_u^A = getseq(A_u, L)$, $Seq_u^B = getseq(B_u, L)$, $Seq_u^G = getseq(G_u, L)$ respectively for songs, artists, albums and genres.

In order to extract the frequent pattern sequences we define the function.

Definition 7 (FreqSeq). *The* freqseq *function returns the closed [13] most frequent sequences with at least minsup occurrences. It is defined as*

$$F = freqseq(Seq_u, minsup) \tag{5}$$

where $F = \{(seq_1, sup_1), \ldots, (seq_n, sup_n)\}$ is a set containing the frequent sub-sequences and their support, seq_i is a sub-sequence properly contained or equals to one of the sequences in Seq_u, $sup_i \geq minsup$ is its support and minsup is the minimum support, for $1 \leq i \leq n$.

By employing the previous functions on L_u, we can obtain for each user the set of frequent sequences $F_{S_u} = freqseq(Seq_u^S, minsup)$, $F_{A_u} = freqseq(Seq_u^A, minsup)$, $F_{B_u} = freqseq(Seq_u^B, minsup)$ and $F_{G_u} = freqseq(Seq_u^G, minsup)$.

By applying the definitions and the functions described above on the user listening L_u we can turn the raw listening data of a user into a complex personal data structure (see Fig. 2) that we call *Personal Listening Data Model* (PLDM). The PLDM characterizes the listening behavior of a user by means of its *indicators, frequencies* and *patterns* (see Fig. 3).

Definition 8 (Personal Listening Data Model). *Given the listening L_u of a user u we define the user* personal listening data model *as*

$$
\begin{aligned}
P_u = \langle |L_u|, |S_u|, |A_u|, |B_u|, |G_u|, \quad & e_{s_u}, e_{a_u}, e_{b_u}, e_{g_u}, e_{d_u}, e_{t_u}, \quad && indicators \\
s_u, a_u, b_u, g_u, d_u, t_u, \quad & && frequencies \\
\hat{s}_u, \hat{a}_u, \hat{b}_u, \hat{g}_u, \quad \tilde{s}_u, \tilde{a}_u, \tilde{b}_u, \tilde{g}_u, \quad & F_{S_u}, F_{A_u}, F_{B_u}, F_{G_u} \rangle \quad && patterns
\end{aligned}
$$

Fig. 3. The PLDM is formed by *indicators* ($|L_u|$, $|S_u|$, $|A_u|$, $|B_u|$, $|G_u|$, and entropy values), by *frequencies* (the support dictionaries) and by *patterns* (most listened preference, most representative preferences and frequent sequences).

It is worth to notice that according to the procedures in [6;8], the PLDM can be extracted through a parameter free approach. The only parameter is *minsup*, but we set *minsup* = 3 to capture all the meaningful frequent subsequence: *minsup* = 1 is useless, *minsup* = 2 is too low because there may by a repetition just by chance.

4   LastFM Case Study

In this section we show the benefits derivable from the application of the PLDMs on the data extracted from a famous music website called Last.Fm. In particular, we will show that the information which is generally reported on the main page of many social network or web services (like the most listened song, artist or genre in Last.Fm) are not good enough to represent the user's preferences. Conversely, a structured data model describing the user behavior like the PLDM can achieve this goal, also providing to the user personal access to her data.

Last.Fm is an online social network, where people can share their own music tastes and discover new artists and genres on the bases on what they, or their friends, like. Each user produces data about her own listening. Through each listening a user expresses a preference for a song, artist, album, genre and take place in a certain time. Using Last.Fm APIs[1] we retrieved the last 200 listening of about 30,000 users U resident in the UK. Given the listening L_u, we calculated the PLDM P_u for each user $u \in U$.

4.1   Data Models Analysis

The first analysis we report is related to the *indicators* of the PLDMs $\{P_u\}$ extracted. In Fig. 4 are reported the distributions of the number of users which have listened a certain number of songs $|S_u|$, artists $|A_u|$, albums $|B_u|$ and genres $|G_u|$. The first distribution is right-skewed, i.e. most of the users have listened about 140 songs. This implies that some tracks have been listened more than once. On the other hand, the other distributions are left-skewed: a typical user listens about 60 artists, 70 albums and 10 genres.

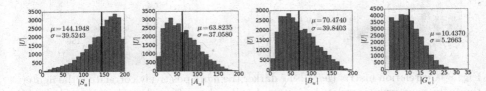

Fig. 4. Distributions of the number of songs $|S_u|$, artists $|A_u|$, albums $|B_u|$ and genres $|G_u|$ respectively. The black vertical lines highlight the means.

---

[1] http://www.last.fm/api/, retrieval date 2016-04-04.

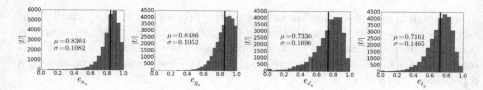

Fig. 5. Distributions of entropy for artists e_{a_u}, genre e_{g_u}, day of week e_{d_u} and time of day e_{t_u} respectively. The black vertical lines highlight the means.

Figure 5 depicts the distributions of the entropy[2]. It emerges that users are much more systematic with respect to the listening time (day of week and time of the day) than with respect to what they listen. This behavior is in opposition to what happens in shopping [5]. Since the artist and genre entropy are right-skewed, it seems that most of the users are not very predictable with respect to the genre or to the artist. This is a first clue that is very unlikely that exists a unique prevalence towards a unique artist or genre.

Figure 6 (left) shows the heat-map of the correlations among the indicators. Some of them like $|A_u|$, $|B_u|$ and $|G_u|$ are highly correlated[3] ($cor(|A_u|, |B_u|) = 0.86$, $cor(|G_u|, |B_u|) = 0.64$): the higher the number of artists or genres, the higher the number of albums listened. Other interesting correlations are $cor(|B_u|, e_{g_u}) = -0.33$ and $cor(|B_u|, e_{a_u}) = 0.55$. Their density scatter plots are reported in Fig. 6 (center, right). They tell us that the higher the number of albums listened, the lower the variability with respect to the genre and the higher the variability with respect to the artists. From this result we understand that a user listening to many different albums narrows its musical preferences toward a restricted set of genres, and that it explores these genres by listening various artists of this genre and not having a clear preference among these artists.

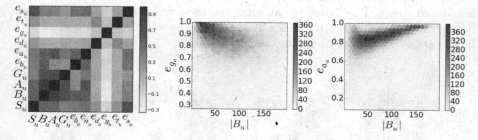

Fig. 6. Correlation matrix (left)): the darker the more positively correlated, the lighter the more negatively correlated. Scatter density plots of number of albums $|B_u|$ and genre entropy e_{g_u} (center) and number of albums $|B_u|$ and artists entropy e_{a_u} (right).

---

[2] Not all of them are reported due to lack of space.

[3] The *p-value* is zero (or smaller than 0.000001) for all the correlations reported.

4.2 Segmentation Analysis

The second analysis we propose investigate the existence of different groups of listeners with respect to their *indicators* in the PLDMs $\{P_u\}$. We applied the clustering algorithm K-Means [13] by varying the number of clusters $k \in [2, 30]$. By observing the trend of the sum of squared error [4] we decided to select 5 as the number of clusters. In Fig. 7 are described the radar charts representing the centroids while in Table 1 are reported the value of the centroids and the size of the clusters.

Table 1. Centroids for the entropy and size of the clusters extracted.

	e_{t_u}	e_{d_u}	e_{s_u}	e_{a_u}	e_{b_u}	e_{g_u}	size
A	0.8067	0.8442	0.9744	0.8591	0.8794	0.8461	0.44
B	0.7092	0.7234	0.9305	0.7001	0.6732	0.8862	0.13
C	0.4672	0.3366	0.9254	0.7438	0.7717	0.8751	0.06
D	0.5568	0.7687	0.9748	0.8666	0.8855	0.8383	0.19
E	0.7484	0.5624	0.9775	0.8739	0.8918	0.8306	0.19

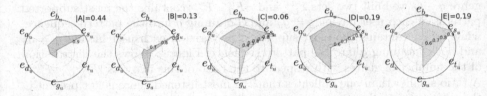

Fig. 7. Radar charts for the centroids of the clusters extracted on the PMDLs.

The most populated cluster is A. It contains the majority of the listeners. It seems that these listeners use the web service without a specific listening schema and that with a high probability they reproduce the tracks using the random function. However, a peculiarity of these users, is that they are more repetitive than users in the other clusters with respect to the genres.

In opposition with A, users in clusters B and C do not have a set of genres which is clearly preferred on top of the others, but they are the most systematic users in terms of albums and artists listened. This means that they like a concise set of artists regardless of their genre and they keep listening only them. The main difference between these two clusters is that users of cluster B are the most systematic in terms of albums and artists, while those of clusters C are the most regular with respect to the use of Last.Fm in specific days and time slots.

Finally, users in clusters D and E are similar to those in cluster A with respect to the level of repetitiveness of listening of genres, artists and albums. On the other hand, how is highlighted by the last two radars in Fig. 7, they are complementary with respect to the day of the week and to time of listening.

Users in cluster D do not have a specific day of the week but use the service constantly at the same time (e.g. during gym session or during specific working areas). Conversely, users in cluster E do not have a specific time slot but use the service periodically in specific days of the week (e.g. during the weekend).

We can conclude that exists a clear distinction among different groups of listeners. From the clustering information originated from the PLDM, a user could learn that is focusing too much on a certain genre or on certain artists and that is not exploring what is outside her "musical confidence zone".

4.3   Sequences Analysis

In this section we make use of the frequent sequences to give a first proof that the most listened genre is not a good candidate to be representative for the user preferences. We remark that a frequent sequence is, for example, a concatenation of genres listened many times in a specific order.

We report in Table 2 the ten most listened genres and artists with the users support, i.e. the percentage of users having that genre or artist as $\hat{g_u}$ or $\hat{a_u}$. To analyze the frequent sequences, for each PLDMs $\{P_u\}$ we considered the most listened genres $\{\hat{g_u}\}$ and the most supported patterns in the genre frequent sequences $\{F_{G_u}\}$ (i.e. the pattern with the highest support). Then, for each genre $g \in G$ we built two sets $F_{G_u}^{\hat{g_u}}$ and $\neg F_{G_u}^{\hat{g_u}}$. $F_{G_u}^{\hat{g_u}}$ contains the most supported patterns of each user having $g = \hat{g_u}$ and containing g into the pattern sequence, while $\neg F_{G_u}^{\hat{g_u}}$ contains the most supported patterns of each user having $g = \hat{g_u}$ and not containing g into the pattern sequence. Figure 8 shows the distribution of the number of genres with respect to the ratio of this two sets $|F_{G_u}^{\hat{g_u}}|/|\neg F_{G_u}^{\hat{g_u}}|$. A ratio smaller than one indicates that the most listened genre is not present in the most supported patterns, vice-versa a ratio greater than one means that the most listened genre is present in the most supported patterns. The higher the ratio the more present is $\hat{g_u}$ in the most supported pattern in F_{G_u}.

Table 2. Ten of most listened genres and artists considering $\{\hat{g_u}\}$ and $\{\hat{a_u}\}$.

	Genre	sup %	Artist	sup %
1	Rock	53.86	The Beatles	0.75
2	Pop	19.64	David Bowie	0.72
3	Hip Hop	5.05	Kanye West	0.56
4	Electronic	2.21	Arctic Monkeys	0.54
5	Folk	2.03	Rihanna	0.51
6	Punk	1.74	Lady Gaga	0.48
7	Indie Rock	1.65	Taylor Swift	0.47
8	Dubstep	0.90	Radiohead	0.43
9	House	0.85	Muse	0.38
10	Metal	0.84	Daft Punk	0.37

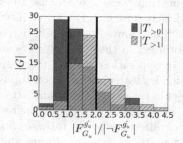

Fig. 8. Distribution of $|G|$ with respect to the ratio of $|F_{G_u}^{\hat{g_u}}|/|\neg F_{G_u}^{\hat{g_u}}|$.

What emerges is that when we consider patterns which have at least two different genres in a sequence (e.g. rock, pop) (labeled with $|T_{>1}|$ in Fig. 8), then for most of the genres the ratio is greater than 1.5. On the other hand, if we consider patterns without any constraint in the number of different genres in a sequence (e.g. rock, rock, rock) (labeled with $|T_{>0}|$ in Fig. 8), than we have that the mode of the distribution is lower than 1.

This result implies that if we consider any kind of sequence, than the most listened genre is among the genres in these patterns but it becomes a significant genre only when patterns with more than a genre are considered. This means that the most listened genre is frequently listened together with other genres.

4.4 Frequency Analysis

In this section we exploit the knowledge of the frequency vectors to demonstrate that the most listened genre, album and artist considered alone do not represent properly the preferences of the users. To this aim we look at the frequency vectors a_u, g_u, the top listened $\hat{a_u}$, $\hat{g_u}$, and the most representative $\tilde{a_u}$, $\tilde{g_u}$. To simplify the following discussion we will refer to the sets $\tilde{a_u}$ and $\tilde{g_u}$ equivalently as $\tilde{x}$ and to the artists and genres contained in such sets as *preferences*.

In Fig. 9 is depicted the result of this analysis for genre (top row) and artist (bottom row)[4]. The first column shows the distribution of the number of users with respect to the number of representative genres $|\tilde{g_u}|$ and artists $|\tilde{a_u}|$. In both cases the smallest value is larger than 1 indicating that each user has more than a preference. On the other hand, a large part of all the genres and artists listened

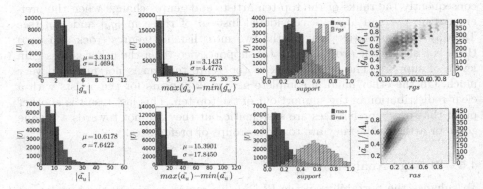

Fig. 9. Frequencies analysis for genre (top row) and artist (bottom row). *First column*: distribution of number of users w.r.t the number of representative preferences. *Second column*: distribution of number of users w.r.t the maximum difference in frequencies between the listening preference. *Third column*: distribution of number of users w.r.t the support given by the representative preferences. *Last column*: density scatter plot between the representative preferences support and the ratio of their number on the number of all the possible artists or genres.

---

[4] Similar results are obtained for album but they are not reported due to lack of space.

are removed when passing from x to $\tilde{x}$. Indeed, the mean for the genres decreases from 10 to 3, the mean for the artist diminishes from 60 to 10.

The second column in Fig. 9 illustrates the distribution of the number of users with respect to the maximum difference in frequencies between the listening preference obtained as $max(\tilde{x}) - min(\tilde{x})$. Both for genres and artists the mode of this value is close to zero. This proofs that the highest preferences are similar in terms of listening for the majority of the users.

The third column shows the distributions of the users with respect to the most listened artist support, mas, and most listened genre support, mgs, defined as:

$$mas = v \text{ s.t. } (a, v) = \hat{a}_u, \; mgs = v \text{ s.t. } (g, v) = \hat{g}_u$$

and the representative artist support, ras, and representative genre support, rgs, defined as:

$$ras = sum(v|(a, v) \in \tilde{a}_u), \; rgs = sum(v|(g, v) \in \tilde{g}_u)$$

From these distributions is evident the increase of the support when not only the top but also all the representative preferences are considered.

The last column reports a density scatter plot of the representative preferences support (rgs and ras) and the ratio of their size on the size of A_u and G_u, i.e. $|\tilde{a}_u|/|A_u|$ and $|\tilde{g}_u|/|G_u|$ respectively. Since the higher concentration of points tends to be $\sim$0.2 with respect to the x-axis and $\sim$0.5 with respect to the y-axis, we have that for most of the users it is sufficient a limited number of preferences (but more than one) to reach a very high level of support. This concludes that each user can be described by few preferences that highly characterize her.

Finally, it is interesting to observe how the total support of the users and consequently the ranks of the top ten artists and genres change when the preferences in $|\tilde{g}_u|$ and $|\tilde{a}_u|$ are considered instead of those in $|\hat{g}_u|$ and $|\hat{a}_u|$ (see Table 3). We can notice how for the two most listened genres (rock and pop) there is a significant drop in the total support, vice-versa the other genres gain levels of support. The overall rank in the genre top ten is not modified very much. On the other hand, a complete new rank appears for the artists with a clear redistribution of the support out of the top ten. This last result is another proof that user's preferences are systematic but they are not towards a unique genre or artist, while they are towards groups of preferences.

4.5   Storage Analysis

To enhance the portability of the PLDM, we report in Fig. 10 the boxplots of the storage occupancy of the data model PLDMs (left) and for the raw listening (right). The storage required by the data model is typically one third of the storage required by the raw data. Moreover, the storage space of the data model will not grow very much when storing more listening because the number of possible genres, artists, albums, songs is limited, while the number of listening grows continuously. Thus, an average storage of 0.01 Mb together with a computational time of max 5 sec per user, guarantees that the PLDM could be calculated and stored individually without the need of a central service.

Table 3. Top ten of the most listened genres and artists considering $\{\tilde{g}_u\}$ and $\{\tilde{a}_u\}$.

	Genre	sup %	Artist	sup %
1	Rock	13.41	David Bowie	0.29
2	Pop	9.73	Arctic Monkeys	0.26
3	Hip Hop	5.16	Radiohead	0.24
4	Indie Rock	4.39	Rihanna	0.24
5	Folk	4.31	Coldplay	0.23
6	Electronic	4.26	The Beatles	0.22
7	Punk	4.07	Kanye West	0.21
8	House	2.63	Muse	0.19
9	R&B	2.53	Florence	0.19
10	Emo	2.11	Lady Gaga	0.19

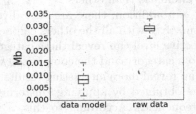

Fig. 10. Data storage for the data model *(left)* and for the raw data *(right)*.

5 Applications

The PLDM described can be easily applied for many purposes and for a wide range of tasks. In this section we will try to structure some application proposals. A first diversification can be made with respect to the main purpose: *analysis* and *services*. Another categorization can be made with respect to the type of data required: *individual* and *collective*. Before going forward it is worth to notice that the computation needed to calculate the PLDM is very small and each user could potentially have it calculated on her own personal device without requiring an external service. Consequently, privacy issues in real applications can be treated by adopting the frameworks in [3,15]: the PLDM only belongs to the user that can decide if she wants or not to disclose it (or part of it) to other users.

The simplest example of *individual analysis* is the user *self-awareness*. Through a smart visualization of the features of the PLDM the user can obtain an unexpected new level of consciousness of her listening behavior. For example a user could discover that is listening a great variety of artists but that they all belong to the same genre and that she always listens to them following the same pattern of songs. A possible reaction could be starting a new listening with an unknown artist belonging to a different genre to enlarge her musical knowledge, possibly discovering new musical preferences. Moreover, due to the continuously growing size of the personal raw listening dataset, the PLDM can be recalculated in different time windows so that the user can observe changes and/or stability in the listening profile.

Nevertheless, sometimes only the self-awareness is not sufficient to realize *who we are* if we do not compare ourselves with the others (*collective analysis*). Thus, if a portion of users agrees to share some features of the PLDM it becomes possible to understand how much we differ from the mass and *where we are* positioned with respect to the others. For example we could discover that our most representative genres are the same of the mass but that we are much more systematic than others.

In addition, there are very diversified categories of listeners and comparing ourselves with all the others can be not meaningful. Users segmentation at a collective level can reveal these categories. Then the knowledge of the membership to a category and the comparison with the users belonging to the same category can reveal more interesting results. As shown in Sect. 4.2, user segmentation can be obtained by applying clustering techniques on the indicators, patterns and frequencies. According to this, a third party *collective service* provider could exploit shared PLDM to offer recommendations services for artists, song, genre etc. Furthermore, different types of recommendations could be provided according to the type of user in the diffusion process [11] and considering if a user is good in discovery novel successful songs.

Finally, each user can make use of the PLDM for *individual services*. Some examples are the creation of personal play-lists coming from the prediction of the desire of the user for a certain genre or artist, and the automatic reproduction in certain days and time of the day. According to the personal data store framework these individual services can be integrated and extended with collective knowledge bringing to the user an upgraded level of services.

6   Conclusion

The endless growing of individual data is requiring efficient models able to store information and tools for automatically transforming this knowledge into a personal benefit. In this paper we have presented the Personal Listening Data Model (PLDM). The PLDM is designed to deal with musical preferences and can be employed for many applications. It is formed by *indicators* of the musical behavior, listening *patterns* and vectors containing the listening *frequencies*. By employing the PLDM on a set of 30k Last.Fm users we proved the potentialities of this model. We have shown how the indicators of PLDM can be exploited to produce a users segmentation able to discriminate between different groups of listeners. Moreover, the patterns and frequency vectors of the PLDM have been used to prove that information like the most listened genre or artist are not enough to represent the musical preferences of a user. Finally, we have proposed a wide set of applications of the PLDMs at individual and collective level both for analytic purposes and for the development of novel services.

In the future, it would be interesting to consider in the Last.Fm PLDM also the friendship dimension in order to estimate and evaluate the level of homophily of each user with respect to different listening and musical aspects. In addition, we would like to implement a real web service where a user can provide her Last.Fm username and a personal dashboard exploiting all the features contained in the PLDM is shown. The dashboard would allow self-awareness and self-comparison with other users, with similar users or with the user's friends. In this way a user could enlarge her musical experience, try novel tracks and increase her musical education because knowledge comes from listening.

Acknowledgements. This work was partially supported by the European Communitys H2020 Program under the funding scheme "INFRAIA-1-2014-2015: Research Infrastructures" grant agreement 654024 *"SoBigData: Social Mining & Big Data Ecosystem"*, http://www.sobigdata.eu, and under the founding scheme "FETPROACT-1-2014: Global Systems Science (GSS)", grant agreement 641191 *"CIMPLEX Bringing CItizens, Models and Data together in Participatory, Interactive SociaL EXploratories"*, https://www.cimplex-project.eu.

References

1. Abiteboul, S., André, B., Kaplan, D.: Managing your digital life. Commun. ACM **58**(5), 32–35 (2015)
2. Bischoff, K.: We love rock 'n' roll: analyzing and predicting friendship links in last.fm. In: Web Science 2012, WebSci 2012, Evanston, IL, USA. 22–24 June 2012, pp. 47–56 (2012)
3. de Montjoye, Y.-A., Shmueli, E., Wang, S.S., Pentland, A.S.: openPDS: protecting the privacy of metadata through safeanswers. PloS one **9**(7), e98790 (2014)
4. Draper, N.R., Smith, H., Pownell, E.: Applied Regression Analysis, vol. 3. Wiley, New York (1966)
5. Guidotti, R., Coscia, M., Pedreschi, D., Pennacchioli, D.: Behavioral entropy and profitability in retail. In: IEEE International Conference on Data Science and Advanced Analytics (DSAA), pp. 1–10. IEEE (2015). 36678 2015
6. Guidotti, R., Trasarti, R., Nanni, M., Tosca: two-steps clustering algorithm for personal locations detection. In: 23rd International Conference on Advances in Geographic Information Systems (ACM SIGSPATIAL 2015). ACM (2015)
7. Guidotti, R., Trasarti, R., Nanni, M.: Towards user-centric data management: individual mobility analytics for collective services. In: MobiGIS Workshop Co-located with ACM SIGSPATIAL 2015. ACM (2015)
8. Keogh, E., Lonardi, S., Ratanamahatana, C.A.: Towards parameter-free data mining. In: Proceedings of the Tenth ACM SIGKDD International Conference on Knowledge Discovery and Data Mining, pp. 206–215. ACM (2004)
9. Moiso, C., Minerva, R.: Towards a user-centric personal data ecosystem the role of the bank of individuals' data. In: 2012 16th International Conference on Intelligence in Next Generation Networks (ICIN), pp. 202–209. IEEE (2012)
10. Pálovics, R., Benczúr, A.A.: Temporal influence over the last.fm social network. Social Netw. Anal. Mining **5**(1), 4:1–4:12 (2015)
11. Pennacchioli, D., Rossetti, G., Pappalardo, L., Pedreschi, D., Giannotti, F., Coscia, M.: The three dimensions of social prominence. In: Jatowt, A., et al. (eds.) SocInfo 2013. LNCS, vol. 8238, pp. 319–332. Springer, Heidelberg (2013)
12. Putzke, J., Fischbach, K., Schoder, D., Gloor, P.A.: Cross-cultural gender differences in the adoption and usage of social media platforms - an exploratory study of last.fm. Comput. Netw. **75**, 519–530 (2014)
13. Tan, P.-N., Steinbach, M., Kumar, V., et al.: Introduction to Data Mining, vol. 1. Pearson Addison Wesley, Boston (2006)
14. Trasarti, R., Guidotti, R., Monreale, A., Giannotti, F.: Myway: Location prediction via mobility profiling. Inf. Syst. (2015)

15. Vescovi, M., Moiso, C., Pasolli, M., Cordin, L., Antonelli, F.: Trust management IX. In: Damsgaard Jensen, C., Marsh, S., Dimitrakos, T., Murayama, Y. (eds.) IFIPTM 2015. IAICT, vol. 454. Springer, Heidelberg (2015)
16. Vescovi, M., Perentis, C., Leonardi, C., Lepri, B., Moiso, C.: My data store: toward user awareness and control on personal data. In: Proceedings of the 2014 ACM International Joint Conference on Pervasive and Ubiquitous Computing: Adjunct Publication, pp. 179–182. ACM (2014)

A High-Level Model Checking Language with Compile-Time Pruning of Local Variables

Giovanni Pardini and Paolo Milazzo[✉]

Dipartimento di Informatica, Università di Pisa,
Largo B. Pontecorvo, 3, 56127 Pisa, Italy
{pardinig,milazzo}@di.unipi.it

Abstract. Among Model Checking tools, the behaviour of a system is often formalized as a transition system with atomic propositions associated with states (*Kripke structure*). In current modelling languages, transitions are usually specified as updates of the system's variables to be performed when certain conditions are satisfied. However, such a low-level representation makes the description of complex transformations difficult, in particular in the presence of structured data.

We present a high-level language with imperative semantics for modelling finite-state systems. The language features are selected with the aim of enabling the translation of models into compact transition systems, amenable to efficient verification via Model Checking. To this end, we have developed a compiler of our high-level language into the modelling language of the PRISM probabilistic model checker.

One of the main characteristics of the language is that it makes a very different treatment of global and local variables. It is assumed that global variables are actually the variables that describe the state of the modelled system, whereas local variables are only used to ease the specification of the systems internal mechanisms. In this paper we describe the procedure for the pruning of local variables that is executed at compile time.

1 Introduction

Expressing the model of a system in order to analyze it by means of model checking can require time. Modelling in itself is often a challenging task, since it requires (i) understanding the mechanisms that govern the dynamics of the system, (ii) performing suitable abstractions that allow such mechanisms to be expressed in a concise way, and (iii) constructing an unambiguous representation of the system mechanisms at the chosen abstraction level, by exploiting a notation that usually depends on the analysis method one wants to apply.

In the case of model analysis by means of model checking, the system dynamics has usually to be formalized as a transition system. Often, such a transition system has the form of a *Kripke structure*, namely it has atomic propositions associated with states, which are used as the basis for the specification of properties to be verified. The way in which a transition system is expressed in the input languages of model checking tools can vary significantly from tool to tool.

© Springer International Publishing AG 2016
P. Milazzo et al. (Eds.): STAF 2016, LNCS 9946, pp. 67–82, 2016.
DOI: 10.1007/978-3-319-50230-4_6

In many cases the input language allows transitions to be specified as updates of the system's variables to be performed when certain conditions are satisfied (as if-then clauses or rewrite rules). However, if-then clauses and rewrite rules are often too low level as a modelling paradigm to express systems' mechanisms in a natural way. Such a low level nature often requires modellers to formulate complex expressions as transition conditions, or to introduce in the model unnecessary variables and transitions just to represent intermediate values for the computation of the next state reached by a transition. This situation is particularly frequent in the case of languages that offer no or few data structures.

The aim of this paper is to propose a new language, called Objective/MC, for the specification of system models to be analysed by means of model checking. We plan to include in Objective/MC rich data structures, object-oriented features and concurrent processes. In this paper, however, we start with the definition of a core version of the language with the main imperative constructs and a basic notion of array and of object.

One of the main characteristics of the language is that it makes a very different treatment of global and local variables. It is assumed that global variables are actually the variables that describe the state of the modelled system, whereas local variables are only used to ease the specification of the system's internal mechanisms. Hence, in this paper we focus on the problem of pruning local variables and generating transitions that correspond to updates of global variables.

The language is developed with the aim of allowing translation of Objective/MC models into the input language of an existing model checking tool. Since in the long term we plan to allow probabilistic and stochastic systems to be dealt with, we choose PRISM as the target model checking tool in this paper. We also include in the language an operator to perform non-deterministic choices that are translated into probabilistic choices in PRISM.

An implementation of the translator from Objective/MC into the modelling language of the PRISM model checker is available [1]. The translator transforms the model in order to make all local variables disappear. Hence, the generated transition system will consist of transitions that correspond to the updates of only the global variables used in the model.

Related Works. Among model checkers with an input language essentially based on if-then clauses or rewrite rules we mention NuSMV [3], PRISM [8] and UPPAAL [9]. In these cases the state of system is merely represented as a set of variables or by simple data structures.

Maude [5] offers a declarative input language based on rewrite rules with the possibility of using complex structures such as terms and objects. The Maude language is presently richer than Objective/MC in terms of functionalities. Differently, Objective/MC is an imperative language and offers compile-time pruning of local variables to combine the ease of specification with the generation of a compact transition system. Moreover, Objective/MC is already designed with the aim of extending it with rich data structures and object oriented features.

Other tools have rich modelling languages, the features of which are often related with the specific kind of systems addressed. This is for instance the case of Software Model Checkers (such as SPIN [7], CBMC [4] or Java Pathfinder [6]) that are based on rich languages for the specification of concurrent processes, or can even executed directly on C or Java source code. In particular, as regards SPIN (and its input language Promela), it includes high level imperative programming constructs and concurrency features. The same holds for Rebeca (Reactive Objects Language) [10], an actor-based language for modelling and verification of reactive systems. With respect to these languages, Objective/MC offers the novelty of the compile-time pruning of local variables.

We remark that the long-term aim of our work is to propose a new high-level modelling language with imperative semantics. The definition of the local variable pruning methodology is a step in this direction. For this reason, we have defined the methodology on a new language rather than on an existing language.

2   The Core Objective/MC Language

In this section, we present a *core* version of the Objective/MC language, which allows us to focus on the foundational aspects of the translation of models into transition systems, in particular as regards the handling of global/local variables. The core language provides only a limited support for object-oriented features; an extensive treatment of those aspects will be the object of a future paper.

The syntax of the Objective/MC language is shown in Fig. 1. For conciseness, we denote a sequence of symbols (of either a syntactical category or terminal symbols) by using an overbar. The concrete syntax follows C-like conventions, such as using semicolons as command terminators.

Declarations

$$Model ::= \overline{D} \; \overline{G} \; \overline{M} \; \textbf{run} \; \{\overline{Com}\} \quad (model)$$

$$D ::= \textbf{class} \; c \; \{\overline{F}\} \qquad\qquad (class)$$

$$M ::= \textbf{void} \; w(\overline{T_v \; I}) \; \{\overline{Com}\} \quad (proc.)$$

$$F, G ::= T \; I \qquad\qquad (field/global \; var)$$

Commands

$$Com ::= T_v \; I = E \qquad\quad (local \; var \; decl)$$
$$\mid \; Loc = E \qquad\qquad\quad (assignment)$$
$$\mid \; \{\overline{Com}\} \qquad\qquad\qquad (block)$$
$$\mid \; \textbf{if} \; (E) \; \{\overline{Com}\} \; \textbf{else} \; \{\overline{Com}\} \quad (if)$$
$$\mid \; \textbf{while} \; (E) \; \{\overline{Com}\} \qquad (while)$$
$$\mid \; \textbf{times} \; (E) \; \{\overline{Com}\} \qquad (times)$$
$$\mid \; w(\overline{E}) \qquad\qquad\qquad (procedure \; call)$$
$$\mid \; \textbf{yield} \qquad\qquad\qquad (yield)$$

Types

$$T_v ::= \textbf{int}(n \mathbin{..} m) \; \mid \; \textbf{bool} \qquad (basic)$$

$$T ::= T_v \; \mid \; c \; \mid \; T[n] \qquad (compound)$$

Expressions

$$Loc ::= I \qquad\qquad\qquad (identifier)$$
$$\mid \; Loc[E] \qquad\qquad\quad (array)$$
$$\mid \; Loc.f \qquad\qquad\qquad (field)$$
$$E ::= v \qquad\qquad\qquad (literal \; value)$$
$$\mid \; Loc \qquad\qquad\qquad (location)$$
$$\mid \; E \; op_b \; E \qquad\qquad (binary \; op.)$$
$$\mid \; op_u \; E \qquad\qquad\quad (unary \; op.)$$
$$\mid \; E \; ? \; E : E \qquad\qquad (conditional)$$
$$\mid \; E \; \textbf{as} \; \textbf{int}(n \mathbin{..} m) \quad (ascription)$$
$$\mid \; \textbf{select}(n, m) \qquad\quad (select)$$

Fig. 1. Syntax of Objective/MC, where v denotes a value in $\mathbb{Z} \cup \{\textbf{true}, \textbf{false}\}$, $op_b \in \{+, -, *, /, <, \leq, >, \geq, ==, !=, \&\&, \|\}$, $op_u \in \{+, -, \neg\}$.

A *Model* is composed of sequences of *class declarations* $\overline{D}$, *global variables declarations* $\overline{G}$, and *procedure declarations* $\overline{M}$ (akin to static methods). In a procedure declaration, the notation $\overline{T_v}\ \overline{I}$ denotes a sequence of pairs $T_v^1\ I^1, \ldots, T_v^k\ I^k$.

The language provides two basic data types: *bounded integers*, declared as **int**$(n \ldots m)$ with $n \leq m$, which can hold any integer value x in the range $[n, m]$[1], and *booleans*, declared as **bool**, holding values {**true**, **false**}. There are also two compound types: fixed-length *arrays*, and *classes*. Each definition of a class introduces a type (different from any other type) which is identified by the name of the class itself. A class contains a number of *fields* $\overline{F}$ of any type. However, only class types which have been declared previously may be referenced, thus ruling out any recursive type.

Global variables are statically allocated, and they are meant to constitute the global state of the system which is updated by the assignment statements occurring in the program model. There are no restriction on the types of the global variables; that is, any valid type according to the grammar, and referring only to classes already declared, may be used. In particular, this allows objects and arrays to be defined as global variables. On the other hand, objects/arrays can be neither defined as local variables nor dynamically allocated. As regards the declaration of procedures $\overline{M}$, they may take any number of parameters, and their types are restricted to the basic types.

The main entry point of the program model is the **run** command block. Commands are executed sequentially, and the canonical control flow commands (*if*, *while*, procedure calls) are provided by the language. Actually, there are two different cycle construct: a standard **while** (E) {...} command which executes its body as long as the guard E evaluates to *true*, and a **times** (E) {...} command which instead executes the body for a fixed number of iterations, obtained by evaluating the integral-type expression E. Recursion is not allowed.

Local temporary variables having basic type **int**/**bool** may be declared and used, and they must be initialized at the same time of their declarations. The syntax of *expressions* is quite standard, where the syntactical category *Loc* for *locations* is used to access: (i) local/global variables from their *identifier* I, (ii) elements of *arrays* as $Loc[E]$, or (iii) *object fields* as $Loc.f$. A *non-deterministic* construct **select**(n, m), with $n, m \in \mathbb{Z}$, is also provided, which "generates" an integral value in the range $[n, m]$ every time the expression is evaluated.

An assignment of the form $Loc = E$ may refer to either a global or local variable, where E is an expression which evaluates to a basic type, and Loc must refer to a variable of a *compatible* type. Formally, either both Loc and E are expressions of type **bool**, or the type of the right hand side expression is an integral type **int**$(n_2 \ldots m_2)$ with range fully contained in the range of the left hand side variable **int**$(n_1 \ldots m_1)$, namely $[n_2, m_2] \subseteq [n_1, m_1]$. In order to fulfil this requirement, the *ascription* construct E **as int**$(n \ldots m)$ may be used

---

[1] The notation $[n, m]$ indicates the integral range of values $\{x \mid n \leq x \leq m\} \subset \mathbb{Z}$.

to force an expression to be considered in the type system as a different (stricter) integral type than the one which can be derived from the subexpressions of E.[2]

Semantics. The semantics of a model M is a transition system, whose *states* are characterized by the all and only global variables defined in the program model (except for a hidden global "program counter" variable needed for the translation of sequential commands). As a consequence, assignments to global variables give rise to transitions in the resulting transition system. A special command **yield** is used to generate a transition for which no declared global variables are modified, and actually only the hidden program counter is updated. Since the Objective/MC language is geared towards the model checking of the resulting transition systems, in defining the semantics we strictly adhere to the following principle:

> *No transitions may be implicitly introduced by the compilation process beyond those transitions which correspond to updates to global variables.*

The motivation for the above principle is that we want to avoid enlarging the state space implicitly. Nevertheless, the modeller may always introduce global variables if necessary to describe an intended behaviour, which *explicitly* enlarge the state space. In the current definition of the language, each *single* assignment to a global variable causes a transition in the resulting transition system.

The language allows *local variables* to be defined and used according to their intuitive imperative semantics. However, rather than storing them in the global state, the compiler instantiates each access to a local variable with an equivalent expression containing only literal values and references to global variables. For this reason, some limitations on their usage apply.

Constraints. Due to the semantics of Objective/MC, there are three constraints on the usage of the language, exemplified by the following model fragments.

```
1 int(0..5) x = g + 1;      1 int (0..5) x = 0;        1 while (g > 0) {
2 if (x > 0)                 2 while (g > 0) {          2     if (q < g) {
3     g = 0; // global assm. 3     if (q == x)          3         g = 0; // global assm.
4 else                       4         x = g;  // error  4     } else {
5     q = 0; // global assm. 5     q = g; // global assm. 5         // empty
6 int(0..6) y = 0;           6 }                         6     }
7 y = x + 1;    // error     7 int(0..6) y = x;        7 } // error in 'while' loop
        (a)                          (b)                          (c)
```

(a) *A local variable cannot be read after the global variables it depends upon may have been modified.* In the example, at line 1, the local variable x is initialized with the global variable g, and it is then *accessed* (i.e. *read*) at line 7. However, since local variables are handled as unevaluated expressions by the compiler, at line 7 its definition may have been invalidated due to the assignment to the dependant global variable g at line 3. A possible solution

---

[2] The formal definition of the type system is omitted due to lack of space.

is to promote variable x into a global variable, thus allowing the previous value of g + 1 to be retained across transitions.

(b) *A local variable declared outside of a while loop cannot be reassigned in the loop body.* Since the loop may be executed an unbounded number of times, it is generally impossible to know the value of a local variable which may be reassigned inside the loop body. In the example above, the local variable x may be assigned at line 4 hence (analogously to the previous case) when it is read at lines 3 and 7, its value cannot be definitely known. Note that *times* loops do not have this limitation.

(c) *Each execution path inside the body of a while loop must contain at least one global variable assignment or a yield.* This constraint is useful to simplify the translation, since it frees the compiler from the need to identify infinite loops at compile-time, as in the example, for which an infinite loop occurs if $0 < g \leq q$. A possible solution is to insert a yield command at line 5, in such a way that a transition is generated for each branch of the if.

Constraints (a) and (b) avoid situations in which one or more transitions in the semantics of the model make it impossible to reconstruct the value of the local variable from current values of the global variables. This could be due either, in case (a), to a change in a global variable upon which the local variable depends, or, in case (b), to the impossibility of knowing the function that allows the local variable to be computed from the global ones. Hence, these language constraints reflect potential constraints arising from the model itself, namely situations in which information needs to be included in the states of the model.

Example 1. Figure 2 contains a model of a *job scheduler* for a fixed number of processors, which may execute jobs of different durations. A processor is characterized by its *load*, modelled as an integer in the range $[0, 10]$. At line 1, an array of 5 processors is declared as a global variable P. Each element of the array is initialized by default at 0. At line 2, a global variable nextjob is declared, representing the duration of the next job to be scheduled (initially 0).

At line 3, a procedure with no parameters is declared. Its purpose is to decrease the load of each processor by one unit each time it is invoked, in order to simulate the progress of the system. A temporary local variable i is used as the index in the array of processors, and as such it will not appear in the translated model. At each iteration of the times cycle, the current processor load P[i], if it is not already nil, is decreased by the assignment at line 6.

The system executes an infinite loop where, at each iteration: (i) procedure execute_step() is called, (ii) if there are no jobs waiting (nextjob = 0), the duration of the next job is selected non-deterministically in the range $[0, 3]$ (line 12), (iii) the index of the least-loaded processor (min_idx) is computed (lines 13–17), and finally (iv) the new job is tentatively assigned to processor P[min_idx] if it can accommodate it and, in this case, nextjob is reset (lines 18–21).

The yield command at line 21 is necessary in order to satisfy constraint (c), since it might be the case that no assignments to global variables are executed in an iteration of the while loop.

```
1   int (0..10)[5] P;            // array of five processors
2   int (0..10) nextjob;          // duration of the next job
3   void execute_step() {         // decreases the load of each processor by one unit
4*      int (0..4) i = 0;
5       times (5) {
6           if (P[i] > 0) { P[i] = P[i]      as int (1..10) - 1; }
7           i = (i < 4 ? i + 1 : i)      as int (0..4); }
8   }
9   run {
10      while (true) {
11          execute_step();
12          if (nextjob == 0) nextjob =      select (0,3);
13          int (0..4) min_idx = 0;
14          int (0..4) i = 1;
15          times (4) {
16              if (P[i] < P[min_idx]) min_idx = i;
17              i = (i < 4 ? i + 1 : i)      as int (0..4); }
18          if (P[min_idx] + nextjob <= 10) {
19              P[min_idx] = (P[min_idx] + nextjob)      as int (0..10);
20              nextjob = 0;
21          } else yield ;
22      }
23  }
```

Fig. 2. An Objective/MC model of a job processor scheduler.

3   Control Flow Graph

The **run** block is translated into a *Control Flow Graph* (CFG), which allows us to abstract from the syntactical representation of the model, and simplify the definition of the subsequent transformations. Let Π_{in} and Π_{out} be countable disjoint sets of *input* and *output endpoints*, respectively. A CFG G is a pair $(N(G), E(G))$ composed of a set of nodes $N(G)$ of the form $[\mathbf{T}]_{\pi_1,\ldots,\pi_k}^{\pi_0}$, with $\pi_0 \in \Pi_{in}$ and $\{\pi_1,\ldots,\pi_k\} \subset \Pi_{out}$, and a set of edges $E(G) \subset \Pi_{out} \times \Pi_{in}$ such that $\forall (\alpha, \beta_1), (\alpha, \beta_2) \in E(G). \beta_1 = \beta_2$. Assuming input($[\mathbf{T}]_{\pi_1,\ldots,\pi_k}^{\pi_0}) = \pi_0$ and outputs($[\mathbf{T}]_{\pi_1,\ldots,\pi_k}^{\pi_0}) = \{\pi_1,\ldots,\pi_k\}$, we define, for any $N \subseteq N(G)$: inputs(N) = $\bigcup_{\mathbf{x} \in N}\{\text{input}(\mathbf{x})\}$; outputs($N$) = $\bigcup_{\mathbf{x} \in N}\text{outputs}(\mathbf{x})$; endpoints($N$) = inputs($N$) $\cup$ outputs(N). For conciseness, we also define outputs(π_0) = $\{\pi_1,\ldots,\pi_k\}$.

Let G be a graph. Given $\pi \in$ inputs($N(G)$), its *predecessors* are defined as $\text{pred}_G(\pi) = \{\alpha \mid (\alpha, \pi) \in E(G)\}$, while, given $\pi \in$ outputs($N(G)$), its *successors* are defined as $\text{succ}_G(\pi) = \{\alpha \mid (\pi, \alpha) \in E(G)\}$. Note that $|\text{succ}_G(\pi)| \leq 1$.

3.1   Construction of the Control Flow Graph

The types of nodes defined for the Control Flow Graph are the following.

$$[\text{let } I = E]_{\pi_1}^{\pi_0} \quad [\ell \Leftarrow E]_{\pi_1}^{\pi_0} \quad [\text{yield}]_{\pi_1}^{\pi_0} \quad [\text{if } E]_{\pi_1,\pi_2}^{\pi_0} \quad [\text{select}_k]_{\pi_1,\ldots,\pi_k}^{\pi_0}$$

$$[\text{begin}]_{\pi_1}^{\pi_0} \quad [\text{end}]^{\pi_0} \quad [\text{skip}]_{\pi_1}^{\pi_0}$$

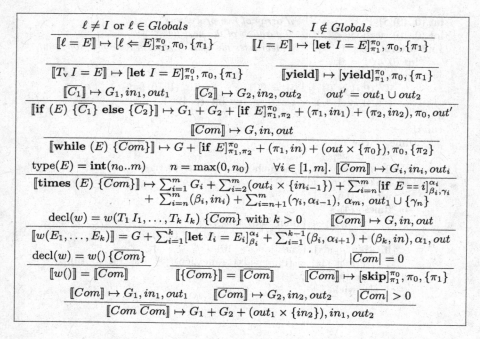

$$\dfrac{\ell \neq I \text{ or } \ell \in \textit{Globals}}{[\![\ell = E]\!] \mapsto [\ell \Leftarrow E]_{\pi_1}^{\pi_0}, \pi_0, \{\pi_1\}} \qquad \dfrac{I \notin \textit{Globals}}{[\![I = E]\!] \mapsto [\textbf{let } I = E]_{\pi_1}^{\pi_0}, \pi_0, \{\pi_1\}}$$

$$\dfrac{}{[\![T_v \, I = E]\!] \mapsto [\textbf{let } I = E]_{\pi_1}^{\pi_0}, \pi_0, \{\pi_1\}} \qquad \dfrac{}{[\![\textbf{yield}]\!] \mapsto [\textbf{yield}]_{\pi_1}^{\pi_0}, \pi_0, \{\pi_1\}}$$

$$\dfrac{[\![C_1]\!] \mapsto G_1, in_1, out_1 \qquad [\![C_2]\!] \mapsto G_2, in_2, out_2 \qquad out' = out_1 \cup out_2}{[\![\textbf{if } (E) \ \{\overline{C_1}\} \textbf{ else } \{\overline{C_2}\}]\!] \mapsto G_1 + G_2 + [\textbf{if } E]_{\pi_1,\pi_2}^{\pi_0} + (\pi_1, in_1) + (\pi_2, in_2), \pi_0, out'}$$

$$\dfrac{[\![Com]\!] \mapsto G, in, out}{[\![\textbf{while } (E) \ \{\overline{Com}\}]\!] \mapsto G + [\textbf{if } E]_{\pi_1,\pi_2}^{\pi_0} + (\pi_1, in) + (out \times \{\pi_0\}), \pi_0, \{\pi_2\}}$$

$$\dfrac{\text{type}(E) = \textbf{int}(n_0..m) \qquad n = \max(0, n_0) \qquad \forall i \in [1, m]. \ [\![\overline{Com}]\!] \mapsto G_i, in_i, out_i}{\substack{[\![\textbf{times } (E) \ \{\overline{Com}\}]\!] \mapsto \sum_{i=1}^{m} G_i + \sum_{i=2}^{m} (out_i \times \{in_{i-1}\}) + \sum_{i=n}^{m} [\textbf{if } E == i]_{\beta_i, \gamma_i}^{\alpha_i} \\ + \sum_{i=n+1}^{m} (\beta_i, in_i) + \sum_{i=n+1}^{m} (\gamma_i, \alpha_{i-1}), \alpha_m, out_1 \cup \{\gamma_n\}}}$$

$$\dfrac{\text{decl}(w) = w(T_1 \, I_1, \ldots, T_k \, I_k) \ \{\overline{Com}\} \text{ with } k > 0 \qquad [\![\overline{Com}]\!] \mapsto G, in, out}{[\![w(E_1, \ldots, E_k)]\!] = G + \sum_{i=1}^{k} [\textbf{let } I_i = E_i]_{\beta_i}^{\alpha_i} + \sum_{i=1}^{k-1} (\beta_i, \alpha_{i+1}) + (\beta_k, in), \alpha_1, out}$$

$$\dfrac{\text{decl}(w) = w() \ \{\overline{Com}\}}{[\![w()]\!] = [\![\overline{Com}]\!]} \qquad \dfrac{}{[\![\{\overline{Com}\}]\!] = [\![\overline{Com}]\!]} \qquad \dfrac{|\overline{Com}| = 0}{[\![\overline{Com}]\!] \mapsto [\textbf{skip}]_{\pi_1}^{\pi_0}, \pi_0, \{\pi_1\}}$$

$$\dfrac{[\![Com]\!] \mapsto G_1, in_1, out_1 \qquad [\![\overline{Com}]\!] \mapsto G_2, in_2, out_2 \qquad |\overline{Com}| > 0}{[\![Com \ \overline{Com}]\!] \mapsto G_1 + G_2 + (out_1 \times \{in_2\}), in_1, out_2}$$

Fig. 3. Construction rules for the Control Flow Graph.

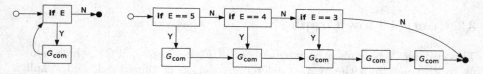

Fig. 4. *While* loop.   **Fig. 5.** *Times* loop, when type$(E) = \textbf{int}(3 \ldots 5)$.

The first two nodes represent assignments to either a *local* variable I or a global variable $\ell \in \textit{Loc}$, respectively, while the third directly corresponds to the *yield* command. The *if* node is used to translate both *if* and *while* commands, where the output endpoints π_1, π_2 denote the branches to follow when the condition E is either satisfied or not, respectively. The *select* node is parameterized by the number of choices $k \geq 1$. There is also a *begin* node, an *end* node (without output endpoints), and a *skip* node for empty command blocks.

Given two graphs G_1, G_2, we define a *union* operation as $G_1 + G_2 = (\text{N}(G_1) \cup \text{N}(G_2), \text{E}(G_1) \cup \text{E}(G_2))$, provided that endpoints$(\text{N}(G_1)) \cap$ endpoints$(\text{N}(G_2)) = \emptyset$. Moreover, we define the *addition* of a set of edges E to a graph G as $G + E = (\text{N}(G), \text{E}(G) \cup E)$, provided that $E \subseteq \text{outputs}(\text{N}(G)) \times \text{inputs}(\text{N}(G))$. Given G_1, G_2 such that $\text{N}(G_2) \subseteq \text{N}(G_1)$ and $\text{E}(G_2) \subseteq \text{E}(G_1)$, we define a *difference* operation as $G_1 - G_2 = (N', E')$ where $N' = \text{N}(G_1) \setminus \text{N}(G_2)$, and $E' = (\text{E}(G_1) \setminus \text{E}(G_2)) \cap (\text{outputs}(N') \times \text{inputs}(N'))$.

```
 1  int (-50..50) pos = 0;
 2  run {
 3      while  (pos != -50 && pos != 50) {
 4          int (0..1) x =    select  (0,1);
 5          if  (x == 0)
 6              pos = (pos - 1)    as int (-50..50);
 7          else
 8              pos = (pos + 1)    as int (-50..50);
 9      }
10  }
```

Fig. 6. A *random walk* model.

The translation of (a sequence of) commands $\overline{Com}$ is obtained through the relation $[\![\overline{Com}]\!] \mapsto \langle G, in, out\rangle$, where $in \in$ inputs(N(G)) and $out \subseteq$ outputs(N(G)) are the designated *input endpoint* and *output endpoints* of the whole graph, respectively. Relation $[\![\cdot]\!]$ is the smallest relation satisfying the rules shown in Fig. 3 (brackets $\langle\ \rangle$ are omitted for clarity) where, for conciseness, a single node $[\mathbf{T}]_{\pi_1,\ldots,\pi_k}^{\pi_0}$ also denotes the graph composed of only such a node. Moreover, we assume local variable names (including parameters) to be unique, and distinct from the global ones (denoted *Globals*); decl(w) to denote the declaration of a procedure w; and type(E) the type of E as inferred by the type system. The definition is quite straightforward. We just point out the different translation of *while* and *times* loops, depicted in Figs. 4 and 5 (the designated *input* and *output* endpoints are depicted with symbols ○ and •, respectively). In the *times* case, the type of E determines the number of copies of the translated loop body G_{com} (obtained from $[\![\overline{Com}]\!]$) in the CFG. Finally, the resulting CFG is obtained by connecting a *begin* node to the designated input endpoint *in*, and by connecting the *out* endpoints to an *end* node. Given a graph G, we denote the input endpoint of the *begin* and *end* nodes by begin(G) and end(G), respectively.

Example 2. Figure 6 shows an implementation of a one-dimensional *random walk*.[3] The position is modelled as a global variable **pos**, initialized at 0, which can vary in the range $[-50, 50]$. The process goes on until the limits of the allowed range for the position are reached. At each iteration of the *while* loop, the position is either decreased or increased by 1, in a non-deterministic way, according to the choice performed by the **select(0,1)** operation. Its CFG is shown in Fig. 7a.

3.2 Transformations

The first transformation consists in the elimination of the *skip* nodes; that is, for all nodes $\mathbf{x} = [\mathbf{skip}]_{\pi_1}^{\pi_0} \in$ N(G), we apply $G \rightsquigarrow G - \mathbf{x} + (\mathrm{pred}_G(\pi_0) \times \mathrm{succ}_G(\pi_1))$.

The second transformation concerns the *expansion* of *select* operators, and consists in replacing each node containing one or more **select**(n, m) operators

---

[3] In this example, we have assumed that global variable **pos** can be initialized inline.

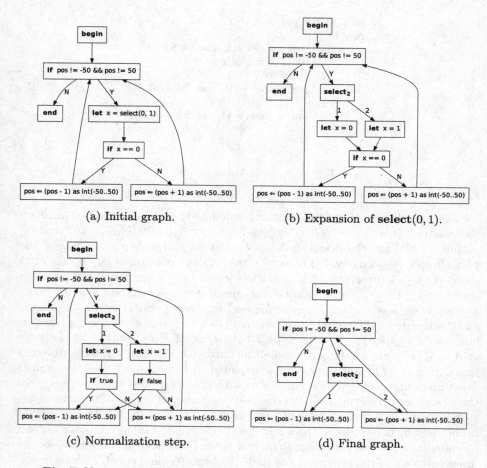

(a) Initial graph.

(b) Expansion of **select**(0, 1).

(c) Normalization step.

(d) Final graph.

Fig. 7. Various transformations of the CFG in the *random walk* example.

with an explicit [**select**$_k$] node, with $k = m - n + 1$. We introduce the function alt : $E \to \mathscr{P}(E)$ which expands an expression E into a set of expressions, one for each different combination of values which can be generated by the all *select* operators appearing in E. We define alt(v) = $\{v\}$, alt(I) = $\{I\}$, alt(**select**(n, m)) = $\{n, \ldots, m\}$ and, for any other expression operator $\varphi \neq$ **select**, alt($\varphi(E_1, \ldots, E_n)$) = $\bigcup \{\varphi(E'_1, \ldots, E'_n) \mid E'_i \in$ alt(E_i), $i = [1, n]\}$. The actual transformations applied are shown in Fig. 8.

Normalization. The next transformations involve *let* nodes for local variables. The aim is to obtain an equivalent *normalized* CFG, namely such that for any node in which a local variable I is *read*, the definition of I is univocally determined. To this purpose, two different transformations are needed, which are based on the duplication of parts of the CFG.

$$\frac{\mathbf{x} = [\mathbf{let}\ I = E]_{\pi_1}^{\pi_0} \in \mathrm{N}(G) \quad \mathrm{alt}(E) = \{E_1, \ldots, E_k\} \quad k > 1}{\begin{aligned} G \rightsquigarrow G - \mathbf{x} + [\mathbf{select}_k]_{\alpha_1, \ldots, \alpha_k}^{\pi_0} + \sum_{i=1}^{k} [\mathbf{let}\ I = E_i]_{\gamma_i}^{\beta_i} + (\mathrm{pred}_G(\pi_0) \times \{\pi_0\}) \\ + \{(\alpha_i, \beta_i) \mid i = [1, k]\} + (\{\gamma_1, \ldots, \gamma_k\} \times \mathrm{succ}_G(\pi_1)) \end{aligned}}$$

$$\frac{\mathbf{x} = [\ell \Leftarrow E]_{\pi_1}^{\pi_0} \in \mathrm{N}(G) \quad \mathrm{alt}(\ell) = \{\ell_1, \ldots, \ell_k\} \quad \mathrm{alt}(E) = \{E_1, \ldots, E_h\} \quad k + h > 2}{\begin{aligned} G \rightsquigarrow G - \mathbf{x} + [\mathbf{select}_{k \cdot h}]_{\alpha_{1,1}, \ldots, \alpha_{k,h}}^{\pi_0} + \sum_{i=1}^{k} \sum_{j=1}^{h} [\ell_i \Leftarrow E_j]_{\gamma_{i,j}}^{\beta_{i,j}} + (\mathrm{pred}_G(\pi_0) \times \{\pi_0\}) \\ + \{(\alpha_{i,j}, \beta_{i,j}) \mid i \in [1, k], j \in [1, h]\} + (\{\gamma_{1,1}, \ldots, \gamma_{k,h}\} \times \mathrm{succ}_G(\pi_1)) \end{aligned}}$$

$$\frac{\mathbf{x} = [\mathbf{if}\ E]_{\pi_1, \pi_2}^{\pi_0} \in \mathrm{N}(G) \quad \mathrm{alt}(E) = \{E_1, \ldots, E_k\} \quad k > 1}{\begin{aligned} G \rightsquigarrow G - \mathbf{x} + [\mathbf{select}_k]_{\alpha_1, \ldots, \alpha_k}^{\pi_0} + \sum_{i=1}^{k} [\mathbf{if}\ E_i]_{\gamma_i, \delta_i}^{\beta_i} + (\mathrm{pred}_G(\pi_0) \times \{\pi_0\}) \\ + \{(\alpha_i, \beta_i) \mid i = [1, k]\} + (\{\gamma_1, \ldots, \gamma_k\} \times \mathrm{succ}_G(\pi_1)) + (\{\delta_1, \ldots, \delta_k\} \times \mathrm{succ}_G(\pi_2)) \end{aligned}}$$

Fig. 8. Transformation rules for the expansion of **select** operators.

We define, for each $\pi \in \mathrm{endpoints}(\mathrm{N}(G))$, the relation $\mathrm{RD}_\pi \subseteq I \times \mathrm{inputs}(\mathrm{N}(G))$ such that $(I, \alpha) \in \mathrm{RD}_\pi$ implies that there exists a path from π to an ancestor α of the form $[\mathbf{let}\ I = E]_\beta^\alpha$, with no other intervening definitions of I along the path. We write $\mathrm{RD}_\pi(I) = \{\alpha \mid (I, \alpha) \in \mathrm{RD}_\pi\}$. Formally, RD is defined by the following equations derived from the nodes of the CFG:

$$[\mathbf{begin}]_{\pi_1}^{\pi_0} \longmapsto \mathrm{RD}_{\pi_1} = \mathrm{RD}_{\pi_0} = \emptyset$$
$$[\mathbf{let}\ I = E]_{\pi_1}^{\pi_0} \longmapsto \mathrm{RD}_{\pi_1} = (\mathrm{RD}_{\pi_0} \setminus \{(I, \alpha) \in \mathrm{RD}_{\pi_0}\}) \cup \{(I, \pi_0)\}$$
$$[\ell \Leftarrow E]_{\pi_1}^{\pi_0}, [\mathbf{yield}]_{\pi_1}^{\pi_0} \longmapsto \mathrm{RD}_{\pi_1} = \mathrm{RD}_{\pi_0}$$
$$[\mathbf{if}\ E]_{\pi_1, \pi_2}^{\pi_0} \longmapsto \mathrm{RD}_{\pi_1} = \mathrm{RD}_{\pi_2} = \mathrm{RD}_{\pi_0}$$
$$[\mathbf{select}_k]_{\pi_1, \ldots, \pi_k}^{\pi_0} \longmapsto \mathrm{RD}_{\pi_1} = \mathrm{RD}_{\pi_2} = \cdots = \mathrm{RD}_{\pi_k} = \mathrm{RD}_{\pi_0}$$

while $\forall \pi \in \mathrm{inputs}(\mathrm{N}(G)) \longmapsto \mathrm{RD}_\pi = \bigcup \{\mathrm{RD}_{\pi'} \mid \pi' \in \mathrm{pred}_G(\pi)\}$. We also assume a function $\mathrm{used}_G(\pi) = \{I_1, \ldots, I_k\}$ giving, for all $\pi \in \mathrm{inputs}(\mathrm{N}(G))$, the set of local variable names *read* in any node reachable from π (including itself).

Definition 1. *A Control Flow Graph G is* normalized *iff, for all* $[\mathbf{T}]_{\pi_1, \ldots, \pi_k}^{\pi_0} \in \mathrm{N}(G)$ *and* $I \in \mathrm{used}_G(\pi_0)$: $|\mathrm{RD}_{\pi_0}(I)| = 1$.

To obtain a *normalized* CFG, for all nodes $\mathbf{x} = [\mathbf{T}]_{\pi_1, \ldots, \pi_k}^{\pi_0}$ violating the above condition, namely such that $|\mathrm{RD}_{\pi_0}(I)| > 1$, two cases need to be considered.

– **Case 1.** This case allows duplicating one node at a time. Given $\alpha \in \mathrm{RD}_{\pi_0}(I)$, let $B_\alpha = \{\beta \in \mathrm{pred}_G(\pi_0) \mid \mathrm{RD}_\beta(I) = \{\alpha\}\}$. Then, if $|\mathrm{RD}_\beta(I)| = 1$ for all $\beta \in \mathrm{pred}_G(\pi_0)$, the following transformation can be applied:

$$G \rightsquigarrow G - (B_\alpha \times \{\pi_0\}) + \mathbf{x}' + (B_\alpha \times \{\gamma_0\}) + \sum_{i=1}^{k} (\{\gamma_i\} \times \mathrm{succ}_G(\pi_i))$$

where $\mathbf{x}' = [\mathbf{T}]_{\gamma_1, \ldots, \gamma_k}^{\gamma_0}$ is a duplicate of $\mathbf{x}$. This transformation detaches parent β from $\mathbf{x}$ and attaches it (as the only parent) to $\mathbf{x}'$. The output endpoints of the duplicate node are connected to the same children of $\mathbf{x}$, in the same manner. This transformation is applied in a maximal way, until its applicability condition is no longer satisfied by any node.

- **Case 2.** After *Case 1*, if there are still nodes for which $|\mathrm{RD}_{\pi_0}(I)| > 1$, it implies that, for some node identified by π_0, its predecessors $\mathrm{pred}_G(\pi_0)$ can be partitioned into two (non-empty) sets $B^{(1)}, B^{(2)}$ such that $\forall\beta \in B^{(1)}.\,|\mathrm{RD}_\beta(I)| = 1$, and $\forall\gamma \in B^{(2)}.\,\mathrm{RD}_\gamma(I) = \mathrm{RD}_{\pi_0}(I)$. Note that $B_\alpha \subseteq B^{(1)}$. Then the following transformation can be performed:

$$G \rightsquigarrow G - (B_\alpha \times \{\pi_0\}) + N' + E' + (B_\alpha \times \{\gamma_0\})$$

which duplicates a subgraph of G which includes $\mathbf{x}$. In particular, N', E', γ_0 are obtained through the function $\mathrm{clone}_G(\mathbf{x}, \pi_0) = (N', E', \gamma_0)$, where: N' are the duplicated nodes, E' are the duplicated edges (which may also point to old nodes still present in G), and γ_0 is entry node of the cloned subgraph, corresponding to π_0.

In order to define the clone function, let us assume a one-to-one mapping $\alpha \mapsto \widetilde{\alpha}$ between endpoints such that $\forall\alpha, \beta.\,\alpha \neq \widetilde{\beta}$. Moreover, let us consider the subgraph G' of G restricted to the nodes $\mathrm{N}(G)\backslash B^{(1)}$, and let $N_0 \subseteq \mathrm{N}(G)$ be the *Strongly Connected Component (SCC)* of G' containing node $\mathbf{x}$ (i.e. $\pi_0 \in \mathrm{inputs}(N_0)$). Assuming $E_c = \mathrm{E}(G) \cap (N_0 \times N_0)$ and $\overline{E_c} = \mathrm{E}(G)\backslash E_c$, we define $\mathrm{clone}_G(\mathbf{x}, \alpha) = (N', E', \widetilde{\alpha})$, where:

$$N' = \left\{ [\mathbf{T}]_{\widetilde{\pi}_1,\ldots,\widetilde{\pi}_k}^{\widetilde{\beta}_2} \;\middle|\; [\mathbf{T}]_{\pi_1,\ldots,\pi_k}^{\beta_2} \in N_0 \wedge \exists\beta_1.\,(\beta_1, \beta_2) \in E_c \right\};$$

$$E' = \left\{ (\widetilde{\beta}_1, \widetilde{\beta}_2) \;\middle|\; (\beta_1, \beta_2) \in E_c \right\} \cup$$
$$\left\{ (\widetilde{\beta}_1, \beta_2) \;\middle|\; (\beta_1, \beta_2) \in \overline{E_c} \wedge \widetilde{\beta}_1 \in \mathrm{outputs}(N') \right\}.$$

Normalization Algorithm. The algorithm alternates between the maximal application of *Case 1* and a single application of *Case 2*, until they are no longer applicable. This alternation is necessary since the transformation performed for one case may enable the application of the other case, for some nodes. Moreover, before the application of each case, the compiler performs a *constant propagation* phase, by instantiating each occurrence of any local variable with its defining expression, whenever such a definition is univocally determined. Precisely, given a node $[\mathbf{T}]_{\pi_1,\ldots,\pi_k}^{\pi_0}$, the instantiation is carried out for each variable I being read in $\mathbf{T}$ such that $|\mathrm{RD}_{\pi_0}(I)| = 1$, which is replaced by an expression containing no references to local variables. At the end, a normalized CFG is obtained, that is then simplified by removing all *let* nodes, and also any *if* node for which its condition has been already reduced to a truth value.

Example 3. Figure 7 shows a few transformation of CFG for the random walk model from Example 2. After the initial construction (Fig. 7a), the first transformation consists in the expansion of the **select** operator present in node [**let** $x = \mathbf{select}(0, 1)$], giving Fig. 7b. The original *let* node is being replaced by a *select* node followed by two new *let* nodes, one for each possible outcome 0 and 1.

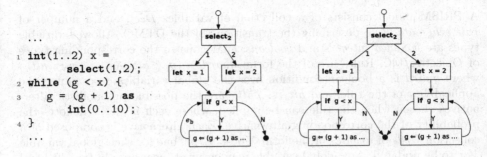

```
1  int(1..2) x =
        select(1,2);
2  while (g < x) {
3      g = (g + 1) as
        int(0..10);
4  }
```

Fig. 9. Example of *while* loop duplication.

Then node [**if** $x == 0$] is duplicated according to *Case 1* of the normalization algorithm, and the subsequent constant propagation causes both occurrences of the local variable x in the *if* nodes to be instantiated, as shown in Fig. 7c. The graph obtained after the final simplification step is shown in Fig. 7d.

Example 4. Consider the model fragment from Fig. 9 (left), in which a variable x is non-deterministically selected and then accessed by the guard of a *while* loop. In the CFG (after the expansion of *select*) the definition of x in the [**if** $g < x$] node cannot be univocally determined; in fact, both definitions of x can be traced back through the backward edge e_b coming from the end of the loop body. Hence, only Case 2 can be applied, which duplicates the SCC composed of the [**if** $g < x$] and [$g \Leftarrow (g + 1) \ldots$] nodes, yielding the CFG depicted in Fig. 9 (right).

4 PRISM Translation

A normalized Control Flow Graph (see Definition 1), containing only assignments to global variables [$\ell \Leftarrow E$], *yield* nodes, *if* nodes, and *select* nodes, is taken as input for the generation of the PRISM model. In the current paper we consider only PRISM models for *Discrete Time Markov Chains* (DTMC).

Definition 2 (PRISM syntax). *Let Var be a countable set of variables' names. The syntax of a subset of PRISM is defined by the following grammar:*

$$PModel ::= \overline{Decl} \ \overline{Rule}$$
$$Decl ::= Var : T_v \ \textbf{init} \ v$$
$$Rule ::= Expr \rightarrow (p_1 : Upds_1 \oplus \cdots \oplus p_n : Upds_n)$$
$$Upds ::= Upd_1 \ \& \ldots \& \ Upd_k$$
$$Upd ::= Var' = Expr$$
$$Expr ::= v \ | \ Var \ | \ Expr \ op_b \ Expr \ | \ op_u \ Expr \ | \ Expr \ ? \ Expr : Expr$$

where T_v, v, op_b, op_u *are as defined for* **Objective/MC** *(see Fig. 1).*

A PRISM model consists of a collection of variables $\overline{Decl}$, and a number of *rule schemata* $\overline{Rule}$ describing the transitions of the DTMC. Allowed variable types are *bounded integers* and *booleans*, analogous to the corresponding types of Objective/MC. Rules are of the form: $guard \rightarrow (p_1 : alt_1 \oplus \cdots \oplus p_n : alt_n)$ where *guard* is a boolean condition over the global variables determining the applicability of the rule, and $alt_1, \ldots, alt_n$ are the possible probabilistic alternatives chosen when the rule can be applied, where each $p_i \in \mathbb{R}^+$ denotes the probability of the corresponding alternative. Each alternative is composed of a collection *Upds* of *updates* of the form $Var' = Expr$, one for each global variable *Var* to be updated. Any global variable may occur at most once in the left hand side of any update in *Upds*. Moreover, rule guards must all be disjoint.

As regards the semantics, the resulting DTMC is obtained from a PRISM model by instantiating its rules for each possible state in the complete state space of the model as determined by the global variables. Since the core Objective/MC language does not currently provide operators for probabilistic choice, in the rest of the paper we assume constant probabilities among rule alternatives, namely for all rules $p_1, \ldots, p_n = 1/n$, and thus omit them from the model descriptions.

Since PRISM only allows variables to be declared as basic types (either integers or booleans), without any structure, the first step in the translation consists in flattening the Objective/MC (structured) global variables into a collection of basic PRISM variables. An array a with $\text{type}(a) = T[n]$ is translated into a set of PRISM variables $a[0], \ldots, a[n-1]$. Similarly, each object o declared among global variables (including those in arrays) is translated into a set of PRISM variables $o.I_1, \ldots, o.I_n$, where $I_1, \ldots, I_n$ are the instance variables of o. Such a translation of objects into PRISM variables is possible since in Objective/MC objects cannot be created dynamically.

First of all, we determine the nodes of the CFG which give rise to transitions in the resulting PRISM model. They are the begin, assignment and yield nodes, and, together with the end node, constitute the set *States*.

We also introduce a special global variable *pc* (*program counter*) of type $\mathbf{int}(-1 \ldots N)$ where $-1 = \mathbf{err}$ denotes an *error* state used to catch violations of integral ranges allowed in expression ascriptions, and $N = |States|$. We assume a one-to-one mapping between *States* and *pc* values in $\{0, \ldots, N-1\}$. For simplicity, we refer to *pc* values with their corresponding endpoints from *States*.

A PRISM rule is generated for each $\alpha \in States$. This requires determining the set of states $\text{next}(\alpha) = \{\beta_1, \ldots, \beta_k\} \subseteq States$ which are *directly* reachable from α in the CFG, namely those states which are reachable through a path containing only *if* and *select* nodes. The generated rules have the following form, for each state α (except for *end* and *error*):

$$pc == \alpha \rightarrow \left(\bigoplus_{i=1}^{k} \{ \mathcal{U} \,\&\, (pc' = \mathcal{C}_{\text{asc}} \,?\, \mathcal{E} : \mathbf{err}) \} \right)$$

while a *deadlock* transition $pc == \alpha \rightarrow (pc' = \alpha)$ is generated for the *end* and *error* states. As regards the first case, each alternative is composed of *(i)* a number of global assignments $\mathcal{U}$, implementing the assignment described in the current node α, and *(ii)* an update of variable *pc*.

The different alternatives to be considered (for $i \in \{1, \ldots, k\}$) emerge from the presence of *select* nodes in the subtree between α and the nodes in next(α). As regards the update $(pc' = \mathcal{C}_{\text{asc}} ? \mathcal{E} : \mathbf{err})$ of the program counter, $\mathcal{C}_{\text{asc}}$ represents the conditions obtained from the ascriptions in the subtree, and $\mathcal{E}$ is a conditional expression that evaluates to the new program counter from the set next(α), which is obtained from the *if* nodes present in the subtree.

Example 5. Consider the CFG of Fig. 7d, and let $pc = 0$ denote the *begin* node, 1 the left assignment node, and 3 the *end* node. Let $\mathcal{C}_{\text{if}} = (pos != -50 \&\& pos != 50)$ be the condition of the *if* node; the rules generated for nodes 0 and 1 are:

$$pc == 0 \rightarrow (pc' = \mathcal{C}_{\text{if}} ? 1 : 3) \oplus (pc' = \mathcal{C}_{\text{if}} ? 2 : 3)$$

$$pc == 1 \rightarrow (pos' = \mathcal{C}_{\text{asc}}^{-1} ? pos - 1 : pos) \& (pc' = (\mathcal{C}_{\text{asc}}^{-1} ? (\mathcal{C}_{\text{if}}^{-1} ? 1 : 3) : \mathbf{err}) \oplus$$
$$(pos' = \mathcal{C}_{\text{asc}}^{-1} ? pos - 1 : pos) \& (pc' = (\mathcal{C}_{\text{asc}}^{-1} ? (\mathcal{C}_{\text{if}}^{-1} ? 2 : 3) : \mathbf{err})$$

where $\mathcal{C}_{\text{if}}^{-1}$ is used to evaluate, from the assignment node 1, the condition $\mathcal{C}_{\text{if}}$ as if the current assignment $(pos' = pos - 1)$ would be already performed, while $\mathcal{C}_{\text{asc}}^{-1}$ checks the ascription in the assignment expression; formally: $\mathcal{C}_{\text{if}}^{-1} = (pos - 1 != -50 \&\& pos - 1 != 50)$, $\mathcal{C}_{\text{asc}}^{-1} = (-50 \leq pos - 1 \&\& pos - 1 \leq 50)$.

Discussion. An implementation of the compiler for the core Objective/MC language into PRISM models is available [1]. We have used the compiler to automatically generate a PRISM model of the job scheduler from Fig. 2, which contains 19 transition specifications. The DTMC built by PRISM (in 0.125 s) consists of 256 states and 343 transitions. Verification of properties can be performed by model checking temporal logic formulas on the variables of the generated PRISM model. A hand-made PRISM model of the job scheduler example is available at [1]. It consists of 5 variables P_0, ..., P_4 representing processors, a `nextjob` variable to store the value of the next processing job to be executed, and a `state` variable for the sequential execution of the steps. The model built by PRISM in this case (in 0.035 s) consists of 264 states and 312 transitions.

In terms of DTMC dimension, the PRISM model obtained from the translation of the Objective/MC model turns out to be similar in size to the hand-made PRISM models. This suggests that the pruning of local variables performed at compile time has actually avoided too many useless states to be introduced by the translation. Note also that in the hand-made PRISM model, changing the range of possible values for the next processing job to be executed requires manually modifying a number of transition specifications in the model source code. Instead, in the Objective/MC model in Fig. 2, the same modification could be done by simply changing the value of the `select` expression at line 12.

5   Conclusions

We have proposed an early version of an object-oriented language, called Objective/MC, for the specification of models to be analysed by model checking.

In particular, we have focused on the imperative constructs of the language and on the handling of global and local variables. As future developments, we plan to formally define the semantics of the language and prove the correctness of the transformations performed on the models. Moreover, we will extend the language with richer object oriented features (methods and inheritance), with richer data structures and operations on them (array filters and a notion of graph), and with probabilistic/stochastic operations (even with uncertain rates [2]). Finally, we plan to add some features to deal with concurrency aspects.

References

1. ObjMC: The Objective/MC compiler. http://www.di.unipi.it/msvbio/ObjMC
2. Barbuti, R., Levi, F., Milazzo, P., Scatena, G.: Probabilistic model checking of biological systems with uncertain kinetic rates. Theor. Comput. Sci. **419**, 2–16 (2012)
3. Cimatti, A., Clarke, E., Giunchiglia, E., Giunchiglia, F., Pistore, M., Roveri, M., Sebastiani, R., Tacchella, A.: NuSMV 2: an opensource tool for symbolic model checking. In: Brinksma, E., Larsen, K.G. (eds.) CAV 2002. LNCS, vol. 2404, pp. 359–364. Springer, Heidelberg (2002). doi:10.1007/3-540-45657-0_29
4. Clarke, E., Kroening, D., Lerda, F.: A tool for checking ANSI-C programs. In: Jensen, K., Podelski, A. (eds.) TACAS 2004. LNCS, vol. 2988, pp. 168–176. Springer, Heidelberg (2004). doi:10.1007/978-3-540-24730-2_15
5. Clavel, M., Durán, F., Eker, S., Lincoln, P., Martí-Oliet, N., Meseguer, J., Quesada, J.F.: Maude: specification and programming in rewriting logic. Theor. Comput. Sci. **285**(2), 187–243 (2002)
6. Havelund, K., Pressburger, T.: Model checking Java programs using Java Pathfinder. Int. J. Softw. Tools Technol. Transf. **2**(4), 366–381 (2000)
7. Holzmann, G.J.: The model checker SPIN. IEEE Trans. Softw. Eng. **23**(5), 279 (1997)
8. Kwiatkowska, M., Norman, G., Parker, D.: PRISM 4.0: verification of probabilistic real-time systems. In: Gopalakrishnan, G., Qadeer, S. (eds.) CAV 2011. LNCS, vol. 6806, pp. 585–591. Springer, Heidelberg (2011). doi:10.1007/978-3-642-22110-1_47
9. Larsen, K.G., Pettersson, P., Yi, W.: UPPAAL in a nutshell. Int. J. Softw. Tools Technol. Transf. (STTT) **1**(1), 134–152 (1997)
10. Sirjani, M., Movaghar, A., Shali, A., De Boer, F.S.: Modeling and verification of reactive systems using Rebeca. Fundamenta Informaticae **63**(4), 385–410 (2004)

Probabilistic Modelling of Station Locations in Bicycle-Sharing Systems

Daniël Reijsbergen[(✉)]

University of Edinburgh, Edinburgh, UK
dreijsbe@inf.ed.ac.uk

Abstract. We present a simulation methodology for generating the locations of stations in Bicycle-Sharing Systems. We present several methods that are inspired by the literature on spatial point processes. We evaluate how the artificially generated systems compare to existing systems through a case study involving 11 cities worldwide. The method that is found to perform best is a data-driven approach in which we use a dataset of places of interest in the city to 'rate' how attractive city areas are for station placement. The presented methods use only non-proprietary data readily available via the Internet.

1 Introduction

Bicycle-Sharing Systems[1] (BSSs) are an increasingly popular phenomenon, as witnessed by the worldwide number of operational systems growing from roughly 350 such systems [7] in 2010 to almost 1,000 at the time of writing [18]. Due to this strong increase, the question of choosing station locations in a new BSS is of increasing relevance to planners, operators, and scientists. A well-studied approach is to optimise some measure of coverage of 'interesting' parts of the city. The choice of Geographic Information System (GIS) dataset to identify interesting locations in the target city depends on the context—e.g., residential and commercial area density are of interest to a commuting-oriented BSS, and proximity to landmarks and restaurants to a BSS focussing on tourism and leisure. In the literature, the best station locations are then typically chosen using some form of deterministic optimisation—e.g., the methods implemented in the geographic analysis tool ArcGIS [10] or the optimisation tool suite XPRESS [8]. This approach will typically return a single optimal solution. In some cases, the user is required to manually determine a set of candidate locations beforehand.

In this paper, we will consider the use of stochastic simulation to generate BSS station locations as an alternative to deterministic optimisation. The probabilities informing the simulation procedure are inspired by the literature on spatial point processes. We will discuss the use of two baseline approaches—in particular the Poisson and Ginibre point process—and compare these to a simulation procedure that incorporates GIS information. The main criterion is correspondence to real-world BSSs, including several major systems such as the

---

[1] Alternatively called Bicycle-Sharing Plans.

© Springer International Publishing AG 2016
P. Milazzo et al. (Eds.): STAF 2016, LNCS 9946, pp. 83–97, 2016.
DOI: 10.1007/978-3-319-50230-4_7

Bicing BSS in Barcelona. The simulation procedure provides insight into how stations are distributed across space - this can inform models of bicycle movement, provide feedback to operators of existing systems, and aid designers of new systems. Executing this approach several times will result in different outcomes, which is typically more informative to planners than the single solution returned by a deterministic optimisation procedure. After all, the GIS data informing the optimality criterion is itself prone to subjectivity and inaccuracies. Additionally, the approach discussed in this paper only uses non-proprietary data and the programming code for the experiments is written in Java and available upon request.

The outline of this paper is as follows. We begin with a discussion of related work and the data sources used in this paper in Sect. 2. We then fix notation and discuss basic simulation procedures in Sect. 3. In Sect. 4, we zoom in on the various techniques to generate station locations. We present the results of a simulation experiment involving a comparison with real-world BSSs in Sect. 5. Section 6 concludes the paper.

2   Background and Data

Before we present this paper's specific contributions, we first elaborate on its position within the wider scientific and societal context. We begin with a discussion of the background and the related scientific literature in Sect. 2.1, and discuss the data sources used to generate the results of this paper in Sect. 2.2.

2.1   Background and Related Work

The recent wave of attention for BSSs from the scientific community is largely due to vast amount of data collected by *third-generation* systems [7]. Third-generation systems combat the theft and vandalism that plagued the previous two generations by employing technologies that allow for bikes and users to be uniquely identified. Data regarding bike availability at stations is collected as a by-product of such systems, and in many cases made available to third-party users, including researchers. One popular research area involves the analysis of bicycle usage patterns [9,11,13,20]. Another area, one that is particularly relevant to his paper, involves the development of algorithms for the positioning of station locations [10,24]. These algorithms can be validated against real-world systems using the station location coordinates that are often provided alongside bike availability data. In the following we present a brief overview of related work concerning both the evaluation of existing systems in terms of their station locations and the design of new systems.

A comprehensive comparison of 38 BSSs worldwide is presented in [21]. Although some of the metrics considered in [21] correspond to usage patterns, some of the metrics solely deal with the geographic position of the stations - two of these metrics will also be considered in Sect. 5. Another research question involves the clustering of stations with similar usage patterns—case studies include Barcelona [9], London [16], and Paris [4]. Of particular interest to this paper is the question of where to position the stations, given a GIS dataset to identify interesting locations: [10] does this for a proposed system in Madrid. The used GIS datasets include the road network, building usages in terms of population and jobs, 'transport zones', and locations of other public transportation hotspots. In [3], a methodology for adding new stations to BSSs is discussed and applied to two BSSs (Washington DC and Hangzhou)—the used GIS datasets here include the Google Places API for identifying Points of Interests (POIs), Location Based Social Network check-in obtained via the Foursquare API, and a demographical dataset. The potential introduction of a BSS in Helsinki, Finland is studied in [15], with a particular focus on open data. A potential BSS in Coimbra, Portugal is studied in [8]. The BSS in New York is studied in [17]; one of the GIS datasets used to identify locations of interest corresponds to taxi GPS transactions. A case study involving data provided by the municipality of Milan is presented in [5]. Naturally, the techniques used to optimise station locations can be applied in many other contexts a well—e.g., placement of defibrillators [22], fire watchtowers [2] or electric taxi charging stations [23]—see also the overview presented in the section on location-allocation models in [10]. For a general overview of location-allocation modelling of bike sharing systems can be found in [24]. Finally, in [12], a methodology for automatically learning patterns in a spatial context is discussed.

2.2   Data

Two main data sources are used in this paper. We use the OpenStreetMap project [14] as a source of geographical information, and use the CityBikes API [1] to obtain data about the locations of bicycle-sharing stations around the world. Both are discussed in more detail below.

OpenStreetMap. OpenStreetMap (OSM) is a project in which users collaborate to create a dataset of roads and places that forms the basis of a non-proprietary map of the world. The database consists of four types of entries: *nodes*, *ways*, *relations* and *tags*. The *nodes* are single latitude-longitude coordinates indicating, e.g., points of interest or corners of larger areas. *Ways* are sequences of nodes, denoting paths and polygons that determine, e.g., the shapes of parks and roads. *Relations* are ordered lists of nodes, ways and other relations, and are used to denote larger geographic entities such as cycling routes or large motorways. The *tags* are used to store metadata about the other three data types. A tag can be used to, for example, indicate that a node corresponds to a convenience store or highway traffic lights.

We use the OSM database for two purposes. First of all, we use it to identify places that are unsuited for BSS station placement, as we discuss in Sect. 3.1. A second purpose for the OSM database is that we use it to collect data about places of interest. In particular, we are interested in nodes that are tagged as a 'shop' or 'amenity'. Note that the latter category is relatively broad, and includes park benches among others. Still we use this as a way of identifying locations of interest, as we discuss in greater detail in Sect. 4.4. The idea behind this choice is that those locations indicate areas that are interesting from a leisure-oriented point of view.

CityBikes. To obtain data about the station locations of existing BSSs, we use the API for the website citybik.es. The project behind this website started as an Android app named CityBikes which helped users plan journeys in a BSS by displaying information about station occupancies. The data used by the app has been made available through a publicly-accessible API. Their system features information about BSSs worldwide, although we will only consider a fraction of those in this paper.

3 Preliminaries

This section combines several topics underlying all of the BSS station placement algorithms of Sect. 4. The structure of this section is as follows. In Sect. 3.1, we discuss the choice of a target area given that a city has been selected. We discuss ways to denote and characterise a configuration of BSS station locations—from now on referred to as a *topology*—in this city in Sect. 3.2, and then discuss a generic simulation procedure for generating a BSS in Sect. 3.3.

3.1 Target Areas and Valid Station Placement Locations

Given a choice of city, the first step in obtaining a BSS topology is determining the *target area*, i.e., the area within the city in which BSS stations can be placed. Initially, this will be (roughly, considering the approximately ellipsoidal shape of the face of the earth) a rectangle $[\lambda_{min}, \lambda_{max}, \phi_{min}, \phi_{max}]$ where λ_{min} and λ_{max} are the minimum and maximum longitudes respectively and ϕ_{min} and ϕ_{max} the minimum and maximum latitudes. The choice of target area has an impact of the accuracy of the method—as we discuss below, we discretise space by projecting the (approximate) rectangles spanning the city onto pixels in an image file. Since we are limited by memory constraints, there is a trade-off between the zoom level (i.e., how big the rectangles are—smaller rectangles capture more detail) and the size of the target area. Since we compare simulation procedures to existing BSSs in this paper, we choose the initial target areas to match the bounding boxes of the existing BSS's station locations, with a margin of 1 km added. If one were interested in designing a BSS for a city that does not currently have one, manual selection of a rectangle as a target area, possibly informed by opening OSM in a web browser, would be the most straightforward approach.

Within a typical initial target area, not all areas will be suited for station placement—particularly bodies of water, parks/forests, and farmland/desert. To identify those areas, we download the pre-generated 256-by-256-pixel tiles used to display OSM maps in a browser. The tiles in the full OSM dataset span the whole world and are generated for each of 20 zoom levels, where level 0 corresponds

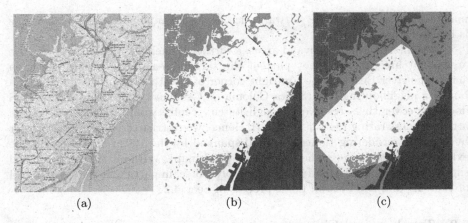

     (a)   (b)   (c)

Fig. 1. Original and filtered versions of the OSM map of the target area in Barcelona. The figure on the far right includes the convex hull spanned by 100 m circles around the stations in the Bicing BSS.

to capturing the entire face of the planet in a single 256-by-256-pixel tile and each subsequent level zooms in further by a factor 2. Given an initial target area in the form of a rectangle, we first identify the tiles corresponding to this area, and obtain an appropriate zoom level. This is done by specifying a maximum of number of pixels in the final image, and then determining the highest zoom level such that the resulting map still has fewer pixels than the maximum. When this is done, we amalgamate all the needed tiles in a single PNG image file— see Fig. 1a for an example involving the Bicing BSS in Barcelona. Finally, we identify the pixels corresponding to bodies of water in the following way: we identify pixel colours ranges[2] that tend to correspond to water bodies, then we identify for each pixel whether it falls inside that range, and finally mark a pixel as 'water' if there are 8 of those pixels within a circle with a radius of 3 pixels around it. These pixels are marked as blue in the filtered image depicted in Fig. 1b. We apply a similar pictures with green pixels for parks/forests and yellow pixels for desert/farmland. The remaining white pixels are then valid for station placement. An alternative to this approach would be to project the generated station locations onto roads, which would also avoid stations being placed in the middle of a building block. Furthermore, as can be seen in Fig. 2, stations are also sometimes placed in tunnels or on islands (e.g., the Holland Tunnel in New York, and Liberty Island), which is also something that can be avoided. This is currently left as future work as the current filtering procedure is accurate enough for illustrative purposes.

Note that the choice to use the pre-generated tiles means that the image files include place names, which causes some distortions—for example, the names of the hilltops in the top-left corner of Fig. 1a result in small patches of white pixels in the top left corner of Fig. 1b. This could be remedied by rendering the tiles

---

[2] In terms of their RGB (Red, Green, Blue) values.

manually using open source software such as, for example, Mapnik[3]. Again, this is left as future research.

After filtering out the invalid areas, a further refinement would be to exclude areas that are otherwise not part of the target area. For example, the area across the river Besòs in the top-right corner of Fig. 1b is not part of Barcelona but of a neighbouring city (Santa Coloma de Gramenet), and the existing BSS does not cover this area even though its city centre would have a fairly large attractiveness rating (as per Sect. 4.4). Hence, we restrict the target area further by instead considering the convex hull spanned by the 100 m areas around the existing BSS stations (in the discretised pixel map). Without this step, several simulation techniques would do considerably worse, in particular the regular grid of Sect. 4.1 and the Poisson point process of Sect. 4.2.

3.2   Topology and Characteristics

A BSS topology can be characterised in many different ways: here, we only discuss characteristics that are purely spatial. A complete spatial characterisation of a BSS topology with N stations is a set of points

$$(\gamma_1, \gamma_2, \ldots, \gamma_N) = ((\phi_1, \lambda_1), (\phi_2, \lambda_2), \ldots, (\phi_N, \lambda_N)),$$

where ϕ_i is the latitude of station i and λ_i its longitude. Since we are mostly interested in these locations as projected onto a map of $I \times J$ pixels (see Sect. 3.1), we will also consider

$$(c_1, c_2, \ldots, c_N) = ((x_1, y_1), (x_2, y_2), \ldots, (x_N, y_N))$$

where

$$x_i = \left\lfloor J \frac{\lambda_i - \lambda_{\min}}{\lambda_{\max} - \lambda_{\min}} \right\rfloor \text{ and } y_i = \left\lfloor I \frac{\phi_i - \phi_{\min}}{\phi_{\max} - \phi_{\min}} \right\rfloor$$

We choose the centre point $c_0 = (x_0, y_0)$ of the BSS to be the point

$$\left(\frac{1}{N} \sum_{i=1}^{N} x_i, \frac{1}{N} \sum_{j=1}^{N} y_j \right).$$

If an existing topology is not available one can alternatively take $(\lfloor J/2 \rfloor, \lfloor I/2 \rfloor)$.

Given two stations' latitude/longitude coordinates $\gamma_i = (\phi_i, \lambda_i)$ and $\gamma_j = (\phi_j, \lambda_j)$, the distance between them is given by the Haversine formula, computed as

$$d(\gamma_i, \gamma_j) = 2R \arcsin \left(\sqrt{\sin^2 \left(\frac{\Delta\phi}{2} \right) + \cos(\phi_i) \cos(\phi_j) \sin^2 \left(\frac{\Delta\lambda}{2} \right)} \right), \quad (1)$$

where $\Delta\phi = \phi_j - \phi_i$, $\Delta\lambda = \lambda_j - \lambda_i$, and R is the radius of the earth, i.e., approximately 6 371 km.

---

[3] http://mapnik.org/.

In Sect. 5, we discuss several more abstract metrics that characterise station topologies, all of which involving the distance between stations. In particular, we will consider the following two measures from [21]:

- $\bar{\delta}$: the average distance over all stations of the distance from a station to its nearest neighbour, given by

$$\delta_i = \min_{\substack{j \in \{1,\dots,N\} \\ j \neq i}} d(\gamma_i, \gamma_j), \text{ and}$$

- the compactness ratio: the ratio between the area of the convex hull to that of a circle with the same circumference.

Additionally, we use the following measures:

- σ_δ: the standard deviation of the nearest neighbour distances,
- $\bar{t}$: the average edge length in the (Euclidean) minimum spanning tree of all the station locations, and
- $\max_t$: the maximum edge length in the (Euclidean) minimum spanning tree of all the station locations.

We consider the minimum spanning tree to identify BSSs that are 'disconnected' is the sense that there exist clusters of stations such that the stations within the clusters may be close together but the clusters themselves are far apart—this information is not captured by the nearest-neighbour distance δ.

3.3 Simulation Methodology

As mentioned earlier, we consider a city map consisting of $I \times J$ pixels, with I representing the height of the image file and J the width. The final number N of stations is assumed to be fixed a priori, and equal to the size of the city's existing BSS in Sect. 5. Each pixel corresponds to a (roughly) rectangular area in the city. The first step of the procedure is to assign to each pixel i, j a probability weight w_{ij}, with a higher weight corresponding to a larger probability of being selected. We also define $\forall i \in \{1, \dots, I\}, j \in \{1, \dots, J\}$, the cumulative weights

$$c_{ij} = \sum_{\substack{(k,l): \ k < i, \text{ or} \\ k = i \wedge l \leq j}} w_{kl}$$

We then generate a (pseudo-)random number u on $[0, 1)$ using (for example) Java's built-in random number generator, and find the first pixel for which $c_{ij}/c_{IJ} > u$. The centre of the rectangle corresponding to this pixel is then selected as the next station's location. We repeat this procedure until we have N stations, and allow the weights to change depending on the locations of the previously sampled stations. For specific applications, this is not necessarily the most efficient procedure, but its appeal is its generality—we apply this procedure for all procedures except the deterministic procedure of Sect. 4.1. In Sect. 4, we discuss various ways to obtain weights w_{ij}. Note that although these processes are typically treated as continuous-space processes in the literature, we evaluate their probabilities on the discrete grid of the pixel map.

4 Topology Generation Models

In this section we discuss the procedure for obtaining station configurations. We discuss four methods: the regular grid (Sect. 4.1), the Poisson point process (Sect. 4.2), the Ginibre point process (Sect. 4.3) and the rating-weighted Poisson process (Sect. 4.4). All procedures except the first can be fully described in terms of the weights w_{ij} that inform the simulation methodology of Sect. 3.3.

4.1 Regular Grid

The idea behind the regular grid is straightforward: we place the stations on a square or hexagonal grid in order to optimise the coverage of the target areas. In principle, this means that each station has 4 or 6 nearest neighbours, with distances δ usually the same across all stations (this is typically not true due to the presence of invalid areas such as water bodies and parks). Given a choice for a square or hexagonal grid, a BSS topology can be defined uniquely using a single value for δ if we require that a station must be placed at the centre point (x_0, y_0). The question is then how to choose δ such that there are N stations in the target area. A complication here is the fact that we want to avoid placing stations in the invalid locations discussed in Sect. 3.1. One possibility is an approach based on bisection: we initialise $\delta_{\max}$ to be some large value (e.g., the length of the diagonal in the bounding box of the target area) and initialise $\delta_{\min} = 0$, then check how many stations are placed within the target area for

$$\delta = \frac{1}{2}(\delta_{\max} - \delta_{\min}).$$

If this number is too large, we set $\delta_{\max} = \frac{1}{2}(\delta_{\max} - \delta_{\min})$, else set $\delta_{\min} = \frac{1}{2}(\delta_{\max} - \delta_{\min})$ and repeat until the new value of δ yields exactly N stations. One complication is that if the target area is not convex, N is not monotonously decreasing as a function of δ. Even if we use the convex hull to narrow the target area as displayed in Fig. 1c, the exclusion of invalid areas such as water bodies will often result in non-convexity. Hence, this approach is approximative at best. When this is finished it is possible to add random noise (e.g., Gaussian noise) to make the topology look less artificial (we will not do this in Sect. 5).

4.2 Poisson Point Process

The Poisson point process is the most straightforward simulation procedure—the idea is to draw station locations uniformly within the target area. In terms of the procedure of Sect. 3.3, this amounts to fixing a constant $k > 0$ and setting $w_{ij} \equiv k \ \forall i \in \{1, \ldots, I\}, j \in \{1, \ldots, J\}$. In continuous space, this approach is called the Poisson point process because the ordered sequence of longitudes forms a realisation of a Poisson process conditional on it having N points within the box, and similarly for the latitudes. To avoid stations being drawn outside the target area or in invalid locations (as discussed in Sect. 3.1), we set w_{ij} to zero for each point (i, j) corresponding to such a pixel. This results in a Poisson process that is *inhomogeneous* across the bounding box. In fact, the two approaches in the remainder of Sect. 4 can also be seen as discrete versions of inhomogeneous Poisson point processes.

4.3 Ginibre Point Process

The origins of the Ginibre point process lie in physics, where it is used to model the locations of particles in a cloud. It has recently been applied in the context of telecommunications systems, namely to model locations of base stations in a cellular network [19]. It can be defined iteratively using the following density (see, e.g., [6]):

$$f(z_k|z_{k-1}\ldots z_1) = \frac{1}{k!} \cdot \frac{1}{\pi} e^{-|z_k|^2} \cdot \prod_{j=1}^{k-1} |z_k - z_j|^2 \tag{2}$$

Generating a sample $(z_1, \ldots, z_N)$ from the standard Ginibre point process is straightforward: let A and B be $N \times N$ matrices filled with realisations of random variables with a normal distribution with mean 0 and variance $\frac{1}{2}$. Then if $\lambda_1, \ldots, \lambda_N$ are the eigenvalues of the complex matrix $A + iB$, then

$$\Big((\mathrm{Re}(\lambda_1), \mathrm{Im}(\lambda_1)), \ldots, (\mathrm{Re}(\lambda_N), \mathrm{Im}(\lambda_N)) \Big) \tag{3}$$

is a realisation of the standard Ginibre point process. It is *scale-invariant*: multiplying the points of a *standard* Ginibre point process by a constant yields a Ginibre point process generated by normally distributed random variables with a different variance. Again, we do not want stations to be placed in rivers or farmland. Our approach is to use (2) to inform the weights w_{ij}, setting w_{ij} to zero for invalid pixels. An alternative approach would be to draw, using (3), a topology of size larger than N, and try to find a scale such that N stations are within the target area and in valid areas. However, this approach does not fit into our general methodology. Note that the procedure based on (2) can be computationally expensive compared to one based on (3) as the weights have to be recomputed each time a station is drawn. This is done efficiently by multiplying the elements of the current matrix by a factor that depends on the distance between each pixel and the station location sampled in the current iteration.

4.4 Rating-Weighted Scheme

The idea behind this approach is to incorporate geographical information into the weights. This is done in the following way. We use a matrix ρ_{ij} to denote the attractiveness of pixel (i, j)—this is initially set to 0. We then download a list of amenities and shops in the target area from the OSM website as discussed in Sect. 2.2. This is followed by going through this list and increasing ρ_{ij} by 5 if the Euclidean distance between the location of the element of the list and the centre of the rectangle corresponding to pixel i, j is smaller than 50 m—if this distance is between 50 and 200 m we increase ρ_{ij} by 2, and if it is between 200 and 1000 m we increase ρ_{ij} by 1. Of course, this is but one of many ways to incorporate the information in the list of places.

Additionally, inspired by the Ginibre point process we will also discourage stations being placed within close proximity of each other. Given that n station locations have already been drawn, let γ_{ij} be the latitude-longitude coordinate corresponding to the centre of pixel (i, j)—we then set

$$w_{ij} = \rho_{ij} \prod_{k=1}^{n} \left(1 - \exp\left(\frac{-(d(\gamma_{ij}, \gamma_k))^2}{\sigma} \right) \right).$$

Like the Ginibre approach, this approach can be computationally expensive: the rating needs to be computed for each pixel, and if we want to let the rating depend on the locations of the stations sampled thus far (to avoid clustering), we need to recompute it after each successful sample. Efficiency can be improved by aggregating pixels, or by using an estimate of $\rho_{\max}$ rather than the exact value.

5   Analysis and Results

In this section we will provide an overview of simulation experiments done using the methodology presented earlier. The case study will feature a selection of 11 cities. The difference between the methods and the real systems will be illustrated using several metrics, to be discussed below.

We begin with an overview of the characteristics discussed in Sect. 3.2 for a number of cities, presented in Table 1. We have made a selection from the close to 400 BSSs available on the citybik.es website, based on a number of basic metrics. First of all, the BSSs of *Barcelona*, *Paris*, *London*, and *New York* were considered because of their (large) size. Furthermore, the New York BSS has the interesting property that the station density is much higher in Manhattan and Brooklyn than in New Jersey. *Brussels* has a very compact BSS, whereas *Nice* is much more strip-like, as evidenced by the high and low compactness ratios respectively. *Melbourne* has a very disconnected BSS, with several southern stations that are very far away from the others, as evidenced by its large value for $\max_t$, the largest edge length in the minimum spanning tree. Finally, we also include *Dublin*, *Glasgow*, *Pisa* and *Tel Aviv*.

In general, there is some degree of variety in terms of the inter-spacing, as evidenced by $\bar{\delta}$ and $\bar{t}$, which are strongly correlated. For example, the average distance to the nearest other station is twice as high in Brussels as it is in London and Paris. There are also considerable differences between the ratios of σ_δ to $\bar{\delta}$, and indication of the standard deviation relative to the mean. For Brussels this ratio is very low (about $\frac{1}{3}$), and much higher for Nice (about $\frac{2}{3}$), meaning that the stations are more evenly spread out in Brussels than they are in Nice. This is also evident if one compares Fig. 2a–b.

Table 1. Comparison of the systems under consideration in terms of the characteristics discussed in Sect. 3.2.

City	# stations	$\bar{\delta}$	σ_δ	$\bar{t}$	$\max_t$	Compactness
Barcelona	465	168.79	99.53	218.61	597.01	.83
Brussels	343	387.11	120.82	431.42	915.01	.93
Dublin	101	196.30	63.95	232.55	438.52	.83
Glasgow	41	420.75	222.77	512.70	1203.02	.79
London	733	213.40	90.65	253.13	700.89	.81
Melbourne	49	431.63	206.95	530.79	1905.63	.80
New York	511	247.98	117.41	283.82	1425.83	.78
Nice	176	237.20	150.86	274.16	1531.63	.55
Paris	1225	218.84	101.94	252.27	1301.27	.88
Pisa	15	644.04	376.21	708.41	1687.53	.75
Tel Aviv	196	339.49	127.04	389.96	1151.84	.73

In Tables 2 and 3, we compare the performance of the topology generation methods in terms of the degree to which their results match the real systems across a range of simulation experiments. In particular, this is done using two different metrics: the coverage overlap and the mean absolute difference. The former metric (the coverage overlap) is calculated as follows: given a city, a coverage radius D, and a topology generation method, we apply the following procedure in each simulation run: we create an image such that each pixel corresponding to an area within D meters of a generated BSS station is marked as 'covered' (e.g., by colouring it pink as in Fig. 2). We also do that for the original BSS, and then check for how many pixels within the target area (the convex hull mentioned earlier, minus the invalid areas) the original and generated BSS give the same result. This is divided by the total number of pixels in this target area to give an overlap score. A comparison in terms of this metric is done in Table 2, for a radius D of 200 m.

For the latter metric (the mean absolute difference), we compute a coverage 'score' for each pixel based on how many stations are in its vicinity. In particular, each station adds a score of 5 to all pixels whose centre is at most 50 m away from it, a score of 2 to all pixels between 50 and 200 m and a score of 1 to all pixels between 200 m and 1 km. The metric is then computed as the absolute difference between the scores for the real system and the generated one, averaged over all pixels (again restricted to the target area). The results in terms of this metric are displayed in Table 3.

In both tables, the numbers are the averages of 10 of such scores, $\pm 1.96 \times$ the standard deviation of the estimator, which gives a rough indication of the accuracy of the estimates in terms of a (rough) 95% confidence interval. Note that high scores are desirable for the coverage overlaps, whereas low values are desirable for the mean absolute differences. The methods which yielded the best results for a given city have been made bold in both tables.

For the 200 m coverage overlaps, the rating-weighted scheme is nearly always the best choice, with Barcelona, Dublin, and Pisa the only exceptions. One possible explanation for the low overlap in Dublin is that its BSS is more commuting-than leisure-oriented. The regular grid does fairly well in all cases. For the mean absolute difference, the rating-weighted method is the best choice in all cases,

Table 2. Comparison of the topology generation methodologies in terms of coverage overlap as discussed in Sect. 5. High values indicate a large overlap—the best-performing methods are marked in bold for each city.

City	Reg. grid	Poisson	Ginibre	Rated
Barcelona	**.64**	.56 ± .01	.59 ± .01	.63 ± .01
Brussels	.54	.57 ± .01	.57 ± .01	**.60 ± .01**
Dublin	**.61**	.54 ± .01	.55 ± .01	.59 ± .02
Glasgow	.63	.64 ± .02	.66 ± .01	**.69 ± .02**
London	.56	.52 ± .01	.48 ± .01	**.59 ± .01**
Melbourne	.62	.64 ± .02	.64 ± .01	**.68 ± .01**
New York	.53	.52 ± .01	.49 ± .01	**.67 ± .01**
Nice	.52	.53 ± .02	.56 ± .01	**.67 ± .02**
Paris	.62	.55 ± .01	.56 ± .01	**.66 ± .01**
Pisa	**.73**	.72 ± .02	.72 ± .02	.72 ± .03
Tel Aviv	.54	.55 ± .01	.58 ± .01	**.61 ± .01**

Table 3. Comparison of the topology generation methodologies in terms of the mean absolute difference as discussed in Sect. 5. Low values indicate a small difference—the best-performing methods are marked in bold for each city.

City	Reg. grid	Poisson	Ginibre	Rated
Barcelona	17.55	18.98 ± .84	24.51 ± .08	**12.29 ± .47**
Brussels	5.88	7.08 ± .33	6.92 ± .06	**5.38 ± .24**
Dublin	9.51	11.07 ± 1.68	15.69 ± .27	**9.06 ± .43**
Glasgow	4.54	5.71 ± .75	4.43 ± .16	**3.23 ± .24**
London	14.39	15.02 ± .39	24.57 ± .03	**9.59 ± .25**
Melbourne	3.69	4.57 ± .33	4.82 ± .08	**3.67 ± .29**
New York	14.39	14.83 ± .54	20.00 ± .04	**5.44 ± .15**
Nice	11.75	13.04 ± .49	18.63 ± .07	**6.55 ± .29**
Paris	19.03	19.42 ± .54	25.69 ± .04	**13.05 ± .33**
Pisa	3.03	3.59 ± .45	4.18 ± .20	**2.93 ± .38**
Tel Aviv	7.71	8.26 ± .42	10.67 ± .06	**5.43 ± .22**

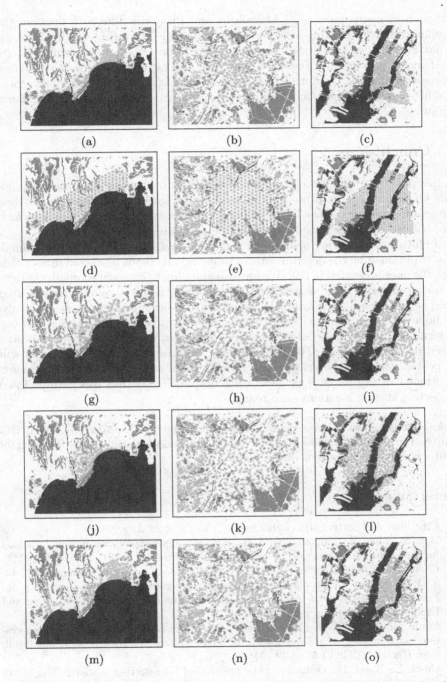

Fig. 2. Left to right: Nice, Brussels, New York. Top to bottom: real system, regular grid (without noise), Poisson, Ginibre, rating-weighted.

although in many cases (e.g., Melbourne and Pisa) the difference between the regular grid and the rating-weighted scheme is small. The rating-weighted scheme is particularly good in cities where the BSS stations are more unevenly distributed across the city, like New York and Nice. The rating-based scheme also does reasonably well for London, Paris and Tel Aviv. It should be noted that there is still substantial room for parameter tuning for some methods (particularly Ginibre).

6   Conclusions

In this paper, we have introduced a new approach for generating station topologies. Of the four methods proposed, the one whose generated topologies matched the existing systems in the best manner was the data-driven approach, in which areas of the city were 'rated' according to popularity.

In future work, we are planning to compare the simulation results to 'optimal' results obtained by the deterministic optimisation methods discussed in Sect. 2.1, e.g., the ones presented in [10]. We are also planning to consider a broader variety of rating methods: e.g., closeness to railway stations for a commuting-oriented BSS, or greater weight to landmarks for a tourism-oriented system. Additionally, we hope to link our methodology to bike movement models: classifying stations in terms of their typical usage behaviour (e.g., during peak hours or weekends) based on their location. The programming code used for the experiments will be posted online in the near future. Finally, there are some minor adjustments mentioned in the texts: e.g., generating bespoke OSM tiles using Mapnik, or projecting station locations onto roads.

Acknowledgments. This work has been supported by the EU project QUANTICOL, 600708. The author would like to thank Vashti Galpin and Jane Hillston for their helpful feedback on an earlier version of this paper.

References

1. CityBikes API. http://api.citybik.es/v2/. Accessed 28 Aug 2015
2. Bao, S., Xiao, N., Lai, Z., Zhang, H., Kim, C.: Optimizing watchtower locations for forest fire monitoring using location models. Fire Saf. J. **71**, 100–109 (2015)
3. Chen, L., Zhang, D., Pan, G., Ma, X., Yang, D., Kushlev, K., Zhang, W., Li, S.: Bike sharing station placement leveraging heterogeneous urban open data. In: Proceedings of the 2015 ACM International Joint Conference on Pervasive and Ubiquitous Computing, pp. 571–575. ACM (2015)
4. Côme, E., Oukhellou, L.: Model-based count series clustering for bike sharing system usage mining: a case study with the Vélib' system of Paris. ACM Trans. Intell. Syst. Technol. (TIST) **5**(3), 39 (2014)
5. Croci, E., Rossi, D.: Optimizing the position of bike sharing stations. The Milan Case (2014)
6. Decreusefond, L., Flint, I., Vergne, A.: Efficient simulation of the Ginibre point process. arXiv preprint arXiv:1310.0800 (2013)

7. Fishman, E.: Bikeshare: a review of recent literature. Transp. Rev. **36**, 92–113 (2016)
8. Frade, I., Ribeiro, A.: Bike-sharing stations: a maximal covering location approach. Transp. Res. Part A Policy Pract. **82**, 216–227 (2015)
9. Froehlich, J., Neumann, J., Oliver, N.: Sensing and predicting the pulse of the city through shared bicycling. IJCAI **9**, 1420–1426 (2009)
10. García-Palomares, J.C., Gutiérrez, J., Latorre, M.: Optimizing the location of stations in bike-sharing programs: a GIS approach. Appl. Geogr. **35**(1), 235–246 (2012)
11. Gast, N., Massonnet, G., Reijsbergen, D., Tribastone, M.: Probabilistic forecasts of bike-sharing systems for journey planning. In: The 24th ACM International Conference on Information and Knowledge Management (CIKM 2015) (2015)
12. Gol, E.A., Bartocci, E., Belta, C.: A formal methods approach to pattern synthesis in reaction diffusion systems. In: 2014 IEEE 53rd Annual Conference on Decision and Control, pp. 108–113. IEEE (2014)
13. Guenther, M.C., Bradley, J.T.: Journey data based arrival forecasting for bicycle hire schemes. In: Dudin, A., Turck, K. (eds.) ASMTA 2013. LNCS, vol. 7984, pp. 214–231. Springer, Heidelberg (2013). doi:10.1007/978-3-642-39408-9_16
14. Haklay, M., Weber, P.: Openstreetmap: user-generated street maps. IEEE Pervasive Comput. **7**(4), 12–18 (2008)
15. Jäppinen, S., Toivonen, T., Salonen, M.: Modelling the potential effect of shared bicycles on public transport travel times in Greater Helsinki: an open data approach. Appl. Geogr. **43**, 13–24 (2013)
16. Lathia, N., Ahmed, S., Capra, L.: Measuring the impact of opening the London shared bicycle scheme to casual users. Transp. Res. Part C Emerg. Technol. **22**, 88–102 (2012)
17. Liu, J., Li, Q., Qu, M., Chen, W., Yang, J., Hui, X., Zhong, H., Fu, Y.: Station site optimization in bike sharing systems
18. Meddin, R., DeMaio, P.: The bike-sharing world map. https://www.google.com/maps/d/viewer?mid=zGPlSU9zZvZw.kmqv_ul1MfkI. Accessed 28 Jan 2015
19. Miyoshi, N., Shirai, T., et al.: A cellular network model with Ginibre configured base stations. Adv. Appl. Probab. **46**(3), 832–845 (2014)
20. Nair, R., Miller-Hooks, E., Hampshire, R.C., Bušić, A.: Large-scale vehicle sharing systems: analysis of Vélib'. Int. J. Sustain. Transp. **7**(1), 85–106 (2013)
21. O'Brien, O., Cheshire, J., Batty, M.: Mining bicycle sharing data for generating insights into sustainable transport systems. J. Transp. Geogr. **34**, 262–273 (2014)
22. Tsai, Y.S., Ko, P.C.I., Huang, C.Y., Wen, T.H.: Optimizing locations for the installation of automated external defibrillators (AEDs) in urban public streets through the use of spatial and temporal weighting schemes. Appl. Geogr. **35**(1), 394–404 (2012)
23. Tu, W., Li, Q., Fang, Z., Shaw, S.I., Zhou, B., Chang, X.: Optimizing the locations of electric taxi charging stations: a spatial-temporal demand coverage approach. Transp. Res. Part C Emerg. Technol. **65**, 172–189 (2016)
24. Zhang, Y., Zuidgeest, M., Brussel, M., Sliuzas, R., van Maarseveen, M.: Spatial location-allocation modeling of bike sharing systems: a literature search. In: Proceedings of the 13th World Conference on Transportation Research (2013)

GCM

On the Definition of Parallel Independence in the Algebraic Approaches to Graph Transformation

Andrea Corradini[(✉)]

Dipartimento di Informatica, Università di Pisa, Pisa, Italy
andrea@di.unipi.it

Abstract. Parallel independence between transformation steps is a basic and well-understood notion of the algebraic approaches to graph transformation, and typically guarantees that the two steps can be applied in any order obtaining the same resulting graph, up to isomorphism. The concept has been redefined for several algebraic approaches as variations of a classical "algebraic" condition, requiring that each matching morphism factorizes through the context graphs of the other transformation step. However, looking at some classical papers on the double-pushout approach, one finds that the original definition of parallel independence was formulated in set-theoretical terms, requiring that the intersection of the images of the two left-hand sides in the host graph is contained in the intersection of the two interface graphs. The relationship between this definition and the standard algebraic one is discussed in this position paper, both in the case of left-linear and non-left-linear rules.

1 Introduction and Background

Graph transformation (GT) is a well-developed computational model suited to describe the evolution of systems. System states are represented by graphs, and rules typically describe local changes of part of the state. One central topic in the theory of GT has been the identification of conditions that guarantee that two transformation steps from a given state are independent, and thus can be applied in any order generating the same result. Interestingly, two transformation steps commute (have the so-called *diamond property*) even if their matches overlap, provided that they overlap only on items that are preserved by both.

In this short paper we start comparing two classical definitions of *parallel independence* of transformation steps proposed for the Double-Pushout (DPO) approach to graph transformation. Not surprisingly, we show that they are equivalent for linear rules. But if rules are non-left-linear, as allowed for example in the [Reversible] Sesqui-Pushout ([R]SqPO) approach where rules can specify the cloning of items, they are not equivalent anymore: The equivalence can be recovered by reinforcing one of the two definitions with an additional condition.

The reader is assumed to be familiar with the DPO approach and recent categorical development of its theory, including the definition and some properties of

P. Milazzo et al. (Eds.): STAF 2016, LNCS 9946, pp. 101–111, 2016.
DOI: 10.1007/978-3-319-50230-4_8

adhesive categories. We briefly recall in the rest of this introductory section a few definitions (final pullback complement, DPO and (Reversible) Sesqui-Pushout approaches).

In order to fix the terminology, let us recall the standard definition of Double-Pushout transformation [13] in a generic category $\mathbf{C}$.

Definition 1 (Double-Pushout transformation). *A production $\rho = (L \xleftarrow{l} K \xrightarrow{r} R)$ is a span of arrows in $\mathbf{C}$. Production ρ is left-linear if l is mono, right-linear if r is mono, and linear if both l and r are monos. A match for a production ρ in an object G is an arrow $m : L \to G$. If the diagram in (1) can be constructed in $\mathbf{C}$, where both squares are pushouts, then we say that there is a transformation step from G to H via (ρ, m), and we write $G \Rightarrow_{(\rho,m)} H$. In this case we call the pair (ρ, m) a redex in G, and we call it (left-, right-) linear if so is ρ. We write $G \Rightarrow_\rho H$ if there is a match m for ρ in G such that $G \Rightarrow_{(\rho,m)} H$.*

$$
\begin{array}{ccccc}
L & \xleftarrow{\ \ l\ \ } & K & \xrightarrow{\ \ r\ \ } & R \\
{\scriptstyle m}\downarrow & & \downarrow{\scriptstyle n} & & \downarrow{\scriptstyle p} \\
G & \xleftarrow{\ \ g\ \ } & D & \xrightarrow{\ \ h\ \ } & H
\end{array}
\qquad (1)
$$

Therefore if (ρ, m) is a redex in G we know that ρ can be applied to match m in G. In diagram (1), K is called the *interface* and D the *context*.

The definition of (Reversible) Sesqui-Pushout transformation [5,7] is very similar to DPO transformation, the only difference being the properties that the left and right squares of diagram (1) have to satisfy. We first recall the definition of final pullback complement.

Definition 2 (final pullback complement). *In diagram (2), $K \xrightarrow{n} D \xrightarrow{a} G$ is a* final pullback complement *of $K \xrightarrow{l} L \xrightarrow{m} G$ if*
1. *the resulting square is a pullback, and*
2. *for each pullback $G \xleftarrow{m} L \xleftarrow{d} K' \xrightarrow{e} D' \xrightarrow{f} G$ and arrow $K' \xrightarrow{h} K$ such that $l \circ h = d$, there is a unique arrow $D' \xrightarrow{g} D$ such that $a \circ g = f$ and $g \circ e = n \circ h$.*

$$
\begin{array}{ccccc}
 & & \overset{d}{\frown} & & \\
L & \xleftarrow{\ l\ } & K & \xleftarrow{\ h\ } & K' \\
{\scriptstyle m}\downarrow & & \downarrow{\scriptstyle n} & & \downarrow{\scriptstyle e} \\
G & \xleftarrow{\ a\ } & D & \xleftarrow{--g--} & D' \\
 & & \underset{f}{\smile} & &
\end{array}
\qquad (2)
$$

Definition 3 ((Reversible) Sesqui-Pushout transformation). *Under the premises of Definition 1, we say that there is an SqPO transformation step from G to H via (ρ, m) if the diagram in (1) can be constructed in $\mathbf{C}$, where the left square is a final pullback complement and the right square is a pushout. Similarly, there is a Reversible SqPO transformation step from G to H via (ρ, m) if the diagram in (1) can be constructed in $\mathbf{C}$, where both the left and the right squares are both final pullback complements and pushouts.*

2 Comparing Definitions of Parallel Independence: The Left-Linear Case

The *Local Church-Rosser Problem* is presented in the following way in [6]:

> Find a condition, called *parallel independence*, such that two alternative direct derivations $H_1 \; {}_{\rho_1}\!\!\Leftarrow G \Rightarrow_{\rho_2} H_2$ are parallel independent iff there are direct derivations $H_1 \Rightarrow_{\rho_2} X$ and $H_2 \Rightarrow_{\rho_1} X$ such that $G \Rightarrow_{\rho_1} H_1 \Rightarrow_{\rho_2} X$ and $G \Rightarrow_{\rho_2} H_2 \Rightarrow_{\rho_1} X$ are equivalent.

Deliberately we leave this statement at a pretty informal level, avoiding to define formally the notion of equivalence of derivation sequence: For the interested reader, several kinds of such equivalences are discussed in [4] and in Sect. 3.5 of [6], the most relevant of which are based on the classical *shift equivalence* [14]. Also, for the sake of simplicity, we do not consider the related notion of *sequential independence* of two consecutive transformation steps.

Relevant for the present discussion is the observation that the above statement fixes a standard pattern for addressing the Local Church-Rosser Problem in the various approaches to algebraic graph transformation: first, a definition of parallel independence for transformation steps has to be provided, next a *Local Church-Rosser Theorem* proves that given two parallel independent transformation steps from a given graph, they can be applied in both orders obtaining the same result (up to isomorphism). Disregarding the proofs of the Local Church-Rosser Theorems, in the following we aim at relating and comparing a few definitions of parallel independence.

In [9], a standard reference for the DPO approach, two definitions of parallel independence are presented. The first one is stated in a set-theoretical way for the category **Graph** of graphs and graph homomorphism, and for *linear* productions. It says that two linear redexes are parallel independent if they satisfy Condition 1.

Condition 1 (preservation of intersection of matches). *In category* **Graph**, (ρ_1, m_1) *and* (ρ_2, m_2) *are two redexes in a graph* G, *as in diagram (3). The intersection of matches* m_1 *and* m_2 *in* G *is preserved along the interfaces, that is,*

$$m_1(L_1) \cap m_2(L_2) \subseteq m_1(l_1(K_1)) \cap m_2(l_2(K_2))$$

or equivalently, since the reverse inclusion always holds,

$$m_1(L_1) \cap m_2(L_2) = m_1(l_1(K_1)) \cap m_2(l_2(K_2)).$$

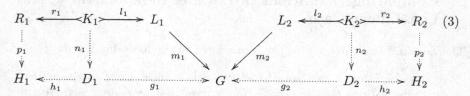

$$R_1 \xleftarrow{r_1} K_1 \xrightarrow{l_1} L_1 \qquad\qquad L_2 \xleftarrow{l_2} K_2 \xrightarrow{r_2} R_2 \quad (3)$$

This definition conveys the precise intuition that two redexes are independent if each preserves the items needed by the other; therefore the match in G of, say, ρ_1 is still available in the result of the transformation step $G \Rightarrow_{(\rho_2, m_2)} H_2$.

Immediately after, a different characterization is presented: two linear redexes are parallel independent if they satisfy Condition 2.

Condition 2 (factorization of matches). *In a category* **C**, (ρ_1, m_1) *and* (ρ_2, m_2) *are two redexes in an object* G, *as in diagram (4). The matches* m_1 *and* m_2 *factorize through the context, that is, there exist arrows* $m_{1d} : L_1 \to D_2$ *and* $m_{2d} : L_2 \to D_1$ *such that* $g_2 \circ m_{1d} = m_1$ *and* $g_1 \circ m_{2d} = m_2$.

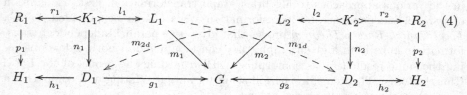

$$R_1 \xleftarrow{r_1} K_1 \xrightarrow{l_1} L_1 \quad\text{-----}\quad L_2 \xleftarrow{l_2} K_2 \xrightarrow{r_2} R_2 \quad (4)$$

The equivalence of Conditions 1 and 2 for linear redexes and for the category of graphs is proved for example in [8] and in Fact 3.18 of [10], by exploiting specific properties of pushouts in **Graph**. The motivation for introducing Condition 2 is pragmatical: it is easier to use in the proof of the *Local Church-Rosser Theorem*, heavily based on diagrammatic constructions.[1]

In subsequent developments of the DPO approach to categories different from graphs (including High Level Replacement (HLR) systems first [11] and DPO transformation in adhesive categories next [15]), Condition 2 has always be taken as the reference definition of parallel independence. But it is obvious that Condition 2 is not a direct translation in categorical terms of the set-theoretical Condition 1, as the authors of [11] implicitly state when they write *"For HLR-systems it is easier to define independence directly by conditions 1 and 2 above* (i.e. Condition 2), *because this avoids to require general pullback constructions generalizing intersections"*. Indeed, a direct categorical formulation of Condition 1 would read as follows.

---

[1] The definitions of parallel independence based on Conditions 1 or 2 date back to the mid seventies of last century. Besides of [8] they also appear in [12]. In [17] parallel independence is defined set-theoretically (see diagram (3)) as $m_1(L_1) \subseteq g_2(D_2) \wedge m_2(L_2) \subseteq g_1(D_1)$, a variant of Condition 2.

Condition 3 (preservation of pullback of matches). *In a category* **C**, *(ρ_1, m_1) and (ρ_2, m_2) are two redexes in an object G. The pullback of the matches m_1 and m_2 in G is preserved along the interfaces, that is, in diagram (5), where both squares are pullbacks, the mediating arrow $i : K_1 \times_G K_2 \to L_1 \times_G L_2$ is an isomorphism.*

$$
\begin{array}{ccc}
K_1 \times_G K_2 & \xrightarrow{\quad \pi_2^K \quad} & K_2 \\
\downarrow \pi_1^K & \searrow i & \downarrow l_2 \\
& L_1 \times_G L_2 \xrightarrow{\pi_2^L} & L_2 \\
& \downarrow \pi_1^L & \downarrow m_2 \\
K_1 \xrightarrow{\;l_1\;} & L_1 \xrightarrow{\;m_1\;} & G
\end{array}
\tag{5}
$$

Therefore Condition 3 is another candidate for a definition of parallel independence, provided that the reference category **C** has the needed pullbacks. To my knowledge, the equivalence of Conditions 2 and 3 was not discussed in the literature. Let us show that the two conditions are indeed equivalent for left-linear productions, and assuming that category **C** is adhesive.

Proposition 1 (matches extend iff their pullback is preserved). *Let* **C** *be an adhesive category. Then for left-linear redexes Conditions 2 and 3 are equivalent.*

Proof. **Condition 2 implies Condition 3.** Suppose that two left-linear redexes (ρ_1, m_1) and (ρ_2, m_2) satisfy Condition 2 and consider diagram (6). We show that the large square is a pullback, from which $L_1 \times_G L_2 \cong K_1 \times_G K_2$ follows (and thus Condition 3). Therefore given an object X with arrows $f : X \to L_2$ and $g : X \to L_1$ such that $m_2 \circ f = m_1 \circ g$, we have to show that there exists a unique arrow $h : X \to K_1 \times_G K_2$ such that $l_2 \circ \pi_2^K \circ h = f$ and $l_1 \circ \pi_1^K \circ h = g$.

$$\tag{6}$$

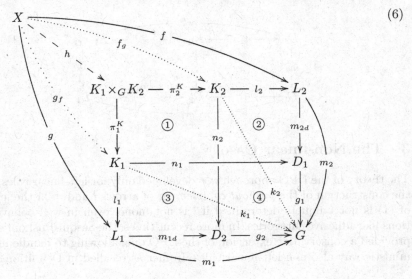

Existence. Square ② + ④ is a pushout by construction, and by adhesivity it is also a pullback, because l_2 is mono by hypothesis. Since $X \xrightarrow{f} L_2 \xrightarrow{m_2} G = X \xrightarrow{m_{1d} \circ g} D_2 \xrightarrow{g_2} G$ and ② + ④ is a pullback, there is a unique arrow $f_g : X \to K_2$ such that $l_2 \circ f_g = f$ and $n_2 \circ f_g = m_{1d} \circ g$. For symmetric reasons, since also ③ + ④ is a pullback there is a unique arrow $g_f : X \to K_1$ such that $l_1 \circ g_f = g$ and $n_1 \circ g_f = m_{2d} \circ f$.

Next observe that by definition $K_1 \xleftarrow{\pi_1^K} K_1 \times_G K_2 \xrightarrow{\pi_2^K} K_2$ is the pullback of $K_1 \xrightarrow{k_1} G \xleftarrow{k_2} K_2$, where k_1 and k_2 are the diagonals of squares ③+④ and ②+④, respectively. Thus since we have $k_2 \circ f_g = m_2 \circ l_2 \circ f_g = m_2 \circ f = m_1 \circ g = m_1 \circ l_1 \circ g_f = k_1 \circ g_f$, we deduce that there is a unique arrow $h : X \to K_1 \times_G K_2$ such that $\pi_2^K \circ h = f_g$ and $\pi_1^K \circ h = g_f$, and thus we obtain $l_2 \circ \pi_2^K \circ h = f$ and $l_1 \circ \pi_1^K \circ h = g$, as desired.

Uniqueness. Suppose that there are arrows $h_1, h_2 : X \to K_1 \times_G K_2$ such that $l_2 \circ \pi_2^K \circ h_1 = f = l_2 \circ \pi_2^K \circ h_2$ and $l_1 \circ \pi_1^K \circ h_1 = g = l_1 \circ \pi_1^K \circ h_2$. Since l_1 and l_2 are mono, we obtain $\pi_2^K \circ h_1 = \pi_2^K \circ h_2$ and $\pi_1^K \circ h_1 = \pi_1^K \circ h_2$. Then $h_1 = h_2$ follows because $K_1 \times_G K_2$ is a pullback object, and $k_1 \circ \pi_1^K \circ h_i = m_1 \circ l_1 \circ \pi_1^K \circ h_i = m_1 \circ g = m_2 \circ f = m_2 \circ l_2 \circ \pi_2^K \circ h_i = k_2 \circ \pi_2^K \circ h_i$, for $i \in \{1, 2\}$.

Condition 3 implies Condition 2. Vice versa, assume that (ρ_1, m_1) and (ρ_2, m_2) satisfy Condition 3. By Proposition 12 of [5] since $l_2 : K_2 \rightarrowtail L_2$ is mono and **C** is adhesive, $K_2 \xrightarrow{-n_2} D_2 \xrightarrow{g_2} G$, is a final pullback complement of $K_2 \xrightarrowtail{l_2} L_2 \xrightarrow{m_2} G$. Thus in diagram (7) the left square is a final pullback complement, the outer square is a pullback by definition, and the upper triangle commutes by (5). By the universal property of final pullback complements there is a unique arrow $m_{1d} : L_1 \to D_2$ making the right square and the bottom triangle commute. Therefore we have $g_2 \circ m_{1d} = m_1$, and by a symmetric argument there exists an arrow $m_{2d} : L_2 \to D_1$ such that $g_1 \circ m_{2d} = m_2$. Thus the two redexes satisfy Condition 2.

$$
\begin{array}{ccccc}
L_2 & \xleftarrow{\quad l_2 \quad} & K_2 & \xleftarrow{\pi_2^k \circ i^{-1}} & L_1 \times_G L_2 \\[2pt]
\llap{m_2}\big\downarrow & & \llap{n_2}\big\downarrow & & \big\downarrow\rlap{π_1^L} \\[2pt]
G & \xleftarrow{\quad g_2 \quad} & D_2 & \xdashleftarrow{\quad m_{1d} \quad} & L_1
\end{array}
\qquad (7)
$$

with π_2^L over the top and m_1 under the bottom.

3   The Non-linear Case

The theory of the DPO approach was developed only for left-linear rules, because the construction of the *pushout complement* of arrows l and m in the left square of (1) is not uniquely determined if l is not mono, even in well-behaved situations like adhesive categories. In more recent times, the Sesqui-Pushout approach provided a conservative extension of the DPO one, allowing to handle in a deterministic way also non-left-linear rules. In fact as recalled in Definition 3 the left square of a transformation step in this case is a final pullback complement of arrows l and m, which (if it exists) is unique up to isomorphisms because it is characterized by a universal property. A definition of parallel independence for SqPO transformation *for linear productions only* has been proposed in [5] by using Condition 2 and assuming adhesivity (and existence of final pullback complements, required for SqPO transformation). Thus by Proposition 1 we now know that Condition 3 would have been equivalent.

More interestingly, in the framework of Reversible SqPO the authors of [7] have considered the Local Church-Rosser Problem for non-linear rules. We consider here only the case of possibly non-left-linear, but right-linear rules, i.e. we assume that morphism $r : K \to R$ is mono. In this case, the definition of [7] can be rephrased as follows: two right-linear redexes are parallel independent if they satisfy both Conditions 2 and 4.

Condition 4 (reflection of matches). *In a category* $\mathbf{C}$, (ρ_1, m_1) *and* (ρ_2, m_2) *are two redexes in an object* G, *as in diagram (4), which satisfy Condition 2. They are reflected identically along the context, that is, the two squares in diagram (8) are pullbacks.*

$$
\begin{array}{ccc}
L_1 \xleftarrow{\ id_{L_1}\ } L_1 & \qquad & L_2 \xrightarrow{\ id_{L_2}\ } L_2 \\
\downarrow m_1 \quad \downarrow m_{1d} & & \downarrow m_{2d} \quad \downarrow m_2 \\
G \xleftarrow{\ g_2\ } D_2 & & D_1 \xrightarrow{\ g_1\ } G
\end{array}
\tag{8}
$$

Essentially, as observed in [7], if productions are non-left-linear, the commutativity requirements for arrows m_{1d} and m_{2d} of Condition 2 are not sufficient and have to be reinforced with the pullback requirements of Condition 4.[2] The same condition is also implied by the definition of parallel independence proposed in [16] in the more general framework of rewriting in categories of spans, where the required pullbacks arise from span composition.

A simple example can clarify this situation. Let $\rho_1 = (L_1 \leftarrow K_1 \to R_1)$ and $\rho_2 = (L_2 \leftarrow K_2 \to R_2)$ be the productions depicted in the following figure, where ρ_1 adds a second loop to a preserved node with a loop, while ρ_2 duplicates the

---

[2] The conditions for parallel independence for non-linear rules in the context of RSqPO, presented in [7], are even stronger. First, besides Condition 2, making reference to diagram (4) it is required that $(\rho_2, h_1 \circ m_{2d})$ and $(\rho_1, h_2 \circ m_{1d})$ are (RSqPO-) redexes. Furthermore, and more interestingly for the present discussion, since productions can also be non-right-linear, besides Condition 4 it is also required that the squares in (9) are pullbacks.

$$
\begin{array}{ccc}
L_1 \xrightarrow{\ id_{L_1}\ } L_1 & \qquad & L_2 \xleftarrow{\ id_{L_2}\ } L_2 \\
\downarrow m_{1d} \quad \downarrow h_2 \circ m_{1d} & & \downarrow h_1 \circ m_{2d} \quad \downarrow m_{2d} \\
D_2 \xrightarrow{\ h_2\ } H_2 & & H_1 \xleftarrow{\ h_1\ } D_1
\end{array}
\tag{9}
$$

node but not the incident loop. Both can be applied using SqPO transformation to the same graph G made of a node with a loop. There are (unique) morphisms $L_1 \to D_2$ and $L_2 \to D_1$ satisfying Condition 2, but the two transformation steps do not enjoy the diamond property, and thus should not be considered as parallel independent. In fact, applying ρ_1 to H_2 one gets a graph with two nodes, one of which has two loops and the other none. Instead applying ρ_2 to H_1 one gets a graph with two nodes, one with two loops and the other with one loop.

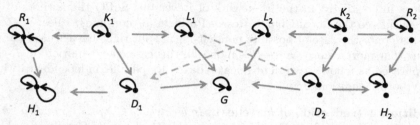

It is easy to show that the depicted redexes do not satisfy neither Condition 3 nor 4. In fact, we show that in the case of non-left-linear productions, Condition 3 is equivalent to the conjunction of Conditions 2 and 4. The last part of the proof exploits results to appear in [3], and requires an additional condition on category **C**, namely that it has a *partial maps classifier* (or equivalently, since **C** is assumed to have final pullback complements, a *subobject classifier*). We refer to [1] for the definition of partial maps classifiers and the relationship with subobject classifiers, and to [2] for their use in the AGREE approach to graph transformation.

Proposition 2 (matches factorize and are reflected identically iff their pullback is preserved). *Let **C** be an adhesive category with final pullback complements and with a sub-object classifier. Then the conjunction of Conditions 2 and 4 is equivalent to Condition 3 for SqPO and RSqPO transformation.*

Proof. **Conditions 2 and 4 imply Condition 3.** Suppose that two redexes (ρ_1, m_1) and (ρ_2, m_2) satisfy Conditions 2 and 4. We proceed as in the proof of Proposition 1 showing that the square of diagram (6) is a pullback.

Given an object X with arrows $f : X \to L_2$ and $g : X \to L_1$ such that $m_2 \circ f = m_1 \circ g$, the *existence* of an arrow $h : X \to K_1 \times_G K_2$ such that $l_2 \circ \pi_2^K \circ h = f$ and $l_1 \circ \pi_1^K \circ h = g$ can be shown as in the proof above, considering that squares ②+④ and ③+④ are now pullbacks by construction, since we consider [R]SqPO transformation. For the uniqueness part, since l_1 and l_2 are not monic in general, we exploit Condition 4.

Thus, making still reference to diagram (6), suppose that there are arrows $h_1, h_2 : X \to K_1 \times_G K_2$ such that $l_2 \circ \pi_2^K \circ h_1 = f = l_2 \circ \pi_2^K \circ h_2$ and $l_1 \circ \pi_1^K \circ h_1 = g = l_1 \circ \pi_1^K \circ h_2$.

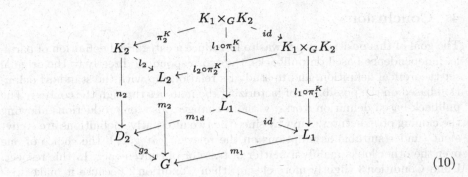

$$(10)$$

Consider the cube in diagram (10): the bottom face is a pullback by Condition 4, the front-left face is a pullback by construction, the back-right face is trivially a pullback, and the front-right and back-left squares commute. Therefore by pullback splitting also the top face is a pullback. By symmetry, also a similar square with indexes 1 and 2 exchanged is a pullback. We exploit these squares in diagram (11): since the outer squares commute by hypothesis, by the pullback property we deduce that $\pi_2^K \circ h_1 = \pi_2^K \circ h_2$ and $\pi_1^K \circ h_1 = \pi_1^K \circ h_2$. Then $h_1 = h_2$ follows by the same argument as in the proof of Proposition 1.

$$(11)$$

Condition 3 implies Conditions 2 and 4. The proof that Condition 3 implies Condition 2 is identical, and even more direct, than the corresponding proof for Proposition 1, because the left square of diagram (7) is a final pullback complement by construction.

For Condition 4, the fact that the squares in (8) are pullbacks is proved in Lemma 1 of [3] by exploiting Condition 3 and an additional condition involving the partial maps classifier, and formulated for the more general framework of AGREE transformation. The latter condition, instantiated to SqPO transformation, requires that the left square of (12) is a pullback. But this follows easily by the observation that the right square of (12) is a pullback thanks to Condition 3, and that the partial maps classifier functor $T : \mathbf{C} \to \mathbf{C}$ preserves pullbacks [1].

$$(12)$$

4   Conclusions

The goal of this position paper was to introduce a categorical definition of parallel independence based on pullbacks, thus corresponding directly to the original set-theoretical definition, and to study its relationship with the standard definition based on the possibility of factorizing the matches through the context. The pullback-based definition works, without changes, also for productions allowing the cloning of structures. Anyway since the two alternative definitions are equivalent (under suitable assumptions on the relevant category), the choice of one over the other looks mainly a matter of taste or of convenience. In this respect, I find Condition 3 slightly more elegant than Condition 2 because it makes reference only to the productions and to the corresponding matches, and not to the context graphs obtained by the application of the productions. But Condition 2 is certainly more convenient in proofs based on diagram constructions and chasing.

Acknowledgments. The idea of spelling out the relationship between the standard algebraic and the pullback-based definitions of parallel independence maturated during stimulating discussions with Dominque Duval, Frédéric Prost, Rachid Echahed and Leila Ribeiro, during the work on the AGREE approach to GT. Hans-Jörg Kreowski provided me some references to the early literature on parallel independence. During the workshop where this work was presented, Michael Löwe suggested several technical improvements, including a new version of the last part of the proof of Proposition 2 that does not need partial maps classifiers: this will be presented in a forthcoming report.

References

1. Cockett, J., Lack, S.: Restriction categories II: partial map classification. Theor. Comput. Sci. **294**(1–2), 61–102 (2003)
2. Corradini, A., Duval, D., Echahed, R., Prost, F., Ribeiro, L.: AGREE – algebraic graph rewriting with controlled embedding. In: Parisi-Presicce, F., Westfechtel, B. (eds.) ICGT 2015. LNCS, vol. 9151, pp. 35–51. Springer, Heidelberg (2015). doi:10.1007/978-3-319-21145-9_3
3. Corradini, A., Duval, D., Prost, F., Ribeiro, L.: Parallelism in AGREE transformations. In: Echahed, R., Minas, M. (eds.) ICGT 2016. LNCS, vol. 9761, pp. 37–53. Springer, Heidelberg (2016). doi:10.1007/978-3-319-40530-8_3
4. Corradini, A., Ehrig, H., Löwe, M., Montanari, U., Rossi, F.: Abstract graph derivations in the double pushout approach. In: Schneider, H.J., Ehrig, H. (eds.) Graph Transformations in Computer Science. LNCS, vol. 776, pp. 86–103. Springer, Heidelberg (1994). doi:10.1007/3-540-57787-4_6
5. Corradini, A., Heindel, T., Hermann, F., König, B.: Sesqui-Pushout rewriting. In: Corradini, A., Ehrig, H., Montanari, U., Ribeiro, L., Rozenberg, G. (eds.) ICGT 2006. LNCS, vol. 4178, pp. 30–45. Springer, Heidelberg (2006). doi:10.1007/11841883_4
6. Corradini, A., Montanari, U., Rossi, F., Ehrig, H., Heckel, R., Löwe, M.: Algebraic approaches to graph transformation - part I: basic concepts and double pushout approach. In: Handbook of Graph Grammars and Computing by Graph Transformations, Foundations, vol. 1, pp. 163–246 (1997)

7. Danos, V., Heindel, T., Honorato-Zimmer, R., Stucki, S.: Reversible Sesqui-Pushout rewriting. In: Giese, H., König, B. (eds.) ICGT 2014. LNCS, vol. 8571, pp. 161–176. Springer, Heidelberg (2014). doi:10.1007/978-3-319-09108-2_11

8. Ehrig, H., Rosen, B.: Commutativity of Independent Transformations on Complex Objects. IBM Thomas J. Watson Research Division (1976)

9. Ehrig, H.: Introduction to the algebraic theory of graph grammars (a survey). In: Claus, V., Ehrig, H., Rozenberg, G. (eds.) Graph Grammars 1978. LNCS, vol. 73, pp. 1–69. Springer, Heidelberg (1979). doi:10.1007/BFb0025714

10. Ehrig, H., Ehrig, K., Prange, U., Taentzer, G.: Fundamentals of Algebraic Graph Transformation. Monographs in Theoretical Computer Science. An EATCS Series. Springer, Heidelberg (2006)

11. Ehrig, H., Habel, A., Kreowski, H., Parisi-Presicce, F.: Parallelism and concurrency in high-level replacement systems. Math. Struct. Comput. Sci. 1(3), 361–404 (1991)

12. Ehrig, H., Kreowski, H.-J.: Parallelism of manipulations in multidimensional information structures. In: Mazurkiewicz, A. (ed.) MFCS 1976. LNCS, vol. 45, pp. 284–293. Springer, Heidelberg (1976). doi:10.1007/3-540-07854-1_188

13. Ehrig, H., Pfender, M., Schneider, H.J.: Graph-grammars: an algebraic approach. In: 14th Annual Symposium on Switching and Automata Theory, Iowa City, Iowa, USA, 15–17 October 1973, pp. 167–180. IEEE Computer Society (1973)

14. Kreowski, H.: Manipulation von Graphmanipulationen. Ph.D. thesis, Technische Universität, Berlin (1977)

15. Lack, S., Sobocinski, P.: Adhesive and quasiadhesive categories. Theor. Inf. Appl. 39(3), 511–545 (2005)

16. Löwe, M.: Graph rewriting in span-categories. In: Ehrig, H., Rensink, A., Rozenberg, G., Schürr, A. (eds.) ICGT 2010. LNCS, vol. 6372, pp. 218–233. Springer, Heidelberg (2010). doi:10.1007/978-3-642-15928-2_15

17. Rosen, B.K.: A Church-Rosser theorem for graph grammars. ACM SIGACT News 7(3), 26–31 (1975)

Approximating Parikh Images for Generating Deterministic Graph Parsers

Frank Drewes[1], Berthold Hoffmann[2], and Mark Minas[3(✉)]

[1] Umeå Universitet, Umeå, Sweden
drewes@cs.umu.se
[2] Universität Bremen, Bremen, Germany
hof@informatik.uni-bremen.de
[3] Universität der Bundeswehr München, Neubiberg, Germany
mark.minas@unibw.de

Abstract. The Parikh image of a word abstracts from the order of its letters. Parikh's famous theorem states that the set of Parikh images of a context-free string language forms a semilinear set that can be effectively computed from its grammar. In this paper we study the computation of Parikh images for graph grammars defined by contextual hyperedge replacement (CHR). Our motivation is to generate efficient predictive top-down (PTD) parsers for a subclass of CHR grammars. We illustrate this by describing the subtask that identifies the nodes of the input graph that parsing starts with.

1 Introduction

The Parikh image of a word abstracts from the positions of letters in the word, by just counting how often these letters occur. Parikh's theorem states that the set of Parikh images of a context-free string language forms a semilinear set that can be effectively computed from its grammar [12]. Another way to put this is to say that, if the order of symbols in strings is disregarded, in effect turning every string into a multiset of symbols, then the context-free languages are effectively equal to the regular ones. This theorem is useful for studying properties of languages, e.g., for proving that some language is not context-free.

In this paper we study the computation of Parikh images for contextual hyperedge replacement (CHR) grammars. Our motivation is the automated generation of efficient parsers for these grammars. In [4], we have devised predictive top-down (PTD) parsers for a class of CHR grammars,[1] a technique similar to top-down $LL(1)$ string parsing. The complexity of PTD parsing is quadratic in general and linear in many practical cases, whereas that of general HR parsing (and thus of CHR parsing as well) is known to be NP-complete. Parikh images are the heart of the PTD parser generation, as they are used to make rule selection deterministic: imagine that the parser is in a situation where it has to expand a nonterminal hyperedge labelled A that is attached to a node v of

---

[1] Due to space restrictions, that paper describes only the HR case.

© Springer International Publishing AG 2016
P. Milazzo et al. (Eds.): STAF 2016, LNCS 9946, pp. 112–128, 2016.
DOI: 10.1007/978-3-319-50230-4_9

the input graph, and there are two rules p, p' with the left-hand side A. Assume further that we have determined the semilinear sets U, V of terminal edge labels that derivations starting with p or p' can attach to v, and that these sets are disjoint. Then the parser can decide whether to apply p or p' by inspecting the part of the input still to be generated, and by checking whether the multiset of labels of edges actually attached to v belongs to U or to V.

Unfortunately, the exact computation of the required Parikh images is computationally far too expensive. Even more importantly, the resulting semilinear expressions become so huge that they cannot be handled in a reasonably efficient manner. Thus, one cannot hope to solve the problem by more efficient algorithms. We therefore propose a procedure which computes an over-approximation of the exact solution that is sufficiently close to the exact solution and sufficiently efficient to be used for PTD parser generation. We illustrate its use by considering the subtask of the parser generator that determines which nodes of the input graph have to be matched when parsing starts.

The remainder of this paper is structured as follows. In Sect. 2, we recall Parikh images, and discuss their exact computation for a given grammar. Since this algorithm is too inefficient for grammars of the size occurring in practical applications, we devise procedures that over-approximate Parikh images, in Sect. 3. That far, we discuss just the simple case of context-free string grammars. In Sect. 4, we introduce CHR grammars, and explain how the start nodes for PTD parsers of CHR grammars can be constructed with the help of the techniques developed in the earlier sections. Finally we mention some related and future work in Sect. 5.

2 Parikh Images and Grammar Graphs

Let Σ be a finite alphabet. We wish to count occurrences of terminal symbols in strings over Σ, but disregard the order of the occurrences of symbols. Thus, in effect, we want to work with finite multisets of elements of Σ rather than with strings. Instead of the usual free monoid Σ^* over Σ, we therefore consider the free *commutative* monoid $\Sigma^\circledast$ over Σ in which the monoid operator $\cdot$ is commutative, i.e., $a \cdot b = b \cdot a$. In other words, $\cdot$ is the union of multisets. If no confusion is likely to arise, we may drop the operator $\cdot$ in expressions, but the reader should keep in mind that the order of the symbols $a_1, \ldots, a_n$ in $a_1 \cdots a_n$ is irrelevant in this case, despite the string-like appearance of the expression. Note that, as a special case of this notation, a denotes the singleton multiset $\{a\}$. Finally, we define the partial ordering $\preceq$ on $\Sigma^\circledast$ to be multiset inclusion, i.e., $u \preceq v$ if v contains every symbol at least as many times as u does.

In the following, let $\Gamma = \langle \Sigma, \mathcal{N}, P, S \rangle$ be a fixed context-free Chomsky grammar with the sets Σ and $\mathcal{N}$ of terminal and nonterminal symbols, respectively, $\Sigma \cap \mathcal{N} = \varnothing$, $P \subseteq \mathcal{N} \times (\mathcal{N} \cup \Sigma)^\circledast$ the set of rules (or productions), and $S \in \mathcal{N}$ the start symbol. Note that we interpret the right-hand sides of rules as elements of $(\mathcal{N} \cup \Sigma)^\circledast$ rather than as strings. Accordingly, the language $\mathcal{L}(\Gamma)$ is a subset of $\Sigma^\circledast$, namely the Parikh image of the traditional string language generated by Γ.

In order to operate on languages $L \subseteq \Sigma^{\circledast}$, we make use of the so-called *counting semiring* over such languages with the addition $+$ of languages being their union and multiplication $\cdot$ being the extension of multiset union $\cdot$ to languages of multisets, i.e., $U \cdot V = \{u \cdot v \mid u \in U, v \in V\}$. Thus, the additive and multiplicative identities are the empty set and $\{\varepsilon\}$, respectively. Again, we write ε instead of $\{\varepsilon\}$. Note that the counting semiring is isomorphic to the one on sets of Parikh vectors counting occurrences of terminal symbols in words over Σ. We define the Kleene operator $\circledast$ on languages $L \subseteq \Sigma^{\circledast}$ as usual: $L^{\circledast}$ is the least set such that $L^{\circledast} = \varepsilon + L \cdot L^{\circledast}$. Since the semiring is commutative as well as idempotent, we have $(K + L)^{\circledast} = K^{\circledast} \cdot L^{\circledast}$ and $(K \cdot L^{\circledast})^{\circledast} = \varepsilon + K \cdot K^{\circledast} \cdot L^{\circledast}$.

Parikh's Theorem [12] states that the commutative language $\mathcal{L}(\Gamma)$ generated by Γ is semilinear, i.e., there are finitely many finite languages $A_1, \ldots, A_n \subseteq \Sigma^{\circledast}$ and $B_1, \ldots, B_n \subseteq \Sigma^{\circledast}$ such that $\mathcal{L}(\Gamma) = A_1 B_1^{\circledast} + \cdots + A_n B_n^{\circledast}$. The languages $A_1, B_1, \ldots, A_n, B_n$ can be effectively computed, e.g., using a generalization of Newton's method [5] but, as explained in the introduction, complexity issues prevent us from using this fact for PTD parser generation. Instead, we devise a procedure that over-approximates the exact Parikh image.

The idea underlying the procedure is to consider all possible derivation trees of Γ and to count the occurrences of terminal symbols in their leaves. We over-approximate the set of derivation trees, thus computing a semilinear set that contains the Parikh image of Γ but is sufficiently close to the exact solution.

A *graph* over our fixed context-free grammar Γ has a set $\dot{G}$ of nodes. Each node $v \in \dot{G}$ is labelled with $\ell(v) \in P \cup \mathcal{N} \cup \Sigma$, i.e., either a rule, a nonterminal, or a terminal symbol of Γ. Instead of explicitly representing edges, each node $v \in \dot{G}$ is assigned a multiset children$(v) \in \dot{G}^{\circledast}$ of children nodes. A *tree* over Γ is just a graph over Γ that satisfies the usual requirements for trees. As a shorthand notation for a tree t we write $\alpha(t_1, \ldots t_n)$ if t has a root node v with label $\alpha = \ell(v)$ and children$(v) = v_1 \cdots v_n$ such that v_i is the root node of the direct subtree t_i, for $i \in [n]$,[2] or just α if v is a leaf.

The set $\mathcal{D}(\alpha)$ of *derivation trees* of Γ with root label $\alpha \in \Sigma \cup \mathcal{N} \cup P$ is inductively defined. If $\alpha \in \Sigma$, the tree consists only of the root as its only node. If $\alpha \in \mathcal{N}$, the tree has a single direct subtree, being a derivation tree whose root is labeled with a rule applicable to α. If α is a rule in P, for each occurrence of a symbol in its right-hand side there is a subtree that is a derivation tree with that symbol as its root label. Formally,

$$\mathcal{D}(\alpha) = \begin{cases} \{\alpha\} & \text{if } \alpha \in \Sigma \\ \{\alpha(t) \mid \exists p = (\alpha, r) \in P : t \in \mathcal{D}(p)\} & \text{if } \alpha \in \mathcal{N} \\ \{\alpha(t_1, \ldots, t_n) \mid \forall i \in [n] : t_i \in \mathcal{D}(a_i)\} & \text{if } \alpha = (A, a_1 \cdots a_n) \in P. \end{cases}$$

We now define the Parikh image $\Psi(t)$ of a derivation tree t as the multiset of the terminal labels of its leaf nodes and the Parikh image $\psi(\alpha)$ of every $\alpha \in \Sigma \cup \mathcal{N} \cup P$ as the set of Parikh images of all derivation trees with root label α:

---

[2] $[n]$ denotes the set $\{1, \ldots, n\}$.

$$\Psi(t) = \begin{cases} a & \text{if } t = a \text{ and } a \in \Sigma \\ \Psi(t_1) \cdot \ldots \cdot \Psi(t_n) & \text{if } t = \alpha(t_1, \ldots, t_n) \text{ and } \alpha \in \mathcal{N} \cup P \end{cases}$$
$$\psi(\alpha) = \{\Psi(t) \mid t \in \mathcal{D}(\alpha)\}.$$

By this, $\psi(S)$ is obviously $\mathcal{L}(\Gamma)$.

In order to approximate the set of all derivation trees, we encode the rules of Γ in a graph G_Γ over Γ, called *grammar graph* of Γ: G_Γ has $\Sigma \cup \mathcal{N} \cup P$ as its node set, and each node is labelled with itself, $\ell(v) = v$ for each node v. The multiset of children of a nonterminal node A consists of just the rules with left-hand side A (in any order), while the multiset of children of a rule node is simply the right-hand side of that rule, and the multiset of children of a terminal node is the empty multiset ε:

$$\text{children}(v) = \begin{cases} p_1 \cdots p_n \text{ if } v \in \mathcal{N} \text{ and } p_1 \cdots p_n \text{ is the multiset of all rules} \\ \qquad\qquad\qquad\qquad \text{with left-hand side } v \\ a_1 \cdots a_n \text{ if } v = (A, a_1 \cdots a_n) \in P \\ \varepsilon \qquad\quad \text{if } v \in \Sigma \end{cases}$$

Clearly, for all $\alpha \in \Sigma \cup \mathcal{N} \cup P$ the derivation trees with root α can be read off G_Γ by starting at the node α and recursively selecting one of its children if $\alpha \in \mathcal{N}$ (thus choosing a rule for α) or all of them if $\alpha \in P$ (thus building sub-derivations that correspond to the nonterminals in the right-hand side of α).

Our aim is to compute $\mathcal{L}(\Gamma) = \psi(S)$ by counting terminal leaves of the derivation trees with root S. Recall that the strongly connected components (SCCs) of the grammar graph are just the maximal subgraphs in which every node can be reached from every other node on a directed path. Thus, nodes belonging to the same cycle are in the same SCC. We identify an SCC with the set C of its nodes. The problem of counting terminal leaves of complete derivation trees can thus be broken down into the simpler problem of considering each SCC of the grammar graph separately, solving the problem for the (possibly infinite) set of all partial derivation trees that can be "read off" this individual SCC, and combining these solutions to obtain one for the derivation trees of Γ.

We now define how to read off trees from C. These trees are called the *component trees* of C. For this, let us call a node v a *successor* of an SCC C if v is a child of a node $u \in C$ but $v \notin C$. We denote the set of all successors of C by $\text{succ } C$. Note that successors can be terminals, nonterminals, as well as rules. The set $\text{trees}_C(v)$ of all component trees that can be read off an SCC C starting at $v \in C \cup \text{succ } C$ is defined as follows:

$$\text{trees}_C(v) = \begin{cases} \{v\} & \text{if } v \in \Sigma \cap C \text{ or } v \in \text{succ } C \\ \{v(t) \mid t \in \text{trees}_C(v_i) \text{ for some } i \in [k]\} \\ \qquad\qquad \text{if } v \in \mathcal{N} \cap C \text{ and } \text{children}(v) = v_1 \cdots v_k \\ \{v(t_1, \ldots, t_k) \mid t_i \in \text{trees}_C(v_i) \text{ for each } i \in [k]\} \\ \qquad\qquad \text{if } v \in P \cap C \text{ and } \text{children}(v) = v_1 \cdots v_k \end{cases}$$

A derivation tree t can be composed from component trees t_1, t_2 if t_1 has a leaf v with the same label as the root r of t_2, i.e., $\ell(v) = \ell(r) = u \in C_2 \cap \text{succ } C_1$ for SCCs C_1, C_2. Then t is obtained from t_1 and t_2 by merging v and r.

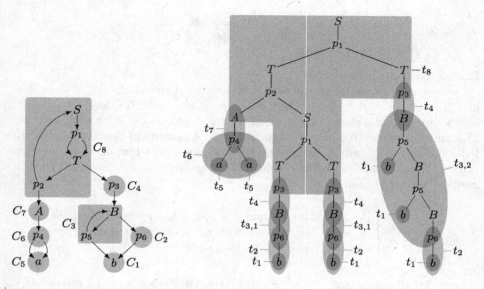

Fig. 1. Grammar graph of the grammar in Example 1 with indicated strongly connected components.

Fig. 2. Derivation tree of a^2b^5.

Example 1. As an example we consider the grammar with $\Sigma = \{a, b\}$, $\mathcal{N} = \{S, A, B, T\}$, and rules $p_1 = \langle S, TT \rangle, p_2 = \langle T, AS \rangle, p_3 = \langle T, B \rangle, p_4 = \langle A, aa \rangle, p_5 = \langle B, bB \rangle, p_6 = \langle B, b \rangle$. Figure 1 shows its grammar graph with indicated strongly connected components and Fig. 2 shows a derivation tree of a^2b^5. The derivation tree is made up of (copies of) the following nine component trees: $t_1 \in \text{trees}_{C_1}(b)$, $t_2 \in \text{trees}_{C_2}(p_6)$, $t_{3,1}, t_{3,2} \in \text{trees}_{C_3}(B)$, $t_4 \in \text{trees}_{C_4}(p_3)$, $t_5 \in \text{trees}_{C_5}(a)$, $t_6 \in \text{trees}_{C_6}(p_4)$, $t_7 \in \text{trees}_{C_7}(A)$, and $t_8 \in \text{trees}_{C_8}(S)$. ◇

The procedure for computing Parikh images (and approximated Parikh images later) of derivation trees runs in three basic steps:

1. The SCCs of the grammar graph are computed.
2. A DAG of SCCs is obtained by contracting each SCC to a single node.
3. This DAG is evaluated in a bottom-up fashion, processing each SCC in turn as described in the following.

The processing of a SCC results in a Parikh image $\psi(v)$ associated with each node v of the SCC. Let C be the next SCC to be processed, assuming that all SCCs containing children of C have already been processed. We determine $\psi(v)$ for each $v \in C$. If v is terminal then $C = \{v\}$ and $\psi(v)$ is a singleton. Hence, the case of $v \in \Sigma \cap C$ does not need to be considered anymore below. For $v \in (\mathcal{N} \cup P) \cap C$, we can determine $\psi(v)$ by collecting the Parikh images of all component trees of C, letting the successor nodes of C act as terminal symbols. Clearly, this component-specific Parikh image of a component tree $t \in \text{trees}_C(v)$ is

$$\Psi_C(t) = \begin{cases} a & \text{if } t = a \in \text{succ } C \\ \Psi_C(t_1) \cdot \ldots \cdot \Psi_C(t_k) & \text{if } t = \alpha(t_1, \ldots, t_k) \text{ and } \alpha \in (\mathcal{N} \cup \mathcal{P}) \cap C. \end{cases}$$

The set of component-specific Parikh images of a node $v \in C$ is then defined as

$$\psi_C(v) = \{\Psi_C(t) \mid t \in \text{trees}_C(v)\}.$$

The actual Parikh image $\psi(v)$ for a node $v \in C$ can then be obtained from $\psi_C(v)$ by substituting each occurrence of any node $u \in \text{succ } C$ by $\psi(u)$, which has been determined previously.

One can compute $\psi_C(v)$ by interpreting the subgraph induced by $C \cup \text{succ } C$ as a system of equations to be solved. Nodes in $\text{succ } C$ are constants representing given Parikh images (that have been determined previously in the bottom-up process). Each node $v \in (\mathcal{N} \cup \mathcal{P}) \cap C$ with its children $v_1, \ldots, v_k$ stands for a variable defined by an equation. If v is a rule, the equation is $v = v_1 \cdot \ldots \cdot v_k$, otherwise it is $v = v_1 + \cdots + v_k$.

Example 2. The system of equations for SCC C_3 of the grammar graph shown in Fig. 1 is

$$B = p_5 + p_6 \qquad p_5 = bB.$$

It has the solution $B = p_6 b^\circledast$, $p_5 = p_6 bb^\circledast$. The system of equations for C_8 is

$$S = p_1 \qquad p_1 = TT \qquad T = p_2 + p_3 \qquad p_2 = AS$$

with the solution $S = p_1 = p_3 p_3 (Ap_3)^\circledast$, $T = p_3 (Ap_3)^\circledast$, $p_2 = Ap_3 p_3 (Ap_3)^\circledast$. $\diamond$

Such a system of equations is called linear if there are no products (by $\cdot$) of more than one variable, i.e., if no rule node in C has more than one child in C (e.g., C_3 in the example above). Therefore we call such an SCC *linear*, too. Each linear system of equations corresponds to a finite automaton and can be algebraically solved using Brzozowski's method [1]. If it is non-linear, i.e., if there is a term involving a product of two variables (e.g., C_8 in the example above), one can solve it using a generalization of Newton's method [5].

3   Approximating Parikh Images

Let us call a tree *repetitive* if there are two distinct but equally labeled nodes on a path from the root to a leaf, and *non-repetitive* otherwise. We now show how to compute approximated Parikh images $\psi'(v)$ instead of $\psi(v)$ by computing $\psi'_C(v)$ as an approximation of $\psi_C(v)$ according to (1) when SCC C is processed:

$$\psi'_C(v) = A_C(v) \cdot (\text{rep } C)^\circledast \tag{1}$$

where

$$A_C(v) = \{\Psi_C(t) \mid t \in \text{trees}_C(v) \text{ and } t \text{ is non-repetitive}\} \tag{2}$$

$$\text{rep } C = \begin{cases} \varnothing & \text{if } |C| = 1 \\ (\text{succ } C) \backslash P & \text{if } |C| > 1 \text{ and } C \text{ is linear} \\ \text{succ } C & \text{if } |C| > 1 \text{ and } C \text{ is not linear} \end{cases} \tag{3}$$

Table 1. Approximated Parikh images for the grammar graph in Fig. 1.

v	SCC	type	rep C	non-repetitive trees	$A_C(v)$	$\psi'_C(v)$	$\psi'(v)$	$\psi''(v)$
b	C_1	elem.	$\varnothing$	$\{b\}$	b	b	b	b
p_6	C_2	elem.	$\varnothing$	$\{p_6(b)\}$	b	b	b	b
B	C_3	linear	$\{b\}$	$\{B(p_6)\}$	p_6	$p_6 b^{\circledast}$	$bb^{\circledast}$	$bb^{\circledast}$
p_3	C_4	elem.	$\varnothing$	$\{p_3(B)\}$	B	B	$bb^{\circledast}$	$bb^{\circledast}$
a	C_5	elem.	$\varnothing$	$\{a\}$	a	a	a	a
p_4	C_6	elem.	$\varnothing$	$\{p_4(a,a)\}$	aa	aa	aa	aa
A	C_7	elem.	$\varnothing$	$\{A(p_4)\}$	p_4	p_4	aa	aa
S	C_8	non-lin.	$\{A,p_3\}$	$\{S(p_1(T(p_3),T(p_3)))\}$	$p_3 p_3$	$p_3 p_3 A^{\circledast} p_3^{\circledast}$	$bb(aa)^{\circledast}b^{\circledast}$	$bba^{\circledast}b^{\circledast}$

Example 3. Table 1 summarizes the results when applying the procedure of computing the approximated Parikh images for the grammar in Example 1. The table shows in each row a node v of the grammar graph in Fig. 1, its SCC C and the type of C where linear SCCs are distinguished from non-linear and elementary ones, the latter being those with $|C| = 1$. Set rep C of the SCC and the set of all non-repetitive component trees with root label v follow. The three remaining entries are the sets $A_C(v)$, $\psi'_C(v)$, and $\psi'(v)$, written as algebraic terms. $\psi'(v)$ is obtained from $\psi'_C(v)$ by substituting each occurrence of any node $u \in \text{succ}\, C$ by $\psi'(u)$, which has been determined previously. (The last column will be explained in Example 4 below.)

Note that the computed approximated Parikh image is $\psi'(S) = bb(aa)^{\circledast}b^{\circledast} = \{a^{2i}b^j \mid i \geqslant 0 \wedge j \geqslant 2\}$ whereas the exact set, as one can see, is $\psi(S) = bb(aab)^{\circledast}b^{\circledast} = \{a^{2i}b^{i+j} \mid i \geqslant 0 \wedge j \geqslant 2\}$, i.e., $\psi'(S) = \psi(S) + aa(aa)^{\circledast}(aab)^{\circledast}$. ◇

We now examine how precise the approximation is. It is immediately clear that $\psi_C(v) = \psi'_C(v)$ if C is elementary, i.e., $|C| = 1$. We now show that the exact component-specific Parikh images are subsets of their approximations (Lemma 1). But the approximation does not contain elements completely unrelated to the exact solution; instead, each approximated element can be extended to one contained in the exact Parikh image (Lemma 2).

Lemma 1. $\psi_C(v) \subseteq \psi'_C(v)$ *for each SCC* C *and* $v \in C$.

Proof. We presume an arbitrary SCC C, node $v \in C$, and tree $t \in \text{trees}_C(v)$, and show that $\Psi_C(t) \in A_C(v) \cdot (\text{rep}\, C)^{\circledast}$. The proof is by induction on the size of t. Thus, assume that $\Psi_C(t') \in A_C(v) \cdot (\text{rep}\, C)^{\circledast}$ for all $t' \in \text{trees}_C(v)$ such that t' is smaller than t. We distinguish three cases.

Case 1 (t is non-repetitive). The proposition follows from $\Psi_C(t) \in A_C(v)$.

Case 2 (t is repetitive and C is linear). As t is repetitive, there are two nodes v_1 and v_2 on a path in t such that $\ell(v_1) = \ell(v_2)$. This decomposes t into three trees t_1, t_2, t_3 as shown in Fig. 3. By the linearity of C all leaves of t_2 except v_2 are in $(\text{succ}\, C) \backslash P = \text{rep}\, C$, which means that $\Psi_C(t_2) \in (\text{rep}\, C)^{\circledast}$. Moreover, the

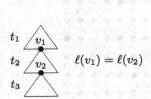

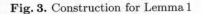

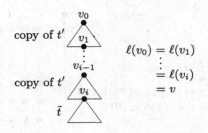

Fig. 3. Construction for Lemma 1   **Fig. 4.** Construction for Lemma 2

tree t' obtained from t_1 and t_3 by identifying v_1 and v_2 is in $\mathrm{trees}_C(v)$ and is smaller than t. Hence, the induction hypothesis yields

$$\Psi_C(t) = \Psi_C(t') \cdot \Psi_C(t_2) \in A_C(v) \cdot (\mathrm{rep}\,C)^{\circledast} \cdot (\mathrm{rep}\,C)^{\circledast} = A_C(v) \cdot (\mathrm{rep}\,C)^{\circledast}.$$

Case 3 (t is repetitive and C is not linear). Decompose t as in the previous case. Again, $\Psi_C(t_2) \in (\mathrm{rep}\,C)^{\circledast}$, this time because all leaves of t_2 except v_2 are in $\mathrm{succ}\,C = \mathrm{rep}\,C$. Consequently, the same argument as above applies.   □

Lemma 2. *For each SCC C, $v \in C$, and $\alpha \in \psi'_C(v)$, there are '$\alpha, \alpha' \in \psi_C(v)$ such that '$\alpha \preceq \alpha \preceq \alpha'$.*

Proof. We presume an arbitrary SCC C, node $v \in C$, and $\alpha \in \psi'_C(v)$. By (1) and (2), there is a non-repetitive tree $\tilde{t} \in \mathrm{trees}_C(v)$ and a $\beta \in (\mathrm{rep}\,C)^{\circledast}$ such that $\alpha = \Psi_C(\tilde{t}) \cdot \beta$ and, therefore, $\Psi_C(\tilde{t}) \preceq \alpha$. In other words, '$\alpha \preceq \alpha$ for '$\alpha = \Psi_C(\tilde{t})$. It remains to be shown that there is a tree $t \in \mathrm{trees}_C(v)$ such that $\alpha \preceq \Psi_C(t)$. We distinguish the three cases in Eq. (3) above.

Case 1 (|C| = 1). In this case $\alpha \in A_C(v)$, and thus $\alpha = \Psi_C(t)$ for a tree $t \in \mathrm{trees}_C(v)$.

Case 2 (|C| > 1 and C is linear). C is strongly connected, i.e., C has a cycle containing each node in C. By following this cycle once, starting at v, one creates a tree t' with both the root and a leaf labelled by v, and such that each node $v \in \mathrm{rep}\,C$ occurs as the label of at least one node. For each $i \geqslant 0$, construct $t_i \in \mathrm{trees}_C(v)$ from $\tilde{t}$ and i isomorphic copies of t' as shown in Fig. 4. By choosing i to be the maximum multiplicity of elements in β, one obtains $\alpha = \Psi_C(\tilde{t}) \cdot \beta \preceq \Psi_C(t_i)$ because $\beta \in (\mathrm{rep}\,C)^{\circledast}$ and $\mathrm{rep}\,C \preceq \Psi_C(t')$.

Case 3 (|C| > 1 and C is not linear). Let n be the maximum multiplicity of elements in α, i.e., $\alpha \preceq (\mathrm{succ}\,C)^n$. By the non-linearity of C, there is a path from v to a rule node r having two distinct nodes $u, u' \in C$ among its children. But there is also a path from u' back to v, which by iteration yields a path starting at v and containing k occurrences of r, for any k. Moreover, again since C is strongly connected, there are $t_1, \ldots, t_k \in \mathrm{trees}_C(u)$ (for a sufficiently large k) such that every node in $\mathrm{succ}\,C$ occurs in at least n of the t_i. Putting these pieces together, we obtain a tree $t \in \mathrm{trees}_C(v)$ such that $\alpha \preceq (\mathrm{succ}\,C)^n \preceq \Psi_C(t)$.   □

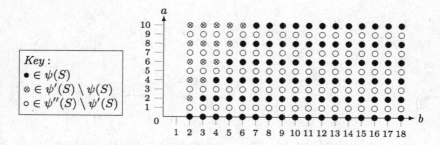

Fig. 5. Parikh images for the grammar in Examples 1–4

The following corollary is an immediate consequence of Lemmas 1 and 2:

Corollary 1. *For each $v \in \Sigma \cup \mathcal{N} \cup P$, the following holds:*

- $\psi(v) \subseteq \psi'(v)$
- *For each $\alpha \in \psi'(v)$, there are '$\alpha, \alpha' \in \psi(v)$ such that '$\alpha \preceq \alpha \preceq \alpha'$.*

In particular, each least element of $\psi'(v)$ is also a least element in $\psi(v)$.

Approximating $\psi(v)$ by $\psi'(v)$ has turned out to be still too inefficient when used for generating parsers for CHR grammars. The most expensive operation is to compute $\psi'(v)$ from $\psi'_C(v)$ by substituting $\psi'(u)$ for each occurrence of any node $u \in \operatorname{succ} C$. This, however, becomes manageable when semilinear sets are approximated by simple semilinear sets. We call a semilinear set M *simple* if there are finitely many finite sets $A_1, \ldots, A_n \subseteq \Sigma^{\circledast}$ and $B_1, \ldots, B_n \subseteq \Sigma$ such that $M = A_1 B_1^{\circledast} + \cdots + A_n B_n^{\circledast}$. (Note that, in contrast to general semilinear sets, $B_1, \ldots, B_n$ are now subsets of Σ rather than of $\Sigma^{\circledast}$.)

Our approximation of Parikh images using simple semilinear sets now works exactly as before, except for an additional simplification step that lets us compute *simple semilinear sets* $\psi''(v)$ instead of $\psi'(v)$: first, in $\psi'_C(v)$, substitute each occurrence of any node $u \in \operatorname{succ} C$ by the recursively computed $\psi''(u)$. Since $\cdot$ distributes over $+$, we can write the resulting expression in the form $A_1 C_1 + \cdots + A_n C_n$, where the A_i are products not containing $\circledast$ and the C_i are products and sums of expressions of the form $E^{\circledast}$. Finally, $\psi''(v) = A_1 B_1^{\circledast} + \cdots A_n B_n^{\circledast}$, where $B_i = \{a \in \Sigma \mid a \text{ occurs in } C_i\}$. One can now verify that Lemmas 1, 2, and Corollary 1 still hold if ψ' is replaced by ψ''.

Example 4. The last column in Table 1 above summarizes the results when applying the procedure of computing the Parikh images for the grammar in Example 1 approximated by simple semilinear sets.

Note that the approximated Parikh image of the generated language is now $\psi''(S) = bba^{\circledast}b^{\circledast} = \{a^i b^j \mid i \geqslant 0 \wedge j \geqslant 2\} = \psi'(S) + abb(aa)^{\circledast}b^{\circledast}$, where $\psi'(S) = bb(aa)^{\circledast}b^{\circledast}$ and $\psi(S) = bb(aab)^{\circledast}b^{\circledast}$ (see Example 3). Figure 5 shows elements of the Parikh images in the (a, b) plane. $\diamond$

4   Application to Deterministic Graph Parsing

In order to illustrate how the approximation of Parikh images can be used to generate predictive top-down (PTD) graph parsers, we recall contextual hypergraph replacement (CHR) as far as it is needed to understand the example. (See [3,4] for details of CHR grammars and PTD parsing, resp.)

We consider a ranked labeling alphabet Σ that comes with an *arity* function $arity\colon \Sigma \to \mathbb{N}$. A *hypergraph* $G = \langle \dot{G}, \bar{G}, att_G, \ell_G \rangle$ over Σ (*graph*, for short) consists of disjoint finite sets $\dot{G}$ of *nodes* and $\bar{G}$ of *hyperedges* (*edges*, for short) respectively, a function $att_G\colon \bar{G} \to \dot{G}^*$ that *attaches* sequences of nodes to edges, and a *labeling* function $\ell_G\colon \bar{G} \to \Sigma$ so that $|att_G(e)| = arity(\ell_G(e))$ for every edge $e \in \bar{G}$. The set of all graphs over Σ is denoted by $\mathcal{G}_\Sigma$. For a graph G and an edge $e \in \bar{G}$, we denote by $G - e$ the graph obtained by removing e from G.

For graphs G and H, a *morphism* $m\colon G \to H$ is a pair $m = \langle \dot{m}, \bar{m} \rangle$ of functions $\dot{m}\colon \dot{G} \to \dot{H}$ and $\bar{m}\colon \bar{G} \to \bar{H}$ preserving labels and attachments: $\ell_H \circ \bar{m} = \ell_G$, and $att_H \circ \bar{m} = \dot{m}^* \circ att_G$; m is *injective* if both $\dot{m}$ and $\bar{m}$ are injective.

We consider edges labeled with a distinguished subset $X \subseteq \Sigma$ as *nonterminals*. A *contextual rule* (*rule*, for short) $L ::= R$ consists of graphs L and R over Σ such that (1) the *left-hand side* L contains exactly one edge x, which is required to be a nonterminal (i.e., $\bar{L} = \{x\}$ with $\bar{\ell}_L(x) \in X$) and (2) the *right-hand side* R is a supergraph of $L - x$. Nodes in L that are not attached to x are the *contextual nodes* of L (and of r); r is *context-free* if it has no contextual nodes.

Let r be a contextual rule as above, and consider some graph G. If there is an injective morphism $m\colon L \to G$, the *replacement* of $m(x)$ by R (via m) is given as the graph H obtained from the disjoint union of $G - m(x)$ and R by identifying every node $v \in \dot{L}$ with $m(v)$. We then write $G \Rightarrow_r H$.

Let $\mathcal{R}$ be a finite set of contextual rules. We write $G \Rightarrow_\mathcal{R} H$ if $G \Rightarrow_r H$ for some rule $r \in \mathcal{R}$, and denote the transitive-reflexive closure of $\Rightarrow_\mathcal{R}$ by $\Rightarrow_\mathcal{R}^*$.

A *contextual hyperedge-replacement graph grammar* (*CHR grammar*, for short) is a triple $\Gamma = \langle \Sigma, \mathcal{R}, Z \rangle$ consisting of a finite labeling alphabet Σ, a finite set $\mathcal{R}$ of contextual rules, and a start graph $Z \in \mathcal{G}_\Sigma$ consisting of a single nonterminal without any attached nodes. The language of terminal graphs generated by Γ is given by $\mathcal{L}(\Gamma) = \{G \in \mathcal{G}_{\Sigma \setminus X} \mid Z \Rightarrow_\mathcal{R}^* G\}$.

Below, following [4], we denote graphs as multisets of literals $a(v_1, \ldots, v_k)$. Such a literal represents an edge that carries a k-ary label $a \in \Sigma$ and connects nodes $v_1, \ldots, v_k$. An isolated node x (such as a context node) is represented by the literal (x).

Example 5 (Flowcharts). A flowchart graph represents the control flow of a program, where nodes (circles) represent program states that are connected by edges representing decisions (diamonds), activities (rectangles), and gotos (thick arrows). An example is the graph in Fig. 6 which, if represented by means of edge literals as introduced above, would be denoted textually as $dec(a, b, c)\ goto(b, d)\ act(c, d)$. (Recall that this should be read as a multiset of literals, despite its string-like appearance.)

Fig. 6. A flowchart graph.

Now consider the rules

$$S() ::\overset{i}{=} D(x) \qquad D(x) ::\overset{a}{=} act(x,y)\ D(y) \qquad\qquad D(x) ::\overset{h}{=} (x)$$
$$D(x) ::\overset{b}{=} dec(x,y,z)\ D(y)\ D(z) \qquad D(x)\ (y) ::\overset{g}{=} goto(x,y)$$

The context-free rules i, a, b, h generate flow *trees* of decisions and activities; the contextual rule, g, inserts gotos to a program state generated elsewhere. Note that these rules can generate unstructured "Spaghetti code"; this cannot be achieved by context-free rules alone.

The flowchart in Fig. 6 is generated as follows:

$$S() \Rightarrow_i D(a)$$
$$\Rightarrow_b dec(a,b,c)\ D(b)\ D(c)$$
$$\Rightarrow_a dec(a,b,c)\ D(b)\ act(c,d)\ D(d)$$
$$\Rightarrow_h dec(a,b,c)\ D(b)\ act(c,d)$$
$$\Rightarrow_g dec(a,b,c)\ goto(b,d)\ act(c,d)$$

Note that the derivation using rule h does not produce an isolated node d. Therefore, literal (d) is omitted. $\diamondsuit$

One obvious task a graph parser must be able to perform is to identify the nodes at which the processing starts, i.e., which nodes correspond to those in the right-hand side of the initial rule applied. For PTD parsing some (or all) of these nodes – they are called *start nodes* in the following – must be determined in a syntactically correct graph by their neighborhood, i.e., their incident edges. We now describe how this can be done using approximated Parikh images.

Let us introduce the notion of neighborhoods first. Given a graph H and any node v (not necessarily of H), the *neighborhood* of v in H is obtained by merging all nodes except v into one. When H is represented by literals, this neighborhood graph $[H]_v$ is obtained by replacing each occurrence of v in a literal by a unique new node •, and all other nodes by a "don't care" node ∘. Isolated nodes are removed, i.e., only edge literals are kept.

It is important to note that the set of literals $a(v_1,\ldots,v_k)$ that appear in $[H]_v$ (for a given CHR grammar) is finite, because a is taken from the finite set of terminal edge labels and $v_1,\ldots,v_k \in \{•,∘\}$. Thus we can view the set of these literals as a complex but finite alphabet Δ, and every $[H]_v$ as an element of $\Delta^\circledast$.

Hence every set of such graphs $[H]_v$ becomes a commutative language over Δ, which allows us to apply the results of Sects. 2 and 3 to these languages.

Example 6. The neighborhood of node d in the graph H shown in Fig. 6 is $[H]_d = dec(\circ, \circ, \circ) \, goto(\circ, \bullet) \, act(\circ, \bullet)$. It represents the fact that d has just one incoming *goto* edge and one incoming *act* edge, and there is just one *dec* edge which is not incident with d. $\Diamond$

Given a syntactically correct graph H, we want to determine for each $v \in \dot{H}$, by just considering its neighborhood, which rule $p = (L :: = R)$ has generated v in the derivation $Z \Rightarrow^* H$. If p generates not just a single node, we also want to know which node $u \in \dot{R} \backslash \dot{L}$ actually corresponds to v. This can sometimes be done by computing, for each rule $p = (L :: = R)$ and node $u \in \dot{R} \backslash \dot{L}$,

$$nh(p, u) = \{[H]_v \in \Delta^\circledast \mid H \text{ is terminal}, \ Z \Rightarrow^* G \Rightarrow_p G' \Rightarrow^* H,$$
$$v \in \dot{H}, \text{ and } v \text{ is the image of } u \text{ created in } G \Rightarrow_p G'\}.$$

The set $nh(p, u)$ contains all possible neighborhoods of copies v of u created by applying p in a derivation of a syntactically correct graph.

The parser can identify node $v \in \dot{H}$ as a start node corresponding to a node u in start rule p if $[H]_v \in nh(p, u)$, but $[H]_v \notin nh(p', u')$ for each $(p', u') \neq (p, u)$. The parser can identify the corresponding start node of every syntactically correct graph if $nh(p, u) \cap nh(p', u') = \varnothing$ for each $(p', u') \neq (p, u)$.

In order to compute neighborhoods, we use the fact that each CHR derivation corresponds to a derivation of neighborhoods. To see this, let $[p]_u$, for any CHR rule $p = (L :: = R)$ and for any node u (not necessarily in $\dot{L} \cup \dot{R}$), be the context-free rule $[L]_u :: = [R]_u$ over Δ. It is clear that $[p]_u$ is context-free because $[L]_u$ is a single literal, and that, for all graphs G, G' with $G \Rightarrow_p G'$ and each node v, there is a node x and a multiset α of literals such that $[G]_v = \alpha [L]_x$ and $[G']_v = \alpha [R]_x$, i.e., a context-free derivation $[G]_v \Rightarrow_{[p]_x} [G']_v$.

Define sets of mapped rules $P^\circ = \{[p]_x \mid p = (L :: = R) \in \mathcal{R} \text{ and } x \notin \dot{R}\}$ and $P^\bullet = \{[p]_x \mid p = (L :: = R) \in \mathcal{R} \text{ and } x \in \dot{L}\}$. Thus, P° consists of all rules not containing $\bullet$ at all and $P^\bullet$ consists of those containing $\bullet$ in both the left-hand side and right-hand side (except for contextual rules where a contextual node x is mapped to $\bullet$, as in this case $[p]_x$ contains $\bullet$ only in its right-hand side).

Now, consider any CHR rule $p = (L_p :: = R_p)$ and any node $u \in \dot{R}_p \backslash \dot{L}_p$. Let G, G' be graphs such that $Z \Rightarrow^* G \Rightarrow_p G'$ and $v \in \dot{G}'$ a node that has been created in the last step, being the image of $u \in \dot{R} \backslash \dot{L}$. Then this means that there is a multiset α of literals, called a *vicinity multiset* of $[L_p]_u$, such that $[Z]_v \Rightarrow_{P^\circ}^* [G]_v = \alpha [L_p]_u$. A neighborhood of v is obtained when G' is derived to a terminal graph H and $[G']_v = \alpha [R_p]_u$ is derived in a corresponding way. Clearly, for every terminal graph H with $G' \Rightarrow^* H$, there are multisets α', α'' such that $[G']_v = \alpha [R_p]_u \Rightarrow_{P'}^* \alpha' \alpha'' = [H]_v$ with $\alpha \Rightarrow_{P'}^* \alpha'$ and $[R_p]_u \Rightarrow_{P'}^* \alpha''$ using the set of rules $P' = P^\circ \cup P^\bullet$. Note that the crucial middle step, which uses the rule $[p]_u$ to create $\bullet$ is not covered by the rules in P'.

Example 7. The sets P° and $P^\bullet$ of context-free rules for the flowcharts rules shown in Example 5 are

$$
P^\circ = \left\{
\begin{array}{ll}
S() \stackrel{[i]_\circ}{::=} D(\circ) & \\
D(\circ) \stackrel{[a]_\circ}{::=} act(\circ, \circ)\, D(\circ) & D(\circ) \stackrel{[b]_\circ}{::=} dec(\circ, \circ, \circ)\, D(\circ)\, D(\circ) \\
D(\circ) \stackrel{[g]_\circ}{::=} goto(\circ, \circ) & D(\circ) \stackrel{[h]_\circ}{::=} \varepsilon
\end{array}
\right\}
$$

$$
P^\bullet = \left\{
\begin{array}{ll}
D(\bullet) \stackrel{[a]_x}{::=} act(\bullet, \circ)\, D(\circ) & D(\bullet) \stackrel{[b]_x}{::=} dec(\bullet, \circ, \circ)\, D(\circ)\, D(\circ) \\
D(\bullet) \stackrel{[g]_x}{::=} goto(\bullet, \circ) & D(\circ) \stackrel{[g]_y}{::=} goto(\circ, \bullet) \\
D(\bullet) \stackrel{[h]_x}{::=} \varepsilon
\end{array}
\right\}
$$

Let us consider rule a and its generated node y in the example derivation shown in Example 5. Rule a is applied to graph $G = dec(a, b, c)\, D(b)\, D(c)$, resulting in graph $G' = dec(a, b, c)\, D(b)\, act(c, d)\, D(d)$ and, after continuing the derivation, in graph $H = dec(a, b, c)\, goto(b, d)\, act(c, d)$, i.e., node y in rule a corresponds to node d in G' and also in H. The neighborhood of d in H, therefore, is derived as follows:

$$
\begin{aligned}
S() &\Rightarrow_{[i]_\circ} D(\circ) \\
&\Rightarrow_{[b]_\circ} \underbrace{dec(\circ, \circ, \circ)\, D(\circ)}_{\alpha}\ \underbrace{D(\circ)}_{[L_a]_y} \\
&\Rightarrow_{[a]_y} \underbrace{dec(\circ, \circ, \circ)\, D(\circ)}_{\alpha}\ \underbrace{act(\circ, \bullet)\, D(\bullet)}_{[R_a]_y} \\
&\Rightarrow_{[h]_x} dec(\circ, \circ, \circ)\, D(\circ)\, act(\circ, \bullet) \\
&\Rightarrow_{[g]_y} \underbrace{dec(\circ, \circ, \circ)\, goto(\circ, \bullet)}_{\alpha'}\ \underbrace{act(\circ, \bullet)}_{\alpha''}
\end{aligned}
$$

Note the correspondence of applied context-free rules and the CHR rules applied in Example 5. Note also that the vicinity multiset $\alpha = dec(\circ, \circ, \circ)\, D(\circ)$ does not contain $\bullet$, but its derived multiset $\alpha' = dec(\circ, \circ, \circ)\, goto(\circ, \bullet)$ does. This is so because rule g uses d as a context node in the CHR derivation.   ◇

We now show that the set of all possible vicinity multisets α of $[L_p]_u$ is actually a context-free language. To see this, we consider the context-free derivation sequence $[Z]_v \Rightarrow_{P^\circ}^* [G]_v = \alpha [L_p]_u . [Z]_v$ and $[L_p]_u$ are nonterminal literals. Therefore, there is a context-free derivation sequence $A_0 \Rightarrow_{P^\circ} \alpha_1 A_1 \Rightarrow_{P^\circ} \alpha_1 \alpha_2 A_2 \Rightarrow_{P^\circ} \cdots \Rightarrow_{P^\circ} \alpha_1 \cdots \alpha_n A_n$ with nonterminal literals $A_0, \ldots, A_n$ and $A_0 = [Z]_v$ as well as $A_n = [L_p]_u$, $(A_i ::= \alpha_{i+1} A_{i+1}) \in P^\circ$ for each i, and $\alpha_1 \cdots \alpha_n \Rightarrow_{P^\circ}^* \alpha$. We introduce a new nonterminal symbol A^v for each nonterminal literal A and define the set P^v of *vicinity rules* as

$$
P^v = \{(B^v ::= \gamma A^v) \mid (A ::= \gamma B) \in P^\circ \text{ and } B \text{ is nonterminal}\} \cup \{[Z]_\circ^v ::= \varepsilon\}.
$$

Note once more that γB is a multiset, so B may be any nonterminal in the right-hand side of $A ::= \gamma B$. Intuitively, if a derivation tree t over P contains a nonterminal node u labelled by B, then P^v allows to derive from B the "context" of u in t, yielding the multiset that consists of all literals generated by t, except for the subtree rooted at u.

One can now verify that the set of all vicinity multisets just consists of each multiset α such that $[L_p]_u^v \Rightarrow_{P''}^* \alpha$ with $P'' = P^\circ \cup P^v$, and, therefore

$$nh(p, u) = \{\alpha \mid [R_p]_u[L_p]_u^v \Rightarrow_{P^s}^* \alpha \text{ and } \alpha \text{ contains terminal literals only}\}$$

where $P^s = P^\circ \cup P^\bullet \cup P^v$. The set of all neighborhoods can thus be computed as the Parikh image of a new nonterminal symbol S_p^u

$$nh(p, u) = \psi(S_p^u)$$

using the set $P^s \cup \{S_p^u :: = [R_p]_u[L_p]_u^v\}$ of rules.

Example 8. The set P^v of vicinity rules for flowcharts (Example 5) is

$$P^v = \left\{ \begin{array}{ll} S()^v :: = \varepsilon & D(\circ)^v ::\stackrel{a^v}{=} act(\circ, \circ) \, D(\circ)^v \\ D(\circ)^v ::\stackrel{i^v}{=} S()^v & D(\circ)^v ::\stackrel{b^v}{=} dec(\circ, \circ, \circ) \, D(\circ) \, D(\circ)^v \end{array} \right\}$$

The only rules in Example 5 that generate any nodes are rules i, a, and b, generating nodes x (rule i), y (rules a and b), and z (rule b). Therefore, we must determine $nh(i, x)$, $nh(a, y)$, $nh(b, y)$, and $nh(b, z)$, which requires the additional nonterminals S_i^x, S_a^y, S_b^y, and S_b^z together with the following rules:

$$S_i^x :: = D(\bullet) \, S()^v \qquad\qquad S_b^y :: = dec(\circ, \bullet, \circ) \, D(\bullet) \, D(\circ) \, D(\circ)^v$$
$$S_a^y :: = act(\circ, \bullet) \, D(\bullet) \, D(\circ)^v \qquad S_b^z :: = dec(\circ, \circ, \bullet) \, D(\circ) \, D(\bullet) \, D(\circ)^v$$

The approximated Parikh images over-approximate the corresponding sets of possible neighborhoods:

$$\psi''(S_i^x) = \varepsilon + goto(\bullet, \circ) + \big(dec(\bullet, \circ, \circ) + act(\bullet, \circ)\big) \cdot U$$
$$\psi''(S_a^y) = act(\circ, \bullet) \cdot Q$$
$$\psi''(S_b^y) = dec(\circ, \bullet, \circ) \cdot Q$$
$$\psi''(S_b^z) = dec(\circ, \circ, \bullet) \cdot Q$$

where

$$Q = \big(\varepsilon + goto(\bullet, \circ) + dec(\bullet, \circ, \circ) + act(\bullet, \circ)\big) \cdot U$$
$$U = goto(\circ, \bullet)^\circledast dec(\circ, \circ, \circ)^\circledast goto(\circ, \circ)^\circledast act(\circ, \circ)^\circledast$$

A careful look at these sets reveals that $\psi''(S_i^x) \cap \big(\psi''(S_a^y) \cup \psi''(S_b^y) \cup \psi''(S_b^z)\big) = \varnothing$, i.e., the start node for parsing H is the unique node $v \in \dot{H}$ whose neighborhood is contained in $\psi''(S_i^x)$. It is the node which has no other incoming edges than *goto* edges. $\diamond$

In general, an analysis such as the one above can easily be made automatically once the simple semilinear sets have been computed, because expressions using union and intersection of such sets can easily be checked for emptiness. If the intersection is nonempty, PTD parsing is not possible, because the parser cannot determine unique start nodes for every input graph.

The neighborhood of a node v contains a literal for each edge in the graph, even for those edges that are not incident with v and, therefore, do not contain $\bullet$ in their literals (e.g., $act(\circ, \circ)$ in Example 8). At the expense of loosing some information, one can omit such literals from the neighborhood and use this modified definition of neighborhoods instead. For the flowchart example, therefore, one can determine the start node of a graph as the node with the following approximated set of (modified) neighborhoods, obtained from $\psi''(S_i^x)$:

$$\varepsilon + dec(\bullet, \circ, \circ)\,goto(\circ, \bullet)^\circledast + act(\bullet, \circ)\,goto(\circ, \bullet)^\circledast + goto(\bullet, \circ).$$

This simple semilinear set determines the start node as the node without any incident edges (first subterm), as the node with a leaving act or dec edge, any number of incoming $goto$ edges, but no other edge (second and third subterm), or as the node that has a leaving $goto$ edge, but does not have any other incident edge (fourth subterm).[3] The parser can actually determine all start nodes in linear time in the number of edges and nodes of the graph when using modified neighborhoods and when storing graphs with adjacency lists. This is so because the parser must check for each node whether it is one of the start nodes. To this end it must visit each of the incident edges and compute the neighborhood by counting the occurrences of literals. Using the resulting representation of the multiset as a tuple of natural numbers, membership of the neighborhood in a simple semilinear set can be checked in constant time. The proposition follows from the fact that each edge is visited as often as indicated by its arity.

5   Conclusions

In this paper we have devised a procedure for approximating Parikh images, and we have shown how this can be used to find the start nodes for PTD parsers of CHR grammars; the procedure is also used for another property of PTD parsers, called neighbor-determined rule choice in [4].

Semilinear sets are studied and applied in various fields such as complexity and computational theory [9,11], formal verification [13], and program analysis [5]. The membership problem for a fixed semilinear set is of linear time complexity [6], but the constants involved would become huge even for small grammars. In fact, the *uniform* membership problem for semilinear

---

[3] Note that a node with just a leaving $goto$ edge can actually not be a starting node although this is indicated by $\psi''(S_i^x)$. The reason for this over-approximation is that rule $[g]_x$ can be be applied to $D(\bullet)$ even if there is no additional node that could be used as a context node, which is actually necessary for applying CHR rule g.

sets is NP-complete [8] even if the sets are represented explicitly in the form $A_1 B_1^\circledast + \cdots + A_n B_n^\circledast$. Furthermore, extracting this explicit form from a context-free Chomsky grammar creates an exponential blow-up in itself. This makes further simplifications mandatory. In practice, it seems that simple approximated Parikh images provide a reasonable compromise between generality and computational efficiency (cf. the experimental evaluation reported in [4]).

Early work on parsing graphs has used little static analysis of grammars [7,10], and the parser generator for positional grammars [2] defers many decisions to parser execution time, and leaves the determination of start nodes to the users of the parsers.

The results of this paper will not only allow us to give a precise definition of the parser generation for CHR grammars; it will also be essential for our future work on generating deterministic bottom-up parsers for CHR grammars, which work analogously to $LR(1)$ string parsers.

Acknowledgements. We thank the anonymous reviewers for the valuable comments.

References

1. Brzozowski, J.A.: Derivatives of regular expressions. J. ACM **11**(4), 481–494 (1964)
2. Costagliola, G., Chang, S.K.: Using linear positional grammars for the LR parsing of 2-D symbolic languages. Grammars **2**(1), 1–34 (1999)
3. Drewes, F., Hoffmann, B.: Contextual hyperedge replacement. Acta Informatica **52**(6), 497–524 (2015)
4. Drewes, F., Hoffmann, B., Minas, M.: Predictive top-down parsing for hyperedge replacement grammars. In: Parisi-Presicce, F., Westfechtel, B. (eds.) ICGT 2015. LNCS, vol. 9151, pp. 19–34. Springer, Heidelberg (2015). doi:10.1007/978-3-319-21145-9_2
5. Esparza, J., Kiefer, S., Luttenberger, M.: Newton's method for *Omega*-continuous semirings. In: Aceto, L., Damgård, I., Goldberg, L.A., Halldórsson, M.M., Ingólfsdóttir, A., Walukiewicz, I. (eds.) ICALP 2008. LNCS, vol. 5126, pp. 14–26. Springer, Heidelberg (2008). doi:10.1007/978-3-540-70583-3_2
6. Fischer, P.C., Meyer, A.R., Rosenberg, A.L.: Counter machines and counter languages. Math. Syst. Theor. **2**, 265–283 (1968)
7. Franck, R.: A class of linearly parsable graph grammars. Acta Informatica **10**(2), 175–201 (1978)
8. Huynh, T.-D.: The complexity of semilinear sets. In: Bakker, J., Leeuwen, J. (eds.) ICALP 1980. LNCS, vol. 85, pp. 324–337. Springer, Heidelberg (1980). doi:10.1007/3-540-10003-2_81
9. Ibarra, O.H., Seki, S.: Characterizations of bounded semilinear languages by one-way and two-way deterministic machines. Int. J. Found. Comput. Sci. **23**(6), 1291–1305 (2012)
10. Kaul, M.: Practical applications of precedence graph grammars. In: Ehrig, H., Nagl, M., Rozenberg, G., Rosenfeld, A. (eds.) Graph Grammars 1986. LNCS, vol. 291, pp. 326–342. Springer, Heidelberg (1987). doi:10.1007/3-540-18771-5_62

11. Lavado, G.J., Pighizzini, G., Seki, S.: Converting nondeterministic automata and context-free grammars into Parikh equivalent deterministic automata. In: Yen, H.-C., Ibarra, O.H. (eds.) DLT 2012. LNCS, vol. 7410, pp. 284–295. Springer, Heidelberg (2012). doi:10.1007/978-3-642-31653-1_26
12. Parikh, R.J.: On context-free languages. J. ACM **13**(4), 570–581 (1966)
13. To, A.W.: Model checking infinite-state systems: generic and specific approaches. Ph.D. thesis, School of Informatics, University of Edinburgh, August 2010

SPO-Rewriting of Constrained Partial Algebras

Michael Löwe[✉]

FHDW Hannover, Freundallee 15, 30173 Hannover, Germany
michael.loewe@fhdw.de

Abstract. Recently, single-pushout rewriting (SPO) has been applied to arbitrary partial algebras (PA). On the one hand, this allows a simple and straightforward integration of (base type) attributes into graph transformation. On the other hand, SPO-PA-rewriting comes equipped with an easy-to-check application condition, namely that an operation cannot be defined twice on the same set of arguments. This provides very natural termination criteria for example in model transformation.

In this paper, we generalise this approach to constrained partial algebras. We allow two different types of constraints, namely (i) requiring some operations to be total and (ii) enforcing some consistency conditions on the algebras by suitable conditional equations. We show that this generalisation again induces an easy to check application condition and provides considerably more expressive power: For example, constraints allow a straightforward algebraic model for the object-oriented concept of inheritance with runtime specialisation and generalisation of objects.

1 Introduction

In [18,20], we introduced single-pushout rewriting (SPO) in categories of partial morphisms over partial algebras (PA) wrt. *arbitrary* signatures. Therefore, we gave up the usual restriction of SPO-rewriting to *graph structures* which are signatures with *unary* operation symbols only, compare [13]. Categories of partial morphisms constructed over graph structures have an initial object and *all* pushouts, which means that all finite co-limits can be constructed. This property leads to a rich theory, compare again [13]. This is no longer the case if we admit constants and operation symbols with more than one argument even if we pass from total to partial algebras.

Partial algebras, however, allow a simple reduction to total graph structures which are constrained by a set of Horn-formulas. The reduction provides an easy to check and characterising condition for the existence of pushouts of partial morphisms, namely that the pushout of partial algebras coincides with the pushout constructed in the underlying graph structure.[1]

In this paper, we discuss which types of *additional* constraints on categories of partial algebras preserve this property that the operational semantics is just well-known rewriting of graph structures. We present two types of such constraints. The first type uses arbitrary conditional equations, which can for example be

---

[1] For details compare [18].

© Springer International Publishing AG 2016
P. Milazzo et al. (Eds.): STAF 2016, LNCS 9946, pp. 129–144, 2016.
DOI: 10.1007/978-3-319-50230-4_10

used to specify that some operations are injective or that different compositions of operations lead to the same result if applied to the same argument.[2]
The second type of constraints discussed in this paper specifies that some unary
operations shall be total, i.e. defined for all arguments. Total and injective operations can be used to model the object-oriented concept of inheritance by sub-type
inclusions, compare Sect. 5.

The paper is structured as follows. In Sect. 2, we recapitulate our notion
of partial algebra and the reduction to hierarchical graph structures. Section 3
presents and generalises the results of [18] concerning existence and characterisation of pushouts in categories of partial morphism over partial algebras. On the
basis of these results, the main Sect. 4 introduces new constraints which preserve
the operational semantics of SPO-rewriting for graph structures and, therefore,
can be interpreted as global application conditions. Section 5 demonstrates the
gain in expressive power which we obtain by using constrained partial algebras.
Finally, Sect. 6 discusses related word and future research issues.

2   Partial Algebras and Hypergraphs

A *signature* $\Sigma = (S, O)$ consists of a set of sort names S and a domain- and
co-domain-indexed family of operation names $O = (O_{w,v})_{w,v \in S^*}$. A *partial Σ-
algebra* $A = (A_S, O^A)$ is a family $A_S = (A_s)_{s \in S}$ of carrier sets together with a
partial map $o^A : A^w \to A^v$ for every operation symbol $o \in O_{w,v}$ with $w, v \in S^*$.[3]

A *homomorphism* $h : A \to B$ between two partial algebras A and B wrt. the
same signature $\Sigma = (S, O)$ is a family of mappings $h = (h_s : A_s \to B_s)_{s \in S}$,
such that, for all operation symbols $o \in O_{w,v}$, the following condition is satisfied: If $o^A(x)$ is defined in A for $x \in A^w$, then $o^B(h^w(x))$ is defined in B and
$h^v(o^A(x)) = o^B(h^w(x))$.[4] A homomorphism $h = (h_s : A_s \to B_s)_{s \in S}$ is *closed*, if
we have for every operation $o \in O_{w,v}$: Whenever o^B is defined for $h^w(x)$ there
is $x' \in A^w$ with $h^w(x) = h^w(x')$ and o^A is defined for x'.[5]

The category of all partial Σ-algebras and all homomorphisms between them
is denoted by $\mathcal{A}_\Sigma$. By $\underline{\mathcal{A}}_\Sigma$ we denote the subcategory of all total Σ-algebras. Note
that all homomorphisms in $\underline{\mathcal{A}}_\Sigma$ are closed.

A (constructive) Σ-*contraint* is given by an epimorphism $c : P \twoheadrightarrow C$ from a
Σ-algebra P, called the *premise*, to a Σ-algebra C which is called the *conclusion*.
A homomorphism $h : P \to A$ *solves* the constraint $c : P \twoheadrightarrow C$, written $h \models c$, if
there is homomorphism $h^* : C \to A$ such that $h^* \circ c = h$. An algebra A satisfies

---

[2] Commutativity in the categorical sense.

[3] By this definition, an operation symbol $o \in O_{w,\epsilon}$ is interpreted in an algebra A as a
partial operation into an one-element-set, i.e. $o^A : A^w \to \{*\}$, which means that o^A
singles out a sub-set of A^w only, namely the sub-set where it is defined. Hence, o^A
is a *predicate*.

[4] Given a sort indexed family of mappings $(f_s : G_s \to H_s)_{s \in S}$, $f^w : G^w \to H^w$ is
recursively defined for every $w \in S^*$ by (i) $f^\epsilon = \{(*, *)\}$, (ii) $f^w = f_s$ if $w = s \in S$,
and (iii) $f^w = f^v \times f^u$, if $w = vu$.

[5] This means that definedness in B stems from definedness in A.

a constraint $c : P \twoheadrightarrow C$, written $A \models c$, if every morphism $h : P \to A$ solves c. Given a set $\mathfrak{C}$ of Σ-constraints, $\mathcal{A}_{\Sigma,\mathfrak{C}}$ denotes the full sub-category of $\mathcal{A}_\Sigma$ of all algebras that satisfy all the constraints $c \in \mathfrak{C}$. Such a category specified by Σ-constraints is called a *quasi-variety*. It is well-known that a full sub-category of $\mathcal{A}_\Sigma$ is a quasi-variety, if and only if it is an epi-reflective sub-category of $\mathcal{A}_\Sigma$.[6] Typically, a constraint is syntactically presented as an implication from a syntactical presentation of the premise to a syntactical presentation of the conclusion.

By contrast to total algebras, epimorphisms in categories of partial algebras need not be surjective in each component.[7] Thus, constraints can express some definedness requirements. Consider as an example the (unconditional) clause $\mathtt{x} \in \mathtt{S} : \mathtt{f(f(x))} = \mathtt{f(x)}$ for a signature Σ with an operation symbol $\mathtt{f} : \mathtt{S} \to \mathtt{S}$. It requires $\mathtt{f}$ to be idem-potent *and total*.

Given a signature $\Sigma = (S, O)$, $\Sigma^{\mathrm{u}} = (S^{\mathrm{u}}, O^{\mathrm{u}})$ denotes the underlying graph structure which is defined on sorts by:

$$S^{\mathrm{u}} = S \uplus \biguplus_{w,v \in S^*} O_{w,v}.$$

For every operation symbol $o \in O_{s_1 \ldots s_j, s_{j+1} \ldots s_{j+k}}$ in Σ with $j, k \geq 0$, O^{u}_{o,s_i} contains an operation symbol d_i^o for $1 \leq i \leq j$ and $O^{\mathrm{u}}_{o,s_{j+i}}$ contains an operation symbol c_i^o for $1 \leq i \leq k$.[8] There are no other operation symbols in O^{u}.

Note that the signature $\Sigma^{\mathrm{u}} = (S^{\mathrm{u}}, O^{\mathrm{u}})$ constitutes a hierarchical graph structure in the sense of [13].[9] In S^{u}, the sorts in S are on level 0 and the sorts in $\biguplus_{w,v \in S^*} O_{w,v}$ are on level 1. All operations in O^{u} are unary and map from sorts on level 1 to sorts on level 0. Thus, a total algebra wrt. $\Sigma^{\mathrm{u}} = (S^{\mathrm{u}}, O^{\mathrm{u}})$ can be interpreted as a hypergraph having vertices typed in S^{u} and hyperedges typed in O^{u}.

Let $\mathcal{G}_\Sigma$ denote the category of all *total* Σ^{u}-algebras and Σ^{u}-homomorphisms, i.e. $\mathcal{G}_\Sigma$ is short for $\underline{\mathcal{A}_{\Sigma^{\mathrm{u}}}}$.[10] Then there is a full and faithful functor $\gamma : \mathcal{A}_\Sigma \to \mathcal{G}_\Sigma$ mapping each partial algebra $A \in \mathcal{A}_\Sigma$ to $\gamma(A) \in \mathcal{G}_\Sigma$ by setting

1. for each sort $s \in S$: $\gamma(A)_s = A_s$ and
2. for each operation $o \in O_{s_1 \ldots s_j, s_{j+1} \ldots s_{j+k}}$ with $j, k \geq 0$:
   (a) $\gamma(A)_o = o^A$ and

---

[6] A category $\mathcal{S}$ is an epi-reflective sub-category of a category $\mathcal{C}$, if it is a sub-category of $\mathcal{C}$, i.e. $\mathcal{S} \subseteq \mathcal{C}$, and for every object $C \in \mathcal{C}$ there is a $\mathcal{C}$-epi-morphism $\eta_C : C \twoheadrightarrow S$ such that $S \in \mathcal{S}$ and for every morphism $f : C \to S'$ with $S' \in \mathcal{S}$, there is a unique morphism $f^* : S \to S'$ with $f^* \circ \eta_C = f$. For the results about epi-reflection, compare [21] for the total case and [1] for the partial case. They can also be found in [14].

[7] Compare [1,14].

[8] d_i^o and c_i^o are short for i-th domain respectively co-domain of operation o.

[9] A signature $\Sigma = (S, O)$ is a *graph structure*, if it contains unary operation symbols only, i.e. $O_{w,v} = \emptyset$, if $|w| = 0$ or $|w| \geq 2$. It is *hierarchical*, if there is no family $(o_i \in O_{s_i, v_i})_{i \in \mathbb{N}}$, such that, for all $i \in \mathbb{N}$, $v_i = x_i s_{i+1} y_i$ with $x_i, y_i \in S^*$.

[10] It is well-known that $\mathcal{G}_\Sigma$ is complete and co-complete.

(b) for all $(x, y) = ((x_1, \ldots, x_j), (y_1, \ldots, y_k)) \in o^A, 1 \le m \le j, 1 \le n \le k$:[11]
  i. $(\mathrm{d}_m^o)^{\gamma(A)}(x, y) = x_m$ and
  ii. $(\mathrm{c}_n^o)^{\gamma(A)}(x, y) = y_n$

and each homomorphism $h : A \to B$ in $\mathcal{A}_\Sigma$ to $\gamma(h) : \gamma(A) \to \gamma(B)$ by setting

1. for each sort $s \in S$: $\gamma(h)_s = h_s$ and
2. for each operation $o \in O_{w,v}$ with $w, v \in S^*$: $\gamma(h)_o(x, y) = (h^w(x), h^v(y))$.

Proposition 1 (Preservation of Epimorphisms). *If $\gamma : \mathcal{A}_\Sigma \to \mathcal{G}_\Sigma$ is the full and faithful functor from partial Σ-algebras to the underlying hierarchical Σ^u-graph-structures, then $\gamma(h) : \gamma(A) \to \gamma(B)$ is epimorphism, if and only if $h : A \to B$ is a closed epimorphism.*

Proof. "$\Leftarrow$": Every closed epimorphism is surjective on all sorts and, by definition of closedness, also on "operations". "$\Rightarrow$": Suppose $\gamma(h) : \gamma(A) \to \gamma(B)$ is epimorphism, i.e. is surjective in each component. Then $h_s = \gamma(h)_s$ is surjective for each sort s. Thus, h is epimorphism. If o^B is defined for $h^w(x)$, $(h^w(x), y) \in o^B$. Since $\gamma(h)_o$ is surjective for every operation o, $(h^w(x), y) = \gamma(h)_o(x', y')$ which means that $h^w(x) = h^w(x')$ and o^A is defined for x'. Therefore, h is closed. □

Unfortunately, the functor γ is not *isomorphism-dense*[12], such that $\mathcal{A}_\Sigma$ and $\mathcal{G}_\Sigma$ are not equivalent. We have to further restrict $\mathcal{G}_\Sigma$ by the following family of constraints which formalises uniqueness of partial maps:

$$\mathcal{U} = \left(\forall e_1, e_2 \in o : (\mathrm{d}_i^o(e_1) = \mathrm{d}_i^o(e_2))_{1 \le i \le |w|} \implies e_1 = e_2 \right)_{w, v \in S^*, o \in O_{w,v}} \tag{1}$$

By $\mathcal{C}_\mathcal{U}$, we denote the constraints (epimorphisms) presented by the implications $\mathcal{U}$. Figure 1 illustrates the correspondence between $\mathcal{U}$ and $\mathcal{C}_\mathcal{U}$ for the sample signature Σ_{f2}. Since there is only one operation, namely $f : S, S \to S$, $\mathcal{C}_\mathcal{U}$ contains a single epimorphism only, which is depicted in Fig. 1 by the dotted arrows.[13]

In the following, $\mathcal{P}_\Sigma \subseteq \mathcal{G}_\Sigma$ denotes the quasi-variety of all algebras in $\mathcal{G}_\Sigma$ satisfying all the constraints in $\mathcal{U}$, i.e. $\mathcal{P}_\Sigma = \mathcal{A}_{\Sigma^u, \mathcal{C}_\mathcal{U}}$. Since $\mathcal{P}_\Sigma$ is an epi-reflection of the category $\mathcal{G}_\Sigma$, we obtain a pair $(F(A) \in \mathcal{P}_\Sigma, \eta_A : A \twoheadrightarrow F(A))$ for every $A \in \mathcal{G}_\Sigma$ such that for every other pair $(X \in \mathcal{P}_\Sigma, f : A \to X)$, there is a unique $f^* : F(A) \to X$ with $f^* \circ \eta_A = f$. Since every image of γ is in $\mathcal{P}_\Sigma$ and γ is isomorphism-dense wrt. $\mathcal{P}_\Sigma$, we have:

---

[11] Note that all operations in $\gamma(A)$ are just projections!

[12] A functor $\gamma : \mathcal{A} \to \mathcal{B}$ between categories $\mathcal{A}$ and $\mathcal{B}$ is isomorphism-dense, if for every $B \in \mathcal{B}$ there is $A \in \mathcal{A}$ such that $\gamma(A) \cong B$.

[13] Note that this visualisation suggests that the constraints in $\mathcal{U}$ can be interpreted as total and non-injective SPO graph rewriting rules. Indeed, applying these rules until every further application leads to an identity trace, provides a constructive way to "execute" the reflection from $\mathcal{G}_\Sigma$ to $\mathcal{A}_\Sigma$.

$\Sigma_{f2} =$
sorts S
opns   f: S,S --> S

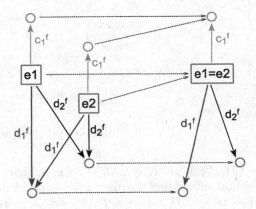

Fig. 1. Example for a uniqueness constraint

Fact 2 (Partial Algebras as Hypergraphs). $\mathcal{A}_\Sigma$ *and* $\mathcal{P}_\Sigma$ *are equivalent.*

Therefore, partial algebras can be considered as special hypergraphs which do not allow multiple edges of the same type between the same domain vertices.

Since $\mathcal{A}_\Sigma$ and $\mathcal{P}_\Sigma$ are equivalent, all results we obtain for $\mathcal{P}_\Sigma$ in the following are also valid in $\mathcal{A}_\Sigma$. Since $\mathcal{P}_\Sigma$ is an epi-reflection of $\mathcal{G}_\Sigma$, $\mathcal{P}_\Sigma$ is closed wrt. sub-objects and products. Thus, pullbacks in $\mathcal{P}_\Sigma$ coincide with pullbacks in $\mathcal{G}_\Sigma$. Pushouts in $\mathcal{P}_\Sigma$ are quotients of pushouts in $\mathcal{G}_\Sigma$ in the following sense: The pushout of $(f : A \to B, g : A \to C)$ in $\mathcal{P}_\Sigma$ is given by $(\eta_D \circ g^* : B \to D', \eta_D \circ f^* : C \to D')$ where $(g^* : B \to D, f^* : C \to D)$ is the pushout of f and g in $\mathcal{G}_\Sigma$ and $\eta_D : D \twoheadrightarrow D'$ is the epi-reflector that transfers the $\mathcal{G}_\Sigma$-object D into $\mathcal{P}_\Sigma$.

3   Partial Morphisms for Algebras and Hypergraphs

The single-pushout approach to rewriting uses partial morphisms as rules, total morphisms as matches, and pushouts in *categories of partial morphisms* as direct derivations. Therefore, we have to proceed from the categories $\mathcal{G}_\Sigma$ and $\mathcal{P}_\Sigma$ with total morphisms to the categories $\mathcal{G}_\Sigma^{\mathrm{P}}$ and $\mathcal{P}_\Sigma^{\mathrm{P}}$ of hypergraphs and partial algebras with partial morphisms.

A *concrete partial morphism* in $\mathcal{G}_\Sigma^{\mathrm{P}}$ is a span of $\mathcal{G}_\Sigma$-morphisms $(p : K \rightarrowtail P, q : K \to Q)$ such that p is monic. Two concrete partial morphisms (p_1, q_1) and (p_2, q_2) are equivalent and denote the same *abstract partial morphism* if there is an isomorphism i such that $p_1 \circ i = p_2$ and $q_1 \circ i = q_2$; in this case we write $(p_1, q_1) \equiv (p_2, q_2)$ and $[(p, q)]_\equiv$ for the class of spans that are equivalent to (p, q). The *category of partial morphisms* $\mathcal{G}_\Sigma^{\mathrm{P}}$ over $\mathcal{G}_\Sigma$ has the same objects as $\mathcal{G}_\Sigma$ and abstract partial morphisms as arrows. The identities are defined by $\mathrm{id}_A^{\mathcal{G}_\Sigma^{\mathrm{P}}} = \left[(\mathrm{id}_A^{\mathcal{G}_\Sigma}, \mathrm{id}_A^{\mathcal{G}_\Sigma}) \right]_\equiv$ and composition of partial morphisms $[(p : K \rightarrowtail P, q : K \to Q)]_\equiv$ and $[(r : J \rightarrowtail Q, s : J \to R)]_\equiv$ is given by

$$[(r, s)]_\equiv \circ_{\mathcal{G}_\Sigma^{\mathrm{P}}} [(p, q)]_\equiv = [(p \circ_{\mathcal{G}_\Sigma} r' : M \rightarrowtail P, s \circ_{\mathcal{G}_\Sigma} q' : M \to R)]_\equiv$$

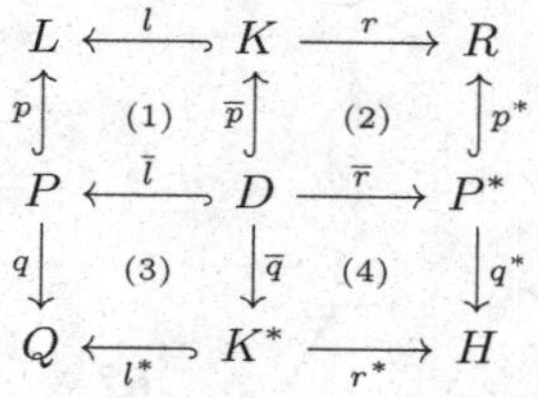

$$L \xleftarrow{\ l\ } K \xrightarrow{\ r\ } R$$

$$\begin{array}{ccccc}
L & \xleftarrow{\ l\ } & K & \xrightarrow{\ r\ } & R \\
p \uparrow & (1) & \bar{p} \uparrow & (2) & \uparrow p^* \\
P & \xleftarrow{\ \bar{l}\ } & D & \xrightarrow{\ \bar{r}\ } & P^* \\
q \downarrow & (3) & \downarrow \bar{q} & (4) & \downarrow q^* \\
Q & \xleftarrow{\ l^*\ } & K^* & \xrightarrow{\ r^*\ } & H
\end{array}$$

Fig. 2. Pushout in $\mathcal{G}_\Sigma^P$

where $(M, r' : M \rightarrowtail K, q' : M \to J)$ is pullback of q and r. Note that there is the faithful embedding functor $\iota : \mathcal{G}_\Sigma \to \mathcal{G}_\Sigma^P$ defined by identity on objects and $(f : A \to B) \mapsto [\mathrm{id}_A : A \rightarrowtail A, f : A \to B]$ on morphisms. We call $[d : A' \rightarrowtail A, f : A' \to B]$ a *total* morphism and, by a slight abuse of notation, write $[d, f] \in \mathcal{G}_\Sigma$, if d is an isomorphism. From now on, we mean the abstract partial morphism $[f, g]_{\equiv}$ if we write $(f : B \rightarrowtail A, g : B \to C)$. If the monic component in a partial morphism is an inclusion, we also write $g : A \overset{B}{\dashrightarrow} C$ for $(f : B \hookrightarrow A, g : B \to C)$. We omit the annotation of the arrow, if the sub-object of the partial morphism is irrelevant or uniquely determined by some universal properties.

It is well-known that $\mathcal{G}_\Sigma^P$ is complete and co-complete.[14]

Construction 3 (Pushout in $\mathcal{G}_\Sigma^P$). For partial morphisms $r : L \overset{K}{\dashrightarrow} R$ and $q : L \overset{P}{\dashrightarrow} Q$, the pushout morphisms $r^* : Q \overset{K^*}{\dashrightarrow} H$ and $q^* : R \overset{P^*}{\dashrightarrow} H$ are constructed as follows, compare Fig. 2:

1. D is the largest sub-algebra in $K \cap P$ satisfying:
   (a) $r(x) = r(y) \wedge x \in D \implies y \in D$ and
   (b) $q(x) = q(y) \wedge x \in D \implies y \in D$.
2. $\bar{l} : D \hookrightarrow P$ and $\bar{p} : D \hookrightarrow K$ are the corresponding inclusions.
3. P^* and K^* are the largest sub-algebras in $R - r(K - D)$ resp. $Q - q(P - D)$.
4. $p^* : P^* \hookrightarrow R$ and $l^* : K^* \hookrightarrow Q$ are the corresponding inclusions.
5. $\bar{r} : D \to P^*$ is defined by $d \mapsto r(d)$ and $\bar{q} : D \to K^*$ by $d \mapsto q(d)$.
6. (q^*, r^*) is the pushout of $(\bar{q}, \bar{r})$ in $\mathcal{G}_\Sigma$.

Remark. Construction 3 leads to the four commutative squares (1)–(4) in Fig. 2. They possess the following properties:

1. Squares (2) and (3) are pullbacks such that $r^* \circ q = q^* \circ r$.
2. Squares (1)–(3) make up a final triple in the sense of [19].
3. Square (4) is hereditary pushout in $\mathcal{G}_\Sigma$ since all pushouts in $\mathcal{G}_\Sigma$ are hereditary, compare Definition 4 below.

Therefore, Construction 3 provides a pushout in $\mathcal{G}_\Sigma^P$ due to the following general fact: A diagram as in Fig. 2 is pushout of partial morphisms over an arbitrary category $\mathcal{C}$, if and only if (1)–(3) make up a final triple in $\mathcal{C}$ and (4) is hereditary pushout in $\mathcal{C}$, compare [19, 20].

---

[14] Compare for example [13].

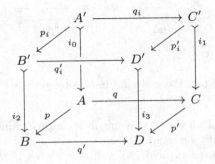

Fig. 3. Hereditary pushout

Definition 4 (Hereditary Pushout). *A pushout (p', q') of (p, q) in an arbitrary category is* hereditary, *if for each commutative cube as in Fig. 3, which has pullback squares (q_i, i_0) and (p_i, i_0) of (i_1, q) and (i_2, p) resp. as back faces with monic i_1 and i_2 the following compatibility between pushouts and pullbacks holds: In the top square, (q'_i, p'_i) is pushout of (p_i, q_i), if and only if, in the front faces, (p'_i, i_1) and (q'_i, i_2) are pullbacks of (i_3, p') and (i_3, q') resp. and i_3 is monic.*[15]

$\mathcal{P}_\Sigma^P$ is the full sub-category of $\mathcal{G}_\Sigma^P$ determined by the object inclusion of $\mathcal{P}_\Sigma \subseteq \mathcal{G}_\Sigma$. $\mathcal{P}_\Sigma^P$ does not possess all pushouts. $\mathcal{P}_\Sigma$ has all final triples but not all pushouts in $\mathcal{P}_\Sigma$ are hereditary. Final triples are constructed as in $\mathcal{G}_\Sigma$, since steps (1)–(5) of Construction 3 produce sub-objects D, P^*, and K^* which satisfy all Horn-formulae in $\mathcal{U}$ (compare (1) on p. x), if L, R, and Q do. Hereditariness of pushouts in $\mathcal{P}_\Sigma$ is characterised by an easy to check condition.

Fact 5 (Hereditrary Pushouts in $\mathcal{P}_\Sigma$). *A pushout in $\mathcal{P}_\Sigma$ is hereditary, if and only if it is pushout in $\mathcal{G}_\Sigma$.*

The proofs for this fact are provided by the proofs for Proposition 7 ($\Leftarrow$) and Proposition 8 ($\Rightarrow$) in [18]. Since all arguments in these proofs do not refer to the concrete structure of the formulae in $\mathcal{U}$, the result can be generalised as follows:

Theorem 6 (Hereditary Pushouts in Reflective Sub-categories of $\mathcal{G}_\Sigma$). *For every epi-reflective sub-category $\mathcal{C}_\Sigma$ of $\mathcal{G}_\Sigma$, we have:*

1. *Pushouts in $\mathcal{C}_\Sigma$ are hereditary, if and only if they are pushouts in $\mathcal{G}_\Sigma$.*
2. *Let $\mathcal{C}_\Sigma^P$ be the full sub-category of $\mathcal{G}_\Sigma^P$ determined by the object inclusion of $\mathcal{C}_\Sigma \subseteq \mathcal{G}_\Sigma$: If a pushout for a pair of morphisms in $\mathcal{C}_\Sigma^P$ exists, then it coincides with the pushout of the pair constructed in $\mathcal{G}_\Sigma^P$.*

4   SPO-Rewriting of Constrained Partial Algebras

Fact 5 shows that SPO-rewriting in $\mathcal{P}_\Sigma^P$ is just SPO-rewriting in graph structures from the operational point of view. It only adds an application condition, namely

---

[15] For details on hereditary pushouts see [11,12].

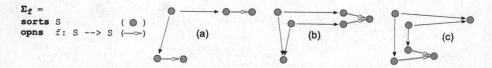

Fig. 4. Examples for impossible rewrites

that rewriting a partial algebra (as a graph structure) must result in a graph structure that represents a partial algebra.

Figure 4 presents three typical impossible rewrites in $\mathcal{P}^{\mathrm{P}}_{\Sigma_f}$. The mappings of the rule morphisms, which are all total in the three examples, are depicted by black straight arrows and the mappings of the match morphisms by dotted arrows. In the situation (a), the rule tries to add a definition of f to an object in the host graph that possesses a definition of f already. Situation (b) wants to add a new object as the result of the application of f for two existing objects. The match identifies the two existing objects. Rewriting in the underlying graph structure produces two parallel "edges" between the old and the new object which does not satisfy the uniqueness condition $\mathcal{U}$, compare (1) on p. x. Situation (c) is kind of symmetric to situation (b). Here two existing objects have the same result under application of f. The rule tries to merge these two objects, which again leads to two parallel "edges" violating $\mathcal{U}$.

If we add more constraints on partial algebras that are subject to SPO-rewriting, we want to preserve this fundamental property, i.e.:

> **Operational Semantics.** *Every SPO-rewrite of a constrained partial algebra coincides with the SPO-transformation of the underlying graph structure.*

Theorem 6 provides a first sort of constraints that satisfy this criteria: namely arbitrary constraints wrt. $\mathcal{G}_\Sigma$.[16] But these constraints do not one-to-one correspond to general constraints on $\mathcal{P}_\Sigma$. Constraints on partial algebras can formulate conditional equalities *and* definedness requirements, since epimorphisms in categories of partial algebras need not be surjective. Therefore, we have to restrict the constraints to those that do not implicitly formulate definedness requirements. By Proposition 1, these constraints are exactly characterised by the epimorphism that are closed. We call a constraint of this type *conditional equation*, since its conclusion in the syntactical presentation as an implication consists of equalities between variables only. Note that the set of constraints presented by $\mathcal{U}$ on p. x is a set of conditional equations.

Corollary 7 (Conditional Equation). *If $\mathcal{A}_\Sigma$ is a category of partial algebras and E a set of conditional equations wrt. Σ, then every pushout in $\mathcal{A}^{\mathrm{P}}_{\Sigma, E}$ coincides with the pushout constructed in $\mathcal{G}^{\mathrm{P}}_\Sigma$.*

Conditional equations provide a rich supply for useful constraints on partial algebras which are subject to rewriting, for example:

---

[16] Recall that $\mathcal{G}_\Sigma$ is the underlying graph structure of $\mathcal{P}_\Sigma$.

Singleton: $x = x'$,
Injectivity: $f(x) = f(x') \implies x = x'$,
Joint-Injectivity: $f_1(x) = f_1(x'), \ldots, f_n(x) = f_n(x') \implies x = x'$,
Commutativity: $f(g(x)) = z, h(x) = z' \implies z = z'$,
Inverse: $f(x) = z, g(z) = x' \implies x = x'$, and
Mutual Inverse: $f(x) = z, g(z) = x', f(x') = z' \implies x = x', z = z'$.

Note that the last five examples require equalities only in situations where the operations are "defined enough", i.e. the premises can be satisfied.

Up to this point, we do not have any means to require some sort of definedness. As it has been shown in [13], requiring definedness of operation symbols having more than one argument or none can lead to situations in which a final triple does not exist, compare steps (1)–(5) of Construction 3. Even worse: If operations with at least two arguments are required to be defined for a certain range of arguments, there are no obvious conditions which decide whether or not the final triple in Construction 3 exists.

Therefore, we restrict definedness requirements to unary operations here as well. Unfortunately, we cannot be as liberal as we want to at this point. This is due to the fact that even definedness requirements for unary operations may heavily interact with other constraints in form of conditional equations in an undesirable way.

Example 8 (Interference of Equations and Definedness). A good example for such an interference is depicted in Fig. 5. The shown specification requires its two unary operations $\underline{f}$ and $\underline{i}$ to be total, i.e. to be defined for all arguments. We – here and in the following – indicate this requirement by underlining the affected operations. Additionally, the operation $\underline{i}$ is forced to be injective.

The right part of the figure shows a pushout of two morphisms from L to R and L to G indicated by the black straight and dotted arrows resp. Note that the pushout does not coincide with the pushout constructed in the underlying graph structure. But it is hereditary.

This is mainly due to the fact, that G admits five sub-algebras only, namely the empty graph, G itself, and the three possible sub-graphs consisting of elements of the sort S' only. Only three of them can occur in a commutative cube

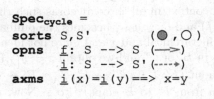
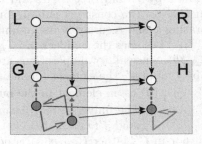

Fig. 5. Operation cycles

as in Fig. 3, namely the empty graph, G, and the sub-graph consisting of the two
S'-elements. And all these three cubes satisfy the hereditariness requirement. □

Example 8 shows a situation that violates our requirement "Operational Semantics" on p. y: We have hereditariness without coincidence of the pushout in the
constrained and the unconstrained category. This is mainly due to the cyclic
structure induced by the operation $\underline{f}$. Therefore, we restrict definedness requirements of unary operations to those that do not lead to cycles, i.e. to those that
produce a hierarchical underlying graph structure.

Definition 9 (Constrained Category of Partial Algebras). *A constrained
category* $\mathcal{R}_{(\Sigma,C,T)}$ *of partial algebras is syntactically given by a triple* (Σ, C, T),
where $\Sigma = (S, O)$ *is a signature,* C *is a set of conditional equations and* $T =
(T_{s,w} \subseteq O_{s,w})_{s \in S, w \in S^*}$ *is a sub-set of the unary operations in* O *satisfying the
following hierarchy condition: There is no family* $(o_i \in T_{s_i, w_i})_{i \in \mathbb{N}}$, *such that, for
all* $i \in \mathbb{N}$, $w_i = v_i s_{i+1} u_i$ *with* $v_i, u_i \in S^*$. *The semantics of* $\mathcal{R}_{(\Sigma,C,T)}$ *is the full
sub-category of* $\mathcal{A}^P_{\Sigma,E}$ *of those algebras in which all operations in* T *are total.*

As a generalisation of Propositions 7 and 8 in [18], we obtain:

Theorem 10 (Hereditariness in Constrained Categories). *A pushout in*
$\mathcal{R}_{(\Sigma,C,T)}$ *is hereditary, if and only if it is pushout in the underlying graph structure* $\mathcal{G}_\Sigma$.

Proof. "$\Leftarrow$": In addition to the arguments in the proof of Proposition 7 in [18], we
have to show that a pushout $(f^* : C \to D, g^* : B \to D)$ in $\mathcal{G}_\Sigma$ for $(f : A \to B, g :
A \to C)$ satisfies the definedness requirements specified by T. So let $o \in T_{s,w}$
and $x \in D_s$. Then $x = f^*(x_c)$ or $x = g^*(x_b)$. Without loss of generality assume
the first. Since C satisfies the definedness requirements, $o^C(x_c)$ is defined. Since
$(f^*)^w (o^C(x_c)) = o^P(f_s^*(x_c)) = o^P(x)$, o^P is defined for x.

"$\Rightarrow$" (Sketch): Here, we can repeat the arguments in the proof of Proposition 8 in [18]. Let $(f : A \to B, g : A \to C)$ be given, $(f^* : C \to D, g^* : B \to D)$
the pushout in $\mathcal{G}_\Sigma$, and $(f' : C \to E, g' : B \to E)$ the pushout in $\mathcal{R}_{(\Sigma,C,T)}$. Since
D satisfies all definedness requirements (see above), E is a quotient of D and
the two pushout morphisms (f', g') are jointly surjective. If the two pushouts
are different, there are two elements $x, y \in B \uplus C$ which are mapped to the same
element z by f' and/or g' in E and to different elements z_1, z_2 by f^* and/or
g^* in D. Now, we construct sub-algebras of $A' \subseteq_A A$, $B' \subseteq_B B$, and $C' \subseteq_C C$
by erasing x and recursively its minimal context in all three algebras such that
$(\subseteq_A, f_{|A'})$ becomes the pullback of $(\subseteq_B, f)$ and $(\subseteq_A, g_{|A'})$ becomes the pullback
of $(\subseteq_C, g)$. Since all total operations are hierarchical and x and y are not identi-
fied by f^* and g^*, the element y remains in B' or C' and we obtain $z' = f'_{|A'}(y)$
or $z' = g'_{|A'}(y)$ as an element in the pushout $(E', f'_{|A'} : C' \to E', g'_{|A'} : B' \to E'$
of $(f_{|A'}, g_{|B'})$. The universal morphism u from E' to E maps z' to z. Now, we
have $u(z') = z$ and $f'(x) = z'$ or $g'(x) = z'$. Since by construction, x is neither
in B' nor in C', either $(\subseteq_B, g'_{|A'})$ is not pullback of (u, g') or $(\subseteq_C, f'_{|A'})$ is not
pullback of (u, f').   □

Having this result about hereditary pushouts, we can conclude:

Corollary 11 (Rewriting in Constrained Categories). *Every pushout in the category* $\mathcal{R}^{P}_{(\Sigma,C,T)}$ *of partial morphisms wrt. a constrained category* $\mathcal{R}_{(\Sigma,C,T)}$ *coincides with the pushout constructed in the underlying graph structure* $\mathcal{G}^{P}_{\Sigma}$.

Remark. Note that step (1) in Construction 3 on p. z needs a marginal modification. Now we construct D as the largest sub-algebra *satisfying all definedness constraints in* T with properties (1a) and (1b). This algebra always exists, since all total operations are unary and the construction ends up in the standard cascade-on-delete behaviour that is well-known from single-pushout rewriting.[17]

The results of this section offer better ways to specify the structures that are subject to single-pushout rewriting. The appropriate framework is provided by the notion of *constrained category of partial algebras*, compare Definition 9. By Corollary 11, a simple operational semantics for rewrites in constrained categories is guaranteed. Therefore, there is a good chance to transfer some SPO-theory from graph structures to partial algebras and even to constrained partial algebras. This is subject of future research. In the rest of the paper, we want to present the gain of expressive power for SPO-rewriting of constrained structures.

5   Inheritance – The Algebraic Way

SPO-rewriting in categories of constrained partial algebras provides mechanisms to model many object-oriented concepts incl. inheritance in a straightforward and appropriate way. The inheritance model which we introduce below goes beyond all existing ones,[18] since it provides easy means for "runtime" type-specialisation and -generalisation of objects. Here is the general recipe how object-oriented class and type models are translated into constrained categories of partial algebras:

Immutable base types, like Integer and String, and the operations on these base types, like concatenation (+) of strings and addition (+), subtraction (-), multiplication (∗), and division (/) of integers are just modelled as a part of the underlying signature by appropriate sort and operation symbols. On the object-level, i.e. on the level of the objects that are subject to SPO-transformation these sort and operation symbols are interpreted by the standard carrier sets and partial operations. Note that the interpretation as *partial* operations provides an adequate model for overflow-situations or division-by-zero. In transformation rules, partial term algebras over a suitable set of variables are used. By

---

[17] Cacade-on-delete is a notion well-known from relational databases: If a row in a relation is deleted, all rows pointing directly or indirectly to it by foreign keys are deleted as well. SPO-rewriting provides exactly the same effect: If a vertex is deleted all edges adjacent to the vertex are deleted as well. In arbitrary graph structure this effect can cascade as well, if we have more than 2 hierarchy levels, see [13] for details.

[18] Compare [4,8,9,17] for the double-pushout, [6,16] for the single-pushout, and [15] for the sesqui-pushout approach.

contrast to total term algebras which are almost always infinite, the partial term algebras used in rules can always be chosen as finite algebras.[19]

Classes are modelled by sorts. So all types (base or not) are modelled by sorts.

An *attribute* a of base type T in a class C is modelled (i) by a partial operation $a : C \to T$, if its multiplicity is zero or one $(0 \ldots 1)$, (ii) a total operation $\underline{a} : C \to T$,[20] if its multiplicity is exactly one (1)[21] (iii) by a predicate $a : C, T \to \{*\}$, if its multiplicity is many incl. none $(*)$ without double assignments of the same value to the same object,[22] and (iii) by an additional sort symbol A and *total* operations $\underline{a_o} : A \to C$ and $\underline{a_t} : A \to T$, if its multiplicity is many incl. none $(*)$ and multiple assignments of the same value to the same object are allowed.[23]

An *association* r between classes C and D is modelled as follows: If the multiplicity of r at both ends is many incl. none $(*)$, we devise a predicate $r : C, D \to \{*\}$ if multiple links between the same pair of objects are forbidden or we add an additional sort R and two *total* operations $\underline{r_C} : R \to C$ and $\underline{r_D} : R \to D$ otherwise. If the multiplicity at the D-end is zero or one $(0 \ldots 1)$, we provide a partial map $r : C \to D$ which obtains an additional injectivity constraint of the form $c \in C : r(c) = r(c') \implies c = c'$, if the C-end has multiplicity $0 \ldots 1$ as well. If the multiplicity at the D-end is exactly one (1), we can devise a total operation $\underline{r} : C \to D$, as long as the signature remains hierarchical.[24]

A *qualified association* q between classes C and D using a T-typed attribute or association a of D as "key" is modelled by a partial operation $q : C, T \to D$.

If a set $a_1, \ldots, a_n$ of $0 \ldots 1$-attributes and/or associations of the same class C is a key to the objects of C, we add an injectivity constraint of the following form:

$$c, c' \in C : a_1(c) = a_1(c'), \ldots, a_n(c) = a_n(c') \implies c = c'$$

Inheritance $S \dashrightarrow G$ of sub-class S from super-class G, is modelled by a total and injective operation $\underline{i_{S,G}} : S \to G$ and for every diamond-situation, defined by $S \dashrightarrow G_1$, $S \dashrightarrow G_2$, $G_1 \dashrightarrow G$, and $G_2 \dashrightarrow G$, we add a commutativity constraint like:

$$x \in S; y, y' \in G : \underline{i_{G_1,G}}(\underline{i_{S,G_1}}(x)) = y, \underline{i_{G_2,G}}(\underline{i_{S,G_2}}(x)) = y' \implies y = y'$$

Let us apply this recipe to the class model for file systems in Fig. 6. We obtain the signature and constraints **File System** below. Note the seamless integration

---

[19] For example, the total term algebra is infinite, if we have a single sort (**Nat**) with a constant (**zero**) and an unary operation (**successor**). In partial algebras, the constant need not be defined and the unary operation need not be defined everywhere. Thus, we can define them as far as they are used in the rule (e. g. to denote constants) and leave them undefined for all values that are not mentioned in the rule.

[20] Note that we indicate the constraint that an operation is total by underlining the operation name.

[21] Note that the attribute automatically becomes **final**, if we model it by a total operation.

[22] Set semantics.

[23] Multi-set semantics.

[24] Note again that the association becomes **final**, if we model it by a total operation.

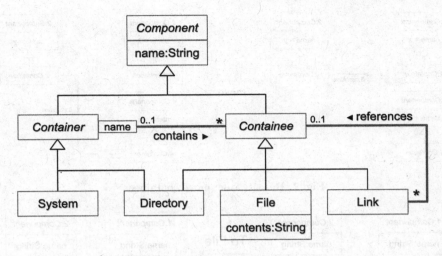

Fig. 6. Class model for file systems

of the "base type" `String`: On the one hand, it is used as "value-provider" for attributes `name` and `contents`. On the other hand, it is integrated in "graphical" structures as in `contains`. The constraints a1 and a2 specify the injectivity of the sub-type embeddings. Constraint a3 specifies the multiple inheritance of `Directory` and the diamond situation wrt. `Component`. Constraint a4 specifies that the index, that is used by a `Container` to manage its `Containees`, is consistent with the naming of the contained `Components`. Constraint a5 stems from the $0 \ldots 1$-multiplicity at the `container`-end of the `contains`-association.

```
File System =
sorts:
  C(omponent), C(ontain)er, C(ontain)ee, S(ystem),
  D(irectory), F(ile), L(ink), Str(ing).
opns:
  i: C'er → C, i: C'ee → C, i: S → C'er, i₁: D → C'er,
  i₂: D → C'ee, i: F → C'ee, i: L → C'ee,
  n(ame): C → Str, c(ontents): F → Str,
  r(erefences): L → C'ee, co(ntains): C'er,Str → C'ee.
axms:
```
> [a1] $(x,x' \in X: \underline{i}(x) = \underline{i}(x') \Longrightarrow x = x')_{X \in \{C'er, C'ee, S, F, L\}}$,
> [a2] $(x,x' \in D: \underline{i}_n(x) = \underline{i}_n(x') \Longrightarrow x = x')_{n \in \{1,2\}}$,
> [a3] $x \in D; y,z \in C: \underline{i}(\underline{i}_1(x)) = y, \underline{i}(\underline{i}_2(x)) = z \Longrightarrow y = z$
> [a4] $x \in C'er; s,s' \in Str: n(\underline{i}(co(x,s))) = s' \Longrightarrow s = s'$
> [a5] $x,x' \in C'er; s \in Str: co(x,s) = co(x',s) \Longrightarrow x = x'$

On the basis of the specification `File System`, operations that change the system's structure can be specified by SPO rewrite rules. Figure 7, for example, specifies the operation that moves a `Containee` (2) from `Container` (1) to

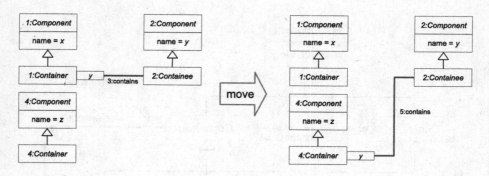

Fig. 7. Rewrite rule: move containee

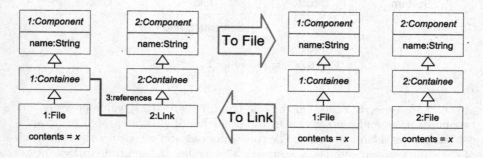

Fig. 8. Rewrite rule: convert to file/convert to link

Container (4). Note that this operation fails, if the receiving container already contains a containee named y. This is due to the fact that the index "contains" is specified as a partial operation that needs to be unique.

The rules in Fig. 8 demonstrate the ability of the chosen inheritance model to change the types of objects at "runtime".[25] The rule read from left to right converts a Link (2) to a File (1) into a file with the same contents as (1). This is possible by exchanging the Link-part of object (2) by a File-part.[26] The rule read from right to left has the inverse effect, namely it converts a file (2) that happens to have the same contents as another file (1) into a link to the file (1). Note that the context (other contains- and references-connections) of the manipulated entity on the Containee-level is not change, since all Containee-parts are preserved.

---

[25] Runtime means here: In the rewrite process.
[26] Note that the rule first generalises the manipulated object by deleting the Link-part. Afterwards it specialises the manipulated object by adding a new File-part.

6   Related Work and Future Research

There are only a few articles in the literature that address rewriting of partial algebras, for example [3] and [2] for the double- and single-pushout approach resp. But, both papers stay in the framework of signatures with *unary* operation symbols only and aim at an underlying category of partial morphisms that is co-complete. Aspects of partial algebras occur in all papers that are concerned with relabelling of nodes and edges, for example [10], or that invent mechanisms for exchanging the attribute value without deleting and adding an object, for example [7]. Most of these approaches avoid "real" partial algebras by completing them to total ones by some undefined-values.

Thus, the approach presented in [18] and further developed in this paper is original. It proposes to start with partial algebras in the first place and to require total operations where needed.[27] This is the other way around as most other approaches do: they start with total algebras and add some partiality where needed. Future research will show which approach is more suitable. Another topic for future research is the transfer of SPO-theory to the presented constrained framework. And finally, bigger case studies must be elaborated in order to confirm practical applicability.

References

1. Burmeister, P.: Introduction to Theory and Application of Partial Algebras - Part I. Mathematical Research, vol. 32. Akademie-Verlag, Berlin (1986)
2. Burmeister, P., Monserrat, M., Rosselló, F., Valiente, G.: Algebraic transformation of unary partial algebras II: single-pushout approach. Theor. Comput. Sci. **216**(1–2), 311–362 (1999)
3. Burmeister, P., Rosselló, F., Torrens, J., Valiente, G.: Algebraic transformation of unary partial algebras I: double-pushout approach. Theor. Comput. Sci. **184**(1–2), 145–193 (1997)
4. Ehrig, H., Ehrig, K., Prange, U., Taentzer, G.: Fundamentals of Algebraic Graph Transformation. Springer, Heidelberg (2006)
5. Ehrig, H., Engels, G., Kreowski, H.-J., Rozenberg, G. (eds.): ICGT 2012. LNCS, vol. 7562. Springer, Heidelberg (2012). doi:10.1007/978-3-642-33654-6
6. Lüdtke Ferreira, A.P., Ribeiro, L.: Derivations in object-oriented graph grammars. In: Ehrig, H., Engels, G., Parisi-Presicce, F., Rozenberg, G. (eds.) ICGT 2004. LNCS, vol. 3256, pp. 416–430. Springer, Heidelberg (2004). doi:10.1007/978-3-540-30203-2_29
7. Golas, U.: A general attribution concept for models in $\mathcal{M}$-adhesive transformation systems. In: Ehrig, H., Engels, G., Kreowski, H.-J., Rozenberg, G. (eds.) ICGT 2012. LNCS, vol. 7562, pp. 187–202. Springer, Heidelberg (2012). doi:10.1007/978-3-642-33654-6_13

---

[27] Note that standard SPO-Rewriting on multi-graphs turns out to be a special case of the set-up presented in this paper: The underlying category is defined by a signature with two sorts, i.e. vertives V and edges E, and two unary operations `source`,`target`:E$\rightarrow$V that are required to be total.

8. Golas, U., Lambers, L., Ehrig, H., Orejas, F.: Attributed graph transformation with inheritance: Efficient conflict detection and local confluence analysis using abstract critical pairs. Theor. Comput. Sci. **424**, 46–68 (2012)
9. Guerra, E., de Lara, J.: Attributed typed triple graph transformation with inheritance in the double pushout approach. Technical report UC3M-TR-CS-06-01, Universidad Carlos III de Madrid (2006)
10. Habel, A., Plump, D.: $\mathcal{M}$, $\mathcal{N}$-Adhesive Transformation Systems. In: Ehrig, H., Engels, G., Kreowski, H.-J., Rozenberg, G. (eds.) ICGT 2012. LNCS, vol. 7562, pp. 218–233. Springer, Heidelberg (2012). doi:10.1007/978-3-642-33654-6_15
11. Heindel, T.: Hereditary pushouts reconsidered. In: Ehrig, H., Rensink, A., Rozenberg, G., Schürr, A. (eds.) ICGT 2010. LNCS, vol. 6372, pp. 250–265. Springer, Heidelberg (2010). doi:10.1007/978-3-642-15928-2_17
12. Kennaway, R.: Graph rewriting in some categories of partial morphisms. In: Ehrig, H., Kreowski, H.-J., Rozenberg, G. (eds.) Graph Grammars 1990. LNCS, vol. 532, pp. 490–504. Springer, Heidelberg (1991). doi:10.1007/BFb0017408
13. Löwe, M.: Algebraic approach to single-pushout graph transformation. Theor. Comput. Sci. **109**(1&2), 181–224 (1993)
14. Löwe, M.L: Algebraic systems, June 2015. http://ux-02.ha.bib.de/daten/Lowe/Master/TheorieInformationssystem/Algebra20150606.pdf
15. Löwe, M.: Polymorphic sesqui-pushout graph rewriting. In: Parisi-Presicce, F., Westfechtel, B. (eds.) ICGT 2015. LNCS, vol. 9151, pp. 3–18. Springer, Heidelberg (2015). doi:10.1007/978-3-319-21145-9_1
16. Löwe, M., König, H., Schulz, C.: Polymorphic single-pushout graph transformation. In: Gnesi, S., Rensink, A. (eds.) FASE 2014. LNCS, vol. 8411, pp. 355–369. Springer, Heidelberg (2014). doi:10.1007/978-3-642-54804-8_25
17. Löwe, M., König, H., Schulz, C., Schultchen, M.: Algebraic graph transformations with inheritance and abstraction. Sci. Comput. Program. **107–108**, 2–18 (2015)
18. Löwe, M., Tempelmeier, M.: On single-pushout rewriting of partial algebras. In: ECEASST, vol. 73 (2016)
19. Monserrat, M., Rossello, F., Torrens, J., Valiente, G.: Single pushout rewriting in categories of spans I: The general setting. Technical report LSI-97-23-R, Department de Llenguatges i Sistemes Informtics, Universitat Politcnica de Catalunya (1997)
20. Tempelmeier, M., Löwe, M.: Single-pushout transformation partieller algebren. Technical report 2015/1, FHDW-Hannover (2015). (in German)
21. Wechler, W.: Universal Algebra for Computer Scientists. EATCS Monographs on Theoretical Computer Science, vol. 25. Springer, Heidelberg (1992)

Attributed Graph Transformation via Rule Schemata: Church-Rosser Theorem

Ivaylo Hristakiev and Detlef Plump[(✉)]

University of York, York, UK
detlef.plump@york.ac.uk

Abstract. We present an approach to attributed graph transformation which requires neither infinite graphs containing data algebras nor auxiliary edges that link graph items with their attributes. Instead, we use the double-pushout approach with relabelling and extend it with rule schemata which are instantiated to ordinary rules prior to application. This framework provides the formal basis for the graph programming language GP 2. In this paper, we abstract from the data algebra of GP 2, define parallel independence of rule schema applications, and prove the Church-Rosser Theorem for our approach. The proof relies on the Church-Rosser Theorem for partially labelled graphs and adapts the classical proof by Ehrig and Kreowski, bypassing the technicalities of adhesive categories.

1 Introduction

Traditionally, the theory of graph transformation assumed that labels in graphs do not change in derivations (see, for example, [2]). But in applications of graph transformation it is often necessary to compute with labels. For instance, finding shortest paths in a graph whose edges are labelled with distances requires to determine the shorter of two distances and to add distances.

Graphs in which data elements of some fixed algebra are attached to nodes and edges have been called attributed graphs since [12], the first formal approach to extend graph transformation with computations on labels. In that paper, graphs are encoded as algebras to treat graph structure and algebra data uniformly. With a similar intention, the papers [6,9] go the other way round and encode the data algebra in graphs. Each data element becomes a special data node and auxiliary edges connect ordinary nodes and edges with the data nodes.

The latter approach has become mainstream but has some serious drawbacks (bemoaned as the *akwardness of attributes* in [17]). Firstly, the way attributes are attached to edges leads to the situation of edges having other edges as sources. This requires non-standard graphs and makes the model unusual. Secondly, and more importantly, there is typically an infinite number of data nodes because standard data algebras (such as integers or lists) have infinite domains.

Supported by a Doctoral Training Grant from the Engineering and Physical Sciences Research Council (EPSRC) in the UK.

© Springer International Publishing AG 2016
P. Milazzo et al. (Eds.): STAF 2016, LNCS 9946, pp. 145–160, 2016.
DOI: 10.1007/978-3-319-50230-4_11

This means that attributed graphs are usually infinite, leading to a discrepancy between theory and practice as graphs are stored using finite representations. In the approach of [6], even rules are normally infinite because they consist of graphs containing the complete term algebra corresponding to the data algebra.

In this paper, we propose an alternative approach to attributed graph transformation which avoids both infinite graphs and auxiliary attribute edges. Instead of merging graphs with the data algebra, we keep them separate. Host graph items simply get labelled with data elements and rule graph items get labelled with terms. To make this work, rules are instantiated by replacing terms with corresponding data values and then applied as usual. Hence our rules are actually *rule schemata* whose application can be seen as a two-stage process.

In order to modify attributes, it is crucial that interface items in rules can be relabelled. We therefore use the double-pushout approach with partially labelled interface graphs as a formal basis [7]. This approach is also the foundation of the graph programming language GP 2 [15]. The fixed data algebra of GP 2 consists of integers, character strings, and heterogeneous lists of strings and integers. In this paper, we abstract from this particular algebra and consider an arbitrary data algebra (see Subsect. 2.2).

In Sect. 3, we define parallel independence of rule schema applications and prove the so-called Church-Rosser Theorem for our setting. Roughly, this result establishes that independent rule schema applications can be interchanged and result in the same graph. Our proof nicely decomposes into the Church-Rosser Theorem for the double-pushout approach with relabelling plus a simple extension to rule schemata (see Subsect. 3.2).

The Church-Rosser Theorem for the relabelling setting was obtained in [8] as a corollary of an abstract result for $\mathcal{M}, \mathcal{N}$-adhesive transformation systems. However, we deliberately avoid the categorical machinery of adhesiveness, van Kampen squares, etc. which we believe is difficult to digest for an average reader. Instead, we merely adapt the classical proof of Ehrig and Kreowski [5] to partially labelled graphs, essentially by replacing properties of pushouts and pullbacks in the unlabelled case by properties of natural pushouts in the setting of partially labelled graphs. (A pushout is natural if it is also a pullback.)

The rest of this paper is organized as follows. In Sect. 2, we describe the general idea of our approach. In Sect. 3, we present the notions of parallel and sequential independence and formalize the Church-Rosser Theorem at the rule schema level. Section 4 contains the relevant proofs. A conclusion and future work are given in Sect. 6.

We assume the reader to be familiar with basic notions of the double-pushout approach to graph transformation (see [3]). An extended version of this paper, along with complete proofs, can be found in [10].

2 Attributed Graph Transformation via Rule Schemata

In this section, we present our approach to transforming labelled graphs by rule schemata. We begin by briefly reviewing labelled graphs and the double-pushout approach to graph transformation with relabelling (see [7] for details).

2.1   Double-Pushout Approach with Relabelling

A *partially labelled graph* G over a (possibly infinite) label set $\mathcal{L}$ consists of finite sets V_G and E_G of *nodes* and *edges*, *source* and *target* functions $s_G, t_G \colon E_G \to V_G$, a partial node labelling function $l_{G,V} \colon V_G \to \mathcal{L}$, and a partial edge labelling function $l_{G,E} \colon E_G \to \mathcal{L}$. Given a node or edge x, we write $l_G(x) = \perp$ to express that $l_G(x)$ is undefined[1]. Graph G is *totally labelled* if $l_{G,V}$ and $l_{G,E}$ are total functions. The classes of partially and totally labelled graphs are denoted by $\mathcal{G}_\perp(\mathcal{L})$ and $\mathcal{G}(\mathcal{L})$, respectively.

A *premorphism* $g \colon G \to H$ consists of two functions $g_V \colon V_G \to V_H$ and $g_E \colon E_G \to E_H$ that preserve sources and targets: $g_V(s_G(e)) = s_H(g_E(e))$ and $g_V(t_G(e)) = t_H(g_E(e))$ for all edges e. Premorphism g is a *graph morphism* if it preserves labels, that is, if $l_G(x) = l_H(g(x))$ for all items x such that $l_G(x)$ is defined.

A graph morphism g *preserves undefinedness* if it maps unlabelled items in G to unlabelled items in H. We call g an *inclusion* if $g(x) = x$ for all items x. Note that inclusions need not preserve undefinedness. Finally, g is *injective (surjective)* if g_V and g_E are injective (surjective), and an *isomorphism* if it is injective, surjective and preserves undefinedness.

Partially labelled graphs and graph morphisms constitute a category (which is $\mathcal{M}, \mathcal{N}$-adhesive [8] if one picks $\mathcal{M}$ to be the injective morphisms and $\mathcal{N}$ to be the injective morphisms that preserve undefinedness). In this category, pushouts need not exist as can be observed in Fig. 2(a).

A *rule* $r = \langle L \leftarrow K \to R \rangle$ over $\mathcal{L}$ consists of two inclusions $K \to L$ and $K \to R$ such that L and R are graphs in $\mathcal{G}(\mathcal{L})$ and K is a graph in $\mathcal{G}_\perp(\mathcal{L})$.

Definition 1 (Direct derivation). A *direct derivation* between graphs G and H in $\mathcal{G}_\perp(\mathcal{L})$ via a rule $r = \langle L \leftarrow K \to R \rangle$ consists of two natural pushouts[2] as in Fig. 1, where $g \colon L \to G$ is an injective graph morphism.

We denote such a derivation by $G \Rightarrow_{r,g} H$. The requirement that the pushouts in Fig. 1 are natural ensures that the pushout complement D in Fig. 1 is uniquely determined by rule r, graph G and morphism g [7, Theorem 1]. Figure 2(b) demonstrates that non-natural pushout complements need not be unique. It is worth noting that in the traditional setting of double-pushout graph transformation with totally labelled graphs, the pushouts are automatically natural by the injectivity of $L \leftarrow K$ and $K \to R$.

Operationally, the application of rule r to graph G proceeds as follows: (1) match L with a subgraph of G by means of an injective graph morphism $g \colon L \to G$ satisfying the *dangling condition*: no node in $g(L) - g(K)$ is incident to an edge in $G - g(L)$; (2) obtain a graph D by removing from G all items in $g(L) - g(K)$ and, for all unlabelled items x in K, making $g(x)$ unlabelled; (3) add disjointly to D all items from $R - K$, keeping their labels, to obtain a graph H; (4) for all unlabelled items x in K, $l_H(g(x))$ becomes $l_R(x)$.

---

[1] We do not distinguish between nodes and edges in statements that hold analogously for both sets.

[2] A pushout is *natural* if it is also a pullback.

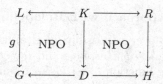

Fig. 1. A direct derivation

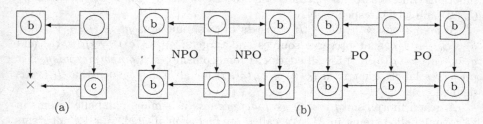

(a)   (b)

Fig. 2. (a) Pushouts need not exist. (b) A natural and a non-natural double pushout.

In [7] it is shown that if G is totally labelled, then the resulting graph H is also totally labelled. Moreover, unlabelled items in the interface graph K have unlabelled images in the intermediate graph D by the naturalness condition for pushouts.

2.2   Rule Schemata

Rule schemata for attributed graph transformation were introduced in the context of the graph programming language GP [16]. We first review signatures and algebras (details can be found, for example, in [3, Appendix B]).

Consider a *signature* Σ consisting of a set S of *sorts* and a family of *operation symbols* $OP = (OP_{w,s})_{(w,s)\in S^* \times S}$. A Σ-*algebra* A consists of a family of carrier sets $(A_s)_{s\in S}$ containing data values, and a set of functions implementing the operations of Σ. A *term algebra* $T_\Sigma(X)$ is built up from terms consisting of constants and variables, where X is a family of variables that is disjoint from OP.

An *assignment* $\alpha\colon X \to A$ is a family of mappings $(\alpha_s\colon X_s \to A_s)_{s\in S}$, giving a value to each variable in X. Its unique extension $\alpha^*\colon T_\Sigma(X) \to A$ evaluates terms according to α.

We assume a fixed Σ-algebra A whose elements are used as host graph labels, and a corresponding term algebra $T_\Sigma(X)$ whose terms are used as labels in rule schemata. To avoid an inflation of symbols, we sometimes equate A or $T_\Sigma(X)$ with the union of its carrier sets.

Definition 2 (Rule schema). A *rule schema* $r = \langle L \leftarrow K \rightarrow R \rangle$ consists of two inclusions $K \to L$ and $K \to R$ such that L and R are graphs in $\mathcal{G}(T_\Sigma(X))$ and K is a graph in $\mathcal{G}_\perp(T_\Sigma(X))$.

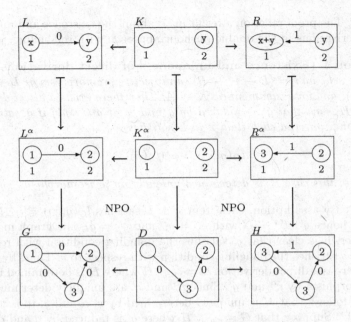

Fig. 3. Example of a rule schema direct derivation

To apply a rule schema r to a graph, the schema is first instantiated by evaluating its labels according to some assignment $\alpha\colon X \to A$.

Definition 3 (Rule schema instance and direct derivation). Consider a graph G in $\mathcal{G}_\perp(T_\Sigma(X))$ and an assignment $\alpha\colon X \to A$. The *instance* G^α is the graph in $\mathcal{G}_\perp(A)$ obtained from G by replacing each label l with $\alpha^*(l)$. The instance of a rule schema $r = \langle L \leftarrow K \to R \rangle$ is the rule $r^\alpha = \langle L^\alpha \leftarrow K^\alpha \to R^\alpha \rangle$.

A *rule schema direct derivation* via r between graphs G and H in $\mathcal{G}_\perp(A)$ is a direct derivation $G \Rightarrow_{r^\alpha, g} H$ via the instance r^α according to Definition 1.

We write $G \Rightarrow_{r,g,\alpha} H$ if there exists a direct derivation from G to H with rule schema r, graph morpshism g and assignment α. Note that we use $\Rightarrow$ for the application of both rule schemata and rules.

Figure 3 shows an example of a rule schema direct derivation, where we assume that algebra A contains the integers with addition $(+)$. The variables x and y are of sort **int** and are mapped by assignment α to 1 and 2, respectively. This allows for the relabelling of node 1 to 3. Note that this rule schema gives rise to infinitely many instances because the carrier set of integers is infinite.

Given an injective premorphism $g\colon L \to G$ and an assignment $\alpha\colon X \to A$, a graph morphism $g'\colon L^\alpha \to G$ is *induced* by g and α if $g'_V = g_V$ and $g'_E = g_E$. In other words, the application of α to L must turn g into a label-preserving graph morphism. The following proposition gives a necessary and sufficient condition for a rule schema with left-hand side L to be applicable with a morphism induced by g and α. The proof relies on a result in [7] about the existence and uniqueness of direct derivations in the double-pushout approach with relabelling.

Proposition 1 (Existence and uniqueness of direct derivations). *Consider a rule schema $r = \langle L \leftarrow K \rightarrow R \rangle$, an injective premorphism $g \colon L \rightarrow G$ with G in $\mathcal{G}_\perp(A)$, and an assignment $\alpha \colon X \rightarrow A$. Then there exists a direct derivation $G \Rightarrow_{r,g',\alpha} H$ such that g' is induced by g and α, if and only if g satisfies the dangling condition and each item x in L satisfies*

$$l_G(g(x)) = \alpha^*(l_L(x)).$$

Moreover, in this case H is determined uniquely up to isomorphism.

Proof. "If": By assumption, each item x in L satisfies $l_G(g(x)) = \alpha^*(l_L(x)) = l_{L^\alpha}(x)$ and hence $g' \colon L^\alpha \rightarrow G$ with $g'_V = g_V$ and $g'_E = g_E$ is a graph morphism.

Moreover, it is clear that g' satisfies the dangling condition with respect to r^α because g satisfies the dangling condition with respect to r. Thus, by [7, Theorem 1], there is a direct derivation $G \Rightarrow_{r^\alpha,g'} H$ where H is determined uniquely up to isomorphism by r^α and g'. Since r^α and g' are uniquely determined by r, α and g, it follows that H is uniquely determined by r, α and g, too.

"Only if": Suppose that $G \Rightarrow_{r,g',\alpha} H$ where g' is induced by g and α. Then, by definition, $G \Rightarrow_{r^\alpha,g'} H$. Hence, by [7, Theorem 1], g' satisfies the dangling condition. Since $g'_V = g_V$ and $g'_E = g_E$, it is clear that g satisfies the dangling condition with respect to r. Moreover, since g' is label-preserving, each item x in L satisfies $l_G(g(x)) = l_G(g'(x)) = l_{L^\alpha}(x) = \alpha^*(l_L(x))$. □

As indicated above, a rule schema $r = \langle L \leftarrow K \rightarrow R \rangle$ may have infinitely many instances. Even if one restricts to instances that are compatible with a given premorphism $g \colon L \rightarrow G$, there may be infinitely many instances to choose from. For example, consider a premorphism that maps a node in L labelled with $x + y$ to a node in G labelled with the integer 3 (assuming the conventions of Fig. 3). There are infinitely many assignments meeting the labelling condition of Proposition 1 because the equation $x + y = 3$ has infinitely many solutions over the integers.

Example 1 (GP 2 rule schemata). Labels in the graph programming language GP 2 [1,15] are integers, character strings or heterogeneous lists of integers and character strings. Lists are constructed by concatenation: given lists x and y, their concatenation is written x:y.

Expressions in the left-hand side L of a GP 2 rule schema are syntactically restricted to ensure that at most one instance of the schema is compatible with a given premorphism $g \colon L \rightarrow G$. To this end, left-hand expressions must neither contain arithmetic operators (except unary minus) nor repeated list variables, and all variables occurring on the right-hand side of a rule schema must also occur on the left-hand side.

Figure 4 shows the declaration of a GP 2 rule schema inc. Its left-hand labels contain typed variables which are instantiated with concrete values during

inc(a,x,y:list; i:int)

Fig. 4. Declaration of a GP 2 rule schema

graph matching. By convention, the interface of the rule schema consists of two unlabelled nodes. The effect of `inc` is to increment the rightmost element in the list of node 2.

In this paper we are not concerned with implementation issues and do not impose any restrictions on rule schemata. Abstracting from GP 2's label algebra, other possible data types for labels include (multi)sets, stacks, queues and records.

3   Church-Rosser Theorem

In this section, we present the notion of parallel independence for direct derivations with relabelling and then extend it to applications of rule schemata.

3.1   Independence of Direct Derivations with Relabelling

Let each of the diagrams in Fig. 5 represent two direct derivations according to Definition 1.

Definition 4 (Parallel and sequential independence). Two direct derivations $H_1 \Leftarrow_{r_1,m_1} G \Rightarrow_{r_2,m_2} H_2$ as in Fig. 5(top) are *parallel independent* if there exist morphisms $i : L_1 \to D_2$ and $j : L_2 \to D_1$ such that $f_2 \circ i = m_1$ and $f_1 \circ j = m_2$.

Two direct derivations $G \Rightarrow_{r_1,m_1} H_1 \Rightarrow_{r_2,m_2} H_2$ as in Fig. 5(bottom) are *sequentially independent* if there exist morphisms $i : R_1 \to D_2$ and $j : L_2 \to D_1$ such that $f_2 \circ i = m_1'$ and $f_1 \circ j = m_2$.

It will turn out that parallel and sequential independence are related: two direct derivations $H_1 \Leftarrow_{r_1,m_1} G \Rightarrow_{r_2,m_2} H_2$ are parallel independent if and only if the direct derivations $H_1 \Rightarrow_{r_1^{-1},m_1'} G \Rightarrow_{r_2,m_2} H_2$ are sequentially independent, where r_1^{-1} denotes the inverse rule of r_1 and m_1' is the comatch of m_1.

Lemma 1 (Characterization of parallel independence). *Two direct derivations $H_1 \Leftarrow_{r_1,m_1} G \Rightarrow_{r_2,m_2} H_2$ are parallel independent if and only if for all items $x_1 \in L_1$ and $x_2 \in L_2$ such that $m_1(x_1) = m_2(x_2)$,*

- *$x_1 \in K_1$ and $x_2 \in K_2$, and*
- *$l_{K_1}(x_1) \neq \bot$ and $l_{K_2}(x_2) \neq \bot$.*

$$R_1 \longleftarrow K_1 \longrightarrow L_1 \qquad L_2 \longleftarrow K_2 \longrightarrow R_2$$

$$\Big\downarrow \text{NPO} \Big\downarrow \text{NPO} \quad {}^{m_1} \quad {}^{m_2} \quad \text{NPO} \Big\downarrow \text{NPO} \Big\downarrow$$

$$H_1 \longleftarrow D_1 \xrightarrow{\ j\ } f_1 \longrightarrow G \longleftarrow f_2 \xrightarrow{\ i\ } D_2 \longrightarrow H_2$$

$$L_1 \longleftarrow K_1 \longrightarrow R_1 \qquad L_2 \longleftarrow K_2 \longrightarrow R_2$$

$$m_1 \Big\downarrow \text{NPO} \Big\downarrow \text{NPO} \quad {}^{m_1'} \quad {}^{m_2} \quad \text{NPO} \Big\downarrow \text{NPO} \Big\downarrow$$

$$G \longleftarrow D_1 \xrightarrow{\ j\ } f_1 \longrightarrow H_1 \longleftarrow f_2 \xrightarrow{\ i\ } D_2 \longrightarrow H_2$$

Fig. 5. Parallel and sequential independence (top and bottom, respectively)

The first condition states that every common item is an interface item. The second condition states that no common item is relabelled by either derivation.

Example 2 (Counterexample to parallel independence). Figure 6 shows two direct derivations $H_1 \Leftarrow G \Rightarrow H_2$ that use instances of the rule schema of Fig. 3. The derivations are *not* parallel independent: there are no morphisms $L_1 \to D_2$ and $L_2 \to D_1$ with the desired properties. The problem is that node 1 gets relabelled, breaking the second independence condition.

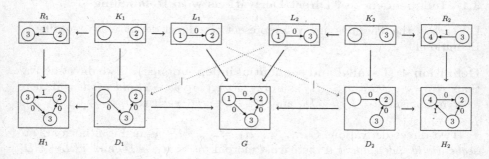

Fig. 6. Counterexample to parallel independence

Our main result (Theorem 2) will show that rule schema direct derivations that are parallel independent can be interchanged to obtain a common result graph. First, we state the Church-Rosser theorem for plain rules in the sense of Definition 1. This has been proved in [8] as a corollary of the Church-Rosser theorem for $\mathcal{M}, \mathcal{N}$-adhesive transformation systems. However, we obtain the result directly without using the notions of adhesiveness and van Kampen square.

The proof follows the original Church-Rosser proof of [5]. At specific points it will be necessary to show that the results for NPO decomposition apply to the given setting. See Sect. 4 for the complete proof.

Theorem 1 (Church-Rosser theorem for plain rules). *Given two parallel independent direct derivations $G \Rightarrow_{r_1,m_1} H_1$ and $G \Rightarrow_{r_2,m_2} H_2$, there are a graph $\tilde{H}$ and direct derivations $H_1 \Rightarrow_{r_2,m_2'} \tilde{H}$ and $H_2 \Rightarrow_{r_1,m_1'} \tilde{H}$. Moreover, $G \Rightarrow_{r_1,m_1} H_1 \Rightarrow_{r_2,m_2'} \tilde{H}$ as well as $G \Rightarrow_{r_2,m_2} H_2 \Rightarrow_{r_1,m_1'} \tilde{H}$ are sequentially independent.*

3.2   Church-Rosser Theorem for Rule Schema Derivations

This subsection lifts the previous independence result to rule schema applications. The main idea is to simply add instantiation on top of plain direct derivations.

Definition 5 (Parallel independence of rule schema derivations). Two rule schema direct derivations $G \Rightarrow_{r_1,m_1,\alpha_1} H_1$ and $G \Rightarrow_{r_2,m_2,\alpha_2} H_2$ are *parallel independent* if the plain derivations with relabelling $G \Rightarrow_{r_1^{\alpha_1},m_1} H_1$ and $G \Rightarrow_{r_2^{\alpha_2},m_2} H_2$ are parallel independent according to Definition 4.

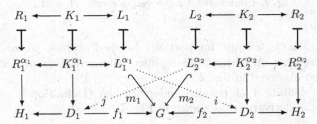

Theorem 2 (Church-Rosser theorem for rule schemata). *Given two parallel independent rule schema direct derivations $G \Rightarrow_{r_1,m_1} H_1$ and $G \Rightarrow_{r_2,m_2} H_2$, there is a graph $\tilde{H}$ and rule schema direct derivations $H_1 \Rightarrow_{r_2,m_2'} \tilde{H}$ and $H_2 \Rightarrow_{r_1,m_1'} \tilde{H}$. Moreover $G \Rightarrow_{r_1,m_1} H_1 \Rightarrow_{r_2,m_2'} \tilde{H}$ as well as $G \Rightarrow_{r_2,m_2} H_2 \Rightarrow_{r_1,m_1'} \tilde{H}$ are sequentially independent.*

Proof. From Theorem 1, we know that independence of the plain derivations with relabelling $G \Rightarrow_{r_1^{\alpha_1},m_1} H_1$ and $G \Rightarrow_{r_2^{\alpha_2},m_2} H_2$ implies the existence of a graph $\tilde{H}$ and direct derivations $H_1 \Rightarrow_{r_2^{\alpha_2},m_2} \tilde{H}$ and $H_2 \Rightarrow_{r_1^{\alpha_1},m_1} \tilde{H}$. This is illustrated in Fig. 7.

The direct derivations $G \Rightarrow_{r_1^{\alpha_1},m_1} H_1$ and $G \Rightarrow_{r_2^{\alpha_2},m_2} H_2$ use instances of the rule schemata r_1 and r_2, and therefore there are rule schema direct derivations $H_1 \Rightarrow_{r_2,m_2'} \tilde{H}$ and $H_2 \Rightarrow_{r_1,m_1'} \tilde{H}$. With Theorem 1 follows that both $G \Rightarrow_{r_1^{\alpha_1},m_1} H_1 \Rightarrow_{r_2,m_2'} \tilde{H}$ and $G \Rightarrow_{r_2^{\alpha_2},m_2} H_2 \Rightarrow_{r_1,m_1'} \tilde{H}$ are sequentially independent.   □

4   Proof of Theorem 1

The proof follows the original Church-Rosser proof of [5]. At specific points it will be necessary to show that the results for NPO decomposition apply to the

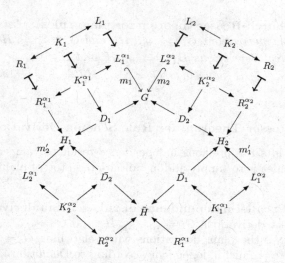

Fig. 7. Church-Rosser theorem for rule schemata

given setting. This is because for partially labelled graphs, pushouts need not always exist, and not all pushouts along injective morphisms are natural. These facts have been observed in Fig. 2.

Using the definition of parallel independence (Definition 4), we start by decomposing the derivations as shown in Fig. 8.

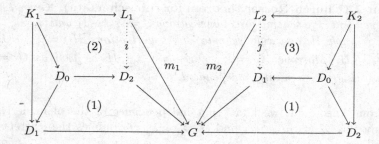

Fig. 8. First decomposition diagram

The graph D_0 is obtained as a pullback of $(D_1 \rightarrow G \leftarrow D_2)$. The universal property of pullbacks gives us that $K_1 \rightarrow D_1$ and $K_2 \rightarrow D_2$ decompose into $K_1 \rightarrow D_0 \rightarrow D_1$ and $K_2 \rightarrow D_0 \rightarrow D_2$ respectively. We also have that $(1+2)$ and $(1+3)$ are NPOs because they are left-hand sides of derivations. Furthermore, $D_1 \rightarrow G$ and $D_2 \rightarrow G$ are injective and jointly surjective which makes (1) an NPO ([10, Lemma 4]).

$D_1 \to G$ and $D_2 \to G$ injective imply that $D_0 \to D_2$ and $D_0 \to D_1$ are also injective. The subsequent parts of the proof contain four claims which are proven afterwards.

Claim 1. The squares (2) and (3) are NPOs.

Next, the pushouts $\overline{D_1}$ of $(D_0 \leftarrow K_1 \to R_1)$ (5) and $\overline{D_2}$ of $(D_0 \leftarrow K_2 \to R_2)$ (6) are constructed. These exist by the following claim:

Claim 2. In Fig. 9, the pushouts $\overline{D_1}$ of $(D_0 \leftarrow K_1 \to R_1)$ (5) and $\overline{D_2}$ of $(D_0 \leftarrow K_2 \to R_2)$ (6) exist.

Again using uniqueness, the morphisms $R_1 \to H_1$ and $R_2 \to H_2$ decompose into $R_1 \to \overline{D_2} \to H_1$ and $R_2 \to \overline{D_1} \to H_2$. We also have that $(5+7)$ and $(6+8)$ are NPOs because they are right-hand sides of derivations.

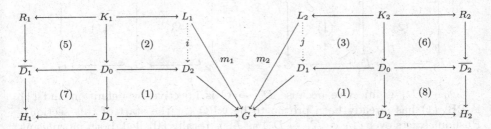

Fig. 9. Second decomposition diagram

Also, (7) and (8) become NPOs by the NPO Decomposition Lemma [10, Lemma 5.3].

Claim 3. In Fig. 9, the squares (7) and (8) are NPOs.

The graph $\tilde{H}$ is constructed as a pushout of $(\overline{D_1} \leftarrow D_0 \to \overline{D_2})$ (4). (See square (4) in Fig. 10.)

Claim 4. The pushout of $(\overline{D_1} \leftarrow D_0 \to \overline{D_2})$ exists.

This pushout becomes NPO by [10, Lemma 3] and the arguments in the proof of Claim 4. Furthermore, the graph $\tilde{H}$ is totally labelled due to the way D_0, $\overline{D_1}$ and $\overline{D_2}$ are constructed - $\overline{D_1}$ can contain unlabelled items only from $D_0 - K_1$ which are labelled in $\overline{D_2}$, and vice versa.

The pushouts can be rearranged as in Fig. 10 to show that $G \Rightarrow_{r_1,m_1} H_1 \Rightarrow_{r_2,m_2'} \tilde{H}$ as well as $G \Rightarrow_{r_2,m_2} H_2 \Rightarrow_{r_1,m_1'} \tilde{H}$ are sequentially independent. Note that the graph $\tilde{H}$ is totally labelled.

This concludes the proof of the Church-Rosser theorem.   □

Next, we present the proofs of the above claims.

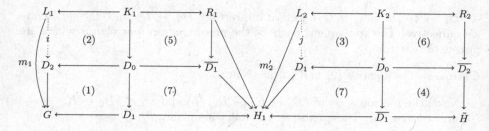

Fig. 10. Rearranged pushouts

Proof of Claim 1. We need to show that the conditions of the NPO Decomposition Lemma [10, Lemma 5.2] hold for the following diagrams.

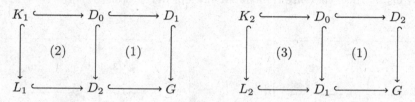

$D_0 \to D_1$ is injective because $D_2 \to G$ is injective by definition and (1) is PB. (1) has already been proven to be NPO (at the start of this section). Pushout exists over $(L_1 \leftarrow K_1 \to D_0)$ as L_1 is totally labelled, both morphisms are injective and $K_1 \to D_0$ preserves undefinedness, all by the definition of direct derivation with relabelling. The square $K_1 L_1 D_0 D_2$ commutes because $(1 + 2)$ and (1) are NPOs. Therefore, all conditions of the NPO Decomposition Lemma [10, Lemma 5.2] hold.

The proof for the second diagram is analogous.

This concludes the proof that the squares (2) and (3) are NPOs.   □

Proof of Claim 2. As in the previous proof, R_1 and R_2 are totally labelled, all morphisms are injective and both $K_1 \to D_0$ and $K_2 \to D_0$ preserve undefinedness, all by the definition of direct derivation with relabelling. Therefore, the pushouts (5) and (6) exist by [10, Lemma 2.2].   □

Proof of Claim 3. In the context of Fig. 11, we need to show that the conditions of the NPO Decomposition Lemma [10, Lemma 5.3] hold.

$D_0 \to D_1$ has already been established as injective. We need that there exists unique NPO complement of $K_1 \to R_1 \to \overline{D_1}$. We have that $K_1 \to R_1$ is injective by definition. $R_1 \to \overline{D_1}$ is injective because $K_1 \to D_0$ and $L_1 \to D_2$ are injective. The pushout (5+7) is a right-hand side of a derivation and $R_1 \to H_1 = R_1 \to \overline{D_1} \to H_1$. Consequently, $R_1 \to \overline{D_1}$ satisfies the dangling condition w.r.t. $K_1 \to R_1$, thus the existence of a unique NPO complement is given by [10, Lemma 2.3]. The proof for the second diagram is analogous.

This concludes the proof that the prerequisites for the NPO Decomposition Lemma [10, Lemma 5.3] hold. Hence, squares (7) and (8) become NPOs.   □

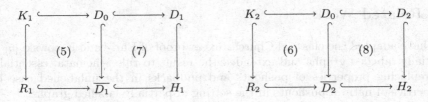

Fig. 11. Pushouts (5), (6), (7) and (8).

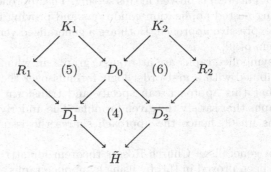

Proof of Claim 4. For a pushout to exist, $\overline{D_1}$ and $\overline{D_2}$ have to agree on the labels of the unlabelled nodes of D_0 ([10, Lemma 2.2]).

$\overline{D_1}$ is constructed as the pushout of $(R_1 \leftarrow K_1 \rightarrow D_0)$ with R_1 being totally labelled. Its node and edge sets and labelling function is as defined in [10, Lemma 2.2]. Moreover, $R_1 \rightarrow \overline{D_1}$ and $D_0 \rightarrow \overline{D_1}$ are injective and jointly surjective.

There are 3 main cases for an item x to be labelled in $\overline{D_1}$:

- the item is created by the first derivation $x \in R_1 - K_1$. This means it does not exist in D_1, D_2 or G. Consequently, this item does not have a preimage in D_0 by pullback construction ([10, Lemma 2.1]). Therefore, it cannot be a source of conflict for pushout existence.
- the item is relabelled by the first derivation, meaning its preimage in D_1 (and D_0) is unlabelled $x \in K_1$ and $l_{K_1}(x) = l_{D_1}(x) = l_{D_0}(x) = \perp$. By the definition of parallel independence, no common items are relabelled making the item not have a preimage in R_2. Therefore it is unlabelled in $\overline{D_2}$ (by definition of pushout), making it a non-conflict w.r.t. pushout existence.
- the item is in $\overline{D_1} - R_1$, i.e. a labelled item of $D_0 - K_1$. We have that $D_0 \rightarrow \overline{D_1}$ and $D_0 \rightarrow \overline{D_2}$ are label preserving, so the label of x in $\overline{D_2}$ is the same as in $\overline{D_1}$.

In all cases, the labels of $\overline{D_1}$ are preserved by the second derivation. The argument for the labelled items of $\overline{D_2}$ is analogous.

This concludes the proof that the pushout (4) over $(\overline{D_1} \leftarrow D_0 \rightarrow \overline{D_2})$ exists.   □

5   Related Work

We have adapted the classical Church-Rosser proof of Ehrig and Kreowski [5] to partially labelled graphs and extended the result to rule schemata, essentially by replacing properties of pushouts and pullbacks in the unlabelled case by properties of natural pushouts in the setting of partially labelled graphs.

In [6], the theory of attributed graph transformation is developed in the framework of so-called adhesive HLR categories. Among other results, the Church-Rosser Theorem is proved in this setting. The approach is further studied in [4] by adding nested application conditions and proving the previous results for this more expressive approach. Both are a generalized version of the Church-Rosser Theorem of [9].

So-called symbolic graphs are attributed graphs in which all data nodes are variables, combined with a first-order logic formula over these variables. In [13] it is shown that this approach can specify and transform classes of ordinary attributed graphs that satisfy the given formula. The underlying graph structure is the same as in [6], hence the approach shares the issues described in the introduction.

Recently, a generalised Church-Rosser theorem for attributed graph transformation has been proved in [11] by using symbolic graphs. A notion of parallel independence is used that takes into account the semantics of attribute operations, in order to reduce the number of "false positives" in conflict checking.

6   Conclusion

In this paper, we have presented an approach to attributed graph transformation based on partially labelled graphs and rule schemata which are instantiated to ordinary rules prior to application. We have defined parallel independence of rule schema applications and have proved the Church-Rosser theorem for our approach. The proof relies on the Church-Rosser theorem for graph transformation with relabelling and adapts the classical proof by Ehrig and Kreowski, bypassing the technicalities of adhesive categories.

Future work includes establishing other classical graph transformation results in our setting, such as embedding and restriction theorems. Furthermore, we aim at studying critical pairs and confluence both for the particular case of the GP 2 language and for attributed graph transformation over arbitrary label algebras. In particular, we plan to give a construction of critical pairs (labelled with expressions) that guarantees the set of critical pairs is both finite and complete. Completeness would mean that all possible conflicts of rule schema applications can be represented as embeddings of critical pairs.

References

1. Bak, C.: GP 2: efficient implementation of a graph programming language. Ph.D. thesis, Department of Computer Science, University of York (2015). http://etheses. whiterose.ac.uk/12586/
2. Ehrig, H.: Introduction to the algebraic theory of graph grammars (a survey). In: Claus, V., Ehrig, H., Rozenberg, G. (eds.) Graph Grammars 1978. LNCS, vol. 73, pp. 1–69. Springer, Heidelberg (1979). doi:10.1007/BFb0025714
3. Ehrig, H., Ehrig, K., Prange, U., Taentzer, G.: Fundamentals of Algebraic Graph Transformation. Monographs in Theoretical Computer Science. Springer, Heidelberg (2006)
4. Ehrig, H., Golas, U., Habel, A., Lambers, L., Orejas, F.: $\mathcal{M}$-adhesive transformation systems with nested application conditions. Part 1: parallelism, concurrency and amalgamation. Math. Struct. Comput. Sci. **24**(4) (2014)
5. Ehrig, H., Kreowski, H.-J.: Parallelism of manipulations in multidimensional information structures. In: Mazurkiewicz, A. (ed.) MFCS 1976. LNCS, vol. 45, pp. 284–293. Springer, Heidelberg (1976). doi:10.1007/3-540-07854-1_188
6. Ehrig, H., Prange, U., Taentzer, G.: Fundamental theory for typed attributed graph transformation. In: Ehrig, H., Engels, G., Parisi-Presicce, F., Rozenberg, G. (eds.) ICGT 2004. LNCS, vol. 3256, pp. 161–177. Springer, Heidelberg (2004). doi:10. 1007/978-3-540-30203-2_13
7. Habel, A., Plump, D.: Relabelling in graph transformation. In: Corradini, A., Ehrig, H., Kreowski, H.-J., Rozenberg, G. (eds.) ICGT 2002. LNCS, vol. 2505, pp. 135–147. Springer, Heidelberg (2002). doi:10.1007/3-540-45832-8_12
8. Habel, A., Plump, D.: $\mathcal{M}$, $\mathcal{N}$-adhesive transformation systems. In: Ehrig, H., Engels, G., Kreowski, H.-J., Rozenberg, G. (eds.) ICGT 2012. LNCS, vol. 7562, pp. 218–233. Springer, Heidelberg (2012). doi:10.1007/978-3-642-33654-6_15
9. Heckel, R., Küster, J.M., Taentzer, G.: Confluence of typed attributed graph transformation systems. In: Corradini, A., Ehrig, H., Kreowski, H.-J., Rozenberg, G. (eds.) ICGT 2002. LNCS, vol. 2505, pp. 161–176. Springer, Heidelberg (2002). doi:10.1007/3-540-45832-8_14
10. Hristakiev, I., Plump, D.: Attributed graph transformation via rule schemata: Church-Rosser theorem (long version) (2016). http://www.cs.york.ac.uk/plasma/ publications/pdf/HristakievPlump.16.Full.pdf
11. Kulcsár, G., Deckwerth, F., Lochau, M., Varró, G., Schürr, A.: Improved conflict detection for graph transformation with attributes. In: Proceedings of Graphs as Models (GaM 2015). Electronic Proceedings in Theoretical Computer Science, vol. 181, pp. 97–112 (2015)
12. Löwe, M., Korff, M., Wagner, A.: An algebraic framework for the transformation of attributed graphs. In: Sleep, R., Plasmeijer, M., van Eekelen, M. (eds.) Term Graph Rewriting: Theory and Practice, pp. 185–199. Wiley, New York (1993)
13. Orejas, F., Lambers, L.: Symbolic attributed graphs for attributed graph transformation. In: Graph and Model Transformation. Electronic Communications of the EASST, vol. 30 (2010)
14. Plump, D.: Confluence of graph transformation revisited. In: Middeldorp, A., Oostrom, V., Raamsdonk, F., Vrijer, R. (eds.) Processes, Terms and Cycles: Steps on the Road to Infinity: Essays Dedicated to Jan Willem Klop on the Occasion of His 60th Birthday. LNCS, vol. 3838, pp. 280–308. Springer, Heidelberg (2005). doi:10. 1007/11601548_16

15. Plump, D.: The design of GP 2. In: Proceedings of the Workshop on Reduction Strategies in Rewriting and Programming (WRS 2011). Electronic Proceedings in Theoretical Computer Science, vol. 82, pp. 1–16 (2012)
16. Plump, D., Steinert, S.: Towards graph programs for graph algorithms. In: Ehrig, H., Engels, G., Parisi-Presicce, F., Rozenberg, G. (eds.) ICGT 2004. LNCS, vol. 3256, pp. 128–143. Springer, Heidelberg (2004). doi:10.1007/978-3-540-30203-2_11
17. Rensink, A.: The edge of graph transformation — graphs for behavioural specification. In: Engels, G., Lewerentz, C., Schäfer, W., Schürr, A., Westfechtel, B. (eds.) Graph Transformations and Model-Driven Engineering: Essays Dedicated to Manfred Nagl on the Occasion of His 65th Birthday. LNCS, vol. 5765, pp. 6–32. Springer, Heidelberg (2010). doi:10.1007/978-3-642-17322-6_2

HOFM

Visual Notation and Patterns for Abstract State Machines

Paolo Arcaini[1], Silvia Bonfanti[2,3(✉)], Angelo Gargantini[2],
and Elvinia Riccobene[4]

[1] Faculty of Mathematics and Physics, Charles University in Prague,
Prague, Czech Republic
arcaini@d3s.mff.cuni.cz
[2] Department of Economics and Technology Management,
Information Technology and Production,
Università degli Studi di Bergamo, Bergamo, Italy
{silvia.bonfanti,angelo.gargantini}@unibg.it
[3] Software Competence Center Hagenberg GmbH, Hagenberg, Austria
[4] Dipartimento di Informatica, Università degli Studi di Milano, Milan, Italy
elvinia.riccobene@unimi.it

Abstract. Formal models are a rigorous way to specify informal system requirements. However, they are not widely used in practice, since they are considered difficult to develop and understand. Visualization is often considered a good means for people to communicate and to get a common understanding. We here make a proposal of a visual notation for Abstract State Machines (ASMs), and we introduce *visual trees* that visualize ASM transition rules. In addition to these graphical components that are based only on the syntactical structure of the model, we also present *visual patterns* that permit to visualize part of the behavior of the machine. A tool is also available to graphically represent ASM models using the proposed notation.

1 Introduction

Formal models are in principle accepted as the only way to specify in a precise and rigorous way the informal system requirements: they help to understand what has to be developed and to prove properties already at the early stages of the system development. However, formal specification languages are not widely used in industry, and practitioners largely consider formal methods "too hard to understand and use in practice". Limiting factors are the lack of *simplicity, learnability, readability, easiness of use* of formal notations [24]. All these qualities are fundamental to achieve easiness of development and comprehension

---

The research reported in this paper has been partly supported by the Charles University research funds PRVOUK, and by the Austrian Ministry for Transport, Innovation and Technology, the Federal Ministry of Science, Research and Economy, and the Province of Upper Austria in the frame of the COMET center SCCH.

© Springer International Publishing AG 2016
P. Milazzo et al. (Eds.): STAF 2016, LNCS 9946, pp. 163–178, 2016.
DOI: 10.1007/978-3-319-50230-4_12

of models, particularly for large, complex software systems. Requirement models should act as a communication medium among customers, users, designers, developers, and this common understanding is fundamental for the success of the system realization. However, since the mathematical notation is not always intuitive, and the size of the specification often consists of several pages of rules and formulas, model comprehension is threatened.

Visualization is considered as a good means for people to communicate and to get a common understanding. Indeed, the use of diagrams and graphical blocks is at the base of the mostly used notations in industry, as FSMs (and their extensions) or UML, the latter nowadays accepted as the industrial standard for system design. However, their shortcomings, as limited expressiveness for FSM w.r.t. other formal notations [5] or semantics lack for UML [6], are well-known.

Ever since UML appeared, many modeling approaches have been developed which try to use UML (or one of its profiles or domain-specific UML-like notations) as front-end of the requirements specification and formal notations as back-end of the process, to provide rigor and preciseness to lightweight models and make model validation and verification possible [13,19,21–23].

Abstract State Machines (ASMs) are an extension of FSMs, obtained by replacing unstructured control states by states comprising arbitrarily complex data [5]. ASMs have been widely used as requirement specification formalism. Despite of their mathematical foundation, a practitioner needs no special training to use the method since ASMs can be correctly understood as pseudo-code (or virtual machines) working over abstract data structures. Furthermore, to ease its use by non-experts, a series of integrated tools (for editing, validation, and verification) have been developed around ASMs [4].

Although the ASM textual notation [10] has been designed with readability in mind, our experience in trying to build and read very large system specifications [1,3] has shown that the complexity of the behavior being described overwhelms the reader, and most users (even the authors of the specification) need help in navigating and understanding it. This also happened while we were developing the ABZ 2016 case study [2], that motivated the current work. We tried, at first, to directly specify the ASM models from the textual description of the requirements. Although the refinement process helped us in managing the complexity of the case study, we still had some problems in discussing among us about the solution. So, we started making some drawings, whose notation was inspired by different sources: control flow graphs, UML state machines, sequence diagrams, etc. The lack of a way to graphically represent ASM models was clear.

A further observation we have made is that most of the new ASM users start developing ASM models as control state ASMs, a particular frequent class of ASMs – proposed by Börger in [5] – useful to model system modes (or control states). Control state ASMs have an intuitive graphical representation by means of FSM-like state diagrams. However, when the system to model is very complex, the resulting control state is too complicated and fails in achieving its main aim, i.e., easily communicating the behavior of the system. Moreover, a systematic use of control state ASMs is missing, and there is no algorithmic support to build or reconstruct such machines from models written in textual notations.

Starting from the motivations that (a) formality is important but also under-standing and communicating among stakeholders is fundamental, (b) visualiza-tion of formal models can surely aid the understanding of model structure and behaviors, (c) visual editing is often used to help designers and developers to graphically build complex models [8], we here propose a graphical notation for ASMs. The overall visualization of a model is given in terms of a graph. In addi-tion, we define *structural* patterns, useful to visualize the structure of a model in a more compact way, and *semantic* patterns to be used when additional infor-mation on the machine workflow can be inferred from the model.

The paper is organized as follows. Section 2 gives a brief background on ASMs. In Sect. 3, we introduce our proposal of a visual notation for ASMs, whose basic constituents (i.e., visual trees) are defined in Sect. 4. Section 5 shows that ASM models usually contain particular recurring patterns of ASM rules that can be visualized in a proper way: some patterns are simply structural, whereas others permit to infer some of the behavioral semantics of the ASM. Section 6 presents the prototypical implementation of a tool supporting the pro-posed visual notation. Section 7 describes a preliminary evaluation of the tool. Section 8 discusses some related work, and Sect. 9 concludes the paper.

2   Abstract State Machines

Abstract State Machines (ASMs) [5] are an extension of FSMs, where unstruc-tured control states are replaced by states with arbitrary complex data. Although the method has a rigorous mathematical foundation, a practitioner can simply understand ASMs as pseudo-code working over abstract data structures.

ASM *states* are algebraic structures, i.e., domains of objects with functions and predicates defined on them. An ASM *location*, defined as the pair (*function-name, list-of-parameter-values*), represents the abstract ASM concept of basic object container. The couple (*location, value*) represents a machine memory unit. Therefore, ASM states can be viewed as abstract memories.

Values of locations can be changed by firing *transition rules*. They express the modification of functions interpretation from one state to the next one. Location *updates* are the basic units of rules construction and are given as assignments of the form $loc := v$, where loc is a location and v its new value. The description of all basic ASM transition rules is given in Table 1.

An ASM *computation* is a finite or infinite sequence $S_0, S_1, \ldots, S_n, \ldots$ of states of the machine, where S_0 is an initial state and each S_{n+1} is obtained from S_n by firing the unique *main rule* which can fire other transitions rules.

There exists a classification of ASM functions that, however, is not relevant for understanding the current work and, therefore, is here skipped.

The ASM modeling process is supported by tools of the ASMETA frame-work[1] [4] that are strongly integrated in order to permit reusing information about models during different development phases. ASMETA provides function-alities for ASM models creation and manipulation (as editing using the AsmetaL

---

[1] http://asmeta.sourceforge.net/.

textual syntax [10], storage, interchange, etc.), and supports model analysis techniques (as validation, (runtime) verification, testing, requirements analysis, etc.).

3   A Visual Notation for ASMs

In this section, we introduce the meaning, the goals, and the possible usage scenarios of the proposed visual notation for ASM models.

The proposed visual notation is defined in terms of a set of construction rules and schemas that give a graphical representation of an ASM and its rules. We assume that the graphical information is represented by a visual graph in which nodes represent syntactic elements (like rules, conditions, rule invocations) or states, while edges represent bindings between syntactic elements or state transitions. We do not introduce a graphical representation for the signature (functions and domains) and properties, since we believe that they can be already easily understood from the textual model.

In the following sections, we propose a set of procedures that allow to automatically derive a *visual graph* from an ASM model. Section 4 introduces procedures that recursively visit the ASM rules and build a *visual tree* representing the syntactical structure of the model. In Sect. 5, we introduce some *visual patterns* that permit to identify recurring graphical schemas, and to obtain a more compact and meaningful representation, possibly capturing some behavioral information. Such representation may be no longer a tree, but a general graph.

The final goal is to have a textual representation together with a graphical visualization as shown in Fig. 1. To be more precise, we have devised two possible usage scenarios of the proposed visual notation.

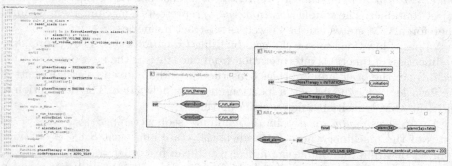

(a) Textual representation   (b) Graphical representation

Fig. 1. Visual notation

Visualization – From Textual to Graphical Representation. The first usage scenario consists in writing an ASM model in a textual representation (AsmetaL) and then derive a graph from it. Such approach can be used when the modeler is familiar with the ASM syntax, but (s)he wants to have a graphical representation of the model for its better understanding and communication. If the ASM model is syntactically correct, also the produced graph is correct. In the visualizer, the user can activate some optimizations (presented in the following sections), in order to have different views of the same model: structural (with different levels of optimization), or semantic (behavioral).

Visual Editing – From Graphical to Textual Representation. The second usage scenario consists in graphically specifying the ASM by drawing the graph. In this way, the modeler can focus on the high level structure of the model, similarly to what is done in code with control flow graphs. Note that the usage of semantic patterns allows the user to also graphically model some evolutions of the system, which are usually difficult to get by writing textual ASM models (at least without simulating it). Of course, the graph produced by the developer is not complete, as it does not specify the signature; moreover, it could also be not correct. Some trivial syntactical violations can be automatically detected on the graph by checking some consistency rules, but other faults may be more difficult to find. Once the modeler has produced the graph, a `translator` can translate the graph in an AsmetaL textual model. The produced model contains (most of) the transition rules, and the modeler is only required to add the signature (and the initialization). Then, the AsmetaL parser may find some faults that passed undetected during graph validation.

4   Visual Trees

We here introduce the relevant concepts which bring to a graphical representation of an ASM model in terms of a navigable forest of tree structures, i.e., a forest of trees connected by navigation links.

Definition 1. *The* visual notation *for ASMs is given by the bijective function* $\mathsf{vis_T}$ *between an ASM rule and a visual tree.*

Definition 2. *The function* $\mathsf{vis_T}$ *is given by Table 1.*

1. *For basic rules (update, skip and macro call) the function simply returns a tree with only one node (the root).*
2. *For compound rules (conditional, block, forall, choose, let), one must apply the schema given in Table 1 and recursively call the function* $\mathsf{vis_T}$ *on component rules.*

Table 1 describes the semantics of ASM transition rules, and shows the proposed graphical representation and the AsmetaL textual notation. The function $\mathsf{vis_T}$ is only based on the syntactical structure of the ASM and it can always be applied. Tree leaves are always skip, update, or call rules, and they are shown in boxes. Note that a call rule invokes a macro rule that has its own tree that, however, is not part of the main tree. At the end, one can obtain a tree for every rule declaration by applying vis$_T$ to its definition. The visualization of an ASM is given by the forest compound of all the trees of the declared rules. To navigate this visual view, the entry point is the tree for the main rule and, from every call rule, one can navigate to the tree of the invoked macro rule by a virtual *navigation link*, which is not visualized in the graphical representation. By considering the navigation links in the visualization, the resulting structure is a graph, as a macro rule can be called by different call rules.

Example 1. For explanation purposes, we use the Hemodialysis Machine Case Study [2]. It describes a hemodialysis device which goes through three phases: the *preparation* in which the device is prepared and the patient is connected, the *initiation* in which the hemodialysis is performed (i.e., the patient's blood is cleaned), and the *ending* in which the therapy terminates and the patient is disconnected. We can abstractly describe the device using the ASM model shown in Code 1[2]. Using the vis$_T$ function, the model can be represented as shown in Fig. 2. Note that the three macro rules r_preparation, r_initiation, and r_ending have their own tree representations that are not part of the tree generated from the main rule, but are connected to their corresponding call rules by navigation links (here rendered as dashed arrows only for presentation purposes).

```
asm Hemodialysis_GM

signature:
  enum domain PhasesTherapy = {PREPARATION |
                 INITIATION | ENDING}
  controlled phaseTherapy: PhasesTherapy

definitions:
  macro rule r_preparation =
    phaseTherapy := INITIATION

  macro rule r_initiation =
    phaseTherapy := ENDING

  macro rule r_ending =
    skip
```

```
main rule r_Main =
par
  if phaseTherapy = PREPARATION then
    r_preparation[]
  endif
  if phaseTherapy = INITIATION then
    r_initiation[]
  endif
  if phaseTherapy = ENDING then
    r_ending[]
  endif
endpar

default init s0:
  function phaseTherapy = PREPARATION
```

Code 1. Hemodialysis case study – AsmetaL model

5   Visual Patterns

We here introduce the notion of *visual pattern* for ASM visual trees. A pattern is a schema of connected tree nodes that is recurring and conveys a *structural* or *semantic* (i.e., behavioral) information. Therefore, identifying a pattern and substituting the entities belonging to it with a simplified structure is of interest.

---

[2] Note that the complete formalization of the case study consists of a sequence of refined models, each one specifying more details of the therapy.

Table 1. vis$_T$: mapping from ASM transition rules to visual trees

Rule	Visual tree	AsmetaL notation
Skip rule do nothing	skip	skip
Update rule update f to v	f := v	f := v
Macro call rule invoke rule r_rule with arguments $\overline{v}$ (if any)	r_rule[] r_rule[$\overline{v}$]	r_rule[] r_rule[$\overline{v}$]

Conditional rule
 execute *rule1* if *guard* holds, otherwise execute *rule2* (if given)
	guard $\longrightarrow$ vis$_T$ (rule1)
	
	 guard $\xrightarrow{\text{true}}$ vis$_T$ (rule1)
	 $\xrightarrow{\text{false}}$ vis$_T$ (rule2)
		if guard **then**
		 rule1
		 endif
		
		 if guard **then**
		 rule1
		 else
		 rule2
		 endif

Block rule execute *rule1 ... rulen* in parallel	par $\longrightarrow$ vis$_T$ (rule1) $\longrightarrow$ vis$_T$ (rule2) ... $\longrightarrow$ vis$_T$ (rule$n$)	**par** rule1 rule2 ... rulen **endpar**
Forall rule execute *rule1* with all values $\overline{v} \in \overline{V}$ for which $d(\overline{v})$ holds	forall $\xrightarrow{\overline{v} \in \overline{V}}$ $d(\overline{v})$ $\longrightarrow$ vis$_T$ (rule1[$\overline{v}$])	**forall** $\overline{v} \in \overline{V}$ **with** d($\overline{v}$) **do** rule1[$\overline{v}$]
Choose rule execute *rule1* with a $\overline{v} \in \overline{V}$ for which $d(\overline{v})$ holds. If no such $\overline{v}$ exists, execute *rule2* (if given)	choose $\xrightarrow{\overline{v} \in \overline{V}}$ $d(\overline{v})$ $\longrightarrow$ vis$_T$ (rule1[$\overline{v}$]) choose $\xrightarrow{\overline{v} \in \overline{V}}$ $d(\overline{v})$ $\longrightarrow$ vis$_T$ (rule1[$\overline{v}$]) ifnone $\longrightarrow$ vis$_T$ (rule2)	**choose** $\overline{v} \in \overline{V}$ **with** d($\overline{v}$) **do** rule1[$\overline{v}$] **choose** $\overline{v} \in \overline{V}$ **with** d($\overline{v}$) **do** rule1[$\overline{v}$] **ifnone** rule2
Let rule execute *rule1* substituting $\overline{t}$ for $\overline{x}$	let $\xrightarrow{\overline{x} = \overline{t}}$ vis$_T$ (rule1[$\overline{x}$])	**let**($\overline{x} = \overline{t}$) **in** rule1[$\overline{x}$] **endlet**

5.1 Structural Patterns

We identify the following structural pattern that permits to obtain a more compact representation of the model structure.

Nested Guards Pattern. The pattern regards the use of *nested conditional rules*. Suppose that you have a conditional rule as shown in Fig. 3a. By applying the visual trees in Table 1, one would obtain the tree shown in Fig. 3b. However, one can visualize the rule in a more compact way as shown in Fig. 3c.

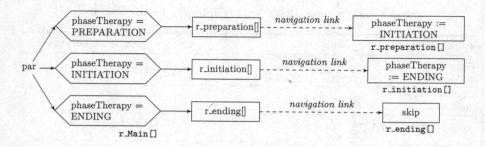

Fig. 2. Hemodialysis case study – visual trees

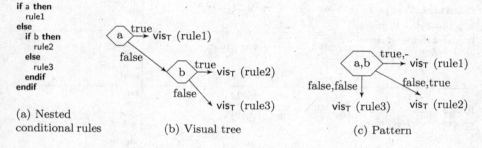

```
if a then
   rule1
else
   if b then
      rule2
   else
      rule3
   endif
endif
```

(a) Nested
conditional rules

(b) Visual tree

(c) Pattern

Fig. 3. Structural pattern – nested guards pattern

The pattern is applicable to any depth of nested conditional rules. One just has to collect all the guards $g_1, \ldots, g_n$, and create only one decision node comprising all the guards separated by commas. The decision node has as many exiting arcs as the number of conditional branches not containing another nested conditional rule, but a different rule rule$i$; each arc is labeled with the evaluations of the guards that permit to take that particular arc and fire rule rule$i$. Evaluations of guards that are not relevant for the firing of a rule rule$i$ are depicted with symbol "–". The decision node has up to $n + 1$ exiting arcs. Note that the pattern does not necessarily produce a tree that is more clear to understand, but it always provides a more compact representation of the nested conditional rules. For this reason, we let the modeler decide if (s)he wants to apply it.

Example 2. Figure 4b shows the application of the pattern to macro rule r_priming (shown in Fig. 4a) of the hemodialysis machine case study.

5.2   Semantic Patterns

Any ASM model can be always represented using visual trees and possibly optimized by applying structural patterns. The resulting tree visualizes the structure of the ASM. However, sometimes it is possible to infer from the model also some hints on the behavior of the machine. For this reason, we introduce *semantic*

```
macro rule r_priming =
   if bp_status_der = STOP then
      bp_status := START
   else
      if bp_fill_fluid and bp_rate_rinsing_150 then
         par
            bp_status := STOP
            tubingPhase := CONNECT_AV_ENDS
         endpar
      endif
   endif
```

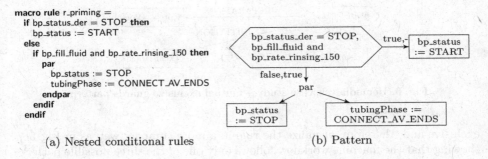

(a) Nested conditional rules   (b) Pattern

Fig. 4. Hemodialysis case study – nested guards pattern

patterns that can be applied when it is possible to infer from the model some information on the workflow of the machine.

We identify here three semantic patterns: *mutual exclusive guards*, *state*, and *state flow* patterns.

Mutual Exclusive Guards Pattern. In case of parallel conditional rules having mutual exclusive guards, it could be useful to represent that the workflow of the machine follows only one of the possible parallel execution paths.

The *mutual exclusive guards pattern* has been defined for this purpose. It is applicable when the rule guards check the current value of a given location that can assume disjoint values. This guarantees mutual exclusion among the guards of the conditional rules.

```
par
   if x = 1 then
      rule1
   endif
   if x = 2 then
      rule2
   endif
   if x = 3 then
      rule3
   endif
endpar
```

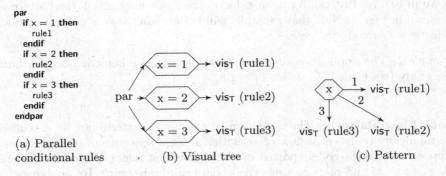

(a) Parallel
conditional rules   (b) Visual tree   (c) Pattern

Fig. 5. Semantic pattern – mutual exclusive guards pattern

Consider, for example, the ASM rule in Fig. 5a. It fires the parallel execution of three conditional rules guarded by the current value of the location x. Applying the visual tree in Table 1 to this rule, we obtain the representation given in Fig. 5b. However, one can understand that the three conditions on x are mutually

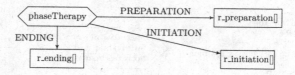

Fig. 6. Hemodialysis case study – mutual exclusive guards pattern

exclusive and, therefore, visualize the rule in a more compact way as in Fig. 5c, showing that the machine workflow follows only one of the three possible paths[3].

Example 3. The application of the mutual exclusive guards pattern to the main rule of Code 1 is shown in Fig. 6.

State Pattern. Often, it could be desirable to represent the machine behavior as a flow of activities along a sequence of states of control, i.e., configurations (or *modes*) in which the machine can be. Therefore, we enrich our visual notation with a special node (an ellipse) representing information about the (control) *state* in which a given rule can be executed.

Suppose the model is as shown in Fig. 7a, where rule$i$ is a macro call rule that might call (directly or indirectly) the update rule state := sj. Using only the visual trees defined in Table 1, the rule would be represented by the schema shown in Fig. 7b. However, supposing the modeler wants to use the function state to identify states of control, if rule$i$ changes the state from si to sj, one can build the graph as shown in Fig. 7c to explicitly represent the state change. In case rule$i$ can bring to different states (e.g., states sj and sk), the pattern is as shown in Fig. 7d. Instead, if rule rule$i$ leaves the mode unchanged, the pattern is as shown in Fig. 7e. Note that rule rule$i$ will be represented as a macro call rule, if this is not already the case.

Example 4. The application of the state pattern to the hemodialysis machine case study (see Code 1) is shown in Fig. 8.

State Flow Pattern. The definition of the state pattern can be extended to graphically represent a flow of activities along a sequence of control states. Suppose to have the code reported in Fig. 9a and that rule$i$ contains the update rule state := sj and rule$j$ contains the update rule state := sk. By applying the state pattern explained above, one would obtain the visual graph in Fig. 9b. However, the evolution of the system from state si to sj and then to sk can be made explicit, and the graph can be rewritten as in Fig. 9c. Note that if rule rule$j$ does not update state, the flow ends with rule$j$. Instead, if rule rule$j$ updates

---

[3] Note that the pattern can be detected by a simple static analysis of the model because of the particular guard structure we consider. If we would like to handle any type of guard, detecting the pattern would require to use a logical solver.

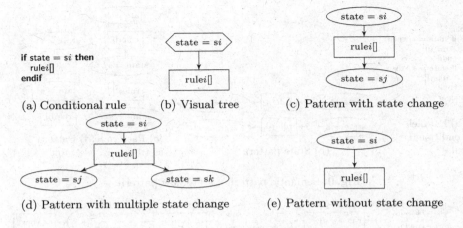

if state = si **then**
 rule$i$[]
endif

(a) Conditional rule   (b) Visual tree   (c) Pattern with state change

(d) Pattern with multiple state change   (e) Pattern without state change

Fig. 7. Semantic pattern – state pattern

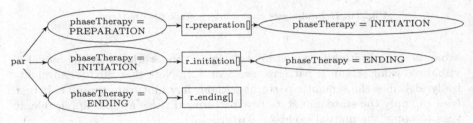

Fig. 8. Hemodialysis case study – state pattern

state to si, the resulting structure is a graph as shown in Fig. 9d. Note that if the state flow pattern is applicable, also the mutual exclusive guards pattern is applicable.

Example 5. The application of the state flow pattern to the hemodialysis machine case study (see Code 1) is shown in Fig. 10.

6   Tool

We have developed a prototypical tool, called `AsmetaVis`, that permits to represent the visual trees and some of the visual patterns we have presented. At the current stage of development, the tool supports the first usage we devised in Sect. 3 for our visual notation, i.e., model *visualization*, that permits to obtain the graphical representation of a specification written in AsmetaL. The tool is currently able to visualize the ASM in two modes:

– *basic visualization* in which the ASM is visualized using only the visual trees presented in Sect. 4; structural patterns (see Sect. 5.1) are not yet supported;

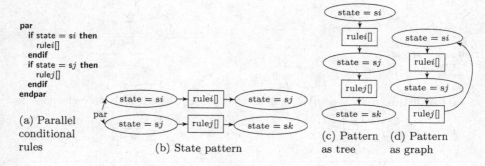

Fig. 9. Semantic pattern – state flow pattern

Fig. 10. Hemodialysis case study – state flow pattern

- *semantic visualization* in which information on the workflow of the model is visualized using semantic patterns (see Sect. 5.2). Note that the tool automatically identifies the semantic patterns without any hint from the user. It first tries to apply the state and state flow patterns; if these are not applicable, it tries to apply the mutual exclusive pattern.

At the beginning, the tool loads the AsmetaL model and shows the graph of the main rule. A double-click on a macro call rule node causes the visualization of the corresponding macro rule graph; in this way, we provide the navigation links described in Sect. 3.

The tool is integrated in the ASMETA framework as eclipse plugin[4] and it uses Zest for implementing the visualization features[5].

Example 6. Figure 11 shows the basic and the semantic visualizations of the model of the hemodialysis machine case study in `AsmetaVis` (see Code 1). In both cases, the main window represents the main rule and the other smaller windows depict the called macro rules.

7   Preliminary Evaluation

We conducted a preliminary experiment to evaluate whether the proposed visual notation can help in understanding a model. We interviewed 15 students who attended a course on formal system modeling and verification at the University of Milan (ten lectures on ASMs), and 11 who attended a course on principles of

---

[4] http://asmeta.sourceforge.net/download/asmetavis.html.
[5] https://www.eclipse.org/gef/zest/.

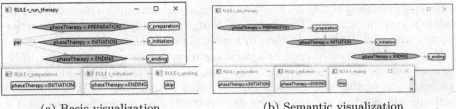

(a) Basic visualization   (b) Semantic visualization

Fig. 11. AsmetaVis tool – hemodialysis case study

programming languages at the University of Bergamo (six lectures on ASMs). We took the (last refined) textual model of the hemodialysis case study [2], that consists of 163 macro rules and 1880 lines of code. We gave the textual model to half of the students and its graphical representation to the other half. Then we asked them a question in order to evaluate their understanding of the model (UQ: Which are the phases of the hemodialysis treatment and in which order are they executed?). We measured the time taken for answering the question. After this experiment, we gave them also the other representation (the textual one for those having the graphical one, and vice versa) and we asked them to identify the same elements in both representations. Then we asked them a question regarding their satisfaction about the notation they used at the beginning (SQ: Are you satisfied with the notation you used at the beginning?).

Table 2 shows the results of the experiment. By UQ, we observe that the graphical notation permits to understand the model semantics better in less time than the textual notation. Regarding the level of satisfaction (SQ), all the students who used the graphical notation were satisfied and they would not have preferred using the textual one. Instead, only 7.6% of those using the textual notation were satisfied and 92.4% of them said that they would have preferred using the graphical one.

8   Related Work

The need of having visualization techniques for easing the work of the modeler is felt in the formal methods community [8,18,25]. Different experiences show that the adoption of such visualization techniques makes the use of formal methods feasible also for non-experts [18], and also helps in teaching formal methods [17].

Table 2. Experimental results

Group	UQ (% correct answers)	Avg. time (s)	SQ (% affirmative answers)
Graphical	92.3	135	100
Textual	76.9	226	7.6

Several graphical notations based on a formal semantics have been defined for modeling system behavior. Examples are Statecharts [12] for modeling reactive systems, and SDL [11] mainly used in telecommunications.

Regarding the visualization of formal notations, some approaches (as in [7, 13]) focus on *model visualization*, while others (as in [15,16]) provide a visual representation of the model execution (or *model animation*). In [13], graphical notations are used as an alternative representation of Z specifications, and a mechanical translation from Z models to diagrams is supported. They share with us the idea of using visualization in two ways. A similar approach is proposed for VDM in [7] where the authors propose two kinds of diagrams: Entry-Structure Diagrams modeling the system state, and Operation-State Diagrams modeling the behavior. ProB [15] allows automatic animation of B models, and can be used for error and deadlock checking, and test-case generation. B-Motion Studio [16] allows to create visualizations for B/Event-B models by using *controls*, which graphically represent some aspects of the model, and *observers* linking controls to the model state and invoking the animator ProB. ViBBA [9] was a tool for building an animator for ASMs. Although very powerful, the approach required a great effort in order to build the animator panel (by adding, from a palette, labels for controlled variables and input widgets, like buttons, for monitored variables) and to connect it to the model. We plan in the future to integrate the animation of behavior in `AsmetaVis`, but we would like to make the process of building animators as automatic as possible.

Our state flow pattern is a conservative generalization of the visualization for *control state machines*, which are an ASMs class with an intuitive (informally defined by examples in [5]) graphical representation in FSM-like diagrams. Our tool automatically provides a correct and precise visualization of those machines.

Other directions of model visualization concern the *use of UML notation as modeling front-end*, due also to the wide use of the UML in industry. For example, UML-B [23] uses the B notation as an action and constraint language for the UML, and defines the semantics of UML entities via a translation into B. Similarly, in [19], transforming rules are given from UML models to Object-Z constructs; therefore, the semantics of UML models is directly expressed in the formal language Object-Z. The tool OZRose has been developed to automate the transforming process. Furthermore, in [21], ArchiTRIO is defined as a formal language which complements UML 2.0 concepts with a logic-based notation to state system properties, both static and dynamic, including real-time constraints. In [22], a framework has been proposed for modeling and executing service-oriented applications. It uses the SCA (Service Component Architecture) notation to express the components architecture, and the ASMs to model services behavior, interactions, orchestration, compensation, and context-awareness. In [14], the method SPACE and its supporting tool Arctis are presented for the development of reactive services. In this method, services are composed of collaborative building blocks that encapsulate behavioral patterns expressed as UML 2.0 collaborations and activities.

Combined approaches have also been studied. In [20], for example, an integration of UML-B and Object-Z has been proposed to define a software development process where UML-B is used as visual modeling notation at early conceptual modeling stage, and Object-Z later when requirements are better understood.

9   Conclusions

With this work we have tried to satisfy a request, felt from long time, to have a way, and a supporting tool, to graphically represent ASM models, from a structural and from a behavioral point of view. We have proposed a graphical notation for ASMs, and we have defined visual patterns that capture, in a concise way, different recurring ASM rule patterns. The representation concerns only the transition rules and not the signature of the model.

As future work, we plan to define visual trees for all the turbo rules, and identify new visual patterns. Regarding the tool, we plan to implement the second usage we devised in Sect. 3 for our visual notation, i.e., the *visual editing* that should allow a modeler to graphically specify the ASM using the visual components (visual trees and visual patterns) we have proposed. Finally, we plan to better evaluate the possible advantages of using the proposed visual notation by means of a controlled experiment.

References

1. Arcaini, P., Bonfanti, S., Gargantini, A., Mashkoor, A., Riccobene, E.: Formal validation and verification of a medical software critical component. In: Proceedings of MEMOCODE 2015, pp. 80–89. IEEE, September 2015
2. Mashkoor, A.: The hemodialysis machine case study. In: Butler, M., Schewe, K.-D., Mashkoor, A., Biro, M. (eds.) ABZ 2016. LNCS, vol. 9675, pp. 329–343. Springer, Heidelberg (2016). doi:10.1007/978-3-319-33600-8_29
3. Arcaini, P., Gargantini, A., Riccobene, E.: Rigorous development process of a safety-critical system: from ASM models to Java code. Int. J. Softw. Tools Technol. Transf. 1–23 (2015)
4. Arcaini, P., Gargantini, A., Riccobene, E., Scandurra, P.: A model-driven process for engineering a toolset for a formal method. Softw. Pract. Exp. **41**, 155–166 (2011)
5. Börger, E., Stärk, R.: Abstract State Machines: A Method for High-Level System Design and Analysis. Springer, Heidelberg (2003)
6. Bryant, B.R., Gray, J., Mernik, M., Clarke, P.J., France, R.B., Karsai, G.: Challenges and directions in formalizing the semantics of modeling languages. Comput. Sci. Inf. Syst. **8**(2), 225–253 (2011)
7. Dick, J., Loubersac, J.: Integrating structured and formal methods: a visual approach to VDM. In: Lamsweerde, A., Fugetta, A. (eds.) ESEC 1991. LNCS, vol. 550, pp. 37–59. Springer, Heidelberg (1991). doi:10.1007/3540547428_42
8. Dulac, N., Viguier, T., Leveson, N., Storey, M.-A.: On the use of visualization in formal requirements specification. In: Proceedings of the 2002 IEEE Joint International Conference on Requirements Engineering, pp. 71–80. IEEE (2002)

9. Gargantini, A., Riccobene, E.: ViBBA: a toolbox for automatic model driven animation. In: Proceedings of SIMVIS 2005, pp. 101–114. SCS Publishing House (2005)

10. Gargantini, A., Riccobene, E., Scandurra, P.: A metamodel-based language and a simulation engine for Abstract State Machines. J. UCS **14**(12), 1949–1983 (2008)

11. Glässer, U., Gotzhein, R., Prinz, A.: The formal semantics of SDL-2000: status and perspectives. Comput. Netw. **42**(3), 343–358 (2003)

12. Harel, D., Politi, M.: Modeling Reactive Systems with Statecharts: The STATE-MATE Approach. McGraw-Hill Inc., New York (1998)

13. Kim, S.-K., Carrington, D.: Visualization of formal specifications. In: Proceedings of APSEC 1999, pp. 102–109. IEEE (1999)

14. Kraemer, F.A., Sltten, V., Herrmann, P.: Tool support for the rapid composition, analysis and implementation of reactive services. J. Syst. Softw. **82**(12), 2068–2080 (2009)

15. Ladenberger, L., Bendisposto, J., Leuschel, M.: Visualising Event-B models with B-Motion studio. In: Alpuente, M., Cook, B., Joubert, C. (eds.) FMICS 2009. LNCS, vol. 5825, pp. 202–204. Springer, Heidelberg (2009). doi:10.1007/978-3-642-04570-7_17

16. Leuschel, M., Bendisposto, J., Dobrikov, I., Krings, S., Plagge, D.: From Animation to Data Validation: The ProB Constraint Solver 10 Years On, pp. 427–446. Wiley, Hoboken (2014)

17. Leuschel, M., Samia, M., Bendisposto, J.: Easy graphical animation and formula visualisation for teaching B. In: The B Method: From Research to Teaching (2008)

18. Margaria, T., Braun, V.: Formal methods and customized visualization: a fruitful symbiosis. In: Margaria, T., Steffen, B., Rückert, R., Posegga, J. (eds.) Services and Visualization Towards User-Friendly Design. LNCS, vol. 1385, pp. 190–207. Springer, Heidelberg (1998). doi:10.1007/BFb0053506

19. Miao, H., Liu, L., Li, L.: Formalizing UML models with Object-Z. In: George, C., Miao, H. (eds.) ICFEM 2002. LNCS, vol. 2495, pp. 523–534. Springer, Heidelberg (2002). doi:10.1007/3-540-36103-0_53

20. Najafi, M., Haghighi, H.: An integration of UML-B and Object-Z in software development process. In: Elleithy, K., Sobh, T. (eds.) Innovations and Advances in Computer, Information, Systems Sciences, and Engineering. Lecture Notes in Electrical Engineering, vol. 152, pp. 633–648. Springer, New York (2013)

21. Pradella, M., Rossi, M., Mandrioli, D.: ArchiTRIO: a UML-compatible language for architectural description and its formal semantics. In: Wang, F. (ed.) FORTE 2005. LNCS, vol. 3731, pp. 381–395. Springer, Heidelberg (2005). doi:10.1007/11562436_28

22. Riccobene, E., Scandurra, P.: A formal framework for service modeling and prototyping. Formal Asp. Comput. **26**(6), 1077–1113 (2014)

23. Snook, C., Butler, M.: UML-B: formal modeling and design aided by UML. ACM Trans. Softw. Eng. Methodol. **15**(1), 92–122 (2006)

24. Spichkova, M.: Design of formal languages and interfaces: "formal" does not mean "unreadable". In: Emerging Research and Trends in Interactivity and the Human-Computer, Interface, pp. 301–314 (2014)

25. Spichkova, M.: Human factors of formal methods. CoRR, abs/1404.7247 (2014)

Visualization of Formal Specifications for Understanding and Debugging an Industrial DSL

Ulyana Tikhonova[✉], Maarten Manders, and Rimco Boudewijns

Technische Universiteit Eindhoven,
P.O. Box 513, 5600 MB Eindhoven, The Netherlands
{u.tikhonova,m.w.manders}@tue.nl, r.c.boudewijns@alumnus.tue.nl

Abstract. In this work we report on our proof of concept of a generic approach: visualized formal specification of a Domain Specific Language (DSL) can be used for debugging, understanding, and impact analysis of the DSL programs. In our case study we provide a domain-specific visualization for the Event-B specification of a real-life industrial DSL and perform a user study among DSL engineers to discover opportunities for its application. In this paper, we explain the rationale behind our visualization design, discuss the technical challenges of its realization and how these challenges were solved using the Model Driven Engineering (MDE) techniques. Based on the positive feedback of the user study, we present our vision on how this successful experience can be reused and the approach can be generalized for other DSLs.

Keywords: Event-B · Visualization · Domain specific language · User study

1 Introduction and Motivation

Domain-Specific Languages (DSLs) are a central concept of Model Driven Engineering (MDE). A DSL is a programming language specialized to a specific application domain. It captures domain knowledge and supports the reuse of such knowledge via common domain notions and notation. In this way, the DSL raises the abstraction level for solving problems in the domain. DSLs are considered to be very effective in software development and are being widely adopted by industry nowadays.

DSL semantics is usually implemented as a translation from the domain concepts to a programming language for an execution platform. From a semantics point of view, the gap bridged by this translation can be quite wide. The DSL translation usually includes complex design solutions and algorithms, which employ both high-level concepts of the DSL and low-level concepts of the execution platform. In traditional MDE, all details of the DSL translation reside in model transformations and code generators. So, to understand how a DSL program works one can either examine the source code of the DSL translation,

© Springer International Publishing AG 2016
P. Milazzo et al. (Eds.): STAF 2016, LNCS 9946, pp. 179–195, 2016.
DOI: 10.1007/978-3-319-50230-4_13

or the source code generated from the DSL program. This poses undesirable challenges when developing, understanding, and debugging DSL programs.

A thorough mathematical-based *formal specification* of a DSL can make the DSL translation more accessible, by expressing the translation on a higher abstraction level than model transformations and code generators [14]. Moreover, tools supporting this formal specification can enhance understanding, developing, and debugging of DSL programs. For example, DSL programs can be explored and debugged by execution (simulation) of their specification using animation tools. However, practical realization of these benefits requires adaptation of the formal specification and supporting tools to the needs and background of engineers who develop or use the DSL.

In this work, we provide a domain-specific visualization for the formal specification of a real-life industrial DSL. This visualization mimics the original graphical notation of the DSL and runs on top of the animation of the DSL specification. As a result, the DSL specification can be used by DSL engineers who are not familiar with the formal notation of the specification. We implemented this visualization by means of model transformations from the DSL to the visualization platform. Thus, a visualization is generated automatically for each concrete DSL program. Furthermore, we investigated the needs and perception of DSL engineers by means of a user study performed with this visualization. The user study indicated that there is a need for such visualization of DSL models; and that it might be challenging to keep the DSL specification consistent with the actual implementation of the DSL, which evolves over time. This challenge is addressed in a framework that we propose as our vision on how successful specification solutions and their visualizations can be reused for other DSLs in the form of specification and visualization templates.

2   Related Work

There exist various approaches for visualizing a formal specification and its execution (animation). It can be a visualization of a state space, or wrapping a formalism into the (standard) graphical notation of UML (such as [10]). In our work we focus on a domain-specific visualization – on a graphical representation tailored for a specific (engineering or application) domain. A number of case studies have proven that a domain-specific visualization of a formal specification can be very useful for creating, validating, and applying the specification by humans, especially by domain experts. For example, in [4] Hansen et al. state that graphical representation of their Event-B specification of a landing gear system was crucial for its development and validation. In [7] Mathijssen and Pretorius use a visualization of their mCRL2 specification of an automated parking garage to discover and fix a number of bugs in the specification. They conclude that the visualized simulation is more intuitively clear and easy to understand, and thus, helps to identify issues that may not have been noted otherwise.

In [12] Stappers specifies the behavior of an industrial wafer handler using mCRL2, obtains a trace to a deadlock state using the mCRL2 toolset, and visualizes this trace using a CAD (Computer Aided Design) model of the wafer handler in a kinematic 3D visualizer. In other words, the visualization animates the 3D virtual model of the physical system by moving its parts along the predefined motion paths. As a result, engineers of the wafer handler could identify the problem that leads to the deadlock state and find a proper solution. Stappers presents his approach from a general point of view, describing the components that are required to realize such a visualization and their architecture. For our work we draw inspiration from his motivation on how system development can benefit from formal specifications and their visualization, and from his overview of how various technological fields connect and interact with each other in order to implement these benefits.

While most of domain-specific visualizations are implemented in an ad-hoc way (for example, a traffic light system presented in [8] is visualized in a prototype simulator developed in Java specifically for this case study); recent developments facilitate the creation of visualizations using dedicated graphical editors integrated with a formalism toolset. For instance, in BMotion Studio [5] (integrated with the ProB animator[1]) one can create an interactive domain-specific visualization for a (single) B or Event-B specification. BMotion Studio has been successfully applied to a number of case studies (see for example [4,6]). In our work we lift this successful tool support to the level of DSLs, automating the creation of BMotion Studio visualizations for multiple (or for a family of) Event-B specifications.

To date, there is a lack of tool support for understanding and debugging an executable DSL on the level of its domain rather than on the level of its target execution platform (such as generated C or Java code). In [3] Chis et al. recognize this problem and propose the Moldable Debugger framework for developing domain-specific debuggers. The Moldable Debugger allows for configuring a domain-specific debugging view as a collection of graphical widgets, such as stack, code editor, and object inspector. In order to visualize the execution of a DSL program in such widgets, a DSL developer needs to specify so-called debugging predicates (capturing an execution state) and debugging operations (controlling the execution of a program). To realize this approach, the Moldable Debugger builds on top of and extends an existing IDE (integrated development environment). In our work we build on top of formal methods, making use of the DSL formal specification. Moreover, we discuss how to design the visualization of a DSL program (*i.e.* domain-specific graphical widgets) based on an explicit definition of the DSL dynamic semantics.

In [2] Bandener et al. visualize behavior of a graphical language in the form of the animated concrete syntax using the Dynamic Meta Modeling (DMM) technique. In DMM, a so-called runtime metamodel enhances the language metamodel with concepts that express an execution state. The language behavior (its dynamic semantics) is specified as a set of graph transformation rules for deriving instances of the runtime metamodel. When applied to a program (*i.e.* instance of the language metamodel), these rules iteratively generate a state space representing the behavior of the given program. Each of these states is

---

[1] http://www3.hhu.de/stups/prob/.

an instance of the runtime metamodel. Bandener et al. enhance the language concrete syntax with the graphical representation of the runtime metamodel. As a result, a graphical representation (*i.e.* a diagram) can be generated for each state of the state space. Their front-end tool allows for choosing a path in such a visualized state space. In our work we also strive for the effect of the animated concrete syntax of the DSL.

3   Visualization of DSL Specifications

In our previous work [13], we employed the Event-B formalism for specifying the dynamic semantics of an industrial DSL. The main motivation for choosing Event-B rather than a formalism designed for specifying dynamic semantics of programming languages (such as Action Semantics or Structural Operational Semantics), was that the Rodin platform offers various supporting tools for Event-B: editors, generator of proof obligations, automatic provers, animators, etc. To be able to apply these tools to a DSL specification, we use Event-B as a back-end formalism for defining the DSL dynamic semantics and develop model-to-model transformations from the DSL to Event-B.

In this work, we apply one of the Rodin tools to Event-B specifications of the DSL. Namely, we employ BMotion Studio for visualizing animation (*i.e.* execution of specifications) of various DSL programs. In this way we help DSL engineers to understand how their programs are executed, *i.e.* we realize specification-based domain-specific debugging. For this, we automate the construction of domain specific visualizations of Event-B specifications using model-to-model transformations from the DSL to BMotion Studio. In what follows, we give an overview of our case study and of our approach to specify the dynamic semantics of the DSL in Event-B (Sect. 3.1), and discuss how we design and implement a visualization of DSL specifications (Sects. 3.2 and 3.3).

3.1   Specification of the LACE DSL

LACE (Logical Action Component Environment) is a mature industrial DSL, developed by and used within ASML[2], a world leading company that produces wafer steppers. LACE is used for (automatic) generation of software that controls ASML lithography machines and orchestrates their numerous subsystems by invoking drivers in a synchronized and effective way. LACE has a graphical notation based on UML activity diagrams. An example of a LACE program is depicted in Fig. 1(a). Here, each column represents a subsystem driver, the rectangles in the columns represent actions of these subsystems, and arrows represent the control (thick arrows) and data (thin arrows) flow. A LACE diagram is translated into C-code, which is executed on a target machine (wafer stepper). Such a translation bridges the wide semantic gap between high-level concepts of the DSL and low-level concepts of the execution platform. Moreover, it includes

---

[2] www.asml.com.

rather complicated design solutions and algorithms. We elicited these design solutions and algorithms by specifying them using the Event-B formalism [1]. The resulting formal specification reveals the complexity of the DSL translation and, thus, facilitates its management.

In Event-B a system is specified as a set of *variables*, that define the state space, and a set of *events*, that define transitions between the states. While in general such a formalism allows for specifying a system on any level of abstraction (from requirements to an implementation), in practice, applying Event-B to the DSL semantics results in a big specification, which is hard to understand, maintain, and verify. There exist a number of techniques that tackle this problem by building on top of Event-B and allowing for (de)composition of an Event-B specification into/of separate Event-B specifications. We apply shared event (de)composition [9] to modularize the specification of LACE.

In the MDE context a DSL resides in two abstraction levels: the DSL meta-model and DSL models (programs). The DSL is designed and implemented on the metamodel level, and it is used via instantiating DSL programs on the model level. While a generic specification of the DSL on the metamodel level can be created and analyzed once, Event-B specifications of many DSL programs need to be constructed for and simulated by DSL users (engineers, who program in LACE). We cannot expect DSL users to create Event-B specifications of their DSL programs and to use Event-B tools themselves. Therefore, we generate such Event-B specifications automatically by instantiating the LACE specification for each concrete LACE program.

Thus, on the meta-model level, we define LACE as a set of separate Event-B *meta-specifications* of different aspects of the semantics. For example, the buffered execution on a subsystem driver is represented and specified as a queue; the mutual dependency of driver operations (such as `AdjustFrame` and `GrabA-Frame` in Fig. 1(a)) is represented and specified as a partial order. On the model level, our DSL-to-Event-B model transformation instantiates and composes such meta-specifications together using an input DSL program as a configuration instruction. For example, for the LACE program depicted in Fig. 1(a) we generate four instances of the queue meta-specification (corresponding to the four subsystems `Laser`, `Sensor`, `Handler`, and `Projector`, as they appear in Fig. 1(a)) and one instance of the partial order meta-specification; and compose these five Event-B specifications together. As a result, an Event-B specification is generated automatically for each concrete DSL program, and the DSL semantics is specified in a clear and modular way.

3.2   Visualization of the LACE DSL

In order to understand how LACE programs are executed, explore the LACE semantics, and even debug the programs, we simulate LACE programs using their Event-B specifications. The simulation of a LACE program is achieved through the execution of the Event-B specification (generated for this program) in an animation tool, for example in the ProB animator. However, DSL engineers

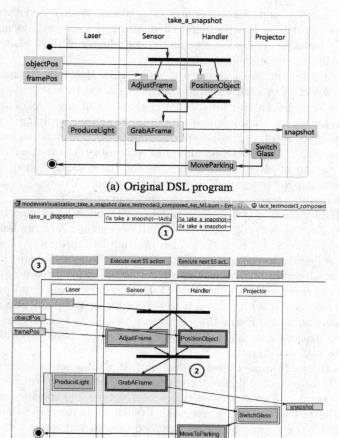

(a) Original DSL program

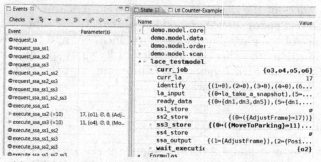

(b) Visualized animation in ProB: (1) subsystem queues, (2) highlighted actions, (3) buttons for executing events

(c) Animation in ProB (running underneath the visualization)

Fig. 1. An example of the LACE DSL program and its visualized animation in ProB (Color figure online)

are hardly familiar with the formal notation of Event-B employed by the animation tools. Moreover, they are hardly familiar with the semantics of the DSL as it is specified in Event-B, and thus, cannot connect Event-B specifications generated from their programs with their original programs.

For example, Fig. 1(c) shows a fragment of the screen shot of how the Event-B specification, which is generated from the LACE program depicted in Fig. 1(a), is executed in the ProB animator. This Event-B specification is composed of the four instances of the same meta-specification representing a subsystem driver (for Laser, Sensor, Handler, and Projector) and of one instance of the partial order meta-specification. The events of these instantiated specifications and, moreover, their combinations can be seen on the left side of Fig. 1(c) (tab "Events"). The variables of the instantiated specifications and their values can be seen on the right side of Fig. 1(c) (tab "State"). It is hard to trace these events and variables back to the original LACE program without knowing the meta-specifications and how they are instantiated and composed.

Consequently, while such a simulation might be useful for a designer who creates Event-B specifications of the DSL; one cannot expect engineers, who program using the DSL notation, to be able to use such a simulation. Therefore, we create a domain-specific visualization for Event-B specifications of LACE. For this we employ BMotion Studio, that provides a graphical editor for creating such visualizations and uses Event-B notation for specifying various details, such as predicate and value expressions.[3] As BMotion Studio is integrated into ProB, a visualization runs together with (or on top of) the ProB animator.

A visualization provides a graphical user interface (GUI) for animating an Event-B specification. For creating such a GUI, BMotion Studio offers a palette of various graphical elements (shapes, connectors, text fields, buttons, etc.) and two concepts responsible for the animation: *controls* and *observers*. Controls are used to execute events of the specification. Observers are used to visualize the current state (*i.e.* current values of the variables). Below we discuss how such a GUI can be designed for a DSL.

The main goal of our DSL visualization is to help a DSL user to grasp how a DSL program is executed. For this, we start from what a user already knows: the DSL concrete syntax. We add to it what a user aims to discover: the DSL dynamic semantics. In other words, we base our visualization on the graphical syntax of LACE; and we project the concepts of the LACE dynamic semantics on it. In general, such concepts represent an execution state and operations that can change this execution state. However, it is not obvious how such concepts can be visualized on top of the graphical syntax of LACE.

For textual programming languages, such as C or Java, an established way to visualize an execution state on the top of the program text is to highlight the code line that is being executed. Moreover, additional views, such as call stack, memory, variables, etc. allow for inspecting other aspects of the execution state. The execution of a program is done step by step using various play-buttons.

---

[3] In this work we use the first version of BMotion Studio. Currently the new version, BMotionWeb, is available.

This way of visualizing a program execution directly links to the concepts that are usually used in descriptions of the dynamic semantics of such languages: execution of a program line-by-line, function calls, memory management.

An example of a graphical language is considered in [2]. In this work the execution of a UML activity diagram is visualized by projecting its dynamic semantics on the diagram. As the dynamic semantics of UML activity diagrams is described using the concept of token (adopted from Petri nets), the visualization consists of tokens (filled black circles) moving between activity nodes.

The dynamic semantics of LACE is defined as a set of meta-specifications (as described in Sect. 3.1).[4] Therefore, we visualize concepts defined in these meta-specifications and project them on the LACE concrete syntax. This allows for breaking down the visualization design and striving towards a modular solution, by focusing on the visualization of meta-specifications rather than on the visualization of the dynamic semantics as a whole. Below we demonstrate this approach on the examples of two meta-specifications (briefly introduced in Sect. 3.1): queue and partial order.

The queue meta-specification represents (models) the buffered execution of subsystem actions on a subsystem driver. An action is enqueued as a result of executing the LACE program, and dequeued when this action is actually executed by the subsystem. We visualize a queue for each subsystem participating in a LACE program as a column showing all elements of the queue (see (1) in Fig. 1(b)). We position the queues above the corresponding subsystems and let them 'grow' downwards: a new element is added to the bottom of the column, and all elements are shifted up when an old element is removed. In the screen shot in Fig. 1(b), the queues of Laser and Projector are empty, the queue of Sensor has one element, and the queue of Handler has two elements.

The partial order meta-specification represents (models) a mutual dependency between subsystem actions (imposed by the control or data flow of a LACE program). Such a dependency influences the throughput of a program and in the combination with the slow execution on a subsystem can cause a bottleneck. Therefore, we visualize the partial order in the interaction with the subsystem queues (where dequeuing can model such a slow execution). For this visualization we use color highlighting ((2) in Fig. 1(b)): red rectangles highlight subsystem actions that are blocked from the execution, and green rectangles highlight subsystem actions that are being executed (*i.e.* are situated at the front/top of the corresponding queues).

To be able to execute the underlying Event-B specification of a LACE program we use buttons integrated into its visualization ((3) in Fig. 1(b)). Such buttons get enabled and disabled based on the current state of the execution, letting a DSL user "discover" the DSL semantics. Each button is attached to

---

[4] Note, that although the graphical notation of LACE is based on UML activity diagrams, the dynamic semantics of LACE does not follow the semantics of UML activity diagrams.

a graphical element of the LACE program in such a way that the user can intuitively associate the enabled or disabled behavior with the corresponding concept of the LACE semantics. For example, each subsystem in Fig. 1(b) has two corresponding buttons attached to its graphical representation (column): "Request SS action" (for enqueuing an action) and "Execute next SS action" (for dequeuing an action).

3.3 Generating LACE Visualizations

The resulting visualization mimics an (arbitrary) LACE program, and thus, needs to be constructed for each concrete LACE program. To make such a visualization design feasible, we automate construction of LACE visualizations using a model-to-model transformation from LACE to BMotion Studio. The transformation derives graphical elements and their layout from a DSL program and generates the corresponding observers (buttons) and controls (shapes, labels, and their attributes) of a visualization. Moreover, the LACE-to-BMS transformation connects elements of the visualization with elements of the underlying Event-B specification.

A BMotion Studio visualization runs on top of an Event-B specification. This means that controls and observers of the visualization query variables and events of the underlying Event-B specification. As the visualization design is determined (shaped) by the concrete syntax rather than by the dynamic semantics of the DSL, querying data from the Event-B specification includes rather non-trivial predicate and value expressions.

For example, to realize highlighting of subsystem actions in green and red (as depicted in Fig. 1(b)), we need to specify two observers for each subsystem action of a LACE diagram. Figure 2 shows the BMotion Studio wizard configuring such observers: an observer sets the background color to red or green when the corresponding predicate is true. The predicates check the mutual dependency between subsystem actions and the execution state of the corresponding subsystem queue. Obviously, writing such predicates manually for all subsystem actions of the LACE program is quite tedious.

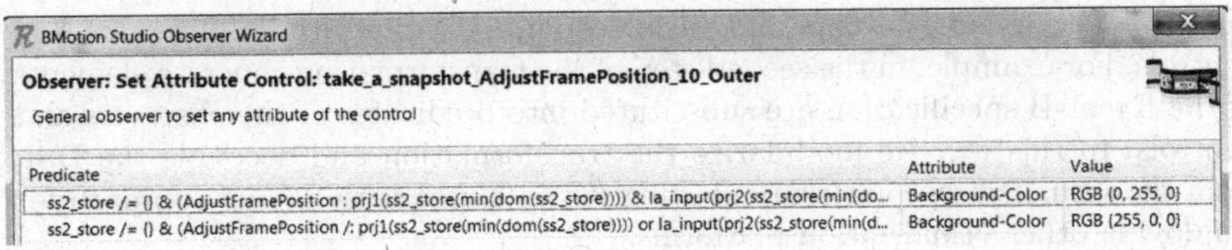

R BMotion Studio Observer Wizard			X
Observer: Set Attribute Control: take_a_snapshot_AdjustFramePosition_10_Outer			
General observer to set any attribute of the control			
Predicate		Attribute	Value
ss2_store /= {} & (AdjustFramePosition : prj1(ss2_store(min(dom(ss2_store)))) & la_input(prj2(ss2_store(min(do...		Background-Color	RGB {0, 255, 0}
ss2_store /= {} & (AdjustFramePosition /: prj1(ss2_store(min(dom(ss2_store)))) or la_input(prj2(ss2_store(min(d...		Background-Color	RGB {255, 0, 0}

Fig. 2. Screen shot of the BMotion Studio wizard for configuring an observer

Buttons (controls) do not map one-to-one on the events either. As described above, to make semantics of buttons intuitively clear to DSL users, we attach them to the graphical elements of a LACE diagram. For example, in Fig. 1(b) there are eight buttons attached to the four subsystem columns, and thus, representing behavior of the subsystems. However, due to another aspect of the LACE semantics, which we do not discuss here, such a behavior of a subsystem can be executed in multiple events and in the combination with the same behavior of another subsystem.[5] This means, that a subsystem button should be able to trigger different events depending on the current execution state, and moreover, some of these events should be triggered by a combination of multiple subsystem buttons. In other words, we need to realize a many-to-many relation between buttons and events.

The LACE-to-BMS transformation overcomes these technical challenges by specifying the mapping between the concrete syntax (shaping the visualization) and the dynamic semantics (driving the visualization) on the level of the LACE metamodel. Thus, all predicate and value expressions and many-to-many relations between elements of the visualization and elements of the Event-B specification are generated automatically for each concrete LACE program.

The scheme of the LACE-to-BMS transformation is depicted in Fig. 3. Within the LACE development environment, a graphical LACE program is parsed into the corresponding LACE *essential model* (*i.e.* abstract syntax tree, AST). This model is used as an input for the LACE-to-Event-B transformation described in Sect. 3.1 (the right part of Fig. 3). Besides a LACE model, the LACE-to-Event-B transformation takes as an input a set of LACE meta-specifications. As an output, this transformation generates an Event-B specification of the LACE program (bottom right corner of Fig. 3) and the corresponding mapping information. The latter is in fact the log of a transformation execution and captures the links between the elements of the resulting Event-B specification and of the original LACE model. The mapping information is necessary for connecting LACE visualizations with the underlying Event-B specifications.

A LACE visualization is generated from the original graphical LACE program (the left part of Fig. 3), as the essential model abstracts from (thus, leaves out) the notation details of the LACE diagram. The LACE-to-BMS transformation uses an intermediate visualization model, which splits the transformation into two separate steps. The first step captures graphical design of the visualization: graphical elements and their layout. The second step takes care of the mapping between Event-B events and variables and BMotion Studio observers and controls. For example, in the second step of the transformation concrete elements of the Event-B specification are substituted into predicates of the observers and controls. In this way we modularize the transformation and decouple the DSL from the visualization platform, allowing for potential reuse of our approach for employing other visualization platforms.

---

[5] One can observe that in Fig. 1(c) "request_ssa_ss1" appears four times in different combinations with other subsystems ("ss2" and "ss3").

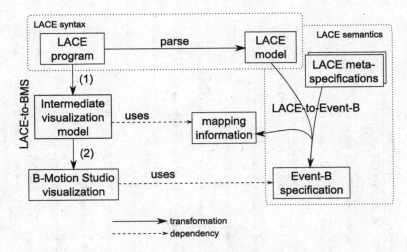

Fig. 3. Transformations from LACE to Event-B and BMotion Studio

4   Discovering Opportunities: User Study

To validate the visualization design and to discover use cases for its application, we performed a user study among LACE end-users (ASML engineers who develop software using LACE). The user study consisted of interviews (with an engineer) and of brainstorming sessions (with few engineers at once). During such an interview or a brainstorming session, we would demonstrate our LACE visualization by animating five existing LACE programs and then collect the feedback using the questionnaire form and personal communication. Ten ASML engineers participated in the user study,[6] with different expertise in LACE and from various application and/or system subdomains.

During the user study we were aiming to achieve the following goals:

– to validate our rationale for designing a DSL visualization;
– to assess how well the level of details is balanced;
– to discover opportunities for applying the visualization in the development process.

Using the GQM (Goal, Question, Metric) method [11], we refine these goals to a more operational level as a set of questions which we need to answer in order to conclude on the results of the user study. Such questions allow for interpreting the data collected during the study. In Table 1 these study questions are shown in the second column next to the goals that they refine. The questions that were asked to the LACE end-users correspond to the Metric category of the GQM method. We show (examples of) these end-user questions in the third column

---

[6] Note that as LACE is a programming language specialized to a specific domain, the community of LACE users is not big. We estimate that the response rate for our user study was 50%.

Table 1. The structure and the results of the user study

Goals	Questions (subgoals)	Metrics (questions asked to the end-users)	Outcome/feedback
Validate the visualization design	Design is intuitive and understandable	Do you understand the visualization of the LACE model?	Yes (3.3 out of 4)
	Observers represent the execution state	Is the visualization intuitive to find the desired information?	Yes (2.9 out of 4)
	Semantics of controls (buttons) is clear	Is the visualization intuitive to execute the desired actions?	Yes (2.9 out of 4)
	Choice of the semantics concepts	What part of LACE should be visualized?	two more concepts were proposed
Assess the level of the details	Overview of an animated diagram	Are you happy with the level of details?	Rather no than yes (1.8 out of 4)
	Insights provided by the visualization	Is highlighting of blocked and queued actions helpful?	Yes (3 out of 4)
		Do queues help to see which actions need to be executed?	Yes (3 out of 4)
	Insights missing in the visualization	Would you find a log of all processed SS actions helpful?	Rather yes than no (2.6 out of 4)
		Would you find the visualization of the data values helpful?	Indifferent (2.1 out of 4)
Discover opportunities for applying the visualization	There is a lack of support for understanding the LACE semantics	Did you have problems learning LACE?	Four people – yes
		Do you still have problems understanding some LACE models?	Mostly not, one person – yes
	The visualization can close this gap	Would this visualization help understanding those models?	Yes (2.9 out of 4)
		How much time would this kind of visualization save you?	15-20%
	What are potential use case scenarios?	How would you apply the visualization in practice?	Prototyping and validation, impact analysis, replay of execution logs and predefined sequences

of Table 1. The corresponding feedback of the users is presented in the rightmost column. Most of the questions in our questionnaire form were closed questions with a grade in the interval [0..4] to indicate the certainty and/or relevance of an answer. In Table 1 we indicate the mean value of the answers, given by the respondents to the corresponding question.

Based on the results of the user study presented in Table 1 and on other feedback of the LACE users, we draw the following conclusions.

- The visualization design is in general acceptable, but can be improved using the feedback provided by the LACE users.
- The approach would benefit from the possibility to configure the level of details of the LACE visualization. For example, a LACE user might want to specify such a configuration for the LACE-to-BMS transformation and in this way adjust the level of details of the generated visualization.
- The LACE users believe that they can use the visualization for understanding and testing behavior of their LACE programs; for replaying real-life system executions; and for checking changes after LACE gets updated (impact analysis).

Moreover, according to the LACE end-users, a crucial requirement of the proposed approach is that the DSL formal specification should be consistent with the actual implementation of the DSL. Without this consistency DSL end-users cannot benefit from the visualized animation of DSL specifications. In Sect. 5 we propose two ideas, that, among other things, allow for realizing this requirement.

5 Future Work: Applying and Reusing LACE Visualizations

Following the positive and constructive feedback of the user study, in this section we elaborate on the potential possibilities for (1) generalizing our approach and making it reusable for other DSLs and for (2) applying our visualization to implement domain-specific debugging. In Sect. 5.1 we propose an idea of reusable specification and visualization templates. In Sect. 5.2 we describe the trace framework that allows for bridging technologically diverse platforms (such as the animation of an Event-B specification and the execution on an ASML machine) through execution traces.

5.1 Specification and Visualization Templates

As described in Sect. 3.1, the dynamic semantics of LACE is defined as a set of meta-specifications and as a model transformation that instantiates and composes these meta-specifications for each concrete LACE program. Note that the examples of such meta-specifications, a queue and a partial order, are not LACE-specific and can be used for defining other DSLs. However, the LACE-to-Event-B model transformation is LACE-specific. To be able to reuse our toolset for defining the dynamic semantics of other DSLs, we need to extract the LACE-specific information from the LACE-to-Event-B model transformation. The extracted LACE-specific information can be lifted until we find a suitable abstraction for configuring a generic DSL-to-Event-B transformation. The resulting abstraction will allow for defining the dynamic semantics of a DSL using existing meta-specifications, identified as reusable and stored in a library. In analogy with generic programming, we call such reusable meta-specifications *specification templates*. Defining the dynamic semantics of a DSL as a composition of such specification templates can facilitate construction of the DSL specification, which is coherent with the actual implementation of the DSL.

In the same way, the BMotion Studio visualizations of the meta-specifications that have been identified as specification templates, can be extracted, parameterized, and collected as their *visualization templates*. To be able to instantiate and compose these visualization templates, we need to find a suitable abstraction for configuring a generic DSL-to-BMS transformation.

An overview of the proposed generic framework is depicted in Fig. 4. This architecture generalizes the transformation scheme depicted in Fig. 3. Here the DSL visualization replaces the intermediate visualization model and specifies how visualization templates can be positioned on the top of the DSL concrete syntax in order to represent the DSL semantics definition. The feasibility of such a framework and its applicability to various DSLs require further research.

5.2   Trace Framework

In order to offer DSL developers the means to quickly implement customizable DSL tooling for inspecting *execution traces* of DSL programs, we propose a *trace framework*. The trace framework uses two kinds of execution traces: *action traces* – sequences of actions executed during the execution of a DSL program, – and *state traces* – sequences of DSL program execution states. The framework defines

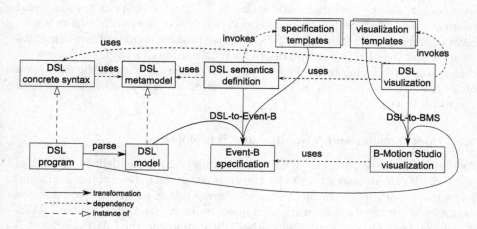

Fig. 4. A generic approach for reusing Event-B specifications and BMotion Studio visualizations

trace operations to (1) capture traces from execution logs (usually through parsing of the execution logs) and to synthesize or edit traces; (2) to visualize, replay and inspect traces; and (3) to compare traces. In order to implement DSL specific tooling, trace operations can be customized and composed into *trace applications*. To validate this approach, we implemented a number of such trace applications. Two examples are briefly described below.

The visualization of LACE programs as described in Sect. 3.2 offers users the possibility to manually play an execution scenario for a specific LACE program. As the user study showed, one of the requested applications of the visualization was the possibility to automatically replay LACE programs as they were executed on a machine. Using our trace framework, we created a trace application that reads an execution log of an actual LACE program and replays this log in ProB using the Event-B specification of this LACE program. For this, the trace application captures action traces from the LACE execution logs by parsing and reordering the data contained in the log files; and then uses these action traces to drive the ProB animator for the Event-B specification of the corresponding LACE program.

Another trace application that was created using our trace framework allows for comparing execution traces. This trace application can be used for several purposes. (1) To find a specific, for instance erroneous, behavior during the execution of a DSL program by comparing an execution trace with a trace containing the expected behavior. (2) Performing impact evaluation on two versions of the same DSL program by comparing an execution trace from a DSL program with an execution trace from a changed version of this program. (3) Finding bottlenecks in the execution of a DSL program by comparing different executions of a single DSL program. (4) To ensure that the Event-B specification of a DSL program is coherent with the generated C code by comparing execution traces obtained from ProB and from a machine.

6   Conclusion

In this work, we provide the domain-specific visualization of DSL formal specifications to support understanding and debugging of DSL programs via animation of their specifications. In general, a design of such a visualization is not obvious and is based on a fine balance between representing the underlying semantics specification in detail and being clear and intuitively understandable to DSL users. Our visualization animates the DSL diagrams by projecting on them the high-level semantics concepts, such as a subsystem buffer and an execution dependency of subsystem actions, – in contrast with the low-level semantics concepts commonly used in debugging, such as call stack, variables, and line-by-line execution. The resulting visualization does not map one-to-one on the underlying Event-B specification, which causes technical challenges in its implementation. We overcome these challenges by developing a model transformation that automatically generates a visualization (file) for each concrete DSL program.

Our user study confirms that a DSL-based development can benefit from having a formal specification of the DSL with an appropriate domain specialization of supporting tools. Following the feedback provided by the DSL users, we demonstrate that debugging of an actual DSL program (*i.e.* generated C code running on the ASML machine) is possible by replaying the execution log in ProB. As a future work, we describe our vision on how our approach can be generalized and reused for other DSLs using libraries of specification templates and the corresponding visualization templates.

Acknowledgements. We would like to thank Lukas Ladenberger (Heinrich-Heine University, Düsseldorf, Germany) for his help with using BMotion Studio. We are very grateful to all ASML engineers who participated in our user study. We also would like to thank Tom Verhoeff and Tim Willemse (both from Eindhoven University of Technology, The Netherlands) for their advice and feedback on this work and this paper.

References

1. Abrial, J.R.: Modeling in Event-B: System and Software Engineering. Cambridge University Press, New York (2010)
2. Bandener, N., Soltenborn, C., Engels, G.: Extending DMM behavior specifications for visual execution and debugging. In: Malloy, B., Staab, S., Brand, M. (eds.) SLE 2010. LNCS, vol. 6563, pp. 357–376. Springer, Heidelberg (2011). doi:10.1007/978-3-642-19440-5_24
3. Chiş, A., Gîrba, T., Nierstrasz, O.: The moldable debugger: a framework for developing domain-specific debuggers. In: Combemale, B., Pearce, D.J., Barais, O., Vinju, J.J. (eds.) SLE 2014. LNCS, vol. 8706, pp. 102–121. Springer, Heidelberg (2014). doi:10.1007/978-3-319-11245-9_6
4. Hansen, D., Ladenberger, L., Wiegard, H., Bendisposto, J., Leuschel, M.: Validation of the ABZ landing gear system using ProB. In: Boniol, F., Wiels, V., Ait Ameur, Y., Schewe, K.-D. (eds.) ABZ 2014. CCIS, vol. 433, pp. 66–79. Springer, Heidelberg (2014). doi:10.1007/978-3-319-07512-9_5
5. Ladenberger, L., Bendisposto, J., Leuschel, M.: Visualising Event-B models with B-motion studio. In: Alpuente, M., Cook, B., Joubert, C. (eds.) FMICS 2009. LNCS, vol. 5825, pp. 202–204. Springer, Heidelberg (2009). doi:10.1007/978-3-642-04570-7_17
6. Ladenberger, L., Dobrikov, I., Leuschel, M.: An approach for creating domain specific visualisations of CSP models. In: Canal, C., Idani, A. (eds.) SEFM 2014. LNCS, vol. 8938, pp. 20–35. Springer, Heidelberg (2015). doi:10.1007/978-3-319-15201-1_2
7. Mathijssen, A., Pretorius, A.J.: Verified design of an automated parking garage. In: Brim, L., Haverkort, B., Leucker, M., Pol, J. (eds.) FMICS 2006. LNCS, vol. 4346, pp. 165–180. Springer, Heidelberg (2007). doi:10.1007/978-3-540-70952-7_11
8. Mauw, S., Wiersma, W.T., Willemse, T.A.C.: Language-driven system design. Int. J. Softw. Eng. Knowl. Eng. **14**(6), 625–663 (2004)
9. Silva, R., Butler, M.: Shared event composition/decomposition in Event-B. In: Aichernig, B.K., Boer, F.S., Bonsangue, M.M. (eds.) FMCO 2010. LNCS, vol. 6957, pp. 122–141. Springer, Heidelberg (2011). doi:10.1007/978-3-642-25271-6_7

10. Snook, C., Butler, M.: UML-B: formal modeling and design aided by UML. ACM Trans. Softw. Eng. Methodol. **15**(1), 92–122 (2006)

11. Solingen, R.V., Berghout, E.: Goal/Question/Metric Method: A Practical Guide for Quality Improvement of Software Development. McGraw-Hill, Cambridge (1999)

12. Stappers, F.P.M.: Bridging formal models: an engineering perspective. Ph.d. dissertation. Chapter 6: Disseminating Verification Results, pp. 109–125. Eindhoven University of Technology (2012)

13. Tikhonova, U., Manders, M., van den Brand, M., Andova, S., Verhoeff, T.: Applying model transformation and Event-B for specifying an industrial DSL. In: MoDeVVa@MoDELS, pp. 41–50 (2013)

14. Watt, D.A., Muffy, T.: Programming Language Syntax and Semantics. Prentice Hall International Series in Computer Science. Prentice-Hall, Englewood Cliffs (1991)

Spatio-Temporal Models for Formal Analysis and Property-Based Testing

Nasser Alzahrani[✉], Maria Spichkova, and Jan Olaf Blech

RMIT University, Melbourne, Australia
s3297335@student.rmit.edu.au,
{maria.spichkova,janolaf.blech}@rmit.edu.au

Abstract. This paper presents our ongoing work on spatio-temporal models for formal analysis and property-based testing. Our proposed framework aims at reducing the impedence mismatch between formal methods and practicioners. We introduce a set of formal methods and explain their interplay and benefits in terms of usability.

1 Introduction

Specifying safety-critical systems, it is not enough to use controlled languages and semiformal languages – the precise and easy-to-read formal specification is essential to ensure that the safety properties of the system really hold. Moreover, the software development process should include aspects of human factors engineering, to improve the quality of software and to deal with human factors in a systematic way, cf. [26]. Human factor aspects usually cover the design of human-computer interface of the software, human-related aspects of the development process, as well as the corresponding automatisation. By the Engineering Error Paradigm [20], humans are seen as a "component of the system" (almost equivalent to software and hardware components in the sense of operation with data and other components), which is the most unreliable in the system.

Software errors can cause wasting of resources [6,19]. An estimate of one trillion US dollars was spent on IT hardware, software and services by governments around the world. Software errors can also be fatal, and in many cases they might be prevented by having a more human-oriented development process and methods. As per statistics presented by Dhillon [8], humans are responsible for 30% to 60% the total errors which directly or indirectly lead to the accidents, and in the case of aviation and traffic accidents, 80% to 90% of the errors were due to humans. Thus, it is necessary to have human factors engineering as a part of the software development process. One of the widely cited accidents in safety-critical systems are the accidents involved massive radiation overdoses by the Therac-25 (a radiation therapy machine used in curing cancer) that lead to deaths and serious injuries of patients which received thousand times the normal dose of radiation [16,17]. The causes of these accidents were software failures as well as problems with the system interface. The error was improbable to reproduce because it required very specific sequence of commands in order to occur.

© Springer International Publishing AG 2016
P. Milazzo et al. (Eds.): STAF 2016, LNCS 9946, pp. 196–206, 2016.
DOI: 10.1007/978-3-319-50230-4_14

The improbability of the sequence makes the error unlikely to be noticed with manual testing because it is almost impossible to think of all combinations of commands and edge cases. Automatisation might solve this problem, but the challenge is to create an automatisation which is not only efficient but also easy-to-use, i.e., is human-oriented.

One of the challenges in software engineering is to develop correct software. The software should meet user requirements, its properties should satisfy the model corresponding to design objective and the implementation should pass all functional tests. Rigorous reasoning is the only way to avoid subtle errors in algorithms, and it should be as simple as possible by making the underlying formalism simple tools [14]. Formal methods (FMs) refer to a class of mathematical techniques used in development of large scale complex systems. These techniques can result in high-quality systems that can be implemented on-time, within budgets and satisfy user requirements [4].

The value of FMs in real systems has far reaching consequences. For instance, FMs help engineers get the code right by getting the design right in the first place. Secondly, FMs help engineers gain a better understanding of the design. Despite all advantages, formal methods are not widely used in large-scale industrial software projects for many reasons [28]. One of the core obstacles is the lack of readability and usability. The syntax of FMs is often too complicated and unreadable for novices, which makes an impression that all the FMs require huge amount of training. There also is a prejudice that the return of investment is very minimal and only justified in critical systems such as medical devices, what is generally not true [18].

Spatio-temporal aspects of safety-critical systems are crucial to verify and to test a system, as in most cases the system properties should be analysed in relation to the time and to the location. To analyse spatio-temporal phenomena, we have to specify the corresponding spatial, temporal and event semantics formally and in a human-oriented way. The goal of our work is to increase usability of the analysis (in the sense of verification and testing) of the spatio-temporal aspects on the base of the corresponding formal models.

Property based testing allows us to generate huge numbers of system operations (e.g. API calls or external events) and permute these operations in ways that is difficult for humans to think of. These combinations are then used to verify the system under test according to the spatio-temporal specification.

Contributions: The proposed framework will help to reduce the impedance mismatch between formal methods and model-based representations and system code, which in turn will help in increasing the adoption rate by practitioners. Our framework aims at providing a set of application programming interfaces (APIs) to map programming language constructs to the formal methods representation. The usability of formal methods will be improved indirectly, as the formal method constructs will be expressed in terms of system code.

2   Background

2.1   Formal Methods

Formal methods were introduced as a means of clearly specifying system requirements. Hinchey [10] argues that although formal methods are essential in the development of critical systems, they have not achieved the level of acceptance, nor level of use, that many believe they should. The uptake of formal methods has been far from ideal because many still believe that formal methods are difficult to use and require great mathematical expertise [10]. Spichkova reports [23] that in many cases simple changes of a specification method can make it more understandable and usable. She argues that such a simple kind of optimisation is often overlooked just because of its obviousness, and it would be wrong to ignore the possibility to optimise the language without much effort. For example, simply adding an enumeration to the formulas in a large formal specification makes its validation on the level of specification and discussion with cooperating experts much easier.

Hinchey [10] also assert that in addition to the benefits of abstraction, clarification, and disambiguation, using formal methods at the formal specification level are invaluable documentation that greatly assist future system maintenance. This research incorporates specifications used in property-based testing to further help in precisely documenting the system. Lamport [14] states two reasons for using formal methods formulas instead of programming language tailored to the specific problem:

- Specialized languages often have limited realms of applicability. A language that permits a simple specification for one system require a very complicated one for a different kind of system. The Duration Calculus seems to work well for real-time properties; but it cannot express simple liveness properties. A formalism like TLA+ that, with no built-in primitives for real-time systems or procedures, can easily specify gas burner for example, it is not likely to have difficulty with a different kind of gas burner.
- Formalisms are easy to invent. However, practical methods must have a precise language and robust tools.

There are many examples where applying formal methods has lead to increasing reliability of systems. For example, a model checker TLC was developed for TLA formula was used to find errors in the cache coherence protocol for a Compaq multiprocessor [27]. In addition, [4] includes many examples of successfully using formal methods to design systems.

2.2   Property-Based Testing

There are many styles in testing software. One popular style is that of *example based testing*. In this style, test cases requires one to provide an example scenario for each feature. That is, each example may exercise one feature of the system under test and the test runs only once with relevant input. Dually, *property based testing* allows for the use of randomly generated tests based on system properties to test systems against their specifications and one test can run hundreds of times with different input values. An example of such library in Haskell programming language is *QuickCheck*. Hughes (inventor of *QuickCheck*) showed that using this library allowed him to discover hundreds of bugs in critical systems such as automobiles and the DropBox file sharing service [7]. However, *QuickCheck* uses Haskell programming language specific constructs (such as arrays, integers) and more complicated data types (such as algebraic data types) to model the specification of a system. Therefore, this research will investigate the possibility to have formal models (BeSpaceD, TLA+ or FOCUS^{ST} formulas) as specifications instead of Haskell constructs, as well as applicability of this approach for property based testing of real systems.

Hughes [12] asserts that Dijkstra was wrong when he claimed that testing can never demonstrate the absence of bugs in software, only their presence. Hughes argues that if we test properties that completely specify a function (such as the properties of reversing a list) then property based testing will eventually find every possible bug. In practice this is not true, since we usually do not have a complete specification, but this style of testing is very effective in exploring scenarios that no human can think of trying.

QuickCheck started as a testing framework for testing pure functional programs [7]. However, recent development in the area of property-based testing [9,13] incorporates the state-fulness of systems. That allowed for the testing of state-ful systems and even test programs written in imperative languages such as C. Hughes assert that testing state-ful systems is challenging. He argues that the state is an implicit argument to and result from every API call, yet it is not directly accessible to the test code. Therefore, his solution was to model the state abstractly and introduce state transition function that model the operations in API under test.

However, the state transition in *QuickCheck* is modelled manually using *pre*, *post* and *next* functions for every operation in the system under test. On the other hand, our framework will generate these transitions automatically using specification formulas.

3   Proposed Framework

Figure 1 depicts the proposed model that will allow for combining formal methods with property-based-testing. The first row (API calls) represents the actual system under test. The second row represents the world in which the specification formulas lives. The time between subsequent API calls is modelled through a function of discreet time. Time functions are mapped to the corresponding state transitions between states. The general idea is to start with specifying the system using human-oriented modelling techniques founded on formal methods. Then, to develop system software according to the specifications. Finally, to run the test suite to verify that the system runs according to the specification. If a test fails, it will be the judgment of the engineer to decide whether the errors

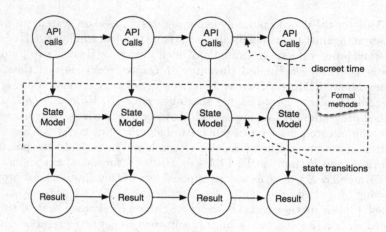

Fig. 1. Proposed framework

were in the system software or in the specification formulas for which the system was not correctly specified.

The implementation language of choice is Scala programming language. It was selected for many reasons. First of all, it is one of the most popular languages on the Java virtual machine. The ecosystem will make it possible to find quick answers for questions that are related to technical aspects. Secondly, BeSpaceD is implemented in Scala. This will lower the impedance mismatch between research model and BeSpaceD. Finally, Scala, is a functional language. This will make working with the concepts of property based testing more natural and simple.

For the property-based testing, we are going to apply the *ScalaCheck library*. However, since the research will investigate the substitution of the simplistic state machine in ScalaCheck with formal methods, the use of this library might be limited.

To relate the different modeling and abstraction layers to each other in the proposed framework, we are using category theory. Category theory helps in illuminating the relations of many aspects of the proposed ingredients that would be unseen otherwise. Figure 1 relates the human actions (API call), system states (state model) and results to each other. Our formal methods-based techniques will only be applied to the State-model level. This will help to stair the direction of future investigation of the proposed model.

4   Initial Set of Modeling Languages and Tools

To create the initial set of formal methods-based modeling languages and tools, we have selected the following ingredients, which have a number of similarities in syntax and semantics and are also covering spatio-temporal aspects of the specifications:

- TLA+: Temporal logic of actions (TLA) is a logic developed by Leslie Lamport, which combines temporal logic with a logic of actions. It is used to describe behaviours of concurrent systems, cf. [15].
- FOCUSST: Formal language providing concise but easily understandable specifications that is focused on timing and spatial aspects of the system behaviour, cf. [24,25].
- BeSpaceD: A framework for modelling and checking behaviour of spatially distributed component systems, cf. [2,3].

The FOCUSST language was inspired by Focus [5], a framework for formal specification and development of interactive systems. In both languages, specifications are based on the notion of streams. However, in the original Focus input and output streams of a component are mappings of natural numbers to single messages, whereas a FOCUSST stream is a mapping from natural numbers to lists of messages within the corresponding time intervals. Moreover, the syntax of FOCUSST is particularly devoted to specify spatial (S) and timing (T) aspects in a comprehensible fashion, which is the reason to extend the name of the language by ST. The FOCUSST specification layout also differs from the original one: it is based on human factor analysis within formal methods [21, 22].

Design goals of BeSpaceD include:

- Ability to model spatial behaviour in a component oriented, simple and intuitive way
- Automatically analyse and verify systems and integration possibilities with other modelling and verification tools.

Blech and Schmidt proposed a process for checking properties of models and described the approach using different examples [3]. In our current work, we only focus on the spatio-temporal aspects of BeSpaceD.

From a programming language perspective, we create BeSpaceD models by using Scala case classes. During the specification process, this gives a functional abstract datatype feeling with a domain specific language flavour. A typical BeSpaceD formula is shown below

```
IMPLIES(AND(TimeInterval(300,605),Owner("AreaOfInterest")),
    OccupyBox(1051,3056,1505,3603))
```

The language constructs comprise basic logical operators (such as AND and IMPLIES). Furthermore special constructs for space, time, and topology are incorporated. In the example, OccupyBox represents a rectangular two-dimensional space while constructs such as TimeInterval allow for the modeling of temporal aspects possible. A variety of different operators exist which facilitates the reasoning about geometric and topological constraints. Furthermore, connections to data sources from cyber-physical systems exists (e.g., lego-trains [11] and event analysis for industrial automation facilities [1]) which facilitates the construction of demonstrators and conduction of experiments.

In our work we are using FOCUSST and TLA+ for modelling the behaviour of systems, whereas the BeSpaceD functionality is invoked at a lower level to check and test properties of the specified systems.

To understand the workflow of the proposed model, we use the example of Therac25 mentioned in the introduction. The machine included VT-100 terminal which controlled the PDP-11 computer. The sequence of user actions leading to the accidents was as follows:

- user selects 25 MeV photon mode
- user enters "cursor up"
- user select 25 MeV Electron mode
- previous commands have to take place in eight seconds

Therefore, we use algebraic data types to model the operations of the machine. Then we provide formal specification formulas and feed them to the framework.

```
sealed abstract class Operation
case object CursorUp extends Operation
case object Select25MevPhotonMode extends Operation
case object Select25MevElectronMode extends Operation
case object OtherKindOfOperation extends Operation

type Therac25 = Sut

val init: TLAInit =  {.. some predicate ...}
val next: TLANext = {.. another predicate ...}

val correctBehaviours: List[TLAState] =
   Therac25.correctBehaviours(init, next)
Therac25.checkAgainst(correctBehaviours, randoms(Operation))
```

The framework would generate large number of *Operation* combinations that are more likely to catch the error that caused the fatal accidents. Frequencies of generated commands can be tailored to match real system behaviour. The example used TLA+ formulas. However, FOCUS^{ST} formulas could have been used instead to specify the system.

To achieve that, we have partially implemented the code that is responsible to generate random BespaceD constructs using techniques from functional programming. The Invariant generator is composed of smaller generators such as integer and string generators as shown in the code below:

```
trait Generator[+T] {
  self =>

  def generate: T

  def map[U](f: T => S): Generator[U] = new Generator[U] {
   def generate = f(self.generate)
  }
}
```

```scala
val integers = new Generator[Int] {
   def generate = scala.util.Random.nextInt()
}

val booleans = integers.map(_ >= 0)

val strings = integers.map(_.toString)

def bSpaceD: Generator[Invariant] = for {
    int1  <- integers
    int2  <- integers
    int3  <- integers
    int4  <- integers
    int5  <- integers
    str   <- strings
} yield IMPLIES(AND(TimeInterval(int1, int2),Owner(str)),
    OccupyBox(int3, int4, int5, int6))
```

5   Evaluation

The evaluation is based on a case study that involves robotics that are installed in the Virtual Experiences Lab(VXLab) at RMIT University, Australia.

Fig. 2. Interacting with robots from the VXLab at RMIT

The implemented model will be installed in the robotic arms or simulations of them. For instance, assuming the existence of the function *initialisePosition()*: *Future[Position]* which is responsible to move a robotic arm to an initial position. The *Future* data type is used because moving arms takes long time and we need to verify the final position the arm reached after the API call. However, since *initialisePosition()* is just returning the initial position, it will return instantly. The framework will call this API function and simultaneously check whether it is in accordance to the specified state. Failing tests for the intended framework might indicate:

– Failure in the software of the system under test. This is one of the benefits of property based testing. The found error may have never been discovered otherwise.
– Wrong specification. The system under test may have been wrongly underspecified. In this case, the engineer might change the formulas to reflect system required properties.

Therefore, the input to the framework is formal-methods formulas and the output is the correct behaviours specified by these formulas. The formulas are written in host programming language (Scala in this research). For example, the initial state for the aforementioned robotic example would be specified as follows:

```
val position: TLAVariable = TLAVariable("Y")
val init: TLAInit =  position
```

For this simple example (the *next* formula has been omitted for simplicity), the only possible correct behaviour for this specification formula is that *position* should equal to "Y". The framework will then check whether the position was indeed "Y" after the call to *initialisePosition()*, otherwise, it reports an error.

Table 1. Evaluating cases with TLA+ init formulas

API code	Init formula	Result	Error?
initialisePosition()	TLAVariable("Y")	"Y"	No
initialisePosition()	TLAVariable("Y")	"K"	Yes
moveToQ()	TLAVariable("Q")	"Q"	Yes
moveToR()	TLAVariable("Q")	"M"	Yes

Table 1 shows some examples for the evaluation of the intended framework using TLA+ formula (Focus^{ST} evaluation will follow similar pattern). The first call to *initialisePosition()* is correctly specified and the actual result reflects the specification (assuming arm initial position is "Y"), as a result, it is regarded as a successful case. The second call to *initialisePosition()* is different from the actual position, therefore, its was reported as an error. Although the result is expected for the call to *moveToQ()* in the third case, the framework reports an error because the specification is not correct (the arm can not logically move to its current position). Finally, *moveToR* is reported as error because the actual result (reached position) is not correct. The result column is calculated by getting the value from the *Future* dataype that each API call returns through *onComplete* callback as follows:

```
initialisePosition() onComplete {
  case Success(position) => println(position)
  case Failure(t) => println("An error has occured:" + t.getMessage)
}
```

6   Conclusions

In this paper, we have presented ongoing work on the use of spatio-temporal models for formal methods-based analysis and testing. We have described different ingredients and their interplay: testing frameworks, TLA+, Focus^{ST} and BeSpaceD. The overall goal of our research is the reduction of the impedance mismatch between formal methods and practitioners.

References

1. Blech, J., Peake, I., Schmidt, H., Kande, M., Rahman, A., Ramaswamy, S., Sudarsan, S., Narayanan, V.: Efficient incident handling in industrial automation through collaborative engineering. In: IEEE 20th Conference on Emerging Technologies Factory Automation (ETFA). IEEE Computer (2015)
2. Blech, J.O.: An example for BeSpaceD and its use for decision support in industrial automation (2015)
3. Blech, J.O., Schmidt, H.: BeSpaceD: towards a tool framework and methodology for the specification and verification of spatial behavior of distributed software component systems (2014)
4. Bowen, J.P., Hinchey, M.G.: Seven more myths of formal methods. IEEE Softw. **12**(4), 34 (1995)
5. Broy, M., Stølen, K.: Specification and Development of Interactive Systems: Focus on Streams, Interfaces, and Refinement. Springer, New York (2001)
6. Charette, R.N.: Why software fails [software failure]. IEEE Spectr. **42**(9), 42–49 (2005)
7. Claessen, K., Hughes, J.: QuickCheck: a lightweight tool for random testing of haskell programs. ACM SIGPLAN Not. **35**(9), 268–279 (2000). doi:10.1145/357766.351266
8. Dhillon, B.: Engineering Usability: Fundamentals, Applications, Human Factors, and Human Error. American Scientific Publishers, Stevenson Ranch (2004)
9. Gerdes, A., Hughes, J., Smallbone, N., Wang, M.: Linking unit tests and properties. In: Proceedings of the 14th ACM SIGPLAN Workshop on Erlang, pp. 19–26. ACM (2015)
10. Hinchey, M.G.: Confessions of a formal methodist. In: Proceedings of the Seventh Australian Workshop Conference on Safety Critical Systems and Software, SCS 2002, vol. 15, pp. 17–20, Australian Computer Society Inc. (2002)
11. Hordvik, S., Øseth, K., Blech, J.O., Herrmann, P.: A methodology for model-based development and safety analysis of transport systems. In 11th International Conference on Evaluation of Novel Approaches to Software Engineering (ENASE) (2016)
12. Hu, Z., Hughes, J., Wang, M.: How functional programming mattered. National Sci. Rev. **2**(3), 349–370 (2015)
13. Hughes, J.: Software testing with quickcheck. In: Horváth, Z., Plasmeijer, R., Zsók, V. (eds.) CEFP 2009. LNCS, vol. 6299, pp. 183–223. Springer, Heidelberg (2010). doi:10.1007/978-3-642-17685-2_6
14. Lamport, L.: Hybrid systems in TLA$^+$. In: Grossman, R.L., Nerode, A., Ravn, A.P., Rischel, H. (eds.) HS 1991-1992. LNCS, vol. 736, pp. 77–102. Springer, Heidelberg (1993). doi:10.1007/3-540-57318-6_25

15. Lamport, L.: The temporal logic of actions. ACM Trans. Prog. Lang. Syst. **16**(3), 872–923 (1994)
16. Leveson, N.G., Turner, C.S.: An investigation of the therac-25 accidents. Computer **26**(7), 18–41 (1993)
17. Miller, E.: The therac-25 experience. In: Conference on State Radiation Control Program Directors (1987)
18. Newcombe, C., Rath, T., Zhang, F., Munteanu, B., Brooker, M., Deardeuff, M.: How amazon web services uses formal methods. Commun. ACM **58**(4), 66–73 (2015)
19. Patra, S.: Worst-case software safety level for braking distance algorithm of a train. In: 2007 2nd Institution of Engineering and Technology International Conference on System Safety, pp. 206–210. IET (2007)
20. Redmill, F., Rajan, J.: Human Factors in Safety-Critical Systems. Butterworth-Heinemann, Oxford (1997)
21. Spichkova, M.: Human factors of formal methods. In: IADIS Interfaces and Human Computer Interaction, IHCI 2012 (2012)
22. Spichkova, M.: Design of Formal Languages, Interfaces: Formal Does not Mean Unreadable. IGI Global, Hershey (2013)
23. Spichkova, M.: Uman factors of formal methods. arXiv preprint arXiv:1404.7247 (2014)
24. Spichkova, M., Blech, J.O., Herrmann, P., Schmidt, H.W.: Modeling spatial aspects of safety-critical systems with focus-st. In: MoDeVVa@ MoDELS, pp. 49–58, Citeseer (2014)
25. Spichkova M. et al.,: Specification and seamless verification of embedded real-timesystems: FOCUS on Isabelle. Ph.D. thesis, Technical University Munich (2007)
26. Spichkova, M., Liu, H., Laali, M., Schmidt, H.W.: Human factors in software reliability engineering. In: Workshop on Applications of Human Error Research to Improve Software Engineering (WAHESE 2015) (2015)
27. Yu, Y., Manolios, P., Lamport, L.: Model checking TLA$^+$ specifications. In: Pierre, L., Kropf, T. (eds.) CHARME 1999. LNCS, vol. 1703, pp. 54–66. Springer, Heidelberg (1999). doi:10.1007/3-540-48153-2_6
28. Zamansky, A., Rodriguez-Navas, G., Adams, M., Spichkova, M.: Formal methods in collaborative projects. In: 11th International Conference on Evaluation of Novel Approaches to Software Engineering. IEEE (2016)

Towards a Developer-Oriented Process for Verifying Behavioral Properties in UML and OCL Models

Khanh-Hoang Doan[✉], Martin Gogolla, and Frank Hilken

Computer Science Department, University of Bremen, 28359 Bremen, Germany
{doankh,gogolla,fhilken}@informatik.uni-bremen.de

Abstract. Validation and verification of models in the software development design phase have a great potential for general quality improvement within software engineering. A system modeled with UML and OCL can be checked thoroughly before performing further development steps. Verifying not only static but also dynamic aspects of the model will reduce the cost of software development. In this paper, we introduce an approach for automatic behavioral property verification. An initial UML and OCL model will be enriched by frame conditions and then transformed into a (so-called) filmstrip model in which behavioral characteristics can be checked. The final step is to verify a property, which can be added to the filmstrip model in form of an OCL invariant. In order to make the process developer-friendly, UML diagrams can be employed for various purposes, in particular for formulating the verification task and the verification result.

Keywords: Validation and verification · Model testing · UML and OCL model · Behavior property verification

1 Introduction

In software development, Model-Driven Engineering (MDE) is playing now a more and more important role. In recent years, the model-based approach has been becoming accepted, in particular by combining the UML (Unified Modeling Language) [15], the OCL (Object Constraint Language) [3] and some efficient tools. Available techniques in tools can be employed for the verification and validation of both static and dynamic properties of a software system.

As model validation and verification have been studied for a long time, a variety of approaches have been introduced. Typical approaches following this line have been discussed, e.g., the Dresden OCL tool [5], a toolset based on Abstract State Machines [17], and the tool USE for UML and OCL model property validation [7,9,19]. In [4] an approach for model consistency checking is introduced, and several correctness properties are automatically checked in [2]. UML model properties such as consistency, independence and consequence are

© Springer International Publishing AG 2016
P. Milazzo et al. (Eds.): STAF 2016, LNCS 9946, pp. 207–220, 2016.
DOI: 10.1007/978-3-319-50230-4_15

validated in [9]. [13, 16] present approaches for OCL constraint validation. However, many of these proposals concentrate on static aspects of the model, e.g., on consistency, independence, and consequences of and between OCL invariants. In order to also validate dynamic aspects, the approach in [8] introduces a transformation from UML and OCL models into so-called filmstrip models that represent sequences of system snapshots in a single object diagram. This filmstripping approach allows to check dynamic properties and will be applied as a central step within the complete verification process as described here.

In technical terms, the context of our work is the tool USE (UML-based Specification Environment) [7]. USE supports the description of a model in terms of a UML class diagram (with e.g. classes, associations) and UML state machines enriched by OCL constraints including class and state invariants as well as pre- and postconditions for operations and transitions. USE can visually represent class, object, sequence, statechart, and communication diagrams of a UML model and animate the model behavior based on command sequences. Offering a precise subset of UML and OCL can support the developer in employing a visual and thus user-oriented language for formulating development artifacts, in particular models and model properties. One central USE component is the so-called model validator that supports the validation and verification of properties based on the Kodkod relational logic [18]. A further USE component that we will employ is the so-called filmstrip transformation. It transforms an application model (with invariants and pre- and postconditions) into an equivalent so-called filmstrip model (with invariants only). This filmstrip model will be checked and tested with the model validator.

The remainder of the paper is organized as follows. Section 2 illustrates the general idea of our approach for a process consisting of several steps, and a simple example is introduced. Details of each verification step are introduced from Sects. 3 to 6. Particularly, Sect. 3 explains frame conditions and how to formulate and add them to the original model. Section 4 describes filmstrip models and how to transform models with frame conditions into filmstrip models. The step for verifying a behavior property is presented in Sect. 5, and in Sect. 6 we introduce the final step, transforming the verification result back into a sequence diagram of the original model. In Sect. 7 we discuss run-times of the verification tasks given in this paper before ending this contribution with some concluding remarks.

2   General Idea and Running Example

2.1   General Idea

Our approach for behavioral property verification can be divided into four steps as illustrated in Fig. 1. The input is a UML model enriched by OCL constraints and the output is a sequence diagram corresponding to a found scenario. The general idea for the verification process can be described as follows:

Step 1: Starting from an application model that describes structure and behavior of a system, add frame conditions. An application model is a UML model

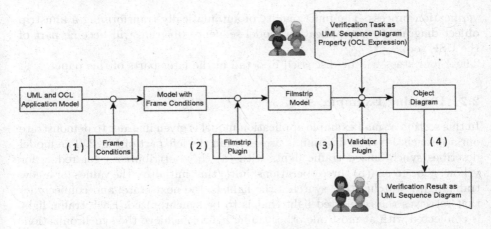

Fig. 1. General idea for the proposed verification process

describing system structure and behavior completely in terms of OCL and consisting of any number of classes, attributes, associations, and operations. The class diagram is enriched by class invariants and operation pre- and postconditions in form of OCL constraints. A frame condition makes the frame of an operation explicit. Particularly, it is a postcondition of an operation to assure that everything that is not in the scope of the operation (the frame) remains unchanged after the operation has been executed. Frame conditions will help the model validator in Step 3 to construct a scenario in a correct way.

Step 2: Transform the frame-conditioned model into a filmstrip model. In a filmstrip model, a single object diagram will describe a sequence of system states and operation calls between them. Roughly speaking, we can use an object diagram of a filmstrip model to describe interactions between objects in sequential order and the state transitions between the objects. Consequently, in the next step, a dynamic property, which is related to state transitions, can be verified in the context of the filmstrip model. The transformation step into the filmstrip model is performed automatically using the filmstrip plugin of USE.

Step 3: Verify a behavioral property of the filmstrip model. A behavioral property can be presented as an application model sequence diagram and can be analyzed by automatically constructing a scenario (an object diagram of the filmstrip model), in which a specified property is satisfied, or by showing that a valid scenario cannot be constructed within a finite search space. This step is performed automatically using the validator plugin of USE employing a configuration file describing the finite search space.

Step 4: Transform the generated object diagram from Step 3 (if the behavior property was satisfied) into a corresponding sequence diagram in the context of the application model. Presenting the verification result as a sequence diagram of the application model will increase readability and understandability of the verification process. The functionality of automatically transforming a filmstrip object diagram to an application model sequence diagram will become part of the USE tool.

These four steps will be discussed in detail in the later parts of this paper.

2.2   Running Example

In this section a small example application model is given in order to demonstrate our approach. Its class diagram is presented in the left part of Fig. 2. The model describes synchronized traffic lights with (a) three attributes: r for red, y for yellow, g for green; (b) three operations: init() that initializes the values for a new traffic light, switch() that switches the light to the next state; and connected() that retrieves the connected light that is to be synchronized. Each traffic light is connected with at most one other traffic light to achieve the synchronization. The full model declaration including all invariants and pre- and postconditions is presented in [6]. The listing below shows the OCL invariants and postconditions of the switch() operation:

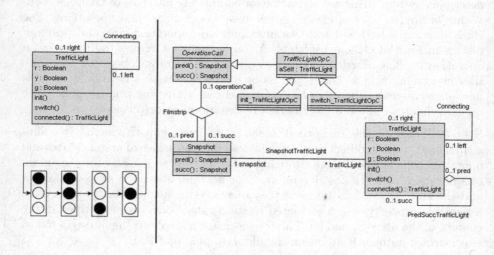

Fig. 2. Class diagram of example application model and switching phases.

```
context TrafficLight
inv Ryg_RYg_ryG_rYg:
    (r=null and y=null and g=null) or
    (r and not y and not g) or (r and y and not g) or
    (not r and not y and g) or (not r and y and not g)
inv oneLight_onePair:
    (left→size()=1 and right→isEmpty()) or (left→isEmpty() and
    right→size()=1)
```

```
inv synchronize:
    (r<>null and y<>null) and
    (r and not y implies not connected().r and not connected().y) and
    (r and y implies not connected().r and connected().y) and
    (not r and not y implies connected().r and not connected().y) and
    (not r and y implies connected().r and connected().y)
context TrafficLight::switch()
post Ryg_2_RYg_2_ryG_2_rYg_2_Ryg:
    (r<>null and y<>null) and
    (r@pre and not y@pre implies r and y) and
    (r@pre and y@pre implies not r and not y) and
    (not r@pre and not y@pre implies not r and y) and
    (not r@pre and y@pre implies r and not y)
```

The first invariant Ryg_RYg_ryG_rYg identifies the states (values of attributes r, y and g) of a traffic light. In particular, a traffic light can only be in one of four states: red (r, not y, not g), red-yellow (r, y, not g), green (not r, not y, g), and yellow (not r, y, not g). The invariant synchronize determines how a pair of traffic lights synchronizes. When the left traffic light changes its state, the right light automatically changes its state respectively, e.g., a traffic light changes from the green state to yellow state when the connected light changes from red to red-yellow. As can be seen, the postcondition Ryg_2_RYg_2_ryG_2_rYg_2_Ryg only defines the changes of the attributes r and y, but does not include the attribute g for specifying the effect after the switch() operation has been executed. In a postcondition, the tag @pre refers to the state given at precondition time. On the other hand, we can see that the relationship between the r, y, and g attributes is fully fixed by the invariant Ryg_RYg_ryG_rYg. Consequently, the value of attribute g is fully determined by the value of r and y. The change of attribute g would be ambiguous if one would consider only the switch() postconditions. The question that comes up now is: what happens to attribute g? How will it be changed by the switch() operation? These questions will be answered by using the verification technique introduced in Sect. 5.

3   Adding Frame Conditions to Application Models

Postconditions typically specify in a declarative way effects of an operation, by expressing what they change. They often implicitly assume that everything else (the frame) remains unchanged. For a verification engine the question comes up how they can infer from postconditions which model elements are *not* allowed to change during an operation execution. This problem is called "*frame problem*" [1] and can be addressed by adding so-called frame conditions in form of OCL expressions. They indicate attributes and association ends that should not be changed after an operation has been executed. To add a frame condition to a model, we formulate it as an OCL expression in form of a postcondition. Various approaches for determining and formulating frame conditions have been introduced [11,12]. In this paper we apply the solution discussed in [14] to specify which properties are not allowed to change during the execution of the operations init() and switch(). Here we only explain how to formulate the frame condition for operation switch(). As can be seen from the postcondition Ryg_2_RYg_2_ryG_2_rYg_2_Ryg presented in Fig. 2, the properties r and y at post-state (i.e., not marked with @pre) are referenced in this postcondition. Consequently, properties r and y are *variable* to the switch() operation, which means that these properties are allowed to change when switch() is executed. Property g is not referenced in any postcondition, however it is referenced in the invariant Ryg_RYg_ryG_rYg with the connection to the variable properties r and y. Therefore, property g is also classified as variable. On the other hand, the state of the other traffic light objects, except the connected one, should not be changed. As the result, the frame conditions of the switch() operation is formulated as follows:

```
context TrafficLight::switch()
post trafficLightUnchangedExcept: let x=self in
  TrafficLight.allInstances@pre=TrafficLight.allInstances and
  TrafficLight.allInstances→forAll(t|
    (t.left@pre = t.left) and (t.right@pre = t.right) and
    (t<>x and t<>x.connected() implies t.r@pre=t.r) and
    (t<>x and t<>x.connected() implies t.y@pre=t.y) and
    (t<>x and t<>x.connected() implies t.g@pre=t.g))
```

In summary, this postcondition says: the switch() operation called on the traffic light object 'self' is only allowed to change the attributes r, y and g of self and its connected traffic light; everything else remains unchanged.

4   Transformation to Filmstrip Model

The application model enriched by frame conditions will be transformed into a so-called filmstrip model. A filmstrip model can describe dynamic aspects of an original application model, i.e., operations and state transitions, by static elements, i.e., UML classes and OCL invariants [10]. Particularly, each operation of classes from the application model is transformed into an OperationCall class, and a Snapshot object is created in the filmstrip model to represent the application model state at a point of time. With a filmstrip model we can describe information on the changes between the application model states and operation calls in one object diagram. It offers many possibilities for validation and verification of dynamic aspects, e.g., behavioral properties. Some elements of the application model are left unchanged, while others are converted with modification compared to the application model [8]. More detail about fimstrip model is introduced in [10]. The right part of Fig. 2 shows the class diagram of the filmstrip model after transforming the frame-conditioned model.

Most importantly, pre- and postconditions from the application model are transformed into invariants of the filmstrip model and realize behavioral properties, which are related to state transitions. These invariants can be checked in a single filmstrip model object diagram. One example of a transformed postcondition is presented as follows:

```
context switch_TrafficLightOpC
inv post_Ryg_2_RYg_2_ryG_2_rYg_2_Ryg:
  (aSelf.succ.r<>null and aSelf.succ.y<>null) and
  ((aSelf.r and not aSelf.y) implies
      (aSelf.succ.r and aSelf.succ.y)) and
  ((aSelf.r and aSelf.y) implies
      (not aSelf.succ.r and not aSelf.succ.y)) and
  ((not aSelf.r and not aSelf.y) implies
      (not aSelf.succ.r and aSelf.succ.y)) and
  ((not aSelf.r and aSelf.y) implies
      (aSelf.succ.r and not aSelf.succ.y))
```

The postcondition Ryg_2_RYg_2_ryG_2_rYg_2_Ryg of the operation switch() is renamed and altered to the invariant post_Ryg_2_RYg_2_ryG_2_rYg_2_Ryg of the new class switch_TrafficLightOpC in the filmstrip model. aSelf is an attribute of the TraffictLightOpC class, from which switch_TrafficLightOpC inherits. This attribute refers to the traffic light object on which the switch() operation is called. And aSelf.succ is the successor of the aSelf object after the switch() operation has been executed (i.e., the self object in the next snapshot).

Some new filmstrip invariants are generated by the filmstrip component. These invariants prevent faulty executions that would have been possible and thus bring the filmstripping model in line with execution of the operations in UML and OCL. In other words, they ensure correct behavior of the filmstrip model, e.g., by forbidding the snapshot object sequence to become a cycle (invariant cycleFree). More details of the complete filmstrip model description can be seen in [6].

5 Verifying Behavioral Properties

A behavioral property is a property related to a behavioral aspect of a design model, typically in connection with the model operations. In other words, checking a behavioral property is a type of verification task, that tries to prove whether a specific property can be reached or not reached under specific conditions, for example, with an operation call sequence. In our approach, first of all, an OCL expression for a behavioral property is added to the filmstrip model. This can be realized by the USE command constraints -load constraintFile, in which constraintFile is name of the file that contains the added OCL expression. Next, we execute the model validator from the USE GUI or on the CLI through the command mv -validate propertyFile. The propertyFile specifies the bounds for the search space of the model validator. For example, in the properties file the number of OperationCall objects, the number of Snapshot objects, or the number of links are stated. The model validator tries to construct a valid system state (object diagram) within the specified bounds. If successful, a system state will be established, that means the property is proved. And if not, the model validator reports that an object diagram cannot be found. This means that the logically negated property has been proved within the given bounds. Specifying proper bound numbers in the propertyFile for the model validator

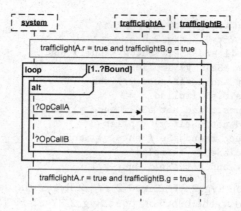

Fig. 3. Verification task for Example 1 as sequence diagram

is important. Bounds must be big enough so that the property can be proved, but not too big so that the model validator can find answers within a small time frame.

Example 1. In this example, the behavior property to be proved is: "Is it possible to construct a scenario (starting in a valid state and having transitions to future states only by operation calls) in which a pair of synchronized traffic light exists that shows initially red and green and after a number of operation calls red and green again?". This property can be expressed with a UML sequence diagram as in Fig. 3. The property can be made precise also with the following OCL expression:

```
context TrafficLight inv rg_And_rg_Again:
   TrafficLight.allInstances→exists(t|t.r and t.connected().g and
     Set{t.succ}→closure(succ)→exists(t1|t1.r and t1.connected().g))
```

After loading this invariant to the filmstrip model by running the command `constraints -load`, we execute the model validator with parameters specified in a property file. Figure 4 presents the found object diagram [6]. The configuration specifies that the generated object diagram has exactly 10 `TrafficLight` objects, 5 `Snapshot` objects and 4 `switch_TrafficLightOpC` objects. As can be seen from the generated object diagram, a pair of synchronized traffic lights, trafficlight1 and trafficlight10 (upper dashed oval), shows red-green and the later incarnation, i.e., trafficlight3 and trafficlight8 (lower dashed oval), shows red-green again. From this we can confirm the claim, that the property can be satisfied for the running example. The protocol in Fig. 5 shows the detailed commands and the result. The run-times for verifying the property are specified within the outputs as well.

There are three run-times that the model validator shows in the result message. The 1st 'Translation time' (1200 ms) is the time needed to translate the

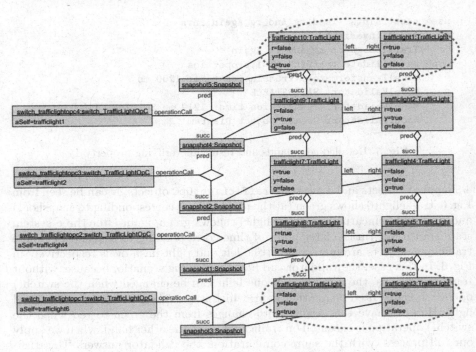

Fig. 4. Generated object diagram for Example 1

class diagram into the relational logic of Kodkod. This translation is only performed one time when executing the model validator the first time in a working session. The validator needs 1212 ms (2nd 'Translation time') to translate the relational formula and the configuration into SAT (this step is performed by Kodkod), and 180 ms (validator 'Solving time') to solve the translated relational formula by the underlying SAT solver. The total time for all verification tasks in this example with the specified bounds parameters is 5941 ms.

Example 2. The behavior property to be checked in the second example is: "Is it possible to construct a scenario in which one traffic light exists so that between two green states we have less than four transitions?". The following listing is the OCL expression for this property:

```
context TrafficLight inv lessthan_4transitions_between_2G:
  TrafficLight.allInstances→ exists (t | t.g and not t.succ.g and
    Set{t.succ}→closure(succ)→exists(t1|t1.g and
      Set{t}→closure(succ)→size() - Set{t1}→closure(succ)→size()<4))
```

To emphasize the important role of frame conditions for a verification task, first we apply our process without Step 2 that adds the frame conditions to the original application model. As the result, the validator finds a satisfying scenario as shown in Fig. 6. The configuration requires exactly 16 TrafficLight objects,

```
use> constraints -load rg_And_rg_Again.invs
     Added invariants:
     TrafficLight:: rg_And_rg_Again
use> mv -validate trafficLight1.properties
     ModelTransformator: Translation time: 1200 ms
     ModelValidator: SATISFIABLE
     ModelValidator: Translation time: 1212 ms Solving time: 180 ms
     ModelValidator: Create object Diagram
```

Fig. 5. Detailed commands and result for verifying property 1

4 Snapshot objects and 3 switch_TrafficLightOpC objects. It can be seen from Fig. 6, trafficlight6 shows green (at the point of time corresponding to snapshot1) and its latest reincarnation, trafficlight7, shows green again after three system state transitions (in the later point of time corresponding to snapshot2). These trafficlight objects are marked with the left and right dash ovals respectively in Fig. 6. In this case, the validator can find a satisfying scenario, because, without frame conditions, the attributes of one light can be changed when the switch() operation is executed on another light, which is not connected to the considered light. Here we have that trafficlight6 changes from the green to red when the switch() operation is executed on trafficlight5. On the other hand, when we apply our full process, with the same configuration, the validator answers 'Unsatisfiable'. That means that such scenario cannot be constructed within the bounds. Figure 7 shows the detailed commands and the result 'Unsatisfiable'.

This example shows the importance of adding frame condition to the original application model in the entire verification process. Frame conditions support the validator to go not into the wrong direction when finding the answer.

6 Transforming Verification Results to Application Model Sequence Diagrams

The result of the model validator, if the verification property is satisfied, is a scenario in form of a filmstrip model object diagram. The ordinary developer, who must not know all details of the filmstripping approach, may find it difficult to understand and use the result in terms of the application model. Therefore, the transformation of the filmstrip model object diagram to an equivalent application model sequence diagram, which is more readable and practical, is helpful. The test case generated by the validator may be used in the later phases of software development. Figure 8 is the application model sequence diagram corresponding to the generated filmstrip model object diagram for Example 1 in Sect. 5.

To built the sequence diagram from the filmstrip model object diagram, firstly, each application object (i.e., an object from a class of the original model) connected to the first snapshot object is considered as an initial object involved in the interaction (here, trafficlight1, trafficlight10). Each OperationCall object in the filmstrip model object diagram is turned into an operation call from the system actor to one of the corresponding initial objects. The sequence diagram is complete when the last operation call has been handled.

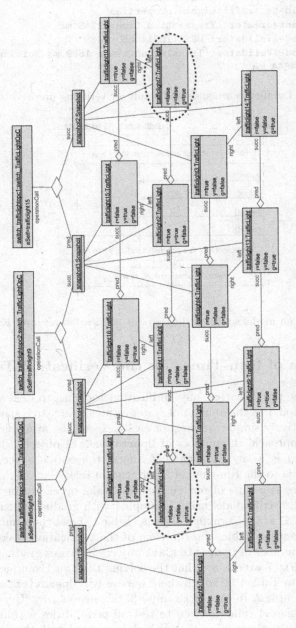

Fig. 6. Generated object diagram for Example 2 without frame conditions

```
use> constraints -load lessthan_4transitions_between_2g.invs
     Added invariants:
     TrafficLight:: lessthan_4transitions_between_2g
use> mv -validate trafficLight2.properties
     ModelTransformator: Translation time: 1248 ms
     KodkodModelValidator: UNSATISFIABLE
     KodkodModelValidator: Translation time: 1689 ms Solving time:
         1964544 ms
```

Fig. 7. Detailed commands and result for verifying property 2

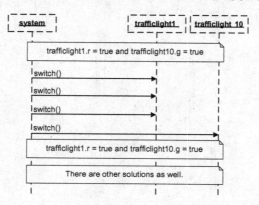

Fig. 8. Application model sequence diagram for verification result of Example 1

7 Evaluation of Run-Times for the Verification Tasks

One of the biggest problem that any verification tool has to deal with is the state-space explosion, i.e., the number of system states (the search space) may be huge even for relatively simple systems, or easily exceed the available computer memory. In our approach, the number of `OperationCall` objects (determining system transitions) is a key element that affects the search space, and that number corresponds to the run-time of a verification task.

We evaluate the run-time of our verification tasks by executing the model validator for the filmstrip model using Example 1 with gradually increasing the number of `switch_TrafficLightOpC` objects. Table 1 shows the resulting times. As can be seen from the table, the run-time of the verification tasks increases rapidly when the number of `OperationCall` objects increases gradually. On the other hand, from Fig. 7 we can see that the solving time for Example 2 is much higher than those in Table 1 although there were only 3 `OperationCall` objects configured for Example 2. In case of Example 2, the answer was "Unsatisfiable", and therefore the model validator had to test all possibilities within the given bounds. Consequently, the solving time is high compared with the solving time for Example 1, for which the answer was "Satisfiable".

The results show that scenarios, i.e., sequence diagrams, with about 20 operation calls can be constructed in less than 10 min.

Table 1. Run-times of verification tasks

Number of operation objects	Translation time [ms]	Solving time [ms]	Total time [m]
4	1 212	180	0.04
8	3 610	2 640	0.12
12	8 402	29 697	0.65
16	20 234	84 963	1.77
20	48 232	462 997	8.54
24	86 946	600 703	11.48

8 Conclusion and Future Work

This contribution has proposed a process for the verification of a behavioral property of a UML model enriched by OCL constraints. The inputs are an application model in form of a USE file and a property that needs to be verified in form of an OCL invariant or in form of a UML sequence diagram; the output is typically a test scenario in form of a sequence diagram. The idea of combining frame conditions, the filmstrip model, and the model validator in a complete process for behavior property verification together with sequence diagrams for verification tasks and verification results has not been discussed before. The last step of our process, the transformation of filmstrip object diagrams to a sequence diagram, will increase the readability and understandability of the verification approach. Most of the steps in our process are automatically performed by the USE tool and its plugins. The process will be adjusted and optimized in later works.

Future work can be done in various directions. First of all, a functionality that allows to automatically transform the generated filmstrip model object diagram to an application model sequence diagram will be worked out. Secondly, the idea for automatically formulating and adding frame conditions to a UML and OCL model should be studied further and supported by tool options. Future work has also to consolidate the approach with larger case studies and has to improve the efficiency of the validator searching process in the presence of filmstrip models.

References

1. Borgida, A., Mylopoulos, J., Reiter, R.: On the frame problem in procedure specifications. IEEE Trans. Softw. Eng. **21**(10), 785–798 (1995)
2. Cabot, J., Clarisó, R., Riera, D.: UMLtoCSP: a tool for the formal verification of UML/OCL models using constraint programming. In: Proceedings of the Twenty-second IEEE/ACM International Conference on Automated Software Engineering, pp. 547–548, ASE 2007, NY, USA. ACM, New York (2007)
3. Cabot, J., Gogolla, Martin: Object constraint language (OCL): a definitive guide. In: Bernardo, M., Cortellessa, V., Pierantonio, A. (eds.) SFM 2012. LNCS, vol. 7320, pp. 58–90. Springer, Heidelberg (2012). doi:10.1007/978-3-642-30982-3_3

4. Dan, C., Mihai, P., Adrian, C., Cristian, B., Sorin, M.: Ensuring UML models consistency using the OCL environment. Electron. Notes Theor. Comput. Sci. **102**, 99–110 (2004). Proceedings of the Workshop, OCL 2.0 - Industry Standard or Scientific Playground?
5. Demuth, B., Wilke, C.: Model and object verification by using Dresden OCL. In: Russian-German WS Innovation Information Technologies: Theory and Practice (2009)
6. Doan, K.H., Gogolla, M., Hilken, F.: Addendum to a complete process for behavioral properties verification. University of Bremen, Technical report (2016). http://www.db.informatik.uni-bremen.de/publications/intern/HOFM2016ADD.pdf
7. Gogolla, M., Büttner, F., Richters, M.: USE: a UML-based specification environment for validating UML and OCL. Sci. Comput. Program. **69**(1–3), 27–34 (2007)
8. Gogolla, M., Hamann, L., Hilken, F., Kuhlmann, M., France, R.: From application models to filmstrip models: an approach to automatic validation of model dynamics. In: Modellierung (MODELLIERUNG 2014) (2014)
9. Gogolla, M., Kuhlmann, M., Hamann, L.: Consistency, independence and consequences in UML and OCL models. In: Dubois, C. (ed.) Tests and Proofs. LNCS, vol. 5668, pp. 90–104. Springer, Heidelberg (2009)
10. Hilken, F., Hamann, L., Gogolla, M.: Transformation of UML and OCL models into filmstrip models. In: Di Ruscio, D., Varró, D. (eds.) Theory and Practice of Model Transformations. LNCS, vol. 8568, pp. 170–185. Springer International Publishing, Heidelberg (2014)
11. Kosiuczenko, P.: Specification of invariability in OCL. Softw. Syst. Model. **12**(2), 415–434 (2011)
12. Krieger, M.P., Knapp, A., Wolff, B.: Automatic and efficient simulation of operation contracts. In: Proceedings of the Ninth International Conference on Generative Programming and Component Engineering, GPCE 2010, pp. 53–62, NY, USA. ACM, New York (2010)
13. Kuhlmann, M., Gogolla, M.: Modeling and validating mondex scenarios described in UML and OCL with USE. Formal Aspects Comput. **20**(1), 79–100 (2007)
14. Niemann, P., Hilken, F., Gogolla, M., Wille, R.: Extracting frame conditions from operation contracts. In: ACM/IEEE 18th International Conference on Model Driven Engineering Languages and Systems (MoDELS 2015) (2015)
15. Object Management Group - OMG: Unified Modeling Language Specification, version 2.5 (2013). http://www.omg.org/spec/UML/
16. Richters, M., Gogolla, M.: Validating UML models and OCL constraints. In: Evans, A., Kent, S., Selic, B. (eds.) UML 2000 The Unified Modeling Language. LNCS, vol. 1939, pp. 265–277. Springer, Heidelberg (2000)
17. Shen, W., Compton, K., Huggins, J.: A toolset for supporting UML static and dynamic model checking. In: 2002 Proceedings of 26th Annual International on Computer Software and Applications Conference, COMPSAC 2002 , pp. 147–152 (2002)
18. Torlak, E., Jackson, D.: Kodkod: a relational model finder. In: Grumberg, O., Huth, M. (eds.) Tools and Algorithms for the Construction and Analysis of Systems. LNCS, vol. 4424, pp. 632–647. Springer, Heidelberg (2007)
19. Ziemann, P., Gogolla, M.: Validating OCL specifications with the USE tool: an example based on the BART case study. Electron. Notes Theor. Comput. Sci. **80**, 157–169 (2003). Eighth International Workshop on Formal Methods for Industrial Critical Systems (FMICS 2003)

Model-Based Generation of Natural Language Specifications

Phan Thu Nhat Vo and Maria Spichkova[✉]

RMIT University, Melbourne, Australia
s3220976@student.rmit.edu.au, maria.spichkova@rmit.edu.au

Abstract. Application of formal models provides many benefits for the software and system development, however, the learning curve of formal languages could be a critical factor for an industrial project. Thus, a natural language specification that reflects all the aspects of the formal model might help to understand the model and be especially useful for the stakeholders who do not know the corresponding formal language. Moreover, an *automated generation* of the documentation from the model would replace manual updates of the documentation for the cases the model is modified. This paper presents an ongoing work on generating natural language specifications from formal models. Our goal is to generate documentation in English from the basic modelling artefacts, such as data types, state machines, and architectural components. To allow further formal analysis of the generated specification, we restrict English to its subset, Attempto Controlled English.

1 Introduction

Model-based development (MBD) is a paradigm in which software and system development focus on high-level executable models, cf. [34]. In the early development phases, formal models allow a wide range of exploration and analysis using domain-specific notations in order to simplify the system design, development or verification/testing. Application of formal models provides many benefits for the software and system development. In "40 years of formal methods" [5], Bjørner and Havelund admit that the gap between academic research on formal methods and its integration in large industrial projects is yet to be bridged. There are a number of hindering factors for adoption of formal methods in industry [33]. As crucial obstacles can be named lack of understandability and readability [29,32], and our aim is to find appropriate ways to avoid these obstacles. Also, human factors play a crucial role and have to be taken into account [28,31].

Application of formal models requires an interplay between formal and informal methods, which use different levels of formality in descriptions. A manual solution to this problem was suggested many years ago: Guiho and Hennebert reported a communication problem in the SACEM project [15] between the verifiers and other engineers, who were not familiar with the formal specification method. The problem was solved by providing the engineers with a natural language description derived *manually* from the formal specification. For a large-scale projects, it would be too time-consuming to derive a natural language

© Springer International Publishing AG 2016
P. Milazzo et al. (Eds.): STAF 2016, LNCS 9946, pp. 221–231, 2016.
DOI: 10.1007/978-3-319-50230-4_16

specification (NLS) manually. In this paper, we propose a framework for *automated generation* of NLS from the basic modelling artefacts, such as data type definitions, State Transition Diagrams (STDs), and architecture specifications.

Contributions: The proposed solution would serve not only increasing the understandability of formal models, but also keeping the system documentation up-to-date. System documentation is an important part of the development process, but it is often considered by industry as a secondary appendage to the main part of the development – modelling and implementation. It is hard to keep the documentation up-to-date if the system model is frequently changing during the modelling phase of the development. Thus, system requirements documents and the general systems description are not updated according to the system's or model's modifications. Sometimes the updates are overlooked, sometimes they are omitted on purpose. For example, it is because of timing or costs constraints on the project. As a result, the system documentation is often outdated and does not describe the latest version of the system model. The question is whether we need to update the documentation *manually*, cf. [32].

Outline: The rest of the paper is organised as follows. Section 2 describes the related work. Section 3 introduces the proposed framework and a small case study to illustrate the ideas of the framework. In Sect. 4 we summarise the paper and propose directions for future research.

2   Related Work

The research field of automated translation from formal modelling languages to natural languages is almost uncovered, however, there are many approaches on automated generation of (semi-)formal specifications from natural language ones. Lee and Bryant [23] presented an approach automatically generate formal specifications in an object-oriented notation from NLS. Cabral and Sampaio [9] suggested to use a Controlled Natural Language (CNL), a subset of English to analyse system characteristics represented by a set of declarative sentences. CNL use restricted vocabulary, grammar rules in defined knowledge based for the aim of formal models generation. This also allows to generate structured models at different levels of abstraction, as well as provides formal refinement of user actions and system responses.

Schwitter et al. [27] introduced ECOLE, an editor for a controlled language called PENG (Process-able English), that defines a mapping between English and First-Order Logic in order to verify requirements consistency, as well as to help writing manuals and system specifications to improve documentation quality, which is our goal of generated specifications in natural language.

As several attempts have been made to automate the requirement capture, there is another approach for the automatic construction of Object-oriented design model in UML diagram from natural language requirement specification. Mala and Uma [24] present a methodology that utilizes the automatic reference resolution and eliminates the user intervention. The input problem statement is split into sentences for tagging by sentence splitter in order to get parts of speech for every word. The nouns and verbs are then identified by tagged texts based on simple phrasal grammars. Reference resolver is used to remove ambiguity by pronouns. The final text is then simplified by the normaliser for mapping the words into object-oriented system elements. The result produced by the system is compared with human output on the basic analysis of the text. The approach is promising to introduce a method to restructure the natural language text into modelling language in respect of system requirements specifications. Although there is a shortage of the efficiency in the tagger and reference resolver that result in unnatural expressions and misunderstandings, it can be improved by building a knowledge base for the system elements generation.

Juristo et al. [20] introduced an approach to formalise the requirement analysis process. The goal of this approach was to generate conceptual models in a precise manner, which provides support for resolving difficulties of misunderstanding the system requirements. The approach is based on examining the information extraction at the beginning of the development process (i.e., describing the problems in natural language sentences), and consists of two different activities: formalisation of the conceptual model and creation of the formal model. The limitation of this approach is in the difficulties to retrieve the rigorous and concise problem descriptions.

Gangopadhyay [14] suggested to design a conceptual model from a functional model, expressed in natural language sentences. Although its application is mainly for database applications, it can be extended to other design problems such as Web engineering and data warehousing. In order to interpret natural language expressions, Gangopadhyay applied the theory of Conceptual Dependencies developed by Schank, cf. [26]. The main goal of this approach was to identify data elements from functional model expressed in NLS, to locate missing information, as well as to integrate all individual data elements into an overall conceptual schema for data model establishment. A prototype system using Oracle database management system has been implemented to contain a parser for information collection. However, the lexicon in use is developed incrementally and semi-automated, so domain specialists still need to manually categorise words and phrases, to ensure non-relevant words are included in the system during the development of the conceptual model and to prevent systematic bias.

Bryant [8] suggested the theory of Two-Level Grammar for natural language requirements specification, in conjunction with Specification Development Environment to allow user interaction to refine model concepts. This approach allows the automation of the process of transition from requirements to design and implementation, as well as producing an understandable document on which software system will base on.

Ilieva and Ormandjieva [19] proposed an approach on transition of natural language software requirements specification into formal presentation. The authors decided their method into three main processing parts: (1) the Linguistic Component as the text sentences to be analysed; (2) the Semantic Network as the formal NL presentation; and (3) modelling as the final phase of formal presentation of the specification. However, the approach of Ilieva and Ormandjieva involves manual human analysis process, to break down problems into smaller parts that are easily understood.

3   Framework

Figure 1 illustrates the general ideas of the suggested framework. To build a prototype for generation of NLS from the basic modelling artefacts, we have selected the AutoFocus3 modelling tool [4,16] as the basis for our models, because this tool (1) embeds the basic modelling artefacts, (2) is open source, as well as (3) has a well defined formal syntax behind all its modelling elements.

AutoFocus3 is developed on system models based on the FOCUS theory [7] that allows to specify system on different levels of abstraction formally and precisely. Source code of AutoFocus3 models are coded in XML, which makes it easy to parse and to analyse. AutoFocus3 has many advantages and is constantly evolving through last 10 years. The tool was applied as a part of tool chain within a number of development methodologies, e.g., for safety-critical systems in general [17,18,30], and for automotive-systems [10,11]. The tool can also be successfully applied for service-oriented modelling [6], which gives us another reason to select AutoFocus3 for the framework we develop.

To allow further formal analysis of the generated specification, we restrict English to its subset, Attempto Controlled English (ACE), cf. [13]. Specifications written in ACE give the impression of being informal, though they are in fact formal and machine executable. ACE provides a set of principles and recommendations for the strategy: to reduce the amount of lexical resources and structural sentences for a specification text to be unambiguously represented, and to fulfil the communication gap between domain specialist and software developer. Basically, the construct of ACE specification is the declarative sentence that is expressive enough to allow both natural usage and computer-processed purpose [12].

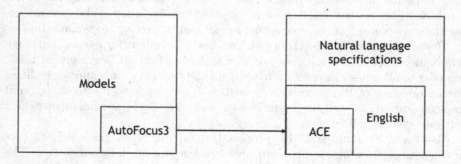

Fig. 1. Framework: generation of natural language specifications from formal models

Implementation: We are currently implementing an automated translator from the AutoFocus3 models to ACE sentences in the Python programming language. Python was chosen as the development language due to its rapid prototyping features, as well as due to its increasing uptake by researchers as a scientific software development language because of good code readability and maintainability. With regard to the Python performance, it is sufficient for many common tasks and turns out to be very close to C language for parsing a file and a tree-like structure, cf. [25]. For the execution environment, we will research on the installation of ACE parsing engine, cf. [21], to execute natural language sentences in Prolog, cf. [3].

XML Code of AutoFocus3 Models. While parsing the XML code of an AutoFocus3 model, we have to identify three core sections:

- Specifications of data types and functions/constants (introduced by the XML-tag *rootElements* with the type *Data Dictionary*, cf. below for an example from the SimpleTrafficLight case study).
- Specifications of the system and components architecture (introduced by the XML-tag *rootElements* with the type *ComponentArchitecture*);
- Specifications of the state machines, used to describe the behaviour of system components (introduced by the XML-tag *containedElements* with the type *StateAutomaton*):

As each of these parts consists of XML representation of the AutoFocus3 elements, we can define a translation schema for each of these elements to generate English sentences out of the XML code. The sentences should be conform to the ACE rules. To validate that this constraint is fulfilled, we have to analyse syntax and semantics of the generated sentences.

Translation Schema. Let us discuss the translation schema in more details, focusing for simplicity on the specifications of data types and functions/constants. The definition of each data type is provided within the XML-tag *typeDefinitions*, where the keyword *Enumeration* indicates that this is an enumeration type. The name of the data type is coded within the attribute *name*. The elements of the type are introduces with the tag *members*. For the case of an enumeration type, we would have the following XML structure, where N is a natural number representing a number of elements in the data type, and $i_1, \ldots, i_{N+1}$ are some natural numbers representing internal identifiers of AutoFocus3 elements:

```
<typeDefinitions xsi:type="org-fortiss-af3-expression-definitions:Enumeration" id="i₁"
name="TypeName">
<members id="i₂" name="MemberName₁" />
...
<members id="iN+1" name="MemberNameN" />
</typeDefinitions>
```

To generate an ACE sentence from this structure, we define two templates:

- For the case we have only one element, i.e., $N = 1$, we would use the template TypeName is a datatype. It consists-of one element that is MemberName$_1$.
- For the case we have more than one element, i.e., $N > 1$, we would use the template TypeName is a datatype. It consists-of N elements that are Member-Name$_1$, ..., MemberName$_N$.

The definition of each function/constant is provided within the tag *function*, where its name and value are coded within the attributes *name* and *value*. For the case of constant function, we would have the following XML structure, where j_1, j_2 are some natural numbers representing internal identifiers of AutoFocus3 elements:

```
<functions id="j₁" >
<function id="j₂" name="ConstantName" />
<definition>
<statements xsi:type="org-fortiss-af3-expression-terms-imperative:Return">
<value xsi:type="org-fortiss-af3-expression-terms:IntConst" value="ConstantVaue" />
</statements>
</definition>
<returnType xsi:type="org-fortiss-af3-expression-types:TInt" />
</functions>
```

To generate an ACE sentence from this structure, we define the following template:

ConstantName is a constant. It is equal to ConstantVaue.

Similar translation patterns apply for architecture specifications and state transition diagram sections.

ACE: Syntax Check. ACE supports declarative sentences, which includes simple sentences, there is/are-sentences, boolean formulas, composite sentences, interrogative sentences, imperative sentences. ACE construction rules determine whether an English sentence is an ACE sentence, cf. [1]. Each ACE sentence is an acceptable English sentence, but not every English sentence is justified as a valid ACE sentence. Thus, to be conformed to ACE construction rules, an NLS in English should be constructed from the following elements:

- Function words: determiners, quantifiers, coordinators, negation words, pronouns, query words, modal auxiliaries, "be", Saxon genitive marker's;
- Fixed phrases: "there is", "it is true that";
- Content words: nouns, verbs, adjectives, adverbs, prepositions.

The function words and fixed phrases are predefined and cannot be changed, whereas content words can be modified by users within the lexicon format, cf. [2]. The content words cannot contain blank spaces. For instance, "interested in" should be reformulated to "interested-in".

ACE: Semantics Check. The mentioned above rules cannot remove all ambiguities in English. To avoid ambiguity, ACE provides a set of interpretation rules. Thus, each ACE sentence can have only one meaning, based on its syntax and on syntax of previous sentences.

The correctness of the generated sentences can be validated by the ACE query sentences, cf. [12]. They can be subdivided into three forms that are *yes/no*-questions (questions that require answer "yes" or "no"), *wh*-questions (questions starting with the words "What", "When", "Where", etc.), and *how much/many*-questions, cf. [1]. For example, we could use the following questions to check the definition of an enumeration data type *XDataType*:

- What is *XDataType*?
- How many elements does *XDataType* have?
- Is *SomeElementName* an element of *XDataType*?

Case Study: SimpleTrafficLight System. We present the core ideas of the framework on example of a small case study, Simple Traffic Lights, introduced by Lam and Teufl in [22]. In the Simple Traffic Lights case study, we the following elements in the data definitions section:

- Functions *tGreen*, *tRed*, and *tYellow* that return a constant integer value to represent the time in seconds for the active pedestrian or traffic light.
- Enumeration data types:

  - *pedastrianColor*: pedestrian lights (*Stop*, *Walk*);
  - *TrafficColor*: traffic lights (*Green*, *Red*, *RedYellow*, *Yellow*);
  - *Signal*: one-element data type to represent the *Present* signal;
  - *IndicatorSignal*: pedestrian requests to pass the street (*Off*, *On*).

Figure 2 illustrates the translation process from the AutoFocus3 data types and the corresponding XML descriptions, to ACE sentences. After translation, we check the definition of each data type as shown on Table 1 and in Fig. 3.

In a similar manner the natural language description of the system and components architecture as well as of state machines, representing components behaviour, are generated and checked.

Table 1. Validation the generated sentences using ACE-questions

Question	Answer
What is IndicatorSignal?	It is a data-type.
How many elements does IndicatorSignal have?	It has 4 elements.
Is On an element of IndicatorSignal?	Yes, it is.

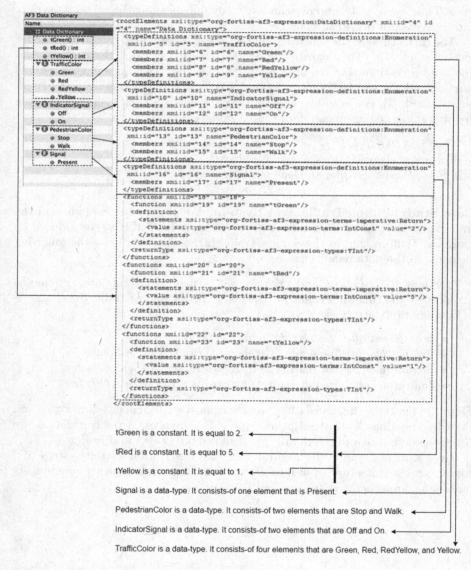

Fig. 2. Mapping from AutoFocus 3 data types to ACE sentences

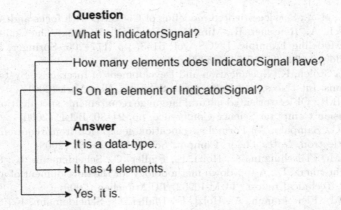

Fig. 3. Validation the generated sentences using ACE-questions

4   Conclusions and Future Work

This paper introduces our ongoing work on NLS from formal models. The goal of our current work is to generate documentation in English from the basic modelling artefacts of the AutoFocus3 modelling language, that are data types, state machines, and architectural components. This would allow to have an easy-to-read and easy-to-understand specifications of systems-under-development, written in English. To allow further formal analysis of the generated specification, we restrict English to its subset, ACE. The proposed framework, in its current version, can be applied to build a prototype for generation of ACE specifications from the AutoFocus3 models.

The future work focuses on the implementation of an prototype translator from AutoFocus3 to ACE, as well as on the extension of the framework to other formal modelling languages.

References

1. ACE   Construction   Rules.   http://attempto.ifi.uzh.ch/site/docs/ace_constructionrules.html. Accessed 28 July 2016
2. ACE Lexicon Specification. http://attempto.ifi.uzh.ch/site/docs/ace_lexicon.html. Accessed 28 July 2016
3. SWI-Prolog. http://www.swi-prolog.org. Accessed 28 July 2016
4. Aravantinos, V., Voss, S., Teufl, S., Hölzl, F., Schätz, B.: AutoFOCUS 3: tooling concepts for seamless, model-based development of embedded systems. In: Joint proceedings of ACES-MB 2015-Model-based Architecting of Cyber-physical and Embedded Systems, p. 19 (2015)
5. Bjørner, D., Havelund, K.: 40 years of formal methods. In: Jones, C., Pihlajasaari, P., Sun, J. (eds.) FM 2014. LNCS, vol. 8442, pp. 42–61. Springer, Heidelberg (2014). doi:10.1007/978-3-319-06410-9_4

6. Broy, M., et al.: Service-oriented modeling of CoCoME with focus and AutoFocus. In: Rausch, A., Reussner, R., Mirandola, R., Plášil, F. (eds.) The Common Component Modeling Example. LNCS, vol. 5153, pp. 177–206. Springer, Heidelberg (2008). doi:10.1007/978-3-540-85289-6_8

7. Broy, M., Stólen, K.: Specification and Development of Interactive Systems: Focus on Streams, Interfaces, and Refinement. Springer, New York (2001)

8. Bryant, B.R.: Object-oriented natural language requirements specification. In: 23rd Australasian Computer Science Conference, pp. 24–30. IEEE (2000)

9. Cabral, G., Sampaio, A.: Formal specification generation from requirement documents. Electron. Notes Theor. Comput. Sci. **195**, 171–188 (2008)

10. Feilkas, M., Fleischmann, A., Hölzl, F., Pfaller, C., Scheidemann, K., Spichkova, M., Trachtenherz, D.: A top-down methodology for the development of automotive software, Technical report, TUM-I0902, TU München (2009)

11. Feilkas, M., Fleischmann, A., Hölzl, F., Pfaller, C., Scheidemann, K., Spichkova, M., Trachtenherz, D.: A refined top-down methodology for the development of automotive software systems - the keylessentry system case study, Technical report, TUM-I1103, TU München (2011)

12. Fuchs, N.E., Kaljurand, K., Kuhn, T.: Attempto controlled english for knowledge representation. In: Baroglio, C., Bonatti, P.A., Małuszyński, J., Marchiori, M., Polleres, A., Schaffert, S. (eds.) Reasoning Web. LNCS, vol. 5224, pp. 104–124. Springer, Heidelberg (2008). doi:10.1007/978-3-540-85658-0_3

13. Fuchs, N.E., Schwitter, R.: Attempto Controlled English (ACE). arXiv preprint cmp-lg/9603003 (1996)

14. Gangopadhyay, A.: Conceptual modeling from natural language functional specifications. Artif. Intell. Eng. **15**(2), 207–218 (2001)

15. Guiho, G., Hennebert, C.: Sacem software validation. In: 12th International Conference on Software Engineering, pp. 186–191. IEEE (1990)

16. Hölzl, F., Feilkas, M.: 13 AUTOFOCUS 3 - a scientific tool prototype for model-based development of component-based, reactive, distributed systems. In: Giese, H., Karsai, G., Lee, E., Rumpe, B., Schätz, B. (eds.) MBEERTS 2007. LNCS, vol. 6100, pp. 317–322. Springer, Heidelberg (2010). doi:10.1007/978-3-642-16277-0_13

17. Hölzl, F., Spichkova, M., Trachtenherz, D.: AutoFocus Tool Chain, Technical report, TUM-I1021, TU München (2010)

18. Hölzl, F., Spichkova, M., Trachtenherz, D.: Safety-critical system development methodology. Technical report, TUM-I1020, TU München (2010)

19. Ilieva, M.G., Ormandjieva, O.: Automatic transition of natural language software requirements specification into formal presentation. In: Montoyo, A., Muñoz, R., Métais, E. (eds.) NLDB 2005. LNCS, vol. 3513, pp. 392–397. Springer, Heidelberg (2005). doi:10.1007/11428817_45

20. Juristo, N., Morant, J.L., Moreno, A.M.: A formal approach for generating OO specifications from natural language. J. Syst. Softw. **48**(2), 139–153 (1999)

21. Kaljurand, K., Fuchs, N.E., Kuhn, T.: APE - ACE Parsing Engine. https://github.com/Attempto/APE. Accessed 30 Mar 2016

22. Lam, P.S., Teu, S.: Simple Traffic Lights tutorial for AutoFocus 3. http://af3.fortiss.org/docs/. Accessed 30 Mar 2016

23. Lee, B., Bryant, B.R.: Automated conversion from requirements documentation to an object-oriented formal specification language. In: Proceedings of the 2002 ACM symposium on Applied computing, pp. 932–936. ACM (2002)

24. Mala, G.S.A., Uma, G.V.: Automatic construction of object oriented design models [UML Diagrams] from natural language requirements specification. In: Yang, Q., Webb, G. (eds.) PRICAI 2006. LNCS (LNAI), vol. 4099, pp. 1155–1159. Springer, Heidelberg (2006). doi:10.1007/978-3-540-36668-3_152

25. Sanner, M.F.: Python: a programming language for software integration and development. J. Mol. Graph. Model. **17**(1), 57–61 (1999)

26. Schank, R.C.: Conceptual dependency: a theory of natural language understanding. Cogn. Psychol. **3**(4), 552–631 (1972)

27. Schwitter, R., Ljungberg, A., Hood, D.: ECOLE - a look-ahead editor for a controlled language. In: EAMT-CLAW 2003, pp. 141–150 (2003)

28. Spichkova, M.: Human factors of formal methods. In: IADIS Interfaces and Human Computer Interaction, IHCI 2012 (2012)

29. Spichkova, M.: Design of formal languages, interfaces: "formal" does not mean "unreadable". In: Blashki, K., Isaias, P. (eds.) Emerging Research and Trends in Interactivity and the Human-Computer Interface. IGI Global (2013)

30. Spichkova, M., Hölzl, F., Trachtenherz, D.: Verified system development with the AutoFocus tool chain. In: Workshop on Formal Methods in the Development of Software (2012)

31. Spichkova, M., Liu, H., Laali, M., Schmidt, H.W.: Human factors in software reliability engineering. In: Workshop on Applications of Human Error Research to Improve Software Engineering (WAHESE 2015) (2015)

32. Spichkova, M., Zhu, X., Mou, D.: Do we really need to write documentation for a system? In: International Conference on Model-Driven Engineering and Software Development (MODELSWARD 2013) (2013)

33. Zamansky, A., Rodriguez-Navas, G., Adams, M., Spichkova, M.: Formal methods in collaborative projects. In: 11th International Conference on Evaluation of Novel Approaches to Software Engineering (ENASE). IEEE (2016)

34. Zhang, J., Cheng, B.H.: Model-based development of dynamically adaptive software. In: Proceedings of the 28th International Conference on Software Engineering, pp. 371–380. ACM (2006)

Human-Oriented Formal Modelling
of Human-Computer Interaction:
Practitioners' and Students' Perspectives

Antonio Cerone[✉]

Department of Computer Science, Nazarbayev University, Astana, Kazakhstan
antonio.cerone@nu.edu.kz

Abstract. Practitioners and students tend to have a negative inclination towards formal methods and consider them hard to learn and unusable in practice. In this paper we analyse the perspectives of practitioners, computer scientists and students to show that a notation developed for modelling interactive systems in previous work and its translations into rewriting logic and process algebra represent an appropriate compromise among such perspectives.

Keywords: Human computer interaction · Formal methods applications · Computer science education

1   Introduction

Formal methods experts are often so much focussed on the investigation of theoretical aspects of formal notations rather than on their applications to real problems, that they often neglect the needs of practitioners. As a result, they produce methods of little use in practice and have to resort to simplified, unrealistic, too abstract versions of application-domain problems while they are also biased in choosing the data that best illustrate the features and potential of their favourite formal languages and analysis techniques [5]. Instead of focusing on usability, formal analysis and the tools that realise it are more and more evolving towards efficient, automatic rather than human-oriented proofs (theorem-proving) [1] or the checking of rich extensions of temporal logic, which are hard to understand by humans (model checking). Nothing of this is of any interest for a practitioner. In addition, formal methods are often presented to students through dry syntax and involved semantics rather than seen in a lively applicative context through lab sessions that allow students to use appropriate, usable tools to experiment both with learning-oriented, fun-making examples and, when familiarity is acquired, with real world case studies [4].

In this paper we consider three human-oriented perspectives in which formal methods can be used to model human-computer interaction.

First, the development of new approaches to the use of formal methods and tools within a specific application domain should address the perspective

© Springer International Publishing AG 2016
P. Milazzo et al. (Eds.): STAF 2016, LNCS 9946, pp. 232–241, 2016.
DOI: 10.1007/978-3-319-50230-4_17

of and provide an effective support to the practitioner (who is normally a domain expert) and should be tested on real case studies from the application domain. This aspect is dealt with in Sect. 2, where modelling and analysis goals and objectives, as well as description level, are established from the perspective of a practitioner, who is, in our context, a cognitive psychologist/scientist. An intuitive but unambiguous notation to model cognitive processes, subset of a more extensive notation presented in previous work [3], is illustrated in the context of the practical use of the practitioner.

Second, the intuitive description of the problem given from a domain expert perspective has to be translated or, technically speaking, implemented into an appropriate formal language, which, on the one hand, is equipped with powerful tools that support the accomplishment of the modelling and analysis objectives of the domain expert, and, on the other hand, is close enough to the intuitive modelling notation used by the domain expert. Section 3 provides another notation, also from our previous work [3], with simple primitives to describe the behaviour of interfaces, which reflects, in a simplified form, the formal methods perspective of modelling a system in terms of transitions between states. Section 4 merges the notations corresponding to the two perspectives into a modelling language for interactive systems, which has been implemented using two distinct formal methods, rewriting logic and process algebra.

Third, it essential to address learners' and practitioners' negative inclination towards formal methods and provide the appropriate educational tools to allow learners, as well as practitioners, to overcome the prejudice that "formal methods are hard to learn and to use". This should be done at the root, by making learning formal methods motivating, appealing and involving for students. Therefore, in Sect. 5 we discuss the role of our modelling language and its translations into rewriting logic and process algebra in the context of an PhD course on applied formal methods.

2   A Perspective from Cognitive Science

Cognitive science is an interdisciplinary field that comprises various research disciplines, including psychology, artificial intelligence, philosophy, neuroscience, linguistics, and anthropology [13]. Moreover, it adopts the so-called *information processing* approach, whereby human cognitive processes are modelled as processing activities that make use of input-output channels, to interact with the external environment, and three main kinds of memory to store information: *sensory memory*, where information perceived through the senses persists for a very short time; *short-term memory (STM)*, where the information that is needed for processing activities is temporary stored; *long-term memory (LTM)*, where information is organised in structured ways for long-term use [6]. In this sense computer scientists and cognitive scientists share the view of a processing system with components for input, output and storage of information, and information streams flowing between different components (*computer analogy*).

In spite of this important commonality, the perspective of a cognitive scientist tends to be very different from the perspective of a computer scientist, especially if the computer scientist is a formal methods expert. In particular, a cognitive scientist tends to see a model as conceptual rather than formal and give it representations that are visual rather than mathematical and/or symbolic. Even when a mathematical representation of the model is conceived, this is envisaged as an operational tool to be used only for description or simulation purposes. Furthermore, even cognitive scientists who work in the area of human-computer interaction are not keen to use formal descriptions, but prefer to adopt instead the scientific method and analyse and evaluate systems using empirical and measurable evidence, systematic observation and usability experiments.

In terms of general goals a domain expert aims at

1. describing domain phenomena with a notation that represents them in an intuitive way by providing a direct representation of the basic components and processes of the domain;
2. using tools that can:
   (a) automatically manipulate such notation to generate simulations of the domain phenomena and map the results on the structure of the domain components;
   (b) extract global information and general properties from an extensive set of simulations.

Therefore, the respective *objective* of a cognitive scientist are

1. a notation to define cognitive processes in terms of how the different components of human cognition (perception, attention, memory, reasoning and action) cooperate to process information, possibly with the support of a digital device or system through its interface, to accomplish specific goals of human behaviour;
2. the availability of tools that:
   (a) allow a simulation mapped on the various cognitive and non cognitive components;
   (b) provide analysis features to conduct in-silico experiments to overcome a major difficulty in cognitive science field studies and lab experiments, that is, that human behaviour, the main object of study, is characterised by multiple aspects, such as unpredictability, ethical issues, individual and cultural diversity, inaccessibility of introspective processes and slow evolution, that hinder the design of the research plan and the validity of the results.

In order to address these human-oriented objectives and link the two distinct perspectives of a cognitive scientist and a computer scientist, we devised an intuitive, formal notation to describe the components of a cognitive system and the information flow among them [3]. We consider only STM as a dynamic memory, that is, supporting both storage and retrieval of information; LTM is, instead, implicitly seen as a container of all knowledge needed for the processing activities, as already given rather than dynamically constructed, with only retrieval and no storage (i.e. no transfer between STM and LTM); sensory memory is not represented at all.

2.1 A Formal Notation for Human Cognition and Behaviour

Input and output occur in humans through senses. We give a general representation of input channels in term of *perceptions*, with little or no details about
the specific senses involved in the perception. We represent output channels in
term of *actions*. Actions are performed in response to perceptions.

Human behaviour is driven by *goals*. In order to accomplish a goal in a specific
domain of action, the human has to carry out a *task*, that is, an operation to
manipulate the concepts of the domain. This is done by performing actions. In
an interactive context, namely while interacting with an interface, each action is
normally executed as an automatic response to a specific perception (*automatic
control* or *automaticity*). For example, automaticity is essential in driving a car:
the driver is aware of the high-level tasks that are carried out, such as driving to
office, turning to the right and waiting at a traffic light, but is not aware about
low-level details such as changing gear, using the indicator and the colour of the
traffic light, amber or red, while stopping at a traffic light. A goal is associated
with a top-level task. A top-level task can be decomposed in a hierarchy of tasks
until reaching basic tasks, which cannot be further decomposed. We model a
basic task as a quadruple

$$info_i \uparrow perc_h \implies act_h \downarrow info_j$$

where perception $perc_h$ triggers the retrieval of information $info_i$ from the STM,
the execution of action act_h and the storage of information $info_j$ in the STM.
We formally denote by *none* when there is no information to retrieve from or
store in the STM.

Information is kept promptly available, while it is needed to perform the
current top-level task, by storing it in the STM. For the purpose of our work
we consider only two kinds of information that can be stored in the STM: *task
goal*, represented as the action that directly accomplishes the goal, and *action
reference*, which refers to a future action to be performed. A task goal is formally
modelled as $goal(act)$ where act is the action that directly accomplishes the goal.

As an example, a simple Automatic Teller Machine (ATM) task, in which
the user has only the goal to withdraw cash, is modelled by the following four
basic tasks

1. $none \uparrow cardR \implies cardI \downarrow cardB$
2. $none \uparrow pinR \implies pinI \downarrow none$
3. $none \uparrow cashO \implies cashC \downarrow none$
4. $cardB \uparrow cardO \implies cardC \downarrow none$

where: $cardR$ denotes the perception that the ATM is ready to receive the card,
$pinR$ that it has requested the pin, $cashO$ that it has delivered the cash and
$cardO$ that it has delivered the card; $cardI$ denotes the action of inserting the
card, $pinI$ inserting the pin, $cashC$ collecting the cash and $cardC$ collecting the
card; $cardB$ is the action reference used as a memory for the card collection (it
refers to action $cardC$). The goal ("to withdraw cash") is identified with the act
of collecting cash (action $cashC$) and is formally modelled as $goal(cashC)$.

3   A Perspective from Formal Methods

We consider one possible formal methods perspective in which the system behaviour is seen as a discrete sequence of state changes. We apply this perspective to the context of a user interacting with an interface. Normally an interface provides an output to the user and waits for the user action (i.e. reaction), which is seen as an input that triggers a change of state. In some cases the current state $state_h$ is associated with a timeout: if user's reaction act_h occurs before the timeout expires, then it triggers the change to state $state_{k'}$, otherwise, at the expiration of the timeout, the state changes to state $state_r$, which may be distinct from $state_k$. In order to associate timeouts with interface states, we decorate interface states as follows.

$state!0$ state not associated with a timeout;
$state!1$ state associated with a timeout that is not expired;
$state!2$ state associated with a timeout that has already expired.

Thus we model a state change as a triple

$$state_h!m \xrightarrow{act_h} state_k!n$$

where interface state $state_h$, with possible timeout characterised by m, triggers the execution of action act_h with a change to state $state_k$, whose possible timeout is charcterised by n. The initial state of the interface is normally an idling state (the interface is available for an interaction), thus it is not associated with a timeout ($state!0$). If we have

$$state_h!1 \xrightarrow{act_h} state_k!n_k$$

and the timeout associated with $state_h$ expires, than $state_h!1$ changes to $state_h!2$ and the state change that occurs at the timeout expiration is modelled by

$$state_h!2 \longrightarrow state_r!n_r$$

where the absence of action denotes that there is no interaction with the user, thus describing an autonomous action of the interface.

4   A Common Perspective

We have seen in Sect. 3 that an action act is performed through a cooperation between the human (the subject performing the action) and the interface (which changes its internal state as a consequence of the human action). Therefore, an action belongs to both a task and an interface transition and represents the basic form of interaction. In the context of an interactive system, a user perception refers to a stimulus produced by an output of the interface with which the human is interacting. We can thus identify the perception with such an output. Moreover, since the output of the interface is associated with the interface state that results from producing that output, we can take a step forward and identify the user perception with the interface state associated with the output that produced that perception. For example, the interface state associated with the interface of a vending machine giving a change is identified with the perception (sound of falling coins or sight of the coins) produced. Thus, in our notation, interface state and corresponding human perception are denoted by the same formal entity (which, assuming the cognitive scientist's perspective, we call "perception" rather than "state"). In this way our formal notation meets Objective 2 presented in Sect. 2.

Identifying interface state and corresponding human perception allows us to merge the two notations presented in Sects. 2 and 3 and attain a modelling language for interactive systems. A state change is thus modelled as

$$perc_h!m \xrightarrow{act_h} perc_k!n$$

where $perc_h$ is the perception that triggers the user to perform action act_h, which causes the interface to change to the state corresponding to perception $perc_k$. As an additional link between the two merged notations, we keep track of the human action act_h, if any, that produced the state $perc_k$ by defining an interface state as a pair $act_h \gg perc_k!n$. The initial state becomes then $\gg perc!0$.

With reference to the ATM example introduced in Sect. 2.1, we model an old interface that sequentially requests a card, requests a pin, delivers the cash and returns the card, and a new interface that returns the card before delivering the cash. The two interface models are as follows.

Old ATM: transitions

1. $cardR!0 \xrightarrow{cardI} pinR!1$
2. $pinR!1 \xrightarrow{pinI} cashO!1$
3. $cashO!1 \xrightarrow{cashC} cardO!1$
4. $cardO!1 \xrightarrow{cardC} cardR!0$
5. $pinR!2 \longrightarrow cardO!1$
6. $cashO!2 \longrightarrow cardO!1$
7. $cardO!2 \longrightarrow cardR!0$

New ATM: transitions

1. $cardR!0 \xrightarrow{cardI} pinR!1$
2. $pinR!1 \xrightarrow{pinI} cardO!1$
3. $cardO!1 \xrightarrow{cardC} cashO!1$
4. $cashO!1 \xrightarrow{cashC} cardR!0$
5. $pinR!2 \longrightarrow cardR!0$
6. $cashO!2 \longrightarrow cardR!0$
7. $cardO!2 \longrightarrow cardR!0$

For both interfaces the initial state is $\gg cardR!0$. In both interfaces, transitions 1–4 model the normal sequences of interactions for the specific design (old or new).

The last three transitions model interface autonomous actions. If the timeout expires after requesting a pin (transitions 5), then in the old ATM the card is returned, whereas in the new ATM the control goes back to the initial state, implicitly modelling that the card is confiscated by the ATM, and in both cases the cash delivery is inhibited. If the timeout expires after delivering the cash (transitions 6), then in the old ATM the card is returned, whereas in the new ATM the control goes back to the initial state, so inhibiting a cash collection action in both cases and implicitly modelling that the cash is taken back by the ATM. Finally, in both interfaces, if the timeout expires after returning the card, then the control goes back to the initial state, so inhibiting a card collection action and, as a result, implicitly modelling that the card is confiscated (transitions 7), obviously, with no cash delivery in the new ATM.

Our modelling language for interactive systems has been translated into rewriting logic [3] and implemented using the MAUDE rewrite system[1], and into the CSP (Communicating Sequential Processes) process algebra [2] and implemented using the Process Analysis Toolkit (PAT)[2]. Both tools, MAUDE and PAT, are equipped with model checkers, thus featuring the potential for meeting Objective 2 from Sect. 2. In reality, the simulators and model-checkers of the two tools produce results that refer to the low-level structures that implement the modelling language with no mechanisms to present the effect of such results on the high-level cognitive and non cognitive components, which the practitioner is familiar with. Therefore, implementing such mechanisms, such as domain specific visualisations [9], would be necessary to accomplish Objective 2.

5   Students' Perspective

There is an ongoing debate on the importance of formal methods to computer science education. This debate links with the wider debate on the centrality of mathematics and logic in computer science curricula: on the one side the claim that rigorous mathematical knowledge is not necessary for computer science practitioners [7] and, on the other side, the belief [14,15] and the empirical evidences [10–12] that learning rigorous discrete mathematics and formal methods has an important impact on problem-solving and programming skills and is perceived by students as useful in practical problems and helpful in improving their mental processes [16].

We agree with the latter position but, in addition, we believe [4] that:

1. instead of tediously going through the semantics of each construct in a formal language, students should be allowed to experiment with an appropriate tool to discover the semantics by themselves;
2. tools for simulation visualisation are essential to allow students to understand the behaviour associated with their models.

Moreover, in order to motivate students, formal methods should be presented in a variety of realistic, applied contexts, not at all limited to computer science and software engineering, and including, why not, examples that can bring some fun [4] in an apparently very serious area. The recent application of formal methods to several disciplines such as biology and cognitive science provides heaps of interesting and motivating examples.

The rewrite systems and CSP translations of our modelling language were presented during a course on "Formal Methods for Interactive Systems", which was held at the IMT School for Advanced Studies Lucca in May 2015 and delivered to four first year PhD students. The double aim of the course, teaching

---

[1]   http://sysma.imtlucca.it/cognitive-framework-maude-hofm-2016/.

[2]   http://sysma.imtlucca.it/cognitive-framework-csp-hofm-2016/.

formal methods and provide an approach for their application to interactive systems, was realised through the use of our practitioner-oriented formal notation and its translations in MAUDE and CSP.

After introducing the two translations but before introducing the tools, the students were asked three questions:

1. "In which of the two approaches did you find easier to get the model right?"
2. "Which of the two translations is more elegant?"
3. "In which of the two approaches the resultant behaviour is easier to guess?"

The PhD students unanimously answered "the rewriting logic approach" to Questions 1 and 3, and "the process algebra approach" to Question 2. It is interesting to notice that, in spite of finding the process algebra approach more difficult, the student unanimously agreed that it is more elegant. These answers, as well as further remarks and opinions that emerged in an open discussion that followed, are an indicator that students have a strong interest for solutions that are concise, elegant and abstract, and that they are happy to tackle challenging problems in order to look for elegant rather than easy solutions. Given the small number of students and the absence of research design we cannot draw empirical conclusions from the students' answers and remarks, although these appear to be in line with the results of previous research [16].

In terms of tools, from the perspective of a student learning formal methods, it is important to see simulation and model-checking results directly on the low-level semantic structures underlying high-level domain structures. This perspective is very different from that of a practitioner, who prefers tools that hide the formal semantic structures underlying domain structures. Moreover, in the case of students' perspective, the presentation of results must aim at highlighting relations between behaviour and semantics and using under-approximation [8], the capability to output only relevant states and/or events, as well as stimulating and developing their abstraction and problem solving skills.

MAUDE and PAT are somehow complementary in terms of presentation of results, also due to the different characteristics of the formal methods on which they are based. MAUDE does not support any form of graphical representation but supports a form of under-approximation, by filtering the output through additional rewrite rules, and allows the designer to easily track which rewrite rule is applied and check the content of all data structures, thus tracking the behaviour back to the architectural view of the designer. PAT facilitates the visual representations of the global behaviour in terms of finite state machines, but the form of under-approximation introduced by the CSP hiding operator is not very effective due to the possible introduction of nondeterminism, while the represented behaviour does not reflect the structure, in terms of concurrent components and synchronisations, from which the global behaviour has been attained. However, the use of both these tools in our course has allowed students to make use of all needed presentation features, visualisation from PAT, under-approximation and behaviour tracking from MAUDE. Moreover, in our class discussions, students showed the perception that the fact that the two tools are based on two distinct modelling paradigms contributed to stimulate and develop their abstraction and problem solving skills.

6   Conclusion and Future Work

We have discussed to which extent the modelling language developed in previous work [3] for modelling interactive systems may represent an appropriate compromise between the perspectives of an HCI practitioner (meets Objective 2 from Sect. 2) and a formal methods expert (can be translated into formal methods and undergo formal analysis). We noted that in order to accomplish Objective 2 from Sect. 2 it would be necessary to implement mechanisms to effectively present the results of simulation and model checking on the high-level cognitive and non cognitive components, for example through domain specific visualisations.

Instead, for students learning formal methods, the presentation of both the rewriting logic translation and the CSP translation and both respective tools, MAUDE and PAT, was perceived by the students themselves as beneficial for their abstraction and problem solving skills. In our future work, we plan to systematically investigate empirical evidence of such student perception.

References

1. Beckert, B., Grebing, S., Böhl, F.: A usability evaluation of interactive theorem provers using focus groups. In: Canal, C., Idani, A. (eds.) SEFM 2014. LNCS, vol. 8938, pp. 3–19. Springer, Heidelberg (2015). doi:10.1007/978-3-319-15201-1_1
2. Cerone, A.: Closure, attention activation in human automatic behaviour: A framework for the formal analysis of interactive systems. In: Proceedings of FMIS 2011, Electronic Communications of the EASST, vol. 45 (2011)
3. Cerone, A.: A cognitive framework based on rewriting logic for the analysis of interactive systems. In: De Nicola, R., Kühn, E. (eds.) SEFM 2016. LNCS, vol. 9763, pp. 287–303. Springer, Heidelberg (2016). doi:10.1007/978-3-319-41591-8_20
4. Cerone, A., Roggenbach, M., Schlingloff, B.-H., Schneider, G., Shaikh, S.: Teaching formal methods for software engineering – ten principles. Informatica Didactica 9 (2015). https://www.informaticadidactica.de/index.php?page=Schlinghoff2015
5. Cerone, A., Scotti, M.: Research challenges in modelling ecosystems. In: Canal, C., Idani, A. (eds.) SEFM 2014. LNCS, vol. 8938, pp. 276–293. Springer, Heidelberg (2015). doi:10.1007/978-3-319-15201-1_18
6. Dix, A., Finlay, J., Abowd, G., Beale, R.: Human-Computer Interaction. Pearson Education, Upper Saddle River (1998)
7. Glass, R.L.: A new answer to "how important is mathematics to the software practitioner?". IEEE Softw. 17(6), 136–136 (2000)
8. Idani, A., Stouls, N.: When a formal model rhymes with a graphical notation. In: Canal, C., Idani, A. (eds.) SEFM 2014. LNCS, vol. 8938, pp. 54–68. Springer, Heidelberg (2015). doi:10.1007/978-3-319-15201-1_4
9. Ladenberger, L., Dobrikov, I., Leuschel, M.: An approach for creating domain specific visualisations of CSP models. In: Canal, C., Idani, A. (eds.) SEFM 2014. LNCS, vol. 8938, pp. 20–35. Springer, Heidelberg (2015). doi:10.1007/978-3-319-15201-1_2
10. Page, R.L.: Software in discrete mathematics. In: Proceedings of ICFP 2003, ACM SIGPLAN Notices, vol. 38, pp. 79–86. ACM (2003)
11. Sobel, A.E.K., Clarkson, M.R.: Formal methods application: an empirical tale of software development. IEEE Trans. Softw. Eng. 28(3), 308–320 (2002)

12. Sobel, A.E.K., Clarkson, M.R.: Response on "Comments on 'Formal methods application: an empirical tale of software development'". IEEE Trans. Softw. Eng. **29**(6), 572–575 (2003)

13. Thagard, P.: Cognitive science. In: Zalta, E.N. (ed.) The Stanford Encyclopedia of Philosophy. Stanford University (2008)

14. Wing, J.M.: Teaching mathematics to software engineers. In: Alagar, V.S., Nivat, M. (eds.) AMAST 1995. LNCS, vol. 936, pp. 18–40. Springer, Heidelberg (1995). doi:10.1007/3-540-60043-4_44

15. Wing, J.M.: Invited talk: weaving formal methods into the undergraduate computer science curriculum (Extended Abstract). In: Rus, T. (ed.) AMAST 2000. LNCS, vol. 1816, pp. 2–7. Springer, Heidelberg (2000). doi:10.1007/3-540-45499-3_2

16. Zamansky, A., Farchi, E.: Exploring the role of logic and formal methods in information systems education. In: Bianculli, D., Calinescu, R., Rumpe, B. (eds.) SEFM 2015. LNCS, vol. 9509, pp. 68–74. Springer, Heidelberg (2015). doi:10.1007/978-3-662-49224-6_7

"Boring Formal Methods" or "Sherlock Holmes Deduction Methods"?

Maria Spichkova[⊠]

RMIT University, Melbourne, Australia
maria.spichkova@rmit.edu.au

Abstract. This paper provides an overview of common challenges in teaching of logic and formal methods to Computer Science and IT students. We discuss our experiences from the course *IN3050: Applied Logic in Engineering*, introduced as a "logic for everybody" elective course at TU Munich, Germany, to engage pupils studying Computer Science, IT and engineering subjects on Bachelor and Master levels. Our goal was to overcome the bias that logic and formal methods are not only very complicated but also very boring to study and to apply. In this paper, we present the core structure of the course, provide examples of exercises and evaluate the course based on the students' surveys.

1 Introduction

Logic not only helps to solve complicated and safety-critical problems, but also disciplines the mind and helps to develop abstract thinking, which is very important for any area of Computer Science and Engineering. Problems in teaching and learning the basic principles of logic lead to the lack of analytical skills and abstract thinking as well as to the problems in understanding of Formal Methods (FMs). The disputes on teaching logic and FMs have been going on for a long time, but most lecturers teaching these subjects agree that they face many challenges specific to these subjects.

Students are strongly focused on the direct relevance of what they study to their daily practice, and are not interested to study more fundamental subjects, especially logic [29,32]. The main obstacle in this case is that the students cannot match logic and FMs (in contrary to Games Development, Programming, Testing, etc.) to real world problems. As curricula becomes more practice-oriented, the mathematical background of the students becomes weaker which provides an additional obstacle in understanding of logic and FMs, cf. [2,5,34]. Also, many students have negative perceptions and even fear of courses that require dealing with complex mathematical notations. This is strongly related to the phenomenon of *mathematical anxiety* [22,31].

The term *mathematical anxiety* was introduced in 1972 by Richardson and Suinn as *"feelings of tension and anxiety that interfere with the manipulation of numbers and the solving of mathematical problems in a wide variety of ordinary life and academic situations,"* [18]. As stressed by Wang et al., mathematical anxiety has attracted recent attention because of its damaging psychological effects and potential associations with mathematical problem solving and

P. Milazzo et al. (Eds.): STAF 2016, LNCS 9946, pp. 242–252, 2016.
DOI: 10.1007/978-3-319-50230-4_18

achievement. From our point of view, this term could be extended to *mathematical and logical anxiety* (or even to *formal methods anxiety*), to cover a similar phenomenon on learning logic and FMs.

Moreover, the term "formal" is for many people just some kind of synonym for "unreadable", however, even small syntactical changes of a formal method can make it more understandable and usable for an average engineer. In the course *IN3050: Applied Logic in Engineering* we aimed to apply the core principles of our research work on *Human Factors of Formal Methods* [24,25], applying the engineering psychology achievements to the design of FMs. However, improving the usability aspects we cannot overcome the preconceived notions about FMs completely. To achieve the goal, we should start by training and teaching of logic not only by presenting its theoretical aspects but also focusing on its real applications, industrial and non-industrial ones, referring to the programming languages where the formal side is almost covered, or to famous fiction books and movies, e.g., to the famous crime stories by A.C. Doyle. We applied these ideas within the course *IN3050: Applied Logic in Engineering* for Bachelor and Master students, and the students' feedback on this matter was very positive.

There also is a great diversity in the students' background and cognitive skills due to the globalisation of higher education, which requires constant adaptation, cf. [7,12]. One possible solution to overcome this problem is to provide courses that require very basic or even no background knowledge in the corresponding areas, having as result a "course for everybody", and providing students with deeper background additional non-compulsory tasks.

Contributions: Our goal was to overcome these problems and to teach the course *IN3050: Applied Logic in Engineering* without expecting any previous knowledge on logics and abstract thinking (in contrary to the many courses on logic and FMs). We introduced this lecture course as a "logic for everybody", to engage pupils studying Computer Science, IT and engineering subjects, to overcome the bias that logic and formal methods are not only very complicated but also "very boring to study and to apply". As per evaluation report [1], the majority of the students agreed that the course was helpful to their understanding of application of logic and FMs in Engineering. We believe that this course would be especially beneficial for Computer Science students, as well as for the IT students who aim to work as Software Requirements Engineers and Software Testers. A general introduction to this course was presented in a technical report [26]. In this paper we are going to focus on generalisation and analysis of the proposed solutions to improve students' learning experience.

Outline: The rest of the paper is organised as follows. Section 2 presents a short overview of the related work on teaching logic and FMs. Section 3 introduces the core structure of the course *IN3050: Applied Logic in Engineering*, where Sect. 4 presents a number of examples we used at the lectures and tutorials. Section 5 concludes the paper evaluating the course based on the results from the students' surveys.

2   Related Work

A symposium to explore and discuss the challenges and successful solutions in teaching of FMs was organised in 2004. After 12 years, the lecturers face very similar problems while teaching logic and FMs: mathematical and logical anxiety as well as understandability and readability of FMs. However, over the last few years there have been number of interesting and promising approaches that we would like to discuss here. In our previous work [28], we discussed the common issues in teaching of FMs and logic, as well as reviewed various approaches for teaching FMs for Software Engineering that have been proposed, and discuss how they address the above mentioned challenges. The focus of our analysis here is on the *collaborative* and *communication* aspects of software development using formal methods and logical modelling.

A novel way to attract students while teaching FMs was presented in [6]. Within the engagement project *cs4fn*, Computer Science for Fun, the authors taught logic and computing concepts using magic tricks, which inspired students to work with logical tasks. Our approach was less revolutionary: we based the course on both practical examples and entertainment examples, such as formal modelling of logical puzzles and the Sherlock Holmes deductions from the modern BBC TV series "Sherlock".

Noble et al. [17] presented a course on *Introduction to Software Modelling*, where Alloy programming language was taught along with introduces the principles and practices of Software Engineering, beginning with domain analysis, specification of classes and use cases, writing invariants, etc. An interesting point about this douse is that the Alloy tool itself and the Alloy language were not introduced until the final two blocks of the course, to allow focusing on software modelling, rather than on the technical tools.

Wang and Yilmaz suggested to group the study programs in three main categories, based on the way logic and FMs are integrated into software engineering curriculum, cf. [30]: programs avoiding FMs, programs having a specific course with emphasis on formal verification of source code, and programs redesigned to have FMs integrated throughout the curriculum. This grouping does not cover another category, which we see as a very promising for integrating logic FMs into software engineering curriculum: to introduce a specific course that

(1) covers basics of logic and FMs, without requiring a deep knowledge in mathematics, and
(2) uses visualisation and gamification/puzzle strategies to make the material more understandable and less boring for the students.

Examples of this kind of courses might be

- the *Logic and FM* course designed for Information Systems students [35],
- a series of courses specifically adapted to the needs of university of applied sciences, described in [29],

– Courses *Computational Thinking* at the Singapore Management University and *Computational Thinking and Design* at the University of Maryland, organised in the spirit of "computational thinking for everybody" envisioned by Wing [33].

The course *IN3050: Applied Logic in Engineering*, which we introduced as a "logic for everybody" course, can be seen as another example of this kind of courses.

3 Course: Applied Logic in Engineering

The course *IN3050: Applied logic in Engineering* (ALE) was introduced at TU Munich, Germany, in Winter Semester 2012/2013 as a face-to-face course on Bachelor and Master levels.[1] The course was designed as an elective without any enforced prerequisites. It contributed 6 credit points to the student curriculum, which corresponds to 4 teacher-directed hours.

In the case of ALE, the teacher-directed hours were divided into weekly lectures (2 h a semester week) and weekly tutorials (2 h a semester week). The course attracted 20 students from the following study programs:

– Computer Science (German, "Informatik"),
– Business Informatics (German, "Wirtschaftsinformatik"),
– Mechanical Engineering (German, "Maschinenwesen").

Introductory courses on Modelling in/for Software Engineering are usually taught in the first or second semester of the first year of study. In contrast to this kind of courses, we

– focused not on principles and practices of Software Engineering, but on logical concepts, representation and analysis of information and problems;
– provided the course without any restriction on the year of study, and as result most of the students enrolled into this course were either at the beginning of their study (1–3 semester) or at their final semesters (7th semester or later).

The exam for this course was organised as an *open book* exam, as our goal was to examine whether the students understand and are able to apply the core principles of logic methods, rather than check they memory.

The *learning outcomes* of this course are that on completion of this course students

(1) will be able to state the basic principles of logic applied in Engineering, and
(2) will experience practical applications of these principles.

The general structure of the course is presented on Fig. 1. ALE is partially based on the book of Schöning [20], which introduces the notions and methods of formal logic from a computer science standpoint, as well as on the book of Russell and Norvig [19]. We also recommended our students to read the textbook of Harrison [11], which focuses on practical application of logic and automated reasoning [11], as well as a number of other books on logic and (semi-)automated theorem proving [4,10,14].

---

[1] http://www4.in.tum.de/lehre/vorlesungen/Logic/WS1213/index.shtml.

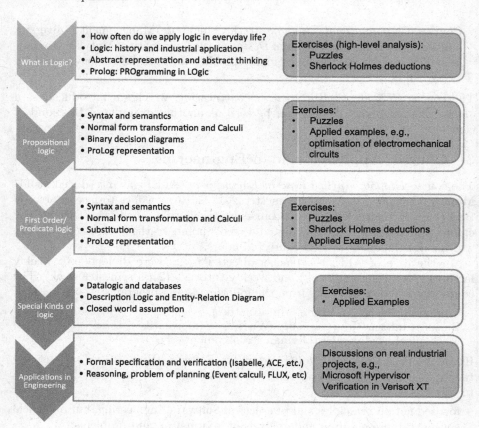

Fig. 1. Structure of the course *Applied logic in Engineering*

To explain the core ideas of Propositional Logic, First Order Logic (FOL) as well as of the special kinds of logics (such as Datalogic, Description logic, etc.), we provided illustrative examples and exercises that were based both

- on application of the logics in Engineering, coming from real industrial problems,
- on puzzles and analysis of situations from famous fiction books and movies, e.g., detective stories like the famous Sherlock Holmes crime stories written by A.C. Doyle.

The second kind of examples and exercises was required to provide more entertainment background for the course and to illustrate that logic is not necessary a very dry subject.

Thus, the course introduces not only the basic principles of Propositional and First Order logic, but also presents the applied nature of logic and FMs, such as

- Reasoning and Planning problems;
- Formal Specifications/models for precise description of systems and requirements and analysis of systems;
- Verification: Proving that a system fulfils its requirements, and that a new version of a system is a refinement of the previous version;
- Theorem proving/Model checking allowing (semi-)automated proofs;
- Design/optimization of digital circuits: Claude Shannon has shown that propositional logic can be used to describe and optimize electromechanical circuits, [21];
- Formalisation of queries in databases.

We also analysed application of FMs in a number of recent research projects, as well as discussed our experience from large scale industrial projects involving FMs, focusing not only on the efficiency features but also on usability aspects and corresponding feedback from industrial partners [3, 8, 9, 13, 15, 16, 23, 27].

4   Examples and Exercises Provided Within the Course

In this section we discuss examples and exercises introduced within the course.
Example: Propositional Logic. This example we used to explain visually how to solve a suggested by Einstein logical puzzle, also in Propositional Logic. Figure 2 presents the task of the puzzle and the initial set up for the suggested visual framework, where the five blocks represent the houses. In the second step, presented on Fig. 3, we apply all the facts highlight hem with light blue, and visualise the corresponding information. In the next step we generate additional rules based on the facts we already know and solve the puzzle, as shown on Fig. 4.

Exercise: Applied Propositional Logic. *Formalise the following sentences S_1 and S_2 as formulas and then show that they are equivalent:*

- The Briton lives in the red house.
- The Swede keeps dogs as pets.
- The Dane drinks tea.
- Looking from in front, the green house is just to the left of the white house.
- The green house's owner drinks coffee.
- The person who smokes Pall Malls raises birds.
- The owner of the yellow house smokes Dunhill.
- The man living in the center house drinks milk.
- The Norwegian lives in the leftmost house.

- The man who smokes Blends lives next to the one who keeps cats.
- The man who keeps a horse lives next to the man who smokes Dunhill.
- The owner who smokes Bluemasters also drinks beer.
- The German smokes Prince.
- The Norwegian lives next to the blue house.
- The man who smokes Blends has a neighbor who drinks water.

Who owns fish?

???	???	???	???	???
Pet?	Pet?	Pet?	Pet?	Pet?
Drink?	Drink?	Drink?	Drink?	Drink?
Cigarettes?	Cigarettes?	Cigarettes?	Cigarettes?	Cigarettes?

Fig. 2. Solving the Einstein puzzle: Step 1

- The Briton lives in the red house.
- The Swede keeps dogs as pets.
- The Dane drinks tea.
- Looking from in front, the green house is just to the left of the white house.
- The green house's owner drinks coffee.
- The person who smokes Pall Malls raises birds.
- The owner of the yellow house smokes Dunhill.
- The man living in the center house drinks milk.
- The Norwegian lives in the leftmost house.

- The man who smokes Blends lives next to the one who keeps cats.
- The man who keeps a horse lives next to the man who smokes Dunhill.
- The owner who smokes Bluemasters also drinks beer.
- The German smokes Prince.
- The Norwegian lives next to the blue house.
- The man who smokes Blends has a neighbor who drinks water.

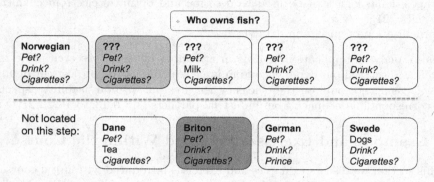

Fig. 3. Solving the Einstein puzzle: Step 2 (Color figure online)

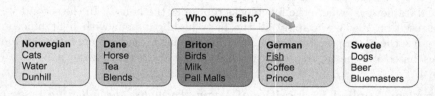

Fig. 4. Solving the Einstein puzzle: Step 3

S_1: *If the communication fails or the battery power gets low, while the system is in sending mode, then the system goes into safety mode.*

S_2: *If the communication fails, then the system must go into safety mode provided that it is in sending mode; and if it is in sending mode, it goes into safety mode, if the battery power gets low.*

To solve this task it is enough to apply Propositional Logic. We define the following four propositions to show that the above sentences are equivalent

$A =$ "communication fails"

$B =$ "battery power gets low"

$C =$ "system is in sending mode"

$D =$ "system gets into safety mode"

Then we will have

$$S_1 : (A \vee B) \wedge C \longrightarrow D$$
$$S_2 \ (A \longrightarrow (C \longrightarrow D)) \wedge (C \longrightarrow (B \longrightarrow D))$$

First step: simplify S_1:

$$(A \vee B) \wedge C \longrightarrow D \equiv$$
$$\neg((A \vee B) \wedge C) \vee D \equiv$$
$$\neg(A \vee B) \vee \neg C \vee D \equiv$$
$$(\neg A \wedge \neg B) \vee \neg C \vee D$$

Second step: simplify S_1:

$$(A \longrightarrow (C \longrightarrow D)) \wedge (C \longrightarrow (B \longrightarrow D)) \equiv$$
$$(\neg A \vee \neg C \vee D) \wedge (\neg C \vee \neg B \vee D) \equiv$$
$$\neg A \wedge (\neg C \vee \neg B \vee D) \vee \neg C \wedge (\neg C \vee \neg B \vee D) \vee D \wedge (\neg C \vee \neg B \vee D) \equiv$$
$$(\neg A \wedge \neg C) \vee (\neg A \wedge \neg B) \vee (\neg A \wedge D) \vee (\neg C) \vee (\neg C \wedge \neg B) \vee (\neg C \wedge D)$$
$$\vee (D \wedge \neg C) \vee (D \wedge \neg B) \vee (D) \equiv$$
$$(\neg A \wedge \neg C) \vee (\neg A \wedge \neg B) \vee (\neg A \wedge D) \vee (\neg C) \vee (\neg C \wedge \neg B) \vee (\neg C \wedge D)$$
$$\vee (D \wedge \neg C) \vee (D \wedge \neg B) \vee (D) \equiv$$
$$(\neg A \wedge \neg B) \vee \neg C \vee D$$

This proves semantical equivalence of the formulas. $\qquad\square$

Example: First Order Logic. Figure 5 provides an example we used to explain the idea of formal notation for syllogisms.

Exercise: Applied First Order Logic. *Formalize the following sentences as formulas and then show that they are equivalent:*

(1) *The following property holds not for all time intervals: If the system gets a signal from its sensors that there is no communication at a time interval t or that the battery power gets low at a time interval t, and exists an information package that have to be send, then at a time interval t there is an information package in the temporal buffer.*

(2) *At some time interval t the following holds for all information packages: there is an information package that have to be send, but there is no information package in the temporal buffer, and the system gets a signal from its sensors that there is no communication or that the battery power gets low.*

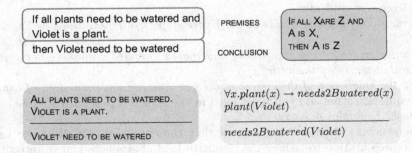

Fig. 5. Visual explanation of formal notation: Introduction to the Syllogisms

One possible solution:

Formalisation of the sentences would be

(1) $\neg \forall t. ((C(t) \vee B(t)) \wedge S(t) \rightarrow T(t))$ and

(2) $\exists t. (S(t) \wedge \neg T(t) \wedge (C(t) \vee B(t)))$.

Proof that both formulas are equal:

$$\neg \forall t. ((C(t) \vee B(t)) \wedge S(t) \rightarrow T(t))$$
$$\equiv \exists t. \neg ((C(t) \vee B(t)) \wedge S(t) \rightarrow T(t))$$
$$\equiv \exists t. \neg (\neg ((C(t) \vee B(t)) \wedge S(t)) \vee T(t))$$
$$\equiv \exists t. (((C(t) \vee B(t)) \wedge S(t)) \wedge \neg T(t))$$
$$\equiv \exists t. (S(t) \wedge \neg T(t) \wedge (C(t) \vee B(t)))$$

Another possible solution:

Formalization of (1): $\neg \forall t. \exists p. ((C(t) \vee B(t)) \wedge S(p,t) \rightarrow T(p,t))$

Formalization of (2): $\exists t. \forall p. (S(p,t) \wedge \neg T(p,t) \wedge (C(t) \vee B(t)))$

Proof that both formulas are equal:

$$\exists t. \forall p. (S(p,t) \wedge \neg T(p,t) \wedge (C(t) \vee B(t)))$$
$$\equiv \neg \forall t. \neg (\forall p. (S(p,t) \wedge \neg T(p,t) \wedge (C(t) \vee B(t))))$$
$$\equiv \neg \forall t. (\exists p. \neg (S(p,t) \wedge \neg T(p,t) \wedge (C(t) \vee B(t))))$$
$$\equiv \neg \forall t. (\exists p. (\neg S(p,t) \vee T(p,t) \vee \neg (C(t) \vee B(t))))$$
$$\equiv \neg \forall t. (\exists p. (\neg S(p,t) \vee \neg (C(t) \vee B(t)) \vee T(p,t)))$$
$$\equiv \neg \forall t. (\exists p. (\neg (S(p,t) \wedge (C(t) \vee B(t))) \vee T(p,t)))$$
$$\equiv \neg \forall t. (\exists p. ((S(p,t) \wedge (C(t) \vee B(t))) \rightarrow T(p,t))) \qquad \square$$

5   Evaluation and Conclusions

This paper presents an overview of common challenges in teaching of formal methods and suggested solutions to them, based on our experiences from the course *Applied Logic in Engineering* taught at TU Munich, Germany.

The course was introduced as an elective course on Bachelor and Master levels and attracted 20 students. As per course evaluation [1], the majority of the students agreed that the provided examples were very helpful, and the learning amount and the amount of the material provided within the course were "exactly right" (German, "genau richting"). For example, we received the following comments from our students:

"Structured logically and builds up stuff part by part; nice additions as Sherlock video";

"The topic presented are interesting and indeed "applied", unlike other logical courses that are more theoretic";

"I liked the small size of the course and I got a deeper understanding of logic".

To the question what did you most liked in the course, the students replied

"Sherlock, Examples during lecture".

The students' feedback highlighted that the examples (for which we used visual representation to reduce the cognitive load of students and to introduce the corresponding ideas more understandable) as well as using puzzles and situations from famous fiction books and movies, not only helps to understand the application of logic and FMs to real world problems, but also makes the leaning experience more interesting and helps to overcome the prejustice that the FMs are *boring per default*. Another point that we took out from the evaluation report is that it would be beneficial for this kind of courses to have a relatively small size of class, which allows teachers to approach each student individually.

References

1. Auswertung zur Veranstaltung Applied Logic in Engineering. TU Munich (2013)
2. Bjørner, D., Havelund, K.: 40 years of formal methods. In: Jones, C., Pihlajasaari, P., Sun, J. (eds.) FM 2014. LNCS, vol. 8442, pp. 42–61. Springer, Heidelberg (2014). doi:10.1007/978-3-319-06410-9_4
3. Botaschanjan, J., Broy, M., Gruler, A., Harhurin, A., Knapp, S., Kof, L., Paul, W., Spichkova, M.: On the correctness of upper layers of automotive systems. Formal Aspects Comput. **20**(6), 637–662 (2008)
4. Büning, H.K., Lettmann, T.: Aussagenlogik: Deduktion und Algorithmen. Teubner (1994)
5. Crocker, D.: Teaching formal methods with perfect developer. In: Teaching Formal Methods: Practice and Experience, Electronic Workshops in Computing (2006)
6. Curzon, P., McOwan, P.W.: Teaching formal methods using magic tricks. In: Fun with Formal Methods: Workshop at the 25th International Conference on Computer Aided Verification (2013)
7. Feast, V., Bretag, T.: Responding to crises in transnational education: new challenges for higher education. High. Educ. Res. Dev. **24**(1), 63–78 (2005)
8. Feilkas, M., Fleischmann, A., Hölzl, F., Pfaller, C., Rittmann, S., Scheidemann, K., Spichkova, M., Trachtenherz, D.: A top-down methodology for the development of automotive software. Technical report TUM-I0902, TU München (2009)
9. Feilkas, M., Hölzl, F., Pfaller, C., Rittmann, S., Schätz, B., Schwitzer, W., Sitou, W., Spichkova, M., Trachtenherz, D.: A refined top-down methodology for the development of automotive software systems - the KeylessEntry-system case study. Technical report TUM-I1103, TU München (2011)
10. Fitting, M.: First-Order Logic and Automated Theorem Proving. Springer, New York (1996)
11. Harrison, J.: Handbook of Practical Logic and Automated Reasoning. Cambridge University Press, New York (2009)
12. Hoare, L.: Swimming in the deep end: transnational teaching as culture learning? High. Educ. Res. Dev. **32**(4), 561–574 (2013)
13. Hölzl, F., Spichkova, M., Trachtenherz, D.: Autofocus tool chain. Technical report TUM-I1021, TU München (2010)
14. Huth, M., Ryan, M.: Logic in Computer Science. Cambridge University Press, New York (2004)
15. Kühnel, C., Spichkova, M.: FlexRay und FTCom: Formale Spezifikation in FOCUS. Technical report TUM-I0601, TU München (2006)
16. Kühnel, C., Spichkova, M.: Upcoming automotive standards for fault-tolerant communication: FlexRay and OSEKtime FTCom. In: Proceedings of EFTS 2006 International Workshop on Engineering of Fault Tolerant Systems (2006)
17. Noble, J., Pearce, D.J., Groves, L.: Introducing alloy in a software modelling course. In: ETAPS 2008 Workshop on Formal Methods in Computer Science Education (FORMED) (2008)

18. Richardson, F.C., Suinn, R.M.: The mathematics anxiety rating scale: psychometric data. J. Couns. Psychol. **19**(6), 551 (1972)
19. Russell, S., Norvig, P.: Artificial Intelligence: A Modern Approach. Prentice Hall, Upper Saddle River (2009)
20. Schöning, U.: Logic for Computer Scienctists. Modern Birkäuser Classics, Secaucus (1989)
21. Shannon, C.E.: A symbolic analysis of relay and switching circuits. Master's thesis (1937)
22. Sherman, B.F., Wither, D.P.: Mathematics anxiety and mathematics achievement. Math. Educ. Res. J. **15**(2), 138–150 (2003)
23. Spichkova, M.: FlexRay: Verification of the FOCUS specification in Isabelle/HOL. A Case Study. Technical report TUM-I0602, TU München (2006)
24. Spichkova, M.: Human factors of formal methods. In: IADIS Interfaces and Human Computer Interaction 2012 (IHCI 2012) (2012)
25. Spichkova, M.: Design of formal languages and interfaces: "formal" does not mean "unreadable". In: Emerging Research and Trends in Interactivity and the Human-Computer Interface. IGI Global (2013)
26. Spichkova, M.: Applied logic in engineering. CoRR, abs/1602.05170 (2016)
27. Spichkova, M., Hölzl, F., Trachtenherz, D.: Verified system development with the autofocus tool chain. In: 2nd Workshop on Formal Methods in the Development of Software (WS-FMDS 2012), vol. 86, pp. 17–24 (2012)
28. Spichkova, M., Zamansky, A.: Teaching formal methods for software engineering. In: 11th International Conference on Evaluation of Novel Approaches to Software Engineering (ENASE) (2016)
29. Tavolato, P., Vogt, F.: Integrating formal methods into computer science curricula at a university of applied sciences. In: TLA+ Workshop at the 18th International Symposium on Formal Methods (2012)
30. Wang, S., Yilmaz, L.: A strategy and tool support to motivate the study of formal methods in undergraduate software design and modeling courses. Int. J. Eng. Educ. **22**(2), 407–418 (2006)
31. Wang, Z., Hart, S.A., Kovas, Y., Lukowski, S., Soden, B., Thompson, L.A., Plomin, R., McLoughlin, G., Bartlett, C.W., Lyons, I.M., Petrill, S.A.: Who is afraid of math? Two sources of genetic variance for mathematical anxiety. J. Child Psychol. Psychiatry **55**(9), 1056–1064 (2014)
32. Wing, J.M.: Weaving formal methods into the undergraduate curriculum. In: Proceedings of Algebraic Methodology and Software Technology, pp. 2–7 (2000)
33. Wing, J.M.: Computational thinking. Commun. ACM **49**(3), 33–35 (2006)
34. Zamansky, A., Farchi, E.: Exploring the role of logic and formal methods in information systems education. In: Proceedings of the 2nd Human-Oriented Formal Methods workshop (HOFM) (2015)
35. Zamansky, A., Farchi, E.: Teaching logic to information systems students: challenges and opportunities. In: Proceedings of the 4th International Conference on Tools for Teaching Logic (TTL) (2015)

Formal Model-Based Development in Industrial Automation with Reactive Blocks

Peter Herrmann[1(✉)] and Jan Olaf Blech[2]

[1] NTNU, Trondheim, Norway
herrmann@item.ntnu.no
[2] RMIT University, Melbourne, Australia
janolaf.blech@rmit.edu.au

Abstract. The use of standard IT equipment to control machines is becoming increasingly popular mostly due to lower costs. Further, trends and initiatives such as Industry 4.0 and smart factories accelerate the use of standard IT components by demanding interconnected controllers and factory equipment communicating with internet services. This development offers new possibilities to use existing software frameworks and software architectural approaches as well as development standards in industrial automation. The formal methods-based support, that already exists for standard IT platforms, can now be applied to industrial control devices as well. In this paper, we look into the application of our Reactive Blocks framework for industrial automation. Reactive Blocks comes with a well established formal semantics and verification approaches tied to it. We demonstrate the advantages of our methodology with an example.

1 Introduction

Industrial automation devices have traditionally been programmed by engineers using standards such as IEC 61131–3 [17] and its derivatives. We see, however, novel trends according to which this well established procedure will change in the near future. One trend is the recent convergence of PC hardware and Programmable Logic Controllers (PLC) with respect to software development. In the past, industrial automation devices mostly relied on techniques and standards that were developed independently from PC hardware and IT technologies. Examples include the IEC 61131 standard for PLC and PROFIBUS [2] on the network technology side. In recent years, some PLC vendors started to integrate standard PC processors. Moreover, smart single-board computers like the Raspberry Pi [30] came into the market offering operating systems close to those of ordinary PCs. These boards are cheap but powerful enough to carry out control functions. For instance, we use Raspberry Pi-based devices to drive a bottling plant deployed in the RMIT's advanced manufacturing precinct [13]. On the network technology side, the Ethernet has gained entry into the world of industrial automation.

Another trend is the growing interconnectivity of controllers. PLCs communicate now with each other and with other external devices and services, not

© Springer International Publishing AG 2016
P. Milazzo et al. (Eds.): STAF 2016, LNCS 9946, pp. 253–261, 2016.
DOI: 10.1007/978-3-319-50230-4_19

just for synchronization and basic control via the Supervisory Control and Data Acquisition (SCADA) level, but also to support maintenance and new production processes making a higher degree of customization possible. The growing interconnectivity also allows for the utilization of novel technologies like cloud computing. For example, services analyzing data streams to determine maintenance intervals are already in place (see, e.g., ABB ServicePort [6]). Initiatives like Industry 4.0 [18] foster these trends as they propose interconnected plants run by controllers coordinating itself using internet-based services.

In our opinion, these trends in industrial automation will have growing relevance also with respect to the application of human-oriented formal methods. In particular, based on the more extended use of standard IT and PC technology, development paradigms from computer science can be applied in this area. This includes the use of model-based development as well as formal specification and verification technologies. Since many engineers have no in-depth experience with the application of the formal methods used in software development, we have to find a way lessening the burden of applying the formalisms in practice. One promising idea is Rushby's concept of "Disappearing Formal Methods" [27] that proposes the wrapping of formal techniques into tools such that they are easy to use. Our model-based engineering technique Reactive Blocks [22] supports Rushby's concept. In this article, we propose its use for the development of control software in industrial automation.

2   Reactive Blocks in Industrial Automation

Reactive Blocks [3,22] is a model-driven engineering technique for reactive Java-based systems. It uses UML activity and state machine diagrams [25] to model systems. Since these diagram types are innately not provided with formal semantics, we defined one ourselves. In [23], we defined an initial formal semantics for

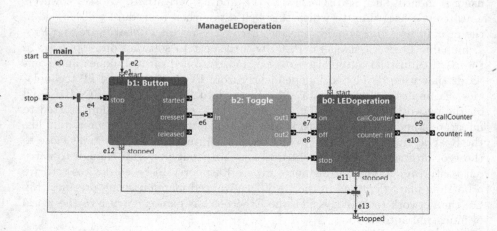

Fig. 1. The UML activity of building block *ManageLEDoperation*.

an early version of the tool based on cTLA [15], a variant of Lamport's Temporal Logic of Actions (TLA) [24]. Becoming more experienced with the tool, we later defined the so-called *reactive semantics* [20]. Since UML activities are basically graphs, we based it on rules in traditional graph theory.

One of the features of Reactive Blocks is that sub-functionality can be specified separately from each other in so-called *building blocks*. That enables us to create models of recurring sub-functionality once and to reuse them in several engineering projects. The reuse is further facilitated by providing each building block with an *External State Machine (ESM)* [19]. This is a behavioral interface allowing us to combine a building block correctly with its environment without having to completely understand its functionality.

A UML activity is used to model the behavior of a building block. The activity depicted in Fig. 1 contains three inner building blocks of type *Button*, *Toggle* and *LEDoperation* that all embed certain sub-functionality. The reactive semantics of the activities resembles Petri nets and corresponds to the flow of tokens via the edges towards the nodes. In this way, control and data flows are nicely visualized and can also be animated by the tool-set. Further, activities may contain operations that represent Java methods executed when a token passes the corresponding node. The flows are run-to-completion (see [20]). That means, a flow passes all nodes on its way in the same atomic step until it reaches one that models the need to wait for a certain stimulus (i.e., a timeout or an external event).

To connect the flows of an activity containing an inner block and the one specifying the behavior of this block, we use so-called parameter nodes and pins. Parameter nodes are the little arrows at the outer edge of the activity. In the node representing an inner building block in an activity, the parameter nodes are shown as pins. For instance, the pins of the inner building block *LEDoperation* in Fig. 1 are identical to the parameter nodes in its activity (see Fig. 2). A flow reaching a pin of an inner building block will continue in the activity of this block from the corresponding parameter node and vice versa in the same run-to-completion step.

Thanks to the formal reactive semantics, we could build a model checker into the tool-set [22] enabling the verification that the UML models fulfill various correctness properties (e.g., the preservation of ESMs by the activities and deadlock freedom). Following the "Disappearing Formal Methods" concept [27] mentioned in the introduction, the formal issues of the verification process are hidden to the user of the tool, and traces towards erroneous states are animated directly on the UML activity graphs. The verification runs scale thanks to the separation of functionality into different building blocks. Moreover, the UML models can be automatically transformed into executable Java code [21].

In our opinion, the features of Reactive Blocks makes it highly suited for the development of control software in industrial automation. The building block concept fits well to the technical engineering disciplines, in which the same physical components are often used in different applications. So, when a particular pump or valve is reused in a certain chemical plant, the building blocks realizing the control of this component may be reused in the software model of the plant as well.

Also the fact that the UML activities visualize control and data flows, is helpful for the industrial automation domain since a typical property of control software is the large number of threads running in parallel. While the coordination of the threads is difficult in classical programming languages, the run-to-completion semantics together with the clearly arranged modelling of the control and data flows facilitates the coordination of the various threads significantly.

Applying the built-in model checker leads to less errors in the generated control software. Moreover, one can couple Reactive Blocks with other analysis tools. Of particular interest for industrial automation is the composition of the tool-set with BeSpaceD [5], a tool suited to verify spatiotemporal properties (see [14]). That allows us to check already on the modelling level that control software guarantees certain cyber-physical properties [16].

Another advantage of the building blocks and the ESMs is that the development of sub-functionality by various teams of experts can be nicely coordinated by embedding the sub-tasks in separate building blocks. Furthermore, the rich set of building block libraries supports the development of technical systems. For instance, the tool-set contains libraries containing various communication protocols as well as blocks supporting the design of Internet of Things applications [3] that play an important role in industrial automation. We show in Sect. 3 that building blocks for control and for communication can be easily combined (see also [12]). This fits nicely with the goals of Industry 4.0 [18].

3   Example

We demonstrate our approach by using a Raspberry Pi equipped with a Berry Clip, i.e., a board provided with six colored LEDs, a buzzer, and a switch. In our toy example, a lucent LED represents a certain production sub-process. To determine the strain of the "plant", the number of changes between the LEDs shall be sent periodically to a remote control center.

We developed the control and communication software for the example by creating three building blocks in Reactive Blocks. Figure 2 depicts the UML activity describing the behavior of the building block *LEDoperation* that realizes the operation of the LEDs on the Berry Clip. The inner block of type *LEDs* contains the functionality to switch on and off the LEDs of the Berry Clip while *TimerPeriodic* realizes a recurring timer that sends flows in even intervals (three seconds in our example).

The ESM of building block *LEDoperation* is shown in Fig. 3. The block is started by a flow through parameter node start which is forwarded to the pin of the same name at the inner block *LEDs*. Thereafter, the ESM is in state *passive*. In this state, a flow through the parameter nodes callCounter and counter is allowed. It can be used by the environment of the building block to retrieve the number of LED changes that are stored in the variable counter.

The rotative lighting of the LEDs is started by a flow through the parameter node on bringing the ESM into state *active*. As shown in the activity, the flow

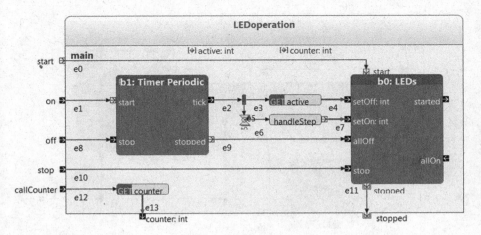

Fig. 2. The UML activity of building block *LEDoperation*.

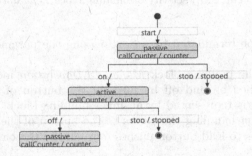

Fig. 3. The ESM of building block *LEDoperation*.

starts the periodic timer. A timeout leads to a flow through pin `tick` of block *TimerPeriodic*. This flow is forked into two flows. One flow retrieves the value of the LED currently switched on, that is stored in variable `active`, and forwards it to pin `setOff` of building block *LEDs*. Thus, the currently lucent LED is switched off. The other flow reaches a flow breaker. That is a special timer without a dedicated duration used to separate a flow into different run-to-completion steps. In our case, we use the flow breaker since the ESM of block *LEDs* does not accept flows through its pins `setOff` and `setOn` in the same run-to-completion step. The flow leaving the flow breaker reaches operation *handleStep* that represents a Java method determining the next LED to switch on, sets the selected value in variable `active` and increments the counter. After terminating the method, the flow forwards to pin `setOn` of building block *LEDs* such that the selected LED is switched on. A flow through parameter node `off` stops the lighting of the LEDs by terminating the periodic timer and switching all LEDs off. The

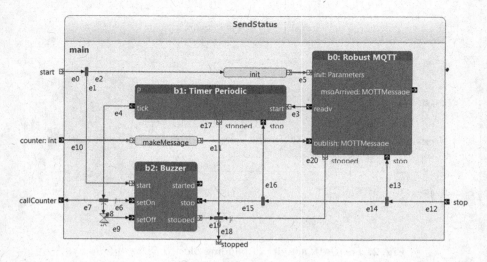

Fig. 4. The UML activity of building block *SendStatus*.

building block can be terminated by a flow passing the parameter nodes `stop` and `stopped`.

Figure 1 shows the building block *ManageLEDoperation* modeling that the LEDs can be switched on and off by pushing the button of the Berry Clip. Here, *LEDoperation* is represented by an inner building block. Further, we use building block *Button* handling the access to the button of the Berry Clip and *Toggle* that allows us to lead button pushes mutually to the `on` and `off` pins of *LEDoperation*.

The transmission of the number of LED changes is realized by building block *SendStatus* depicted in Fig. 4. We use the popular MQTT protocol, the functionality of which is handled by the inner block *RobustMQTT*. Further, *SendStatus* uses another periodic timer initiating a transmission every 30 s. A timeout leads to a retrieval of the current counter value by a flow through parameter node `callCounter`. The value is received via parameter node `counter` that is forwarded to operation *makeMessage*. The corresponding Java method creates an object containing the MQTT message format that is forwarded to the pin `publish` of block *RobustMQTT* triggering the transmission of the counter value. Moreover, the building block contains the inner block *Buzzer* that is used to give a short audio signal using the buzzer of the Berry Clip in order to show that the status value was sent.

The activity of the overall system model is quite simple. It consists of instances of building blocks *ManageLEDoperation* and *SendStatus*, initial triggers for these blocks, and edges connecting their pins `callCounter` resp. `counter`. We automatically transformed this system description into a runnable JAR file that can be directly executed on the Raspberry Pi. Moreover, we created another simple system model enabling us to receive and print out MQTT messages at a remote control station.

The toy example substantiates two of the advantages named in Sect. 2. One is reusability. The complex functionality, i.e., the activation of the various units of the Berry Clip as well as the transmission via MQTT had not to be programmed manually but could be reused by simply adding already existing building blocks. Thus, the only creative task was the link of the various building blocks. Therefore the models for the Berry Clip controller and the remote station could be created by one of the authors within less than an hour. The undertaking was supported by the model checker built into Reactive Blocks since we could easily find out if all the blocks were indeed correctly coupled preserving their ESMs.

The other advantage affirmed by the example is the coordination of development teams since one can hand the creation of the building blocks *LEDoperation* and *ManageLEDoperation* over to a team of control software experts and *SendStatus* to people with in-depth knowledge about communication. Also here the model checker is of great help since it guarantees that the teams realize the ESM-based behavioral interface descriptions of the particular blocks correctly such that the results of their work can be seamlessly coupled.

4   Related Work

Formal specification of Programmable Logic Controllers (PLC) is not new but most work is based on PLC specific programming and specification techniques (see, e.g., [26, 29]). Summaries of earlier approaches to use formal methods for the specification and verification of PLC programs is given in [1, 9].

One of the main disadvantages of the IEC standard 61131 [17] is that it leaves some implementation and semantics aspects open to the PLC vendors. This makes formal specification and verification work difficult, but it also hinders cross platform development efforts. Some approaches such as the UNICOS toolset [10] were developed to address these shortcomings. A comprehensive model checking approach for IEC 61131–3 programs in connection with UNICOS can be found in [8]. A transformation from UML into IEC 61131 has been studied in [31]. In [11], UML is used to model control software and analysis patterns together with cTLA (see [15]) to verify their correctness. We established Coq descriptions of IEC 61131–3 programs (see [4]) to facilitate human directed verification of PLC programs (see also [7]). Another formal approach based on IEC 61499 was proposed in [32]. Formal methods are also used to analyze Ethernet-based real-time communication [28].

5   Conclusion

In this paper, we motivated that systems bridging control automation with the classical IT world will become more mainstream in the close future. That opens the door for the application of model-based and formal methods in this application domain as well. In particular, we propose the use of Reactive Blocks for control applications in the industrial automation domain. We believe that, due to the easy use of the UML diagrams for modeling and the model checker for analysis, it facilitates the application of formal methods in the practical development of control system software also by users that are not experts in formal techniques. We exemplified our approach by discussing the development of a small Raspberry Pi-based system that, in spite of its size, is sufficient to point out some of the expected advantages.

References

1. Bauer, N., Engell, S., Huuck, R., Lohmann, S., Lukoschus, B., Remelhe, M., Stursberg, O.: Verification of PLC programs given as sequential function charts. In: Ehrig, H., Damm, W., Desel, J., Große-Rhode, M., Reif, W., Schnieder, E., Westkämper, E. (eds.) Integration of Software Specification Techniques for Applications in Engineering. LNCS, vol. 3147, pp. 517–540. Springer, Heidelberg (2004). doi:10.1007/978-3-540-27863-4_28

2. Bender, K., Katz, M.: PROFIBUS: der Feldbus für die Automation. Hanser (1990)

3. Bitreactive, A.S.: Reactive Blocks. www.bitreactive.com. Accessed 28 Jan 2016

4. Blech, J.O., Ould Biha, S.: Verification of PLC properties based on formal semantics in Coq. In: Barthe, G., Pardo, A., Schneider, G. (eds.) SEFM 2011. LNCS, vol. 7041, pp. 58–73. Springer, Heidelberg (2011). doi:10.1007/978-3-642-24690-6_6

5. Blech, J.O., Schmidt, H.: BeSpaceD: towards a tool framework and methodology for the specification and verification of spatial behavior of distributed software component systems. Technical report 1404.3537. arXiv.org (2014)

6. Boo, P.: A service tool grows up - ABB ServicePort. In: ABB Review (2015)

7. Canet, G., Couffin, S., Lesage, J.J., Petit, A., Schnoebelen, P.: Towards the automatic verification of PLC programs written in instruction list. In: Systems, Man, and Cybernetics, vol. 4, pp. 2449–2454. IEEE (2000)

8. Fernandez Adiego, B., Darvas, D., Vinuela, E.B., Tournier, J.C., Bliudze, S., Blech, J.O., Gonzalez Suarez, V.M.: Applying model checking to industrial-sized PLC programs. IEEE Trans. Ind. Inform. 11(6), 1400–1410 (2015)

9. Frey, G., Litz, L.: Formal methods in PLC programming. In: Systems, Man, and Cybernetics, vol. 4, pp. 2431–2436. IEEE (2000)

10. Gayet, P., Barillere, R.: UNICOS a framework to build industry like control systems: principles and methodology. In: International Conference on Accelerator and Large Experimental Physics Control Systems, Genève, Suisse (2005)

11. Graw, G.: Korrekte Steuerungssoftware. Dissertation, Technische Universität Dortmund (2010) (in German)

12. Han, F., Blech, J.O., Herrmann, P., Schmidt, H.: Model-based engineering and analysis of space-aware systems communicating via IEEE 802.11. In: 39th Annual International Computers, Software and Applications Conference (COMPSAC), pp. 638–646. IEEE Computer (2015)

13. Harland, J., Blech, J.O., Peake, I., Trodd, L.: Formal behavioural models to facilitate distributed development and commissioning in industrial automation. In: Evaluation of Novel Approaches to Software Engineering, COLAFORM Track (2016)

14. Herrmann, P., Blech, J.O., Han, F., Schmidt, H.: A model-based toolchain to verify spatial behavior of cyber-physical systems. Int. J. Web Serv. Res. (IJWSR) 13(1), 40–52 (2016)

15. Herrmann, P., Krumm, H.: A framework for modeling transfer protocols. Comput. Netw. 34(2), 317–337 (2000)

16. Hordvik, S., Øseth, K., Blech, J.O., Herrmann, P.: A methodology for model-based development and safety analysis of transport systems. In: 11th International Conference on Evaluation of Novel Approaches to Software Engineering (ENASE) (2016)

17. IEC: IEC Standard IEC 61161-3. Programmable Controllers – Programming Languages, 2.0 edn. (01 2003)

18. Kagermann, H., Wahlster, W., Helbig, J.: Umsetzungsempfehlungen für das Zukunftsprojekt Industrie 4.0. Abschlussbericht des Arbeitskreises Industrie 4, 5 (2013) (in German)

19. Kraemer, F.A., Herrmann, P.: Automated encapsulation of UML activities for incremental development and verification. In: Schürr, A., Selic, B. (eds.) MODELS 2009. LNCS, vol. 5795, pp. 571–585. Springer, Heidelberg (2009). doi:10.1007/978-3-642-04425-0_44

20. Kraemer, F.A., Herrmann, P.: Reactive semantics for distributed UML activities. In: Hatcliff, J., Zucca, E. (eds.) FMOODS/FORTE -2010. LNCS, vol. 6117, pp. 17–31. Springer, Heidelberg (2010). doi:10.1007/978-3-642-13464-7_3

21. Kraemer, F.A., Herrmann, P., Bræk, R.: Aligning UML 2.0 state machines and temporal logic for the efficient execution of services. In: Meersman, R., Tari, Z. (eds.) OTM 2006. LNCS, vol. 4276, pp. 1613–1632. Springer, Heidelberg (2006). doi:10.1007/11914952_41

22. Kraemer, F.A., Slåtten, V., Herrmann, P.: Tool support for the rapid composition, analysis and implementation of reactive services. J. Syst. Softw. 82(12), 2068–2080 (2009)

23. Kraemer, F.A., Herrmann, P.: formalizing collaboration-oriented service specifications using temporal logic. In: Networking and Electronic Commerce Research Conference (NAEC), pp. 194–220. ATSMA, Riva del Garda, October 2007

24. Lamport, L.: Specifying Systems: The TLA$^+$ Language and Tools for Hardware and Software Engineers. Pearson Education Inc, London (2002)

25. Object Management Group: OMG Unified Modeling LanguageTM (OMG UML), Superstructure – Version 2.4.1 (2011). www.omg.org/spec/UML/2.4.1/Superstructure/PDF/. Accessed 28 Jan 2016

26. Rausch, M., Krogh, B.H.: Formal verification of PLC programs. In: American Control Conference, vol. 1, pp. 234–238. IEEE (1998)

27. Rushby, J.: Disappearing formal methods. In: High-Assurance Systems Engineering Symposium, pp. 95–96. ACM. Albuquerque (2000)

28. Steiner, W., Dutertre, B.: SMT-Based formal verification of a *TTEthernet* synchronization function. In: Kowalewski, S., Roveri, M. (eds.) FMICS 2010. LNCS, vol. 6371, pp. 148–163. Springer, Heidelberg (2010). doi:10.1007/978-3-642-15898-8_10

29. Stursberg, O., Kowalewski, S., Hoffmann, I., Preußig, J.: Comparing timed and hybrid automata as approximations of continuous systems. In: Antsaklis, P., Kohn, W., Nerode, A., Sastry, S. (eds.) HS 1996. LNCS, vol. 1273, pp. 361–377. Springer, Heidelberg (1997). doi:10.1007/BFb0031569

30. Upton, E., Halfacree, G.: Raspberry Pi User Guide. Wiley, Cambridge (2014)

31. Vogel-Heuser, B., Witsch, D., Katzke, U.: Automatic code generation from a UML model to IEC 61131-3 and system configuration tools. In: International Conference on Control and Automation (ICCA), vol. 2, pp. 1034–1039. IEEE (2005)

32. Vyatkin, V., Hanisch. H.M.: Formal modeling and verification in the software engineering framework of IEC 61499: a way to self-verifying systems. In: Emerging Technologies and Factory Automation (ETFA), vol. 2. IEEE Computer (2001)

MELO

Computational Design Synthesis
Using Model-Driven Engineering
and Constraint Programming

Raphael Chenouard[1]([✉]), Chris Hartmann[1,2], Alain Bernard[1],
and Emmanuel Mermoz[2]

[1] Ecole Centrale de Nantes, IRCCyN UMR CNRS 6597, 1 Rue de la No BP 92101,
44321 Nantes Cedex 3, France
`{raphael.chenouard,alain.bernard}@irccyn.ec-nantes.fr`,
`chris.hartmann@airbus.com`
[2] Airbus Helicopters, Aéroport de Marseille Provence, 13700 Marignane, France
`emmanuel.mermoz@airbus.com`

Abstract. This paper introduces a new process for computational
design synthesis. It starts from functional requirements to generate one
or more topologies of components. This process is implemented using
Model-Driven Engineering techniques and Constraint Programming solving capabilities. Model transformations are used to transform functions
and available components to a CSP. This problem is solved with a CSP
solver, which solutions are transformed to topological architectures. The
process is successfully applied on the design synthesis of an autonomous
generator. It produces about 60 relevant solutions from which we found
some existing product architectures.

1 Introduction

Design synthesis is a hard task in the design process of a product. It is one step
within the preliminary design phase of a system of interest, when considering
a common design process [10]. The design synthesis task ends-up with a set
of architectures related to a functional decomposition derived from the stakeholders' needs. The modeling of products during preliminary design phases is
generally based on three aspects: function, behavior and structure [4].

Some previous works in design synthesis are based on graph grammars and
rules to build graphs corresponding to relevant topologies of components [6].
These rules are based on well-known principles of solutions or functional decomposition in a given context. The major advantages of this kind of approaches
is that it generates solutions that fit good practices and designer experience.
However, the search space of possible solutions may be only partially explored.
Thus, some innovative and efficient solutions may not be found.

Some recent works mainly in the field of embedded systems investigate this
kind of problem as Design Space Exploration (DSE) [8,16]. These works use
as well model-driven engineering and optimization techniques to automate the

P. Milazzo et al. (Eds.): STAF 2016, LNCS 9946, pp. 265–273, 2016.
DOI: 10.1007/978-3-319-50230-4_20

definition of a valid solution. [8] like [6] uses graph theory to define rules that guide the building of solutions. Some cut-off criteria are used to improve the exploration procedure which defines new states by applying graph transformation rules using a selection heuristic. In [16], the aim is to define a more generic framework being able to address various kinds of DSE like resource allocation problems, routing problems or configuration problems. One of the major benefits of this approach is its wide application range and its solver independence. However, the designer has to define a metamodel template used for the exploration. Obviously it makes the exploration easier, but it requires to know in advance the main structure of valid solutions even if their language propose mechanisms to deal with alternatives or optional elements.

Another previous approach also mixed Model-Driven Engineering (MDE) and Constraint Programming (CP) [2] to define a framework for modeling problems independently from a solver like in the Model-Driven Architecture philosophy, but applied here to mathematical problem modeling and solving. This work was also followed by the definition of high level modeling concepts to ease the definition of Constraint Satisfaction Problems (CSPs) in order to represent design problems [3]. The behavioral aspect of a product was the main target, whereas functional and structural concerns were not really investigated.

In this paper, we propose a method based on MDE and CP to compute product topologies from a brief functional description. The generation of topologies must only satisfy the functional requirements. We do not take into account, at this step, the behavioral aspect of a product and we restrict the structure definition to a topological architecture: a set of inter-connected components. Our aim is to explore all possible solutions and provide more innovative architectures that may not be found using classical design processes. Moreover, we do not want to use pre-defined rules or patterns that will always lead to the same kinds of solution principles and exclude possible promising solutions.

The next section introduces the main process and modeling elements regarding designers activities for design synthesis. Section 3 deals with automated solving of a computational design synthesis problem. Section 4 presents an application of the method on a concrete case with a discussion of the proposed process issues, before ending with a conclusion and the future works description.

2   Design Synthesis Automated Process

As said previously, design synthesis aims at generating a product architecture from needs and requirements [1]. In this paper, we focus on the transformation of functional needs to topological architectures, namely networks of components. In most existing work, designers first decompose functions to define a functional architecture [6], then allocate functions to physical components and check feasibility and performances [17].

We propose in this paper to directly compute a topological architecture without investigating too deeply the functional architecture. Our aim is to maximize innovative solutions without using classical design patterns that will always produce the same solution principles. Thus, we just want to use high-level functions

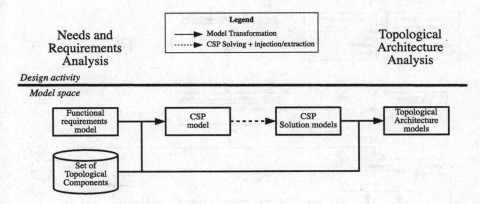

Fig. 1. Main process of the proposed method.

- issuing from stakeholders needs - and a database of allowed topological components (see Fig. 1). These high-level functions define the functional requirements from which we compute satisfying architectures. The following subsections presents the two main metamodels we used as input and output of our automated process implemented in the Eclipse environment with ATL transformation Language [11]. The solving is done using CSP formalism with classical CP solving methods [12]. Computed solutions are transformed into topological architectures and finally designers can analyse and investigate the best one(s) for physical feasibility analysis.

2.1   Functional Requirements Modeling

Since more than a decade, researchers investigate the best manner to represent functions within a design process. The kind of words or verbs to use is out of the scope of this paper. We refer to this previous work [9] to deal with this issue. We want to define the main concepts that are used in the proposed transformation process to state input models like in [7].

Then, a function is defined by a name (that should be an action verb) and a set of flows (oriented or not). Flows can be of three main categories: material, energy and signal. Functions and flow may have some properties defined by a name and a unit (e.g. an electrical flow is often defined with 2 properties: *current* with unit *A* and *voltage* with unit *V*). A model of functional requirements is simply a set of functions and flows instances as shown in Fig. 2.

2.2   Topological Architecture Modeling

We consider that a topological architecture is a network of components, namely a set of inter-connected components. This definition is similar to the definition in the systems engineering domain [14]. Then, a component is mainly defined by its name and its interfaces relating to flows (see Fig. 3). Components are

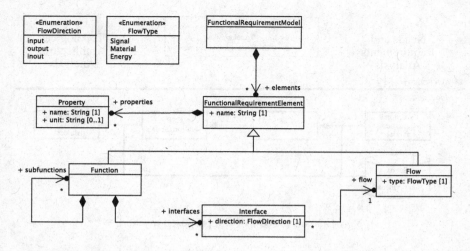

Fig. 2. Metamodel for simplified functional requirements definition.

connected through their interfaces which must be of compatible flows. Some concepts are similar to those defined in the functional requirements metamodel, like flow and property. Components are close to functions, but the function concept relates to main functions, whereas components may integrate additional flows corresponding to induced effects and they are connected to form a network. Moreover, they are defined as generic abstractions of real components like for instance a generic piston engine or an electrical battery.

Components are not considered as composite since we only consider atomic ones. We focus on their connections within an architecture at a given level of decomposition. Following a systemic approach, one can easily define functional requirements for a component and apply recursively this process to define its composition. In fact, we consider that a component only refers to a physical element that interacts with other elements of the same decomposition level. In this way, several components of the same type are just considered as different components with same properties and interfaces definition. For instance, we may have several piston engines with identical characteristics (maximum power, efficiency curve, input/output interfaces), but we consider them as different components in a topological architecture.

3   Solving a Design Synthesis Problem

Passing from functional requirements to a physical architecture is not obvious and cannot be processed using a simple model transformation. We propose in this paper to formulate a graph problem that can be solved using CP solvers. The objective is to find a set of connected nodes (i.e. used component interfaces) and a set of isolated ones (i.e. unused component interfaces) with respect to a set of constraints related to the possible connections.

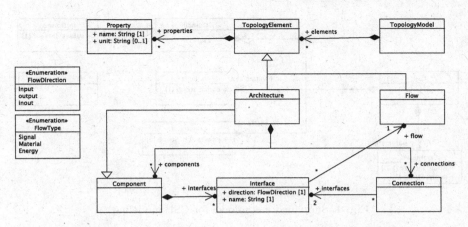

Fig. 3. Metamodel for topological architecture definition.

Given a database of allowed components and the set of functions to satisfy, we generate a mathematical problem which solutions are connected graphs compatible with the following constraints:

1. connections can only exist between compatible interfaces,
2. function flows must be satisfied by input/output interfaces of the whole system,
3. all interfaces of a component must be connected or none of them.

In our CSP, decision variables are the connections between interfaces (components and functional requirements). Thus, we use a matrix of binary variables to represent these decision variables. We can easily pre-compute the compatible and incompatible interfaces of each given interface using its flow description to eliminate some trivial decision variables. Concretely, we compute a matrix of binary values defining allowed and not allowed connections and we set constraints fixing these decision variables if the connection is not allowed. Thus, only the second and third set of constraints are used to restrict the domain of variables during the solving process [15].

We use a simplified metamodel to define CSPs as shown in Fig. 4. A CSP is defined as three sets: domains, variables and constraints. Since we only use integer and binary variables, no additional domain kinds are considered. Constraints are not detailed here, but consist of classical logical and arithmetical expressions [2]. Since we use MiniZinc concrete syntax, we take advantage of some additional high-level constructs like matrices of variables or parameters, forall and if-else constraints or sum function calls [13]. The solving is carried out with the default solver of MiniZinc 2.0.12 distribution.

After the solving phase, we get a set of solutions. A solution is simply a list of couples (value, variable) for which all constraints are satisfied (see Fig. 5). Obviously all variables must have a value to get a complete solution. Since decision variables are connections between interfaces of components, it is easy to identify

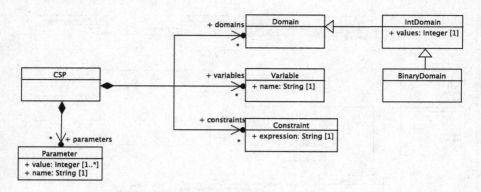

Fig. 4. Simplified metamodel for CSP modeling.

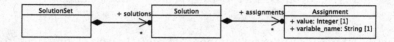

Fig. 5. Metamodel for solution modeling.

which ones are used and how they are linked to each others. A last transformation step is used to generate a topology from the set of used components and a CSP solution.

One drawback of this modeling, is the possible huge number of variables. For n interfaces (from a given set of allowed components) and m interface from input and output functions to satisfy, we have more than $n^2 + m * n$ variables. Nevertheless, we use binary variables and the scaling of CP solving algorithms stays satisfactory.

4   Application and Discussion

We applied our approach to an autonomous generator design synthesis problem. We consider three high-level functions:

- the system must start/stop on demand,
- the system must produce electrical energy,
- the system must follow a voltage order (e.g. between 110 V, 220 V and 370 V),

These three functions imply two input flows: (1) the voltage order and (2) an on/off signal; and only one output flow: electrical energy.

We use a set of 10 allowed components corresponding to 39 interfaces. So, we get $1521 + 117$ binary variables. These components include the environment as a source for air and a sink for (exhaust) gas and thermal energy.

We obtain about 60 solutions. Figure 6 shows one solution that uses all allowed components. A turbine and a piston engine are used to produce the mechanical energy for an alternator which produces electrical energy. An electrical engine is used, since it is required to start the turbine and the piston engine. It produces mechanical energy and it receives the start signal and electrical energy. No electrical energy flow is defined in the input functional requirements, so a battery is used to feed the electrical engine. This battery can also be used to store and deliver the produced electricity. It also may improve the electricity quality as the battery can soften the power demand.

For each solution and the corresponding selected component descriptions, an architectural topology is generated. For printing purposes, we also generate a DOT model processed with the GraphViz compiler [5] as it can be seen on Fig. 6.

We apply our process to an autonomous generator problem. We only consider 10 topological components, but we get more than 60 topologies. All these

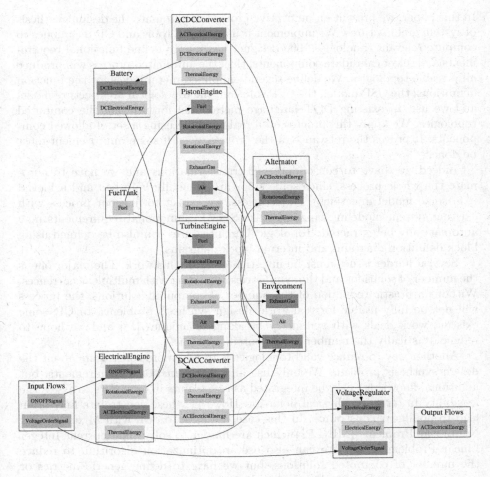

Fig. 6. Example of a solution obtained by the solving process.

solutions are valid in terms of flow connections and we were able to find some architectures used in existing products.

On this example, we do not use several occurrences of components. Some other experiments show that many similar (i.e. symmetrical) solutions are computed and we can expect an exponential rise of the solution number according to the number of allowed components (and their number of interfaces). The next step for the designer is to check the physical feasibility of a topological architecture. Working with so much solutions is not realistic on bigger design synthesis problems even if we can automate many steps, but additional constraints can be easily integrated in our approach to take into account other requirements or performance criteria.

5   Conclusion and Future Work

In this paper, we present an innovative process to automate the design synthesis of system architectures. We implement it using MDE tools and CP techniques to compute relevant topologies. The designer has just to define functional requirements and select candidate components, then the automated process will produce all possible topologies. We define several simplified metamodels for the function definitions, the CSP model, the CSP solution, the topological architecture model and we use an existing DOT language metamodel for printing the computed topologies. We apply this process on a real example using a set of allowed components. It proves the relevance of the process, even if some improvement must be done.

Indeed, we have to consolidate our transformations and we have to automate the whole process, since some steps are manually launched and achieved (e.g. some model injections). Nevertheless, we expect to link our process with existing system modeling languages like SysML. Functional requirements may automatically be extracted. Topological architectures can also be defined using block definition diagrams and internal block diagrams.

Several harder issues must be investigated after this work. The major one is the number of solutions and the symmetries appearing with multiple occurrences. Without a drastic reduction of the number of computed solutions, the process will not be fully usable for real-world design synthesis problems. In CP, some existing work deals with symmetry breaking techniques [18] and we hope to reduce drastically the number of computed solutions.

Another way to reduce valid topologies is to add more constraints about the design synthesis problem. We only use high-level functional requirements, but additional knowledge may be integrated as constraints in our CSPs to assess the feasibility in terms of physical behavior. However, these constraints may often lead to nonlinear constraints. In this case, we have to deal with Mixed-Integer NonLinear Problems (MINLPs) which are harder to solve than current Integer Linear Problem (ILP). We can also use an optimization algorithm to reduce the number of computed solutions, but we have to define generic metrics or performance criteria related to the topological aspects of the computed solutions.

Some additional knowledge may also be integrated to deal with performance criteria coming from needs and requirements.

References

1. Cagan, J., Campbell, M.I., Finger, S., Tomiyama, T.: A framework for computational design synthesis: model and applications. ASME. J. Comput. Inf. Sci. Eng. **5**(3), 171–181 (2005)
2. Chenouard, R., Granvilliers, L., Soto, R.: Model-driven constraint programming. In: Proceedings of the 10th International ACM SIGPLAN Conference on Principles and Practice of Declarative Programming (PPDP), pp. 236–246 (2008)
3. Chenouard, R., Granvilliers, L., Soto, R.: High-level modeling of component-based CSPs. In: Rocha Costa, A.C., Vicari, R.M., Tonidandel, F. (eds.) SBIA 2010. LNCS (LNAI), vol. 6404, pp. 233–242. Springer, Heidelberg (2010). doi:10.1007/978-3-642-16138-4_24
4. Gero, J.S.: Design prototypes: a knowledge representation schema for design. AI Mag. **11**(4), 26 (1990)
5. Graphviz: Graph visualization software. http://www.graphviz.org
6. Helms, B., Shea, K.: Computational synthesis of product architectures based on object-oriented graph grammars. J. Mech. Des. **134**(2), 1–14 (2012)
7. Hartmann, C., Chenouard, R., Mermoz, E., Bernard, A.: Formulation of a design problem for computational pre-design. In: Virtual Concept Workshop (2016)
8. Hegeds, A., Horvth, A., Varr, D.: A model-driven framework for guided space exploration. Autom. Softw. Eng. **22**(3), 399–436 (2015)
9. Hirtz, J., Stone, R.B., McAdams, D.A., Szykman, S., Wood, K.L.: A functional basis for engineering design: reconciling and evolving previous efforts. Res. Eng. Des. **13**(2), 6582 (2002)
10. Pahl, G., Beitz, W.: Engineering Design: A Systematic Approach. Springer, London (1995)
11. Jouault, F., Allilaire, F., Bézivin, J., Kurtev, I.: ATL: a model transformation tool. Sci. Comput. Program. **72**(12), 3139 (2008)
12. Kumar, V.: Algorithms for constraint satisfaction problems: a survey. AI Mag. **13**(1), 32–44 (1992)
13. Nethercote, N., Stuckey, P.J., Becket, R., Brand, S., Duck, G.J., Tack, G.: MiniZinc: towards a standard CP modelling language. In: Bessière, C. (ed.) CP 2007. LNCS, vol. 4741, pp. 529–543. Springer, Heidelberg (2007). doi:10.1007/978-3-540-74970-7_38
14. Rechtin, E.: Systems Architecting: Creating and Building Complex Systems. Prentice Hall, Englewood Cliffs (1991)
15. Rossi, F., Van Beek, P., Walsh, T.: Handbook of Constraint Programming. Elsevier, New York (2006)
16. Saxena, T., Karsai, K.: Towards a generic design space exploration framework. In: IEEE 10th International Conference on Computer and Information Technology (CIT), pp. 1940–1947 (2010)
17. Umeda, Y., Tomiyama, T., Yoshikawa, H.: FBS modeling: modeling scheme of function for conceptual design. In: Proceedings of the 9th International Workshop on Qualitative Reasoning (1995)
18. Walsh, T.: General symmetry breaking constraints. In: Benhamou, F. (ed.) CP 2006. LNCS, vol. 4204, pp. 650–664. Springer, Heidelberg (2006). doi:10.1007/11889205_46

Incremental Consistency Checking
of Heterogeneous Multimodels

Zinovy Diskin[1,2] and Harald König[3(✉)]

[1] NECSIS, McMaster University, Hamilton, Canada
[2] Generative Software Development Lab, University of Waterloo, Waterloo, Canada
zdiskin@uwaterloo.ca
[3] University of Applied Sciences FHDW Hannover, Hannover, Germany
harald.koenig@fhdw.de

Abstract. The local approaches to global consistency checking (GCC) of heterogeneous multimodels strive to reduce the model merging and matching workload within GCC. The paper's contribution to such approaches is a framework allowing the user to do matching incrementally: to build the match required for checking the multimodel w.r.t. a new constraint, the user employs matches produced in previous GCC sessions.

1 Introduction

Modeling a complex system normally results in a *(heterogeneous) multimodel*, i.e., a set of heterogenous (component) models each one conforming to its own metamodel. A fundamental fact about multimodeling is that if even each of the component model perfectly conforms to its metamodel, taken together they may violate some global consistency (GC) rules, i.e., be globally inconsistent [2,7]. An accurate mathematical definition of GC based on model merge was proposed in [9] for the homogeneous case, and extended for the heterogeneous multimodeling in [1]. Moreover, while in [9], the merge-based definition of GC was also used as a practical procedure for GC checking (GCC), in [1] we proposed a more efficient *local* approach, in which consistency is only checked at the overlaps of the component metamodels, which reduces the model merge workload in GCC. The local idea was significantly developed in our paper [4], in which we proposed to check each global constraint c individually, and correspondingly do matching and merging as minimally as required for checking c, i.e., only using those (meta)model elements that affect the validity of c. In this way, not only model merging, but also matching workload is reduced. As model matching is a very expensive procedure, the local approach of [4] provides significant gains for GCC.

The present paper makes a new contribution to the local GCC by reducing the model matching workload even more by doing it incrementally. Suppose that

This work is supported by the Automotive Partnership Canada via the Network on Engineering Complex Software Intensive Systems (NECSIS).

P. Milazzo et al. (Eds.): STAF 2016, LNCS 9946, pp. 274–288, 2016.
DOI: 10.1007/978-3-319-50230-4_21

the user performed GCC of a given multimodel w.r.t. a set of global constraints C, but after that the user needs to make yet another GCC session for a bigger set of constraints $C' \supset C$. We show how the user can effectively perform the new matching procedure required for the latter GCC by using results of the former match rather than building the new match from scratch. In a nutshell, the mathematical framework we develop allows us to transform a constraint increment $C' - C$ into a respective increment in the inter-model correspondence specification.

The paper is structured as follows. Sections 2 and 3 provide the required background: in Sect. 2, we explain the main concepts and challenges of GCC of heterogeneous multimodels with a simple example, and in Sect. 3, we outline our mathematical framework, particularly, the machinery of diagrammatic constraints. Section 4 presents the contribution of the paper—incremental model matching within GCC. In Conclusion we outline directions for future work.

2   Background I: Multimodeling, Global Constraints and Global Consistency

Modeling a complex system normally results in a *multimodel*, i.e., a set of heterogenous models (class diagrams, sequence diagrams, statecharts, activity diagrams, etc.), each one conforming to its own metamodel. For illustrating the main concepts, we will consider a toy example in Fig. 1, which shows two class diagrams $A_{1,2}$, each one conforming to its own metamodel $M_{1,2}$. Metamodel M_1 specifies classes implementing interfaces with operations implemented by methods. Metamodel M_2 says that classes can be abstract, they have attributes, and also implement interfaces. Each of the metamodels has its own constraints, e.g., all directed association are assumed to have multiplicities [0..1] at the target

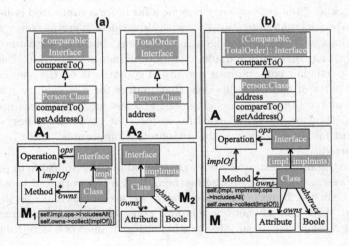

Fig. 1. Sample multimodel

end by default, and the OCL constraint in M_1 prescribes that each implemented operation in a class belongs to this class' implemented interface. In addition, we may want to require that every class owns at least one either method or attribute (or have both). This constraint cannot be declared in any of the two metamodels as M_1 knows nothing about attributes while M_2 knows nothing about methods. Following [1], we call such constraints *inter-metamodel* or *global*; correspondingly, metamodels $M_{1,2}$ and their constraints are called *local*.

What is the metamodel to which a global constraint can be attached? A reasonable answer seems obvious: we need to merge local metamodels into a *global* metamodel M, which in our case can be easily done manually as shown in Fig. 1(b). For this merge, we have silently assumed (1) merging elements of $M_{1,2}$ (i.e., glueing them together) with the same names except two associations *owns*, and (2) merging associations *impl@M_1* and *implmnts@M_2* even though they have different names (elements to be merged as well as their merge are shaded in grey). The merged metamodel M clearly violates two basic constraints of the metametamodel: (C1) different associations from the same metaclass must be named differently, and (C2) any element only has one name. Thus, while local metamodels do conform to the metametamodel, their merge does not, and we say that metamodels $M_{1,2}$ are *globally* inconsistent. Fixing global inconsistency in our case is easy: we need to rename homonymic elements (say, into *owns_a* and *owns_m*), and choose one of the synonymic names (say, *impl*) or generate a new one. These fixes are not shown in Fig. 1(b), but below we will assume them done. After the merged metamodel M is built and fixed, we can attach global constraints to it, and check global consistency of the multimodel (A_1, A_2). For this, we need first to merge the local models into a global model A as shown in Fig. 1(b) (again shaded in grey in $A_{1,2}$ and A_0), and then check validity of global constraints for A. Specifically, we see that the "one method or attribute"-constraint described above is satisfied by model A.

In the toy example above, all manipulations were easy, but in practice, merging and checking global consistency may be a far more complicated issue. Specifically, (meta)model matching (together with subsequent merging) are very expensive operations which need intelligent tool support, but anyway cannot be fully automated. A key observation made in [1] and further developed in [4] is that for checking a particular constraint or a group of constraints C, the user can match only small parts of the (meta)models that matter for C's validity rather than match and merge the entire (meta)models. For instance, in the example above, the "one method or attribute"-constraint does not cover interfaces, such that manual effort for the decision whether to match "Comparable" and "TotalOrder" can be omitted.

To make the simple example above generalizable and applicable to practically interesting cases, we need a precise mathematical framework and tools built on the base of such a framework. Specifically, we need a formal specification of models and their merge, metamodels and constraints, and conformance of a model to a metamodel. A suitable mathematical framework is outlined in the next section.

3   Background II: Mathematical Framework

We assume the reader to be familiar with the concept of (directed multi-)graphs and graph morphisms (mappings), which together constitute the category $\mathbb{G}$ of graphs. We also assume some basic knowledge of categories and functors. In Sect. 3.1, we explain model mappings and spans, and in Sect. 3.2 model merge. Section 3.3 explains the fundamental tool for our considerations — diagrammatic constraints, and Sect. 3.4 explains local checking of global constraints in detail. To make the paper self-contained, we sketched some technical material heavily used in the paper in the appendix.

3.1   Model Mappings and Spans

Models' structures are governed by metamodels. Since many models are graphical, this can be formalized via typed graphs by defining a model A as a triple (M_A, G_A, τ_A) with M_A a graph of *types* or A's *metamodel graph*, G_A a graph specifying model's data, and $\tau_A : G_A \to M_A$ a graph morphism called *typing*, which assigns to each model element its type in the metamodel graph M_A (see, for example, models A_1 and A_2 in Fig. 2). We will often omit subindex $_A$ near model's components. In a homogeneous environment determined by a single metamodel M, all models are typed over M and thus are pairs (G, τ). We will also use the latter notation if M is clear from the context. We will denote the class of all models over M by $\text{MODEL}[M]$.

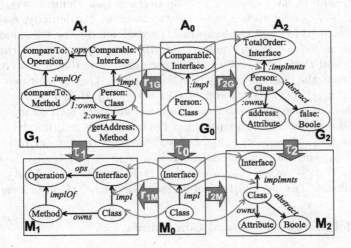

Fig. 2. Model overlapping via spans

The following notion is fundamental for our work with hetero-geneous models. A *model mapping* or *morphism* $r: A \to A'$ is a pair (r_G, r_M) of graph morphisms $r_G: G \to G'$ and $r_M: M \to M'$ such that the inset diagram commutes, i.e. $\tau; r_M = r_G; \tau'$. For example, Fig. 2 presents two model mappings, $r_1 = (r_{1G}, r_{1M}):$ $A_1 \leftarrow A_0$ and $r_2 = (r_{2G}, r_{2M}): A_0 \to A_2$. Note the importance of commutativity, which enforces mapping models' data elements to preserve their types. We will often omit subindexes $_{M,G}$ if they are clear from the context.

$$\begin{array}{ccc} A & \xrightarrow{\ r\ } & A' \\ & = & \\ G & \xrightarrow{\ r_G\ } & G' \\ \tau \downarrow & & \downarrow \tau' \\ M & \xrightarrow{\ r_M\ } & M' \end{array}$$

Three special types of model maps are important. Two models are *isomorphic*, written $A \cong A'$, if both mappings r_M and r_G are isomorphisms. Model A is a *submodel* of A', written $A \hookrightarrow A$, if both r_M and r_G are inclusions. Finally, if the square in the inset diagram above is a pullback (see Appendix), then we write $r: A \xrightarrow{\text{pb}} A'$ and call model A the *(retyped) restriction* (or *reduction*) of model A' *along* map r_M.

Model overlap can be specified by a pair of model mappings $A_1 \xleftarrow{r_1} A_0 \xrightarrow{r_2} A_2$ with a common source as illustrated in Fig. 2 (curved arrows denote mapping behavior). Such a configuration of models and mappings is called a *span*; the common model is the *head* of the span, and the two mappings are its *legs*. In more detail, a model span consists of two graph spans: a metamodel span $M_1 \xleftarrow{r_{1M}} M_0 \xrightarrow{r_{2M}} M_2$ and a data span $G_1 \xleftarrow{r_{1G}} G_0 \xrightarrow{r_{2G}} G_2$. In each of the graph spans, an element x in the head represents a common/shared concept, while legs show how this concept is represented in each of the components. For example, each element $x \in M_0$ declares that elements $r_{1M}(x) \in M_1$ and $r_{2M}(x) \in M_2$ refer to the same (meta)classifier. Particularly, associations *impl* in metamodel M_1 and *implmnts* in M_2 are declared to be the same in Fig. 2 despite their different names. Analogously, the upper span declares that classes *Person@A_1* and *Person@A_2* refer to the same class. Note that it is no restriction to assume that the overlap span is *jointly injective*, i.e., for any two elements $x, x \in M_0$, if $r_{1M}(x) = r_{1M}(x')$ and $r_{2M}(x) = r_{2M}(x')$, then $x = x'$.

When a span specifies a model overlap, we will refer to it as an *overlap* or *correspondence* span. Thus, the metamodel of our sample multimodel is actually a span $\mathcal{M} = (M_1, M_2, M_0, r_{1M}, r_{2M})$ or shorter $\mathcal{M} = (r_{1M}, r_{2M})$ rather than a pair (M_1, M_2), and the multimodel itself is a span $\mathcal{A} = (A_1, A_2, A_0, r_1, r_2)$ or shorter $\mathcal{A} = (r_1, r_2)$ rather than a pair (A_1, A_2). We will call (A_1, A_2) the *base* of multimodel $\mathcal{A}$. Thus, a multimodel is essentially richer than its base (cf. [1]).

3.2   Model Merge and Global Constraints

After model overlap is specified by a span, we can merge the component models in an entirely automatic way by employing an operation called *pushout (PO)*. Figure 3 explains the idea by showing how the two metamodels are merged. Intuitively, we first take the disjoint union of M_1 and M_2, and then glue together those elements, which are declared to be the same by the span. The result is a merged graph M together with two mappings $\overline{r_1}: M_1 \to M$ and $\overline{r_2}: M \leftarrow M_2$

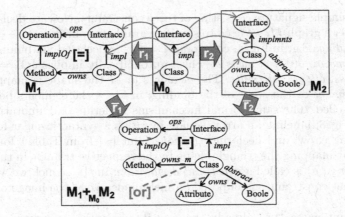

Fig. 3. Merging metamodels (Color figure online)

specifying embedding of the local metamodel graphs into the merge. We will denote it by $M_1 +_{M_0} M_2$.

Local constraints are directly carried into the merged graph along the maps $\overline{r_1}$ and $\overline{r_2}$, in this way the commutativity constraint (note the label [=]) and multiplicities (not shown) are carried into the merge. Thus, PO takes a span of metamodels as its input, and outputs a cospan (two mappings with a common target), encompassing all data from the local metamodels without duplication. Models' data graphs are also merged with PO, and it can be shown that the result of data graph PO is properly typed over the metamodel graph PO (we omit the figure to save space). However, as our discussion in Sect. 2 shows, some constraints can be violated and have to be checked. In addition, inter-metamodel constraints may be added to the merged metamodel, e.g. the above mentioned "one method [or] attribute" constraint shown in green in Fig. 3.

3.3   Diagrammatic Constraints

A key feature of constraints used in metamodeling is their *diagrammatic* nature: the set of elements over which a constraint is declared is actually a diagram of some shape specific for the constraint. For example, the shape of any multiplicity constraint is a single arrow, while the shape of constraint [or] discussed above is a span of two arrows.

To declare a constraint named c over a metamodel graph M, we recognize the constraint shape in the graph and label the respective configuration by constraint name c. Formally, we first declare a

Table 1. Sample constraints

Name	Shape
[0..1]	①—$\xrightarrow{12}$—②
[or]	①←$\underset{01}{}$—⓪—$\underset{02}{\longrightarrow}$②
[=]	⓪—$\xrightarrow{01}$—① ... $\underset{02}{}$ ... $\xrightarrow{12}$ ... ②

signature of constraints, i.e., a set of constraint names/labels, each one assigned with its *(arity) shape* denoted, for a constraint c, by S^c. For example, Table 1 specifies a simple signature consisting of three constraints. Now, to declare a constraint c over a graph M, we need to specify a graph morphism $\delta : S^c \to M$ called *(shape) binding*. E.g. in Fig. 4, constraint $c = [or]$ is declared via binding δ with $\delta(01) = owns\_m$, $\delta(02) = owns\_a$, which automatically implies $\delta(1) = Method$, $\delta(0) = Class$, $\delta(2) = Attribute$. The elements in M the shape is mapped to, is called the *image* or the *scope* of the binding; in Fig. 4 the elements beyond the scope are veiled. The same formal mechanisms underlines commutativity constraint in Fig. 3: labeling an arrow square by $[=]$ is a syntactic sugar for adding the diagonal arrow, and declaring the constraint $[=]$ from Table 1 for the two triangles (by mapping the triangle shape to the respective triangle in the graph).

The pair (c, δ) is called a *constraint declaration*. In the sequel, we write $c@\delta$, meaning that constraint c is imposed on metamodel M at the image of binding map δ.

Constraint name "or" already suggests its semantic interpretation in this context: "Each class shall own at least a method *or* an attribute". Importantly, *semantics* of a constraint is, in general, defined irrespective to the binding by defining a *validating* function VALIDATE$_c$(X : MODEL[S^c]): BOOLEAN which inputs a typed graph $X = (G_X, \tau_X : G_X \to S^c)$, i.e. a model typed over c's shape, and outputs Boolean truth iff the model is considered to be satisfying the constraint. The validating function must be stable under isomorphism: if $X \cong X'$, then VALIDATE$_c$(X) = VALIDATE$_c$(X').

Now checking consistency of model $A = (G, \tau : G \to M)$ against a fixed constraint declaration $c@\delta$ in M is performed by function

$$\text{CHECK}(A: \text{MODEL}[M], c@\delta : \text{CONSTR}): \text{BOOLEAN}$$

which performs three steps:

1. *Restrict* A to elements, whose types are in the image of δ in M.
2. *Retype* elements of this new structure to formal typing over S^c. This yields typed graph $A^{c@\delta} = (G^{c@\delta}, \tau^{c@\delta})$.
3. Return the result of VALIDATE$_c$($A^{c@\delta}$).

In Fig. 4 the steps of function CHECK can be tracked: VALIDATE$_c$ acts on models typed over S^c: It returns true if each element of type 0 in $G^{c@\delta}$ has an outgoing edge to some element of type 1 or to some element of type 2. Graph G is restricted and retyped by pulling back τ along δ, $\tau^{c@\delta}$ is the retyping.

Model A satisfies $c@\delta$, written $A \models c@\delta$, if

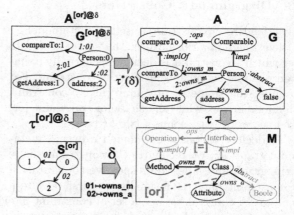

Fig. 4. Constraint declaration and check

CHECK$(A, c@\delta)$=*true*. A is a *legal* model over metamodel M, if $A \models c@\delta$ for all constraints $c@\delta$ declared in M.

The framework described above allows us to give an accurate formal *definition* of global consistency. In a nutshell, we specify local (meta)model overlap by a span, then merge using PO, specify global constraints over the the merged metamodel, and finally check the merged model against global constraints.

3.4   Global Consistency Revisited: Local Constraint Checking

As mentioned above, using this definition of global consistency as an algorithm for consistency checking is very inefficient due to the expensive operation of model matching. A better technique is given in [4]: Let $\mathcal{A}$ be a multimodel with base (A_1, A_2), $A_i = (G_i, \tau_i: G_i \to M_i)$ $(i = 1, 2)$ defined over a multimetamodel $\mathcal{M} = (M_1, M_0, M_2, r_1, r_2)$. An inter-metamodel constraint $c@\delta$ is verified as follows (see Appendix for how the pullback operation works).

1. *Binding projection:* Identify those fragments of M_1, M_2, and M_0, that matter for checking, by pulling δ back along $\bar{r}_1$, along $\bar{r}_2$, and along $r_1; \bar{r}_1$ (or, equivalently, along $r_2; \bar{r}_2$ as the square is commutative), cf. Fig. 4. This results in mappings $\bar{r}_1^*(\delta) : S_1^{c@\delta} \to M_1$, $\bar{r}_2^*(\delta) : S_2^{c@\delta} \to M_2$, and $(r_1; \bar{r}_1)^*(\delta) : S_0^{c@\delta} \to M_0$. Let's call these maps *localised bindings* (of δ to M_1, M_2, M_0. resp.). Let

$$S_i^{c@\delta} \xrightarrow{k_{iM}} I_i^{c@\delta} \lhook\joinrel\longrightarrow M_i \text{ for } i = 1, 2, 0$$

be their epi-mono-factorisations, i.e.$I_i^{c@\delta}$is the image of δ's localised binding to M_i.

2. *Model restriction and retyping:* Carry out steps one and two of the constraint checking algorithm of Sect. 3.3 *locally*, i.e. construct consecutive pullbacks of τ_i along the two morphisms of the above epi-mono-factorisation, yielding

$$B_i^{c@\delta} \text{ pb} \xrightarrow{k_i} A_i^{c@\delta} \text{ pb} \lhook\joinrel\longrightarrow A_i$$

The right pullback yields subgraph $A_i^{c@\delta}$ of A_i comprising those model elements that are typed in $I_i^{c@\delta}$, the left pullback retypes elements of $A_i^{c@\delta}$ such that they are typed over $S_i^{c@\delta}$. Let $A_i^{c@\delta} = (G_i^{c@\delta}, \tau_i^{c@\delta}: G_i^{c@\delta} \to I_i^{c@\delta})$ and provide the modeler with model data $G_1^{c@\delta}$ and $G_2^{c@\delta}$.[1, 2]

3. *Matching:* Determine compatibly typed overlap $A_0^{c@\delta} = (G_0^{c@\delta}, \tau_0^{c@\delta}: G_0^{c@\delta} \to I_0^{c@\delta})$ of these two data graphs, including correspondence span $r_1': A_0^{c@\delta} \to A_1^{c@\delta}$ and $r_2': A_0^{c@\delta} \to A_2^{c@\delta}$.[3] We will refer to the triple $(A_0^{c@\delta}, r_1', r_2')$ as a *constraint specific (correspondence) span* and denote it by span$(c@\delta)$.

---

[1] In Fig. 3, $G_1^{c@\delta}$ comprises classes, interfaces, and operations; $G_2^{c@\delta}$ contains classes, interfaces, and attributes.

[2] Recall the fact that $B_i^{c@\delta}$, $A_i^{c@\delta}$, and A_i are typed graphs, such that the arrows of the form $\xrightarrow{pb}$ depict morphism *pairs* in a pullback square, cf. Sect. 3.1.

[3] Hence, in Fig. 3, $G_0^{c@\delta}$ contains only certain classes.

4. *Validation:* Compute pullback $B_0^{c@\delta} = (H_0^{c@\delta}, \sigma_0^{c@\delta}: H_0^{c@\delta} \to S_0^{c@\delta})$ of this overlap along k_{0M} and apply $validate_c(B_1^{c@\delta} +_{B_0^{c@\delta}} B_2^{c@\delta})$.

The key point of this algorithm is that the constraint-tailored correspondence span $\mathsf{span}(c@\delta)$ can be much smaller than the span specifying all correspondences between the component models. E.g. checking our sample multimodel against the constraint "One attribute or one method" specified in Sect. 2 requires to match classes in models A_1 and A_2 while matching interfaces is not necessary. For this toy example, the difference is not significant, but for practical models comprising thousands of elements, the performance gain is essential.

4   From Constraints to Model Matching, Incrementally

This section introduces the main contribution of the paper. Since the most expensive step in the algorithm of Sect. 3.4 is model matching (Step 3), we focus on minimizing this effort by computing the required correspondence span incrementally. The idea is briefly explained in Sect. 4.1, Sect. 4.2 describes our main technical vehicle for the constraint grouping task, and Sect. 4.3 explains incrementality in detail.

4.1   Incrementality in a Nutshell

Suppose we need to check global consistency wrt. a set of constraints

$$C = \{c_1@\delta_1, ..., c_n@\delta_n\}.$$

In the next section we will show that any such set gives rise to a constraint declaration $c@\delta$ for some new constraint symbol c with a new binding map δ such that for any multimodel A we have $A \models c@\delta$ iff $A \models C$ (where, as usual, $A \models C$ means $A \models c_i@\delta_i$ for all $i = 1, .., n$). We will denote this new constraint declaration by $\bigwedge C$ and call it *consolidation* of C. Thus, we can replace checking A against C by checking it against a single constraint $\bigwedge C$ with our algorithm in Sect. 3.4, so that model matching is reduced to discovering the correspondence span $\mathsf{span}(C) \stackrel{\text{def}}{=} \mathsf{span}(\bigwedge C)$.

Assume now that new constraints are added to group C resulting in a bigger group $C' \supseteq C$. To check A against C', we need to build a correspondence span $\mathsf{span}(C')$, which, as we mentioned several times, is an expensive procedure. Our idea is to build $\mathsf{span}(C')$ incrementally (rather than from scratch) using the previously built correspondence span $\mathsf{span}(C)$. Indeed, we will define a "delta" span $\mathsf{span}(C, C')$ and an operation $\uplus$ of span union such that $\mathsf{span}(C') = \mathsf{span}(C) \uplus \mathsf{span}(C, C')$, so that GCC can be done incrementally with an effective reuse of the model matching knowledge.

4.2 Constraint Grouping

Logical programming enables definition of new formulas with the help of conjunction of already known formulas, e.g.

$$pythagoreanTriple(x, y, z) := (x^2 + y^2 = z^2) \wedge isInteger(x) \wedge isInteger(y).$$

This classical *consolidation* of three small formulas by defining their conjunction can be carried out in the same way with diagrammatic constraints: For the sake of simplicity we explain the idea for two constraint declarations only. The general case of an arbitrary (finite) number is straightforward. Let $c_1@\delta_1$ and $c_2@\delta_2$ be imposed on metamodel M. We can define a new constraint symbol $c_1 \wedge c_2$ (read "c_1 and c_2") with arity graph $S^{c_1 \wedge c_2} := S^{c_1} + S^{c_2}$, i.e. the *coproduct* of the two arity graphs (whenever, in the sequel, a term is printed in italics, we refer to the appendix' terminology). In the classical case this corresponds to the disjoint union of all variable slots in the atomic formulae: We obtain 5 slots $s_1, \ldots, s_5$ for the arity of the consolidated formula. For the diagrammatic conjunction of $c_1@\delta_1$ and $c_2@\delta_2$ we take $[\delta_1, \delta_2] : S^{c_1} + S^{c_2}$ (*universal* morphism) to be the corresponding binding map. In the classical example above, this means that the slots are mapped $s_1 \mapsto x$, $s_2 \mapsto y$, $s_3 \mapsto z$, $s_4 \mapsto x$, $s_5 \mapsto y$, placing x, y, z accordingly into the slots.

Semantics of $c_1 \wedge c_2$ is defined as follows. For any model X with $\tau_X : G_X \to S^{c_1 \wedge c_2}$, we set $X \models c_1 \wedge c_2$ iff $i_{c_1}^*(X) \models c_1$ and $i_{c_2}^*(X) \models c_2$, where $i_{c_1} : S^{c_1} \to S^{c_1 \wedge c_2}$ and $i_{c_2} : S^{c_2} \to S^{c_1 \wedge c_2}$ are the coproduct's *canonical injections* (recall that $S^{c_1 \wedge c_2} = S^{c_1} + S^{c_2}$), and $i_{c_1}^*(\_)$, $i_{c_2}^*(\_)$ are the respective PB operations (acting, in fact, on τ_X — see Appendix). Stability under isomorphisms is obvious.

$(c_1 \wedge c_2)@[\delta_1, \delta_2]$ is called a *consolidated constraint declaration* (composed of $c_1@\delta_1$ and $c_2@\delta_2$). Note that in the partially ordered (by $\models$) set of all constraint declarations, $(c_1 \wedge c_2)@[\delta_1, \delta_2]$ is the g.l.b. of $c_1@\delta_1$ and $c_2@\delta_2$.

The construction defined above for the case of two constraint declarations in the group, is directly generalized for the case of any finite number of constraints $C = \{c_1@\delta_1, \ldots, c_n@\delta_n\}$. We will denote the corresponding consolidated constraint by $\bigwedge C$.

Theorem. Given a set of global constraints $C = \{c_1@\delta_1, \ldots, c_n@\delta_n\}$ (declared over the metamodel merge), let $\bigwedge C$ be its consolidated constraint declaration as defined above. Then $\mathcal{A} \models C$ iff $\mathcal{A} \models \bigwedge C$.

4.3 From Constraints to Correspondence Spans

Given a constraint declaration $c@\delta$, let $S^{c@\delta} \xrightarrow{k_M} I^{c@\delta} \hookrightarrow M$ be its epi-mono factorisation as described in Sect. 3.4.

Definition. Given two constraints, $c@\delta$ and $c'@\delta'$, we say the latter *(semantically) entails* the former, and write $c'@\delta' \models c@\delta$, if $I^{c@\delta} \subset I^{c'@\delta'}$ and $\mathcal{A} \models c@\delta$ for any multimodel $\mathcal{A}$ with $\mathcal{A} \models c'@\delta'$.

Corollary. Given a metamodel M, the space of all constraint declarations over M is a (thin) category, say, $\text{CONSTR}(M)$, whose arrows are entailments. [4]   □

Specifically, it is easy to see that given two groups of constraints such that $C \subset C'$, we have $\bigwedge C' \models \bigwedge C$ for their consolidations. This is our main motivating example, but proofs are easier to build in a bit more general situation of semantic entailment.

Given entailment $c'@\delta' \models @\delta$, we have a diagram

$$S^{c'@\delta'} \qquad S^{c@\delta} \longrightarrow I^{c@\delta} \hookrightarrow I^{c'@\delta'} \hookrightarrow M \qquad (1)$$

with $I^{c@\delta}$ and $I^{c'@\delta'}$ being images of δ and δ' resp., which gives rise (through backward propagation) to inclusions

$$A_1^{c@\delta} \subseteq A_1^{c'@\delta'} \text{ and } A_2^{c@\delta} \subseteq A_2^{c'@\delta'}$$

where models A with subindexes are constraint-specific restrictions of local models produced in Step 2 of the algorithm (Sect. 3.4). Thus, there will be further automation potential for matching in Step 3, if two elements $x_1 \in A_1^{c@\delta}$ and $x_2 \in A_2^{c@\delta}$ are declared to be the same: In this case neighbors (reachable via an edge in the data graph) $y_1 \in A_1^{c'@\delta'} - A_1^{c@\delta}$ (of x_1) and $y_2 \in A_2^{c'@\delta'} - A_2^{c@\delta}$ (of x_2) are likely to be identical, too.

We demonstrate the effects for the simple situation of a singleton $C = \{c_1@\delta_1\}$ and $C' = C \cup \{c_2@\delta_2\}$. Consider for this the metamodel merge M in Fig. 3. Suppose again that classes shall either possess an attribute or a method (constraint $c_1@\delta_1$), and, additionally, the following property (constraint $c_2@\delta_2$) has to hold for any class c:

$$(\sim c.abstract \wedge c.impl = i) \text{ implies } (\forall op \in i.ops: \exists m \in c.owns\_m: m.implOf = op)$$

i.e. each operation of an implemented interface has to be instantiated in each concrete class. Let $c'@\delta'$ be the consolidation of C'. Its scope consists of the complete merge M in Fig. 3. For applying our algorithm for checking validity of (A_1, A_2) against $c_1@\delta_1$, the user has to specify sameness of model elements. Since the image of δ_1 only covers *Class* in the complete overlap of M_1 and M_2, the user only needs to match classes. Thus, in Fig. 2, he will declare classes *Person* to be the same. In contrast, extended constraint declaration $c'@\delta'$ covers the complete overlap M_0 in Fig. 3. Hence the user, additionally, has to specify sameness of interfaces. Since *Person*-classes have already been matched, it is likely that interfaces *Comparable* and *TotalOrder* are the same, and the system can propose their matching to the user, which he can confirm or reject.

In the rest of the section, we investigate the nature of mapping span, which maps a constraint $c@\delta$ to its specific correspondence span. We will show that it can be extended to arrows by mapping an entailment $c'@\delta' \models c@\delta$ to the respective inclusion of correspondence spans. The latter can be seen as an increment for model matching.

---

[4] A thin category is nothing but a partially preordered (big) set: for any pair of objects, the set of mediating arrows between them is either empty or a singleton.

It is easy to verify that image inclusion of two constraints faithfully propagates back to the local metamodels and its overlap by *Preservation* properties of pullbacks. Thus diagram (1) is fully propagated back to mappings with codomain M_1, M_2, and M_0 in step 1 of the algorithm in Sect. 3.4, meaning that we get the same shaped diagram (including image properties) for the localised bindings:

$$S_i^{c'@\delta'} \longrightarrow S_i^{c@\delta} \longrightarrow I_i^{c@\delta} \hookrightarrow I_i^{c'@\delta'} \hookrightarrow M_i \qquad (2)$$

for all $i \in \{0, 1, 2\}$. In step 2, pullback of τ_i along these mappigs ($i \in \{1, 2\}$) is carried out. If verification of $c@\delta$ and $c'@\delta'$ would be performed simultaneously, the system would present to the modeler typed graphs $(A_i^{c@\delta})$ $^{pb} \hookrightarrow (A_i^{c'@\delta'})$ for $i \in \{1, 2\}$ where inclusion is provided by *preservation* properties and one can show that the pullback property arises from its *decomposition* property (see Appendix). Suppose the modeler has already specified model overlap $A_0^{c@\delta} = (G_0^{c@\delta}, \tau_0^{c@\delta})$ for checking $c@\delta$, then the question is, how to efficiently fill the gaps (question marks and dashed arrows) in

$$
\begin{array}{ccccccc}
A_1^{c@\delta} & \xleftarrow{\ \ r_1'\ \ } & A_0^{c@\delta} & \xrightarrow{\ \ r_2'\ \ } & A_2^{c@\delta} & = & \mathsf{span}(c@\delta) \\
{\scriptstyle pb}\ \Big\uparrow & & {\scriptstyle pb}\ \Big\uparrow\ {\scriptstyle ?} & & {\scriptstyle pb}\ \Big\uparrow & & \Big\uparrow \\
A_1^{c'@\delta'} & \xleftarrow{--?--} & A_0^{c'@\delta'}\ {\scriptstyle ?} & \xdashrightarrow{--?--} & A_2^{c'@\delta'} & = & \mathsf{span}(c'@\delta')
\end{array}
$$
$$(3)$$

Whereas the two horizontal dashed correspondence morphisms declare the extended overlap, the vertical dashed line guarantees coherence with the overlap w.r.t. $c@\delta$.

Note that for any solution $A_0^{c'@\delta'} := (G_0^{c'@\delta'}, \tau_0^{c'@\delta'} : G_0^{c'@\delta'} \to I_0^{c'@\delta'})$ the codomain $I_0^{c'@\delta'}$ is already known, cf. (2). Thus, we have to find $G_0^{c'@\delta'}$ and its typing. We claim that $G_0^{c'@\delta'}$ is of the form $G_0^{c@\delta} + G_0$, where G_0 can be any subset of elements of

$$\{(x_1, x_2) \in G_1^{c'@\delta'} \times G_2^{c'@\delta'} \mid \exists t_0 \in I_0^{c'@\delta'} - I_0^{c@\delta} : \tau_1^{c'@\delta'}(x_1) = r_1(t_0) \wedge \tau_2^{c'@\delta'}(x_2) = r_2(t_0)\},$$

which turns $G_0^{c'@\delta'}$ into a legal graph. We call G_0 the *match-extension* and define $\tau_0^{c'@\delta'} = \tau_0^{c@\delta}$ on $G_0^{c@\delta}$ and $\tau_0^{c'@\delta'}(x_1, x_2) = t_0$. Note that this is unique since we assumed in the beginning of Sect. 3.2 r_1 and r_2 to be jointly injective. Moreover the correspondence maps must be taken to be projections $(x_1, x_2) \mapsto x_1$ and $(x_1, x_2) \mapsto x_2$ on match-extension and such that they coincide with r'_{1G} and r'_{2G} on $G_0^{c@\delta}$. Finally the model part of the vertical dashed map is the inclusion of $G_0^{c@\delta}$ into $G_0^{c'@\delta'}$. It can now be shown that $G_0^{c'@\delta'}$ is indeed a graph, the above diagram becomes commutative, all mappings on the model level are proper graph morphisms and are compatibly typed, and the three vertical arrows are inclusion pullbacks, as desired.

Thus, in the example above, $G_0^{c'@\delta'} = G_0^{c@\delta} + G_0$, where graph $G_0^{c@\delta}$ has exactly one node *Person*. For graph G_0, there are three cases:

1. $G_0 = \emptyset$ (no extension)
2. $G_0 = \{(Comparable : Interface, TotalOrder : Interface)\}$.
3. $G_0 = \{(Comparable : Interface, TotalOrder : Interface), (impl_1, impl_2)\}$, where $impl_1$ specifies that *Person* implements *Comparable* and $impl_2$ specifies that *Person* implements *TotalOrder*.

The second case results in a double declaration of $Comparable = TotalOrder$ to be implemented by *Person*, which can automatically be rejected by the algorithm. In addition to that, the algorithm can propose the third case, because it is likely that *Comparable* and *TotalOrder* can be declared to be the same, since otherwise *Person* should not be in the original overlap (because then it implements different behavior). The user must only confirm this choice. If he rejects, the algorithm outputs case 1.

Given a multimodel base (A_1, A_2) over the multimetamodel $\mathcal{M}$, the construction described by diagram (3) defines mappings between model correspondence spans over $\mathcal{M}$, which makes the space of spans a category $\text{SPAN}(\mathcal{M})$. We can summarize our discussion by formulating an important requirement to the model matching tool: in order to preserve the matching knowledge, mapping span : $\text{CONSTR}(M) \to \text{SPAN}(\mathcal{M})$ should be a functor. This requirement is well aligned with matching algorithms based on similarity flooding [6]: global constraints provide information about model correspondences, which can be used for matching (e.g., as it was done in our example above).

5   Conclusion: Future Work

We plan to extend the functorial nature of mapping span : $\text{CONSTR}(M) \to \text{SPAN}(\mathcal{M})$ towards a richer structure over the spaces. Namely, we want to make them lattices formed by Boolean logical operations for the former space, and by Boolean operations over spans for the latter space. Then it should be possible to establish a structure compatible map (homomorphism) from the former algebra to the latter, which would allow the user to do matching in a compositional way with extensive reuse. Another direction is to investigate interaction between our incremental approach and similarity flooding matching algorithms, which potentially can enhance tools for both model matching and global consistency checking. We also plan to develop a tool support for the approach in collaboration with the Bergen group, whose ongoing work on tooling for diagrammatic constraint checking, and subsequent model repairing [5,8] looks very promising.

A   Appendix. Some Operations Over Graphs and Models

Two operations over graphs and graph morphisms heavily employed in the paper are sketched below; a detailed specification can be found in, say, [3].

Coproducts. The *coproduct* $G_1 + G_2$ of two graphs G_1, G_2 is their disjoint union. Importantly, any coproduct is endowed with two canonic injections $i_k :$ $G_k \hookrightarrow G_1 + G_2$, $k = 1, 2$, which map each element to itself in the union.

Any pair of graph morphisms $f_{1,2} : G_{1,2} \to H$ gives rise to a unique morphism $[f_1, f_2] : G_1 + G_2 \to H$ compatible with injections: $i_{1,2}; [f_1, f_2] = f_{1,2}$. This property of coproducts is called *universality* and morphism specified above *universal*. It is easy to see that universality allows us to define the following operation over models (typed graphs): having typed graphs A_1, A_2 we define $A = A_1 + A_2$ by setting $G_A = G_1 + G_2$, $M_A = M_1 + M_2$ and $\tau_A = [\tau_1; i_1, \tau_2; i_2]$ where $i_{1,2} : M_{1,2} \hookrightarrow M_A$ are coproduct injections.

Restriction/Retyping and Pullbacks. Given a model $A = (M, G, \tau)$ and a type graph map as shown in the inset diagram, we can define a new model $A' = (G', \tau')$ over M' by setting $G' = \{e = (t, x) | t \in M', x \in G, f(t) = \tau(x)\}$ [5] with projection mappings $\tau'(e) = t$ and $f'(e) = x$. Further in the paper, we will often denote map f' by $\tau^*(f)$ and say that it is obtained by *pulling f back along τ*, and similarly $\tau' = f^*(\tau)$ is obtained by pulling τ back along f; correspondingly, the entire operation of producing a span (τ', f') from cospan (τ, f) is called *pull-back(PB) (of graphs)*.

$$\begin{array}{ccc} G' & \xrightarrow{f'} & G \\ {\scriptstyle \tau'} \downarrow & & \downarrow {\scriptstyle \tau} \\ M' & \xrightarrow{f} & M \end{array}$$

If f is inclusion, then PB provides the *(retyped) restriction* of model A over the M' part of the metamodel graph. Pullback operation can be seen as a generalization of model restriction for arbitrary mappings f, and we will often call it so. As any PB square is commutative, we can consider it as a special model morphism, which we will denote by a special arrow $f : A' \xrightarrow{pb} A$.

Preservation properties. It is known that If f is inclusion, injective or surjective, then f' is, resp., inclusion, injective or surjective as well.

Pullback composition and decomposition. Given $f : A \xrightarrow{pb} B$ and $g : B \xrightarrow{pb} C$, their composition is also PB, i.e., $f; g : A \xrightarrow{pb} C$. Moreover, given that the second arrow and the composition are PBs, $f; g : A \xrightarrow{pb} C$ and $g : B \xrightarrow{pb} C$, it is possible to prove that the first arrow is also PB, $f : A \xrightarrow{pb} B$.[6]

Coproducts and pullbacks (Extensivity). Given three typed graphs and morphism pairs $A_1 \longrightarrow A_0 \longleftarrow A_2$, then $A_1 {}^{pb} \dashrightarrow A_0 \dashleftarrow {}^{pb} A_2$ if and only if $A_0 \cong A_1 + A_2$.

References

1. Diskin, Z., Xiong, Y., Czarnecki, K.: Specifying overlaps of heterogeneous models for global consistency checking. In: Dingel, J., Solberg, A. (eds.) MODELS 2010. LNCS, vol. 6627, pp. 165–179. Springer, Heidelberg (2011). doi:10.1007/978-3-642-21210-9_16

---

[5] It is easy to show that G' is equipped with a graph structure in a unique way, see, e.g., [3].

[6] But $f; g : A \xrightarrow{pb} C$ and $f : A \xrightarrow{pb} B$ do not, in general, imply $g : B \xrightarrow{pb} C$.

288   Z. Diskin and H. König

2. Egyed, A.: Fixing inconsistencies in UML design models. In: ICSE. pp. 292–301 (2007)
3. Ehrig, H., Ehrig, K., Prange, U., Taentzer, G.: Fundamentals of Algebraic Graph Tranformations. Springer, Heidelberg (2006)
4. König, H., Diskin, Z.: Advanced local checking of global consistency in heterogeneous multimodeling. In: Modelling Foundations and Applications - 12th European Conference, ECMFA 2016, Held as Part of STAF 2016, Vienna, Austria, July 6-7, 2016, Proceedings, pp. 19–35 (2016). http://dx.doi.org/10.1007/978-3-319-42061-5_2
5. Lamo, Y., Wang, X., Mantz, F., Bech, Ø., Sandven, A., Rutle, A.: DPF workbench: a multi-level language workbench for MDE. In: Proceedings of the Estonian Academy of Sciences, vol. 62, pp. 3–15 (2013)
6. Melnik, S., Garcia-Molina, H., Rahm, E.: Similarity flooding: a versatile graph matching algorithm and its application to schema matching. In: ICDE, pp. 117–128. IEEE Computer Society (2002)
7. Nentwich, C., Emmerich, W., Finkelstein, A.: Consistency management with repair actions. In: ICSE, pp. 455–464 (2003)
8. Rutle, A., Rabbi, F., MacCaull, W., Lamo, Y.: A user-friendly tool for model checking healthcare workflows. In: (EUSPN-2013) and ICTH, pp. 317–326 (2013). http://dx.doi.org/10.1016/j.procs.2013.09.042
9. Sabetzadeh, M., Nejati, S., Liaskos, S., Easterbrook, S., Chechik, M.: Consistency checking of conceptual models via model merging. In: RE, pp. 221–230 (2007)

Continuing a Benchmark for UML and OCL Design and Analysis Tools

Martin Gogolla[1(✉)] and Jordi Cabot[2,3]

[1] University of Bremen, Bremen, Germany
gogolla@informatik.uni-bremen.de
[2] ICREA, Barcelona, Spain
jordi.cabot@icrea.cat
[3] Internet Interdisciplinary Institute, UOC, Barcelona, Spain

Abstract. UML and OCL are frequently employed languages in model-based engineering. OCL is supported by a variety of design and analysis tools having different scopes, aims and technological corner stones. The spectrum ranges from treating issues concerning formal proof techniques to testing approaches, from validation to verification, and from logic programming and rewriting to SAT-based technology.

This paper presents steps towards a well-founded benchmark for assessing UML and OCL validation and verification techniques. It puts forward a set of UML and OCL models together with particular questions centered around OCL and the notions consistency, independence, consequences, and reachability. Furthermore aspects of integer arithmetic and aggregations functions (in the spirit of SQL functions as COUNT or SUM) are discussed. The claim of the paper is not to present a complete benchmark. It is intended to continue the development of further UML and OCL models and accompanying questions within the modeling community having the aim to obtain an overall accepted benchmark.

Keywords: OCL · Model-driven engineering · Benchmark · Verification and validation · SAT

1 Introduction

Model-driven engineering (MDE) as a paradigm for software development is gaining more and more importance. Models and model transformations are central notions in modeling languages like UML, SysML, or EMF and transformation languages like QVT or ATL. In these approaches, the Object Constraint Language (OCL) can be employed for expressing constraints and operations and therefore OCL plays a central role in MDE.

A variety of OCL tools and verification/validation/testing techniques around OCL are currently available (e.g. [1–4,6,8–11,14–17,19,21–23]) but it is an open issue how to compare such tools and support developers in choosing the OCL tool most appropriate for their project. In many other areas of computer science this comparison is performed by evaluating the tools over a set of standardized

© Springer International Publishing AG 2016
P. Milazzo et al. (Eds.): STAF 2016, LNCS 9946, pp. 289–302, 2016.
DOI: 10.1007/978-3-319-50230-4_22

benchmark able to provide a somewhat fair comparison environment. Unfortunately, such benchmarks are largely missing for UML and practically inexistent for OCL.

In this sense, this paper continues the initial proposal of a set of UML/OCL benchmarks [13] and puts forward a couple of complementary benchmark models and a few ideas to encourage the community to have an active participation in this benchmark creation and acceptance process. The two new scenarios focus on integer arithmetic (area that has a significant effect on the tool efficiency depending on the underlying formalism used in the reasoning tasks) and large models with heavy use of aggregated functions, a topic for which the OCL language itself has limited coverage [7].

The structure of the rest of this paper is as follows. The next section gives a short introduction to OCL. Section 3 reviews the initial set of models in our benchmark. Section 4 puts forward additional benchmark models while Sect. 5 discusses possible actions to take to further extend the benchmark. The paper is finished in Sect. 6 with concluding remarks.

2   OCL in a Nutshell

The Object Constrains Language (OCL) is a textual, descriptive expression language. OCL is side effect free and is mainly used for phrasing constraints and queries in object-oriented models. Most OCL expressions rely on a class model which is expressed in a graphical modeling language like UML, MOF or EMF. The central concepts in OCL are objects, object navigation, collections, collection operations and boolean-valued expressions, i.e., formulas. Let us consider these concepts in connection with the object diagram in Fig. 1 which belongs to the class diagram in Fig. 2. This class diagram captures part of the submission and reviewing process of conference papers. The class diagram defines classes with attributes (and operations, not used in this example) and associations with roles and multiplicities which restrict the number of possible connected objects.

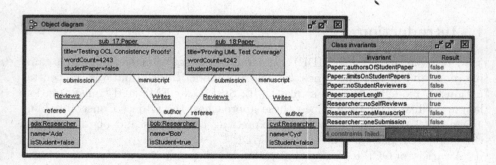

Fig. 1. Object diagram for WR

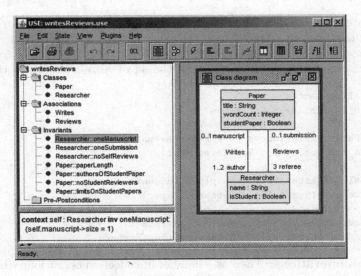

Fig. 2. Class diagram for WR

Objects: An OCL expression will often begin with an object literal or an object variable. For the system state represented in the object diagram, one can use the objects `ada`, `bob`, `cyd` of type `Researcher` and `sub_17`, `sub_18` of type `Paper`. Furthermore variables like `p:Paper` and `r:Researcher` can be employed.

Object navigation: Object navigation is realized by using role names from associations (or object-valued attributes, not occurring in this example) which are applied to objects or object collections. In the example, the following navigation expressions can be stated. The first line(s) shows the OCL expression and the last line the evaluation result and the type of the expression and the result.

```
bob.manuscript
sub_17 : Paper

bob.manuscript.referee
Set{ada} : Set(Researcher)

cyd.manuscript.referee.manuscript.referee
Bag{ada} : Bag(Researcher)

sub_17.author->union(sub_17.referee)
Set{ada,bob} : Set(Researcher)
```

Collections: Collections can be employed in OCL to merge different elements into a single structure containing the elements. There are four collection kinds: sets, bags, sequences and ordered sets. Sets and ordered sets can contain an elements at most once, whereas bags and sequences may contain an element more than once. In sets and bags the element order is insignificant, whereas sequences and ordered sets are sensitive to the element order. For a given class, the operation allInstances yields the set of current objects in the class.

```
Paper.allInstances
Set{sub_17,sub_18} : Set(Paper)

let P=Paper.allInstances in P.referee->union(P.author)
Bag{ada,bob,bob,cyd} : Bag(Researcher)

Paper.allInstances->sortedBy(p|p.wordCount)
Sequence{sub_18,sub_17} : Sequence(Paper)

Sequence{bob,ada,bob,cyd,ada}->asOrderedSet
OrderedSet{bob,ada,cyd} : OrderedSet(Researcher)
```

Collection operations: There is a number of collection operations which contribute essentially to the expressibility of OCL and which are applied with the arrow operator. Among further operations, collections can be tested on emptiness (isEmpty, notEmpty), the number of elements can be determined (size), the elements can be filtered (select, reject), elements can be mapped to a different item (collect) or can be sorted(sortedBy), set-theoretic operations may be employed (union, intersection), and collections can be converted into other collection kinds (asSet, asBag, asSequence, asOrderdSet). Above, we have already used the collection operations union, sortedBy, and asOrderedSet.

```
Paper.allInstances->isEmpty
false : Boolean

Researcher.allInstances->size
3 : Integer

Researcher.allInstances->select(r | not r.isStudent)
Set{ada,cyd} : Set(Researcher)

Paper.allInstances->reject(p | p.studentPaper)
Set{sub_17} : Set(Paper)

Paper.allInstances->collect(p | p.author.name)
Bag{'Bob','cyd'} : Bag(String)
```

Boolean-valued expressions: Because OCL is a constraint language, boolean expressions which formalize model properties play a central role. Apart from typical boolean connectives (and, or, not, =, implies, xor), universal and existential quantification are available (forAll, exists).

```
Researcher.allInstances->forAll(r, s |
```

```
    r<>s implies r.name<>s.name)
true : Boolean

Paper.allInstances->exists(p |
    p.studentPaper and p.wordCount>4242)
false : Boolean
```

Boolean expressions are frequently used to describe class invariants and operation pre- and postconditions.

3   Previous Benchmarks

The previous benchmark posed general questions that concerned the validation and verification of properties in UML and OCL models. The questions came hand in hand with precise models in which the questions were made concrete. Questions were given names in order to reference them. The following questions were stated:

ConsistentInvariants: Is the model consistent? Is there at least one object diagram satisfying the UML class model and the explicit OCL invariants?

Independence: Are the invariants independent? Is there an invariant which is a consequence of the conditions imposed by the UML class model and the other invariants?

Consequences: Is it possible to show that a stated new property is a consequence of the given model?

LargeState: Is it possible to automatically build valid object diagrams in a parameterized way with a medium-sized number of objects, e.g. 10 to 30 objects and appropriate links, where all attributes take meaningful values and all links are established in a meaningful way? These larger object diagrams are intended to explain the used model elements (like classes, attributes and associations) and the constraints upon them by non-trivial, meaningful examples to domain experts not necessarily familiar with formal modeling techniques.

InstantiateNonemptyClass: Can the model be instantiated with non-empty populations for all classes?

InstantiateNonemptyAssoc: Can the model be instantiated with non-empty populations for all classes and all associations?

InstantiateDisjointInheritance: Can all classes be populated in presence of UML generalization constraints like disjoint or complete?

InstantiateMultipleInheritance: Can all classes be populated in presence of multiple inheritance?

ObjectRepresentsInteger: Given a representation of the integers in terms of a UML class model where an integer is captured as a connected component in an object diagram. Is it true that any connected component of a valid object diagram either corresponds to the term *zero* or to a term of the form $succ^n(zero)$ with $n > 0$ or to a term of the form $pred^n(zero)$?

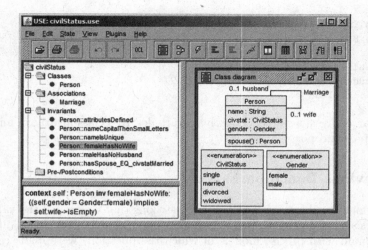

Fig. 3. Class diagram for CS

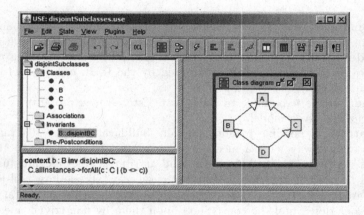

Fig. 4. Class diagram for DS

IntegerRepresentsObject: Is it true that any term of the form *zero* or of the form $succ^n(zero)$ or of the form $pred^n(zero)$ corresponds to a valid object diagram for the model?

The concrete four UML and OCL models that were used to make the questions precise were: CivilStatus (CS) [see Fig. 3], WritesReviews (WR) [see Fig. 2], DisjointSubclasses (DS) [see Fig. 4], and ObjectsAsIntegers (OAI) [see Fig. 5]. All details can be found in [13].

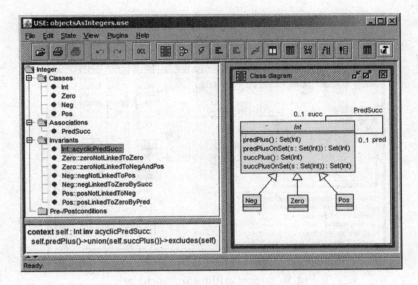

Fig. 5. Class diagram for OAI

4 Additional Benchmarks

The two new benchmarks described in this section complement the old benchmarks with regard to the use of integer arithmetic and the construction of larger models for which aggregate functions (in the sense of SQL functions as count or min) are needed.

4.1 Integer Arithmetic

As indicated in Fig. 6, for the integer arithmetic benchmark the respective class diagram only has one class with three integer attributes a, b, and c. Basically in this benchmark solutions for the equation a = b op c have to be found. The operator op is one of the basic OCL integer operators +, -, *, div. Exactly one of the four invariants from the lower left of Fig. 6 will be active.

The benchmark asks for the construction of a number of C objects (in the example exactly 31) in which the respective operator invariant is valid. The other two invariants guarantee that the solutions in the found C objects are mutually distinct solutions, i.e., each solution appears only once.

We have used this benchmark to compare the efficiency of different SAT solvers that can be employed for the model validator available in the USE tool. The different SAT solvers (SAT4J, LightSAT4J, MiniSat, MiniSatProver) available under Windows show significantly different performance under this benchmark. Another instantiation of the benchmark for available SAT solvers under Linux confirmed the observations made for Windows.

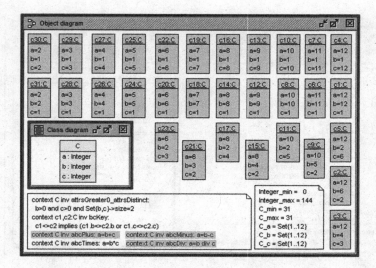

Fig. 6. Integer arithmetic benchmark

4.2 Larger Model with Aggregation Functions

The second new benchmark handles global invariants restricting many classes and concerns the construction of object diagrams for a State-Distict-Community world as shown in Fig. 7. States consist of districts that in turn consist of communities. Individual persons with four statistical attributes (female, young, degree, married) live in communities. The task is to construct an object diagram where in each geographical area (State, District, Community) the statistical distribution of the attributes follows the percentages (Pc) stated in the Config object.

An example object diagram is presented in Fig. 8. For example, there the Config object requires that in each state, district and community the percentage of young people lies between 25% and 75% (minPcYoung and maxPcYoung). This example object diagram used 2 states, 3 districts, and 4 communities. The number of Person objects is also stated in the Config object.

The underlying invariants concern the three geographical areas and the four statistical attributes. The invariants also include a decent degree of integer arithmetic in order to restrict the statistical distribution of the attributes correctly. It took the USE model validator about 6 min to construct the example object diagram. This benchmark is well-suited for comparing the abilities of a UML and OCL analysis tool with regard to global constraints, integer arithmetic and the construction of middle-sized object diagrams.

5   Community Roadmap

Completing the benchmark is not something we can do on our own. And we shouldn't either. The next subsections discuss three different community-driven actions to bring our proposal closer to reality.

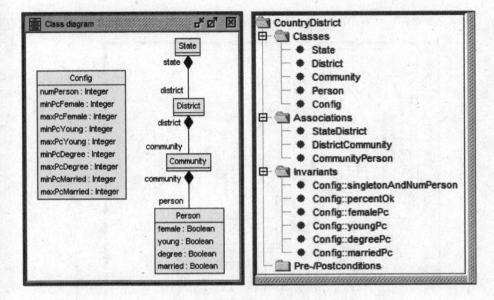

Fig. 7. Class diagram for state-district

5.1 Improving Benchmark Coverage

Our initial collection of benchmark models covers already a good number of interesting OCL expressions and scenarios but it is far from being complete. Speaking generally, for an OCL tool there are challenges in two dimensions: (a) challenges related to the expressiveness of OCL (i.e., the complete and accurate handling of OCL) and (b) challenges related to the computational complexity of the evaluating OCL for a given problem (verification, testing, code-generation,...).

Therefore, beyond increasing the number of benchmark models, we also require several variations of the same model, e.g. in terms of size and specific constructs used in the OCL constraints, to be part of the benchmark and improve this way it's coverage. And each of these variations can be decomposed in a number of subvariations that are relevant too. For instance, wrt size variations, we can increase a model by adding more classes, more attributes per class, increasing its density (number of associations between classes), the number of constraints, or all of them at the same time. Some underlying formalisms are more sensitive than others to some of these variations so fair evaluations would require to play with all these extension variables.

This could easily lead to a combinatorial explosion. Still, based on our own experience we believe that at least the following scenarios should be added to our current collection of benchmark models:

1. Models with tractable constraints, i.e., constraints that can be solved 'trivially' by simple propagation steps.

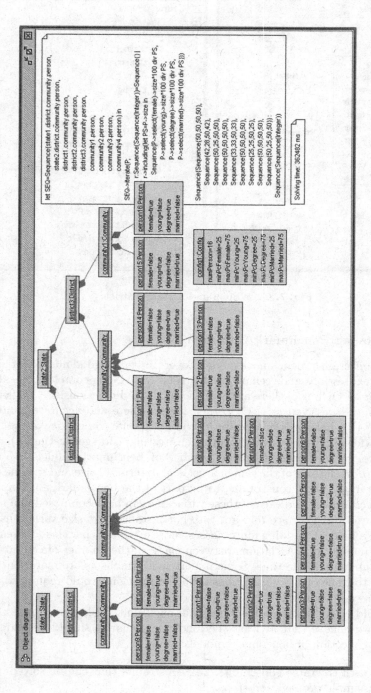

Fig. 8. Object diagram for country-district

2. Models with hard, non-tractable constraints, e.g., representations of NP-hard problems.
3. Unsatisfiable models, i.e. models that cannot be even instantiated in way that all constraints are satisfied.
4. Highly symmetric problems, i.e., that require symmetry breaking to efficiently detect unsatisfiability.
5. Intensive use of Real arithmetic.
6. Intensive use of String values and operations on strings. So far, String attributes are mostly ignored [5] or simply regarded as integers which prohibits the verification of OCL expressions including String operations other than equality and inequality.
7. Many redundant constraints: is the approach able to detect the redundancies and benefit from them to speed up the evaluation?
8. Sparse models: instances with comparably few links offer optimization opportunities that could be exploited by tools.
9. Support for recursive operations, e.g. in form of fixpoint detection or static unfolding.
10. Intensive use of the 'full' semantic of OCL (like the undefined value or collection semantics); this poses a challenge for the lifting to two-valued logics.

Recent research developments (e.g. [20]) could be enhanced to deal with OCL expressions and be employed to automatically generate some of these benchmark models, specially variations in size or density given a "seed" model. Nevertheless, making an effort to find and contribute industrial models is still key to make sure that tools face realistic models.

5.2   OCL Repository

The easiest way to share and contribute models to a common benchmark is by storing them all in a single repository. This is not a new idea, several initiatives like MDEForge [18] or ReMODD [12] have been proposed before but with limited success, mainly due to their ambitious goal: a repository for all kinds of models (and other modeling artifacts) in any format, shape or size.

We aim for a less ambitious but more feasible goal, a repository for OCL-focused models. Being a textual language, the standard infrastructure for code hosting services/version control systems can be largely reused. We still need to store the models accompanying those OCL expressions but, in our scenario, they are basically only UML models and, mostly, limited to class diagrams which simplifies a lot their management.

Nowadays, the online coding platform GitHub (with over 30 million hosted projects) is the only reasonable choice to host such repository since it offers all the functionality we need and it is very well-known which reduces the entry barrier of possible contributors that are not forced to invest time learning a new environment. Therefore we have initialized our OCL repository there[1] and added some basic instructions on how to contribute new UML/OCL models there.

---

[1] https://github.com/jcabot/ocl-repository.

5.3 OCL Competitions

Competition is in our blood. Therefore, one way to increase awareness on the benchmark is to organize yearly competitions of OCL tools where tool vendors evaluate their tools against each other by executing them on the same set of benchmark models.

This format is very successful in the SAT community (e.g. see[2]) where winning a competition is considered a very prestigious achievement for a SAT solver and therefore something that vendors/researchers strive for. In the MDE community we have the successful example of the Tool Transformation Contest[3], focusing on comparing the expressiveness, usability and performance of transformation tools to get a deeper understanding of their relative merits and identify open problems. We propose to replicate these successes in the OCL community.

Typically, competitions are organized in different tracks depending on the properties we want to measure and, more importantly, include an initial call for problems/case studies to use in the competition itself. These proposals are perfect candidates to extend our benchmark.

6 Conclusions

This paper emphasizes the increasing need for a reliable set of OCL Benchmarks that can be used to consistently evaluate and compare OCL tools. We believe such benchmarks would encourage the development of new OCL tools (that now would have a way to evaluate their progress and contrast it against more established tools and a chance to distinguish themselves by focusing on those aspects where others may be failing) and increase the user base of OCL and other similar languages since users would be more confident on the tools' capabilities.

This is still work in progress, and thus, we have also outlined how the community as a whole should (and could) push forward these ideas by, for instance, contributing to a common repository or organizing and participating in specific events on this topic. We hope to see these actions taking place in a near future.

References

1. Anastasakis, K., Bordbar, B., Georg, G., Ray, I.: On challenges of model transformation from UML to alloy. Softw. Syst. Model. **9**(1), 69–86 (2010)
2. Beckert, B., Giese, M., Hähnle, R., Klebanov, V., Rümmer, P., Schlager, S., Schmitt, P.H.: The KeY system 1.0 (Deduction Component). In: Pfenning, F. (ed.) CADE 2007. LNCS (LNAI), vol. 4603, pp. 379–384. Springer, Heidelberg (2007). doi:10.1007/978-3-540-73595-3_26
3. Boronat, A., Meseguer, J.: Algebraic semantics of OCL-constrained metamodel specifications. In: Oriol, M., Meyer, B. (eds.) TOOLS EUROPE 2009. LNBIP, vol. 33, pp. 96–115. Springer, Heidelberg (2009). doi:10.1007/978-3-642-02571-6_7

---

[2] http://www.satcompetition.org/.

[3] http://www.transformation-tool-contest.eu.

4. Brucker, A.D., Wolff, B.: HOL-OCL: a formal proof environment for UML/OCL. In: Fiadeiro, J.L., Inverardi, P. (eds.) FASE 2008. LNCS, vol. 4961, pp. 97–100. Springer, Heidelberg (2008). doi:10.1007/978-3-540-78743-3_8

5. Büttner, F., Cabot, J.: Lightweight string reasoning for OCL. In: Vallecillo, A., Tolvanen, J.-P., Kindler, E., Störrle, H., Kolovos, D. (eds.) ECMFA 2012. LNCS, vol. 7349, pp. 244–258. Springer, Heidelberg (2012). doi:10.1007/978-3-642-31491-9_19

6. Cabot, J., Clarisó, R., Riera, D.: UMLtoCSP: a tool for the formal verification of UML/OCL models using constraint programming. In: Stirewalt, R.E.K., Egyed, A., Fischer, B. (eds.) ASE, pp. 547–548. ACM (2007)

7. Cabot, J., Mazón, J.-N., Pardillo, J., Trujillo, J.: Specifying aggregation functions in multidimensional models with OCL. In: Parsons, J., Saeki, M., Shoval, P., Woo, C., Wand, Y. (eds.) ER 2010. LNCS, vol. 6412, pp. 419–432. Springer, Heidelberg (2010). doi:10.1007/978-3-642-16373-9_30

8. Calì, A., Gottlob, G., Orsi, G., Pieris, A.: Querying UML class diagrams. In: Birkedal, L. (ed.) FoSSaCS 2012. LNCS, vol. 7213, pp. 1–25. Springer, Heidelberg (2012). doi:10.1007/978-3-642-28729-9_1

9. Castillos, K.C., Dadeau, F., Julliand, J., Taha, S.: Measuring test properties coverage for evaluating UML/OCL model-based tests. In: Wolff, B., Zaïdi, F. (eds.) ICTSS 2011. LNCS, vol. 7019, pp. 32–47. Springer, Heidelberg (2011). doi:10.1007/978-3-642-24580-0_4

10. Chimiak-Opoka, J.D., Demuth, B.: A Feature Model for an IDE4OCL. ECEASST 36 (2010)

11. Clavel, M., Egea, M., de Dios, M.A.G.: Checking unsatisfiability for OCL constraints. Electron. Commun. EASST 24, 1–13 (2009)

12. France, R.B., Bieman, J.M., Mandalaparty, S.P., Cheng, B.H.C., Jensen, A.C.: Repository for model driven development (ReMoDD). In: 34th International Conference on Software Engineering, ICSE 2012, pp. 1471–1472 (2012)

13. Gogolla, M., Büttner, F., Cabot, J.: Initiating a benchmark for UML and OCL analysis tools. In: Veanes, M., Viganò, L. (eds.) TAP 2013. LNCS, vol. 7942, pp. 115–132. Springer, Heidelberg (2013). doi:10.1007/978-3-642-38916-0_7

14. Gogolla, M., Büttner, F., Richters, M.: USE: a UML-based specification environment for validating UML and OCL. Sci. Comput. Prog. 69, 27–34 (2007)

15. Gonzalez, C.A., Büttner, F., Clarisó, R., Cabot, J.: EMFtoCSP: a tool for the lightweight verification of EMF models. In: Gnesi, S., Gruner, S., Plat, N., Rumpe, B. (eds.) Proceedings of ICSE 2012 Workshop Formal Methods in Software Engineering: Rigorous and Agile Approaches (FormSERA) (2012)

16. Hußmann, H., Demuth, B., Finger, F.: Modular architecture for a toolset supporting OCL. Sci. Comput. Program. 44(1), 51–69 (2002)

17. Queralt, A., Artale, A., Calvanese, D., Teniente, E.: OCL-lite: finite reasoning on UML/OCL conceptual schemas. Data Knowl. Eng. 73, 1–22 (2012)

18. Rocco, J.D., Ruscio, D.D., Iovino, L., Pierantonio, A.: Collaborative repositories in model-driven engineering. IEEE Softw. 32(3), 28–34 (2015)

19. Roldán, M., Durán, F.: Dynamic Validation of OCL Constraints with mOdCL. ECEASST 44 (2011)

20. Semeráth, O., Vörös, A., Varró, D.: Iterative and incremental model generation by logic solvers. In: Stevens, P., Wąsowski, A. (eds.) FASE 2016. LNCS, vol. 9633, pp. 87–103. Springer, Heidelberg (2016). doi:10.1007/978-3-662-49665-7_6

21. Wille, R., Soeken, M., Drechsler, R.: Debugging of inconsistent UML/OCL models. In: Rosenstiel, W., Thiele, L. (eds.) DATE, pp. 1078–1083. IEEE (2012)

22. Willink, E.D.: Re-engineering eclipse MDT/OCL for Xtext. ECEASST **36** (2010)
23. Yatake, K., Aoki, T.: SMT-based enumeration of object graphs from UML class diagrams. ACM SIGSOFT Softw. Eng. Notes **37**(4), 1–8 (2012)

An Experience Integrating Response-Time Analysis and Optimization with an MDE Strategy

Juan M. Rivas[1]([⊠]), J. Javier Gutiérrez[1], Mario Aldea[1], César Cuevas[1],
Michael González Harbour[1], José María Drake[1], Julio L. Medina[1],
Laurent Rioux[2], Rafik Henia[2], and Nicolas Sordon[2]

[1] Software Engineering and Real-Time Group,
University of Cantabria, Santander, Spain
{rivasjm,gutierjj,aldeam,cuevasce,
mgh,drakej,medinajl}@unican.es
[2] Thales Research and Technology, Palaiseau, France
{laurent.rioux,rafik.henia,
nicolas.sordon}@thalesgroup.com

Abstract. The objective of this experience is applying Model-Driven Engineering (MDE) to the development of complex design toolchains for distributed real-time systems by integrating stand-alone tools for this kind of system. MDE provides the capability to present to each tool the view of the design that is required in each case and also provides the traceability between models to return the results of applying a tool to the original model where the whole information of the developed system persists. Since the tools require complex and interrelated scenarios of model transformation processes they need to be programmed and optimized to obtain acceptable execution times and scalability. The experience described in this paper is the development of a Model-Driven Engineering (MDE) toolchain to support the design of distributed real-time systems using stand-alone tools for calculating response times, assigning priorities to tasks and allocating tasks to processors. The process starts from a base design described with a model that follows the OMG MARTE specification. This toolchain can be applied at any stage of the design process using timing parameters with different degrees of refinement, thus allowing the exploration of different design solutions when needed.

Keywords: MDE tools · IDE · Schedulability analysis · Optimization · Real-time · Design space exploration

1 Introduction

Development toolchains for embedded real-time systems require exploring multiple optimization aspects at the design phase, before their implementation. Aspects like the architectural design, the concurrency model, the deployment on the distributed platforms, the timing behavior, security and others require the description of specific system information and are heavily interrelated. Each of these aspects is supported by a

© Springer International Publishing AG 2016
P. Milazzo et al. (Eds.): STAF 2016, LNCS 9946, pp. 303–316, 2016.
DOI: 10.1007/978-3-319-50230-4_23

community of experts that generates knowledge and provides tools to manage it. A challenge of current software engineering is to facilitate the integration of this knowledge and the resources produced by the experts in different domains in such a way that the engineers developing the system can use them in an efficient and easy way.

Model-Driven Engineering (MDE) [1] is the methodology that currently provides the most promising approach to manage the complexity and multi-aspect nature of embedded real-time systems development:

- In MDE all the information on the system is formulated as models and the development and design processes are specified in terms of model transformations. A system may be represented by a large number of models, some of which have the objective of storing a persistent description of the system, but others are temporarily generated to extract and adapt the information required by the specific tools used during the development to handle each aspect of the design.
- In MDE each model is defined as an instance of a meta-model that describes the contents, structure and format of the terminal model containing the system information. This formalization allows generating transformation tools that are generic and reusable over many kinds of models by using the meta-models as reflective information.
- The use of references between the elements of different models avoids duplicating information and facilitates the global coherence and maintenance of the system information.

Conventional MDE toolchains are sequences of model transformations. However, a toolchain for embedded real-time systems must contain different branches working on the aspects of the design supported by stand-alone tools. In this case we find the following requirements:

- The transformation branches are usually of double direction. The direct branch adapts the information stored in the base design models to the representation required by the stand-alone tool, while the reverse branch returns the results generated by the tool to the system base description. Since these branches are interdependent they need to be co-designed and co-maintained, and they need to exchange transversal configuration information among them.
- Sometimes the transformation processes are iterative rather than linear, since the transformation branch must be repeated until a particular objective is achieved.
- Efficiency is a concern, especially in these iterative processes, and this requires finding imaginative ways to store the models and avoid repeating transformations as much as possible.

The experience described in this paper is the implementation of a toolchain for designing embedded real-time distributed systems starting from a base description of the system that follows the OMG MARTE standard profile (The UML Profile for Modelling and Analysis of Real-Time and Embedded Systems) [2]. The Schedulability Analysis Modeling chapter (SAM) of this standard supports all the necessary modelling elements to perform the schedulability analysis or optimization of a real-time system. The process followed by the toolchain includes the schedulability analysis of the system, which allows ensuring whether the timing requirements imposed in the software can be met or not. When a system meets all its timing requirements, we say that the system is schedulable. In common real-time distributed systems, like those that can be found on cars or airplanes, the schedulability analysis normally consists on the calculation of worst-case response times in order to compare them with the timing requirements imposed on specific actions of the software.

On the other hand, the toolchain pays attention to two particular optimization aspects: (1) finding the scheduling parameters (usually priorities) that allow the system to be schedulable, and (2) in a distributed system finding a suitable allocation of tasks and messages to processors and networks, respectively. This is what we call the architecture optimization. During the optimization process these two aspects can be combined in order to find the best possible solution. The schedulability analysis and optimization of a real-time distributed system are supported by complex techniques that are implemented in the appropriate stand-alone tools.

In this paper, we propose the integration of schedulability analysis and optimization tools within an MDE strategy with the following characteristics:

- A general meta-model based on the MARTE standard is used at the base design level. This meta-model allows modelling systems independently of the application domain.
- An intermediate model particularly suitable for analysis will allow the connection (through the appropriate transformations) between the general model coming from the design phase and the specific model used by the selected analysis tool. Therefore, any existing analysis tool can be integrated in the toolchain through the adequate model transformation.
- A special-purpose tool is created to optimize (1) the priority assignment for the tasks and messages (the latter only if fixed-priority communication networks are specified), and (2) the allocation of tasks and messages to processors and networks.

As a proof of concepts, in a previous work [3] we presented a prototype of the toolchain described in this paper. In the current work, the integration of the stand-alone tools has been completed and implementation details are presented.

This document is organized as follows. Section 2 reviews some tools that are related with the approach we present in this paper. In Sect. 3 we review the real-time system model and current schedulability analysis and optimization techniques. In Sect. 4, we provide an overview of the architecture proposed for the integration of the tools in the MDE toolchain. Section 5 describes the integration of an available schedulability analysis tool in our MDE strategy. In Sect. 6, we describe the design of the optimization tool for priorities and architecture. Section 7 provides an industrial case study to which the tools have been applied. Finally, Sect. 8 draws the conclusions.

2   Related Work

There are other recent works in line with this approach. For example, [4] presents Optimum, a MARTE-based methodology for designing real-time applications in a schedulability-aware fashion, i.e., enabling schedulability analysis of UML models at early stages. In [5], the MoSaRT analysis repository is presented as a helpful modelling support to avoid wrong design choices at an early design phase, thus helping designers to cope with the scheduling analysis difficulties. The work in [6] proposes an integrated approach for prediction of performance in the context of distributed real-time embedded defense systems. In this case, performance prediction aims at addressing issues related to the integration of realistic data sources or the visualization of the causes of performance issues. In [7], model-driven development is applied to the integration of schedulability analysis in the development process of high-integrity distributed real-time systems programmed in the Ada programming language.

The main difference with previous works is that our MDE approach is more complete and modular in the sense that the tools for analysis, priority optimization, or architecture optimization, are independent and could be easily changed if, for example, a better tool is available. On the other hand, our approach can be applied to any application domain that would need verifying real-time properties or optimizing the whole or a part of the application, once it has been designed following the general base model.

3   Real-Time Model

This section gives a high-level overview of the real-time model behind the presented MDE strategy, along with the different versions of this model used by the schedulability analysis and optimization tools integrated in the toolchain. We follow the OMG MARTE standard [2] in which the system's software is described as a set of distributed end-to-end flows executing in multiple processors that can be communicated through one or more networks. This model is commonly used by schedulability analysis and optimization algorithms for distributed real-time systems.

The model follows an event-driven approach, in which each end-to-end flow is re-leased by an event that can be periodic or sporadic. Sporadic events must have a minimum inter-arrival time. Each end-to-end flow is composed of a series of steps that execute sequentially. A step represents the execution of a thread in a processor, or the transmission of a message through a network. Each step has a worst-case execution time (WCET), which specifies the maximum amount of time (or an upper bound on it) that the step needs to execute if it were alone in the system. Likewise, a step can also have a best-case execution time or lower bound on it (BCET). Each step is scheduled by using the scheduling parameters assigned according to the scheduling policy used. In this work we consider a fixed-priority policy.

Figure 1 shows an example of one end-to-end flow with 6 steps executing in two processors and one network. After the first step, there is a forking action that simultaneously releases two different branches of the end-to-end flow. The timing requirements are given as end-to-end deadlines which reference the event triggering the end-to-end flow, and must be met by the last step in the corresponding end-to-end flow branch. As a result of applying a schedulability analysis technique, a worst-case response time (WCRT) is calculated for each step. If the WCRT of the last step of each end-to-end flow branch is less than or equal to its deadline, the system is said to be schedulable, that is, it is guaranteed to meet its deadlines in all cases, including the worst one.

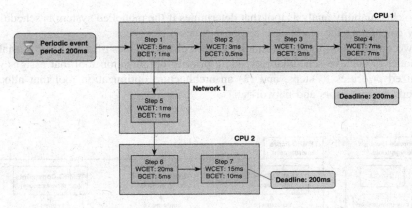

Fig. 1. Example of an end-to-end flow

At the base design level we will use the TEMPO-MARTE meta-model presented in a previous work [8] which enables the description of the real-time system design. This meta-model is suitable for different application domains, and it has been successfully applied to the industrial design of on-board satellite software. This design model can be transformed into another one, compliant to another meta-model called TEMPO-Analysis, which contains the relevant information (concurrency and real-time aspects) organized in a format more suitable for the schedulability analysis and optimization tools. Finally, this analysis model should be transformed into the specific model of the selected analysis tool.

In this paper, we present the integration of MAST (Modeling and Analysis Suite for Real-Time Applications) in the proposed toolchain for the schedulability analysis of the system. MAST defines a meta-model [9, 10] to describe the timing behavior of real-time systems which is aligned with the MARTE standard, and it also provides a selection of techniques [11] to perform schedulability analysis, priority optimization, or sensitivity analysis (assessment of how far or close is the system from meeting its timing requirements). Regarding schedulability analysis, this selection includes representative algorithms such as: the classic holistic analysis [12] that considers the steps as if they were independent; (2) an offset-based technique [13] that exploits the interdependencies among the steps of the same end-to-end flow through the use of task offsets; and (3) another offset-based technique [14] that exploits the precedence relations among the steps.

4 Toolchain Architecture Overview

We propose an MDE toolchain that implements the necessary underlying infrastructure to perform schedulability analysis and optimization of real-time systems inside an EMF/Ecore environment based on the TEMPO meta-model aforementioned. An overview of the architecture of the toolchain is shown in Fig. 2. The toolchain is composed of two different interoperable tools:

1. A schedulability analysis tool that determines if the modelled system is schedulable by calculating the worst-case response times of the steps.
2. Two optimization tools that modify certain characteristics of the TEMPO-Analysis model to achieve schedulability: (1) a priority optimization tool that assigns optimized priorities to steps, and (2) an architecture optimization tool that allocates steps to processors and networks.

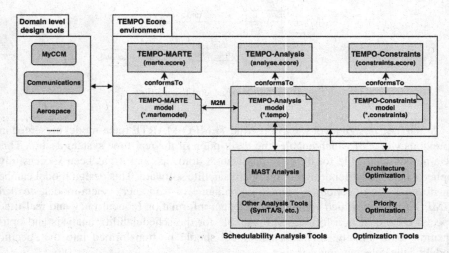

Fig. 2. Architecture of the TEMPO analysis and optimization toolchain

While TEMPO-MARTE represents the basis for the design view, its SAM-like derivative (TEMPO-Analysis) specifically targets schedulability analysis and optimization tools. Hence, the toolchain we propose operates on the TEMPO-Analysis models directly, thus avoiding unnecessary TEMPO-MARTE to TEMPO-Analysis (and vice versa) transformations.

The architecture optimization tool relies on the priority optimization tool to calculate a priority assignment for each allocation of steps to processors tested. Similarly, the priority optimization tool uses a schedulability analysis tool that accepts a TEMPO-Analysis model as input. In this experience we use MAST as the schedulability analysis tool inside this Ecore environment, but the toolchain is designed to work with any other TEMPO-Analysis compatible tool. In this way, the optimization tools can be used in conjunction with other analysis tools such as SymTA/S [15].

In order to allow the specification of other parameters not included in the TEMPO-Analysis meta-model but necessary for the optimization process, the input model for the optimization tool is complemented with an additional constraints model that is compliant to the TEMPO-Constraints meta-model. This model contains information such as valid priority ranges, which step priorities cannot be modified, or step-to-processor affinities.

The toolchain implements the necessary model-to-model (M2M) transformations to operate with the different meta-models involved. All these transformations work under the Eclipse Modeling Framework (EMF). Some of them are implemented in Java, while others rely on ATL [16]. The following sections explain in more detail the design of these tools and their interconnections. Details on the TEMPO-MARTE to TEMPO-Analysis transformations and back can be found in [8].

5   Integration of the Schedulability Analysis Tool

The goal of the schedulability analysis tool is to determine if the system is schedulable. This is carried out by calculating the WCRTs of the steps and comparing them with the imposed deadlines. In this work we define a tool to perform the schedulability analysis on models compliant to the TEMPO-Analysis meta-model using the MAST analysis tools. The link between the TEMPO-Analysis input model and MAST is automatically established using ATL M2M transformations. Two transformation chains are defined in this link:

1. A TEMPO-Analysis to MAST transformation to create the input model for the MAST analysis tool.
2. A return transformation, in which the worst-case response times obtained by MAST are incorporated into the TEMPO-Analysis model.

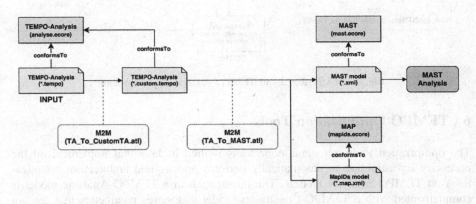

Fig. 3. TEMPO-Analysis to MAST transformation

The TEMPO-Analysis to MAST transformation chain is depicted in Fig. 3, and is composed of two ATL transformations applied sequentially. In the first ATL transformation (TA_To_CustomTA.atl), a new TEMPO-Analysis customized model is generated from the TEMPO-Analysis input model. This new model adds the information that is optional in TEMPO but is mandatory in a MAST model, such as names for every element. Afterwards, the second transformation is applied to this intermediate customized TEMPO-Analysis model (TA_To_MAST.atl). This transformation generates two models, (1) a MAST model that can be used as input to the MAST analysis tool, and (2) a mappings model (compliant to the MapIDs meta-model) that maps the names of the TEMPO-Analysis model elements to the names of their counterpart MAST model elements.

A diagram of the return MAST to TEMPO-Analysis transformation is shown in Fig. 4. It consists of one transformation (TA_MASTResults_MAPIDS_to_TA.atl). This transformation has three inputs, (1) a MAST-Results model that contains the worst-case response times of the steps, (2) the MapIDs model generated previously, and (3) the TEMPO-Analysis custom model that has also been generated previously. The output of this transformation is a TEMPO-Analysis model which now includes the worst-case response times of the steps.

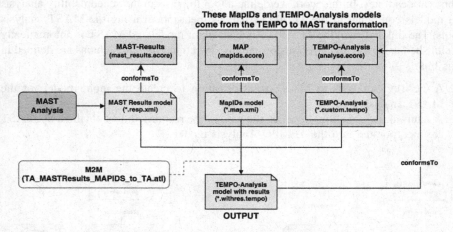

Fig. 4. MAST-Results to TEMPO-Analysis transformation

6   TEMPO Optimization Tools

The optimization tools are stand-alone tools written in Java that implement all the necessary infrastructure to automatically perform priority and architecture optimizations on TEMPO-Analysis models. The information in a TEMPO-Analysis model is complemented with a TEMPO-Constraints model that stores parameters that are not modelled by TEMPO-Analysis but must be specified for the optimization process.

6.1   Priority Optimization

The goal of the priority optimization is to find a suitable assignment of priorities (if possible) that makes the system schedulable. This assignment assumes that steps have been statically allocated to processors or networks.

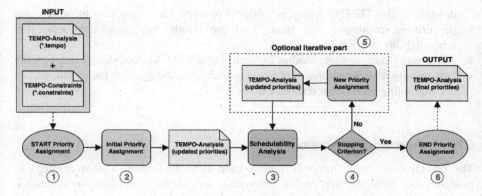

Fig. 5. Design of the priority optimization tool

The priority optimization uses an iterative process that implements the HOSPA heuristic algorithm [17] included in the MAST tools. The flow of this optimization algorithm is depicted in Fig. 5, and is composed of the following stages:

1. The input of the priority optimization tool is a pair of TEMPO-Analysis and TEMPO-Constraints models. The parameters of the TEMPO-Constraints model relevant to the priority optimization are (1) the priority ranges from which the priorities of the steps can be selected, and (2) the list of steps that have pre-assigned priorities that cannot be changed.
2. The priority optimization process starts with an initial priority assignment. As with HOSPA, this initial assignment is a fast non-iterative algorithm that distributes the deadlines of the end-to-end flows among the tasks, and then the Deadline Mono-tonic criterion is applied. The TEMPO-Analysis input model is updated with these initial priorities.
3. The next step is to determine if this new priority assignment makes the system schedulable. This is achieved by applying a schedulability analysis tool on the TEMPO-Analysis model with the updated priorities.
4. Once the schedulability analysis has been performed, the priority optimization process finishes if any of the following stopping criteria is met:
   (a) The last priority assignment makes the system schedulable.
   (b) Two consecutive priority assignments were identical.
   (c) A pre-established maximum number of iterations have been reached. This number of iterations can be set to zero, thus making the priority optimization process non iterative, finishing with the initial assignment.
   (d) A pre-established maximum number of iterations on an already schedulable solution are reached. The priority optimization process has the capability of improving an already schedulable solution by iterating over it.
5. If no stopping criterion is met, a new priority assignment is made by using the same formulation as in HOSPA. This new assignment takes into account the previously calculated worst-case response times of the steps to reorganize the priorities in the system, giving higher priorities to those tasks that are farther from meeting their

deadlines. The TEMPO-Analysis model is updated with these new priorities, and the process continues with stage 3 of the priority optimization process (the schedulability analysis).

6. The priority optimization finishes by returning a TEMPO-Analysis model with the best priority assignment that was found, which could be schedulable or not, and its corresponding worst-case response times.

6.2   Architecture Optimization

The objective of the architecture optimization is to find an allocation of steps to processors or networks that makes the system schedulable. Secondary optimization criteria can be set, i.e., to balance the workload among the processors, or to minimize the inter-processor communications.

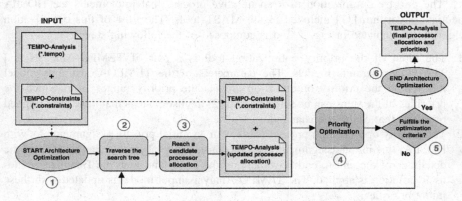

Fig. 6. Design of the architecture optimization tool

As with the priority assignment, the architecture optimization process operates on a TEMPO-Analysis model complemented with a TEMPO-Constraints model. A diagram of the architecture optimization algorithm is depicted in Fig. 6 and comprises the following stages:

1. The input is a pair of TEMPO-Analysis and TEMPO-Constraints models. The parameters of the constraints model relevant to the architecture optimization are: (1) the step to processor affinities (subset of processors to which each step can be assigned to); (2) inter-processor latencies (communication latencies of messages between pairs of processors); and (3) default inter-processor latencies for processor pairs whose latencies were not explicitly specified. These inter-processor latencies can be interpreted as message transmission times if a full schedulability analysis of the networks is specified.

2. A brute-force search algorithm is intractable for non-trivial systems, thus an advanced algorithm is required. We are experimenting with a backtracking algorithm

that is providing promising results. The search tree is traversed and nodes are pruned according to their *a priori* likelihood of satisfying the optimization criteria (nodes with low *a priori* likelihood are pruned). This likelihood is determined taking into consideration indications such as the utilization in the processors, the number of messages that need to be transmitted, or a quick estimation of the worst-case response times.

3. By traversing the search tree, the algorithm reaches a candidate allocation. The input TEMPO-Analysis model is updated with this candidate step to processor or network allocation.

4. The priority optimization tool described in Sect. 6.1 is applied on the TEMPO-Analysis model with the updated architecture. The TEMPO-Constraints model is also provided. The priority optimization returns a TEMPO-Analysis model with the best priority assignment that could be found for this allocation, together with the associated worst-case response times.

5. The optimization process finishes when the resulting TEMPO-Analysis model meets the optimization criterion set by the user. The main criterion is that the system has reached schedulability. Secondary criteria that can be set are: (1) to minimize the number of processors used, (2) to balance the load, or (3) to minimize the inter-processor communications. A maximum number of iterations can also be set. If no criterion is met, the process continues on stage 2, continuing the tree traversal until another candidate allocation is reached.

6. When a stopping criterion is satisfied, the architecture optimization finishes by returning a TEMPO-Analysis model with an updated allocation, a priority assignment for this allocation, and the associated worst-case response times for this system configuration.

7 Industrial Case Study

In this section we present a case study consisting on the application of our MDE analysis and optimization strategy on a simplified version of an industrial system. The system is a robot controller composed of two specialized nodes (Teleoperation Station and Local Controller) connected via Ethernet. Both nodes and use fixed priority (FP) scheduling while the network has no contention given the offsets of the messages sent. The software consists of one end-to-end flow crossing both nodes and the network, and two independent tasks. Figure 7 shows an overview of the system, including the worst-case execution times (WCET) of each task.

The end-to-end flow is triggered by a periodic event with a period of 50 ms. The first task in the end-to-end flow is Trajectory Planner, executing in the Teleoperation Station. Once finished, this task sends a message to the Local Controller which launches the execution of task Command Manager. The flow continues with the execution of task Data Sender on the Local Controller, which sends a message to the Teleoperation Station, launching task Reporter, which is the last task in the flow. This task must finish at the latest 50 ms after the external event that triggered the flow arrived. Additionally, the system has a task (GUI) with a period of one second executing in the

Teleoperation Station, and another task (Servo Control) with a period of 5 ms executing in the Local Controller. These two tasks must finish before their next activation (deadline equal to their periods). The system also has three shared resources (mutual exclusion resources) that are accessed via the immediate ceiling protocol. These shared resources are named Commands, Servo Data, and Status. Which tasks access each shared resource, and for how long, is also shown in Fig. 7.

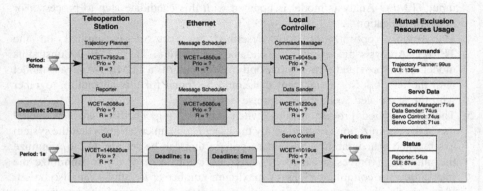

Fig. 7. Robot controller system

During the design phase inside our MDE strategy, the system is modeled with the TEMPO-MARTE meta-model. During this phase, the priorities (Prio) and associated worst-case response times of the tasks (R) are still unknown. Once all the tasks and timing requirements have been laid out, a designer of such system must determine these values of the system, so it can be guaranteed whether deadlines are going to be met in the worst-case. For this purpose, the TEMPO-MARTE model is transformed into another model that conforms to the TEMPO-Analysis meta-model, which is suited for the schedulability analysis. We now use the proposed analysis and optimization toolchain to achieve this goal.

The schedulability analysis tool is implemented as an Eclipse plug-in that operates on TEMPO-analysis (*.tempo) models. The optimization tool uses the same internal functionality as the schedulability analysis tool, but is implemented as a stand-alone tool that can operate without Eclipse. We model the robot controller system using the TEMPO-analysis meta-model, and then use this stand-alone tool to calculate a priority assignment and its associated worst-case response times. We also define a TEMPO-Constraints model specifying that the priorities should be selected in the range [1, 10]. Since each processor has at most three tasks, this range is large enough to guarantee that tasks don't share the same priority level. No architecture optimization is needed in this case because the tasks have a fixed allocation driven by their hardware requirements. The priorities and worst-case response times calculated by the tool are depicted in Fig. 8. Since the worst-case response times of the tasks (R) are lower than the associated deadlines, we can now determine that the system, with the priorities provided by the tool, is schedulable. It is worth noting that the worst-case response

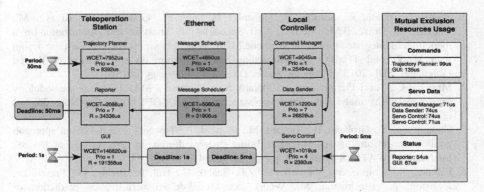

Fig. 8. Robot controller system with results (priorities and response times)

times are given as an upper bound of the latency from the arrival of the external event until the task finishes its execution.

Including all the underlying M2M transformations, the schedulability analysis of this system required approximately 1 s, while the priority assignment required 2 s.

8 Conclusions

We have presented a toolchain to perform, inside the Thales' TEMPO Ecore environment, three of the most important actions in the development of real-time systems: the schedulability analysis, the optimization of the priorities and the optimization of the allocation of tasks and messages to processors and networks. This toolchain implements the necessary M2M transformations to take advantage of the widely used MAST analysis tool, although the optimization tools can use any TEMPO-Analysis compatible schedulability analysis tool.

This toolchain is a result of the fruitful collaboration between Thales Research & Technology and the University of Cantabria (industry and academia). It represents a contribution to the industrial exploitation of model-driven technologies, schedulability analysis and optimization in the design of real-time systems in a variety of application domains.

Acknowledgment. This work has been funded in part by the Spanish Government under grant number TIN2014-56158-C4-2-P (M2C2).

References

1. Schmidt, D.C.: Model-driven engineering. IEEE Comput. **39**(2), 26–31 (2006)
2. Object Management Group: UML profile for MARTE: modeling and analysis of real time embedded systems, version 1.1. OMG document formal/2011-06-02 (2011)

3. Rioux, L., Henia, R., Sordon, N., González Harbour, M., Gutiérrez, J.J., Rivas, J.M., Cuevas, C., Drake, J.M., Medina, J.L.: Schedulability analysis and optimization in a model-based integrated toolchain: synthetic MARTE models for optimizing real-time design with MAST and TEMPO. In: Proceedings of the Forum on specification & Design Languages, FDL 2015, Barcelona, Spain, Demo Night Session (2015)

4. Mraidha, C., Tucci-Piergiovanni, S., Gérard, S.: Optimum: a MARTE-based methodology for schedulability analysis at early design stages. ACM SIGSOFT Softw. Eng.Notes **36**, 1–8 (2011)

5. Ouhammou, Y., Grolleau, E., Richard, M., Richard, P.: Towards a model-based approach guiding the scheduling analysis of real-time systems design. In: Proceedings of the 5th International WATERS Workshop, pp. 19–24 (2014)

6. Falkner, K., Chiprianov, V., Falkner, N.J., Szabo, C., Hill, J., Puddy, G., Fraser, D., Johnston, A., Rieckmann, M., Wallis, A.: Model-driven performance prediction of distributed real-time embedded defense systems. In: Proceedings of the 18th International Conference on Engineering of Complex Computer Systems (ICECCS), pp. 155–158 (2013)

7. Pérez, H., Gutiérrez, J.J., Asensio, E., Zamorano, J., de la Puente, J.A.: Model-driven development of high-integrity distributed real-time systems using the end-to-end flow model. In: Proceedings of the 37th Euromicro SEAA Conference, pp. 209–216 (2011)

8. Henia, R., Rioux, L., Sordon, N., Garcia, G.-E., Panunzio, M.: Integrating formal timing analysis in the realtime software development process. In: WOSP 2015, pp. 35–40 (2015)

9. González Harbour, M., Gutiérrez, J.J., Palencia, J.C., Drake, J.M.: MAST: modeling and analysis suite for real time applications. In: Proceedings of the 13th Euromicro Conference on Real-Time Systems, Delft, The Netherlands, pp. 125–134 (2001)

10. González Harbour, M., Gutiérrez, J.J., Drake, J.M., López, P., Palencia, J.C.: Modeling distributed real-time systems with MAST 2. J. Syst. Architect. **56**(6), 331–340 (2013). Elsevier

11. MAST. http://www.mast.unican.es

12. Tindell, K.W., Clark, J.: Holistic schedulability analysis for distributed hard real-time systems. Microprocessing Microprogramming **40**(2–3), 117–134 (1994)

13. Mäki-Turja, J., Nolin, M.: Efficient implementation of tight response-times for tasks with offsets. Real-Time Syst. J. **40**(1), 77–116 (2008)

14. Palencia, J.C., González Harbour, M.: Exploiting precedence relations in the schedulability analysis of distributed real-time systems. In: Proceedings of the 20th Real-Time Systems Symposium, Phoenix, AZ, USA, pp. 328–339. IEEE (1999)

15. SymTA/S. https://www.symtavision.com/

16. Frédéric, J., Allilaire, F., Bézivin, J., Kurtev, I.: ATL: a model transformation tool. Sci. Comput. Program. **72**(1), 31–39 (2008)

17. Rivas, J.M., Gutiérrez, J.J., Palencia, J.C., González Harbour, M.: Schedulability analysis and optimization of heterogeneous EDF and FP distributed real-time systems. In: Proceedings of the 23rd Euromicro Conference on Real-Time Systems, Porto, pp. 195–204 (2011)

Towards Model-Based Optimisation:
Using Domain Knowledge Explicitly

Steffen Zschaler[1]([✉]) and Lawrence Mandow[2]

[1] Department of Informatics, King's College London, London, UK
szschaler@acm.org
[2] Departamento de Lenguajes y Ciencias de la Computación,
Universidad de Málaga, Málaga, Spain
lawrence@lcc.uma.es

Abstract. Search-based software engineering (SBSE) treats software-design problems as search and optimisation problems addressing them by applying automated search and optimisation algorithms. A key concern is the adequate capture and representation of the structure of design problems. Model-driven engineering (MDE) has a strong focus on domain-specific languages (DSLs) which are defined through meta-models, capturing the structure and constraints of a particular domain. There is, thus, a clear argument for combining both techniques to obtain the best of both worlds. Some authors have proposed a number of approaches in recent years, but these have mainly focused on the optimisation of transformations or on the identification of good generic encodings of models for search. In this paper, we first provide a structured overview of the current state of the art before identifying limitations of the key proposals (transformation optimisation and generic genetic encodings of models). We then present a first prototype for running search algorithms directly on models themselves (rather than a separate representation) and derive key research challenges for this approach to model optimisation.

Keywords: Evolutionary optimisation · Object space · Model-driven engineering · Model transformations

1 Introduction

Search-based software engineering (SBSE) is about using optimisation techniques for automating the search for (near-)optimal software designs [1]. More recently, the use of search-based approaches has also been extended to software adaptation (e.g., [2,3]). Using search-based techniques allows the exploration of much larger design spaces than could be explored manually by developers. As a result, better solutions can be identified more quickly.

However, as has been recognised before [4,5], the problem domains in software engineering are too complex to be effectively captured with traditional problem representations as they are typically used in search-based systems. Model-driven

© Springer International Publishing AG 2016
P. Milazzo et al. (Eds.): STAF 2016, LNCS 9946, pp. 317–329, 2016.
DOI: 10.1007/978-3-319-50230-4_24

engineering (MDE) offers good techniques for capturing complex domains including their structural constraints by using meta-models. As a result, there has recently been increased interest in combining the advantages of SBSE and MDE [6–15].

Much of this work has focused on finding good generic representations of models that are tailored towards the needs of standard optimisation algorithms (most typically, genetic algorithms, e.g. [16]). As we will discuss in detail in Sect. 3, these generic encodings introduce their own challenges. Most importantly, they make it easy for search steps to produce invalid candidate solution; that is, models that do not satisfy the constraints expressed by the meta-model or its well-formedness rules.

We propose an alternative approach: instead of defining a secondary encoding for candidate solutions, we propose to run optimisation algorithms directly on models represented in standard meta-modelling data structures. We argue that given that developers have spent substantial time and effort designing meta-models that are a good representation of the domain, we should make use of as much of this information as possible during search and optimisation. We present a first prototype of a tool for running population-based optimisations directly on models and discuss some of the research challenges that need to be addressed to make this vision a reality.

The remainder of this paper is structured as follows: In the next section, we give an overview of existing work defining generic approaches to SBSE in an MDE context. We then discuss some of the limitations of these existing works in Sect. 3, before presenting our own proposal in Sect. 4. Our work is only an initial exploration, highlighting more problems than providing definitive solutions, so in Sect. 5, we outline some of the key research challenges in this area.

2   Related Work

Table 1 summarises the current literature on optimisation in MDE.[1] We use two orthogonal sets of categories for characterising the different approaches that have been explored so far:

1. *By optimisation target.* Some approaches focus on selecting optimal *transformations* (producing optimal models), while other approaches focus on finding optimal *models* directly without considering optimality of transformations (and, possibly, without explicitly specified transformations).
2. *By encoding approach.* Two general approaches have emerged: (1) general encoding of MDE artefacts using standard genetic encodings and applying genetic optimisation algorithms, and (2) techniques that work directly on the structure of the MDE artefacts themselves (possibly with annotations).

We will briefly discuss these categories in more detail below.

---

[1] Some other approaches exist, but they have only been defined for a specific problem. Here, we focus on approaches that aim to be generic.

Table 1. Overview of related work

	Optimisation of models	Optimisation of transformations
Genome encoding	[5,10,11]	[6,13]
Direct search	[4,12,17]	[7–9,15]

2.1 Optimisation of Transformations

A number of authors have proposed approaches that aim to search for optimal transformations instead of looking only for optimal models. Optimality of the models produced is still of interest, but they are only indirectly manipulated by searching the space of viable model transformations. This indirect approach is chosen for one of three reasons:

1. There may be optimality criteria directly on the transformations themselves. For example, when optimising cloud data centre configurations based on a current configuration [3], we are not only interested in finding the optimal new configuration, but also the shortest or least costly path there. Searching for transformations rather than for models directly allows these objectives to be expressed and incorporated into the search process.
2. There might be reachability constraints requiring valid solutions to be reachable from an initial model through a sequence of model transformations. Optimising transformation chains enables these constraints to be expressed.
3. The transformations encode developer choices, but may need to be rerun for other source models at a later stage. In other words, the transformations are the actual optimisation object, their application to models is separate to the optimisation process.

Using genome encodings. Abdeen *et al.* [13] propose encoding different transformation sequences as genomes so that they become amenable to search with a genetic algorithm. Their approach is based on Viatra. Each candidate solution is a tuple made from a start model and a sequence of applications of small, predefined Viatra transformations. The paper provides some good discussion of the issue of invalid individuals: these may be the result of crossover or mutation, making transformation chains invalid or causing them to create invalid models. [13] uses a specific ranking mechanism to handle these cases.

Fleck *et al.* [6], propose MOMoT. MOMoT uses base transformations expressed in Henshin and optimises chains of applications of these transformations to a base model. Fleck *et al.* handle invalid candidate solutions with a repair mechanism, effectively reducing the population size for these situations.

Using direct search. Drago *et al.* [7–9] proposed QVT-R^2, an extension of QVT-Relational. In QVT-R^2, transformation developers create non-deterministic transformations by providing multiple rules matching the same structure in the source model. The rules are then annotated with information about relevant quality analysis (e.g., information about how to invoke an external performance analysis). Each choice point is then incrementally and interactively fixed for a given source model by running all transformation options and asking the developer to choose the best resulting model based on the automatically invoked quality analyses.

Hegedüs *et al.* [15] describe an approach to the guided exploration of transformation chains, using a single-state, back-tracking algorithm guided by dependency graphs between the individual transformations. Their work is based on their earlier work on CPS(M) [14], where they introduced an approach to search-based constraint solving directly over models.

2.2   Optimisation of Models

Using genome encodings. Williams [10] proposes Crepe, a generic encoding of models as sequences of integers. Given a meta-model and a so-called "finitisation model" (containing information about the range of attributes), Crepe provides a unique, bi-directional transformation between instances of the meta-model and integer-vector representations of these models. The integer vectors can be used as genomes in the context of genetic algorithms using standardised, domain-independent operators for mutation and crossover. In [11], the authors provide some extensions to the approach as well as a first comparative evaluation of its performance compared to a manually implemented optimisation.

Kessentini *et al.* [5], give a high-level overview of an architecture for reusing SBSE techniques in the context of MDE. A key ingredient of their approach is also a generic meta-model for encoding models as genomes, making them amenable to standard genetic operators such as mutation and crossover.

Using direct search. Burton and Poulding [4] were the first to describe an idea for running optimisation directly on models.[2] They create separate domain-specific modelling languages describing a search problem and candidate solutions and run search to find near-optimal solutions. As described in [17], their solutions are mappings between solution and problem models, effectively limiting the problem to the optimisation of vectors of binary associations. This enables them to easily define general mutation and crossover operators so that standard evolutionary search can be applied.

Denil *et al.* [12] present a general approach for model-based optimisation using their Formalism Transformation Graph and Process Model (FTG+PM). Their main focus is implementing different search algorithms as transformation scheduling programs, fully integrating them into a general MDE approach. They show how to implement a number of single-state search algorithms in this way, applying them to a problem in circuit design. Candidate solutions are implicit in the transformation scheduling language, which may make it difficult to extend this approach to population-based search algorithms.

---

[2] In earlier work, Horvath *et al.* [14] introduce the idea of search over models, but without support for optimisation.

3   Issues with Generic Encoding of Models

We are interested in optimisation of models rather than transformations. While the latter is useful when we have optimality requirements over transformation chains (or reachability constraints expressed through such chains), more typically, we are interested simply in deriving optimal models. In such a case, optimising transformations incurs too much overhead in repair and through redundant representations of the same model through different transformation chains (effectively reducing the size of the search population).

Generic genetic encodings of models as proposed in [5,10,11], however, have their own problems. In particular, it seems very difficult to ensure locality and preservation of well-formedness as we will demonstrate in an example. Figure 1(a) shows the meta-model of a simple Zoo DSL. This DSL allows the description of zoo configurations, where there are cages with animals, some of which may eat other animals. An optimisation problem of interest would be to find the minimum number of cages to keep all the animals in so that there are no animals that eat each other in the same cage. Note that cages have a maximum capacity and animals require a certain amount of space. The meta-model has been annotated to indicate how it would be encoded by the algorithm proposed in [10]. There, models are encoded as integer strings, where each model element is started by an integer identifying its meta-class (shown in dashed rectangles in Fig. 1(a)). This is then followed by pairs of integers where the first identifies the structural feature (indicated by dashed circles in the figure) and the second provides the value for this feature. For associations, the values are provided by numbering all instances of the target type in sequence of appearance in the gene.

Figure 1(b) shows an example model[3] and its encoding as a gene using this algorithm. To ensure smooth applicability of the standard mutation and crossover operators, genetic encodings should be local; that is, changes in one part should not affect other parts of the represented object. This is not the case

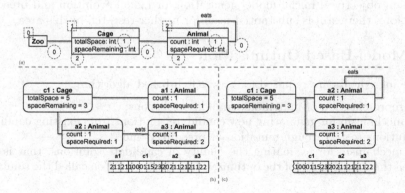

Fig. 1. Zoo DSL example (based on [10])

---

[3] We leave out the recurring Zoo object for simplicity.

for this generic encoding. For example, Fig. 1(c) shows the same gene after it has been split in preparation of a standard single-point crossover operation, removing the representation for object a1 only. The remainder of the gene is exactly as before, but the model fragment encoded by it has changed dramatically: the eat relationship between the two animals has been lost and a3 has been moved into the cage. Note that the latter change has also led to a violation of the model's well-formedness rules, which require that spaceRemaining should always indicate the space left to place additional animals in a cage (and so should now be 2). We are not aware of any generic genetic encoding of models that has overcome this problem using generic mutation and crossover operators. As a result, such approaches require a lot of repair of candidate solutions, substantially worsening the optimisation performance [11].

The problem could be resolved by defining domain-specific mutation and crossover operators. However, these are difficult to implement on the level of genotypes; they will effectively have to constantly reinterpret the genes as the corresponding model fragments. We have explored this in [18], showing that such specific operators do indeed have a positive effect on the performance of the optimisation algorithm.

In the next section, we propose that using optimisation directly on models makes it much easier to define such domain specific operators, substantially reducing the need for repair. As discussed in Sect. 2, we are not the first to propose this: Burton *et al.* [4,17] first proposed the idea and gave an example. They do not, however, provide a general implementation. Denil *et al.* [12] provide a first generic implementation using a transformation scheduling language. However, it is difficult to see how their approach would generalise to population-based algorithms as typically used for multi-objective optimisation as the actual candidate-solution model is implicit in the specification. As a result, their implementation works well for single-state search algorithms, including with backtracking, but cannot easily represent populations of more than one candidate solution. Moreover, they do not provide general mechanisms for encoding optimisation objectives, initial model generation, or model evolution and breeding. Therefore, there still is substantial need for further research in this area.

4   Model-Based Optimisation

Three ingredients are required for any search-based algorithm:

1. A representation of individual candidate solutions;
2. A mechanism for generating new candidate solutions from existing candidate solutions (e.g., through mutation or breeding); and
3. A mechanism for evaluating the quality of candidate solutions; that is how well they satisfy each of the optimisation objectives (often called the solution's fitness).

Most search algorithms also require a means of generating an initial population of candidate solutions. Once these ingredients have been defined for a specific problem, we can apply standard search-based algorithms.

As discussed above, we will use models to represent individual candidate solutions. Therefore, the overall search space is defined through a meta-model. An initial population of candidate solutions can be provided in a number of ways—for example, it could be provided as a set of explicit model files or we could use constraint solvers like Alloy [19] to generate a suitable set of initial models (e.g., using the Cartier tool originally developed for transformation testing [20, 21]).

To generate new solutions from existing ones, endogenous model transformations are an obvious candidate. In particular, we propose to use graph transformations, as they have a clear and simple syntax for easily expressing endogenous transformations. For example, Fig. 2 shows a simple Henshin rule that can be used for the search problem described in the previous section. Because these rules are defined on the model level, we will often be able to easily write them in a way that ensures well-formedness rules are preserved.

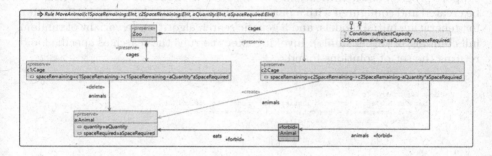

Fig. 2. Henshin rule for moving animals between cages

Evaluating the fitness of candidate solutions can take many different forms. In the simplest case, fitness may be determined by a model query—for example expressed in OCL. In other cases, we may require to run a simulation of the candidate solution, which may involve further transformations etc. (e.g., [2, 3]).

To test out these ideas, we are currently developing a prototype tool for model optimisation.[4] Our tool provides a simple Xtext-based DSL to allow describing model-based search problems together with an interpreter for running searches. Search algorithms, fitness functions, and initial model provision are modularised behind Java interfaces. For search algorithms this means that it is easy to incorporate existing implementations, such as the MOEA framework[5]. We currently have no DSL-level support for fitness functions and initial model generation, but plan to add these features. For now, they are specified by providing Java implementations. Solution evolution is realised by Henshin transformations.

Figure 3 shows an example specification of the Zoo example in our tool. After some configuration information in the first line, this code declares the structure

---

[4] See https://github.com/mde-optimiser/mde_optimiser.
[5] See http://moeaframework.org/.

of the search space by indicating a meta-model, and then defines relevant fitness functions and model evolvers. Fitness functions are currently provided by implementing a specific Java interface; we are planning to provide full OCL integration in the language for simple model queries. Evolvers are defined by specifying a Henshin model and naming a rule in this model.

```
1  basepath <src/uk/ac/kcl/MDEOptimise/tests/models/zoo/>
2  metamodel <zoo.ecore>
3  fitness "uk.ac.kcl.MDEOptimise.tests.models.zoo.ZooFitnessFunction"
4  evolve using <zoo_evolution.henshin> unit "MoveAnimal"
```

Fig. 3. Specification of the Zoo search problem

Figure 4 shows how to run a search using our tool. At this point, we only support programmatic invocation. For this, a new **Interpreter** object needs to be created and configured with a parsed version of the problem, a **ModelProvider** for generating initial models, and a generic search algorithm (a variant of random hill climbing in this example). Invoking **execute** runs the search as specified and returns the set of solutions found.

```
1  class PaperSample {
2      def Set<EObject> runSearch (Optimisation model, ModelProvider mp) {
3          val interpreter = new OptimisationInterpreter(model, new RandomHillClimbing (10), mp)
4          return interpreter.execute();
5      }
6  }
```

Fig. 4. Basic code for running model-based search algorithms

As a tool, our prototype is closest to MOMoT [6], which also uses meta-models to represent search spaces and Henshin rules to represent evolution. However, they are searching for transformation chains using a genetic encoding, while we are searching directly on models.

5   Research Challenges

Our initial work has identified a number of challenges requiring further research to enable model-based optimisation to be used effectively.

5.1   Reuse of Existing Optimisation Algorithms

Some existing optimisation algorithms make particular assumptions about the search space. For example, hill climbing, a basic single-objective search algorithm, expects to be able to identify the complete "neighbourhood" of a given candidate solution so that this can be systematically explored. Similarly, swarm-based search algorithms expect to be able to identify a "direction" vector between solutions and to use this to guide the derivation of one solution from another. These notions are easily defined in classic search-based approaches, where solutions are represented by (high dimensional) numerical vectors. It is less obvious what they mean for models, which are only indirectly related by model transformation chains. Providing appropriate interpretations of these notions will make it possible to reuse more existing search and optimisation algorithms. Beyond that, however, there is an opportunity to explore novel search algorithms that take guidance from the structure and constraints encoding the search space in a model-driven context.

5.2   Model Evolution

Generating new candidate solutions from existing ones is a key part of any search algorithm. In model-based search, a number of challenges need to be addressed:

Model breeding. Many population-based algorithms rely on a notion of "breeding", which allows creating new candidate solutions by combining two good parent solutions. This is useful because it allows the search to reach new areas of the search space, hopefully benefiting from the advantages of both parent solutions. For example, in genetic algorithms, "breeding" is realised through so-called crossover operators, which combine two genes by swapping sub-sequences. While mutation of solutions is easily captured by model transformations as discussed, it is less clear how to express breeding. Two approaches seem worth exploring:

1. *Domain-specific breeders.* As with model mutation, we could use model transformations to express domain-specific breeding. These transformations would take in two models and produce a new model. For example, in our Zoo problem, we could consider developing a transformation that takes two cage–animal allocations and produces a new one mixing allocations from both sources while making sure that constraints are not violated (e.g., updating spaceRemaining values and checking for eats relationships). Burton *et al.* [17] show a first example of this for problems where solutions are essentially sets of links between pre-existing model elements.

2. *Generic breeding through model merging.* Model breeding essentially requires identifying the common and different parts of two models so that the common parts can be retained in the new solution and the different parts can be mixed suitably. This is very similar to what has been developed in the context of work on model differencing and model merging [22–25]. It should be possible to reuse ideas from this field to develop generic model breeders. The key challenge here is that mixing of differences should lead to a new model that is (a) different from both parent models, and (b) well-formed. This will require suitable adjustments to be made to existing diff/merge algorithms for models.

It is very likely that in either case we will not be able to produce breeders that are guaranteed to produce well-formed models, introducing the need to deal with invalid solutions in the search. Abdeen *et al.* [13] give a good discussion of these issues in the context of genetic optimisation of model-transformation chains, where they use repair as well as customised ranking rules. Similar techniques could be applied to model-based optimisation, too.

Efficient model evolution. Our current prototype first establishes all matches for all evolvers and then randomly selects one of them when asked to produce a new candidate solution. Especially where rules have similar pre-conditions or will often not be applicable this seems an inefficient approach. We should explore mechanisms for selecting evolvers (and matches) more efficiently. Denil *et al.* [12] provide some initial insights into this problem by considering optimisation algorithms to be a kind of transformation scheduling specification. This enables them to use different sets of evolvers at different stages of the optimisation process.

Non-deterministic matching in graph transformation engines. Search-based algorithms rely on an amount of randomness underlying the exploration process. Using graph transformations as model evolvers requires the matching process to be non-deterministic. In other words, if there are multiple potential matches for a graph-transformation rule in a model, the choice of match to apply should be non-deterministic. Otherwise, we risk excluding large parts of the search space from the search as a result of an accidental systematic effect of how models happen to be stored in memory or of how model elements are enumerated to find potential matches. Henshin is currently not non-deterministic in this sense, requiring us to explicitly establish all matches and make a random selection. It would be more efficient if Henshin were to non-deterministically select matches on its own.

Compact representations of solutions and evolvers. Typically, a substantial part of a candidate solution will remain constant, as it essentially describes problem constraints rather than solution elements. Burton *et al.* [17] use different models to represent these static parts independently of the parts that change during search. This makes for a very compact solution representation, but requires a separate composition transformation whenever a solution's fitness is to be evaluated or when a new solution needs to be generated. There is a need to understand other similarly compact representations of candidate solutions and how they affect solution evolution and fitness evaluation. Similarly, we should explore ways in which evolvers can be represented more compactly and executed more efficiently knowing that large parts of a candidate solution never change. This has been partially explored in the context of single-state search in the work on design-space exploration [15], where critical-pair analysis is used to establish a dependency graph between evolvers and use this as a basis for guiding the selection of the next evolver to apply.

5.3   Performance

Search algorithms are computationally expensive. Typically, they require a large number of iterations to be run for large populations of candidate solutions. Each iteration requires each candidate solution in the population to be evolved to a new solution and the fitness of these solutions to be evaluated. The performance of search algorithms is therefore substantially influenced by the performance of solution evolution and fitness evaluations. Depending on the size of the models, model transformations can be computationally expensive to execute. There has been recent interest in increasing the efficiency of model transformation execution [26,27]. We need to explore how this could be integrated into model-based optimisation. Ideally, we would like to be able to run model-based search even at system run time to support self-aware system adaptation.

5.4   Flexible Definition of Model Providers

As discussed above, candidate solutions in model-based optimisation are particular in that substantial parts of the model will remain constant as they are describing the search problem. When using constraint solvers like Alloy [19], this would result in a large number of constraints, potentially impacting the performance of initial model generation. Better techniques need to be studied that can limit the performance impact on model generation. It would be useful to identify what are the key constraints that must be available to the constraint solver for it to construct valid instance *of the variable model part* without necessarily recreating the complete constant part every time.

5.5   Expressing Fitness Evaluations

Some fitness functions are essentially model queries, which can be efficiently expressed in languages like OCL. However, other evaluations will be more complex, including simulations and model analyses. At the moment, these are handled by providing a general Java interface to be implemented for specific fitness evaluations. Techniques better aligned with model-driven approaches need to be developed. Kessentini *et al.* [5] have made some interesting first proposals in this area, which need to be explored further.

6   Conclusions

Search-based software engineering (SBSE) and model-driven engineering (MDE) are highly complementary approaches to software engineering. As a result, there has been substantial interest recently in exploring the combination of both approaches, in particular using MDE technologies to simplify and streamline the application of SBSE. This paper adds to the debate by

1. Providing an overview and initial classification of the current state of the art;
2. Identifying issues with generic genetic encodings of models;
3. Presenting an initial prototype for model-based optimisation; and
4. Identifying a catalogue of research challenges towards complete support for model-based optimisation.

References

1. Harman, M., Jones, B.F.: Search-based software engineering. Inf. Softw. Technol. **43**(14), 833–839 (2001)
2. Efstathiou, D., McBurney, P., Zschaler, S., Bourcier, J.: Efficient multi-objective optimisation of service compositions in mobile ad hoc networks using lightweight surrogate models. JUCS **20**(8), 1089–1108 (2014). Special issue on WAS4FI 2013
3. Chatziprimou, K., Lano, K., Zschaler, S.: Surrogate-assisted online optimisation of cloud iaas configurations. In: IEEE 6th International Conference on Cloud Computing Technology and Science (CloudCom), pp. 138–145 (2014)
4. Burton, F.R., Poulding, S.: Complementing metaheuristic search with higher abstraction techniques. In: 1st International Workshop Combining Modelling and Search-Based Software Engineering (CMSBSE 2013), pp. 45–48 (2013)
5. Kessentini, M., Langer, P., Wimmer, M.: Searching models, modeling search: on the synergies of SBSE and MDE. In: 1st International Workshop Combining Modelling and Search-Based Software Engineering (CMSBSE 2013), pp. 51–54 (2013)
6. Fleck, M., Troya, J., Wimmer, M.: Marrying search-based optimization and model transformation technology. In: Proceedings of 1st North American Search Based Software Engineering Symposium (NasBASE 2015) (2015). http://martin-fleck.github.io/momot/downloads/NasBASE_MOMoT.pdf
7. Drago, M.L., Ghezzi, C., Mirandola, R.: QVTR^2: a rational and performance-aware extension to the relations language. In: Dingel, J., Solberg, A. (eds.) MODELS 2010. LNCS, vol. 6627, p. 328. Springer, Heidelberg (2011). doi:10.1007/978-3-642-21210-9_31
8. Drago, M.L., Ghezzi, C., Mirandola, R.: Towards quality driven exploration of model transformation spaces. In: Whittle, J., Clark, T., Kühne, T. (eds.) MODELS 2011. LNCS, vol. 6981, pp. 2–16. Springer, Heidelberg (2011). doi:10.1007/978-3-642-24485-8_2
9. Drago, M.L., Ghezzi, C., Mirandola, R.: A quality driven extension to the QVT-relations transformation language. Comput. Sci. Res. Dev. **30**(1), 1–20 (2015). First online: 24 November 2011
10. Williams, J.R.: A Novel Representation for Search-Based Model-Driven Engineering. Ph.d. thesis. University of York (2013)
11. Efstathiou, D., Williams, J.R., Zschaler, S.: Crepe complete: multi-objective optimisation for your models. In: Proceedings of 1st International Workshop on Combining Modelling with Search- and Example-Based Approaches (CMSEBA 2014) (2014)
12. Denil, J., Jukss, M., Verbrugge, C., Vangheluwe, H.: Search-based model optimization using model transformations. In: Amyot, D., Fonseca i Casas, P., Mussbacher, G. (eds.) SAM 2014. LNCS, vol. 8769, pp. 80–95. Springer, Heidelberg (2014). doi:10.1007/978-3-319-11743-0_6
13. Abdeen, H., Varró, D., Sahraoui, H., Nagy, A.S., Debreceni, C., Hegedüs, Á., Horváth, Á.: Multi-objective optimization in rule-based design space exploration. In: Crnkovic, I., Chechik, M., Grünbacher, P. (eds.): Proceedings of 29th ACM/IEEE International Conference Automated Software Engineering (ASE 2014), pp. 289–300. ACM (2014)
14. Horváth, Á., Varró, D.: CSP(M): constraint satisfaction problem over models. In: Schürr, A., Selic, B. (eds.) MODELS 2009. LNCS, vol. 5795, pp. 107–121. Springer, Heidelberg (2009). doi:10.1007/978-3-642-04425-0_9

15. Hegedüs, Á., Horváth, Á., Ráth, I., Varró, D.: A model-driven framework for guided design space exploration. In: Proceedings of 26th IEEE/ACM International Conference Automated Software Engineering (ASE 2011), pp. 173–182, November 2011

16. Deb, K., Pratap, A., Agarwal, S., Meyarivan, T.: A fast and elitist multiobjective genetic algorithm: NSGA-II. IEEE Trans. Evol. Comput. **6**(2), 182–197 (2002)

17. Burton, F.R., Paige, R.F., Rose, L.M., Kolovos, D.S., Poulding, S., Smith, S.: Solving acquisition problems using model-driven engineering. In: Vallecillo, A., Tolvanen, J.-P., Kindler, E., Störrle, H., Kolovos, D. (eds.) ECMFA 2012. LNCS, vol. 7349, pp. 428–443. Springer, Heidelberg (2012). doi:10.1007/978-3-642-31491-9_32

18. Mandow, L., Montenegro, J.A., Zschaler, S.: Mejora de una representación genética genérica para modelos. In: Actas de la XVII Conferencia de la Asociación Española para la Inteligencia Artificial (CAEPIA 2016) (2016, in press)

19. Jackson, D.: Alloy: a lightweight object modelling notation. ACM Trans. Softw. Eng. Methodol. **11**(2), 256–290 (2002)

20. Sen, S., Baudry, B., Mottu, J.M.: On combining multi-formalism knowledge to select models for model transformation testing. In: Proceedings of 1st International Conference on Software Testing, Verification, and Validation, pp. 328–337 (2008)

21. Sen, S., Baudry, B., Mottu, J.-M.: Automatic model generation strategies for model transformation testing. In: Paige, R.F. (ed.) ICMT 2009. LNCS, vol. 5563, pp. 148–164. Springer, Heidelberg (2009). doi:10.1007/978-3-642-02408-5_11

22. Kolovos, D.S.: Establishing correspondences between models with the epsilon comparison language. In: Paige, R.F., Hartman, A., Rensink, A. (eds.) ECMDA-FA 2009. LNCS, vol. 5562, pp. 146–157. Springer, Heidelberg (2009). doi:10.1007/978-3-642-02674-4_11

23. Kolovos, D.S., Ruscio, D.D., Pierantonio, A., Paige, R.F.: Different models for model matching: an analysis of approaches to support model differencing. In: Proceedings of ICSE Workshop on Comparison and Versioning of Software Models (CVSM 2009). IEEE Computer Society, pp. 1–6 (2009)

24. Maoz, S., Ringert, J.O., Rumpe, B.: A manifesto for semantic model differencing. In: Dingel, J., Solberg, A. (eds.) MODELS 2010. LNCS, vol. 6627, pp. 194–203. Springer, Heidelberg (2011). doi:10.1007/978-3-642-21210-9_19

25. Langer, P., Mayerhofer, T., Kappel, G.: Semantic model differencing utilizing behavioral semantics specifications. In: Dingel, J., Schulte, W., Ramos, I., Abrahão, S., Insfran, E. (eds.) MODELS 2014. LNCS, vol. 8767, pp. 116–132. Springer, Heidelberg (2014). doi:10.1007/978-3-319-11653-2_8

26. Amstel, M., Bosems, S., Kurtev, I., Ferreira Pires, L.: Performance in model transformations: experiments with ATL and QVT. In: Cabot, J., Visser, E. (eds.) ICMT 2011. LNCS, vol. 6707, pp. 198–212. Springer, Heidelberg (2011). doi:10.1007/978-3-642-21732-6_14

27. Mészáros, T., Mezei, G., Levendovszky, T., Asztalos, M.: Manual and automated performance optimization of model transformation systems. Int. J. Softw. Tools Technol. Transf. **12**(3), 231–243 (2010)

SEMS

On the Emergence of Patterns for Spreadsheets Data Arrangements

Ricardo Teixeira[✉] and Vasco Amaral

NOVA LINCS, DI, FCT, Universidade Nova de Lisboa, Lisbon, Portugal
rd.teixeira@campus.fct.unl.pt,
vasco.amaral@fct.unl.pt

Abstract. Spreadsheets are widely used both by individuals as well as large companies in a vast plethora of application domains. One of the reasons for this popularity is the general purpose flexibility spreadsheets offer to the end user. This flexibility favors the existence of multiple spreadsheet designs regarding the physical organization of the data presented by a spreadsheet. Nevertheless, to the best of our knowledge, little is still known about patterns of spreadsheet data arrangements. Works refer the emergence of commonalities and templates but it is hard to find a systematic study on the topic that presents us catalogues. It is known that spreadsheets are extremely error-prone. Therefore, to know the typical data arrangement patterns can be very useful insight on how to build mechanisms and strategies in order to prevent errors regarding spreadsheets specification and maintenance. The present work aims at present data arrangement patterns that emerged from our studies and direct observation of real-world spreadsheet samples from two large datasets, and, additionally, a formal representation of the patterns identified through the use of conceptual models.

Keywords: Spreadsheets · Data arrangements · Patterns · Conceptual model · UML

1 Introduction

Being the first "programmer in a box" to come along for technology users, spreadsheets are widely used both by individuals to cope with simple needs like tracking personal finances, training plans, to-do lists, supplier databases, or any purpose that requires input of data and/or performing calculations; as well as large companies as integrators of complex systems and as support for informing business decisions especially in areas like marketing, business development, sales, and finance. As result of this general purpose flexibility, a plenty of spreadsheet layout designs are possible towards the physical organization of the data composing a spreadsheet.

Works proposing spreadsheet models [1, 2] already systematize common templates of table structures. Other works created a library containing common spreadsheet patterns [3] for later use of pattern matching algorithms in order to extract models from them. Other works implemented a header inference system for spreadsheets [4], describing the relation between the headers and their association with data.

© Springer International Publishing AG 2016
P. Milazzo et al. (Eds.): STAF 2016, LNCS 9946, pp. 333–345, 2016.
DOI: 10.1007/978-3-319-50230-4_25

However, these patterns are quite far from covering all existing kinds of spreadsheet's data arrangements and do not take in consideration the domains those patterns are generally applied.

Knowing more about the typical data arrangement patterns, in other words, what people usually want to model in a spreadsheet and what they usually expect to see in a spreadsheet, can be very useful insight in how to build mechanisms and strategies to specify and maintain less erroneous spreadsheets.

This work intends to take a step on extending the current perception of the emerged spreadsheet patterns regarding the data arrangements. For this purpose, two large repositories of spreadsheets used in spreadsheet studies were directly observed and analyzed, namely:

- The EUSES corpus [5] – published in 2005 and made available only to researchers, it is a dataset of over 4,500 spreadsheets gathered from the public world-wide-web;
- Enron corpus [6, 7] – a recent large dataset containing around 15,000 industrial spreadsheets extracted from the Enron Corporation e-mail archive made public during the legal investigation concerning the company after it went bankrupt.

The analysis method consisted of manually selecting random spreadsheet samples from the datasets, until the patterns observed were becoming redundant. Due to the low diversity verified, only 80 spreadsheets representative of all of the spreadsheets existing in the datasets were selected and reunited. With them, a formal systemization of data arrangement patterns was made using the UML conceptual model, namely, class diagrams, which is one of the most proliferated conceptual models, having a high level of understanding.

The rest of the paper is organized as follows: in Sect. 2 we present the identified patterns, cataloging them and presenting related insights. Then, in Sect. 3 we present a metamodel of a spreadsheet concerning its data arrangement, and in Sect. 4 we conclude the paper.

2   Patterns

2.1   Table Structures

When thinking about spreadsheets we immediately conceive tabular forms constituted by a set of labels – usually called "headers" – associated with a set of values. Based on the spreadsheets observed, we can catalogue the common tables structures into three distinct groups which are defined by the table growth orientation and their purpose.

Vertical Tables. The most linear table structure consists of a simple grown-vertically table, where there is a header in the first row; this structure is commonly associated with inventory, database (Fig. 1), or statistical data (Fig. 2). A header can represent a formula referring other row's entry values.

Also, sometimes there is an additional bottom row that applies an aggregation function to some specific column, as we can see in Fig. 2.

	A	B	C	D	E	F	G	H	I
1	Title	First Name	Last Name	Country	Nationality	Age Group	Sex	Address_1	Address_2
2	Ms.	Maxine P.	McClean	BARBADOS	Barbadian	35 - 44	Female	22 Oxnards Heights	St. James
3	Ms.	Jeanette	Bell	BARBADOS	Barbadian	45 - 54	Female	Women and Development Unit	School of Continuing Studies
4	Mr.	Anthony	Bovel	BARBADOS	Barbadian	45 - 54	Male	2nd Avenue Promenade Road	Kew Land
5	Dr.	Judith W.	Edwin	VIRGIN IS.	U.S.	> 55	Female	P.O. Box 306935	St. Thomas
6	Mr.	Raymond	Joseph	ST. LUCIA	St. Lucian	45 - 54	Male	Teacher Education Division	Sir Arthur Lewis Com. College
7	Ms.	Desiree V.	Edwards	ANTIGUA	Antiguan	35 - 44	Female	P.O. Box 1430	St. John's
8	Dr.	Edris L.	Bird	ANTIGUA	Antiguan	> 55	Female	P.O. Box 1810	St. John's
9	Ms.	Brenda C.	Carrott	ANTIGUA	Antiguan	25 - 34	Male	Lower Fort Road	St. John's
10	Ms.	Angela	Brice	ST. LUCIA	St. Lucia	> 55	Female	P.O. Box 4005	Castries
11	Ms.	Maureen	Lucas	BARBADOS	Barbadian	45 - 54	Female	Spooners Hill	St. Michael
12	Ms.	Martina	Augustin	ST. LUCIA	St. Lucian	45 - 54	Female	Sir Arthur Lewis Com. College	Morne Fortune
13	Ms.	Ruby	Yorke	ST.LUCIA	St. Lucian	> 55	Female	P.O. Box 1553	Castries
14	Ms.	Gem	Lynch	BARBADOS	Barbadian	45 - 54	Female	"Der-Land"	Upper Golf CLub Road
15	Ms.	Patricia E.	Linton	BARBADOS		45 - 54	Female	Lot # 2 Kirtons	St. Philip

Fig. 1. Vertical table used as a database

	A	B	C	D
1	Database Name	Searches	Full-text	PDF
2	Academic Search Premier	118 964	101 189	32 644
3	American Heritage Children's Dictionary	2	1	0
4	Business Source Premier	26 768	21 656	7 353
5	Clinical Pharmacology	38	21	0
6	Funk & Wagnalls New World Encyclopedia	712	156	0
7	Health Source - Consumer Edition	5 297	980	125
8	Health Source: Nursing/Academic Edition	11 293	2 019	941
9	Image Collection	168	184	0
10	MAS Ultra - School Edition	4 180	1 829	59
11	MEDLINE	16 346	89	0
12	Military & Government Collection	3 325	609	44
13	Psychology and Behavioral Sciences Collection	32 346	7 536	3 567
14	Regional Business News	6 345	2 718	464
15	Religion and Philosophy Collection	5 827	682	186
16	Total	231 611	139 669	45 383

Fig. 2. Vertical table used to display statistical data

Horizontal Single Entry Tables. A second table structure is a table whose headers are disposed vertically, and in which there is only one entry. Typically, the purpose of this kind of tables is to display summary data, and usually an aggregation function is applied on the solo entry values.

In Fig. 3, a SUM function is used to calculate the "TOTAL INCOME" from the above entry values.

	A	B
1	The American Society of Hematology	
2	2002 Audited Financial Statement	
3		
4		
5	INCOME	
6		
7	Administrative	1 017 768
8	Annual Meeting	9 316 889
9	Awards	252 592
10	BLOOD Journal - Editorial	619 595
11	BLOOD Journal - Publishing	8 730 190
12	Clinical Research Training Institute	15 000
13	Education & Communications	111 759
14	Self Assessment Program	325 160
15		
16	TOTAL INCOME:	20 388 953

Fig. 3. Horizontal single entry table example

Relationship Tables. A third group of table structures are the relationship tables, consisting of tables that grow horizontally, with a highlighted header – the top one. The top header values are themselves headers, that is, without that header's entry value, the other header entry values are meaningless. Sometimes the top header label is omitted, being only displayed its values. Aggregation functions are also commonly used on this tables, both vertically (see row "8" in Fig. 4) and horizontally (see column "F" in Fig. 5 of Sect. 2.2).

	A	B	C	D	E	F
1	Calendar Year	2002	2003	2004	2005	2006
2						
3	Volume / Day	100 000	100 000	100 000	100 000	100 000
4	Days/Year	365	365	365	365	151
5	Demand Charge/MMbtu	$ 0,356480	$ 0,356480	$ 0,299080	$ 0,299080	$ 0,299080
6	Gas Research Institute (GRI)	$ 0,001970	$ 0,001640	$ -	$ -	$ -
7						
8	Total Calendar Demand Charge	$ (13 083 425,00)	$ (13 071 380,00)	$ (10 916 420,00)	$ (10 916 420,00)	$ (4 516 108,00)

Fig. 4. Relationship table using calendar years

This table structure pattern dominates spreadsheets used for financial modeling and analysis, with the top header usually representing calendar years (Fig. 4), year quarters, months, etc.

2.2 Header Composition

In horizontal tables, it is usual to see headers composed by other headers. The main headers – the ones who are composed – typically represent categories, and the coupled ones are headers belonging to the category of the main header where they are attached.

	A	B	C	D	E	F
1	2004 FINANCIAL ANALYSIS					
2		Q1	Q2	Q3	Q4	TOTAL
3						
4	Expected number of purses sold:	500	600	700	800	2600
5						
6	COSTS					
7	Cigar Boxes	$ 250,00	$ 300,00	$ 350,00	$ 400,00	$ 1 300,00
8	retaurants (1000 boxes for free)	$ -	$ -	$ -	$ -	
9	tobacco shops (1000 boxes for $1.00 each)	$ 250,00	$ 300,00	$ 350,00	$ 400,00	
10						
11	Cigar Box Accessories ($3.00/box)	=(B4*3)	$ 1 800,00	$ 2 100,00	$ 2 400,00	$ 7 800,00
12						
13	Resourses	$ 13 850,00	$ 13 850,00	$ 13 850,00	$ 13 850,00	$ 55 400,00
14	CEO/CIO ($25,000 each)	$ 12 500,00	$ 12 500,00	$ 12 500,00	$ 12 500,00	
15	Purse maker ($6.00/hour)	$ 1 350,00	$ 1 350,00	$ 1 350,00	$ 1 350,00	
16						
17	Technology	$ 704,00	$ 30,00	$ 30,00	$ 30,00	$ 794,00
18	Web Site					
19	domain name	$ 35,00	$ -	$ -	$ -	
20	hosting	$ 30,00	$ 30,00	$ 30,00	$ 30,00	
21	digital camera	$ 300,00	$ -	$ -	$ -	
22	MS Access database	$ 339,00	$ -	$ -	$ -	
23	Macromedia Dreamweaver	$ 399,00	$ -	$ -	$ -	
24						
25	Marketing	$ 1 250,00	$ 1 250,00	$ 1 250,00	$ 1 250,00	$ 5 000,00
26						
27	Micellaneous Costs	$ 1 000,00	$ 1 000,00	$ 1 000,00	$ 1 000,00	$ 4 000,00
28						
29	Total Costs	$ 18 654,00	$18 230,00	$18 580,00	$18 930,00	$ (74 294,00)
30						
31	REVENUE ($60/purse)	$ 30 000,00	$ 36 000,00	$ 42 000,00	$ 48 000,00	$ 156 000,00
32						
33	Total Revenue	$ 30 000,00	$36 000,00	$42 000,00	$48 000,00	$156 000,00
34						
35	TOTAL PROFIT	$ 11 446,00	$17 770,00	$23 420,00	$29 070,00	$ 81 706,00

Fig. 5. Relationship table with coupling

Commonly, a main header's entry value consists of an aggregation function – usually SUM – applied to the coupled headers' entry values.

In Fig. 5, we can see a relationship table composed by six main headers: "Expected number of purses sold:", "COSTS", "Total Costs", "REVENUE ($60/purse)", "Total Revenue" and "TOTAL PROFIT", with the last four ones consisting of formulas. The main header "COSTS" is composed by other six headers, with three of them – namely: "Cigar Boxes", "Recourses" and "Technology" – having attached headers of their own. It is also possible to verify that "COST" has no table entry values associated, functioning as a pure categorization label, meanwhile the lower level main headers, such as "Cigar Boxes", have entry values consisting of a SUM aggregation function applied to the headers' values they have attached.

2.3 Header Hierarchy

Similar to the composed headers, there are the hierarchically organized headers. Although in the header composition is express some sort of hierarchy, there are actually some major differences between the two header arrangements: in this type of header arrangement, the hierarchy is explicit, that is, the headers are not physically on the same level; also, unlike composed headers, in this arrangement the top headers (the ones who have at least one header below in the hierarchy) do not have any values in the table associated to them; lastly, a header hierarchy appears in both vertical and horizontal table structures, although it is very uncommon to see it in a horizontal one.

In Fig. 6 it is possible to see a vertical table with two header hierarchies ("Dimensions" and "Location") which have a mere organizational purpose, with the intend to offer a clearer and focused table understating. However, header hierarchies

	A	B	C	D	E	F	G	H	I
1	IDAHO STATE CAPITOL ARTWORK AND DISPLAY INVENTORY								
2									
3	Category	Dimensions			Location			Description	Photo
4		Height	Width	Depth	Floor	Wing	Notes		
5	portraits (10)	50"	35"		1	R	on walls between pillars; 8 on inside; 2 on outside, N side.	Territorial Governor portraits, there is a descriptive plaque under the William Wallace portrait on north side (plaque is 13"x10.5"). All belong to Historical Society.	none
6	sculpture	10'-6"	3'-1"	5'-6"	1	R	NE corner near stairway down	Miner statue, titled "The Patriot." Text on base reads, "Created by Kenneth Lonn, a Bunker Hill Mine Mechanic. This sculpture in steel is dedicated to the man and women of Idaho's mining industry. On loan to the State of Idaho By The Bunker Hill Company, Kellogg, Idaho A Subsidiary of Gulf Resources & Chemical Corporation." Height is approximate, to top of drill.	P002
7	display case	3'-3"	8'	5'-3.75"	1	R	NE corner near stairway down	Idaho State Capitol Plan, diorama under glass, on wood base.	P003
8	plaque	19"	18"		1	R	NE corner near stairway down	Detail about miner sculpture. Black plastic frame and cracked plexiglass cover.	P001
9	plaque	24"	20"		1	R	NE corner near stairway down	engraved bronze, "We Were Miners Then" by Gov. Phil Batt, next to miner detail plaque.	P001
10	plaques	18"	22"		1	R	outside of between-pillar wall, NW corner near Cap. Ed. Cntr.	Smaller engraved bronze plaque (3.75"x18.5") above says "In Memory of JFK." Larger plaque has Prayer of St. Francis of Assissi.	P004
11	picture	18.25"	22.5"		1	R	NW corner near Cap. Ed. Cntr.	Wood framed photo of USS Boise CL-47 ship. Back of item has very faded paper (unreadable) and stamp that says "Official United States Navy Photograph."	P005
12	picture	18.25"	22.5"		1	R	NW corner near Cap. Ed. Cntr.	Wood framed photo of USS Idaho BB-42 ship. Back has stamp that says "Official United States	P006
13	display case	37.5"	25.5"		1	R	wall on N side of entrance to W hallway	"Idaho Peace Officers Association" dark-stained wood display case with glass front. Contains 4 badges and several engraved name plates.	P007
14	plaque	33"	33"		1	R	outside of between-pillar wall, SW corner	Engraved bronze, "In memory of the deceased Idaho volunteers" who died in war of 1898-99 with Spain.	P008
15	plaque	32.75"	25"		1	R	outside of between-pillar wall, SW corner	Engraved bronze plaque with Gettysburg Address. Bottom dedication: "Presented by the Woman's Relief Corps Department of Idaho, to the State of Idaho, in honor of the grand army of the republic, September 11, 1928."	P009
16	plaque	32.75"	25"		1	R	outside of between-pillar wall, SE corner	Engraved bronze plaque, "Memorial Day Order" and description. Bottom dedication: "Presented by the Woman's Relief Corps Department of Idaho, to the State of Idaho, in honor of the grand army of the republic, September 11, 1928."	P010
17	sculpture	5'	3'	2'-3"	1	R	under stairwell in SE corner	Large stone on pedastal (dimensions 2'-5.5" tall x 2'-8" wide x 1'-8" deep). Plaque says "Dedicated 3/22/99, to be opened in year 2010." Another plaque says "Base dontated by CI."	P011
18	sculpture	6'	3'	3'	1	R	under stairwell in SE corner	bronze sundial on circular bronze base, some stones inside the "stalk" of the base, says "Anno 1974 on stalk	P012
19	display case	7'-3"	4'-1/2"	11.5"	1	R	SE corner by elevator	"Idaho Sheriffs Association," medium-stained wood case sitting on floor, glass front, contains sheriffs badges from all Idaho counties with large wood Idaho carving in center.	P013
20	plaque	32.5"	26.5"		1	R	SE corner by elevator	"American Mothers Inc. Idaho Mothers Hall of Fame" framed plaque	P014

Fig. 6. Vertical table with a header hierarchy

	A	B	C	D	E	F	G	H	I	J	K	L	M
1													
2		**Quarterly Financial and Stock Information**											
3		Sony Corporation and Consolidated Subsidiaries											
4		Year ended March 31											
5		(Unaudited)											
6													
7							Yen in billions except per share amounts						
8			1st Quarter			2nd Quarter			3rd Quarter			4th Quarter	
9			2002	2003		2002	2003		2002	2003		2002	2003
10		Sales and operating revenue. . . .	\1 633,50	\1 721,80		\1 780,90	\1 789,70		\2 279,30	\2 307,70		\1 884,60	\1 654,40
11		Operating income (loss).	3,0	51,9		(3,4)	50,5		158,6	199,5		(23,6)	(116,5)
12		Income (loss) before											
13		income taxes	(14,3)	116,6		0,6	48,8		119,3	201,9		(12,8)	(119,7)
14		Income taxes	20,3	53,6		14,8	(14,9)		39,0	65,5		(8,9)	(23,4)
15		Income (loss) before cumulative											
16		effect of accounting changes . .	(36,1)	57,2		(13,2)	44,1		64,0	125,4		(5,5)	(111,1)
17		Net income (loss)	(30,1)	57,2		(13,2)	44,1		64,0	125,4		(5,5)	(111,1)
18		Per share data of common stock											
19		Income (loss) before cumulative											
20		effect of accounting changes											
21		-Basic	(\39,26)	\62,23		(\14,34)	\47,89		\69,72	\136,19		(\5,91)	(\120,47)
22		-Diluted	(39,26)	57,90		(14,34)	44,70		64,87	126,05		(5,91)	(120,47)
23		Net income (loss) –											
24		-Basic	(32,75)	62,23		(14,34)	47,89		69,72	136,19		(5,91)	(120,47)
25		-Diluted	(32,75)	57,90		(14,34)	44,70		64,87	126,05		(5,91)	(120,47)

Fig. 7. Relationship table with a header hierarchy

can be use with a comparison purpose in mind. As we can see in Fig. 7, there is a hierarchy for each header naming a year quarter ("1st Quarter", "2nd Quarter", "3rd Quarter" and "4th Quarter") with all of them sharing the same semantic yet physically different sub-headers. Using this kind of arrangement obviates the need for multiple tables, whose physical separation makes it difficult to compare the analogous data from the distinct tables; or obviates the need for unique header labels – for instance, using "1st Quarter 2002", "2nd Quarter 2002", etc., that also complicates the data analysis.

2.4   Table Replication

In a spreadsheet, it is often observed the replication of table structures, only differing semantically in a certain aspect. In Fig. 8 we can see two structure replicas of a total of five replicas of a relationship table, only differing in the year in which the table data concerns. In this case, the replicas are distributed by different worksheets, however, the replication can also occur on a single worksheet as shown in the example in Fig. 9, where to calculate the "INCOME" and the "EXPENSES" the same table structure can be used.

The choice between the two replication options seem to depend on the table dimensions: larger table structures will naturally fit better in a spreadsheet on distinct worksheets (Fig. 8), while smaller ones can perfectly fit on the same worksheet (Fig. 9); and on the table purpose: if the spreadsheet analysis mainly relies on the comparison of the output data from the distinct replicas, it is convenient that the replicas stay physically close, which is the case of the example in Fig. 9 – besides the fact that the structures are quite small, the obvious object of analysis of the worksheet is the comparison between the "TOTAL INCOME" and the "TOTAL EXPENSES.

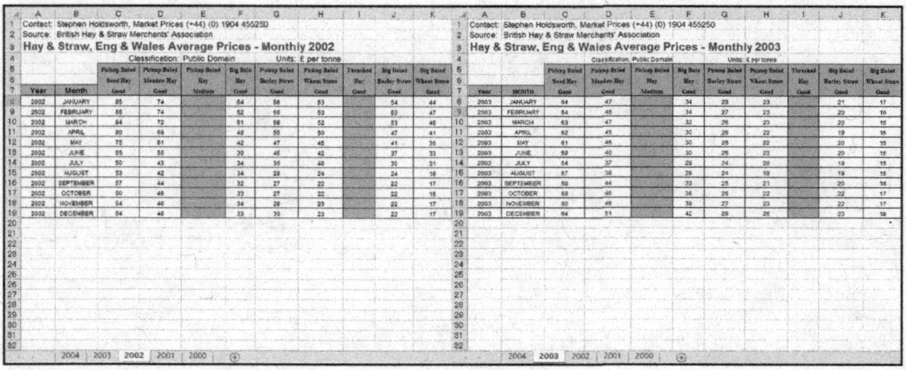

Contact: Stephen Holdsworth, Market Prices (+44) (0) 1904 455250										
Source: British Hay & Straw Merchants' Association										
Hay & Straw, Eng & Wales Average Prices - Monthly 2002										
		Classification: Public Domain				Units: £ per tonne				
Year	Month	Pickup Baled Seed Hay Good	Pickup Baled Meadow Hay Good	Pickup Baled Hay Medium	Big Bale Hay Good	Pickup Baled Barley Straw Good	Pickup Baled Wheat Straw Good	Thrashed Hay Good	Big Baled Barley Straw Good	Big Baled Wheat Straw Good
2002	JANUARY	85	74		54	56	53		54	44
2002	FEBRUARY	86	74		52	60	53		53	47
2002	MARCH	84	72		51	58	52		53	46
2002	APRIL	80	69		48	55	50		47	41
2002	MAY	75	61		42	47	46		41	36
2002	JUNE	65	55		39	45	42		37	33
2002	JULY	50	43		34	35	40		30	31
2002	AUGUST	53	42		34	28	24		24	18
2002	SEPTEMBER	57	44		32	27	22		22	17
2002	OCTOBER	50	46		33	27	22		22	16
2002	NOVEMBER	54	46		34	28	23		22	17
2002	DECEMBER	54	46		33	30	23		22	17

2004 | 2003 | 2002 | 2001 | 2000

Contact: Stephen Holdsworth, Market Prices (+44) (0) 1904 455250										
Source: British Hay & Straw Merchants' Association										
Hay & Straw, Eng & Wales Average Prices - Monthly 2003										
		Classification: Public Domain				Units: £ per tonne				
Year	MONTH	Pickup Baled Seed Hay Good	Pickup Baled Meadow Hay Good	Pickup Baled Hay Medium	Big Bale Hay Good	Pickup Baled Barley Straw Good	Pickup Baled Wheat Straw Good	Thrashed Hay Good	Big Baled Barley Straw Good	Big Baled Wheat Straw Good
2003	JANUARY	64	47		34	28	23		21	17
2003	FEBRUARY	64	48		34	27	23		20	16
2003	MARCH	63	47		32	26	23		20	15
2003	APRIL	62	45		30	26	22		19	15
2003	MAY	61	46		30	26	22		20	15
2003	JUNE	59	40		30	26	22		20	15
2003	JULY	54	37		29	24	20		19	15
2003	AUGUST	57	38		29	24	19		19	15
2003	SEPTEMBER	58	44		33	25	21		20	16
2003	OCTOBER	58	46		36	26	22		22	17
2003	NOVEMBER	60	48		39	27	23		22	17
2003	DECEMBER	64	51		42	29	25		23	18

2004 | 2003 | 2002 | 2001 | 2000

Fig. 8. Relationship table replicated in different worksheets

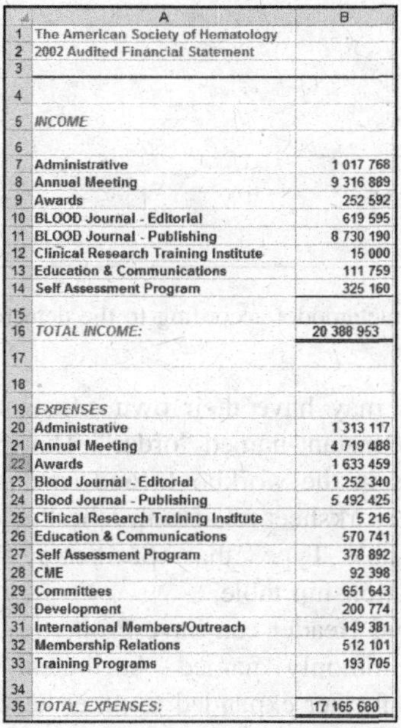

	A	B
1	The American Society of Hematology	
2	2002 Audited Financial Statement	
3		
4		
5	*INCOME*	
6		
7	Administrative	1 017 768
8	Annual Meeting	9 316 889
9	Awards	252 592
10	BLOOD Journal - Editorial	619 595
11	BLOOD Journal - Publishing	8 730 190
12	Clinical Research Training Institute	15 000
13	Education & Communications	111 759
14	Self Assessment Program	325 160
15		
16	*TOTAL INCOME:*	20 388 953
17		
18		
19	*EXPENSES*	
20	Administrative	1 313 117
21	Annual Meeting	4 719 488
22	Awards	1 633 459
23	Blood Journal - Editorial	1 252 340
24	Blood Journal - Publishing	5 492 425
25	Clinical Research Training Institute	5 216
26	Education & Communications	570 741
27	Self Assessment Program	378 892
28	CME	92 398
29	Committees	651 643
30	Development	200 774
31	International Members/Outreach	149 381
32	Membership Relations	512 101
33	Training Programs	193 705
34		
35	*TOTAL EXPENSES:*	17 165 680

Fig. 9. Horizontal single entry replicated in the same worksheet

3 A Metamodel for Spreadsheet Arrangement

The patterns identified in Sect. 2 can be formally systemized using and extending the UML conceptual model, specifically the UML class diagram metamodel. In Fig. 10, we present the metamodel in which spreadsheet elements – represented as entities – such as worksheets, tables, headers, etc., are an extension of the entity Class, and inherit some of its relations with other entities, namely, Association (with Aggregation and Composition specializations), Property and Usage.

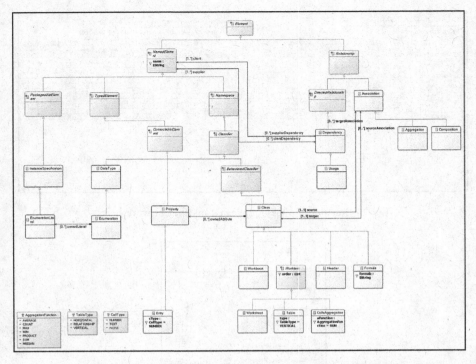

Fig. 10. Spreadsheet metamodel according to the detected patterns identified

The spreadsheet entities may have their own constants, for instance, the entity Worksheet have an integer constant named "order". That constant indicates in which order the worksheet appears in the workbook, and so does the entity Table, but to indicate its placement in the worksheet relative to other tables. Additionally, Table has another constant named "Table Type" that specifies if the table grows vertically, horizontally, or if it is a relationship table.

Entities such as Table and Header can have Properties, which in the context of a class diagram are the commonly named Attributes. Those attributes specify child-headers, which can be further expanded to other headers, or be "leaf" headers.

With Association and its two extensions we can specify to which the spreadsheets entities connect and how this connection is done in terms of data arrangement. For instance, in Fig. 11 we can see a model (according to the metamodel) of the spreadsheet table shown in Fig. 6 of Sect. 2.3, where the header hierarchies are expressed through two aggregations. If there were no hierarchies, that is, all the headers placed on the same row, a composition would be used instead.

Using the entity Usage it is possible to specify usage dependencies among instances of the spreadsheet entities. For instance, as we see in Fig. 12 – a partial model of the table presented in Fig. 5 of Sect. 2.2 – there is an entity Formula to specify a formula associated to the attribute of the same name of the class to which this entity Formula is associated by a composition. This entity has a string constant to express the formula

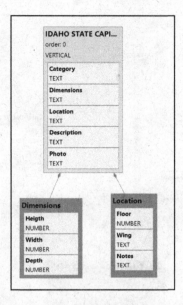

Fig. 11. Model representation of the table presented in Fig. 6 of Sect. 2.3

text with the header reference between brackets. Moreover, there is expressed a dependency between the Formula entity and the corresponding header that is referenced, using Usage.

Furthermore, for a particular group of formulas, more specifically, the aggregation functions, there is a proper entity associated to the header of which attributes are input for the aggregation function specified in the entity CellsAggregation (see Fig. 13).

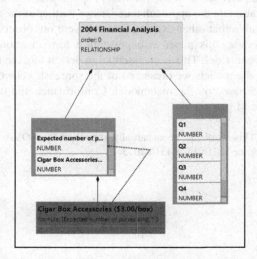

Fig. 12. Partial model representation of the table presented in Fig. 5 of Sect. 2.2

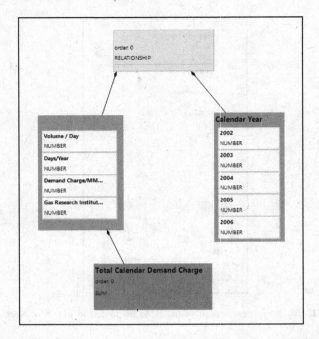

Fig. 13. Model representation of the table presented in Fig. 4 of Sect. 2.1

4 Conclusions

This paper presented a brief catalog of spreadsheet patterns regarding data arrangements layouts observed from two real-world spreadsheets datasets, extending and confirming the actual perceptions of the patterns in spreadsheets designs. Nevertheless, there is a major limitation on the approach taken, since neither of the datasets were fully covered, so it is possible that other existing patterns were not observed and, therefore, not registered. Moreover, this paper also presents a formalization of the identified patterns as a UML metamodel. This is an essential to design tools to build on top of the UML realm. In fact, the models we presented of the spreadsheets were created using a tool we implemented based on the metamodel. Conformance and other model-driven features are thus free to get.

Acknowledgements. This work has been partially supported by NOVA LINCS through the FCT project with reference UID/CEC/04516/2013.

Attachments

Attachment 1. EUSES' Spreadsheet Files

Database
01_20_04.xls
consultants.xls
Database_excel95.xls
datadict.xls
dist_ed_courses_Jan2000.xls
document_de_reference#A828A.xls
EbscohostByDb2002-03.xls
epcdata2002.xls
FeatureList.xls
flip_usd5.XLS
FS_Upgrade_Plan_v3_111502.xls
FS_Upgrade_Proj_Mgmt_#A829F.xls
haymth.xls
haymth_old.xls
ps-cs-msc-new.xls
topconschedtemplate.xls

Financial
02rise.xls
costfactors.xls
departmental_sales_e.xls
FinancialReport.xls
hist4q_e.xls
hist_e.xls
PersonalFinanceScope.xls
Prq403.xls
Q3_Final.xls
Q4_02.XLS
quaterly.xls
tab004.xls
treasurers_report_aud#A7EA4.xls
UF_Genetics_Financial#A7E51.xls
USFAthleticFinancialSummary.xls
W_SBT_financial.xls

Grades
1A6EGrades.xls
262grades.xls
310Grades.xls
483_grades_web.xls
511Grades.xls

Inventory
am-template-inventory.xls
capitol_art_inventory.xls
ColdStorage.xls
inventor.xls
Inventory%20Schedule%202004.xls
Inventory-Emergency_C#A84CC.xls
InventoryList.xls
NMfgInventory04.xls
nonstandby_inventory_#A8712.xls
Overview.xls
Software_inventory_sheet.xls
temp_videos0304.xls
TuftsGHGInventory.xls
VRSinventory01.xls
VRSinventory03.xls

Attachment 2. EURON's Spreadsheet Files

andrea_ring__4__BRLH Storage.xlsx
andrew_lewis__84__Notification Rpt 1200.xlsx
andy_zipper__109__Cost Allocation 02-21-01.xlsx
andy_zipper__112__mODEL 3 7 01 Base.xlsx
andy_zipper__115__DYNEGY-ICE VOL Jun1.xlsx
andy_zipper__266__Broker detail 5-29-01.xlsx
andy_zipper__290__AGA.xlsx
andy_zipper__342__COF Curves for Andy Zipper.xlsx
barry_tycholiz__870__EPNG BP Tariff Sheet.xlsx
benjamin_rogers__1003__NEPOOL-ZoneG Dailies.xlsx
benjamin_rogers__1024__TLR Analysis.xlsx
benjamin_rogers__1052__FPLE model.xlsx
benjamin_rogers__1058__newco development cash flow.xlsx
benjamin_rogers__1108__Wheatland O&M.xlsx
benjamin_rogers__1231__Comparison2.xlsx
benjamin_rogers__911__PJM Eastern Hub Pricing.xlsx
benjamin_rogers__936__PJM Model.xlsx
bill_williams_iii__1373__EOL 5-11.xlsx
bill_williams_iii__1395__EES September Daily.xlsx
chris_germany__2124__DecCohCHOICE-ENA.xlsx
chris_stokley__3947__NP15 DJ Charts.xlsx
darrell_schoolcraft__7827__imbalsumm0110.xlsx
larry_may__21636__ed052501.xlsx
louise_kitchen__22676__BGM 1024 ngpl.xlsx
phillip_m_love__30520__Paulacustomerlist.xlsx

stacey_white__39052__Summary Oct 15.xls
steven_p_south__39352__04-23-01 Earnings 2 of 2.xlsx
vladi_pimenov__41075__VLADI-GASDAILY-CURVEFETCH.xlsx

References

1. Engels, G., Erwig, M.: ClassSheets: automatic generation of spreadsheet applications from object-oriented specifications. In: Proceedings of the 20th IEEE/ACM International Conference on Automated Software Engineering, ASE 2005, pp. 124–133. ACM, New York (2005)
2. Cunha, J., Fernandes, J.P., Mendes, J., Saraiva, J.: Embedding and evolution of spreadsheet models in spreadsheet systems. In: Proceedings of the 2011 IEEE Symposium on Visual Languages and Human-Centric Computing, Pittsburgh, pp. 179–186 (2011)
3. Hermans, F., Pinzger, M., Deursen, A.: Automatically extracting class diagrams from spreadsheets. In: D'Hondt, T. (ed.) ECOOP 2010. LNCS, vol. 6183, pp. 52–75. Springer, Heidelberg (2010). doi:10.1007/978-3-642-14107-2_4
4. Abraham, R., Erwig, M.: Header and unit inference for spreadsheets through spatial analyses. In: Proceedings of the 2004 IEEE Symposium on Visual Languages and Human-Centric Computing, Rome, pp. 165–172 (2004)
5. Fisher, M., Rothermel, G.: The EUSES spreadsheet corpus: a shared resource for supporting experimentation with spreadsheet dependability mechanisms. In: 1st Workshop on End-User Software Engineering, pp. 47–51. ACM, New York (2005)
6. Hermans, F., Murphy-Hill, E.: Enron's spreadsheets and related emails: a dataset and analysis. In: 37th International Conference on Software Engineering, ICSE 2015, Florence, pp. 7–16 (2015)
7. Jansen, B.: Enron versus EUSES: a comparison of two spreadsheet Corpora. In: Second Workshop on Software Engineering Methods in Spreadsheets, SEMS 2015, Florence, pp. 41–47 (2015)

Towards an Automated Classification of Spreadsheets

Jorge Mendes[1,2]($\boxtimes$), Kha N. Do[3], and João Saraiva[1,2]

[1] HASLab, INESC TEC, Porto, Portugal
[2] HASLab, Universidade do Minho, Braga, Portugal
{jorgemendes,jas}@di.uminho.pt
[3] University of Science, Vietnam National University,
Ho Chi Minh, Vietnam
dnkha@fit.hcmus.edu.vn

Abstract. Many spreadsheets in the wild do not have documentation nor categorization associated with them. This makes difficult to apply spreadsheet research that targets specific spreadsheet domains such as financial or database.

We introduce with this paper a methodology to automatically classify spreadsheets into different domains. We exploit existing data mining classification algorithms using spreadsheet-specific features. The algorithms were trained and validated with cross-validation using the EUSES corpus, with an up to 89% accuracy. The best algorithm was applied to the larger Enron corpus in order to get some insight from it and to demonstrate the usefulness of this work.

Keywords: Spreadsheets · Data mining · Classification

1 Introduction

Spreadsheets are widely used at all levels of organizations. In fact, they are used both from professional programmers at large worldwide organizations, to non-professional programmers in small family-run businesses. As recent research studies [1,8] and frequent reports of horror stories[1] show, spreadsheets are prone to errors. Recently advanced techniques have been proposed (some of them already incorporated in regular programming languages), in order to improve both the efficiency and productivity of spreadsheet users. To support such ongoing research activity, several spreadsheet corpora have been proposed in the literature [3,4,7] so that researchers can experiment their techniques in a corpus that represent real-world spreadsheet applications. For example, the EUSES corpus [4] divides its 5607 spreadsheets in 11 distinct categories, including *finances*, *databases*, etc. As a consequence, researchers can apply their techniques to one specific application domain of spreadsheets.

---

[1] Please see the spreadsheet horror stories available at http://www.eusprig.org/horror-stories.htm.

P. Milazzo et al. (Eds.): STAF 2016, LNCS 9946, pp. 346–355, 2016.
DOI: 10.1007/978-3-319-50230-4_26

The classification of software artifacts, in particularly source code files, are usually performed by the administrator of a repository [15]. The EUSES corpus is no exception, and its creators gathered spreadsheets from different sources and put them together in a single repository for easy access by researchers. When dealing with large corpora, this process can be tedious and time consuming. Thus, it is not surprising that the large Enron spreadsheet repository [7] is not classified yet.

This paper presents the use of automated software classification algorithms in determining the appropriate application domain for a particular spreadsheet. We configure well-known classification algorithms with spreadsheet-specific properties. The EUSES corpus is used as the basis for training and testing the classification algorithms. In this training study we considered five different classification algorithms, which are provided by the widely used Java-based Weka machine learning suite [6,14]. Our first experimental results show that the best spreadsheet classification algorithms are based on decision trees, which correctly classifies 89% of the spreadsheets during cross-validation.

In order to perform the feature extraction and data preprocessing, we developed a Java-based tool to interact directly with both spreadsheets and Weka. This helps to automate the whole process: spreadsheets have their features automatically extracted and then packed in a file format compatible with the Weka machine learning suite.

Having defined the best classification algorithm for spreadsheets, we then automatically applied the classification process to the Enron repository. We were able to: evaluate the performance of the process, get some information about biases from the EUSES training, get some insight on the Enron corpus from the point of view of the EUSES corpus. These results are available to the spreadsheet research community and show that further work on this subject is required.

The remaining of this paper is structured as follows: Sect. 2 describes the spreadsheet classification process: the EUSES spreadsheet corpus, the spreadsheet specific features used in the classification algorithms, and the five used classification algorithms. Section 3 briefly describes our spreadsheet classification framework. Section 4 contains the experiments we performed and the results obtained with the five classification algorithms and the spreadsheet specific features. Section 5 presents the results of classifying the Enron corpus. Section 6 discusses our results and, finally, we conclude with Sect. 7.

2   Classification Environment

The classification of software artifacts [14] is usually performed in the following steps:

- select data to train classification algorithms
- preprocess the data
- train the algorithms
- evaluate the derived models
- classify new artifacts

In the classification of spreadsheets we also followed these steps. First, we sampled the EUSES corpus to obtain a training set (Sect. 2.1). Then, we pre-processed the spreadsheet data to extract features from the training set spreadsheets (Sect. 2.2). Next, we considered and applied several classification algorithms to the training set to obtain different classification models (Sect. 2.3). After, we evaluated all models using a five fold cross validation with this sampled dataset (Sect. 4). Then, the best classifier will be used to classify new spreadsheet instances, namely the Enron dataset (see Sect. 5).

2.1   The EUSES Spreadsheet Corpus

The data used to classify the algorithms is extracted from the EUSES spreadsheet corpus [4]. Most of the spreadsheets in this corpus were obtained from the Internet through searches using the Google search engine [5], but some of them result from other researchers or individuals. It has a total of 5607 spreadsheet files, organized in 11 distinct categories:

- cs101   - forms3   - jackson
- database   - grades   - modeling
- filby   - homework   - personal
- financial   - inventory

Some processing was already applied to this corpus. Each of these categories has up to three directories: *bad*, *duplicates*, and *processed*. The *bad* directories contain files that the authors of the EUSES corpus were unable to use for some reason[2]. The *duplicates* directories, as the name suggests, contain duplicate files. The *processed* directories contain the remaining files.

From the available categories, only six were kept for classification due to the reduced number of spreadsheets in the other categories (see Table 1). The six categories kept are: *database, financial, grades, homework, inventory*, and *modeling*. All the spreadsheets in these categories are from the Internet searches. Moreover, only the files in the *processed* directories were taken into account for the classification, resulting in a total of 4402 spreadsheet files, with an average of 734 files per category.

2.2   Feature Extraction

Sets of spreadsheet files are not directly usable to train a classifier. Thus, a preliminary step that extracts features from the spreadsheets is required.

Spreadsheets have many attributes that can be extracted as features, hence a selection must be made. Starting from common knowledge, having in mind the selection of attributes that could distinguish spreadsheet categories, only the words present in cell contents were extracted. Each word is considered an

---

[2] This information is not clearly specified by the authors, but range from password protected files to spreadsheets with disruptive macros [4].

Table 1. Spreadsheet file count in the EUSES corpus.

	Total	*bad*	*duplicates*	*processed*
cs101	9	1	0	8
database	904	59	125	**720**
filby	45	0	0	45
financial	902	31	91	**780**
forms3	26	0	0	26
grades	895	17	148	**731**
homework	951	29	239	**683**
inventory	891	49	86	**756**
jackson	13	0	0	13
modeling	966	51	183	**732**
personal	5	0	0	5
Total	5607	236	872	4499

attribute, and its value for each spreadsheet is the number of occurrences of that word in it. This makes the *words* feature.

The extraction process is as follows. If a cell contains a sentence, this sentence is split into the several words that compose it. The resulting set of words passes then through a cleaning process, where words that are present in all the categories are removed from the set. Moreover, words that appear in less than 10% of the spreadsheets in a given category are removed from the set of words in that category.

2.3   Algorithm Selection

Several algorithms are available to classify software artifacts based on the extracted features. In order to select the one that best suits spreadsheet classification based on the mentioned features, several experiments were performed with Weka. The following algorithms from the Weka suite were used in these experiments:

- DecisionTable – Implementation of the IDTM algorithm [11]
- J48 – Java implementation of the C4.5 algorithm to generate decision trees [13]
- REPTree – A decision tree learner
- NaiveBayes – Implementation of a Naive Bayes classifier [9]
- NaiveBayesMultinomial – Implementation of a multinomial Naive Bayes classifier [12].

3   SSClassifier: A Java/Weka-Based Spreadsheet Classifier

In order to automatically classify large data sets of spreadsheets, like the EUSES and Enron corpora, we developed a Java-based tool to process in

350 J. Mendes et al.

batch textual spreadsheets. This was accomplished using the Apache POI [2] library to read the spreadsheet files and access their contents. The extraction of spreadsheet features, as described in Sect. 2.2, was directly implemented in the Apache POI spreadsheet representation. Then, we implemented a bridge between the Apache POI and the Weka data representations, so that we could experiment with different classification algorithms and spreadsheet features. The architecture of the developed framework, named SSClassifier, is presented in Fig. 1.

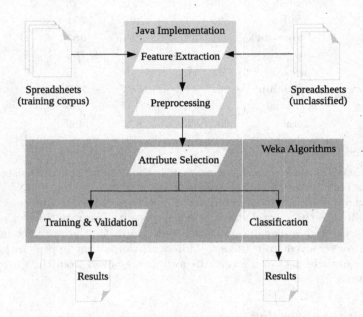

Fig. 1. Architecture of SSClassifier.

The SSClassifier is publicly available from: https://bitbucket.org/SSaaPP/spreadsheet-classification/.

4 Experiments

Several experiments were performed to select the best set of attributes and algorithms from the ones defined in the previous section. A common flow was defined for the several algorithms (depicted in Fig. 2), where we then experimented with different inputs using five-fold cross-validation.

The attributes in the *words* feature consist in counts of words. The words are the ones present in the spreadsheet contents, and some filtering is required in order to obtain better results, much like with Natural Language Processing (NLP). Some filtering was already applied, as described in Sect. 2.2, namely

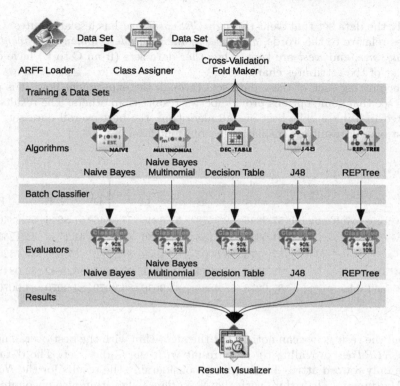

Fig. 2. Experiment flow layout.

removing words present in all categories and that do not provide any new information (analogously to stop words in NLP), and discarding words that appear only in a small subset of spreadsheets from a category.

The attributes used and their order is important in order to generate better models. Thus, a selection of the attributes and a reordering was performed to select the best option. The different sets of data based on the set of all the word counts present in spreadsheets used are:

A full set of data;

B selection using the *CfsSubsetEval* attribute evaluator and *BestFirst* search method;

C selection using the *CorrelationAttributeEval* attribute evaluator and *Ranker* search method;

D selection using the *GainRatioAttributeEval* attribute evaluator and *Ranker* search method;

E selection using the *InfoGainAttributeEval* attribute evaluator and *Ranker* search method;

F selection using the *ReliefFAttributeEval* attribute evaluator and *Ranker* search method.

Only the data set that went through *CfsSubsetEval* has less attributes. Only the ones relative to the words, *database, financial, grades, homework, inventory, modeling, size,* and *west* are kept. The other data sets (from C to F) have only the order of the attributes changed.

After putting each of these data sets through the experiment flow, it is possible to see that some options provide better results than others. The results are presented in Table 2. The best overall algorithm, the best overall data set, and the best overall result are displayed in bold font face.

Table 2. Five-fold cross-validation results using the *words* feature.

	A	B	C	D	E	F
NaiveBayesMultinomial	57.8846	82.3473	57.8846	57.8846	57.8846	57.8846
NaiveBayes	41.0046	50.6158	41.1736	41.1736	41.1736	41.1253
J48	87.8773	88.0705	87.4909	87.8532	87.829	87.7324
REPTree	88.9882	87.8049	**89.1331**	89.0365	88.9882	89.0848
DecisionTable	85.0278	85.4866	84.9070	84.9070	84.9070	84.9070

From the results, we can notice that the algorithm with the best overall accuracy is *REPTree*, providing the best result with the C data set. The data set B, with only 8 word attributes, improves considerably the results for the *NaiveBayesMultinomial* algorithm, with the *NaiveBayes* algorithm also encountering some improvements. However, the other algorithms suffer in terms of accuracy, but only slightly. Nevertheless, this data set provides a lot of improvements in terms of time for model training. All the resulting data from this work is provided with the source code of the tool.[3]

5 . Classifying the Enron Corpus

The Enron corpus [10] is an email data set that was released to the public. This data set was processed in order to remove private and confidential data, but many emails and respective attachments still remain.

Hermans and Murphy-Hill [7] analyzed the Enron email data set and found spreadsheets as attachments in those emails. They extracted those spreadsheets and provided it as its own corpus[4].

The Enron spreadsheets have been submitted through a similar process than the one applied to the EUSES corpus in order to classify them. First, all spreadsheets were preprocessed in order to extract the *words* feature. Some of the spreadsheets were not analyzed due to size limits or due to not being supported by our toolset; 210 spreadsheets were left out. Then, this data was classified

---

[3] https://bitbucket.org/SSaaPP/spreadsheet-classification/src/2259e60/paper/data/.

[4] The Enron spreadsheet corpus is available through here: www.felienne.com/enron.

using the *REPTree* algorithm that was trained with the data from the EUSES corpus after the *CorrelationAttributeEval* attribute selection process. The results are presented in Table 3.

Table 3. Results of the prediction on the Enron corpus.

Prediction	Count
database	2039
financial	3176
grades	448
homework	8915
inventory	1057
modeling	83
Total result	15718

The results of the classification of the Enron corpus are very preliminary and need a proper validation that due to time limitations we were unable to include in this paper. As we can notice, most of the spreadsheets are classified as *homework*. In fact, the *homework* class in the EUSES original classification includes a large set of different domains. This results in a large vocabulary for that category in the training of the classification algorithms. Of course, the original data set (the EUSES corpus) and its classification, that we use to train the algorithms, does influence the results. A proper validation of our preliminary results is needed, indeed.

6   Discussion

The Apache POI [2] library was used to read the spreadsheet files and access their contents. However, it several limitations. Its Excel file support is considerably limited, with support only for recent file formats:

– Excel'97(-2007)
– 2007 OOXML

From the *processed* spreadsheets in the EUSES corpus, 261 spreadsheets were discarded (around 6%) due to the lack of support for them from Apache POI. Even for the supported file formats, many features are not available or are very limited, e.g., charts and pivot tables. Thus, we were highly constrained in the features to extract for classification. The issues of using Apache POI can be solved by switching to LibreOffice Calc or Microsoft Excel extensions[5], which have better support for these file formats. Nevertheless, Apache POI is a relatively simple point of entry for spreadsheet analysis, thus its use in this work.

---

[5] Only tools that can be used locally were considered to avoid issues related to transfering much data across networks.

The EUSES corpus was used as a basis for this work. This corpus already has some kind of categorization and contains many spreadsheets. However, the categories for the spreadsheets gathered from Internet searches (i.e., the ones that were used in this work) are not based on spreadsheet characteristics, but on keywords that the EUSES creators thought being commonly associated with spreadsheets. This does not make the categories invalid, but might not reflect what people think about the spreadsheets in those categories. Moreover, some categories may contain some overlap. For example, one expects the *homework* category to contain spreadsheets from different domains since homework can be on diverse subjects.

Hence, two possible issues might arise:

- the categories do not match with what one can find from a random set of spreadsheets;
- the categorization of the spreadsheets was dependent on an Internet search, thus the contents/categorizations might be questionable.

In order to overcome these issues, a large set of spreadsheets can be gathered and then clustering algorithms be ran on them. This would allow to organize the spreadsheets based on their characteristics. Another option is to find spreadsheets with a clear categorization (e.g., from the intended purpose by their creators) and then perform a new classification based on these new spreadsheets and categories. Both of these possible solutions can provide a better training corpus. However, the second solution might not yield a large enough data set to apply data mining techniques.

Nevertheless, the work herein presented allows to augment the EUSES corpus in an automated way with spreadsheets which do not have a category associated with them, but are close to the ones already present in the corpus.

The classification model obtained from the EUSES corpus was applied to the Enron spreadsheet repository in order to try obtaining insight on both the classification process and the spreadsheets in the Enron repository. The high number of *homework* spreadsheets found suggests that the EUSES classification model is inappropriate to classify generically any spreadsheet.

The algorithms used make only a small subset of the available algorithms for classification. This work can be easily expanded to include other algorithms. Moreover, more than a selection and ranking of algorithms for spreadsheet classification, this work provides a methodology and work flow to extract features from spreadsheets, filter them, train and then test classification algorithms.

Another close point is the selection of attributes. Much work can still be done in order to find the best set of attributes for a classification algorithm. Improvements are left for future work.

7   Conclusion

This paper presents an automatic classification technique for spreadsheets. We considered five well-known data mining classification algorithms available in the widely used software classification framework Weka. We considered spreadsheet-specific features when we trained and validated such algorithms with the EUSES spreadsheet corpus. The decision tree learner algorithm *REPTree* correctly classified 89% of the EUSES corpus using the *words* spreadsheet feature during cross-validation. In order to train and validate the classification algorithm, we developed a Java tool to extract spreadsheet features in order to use them with Weka to process and classify spreadsheet corpora.

References

1. Abreu, R., Cunha, J., Fernandes, J.P., Martins, P., Perez, A., Saraiva, J.: Smelling faults in spreadsheets. In: 2014 IEEE International Conference on Software Maintenance and Evolution (ICSME), pp. 111–120, September 2014
2. Apache Software Foundation: Apache POI. http://poi.apache.org
3. Aurigemma, S., Panko, R.R.: The detection of human spreadsheet errors by humans versus inspection (auditing) software. In: Proceedings of EuSpRIG Conference (2010)
4. Fisher, M., Rothermel, G.: The EUSES spreadsheet corpus: a shared resource for supporting experimentation with spreadsheet dependability mechanisms. In: Proceedings of the First Workshop on End-User Software Engineering (WEUSE I), pp. 1–5. ACM (2005)
5. Google: Google. https://www.google.com
6. Hall, M., Frank, E., Holmes, G., Pfahringer, B., Reutemann, P., Witten, I.H.: The weka data mining software: an update. SIGKDD Explor. Newsl. **11**(1), 10–18 (2009)
7. Hermans, F., Murphy-Hill, E.: Enron's spreadsheets and related emails: a dataset and analysis. In: Proceedings of the 37th International Conference on Software Engineering, ICSE 2015, vol. 2. pp. 7–16. IEEE Press, Piscataway (2015)
8. Jannach, D., Schmitz, T., Hofer, B., Wotawa, F.: Avoiding, finding and fixing spreadsheet errors - a survey of automated approaches for spreadsheet QA. J. Syst. Softw. **94**, 129–150 (2014)
9. John, G.H., Langley, P.: Estimating continuous distributions in Bayesian classifiers. In: Eleventh Conference on Uncertainty in Artificial Intelligence, pp. 338–345. Morgan Kaufmann, San Mateo (1995)
10. Klimt, B., Yang, Y.: Introducing the Enron corpus. In: 1st Conference on Email and Anti-Spam (CEAS) (2004)
11. Kohavi, R.: The power of decision tables. In: Lavrac, N., Wrobel, S. (eds.) Machine Learning, vol. 912, pp. 174–189. Springer, Heidelberg (1995)
12. Mccallum, A., Nigam, K.: A comparison of event models for Naive Bayes text classification. In: Workshop on Learning for Text Categorization, AAAI 1998 (1998)
13. Quinlan, R.: C4.5: Programs for Machine Learning. Morgan Kaufmann Publishers, San Francisco (1993)
14. Witten, I.H., Frank, E.: Data Mining: Practical Machine Learning Tools and Techniques. Morgan Kaufmann Series in Data Management Systems, 2nd edn. Morgan Kaufmann Publishers Inc., San Francisco (2005)
15. Yusof, Y., Rana, O.F.: Classification of software artifacts based on structural information. In: Setchi, R., Jordanov, I., Howlett, R.J., Jain, L.C. (eds.) KES 2010. LNCS, vol. 6279, pp. 546–555. Springer, Heidelberg (2010). doi:10.1007/978-3-642-15384-6_58

Programming Communication with the User in Multiplatform Spreadsheet Applications

Jerzy Sikora[1], Jacek Sroka[2], and Jerzy Tyszkiewicz[2(✉)]

[1] Institute of Archaeology, University of Lodz, Łódź, Poland
jerzy.sikora@uni.lodz.pl
[2] Institute of Informatics, University of Warsaw, Warsaw, Poland
{sroka,jty}@mimuw.edu.pl

Abstract. It is quite common that the same person uses many different devices, depending on the situation: smartphones and tablets in the field, laptops in the office, switching between operating systems and Web-based applications. A spreadsheet user in this situation needs a *multiplatform spreadsheet*, one which will work equally well on all types of devices. The alternative of having many spreadsheets and copying data between them is clearly inferior, because it is a well-known source of errors.

The topic we want to address in the present paper is programming the interaction with the user in a multiplatform spreadsheet, using only the core spreadsheet functionalities, which are implemented in the majority of spreadsheet systems.

We report here on our experiences with creating the user interface of a multiplatform spreadsheet application for archaeologists working in the field.

1 Introduction

1.1 Early History

The initial challenge came from one of the authors of the present paper (J. Si.), who needed a mobile application for Android, capable of storing stratigraphic data collected during excavations, consisting of textual descriptions of archaeological contexts, and chronological *earlier-than* and *later-than* relations between them. The data was intended to be transferred for further analysis to a standard, Windows-based application (running under Wine on a Linux machine). So from the very beginning the application was intended to be used in an environment with at least two (or perhaps even three) operating systems involved. This is nothing particular. Nowadays users routinely switch between devices, operating systems, and between online and offline mode of work.

We decided to implement the archaeological application, later named *Strati5*, as a multi-platform spreadsheet. The application was described from the user's point of view in [10]. We also published a short, nontechnical paper [9], advocating the general idea of rapid development of mobile multiplatform applications in the form of spreadsheets with Strati5 as a working example.

© Springer International Publishing AG 2016
P. Milazzo et al. (Eds.): STAF 2016, LNCS 9946, pp. 356–371, 2016.
DOI: 10.1007/978-3-319-50230-4_27

1.2   Why a Spreadsheet?

In the paper [11] the other two of us (J. Sr. and J. Ty., with other co-authors) made a claim, that spreadsheet formulas in fact constitute a platform-independent programming language, even though there is no common formal standard in this respect. Applications written in this language run on virtual machines, which are spreadsheet management systems, like *Microsoft Excel* (available for Windows desktop and phone, Mac, Android and iOS), *Apache OpenOffice* and *LibreOffice calc* (available for Windows, Mac and Linux), *WPS Office* spreadsheet (available for Windows desktop, Linux, iOS and Android), and many other.[1]

When we had a chance to verify our belief in practice, we did so, treating the archaeological application as a test, if spreadsheet technology can indeed serve for multi-platform programming.

Next, using spreadsheet as an application saved us a lot of implementation work. Programming the user interface is typically one of the most laborious parts of each project. In our case, a vast majority of the user interface is always provided directly by the spreadsheet system used. It is responsible for all functionalities related to data navigation, typing, editing, undo, redo, file opening and saving, etc. It also adapts the application to different screen sizes and resolutions, mouse or touch as a pointing device, etc. Finally, it seems almost impossible to find another technology which would make the very same code run on Android, iOS, Windows, Linux and MacOS.

Having one application for all systems, we did not have to implement any protocols to facilitate data transfer between different applications. Copying data between spreadsheets is generally considered to be error-prone, so sharing the same spreadsheet between devices and systems prevents many potential errors and risks.

Last but not least, spreadsheet technology is very conservative and backward compatibility has always been a major concern. Therefore, we expect our application to remain fully functional for many years without any need of modifications, and even to get ported to new operating systems, should they appear on the market—most likely without a single keystroke on our part.

1.3   Development History

After testing a few systems, WPS Office for Android was chosen as the optimal one to start with and within a few days the first working version of Strati5 for the tablet was available.

Tests took place during regular archaeological excavations in Ostrowite (Pomerania, Poland) led by J. Si. A number of improvements resulted in a tool, running on Android tablet (for collecting data in the field) and on Linux laptop

---

[1] A *Spreadsheet management system* (or spreadsheet system) is a software used to create, manage and execute individual *spreadsheets*. This distinction resembles the relation between a *database management system* and individual *databases*.

at the base camp (for exporting the data to an external application). The whole spreadsheet was routinely used and transferred between the devices, causing no problems during many months of excavations. Strati5 proved to be reasonably comfortable and intuitive in everyday operation.

Then we decided to offer the application to other users, making it as independent of the operating system as possible. Achieving this goal required a number of changes and appeared to be an interesting programming experience.

In the present paper we discuss the technical issues of programming the interaction with the user in a spreadsheet intended to be transferred between many platforms. We hope that this knowledge and developed know-how will be useful in other cases. Requests for help in porting existing spreadsheets into mobile environments already show up at MrExcel.com, a very active spreadsheet-related forum, as witnessed by recent posts [1,3,7,8]. We expect that this demand will grow. There have been a few papers which deal with the usability of mobile spreadsheets [2,4,5], but they all discuss spreadsheet management systems rather than individual spreadsheets, so we are probably pioneers in this respect.

As a by-product of our technical developments, in Sect. 3.2 we describe a simple design pattern, which can be used to control location of cyclic references in all types of Excel: desktop, mobile and online.

2   The Overall Structure of the Interface – Strati5

In this section we describe the spatial organization of the interface and spreadsheet functionalities necessary to implement it. Our working example is Strati5.

2.1   Fundamental Requirements

The requirement was to develop a mobile application, capable of storing stratigraphic data, consisting of archaeological contexts with textual descriptions, a set of chronological *earlier-than* and *later-than* relations between the contexts, which are edges of a directed acyclic graph of interest to archaeologists, called Harris matrix. Later we added groups, i.e., named sets of contexts, to the data model. We identified the following main requirements:

A. Entry and storage of the data, with estimated growth rate of at most 20 records a day and average of 200 records per month.
B. Warn about/prevent duplicated context id.
C. Warn about/prevent cycles in the relations between contexts.
D. Warn about/prevent using undefined contexts in the relations.
E. Warn about/prevent duplicate group id.
F. Warn about/prevent assigning contexts to undefined groups.
G. Operating on a mobile devices and laptops, with strong preference toward network-independent operation.
H. Automatic or semi-automatic data export in a format accepted by *Stratify* [6], a popular free desktop application for maintaining and processing stratigraphic data.

I. Low resource consumption, to enable smooth operation on a tablet and prevent draining the battery, assuming load from item A above.

As it can be recognized, most of the above items were related to data validation. While analyzing the methods to implement them, we came up with the conclusion, that **it was impossible to support all popular spreadsheet systems**.

Instead, we decided to work toward a more realistic goal of **supporting sufficiently many spreadsheet systems to offer our tool on all major operating systems, and to cover a few most important spreadsheet systems**: Microsoft Excel for Windows desktop and Mac, LibreOffice and Apache OpenOffice for Windows, Linux and Mac, and Google sheets.

2.2 Structure of the Interface

After some consideration, we decided that the key services we needed from the spreadsheet systems were:

- Reporting emergence of cyclic references (required for reporting cyclic relations between contexts);
- Support for array formulas;
- Support for "freeze panes" (i.e., making the top row(s) and/or the leftmost column(s) always visible on the screen);
- Support for data validation by a list of allowed values;
- Support for conditional formatting.

They were needed for a very schematic idea of the interface, shown on Fig. 1. It was based on the *freeze panes* function applied to a few rows and columns.

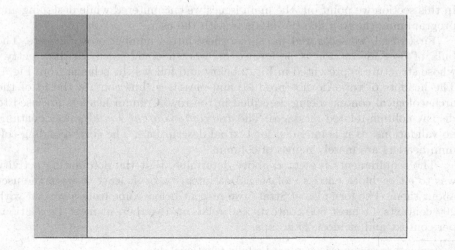

Fig. 1. Schematic structure of the user interface. The gray top row(s) and leftmost column(s) are frozen panes.

Referring to the colors on the figure, the roles of the particular areas are as follows:

- The dark gray area in the top left corner is always present on the screen. It can display messages about spreadsheet's global state, by formulas producing texts of messages and conditional formatting indicating their presence.
- The medium gray area on the top edge consists of cells which are visible whenever any fragment of their column is visible. They can be used to display column-related messages.
- The medium gray area on the left edge consists of cells which are visible whenever any fragment of their row is visible. They can be used to display row-related messages.
- The light gray area are individual cells and the functions used in them are most likely data validations and perhaps conditional formatting.

Eventually, the following operating systems and spreadsheet systems passed tests of compliance with the above requirements:[2]

Windows Excel, LibreOffice, OpenOffice, WPS Office
MacOS X Excel, LibreOffice, OpenOffice, WPS Office
Linux LibreOffice, OpenOffice, WPS Office
Android WPS Office
iOS WPS Office
Windows mobile MS Office
All systems Google sheets.

3   Interaction with the User

In this section we point out the main issues we encountered while designing and programming the way Strati5 interacts with the user.

First of all, we separated the spreadsheet into a number of worksheets. The bulk of user interaction is performed on worksheet intended for data entry,[3] whose structure is presented in Fig. 2 below and follows the schema from Fig. 1. The headers of rows do not produce any messages, but contain the id of the archaeological context being described in the row. Column headers are used to display column-related messages. The *descriptions of the contexts* area contains no validations, as it is intended for textual descriptions. The corresponding column headers are merely names of columns.

The requirements presented above determine, that the dominating activity was to either block entries violating data integrity, or at least to warn the user about them. The formulas of Strati5 we present below come from a variant with 200 contexts, at most 500 contexts and relations together, at most 12 relations per context and at most 20 groups.

---

[2] Some other combinations might be fully functional, too.
[3] In fact, the remaining worksheets are almost never used in the field, and relatively seldom at the base camp.

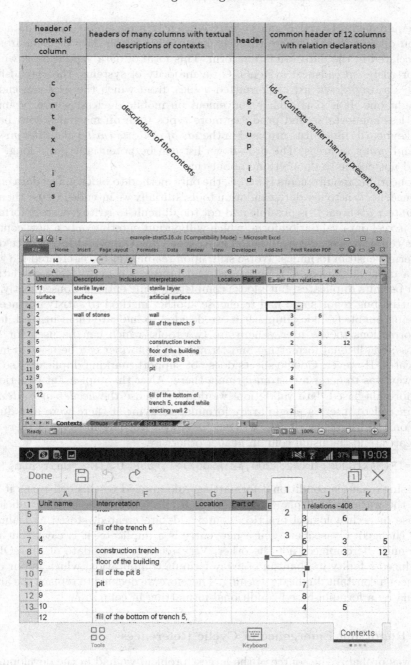

Fig. 2. The structure of the data entry worksheet of Strati5 (top). The colors follow Fig. 1. There are no global state messages. The cells in the white areas undergo no validation. Below Strati5 in Microsoft Excel under Windows 7 desktop (middle) and in WPS Office under Android on a smartphone (bottom).

Requirements D and F can be very efficiently programmed using data validation of type "List", where the user has to choose the data element from a list declared in the data validation form. This form of data validation is widely supported by spreadsheet systems. On a majority of systems, the spreadsheet displays a drop-down list of permitted values, from which the user can choose the right one. It is particularly convenient on mobile devices, where typing is much less comfortable and produces more typos than on machines with hardware keyboards. Such lists are used in the *ids of contexts earlier than the present one* and *group id* areas. The drop-down list can be potentially quite long, but we did not decide to do anything about that.

Concerning requirements B and E, the only method to block a new data entry in spreadsheets is to use data validation tools. Initially we intended to use them in the *context ids* area. It is possible and not too difficult to write a custom formula in the Excel data validation form, which will permit entering only a new context id in a cell. However, data validation in Apache OpenOffice and LibreOffice does not permit custom formulas. Worse still, upon reading an Excel-created file with such a data validation, it is corrupted and produces a faulty data validation, which permits duplicates, but blocks completely some entries. Consequently, we submitted bug reports and had to choose another method to satisfy our need.

Being unable to block duplicates, we decided to indicate them instead, leaving corrections to the user. There are two tools, which can be used for this purpose: conditional formatting and formulas. The former can be used to mark duplicates. However, Google sheets does not support marking duplicates, so the only way was to enter a custom formula there. After the unpleasant experience with formula-based data validation, we decided to use the *header of context id column* cell to insert a single array formula, verifying if there were any duplicates on the list below. It was written to yield a warning message if there are duplicates, and the usual column header otherwise:

```
A1 {=IF(MAX(COUNTIF(A2:A200,A2:A200))>1,"DUPLICATE","Unit name")}
```

A single simple conditional formatting rule applied to this cell turns it red when the warning is displayed, to increase its visibility. This form is sufficient, because in archaeological practice, context ids are created, stored and almost never changed. Consequently, if a new entry is a duplicate, it is clear that this entry must be changed, not the other. Very recently an update of LibreOffice introduced a faulty mechanism of array formula computation, which in our case produces a constant duplicate warning. Therefore we decided to replace the array formula by a formula-based conditional formatting in column A.

3.1   Reporting Emergence of Cyclic References

This was probably the source of the largest problem we had in the development of Strati5. Our implementation of breadth-first-search (BFS) graph traversal (presented for completeness in Appendix A) produces a cyclic reference between spreadsheet cells as a manifestation of a cycle in the "earlier than" relation created by the user. Therefore, we needed to notify the user of this event. Unfortunately, the way spreadsheet management systems react on cyclic references is very diverse. We have noted the following basic groups:

pop-up Displaying a pop-up window with an appropriate message. This form is exhibited by Microsoft Excel for Windows desktop and Mac OS, WPS Office for Windows and for Android. Additionally, the cells which are lying on the cycle, as well as those which depend on them, are not recomputed.

error Evaluating the cells which are lying on the cycle to an error value. This form is exhibited by OpenOffice, LibreOffice and Google sheets.

stop The cells on the cycle, as well as those which depend on them, are not recomputed. This form is exhibited by Microsoft Excel for Windows Mobile, Microsoft Excel Online, WPS Office for iOS.

Systems exhibiting **pop-up** message notify the user themselves.

For **error** group we used the top row to display the message. The common header of the columns where the user was supposed to enter the ids of later contexts were a single cell merged from several individual ones, whose text was constructed by a formula of the form `=IF(ISERROR(SUM('Cycle test'!I2:I500)),"Cycle detected!", "Earlier than")`. The column I on the worksheet `Cycle test` is the place where cyclic references, and consequently, error values, emerge (see Appendix A). SUM function evaluates to an error if there are any errors in the summation area, and to a number otherwise. The whole formula thus produces the message, whose visibility is increased by conditional formatting. This gave us a common solution for **pop-up** and **error** systems.

Supporting **stop** was very important for us, because all available spreadsheet management systems for iOS and Windows Phone were of this type.

We divided the header into two cells. The first of them contains the formula
`=IF(ISERROR(SUM('Cycle test'!I2:I500)),"Cycle detected!",`
`"Earlier than relations"&SUM('Cycle test'!H2:H500))`,
while the other cell contains
`="Earlier than relations"&SUM('Cycle test'!H2:H500))`.

Then conditional formatting is applied to both cells, turning them red if their values differ.

The cells in the range `'Cycle test'!H2:H500` contain numbers related to each tuple in the *earlier-than* relation such that any *single* change of the relations causes a change of their sum. `'Cycle test'!I2:I500` contains distances of the contexts from the sterile layer and is, as before, the place where cyclic references emerge.

In systems with **pop-up** and **error** responses the new formulas work very much as before. In systems with **stop** response, the two results are obviously equal if there are no cyclic references. However, if the user adds to, or modifies a tuple in the relation creating a cyclic reference, the system stops the evaluation of some cells in the range `'Cycle test'!I2:I500`. One of the header formulas depends on this range, the other does not. The latter is computed normally and its value changes. The former is not recomputed due to its dependence on unevaluated cells. Crucially, after the recomputation is finished, conditional

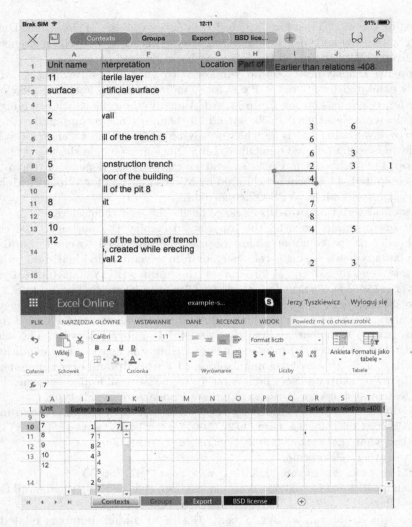

Fig. 3. Strati5 in WPS Office under iOS (top) and in Excel Online (bottom), showing a warning about cyclic references. They are **stop** systems, so the indication is the red color of the header. The bottom screenshot shows the the second cell of the header, with a different value in it, triggering the conditional formatting.

formatting is applied to all cells, irrespectively of their evaluation status and the two cells become red and issue a visual warning to the user, although no text message is produced.

3.2   By-Product: A Cycle Indicator

A by-product of the above mechanism is our construction of a universal detector of cyclic references in Excel desktop and online.

Excel desktop reports the emergence of cyclic references by a pop-up window and indicates one, more-or-less randomly selected cycle, among all that are created. This gives access to one cycle at a time. If such references are not enabled, but already present somewhere in the workbook, there will be no warning or indication of the subsequently created ones. This is especially likely if formulas with OFFSET or INDIRECT are used and edited, but INDEX function used in the reference form can cause the same effect.

Excel online does not report emergence of cyclic references in any way and have no error checking tool.

The design pattern described below allows the user to set up cycle warnings for any number of cells. All of them are activated simultaneously and visually indicate ones which lie on cycles or depend on such cells. The form presented here works for cells which do not evaluate to error values, but this can be overcome with minor modifications.

As a matter of example, let us assume that the range A1:A10 are the cells suspect of becoming elements of cycles we want to monitor.

We set up a single reference cell, let it be

C1	=NOW()

The monitors are installed by formulas (we assume that the formula is entered into the top cell of the range and copied down, with automatic modifications introduced by the spreadsheet)

B1:B10	=IF(A1=A1,C1)

and conditional formatting rules applied to cells in B1:B10, so that they change the formatting of cell Bi iff its value is **smaller** than the value of the reference C1.

Let us assume the user makes an edit, which might cause some of the cells to become members of cycles themselves or to depend on cells which are now on cycles. Then the following events happen:

- Some of the cells in A1:A10 are attempted to be recomputed. Ones which are now on cycles are not recomputed and the recomputation of their dependents, including those in B1:B10, is also blocked[4].
- The formula in C1 is volatile, hence it is recomputed and its value increases.
- Formulas in B1:B10 depend on cell C1 whose value has changed, hence their recomputation is attempted. It succeeds for Bi iff Ai is not on a cycle and does not depend on a cycle, otherwise it is blocked and the old timestamp is retained.

---

[4] Excel for Android recomputes all cells which are not elements of cycles, even if they depend on cells which are elements of cycles. Therefore our solution does not work in Excel for Android.

– Conditional formatting is applied to all cells in `B1:B10`. Those which have been recomputed are equal to `C1` and are not formatted; those which have not been recomputed contain a timestamp older than the present value of `C1` and are therefore formatted.

A small variation allows a single monitor to be applied to several cells, e.g.,

`B1` `=IF(COUNT(A1:A10)=COUNT(A1:A10),$C$1)`

collectively monitors the whole range `A1:A10`.

This design pattern incurs only low computational overhead and does not require modifying the monitored spreadsheet computation. In particular, it can be easily removed, when it is no longer needed.

3.3 Data Export

Requirement H was to provide data export from Strati5 to Stratify [6]. This tool can read csv files of a specific structure, defined by the number of columns, their data types and headers. The solution we implemented was to produce such a csv file by concatenating values of certain cells, in a worksheet intended for data export. The user is supposed to either copy and paste its content into a text editor, or save it directly from the spreadsheet system as a csv file. Subsequently Stratify can import such a file.

3.4 "Soft" Methods to Reduce Resource Consumption

We used two "soft" tricks to reduce the resource consumption of Strati5, both related to the interaction with the user. This was done to satisfy requirement I.

The first one is that the user, while describing a context, is allowed to specify only contexts which are later than the present one, while relations in both directions make perfect sense in archaeology, and Stratify permits them to be specified. Specifying that a context c is earlier than the presently edited context d can still be done: by going to the row with context c and entering there d as a later context. This way we avoided expensive sorting by spreadsheet formulas to group the tuples of the *earlier-than* relation by the first coordinate, which is crucial for our implementation of BFS.

The next trick is that we introduced two predefined contexts: the chronologically oldest context "sterile layer" and the top context "surface", which are crucially *not processed* in the acyclicity test (but are processed in the duplicate-freeness test). The typical structure of many archaeological sites causes these two contexts to be present in a very large fraction of the *earlier-than* tuples, while they have no impact on the cyclicity of the relation. By eliminating them, we get a significant reduction of the number of tuples Strati5 must process.

We expect that in many other contexts, domain-specific knowledge about data to be processed can help devising analogous layout solutions to reduce the computational cost of the spreadsheet application.

4   Scalability Problem

This is a problem we did not find any good solution for. Spreadsheets come always with certain fixed number of rows and columns of formulas, and thus are capable of processing a predefined maximal number of data items. Too small a spreadsheet is therefore bad, too large one slows down the applications and drains the battery—the opposite of requirement I. The designer has two basic methods to overcome this problem: either to produce a couple of spreadsheets of different sizes and let the user transfer the data between them when necessary (which is error prone), or to assume that the user will modify the spreadsheet, adding or removing rows of formulas. Preparing the spreadsheet for the latter action is not trivial and requires a good deal of additional design work. It also interferes with the good practice of hiding or locking those portions of the spreadsheet which are not supposed to be edited by the end user.

5   Availability

Strati5 is available from http://bit.ly/Strati5, and is an open-source software with a BSD license. Let us note here that, as far as we know, there is no technology to close the code of a multiplatform spreadsheet application, so multiplatform spreadsheets are open source by necessity.

6   Standardization Issues

We were asked by the anonymous reviewers to discuss the issue of standardization between spreadsheet management systems.

The following list indicates the main difficulties encountered while developing our multiplatform spreadsheet:

a. Limited mutual compatibility of spreadsheet systems.
b. Highly insufficient documentation.
c. Technical and legal problems with using SDK tools for mobile systems.

It is clear that the more functionalities are compatible between spreadsheet systems, the easier is to program multiplatform spreadsheets. Issues a and b are two sides of the same coin. Definitely, they are real: during the whole development process of Strati5 we had problems with mutual compatibility between spreadsheet management systems and with their (lack of) documentation. Therefore we had to rely on experiments choosing solutions in many cases, and we could not use SDK tools for that.

A lot of work was necessary to find a workaround (not a solution!) of the problem that cyclic references, a fundamental property of a spreadsheet, are reported in so many different ways. Even spreadsheet systems coming from the same vendor differ in this respect: Microsoft Excel for Windows (pop-up) differs from its Online and Windows mobile versions (stop), WPS Office for Android and Windows (pop-up) differ from WPS Office for iOS (stop).

Cross-vendor problems concern other fundamental issues: LibreOffice and OpenOffice do not permit formula-based data validations. Even the syntax and behavior of formulas tends to differ from vendor to vendor like, e.g., error encoding and handling between various Excel variants and LibreOffice on the one hand and OpenOffice on the other hand.

The methods to create references to external workbooks are not transferable between spreadsheet systems, in particular if one wants to use INDIRECT or some other programmable, foolproof mechanism.

Indeed, as commented during the workshop, the relations between different spreadsheet systems and their vendors seem to resemble those between Web browsers and their vendors during the browser wars, with similar consequences for the users and programmers.

A significant problem is related to the performance of the whole systems and of their particular functions. Working with hardware of potentially low performance, the programmer must know how spreadsheet systems implement specific functions.[5] E.g., in desktop Excel =MATCH(val,rng,0) is of linear time complexity, while =MATCH(val,rng,1) is logarithmic, assuming that rng is sorted. It would be desired to have guarantees that these complexities carry over to other spreadsheet systems. In desktop Excel =COUNTIFS(rng1,val1,rng2,val2) is much faster than =SUMPRODUCT((rng1=val1)*(rng2=val2)). Again, one would like to know that the same relation holds in other systems. If many formulas are being evaluated, the ability of the spreadsheet systems under consideration to perform multi-threaded computations becomes an important factor, too.

We can also list two particular functionalities which would be very useful in programming multiplatform spreadsheets.

Widely adopted and extended INFO function to determine the identity of the spreadsheet system. That would help in programming spreadsheets in a clean way, with clearly indicated portions of the code to be executed on particular spreadsheet systems. The present functionality of INFO is insufficient: it returns the version number of the system, but not its identity. E.g., =INFO("RELEASE") returns the same value 11 in the latest WPS Office on Windows and on Android, even though both spreadsheet systems differ in behavior and functionality, and in quite different and much older Excel 2003. The situation is even worse with Excel, whose online and Android versions do not support this function at all.

Row-wide and column-wide conditional formatting – in particular, setting conditionally the width of columns and height of rows. This way one could set a column to be a (part of a) frozen pane and be always present on the screen, fill it with formulas computing warning messages, and set its width conditionally to be 0 if it does not contain any warnings. Effectively, the column would then play the role of a pop-up window produced without any scripts or macros.

Built-in array function sorting its input (like the one present in Google sheets) in $O(n \log n)$ time would be a great tool to reduce resource consumption by many

---

[5] We would like to thank one of the anonymous reviewers, who has pointed to us the importance of this topic.

algorithms implemented by spreadsheet formulas. The typical sorting algorithms built from formulas are quadratic. There is a spreadsheet sorting algorithm of $O(n \log^2 n)$ time complexity, but it requires $O(n \log n)$ formulas and is quite complex [11]. Reducing resource consumption is particularly important on mobile systems, due to their relatively low performance and dependence on battery.

Acknowledgments. We would like to thank the anonymous reviewers of our paper and all participants of SEMS 2016, whose comments influenced this post-proceedings paper.

The research project in Ostrowite, where J. Si. tested Strati5, was financed by the National Science Centre grant based on the decision 2015/19/B/HS3/02124. The research of J. Sr. was sponsored by National Science Centre grant based on the decision 2012/07/D/ST6/02492.

A   BFS by Spreadsheet Formulas

Below we describe our implementation of the cyclicity test, which is based on BFS graph traversal of [11], for Strati5 with the size limits we have indicated. The way it is programmed is important for the generation of messages about cyclicity of the relation.

Initial data is located in the worksheet **Contexts**. The range with contexts is **Contexts!A2:S200**, with two contexts predefined: the top and the bottom layer. The range **Contexts!I4:T200** contains the relations: in row i (i.e., the range **Contexts!Ii : Ti**) contains the list of contexts which are later than the context in cell **Contexts!Ai**. The formulas below are located in the worksheet **Cycle test**, which is hidden by default, because it is not intended to be edited by the end user.

Below we indicate ranges and formulas. Each time, if the range consists of more than one cell, we assume that the formula is entered into the top cell of the range and copied down, with automatic modifications introduced by the spreadsheet.

The formulas below ignore rows 1, 2 and 3 of the tab **Contexts**. The first of them contains the headers, the other two contain two predefined contexts: the sterile layer and the present surface, which are the bottom and top contexts in the *earlier-than* relation. We do not process them.

First we count later contexts in each row, to know how many tuples it will produce.

| A2:A200 | =COUNTA(Contexts!I4:T4) |

Now we compute the incremental sum of the tuples to be created, adding one dummy tuple for each context.

| B2 | =1 |

| B3:B500 | =B2+A2+1 |

This is the total number of all tuples:

`C2` =SUM(B2:B200)

And this is the total number of all contexts:

`D2` =COUNTA(Contexts!A4:A200)

Next we produce the number of the row in which the first coordinate of the tuple is located. The count of rows refers to the area starting in row 4 in tab Contexts, hence here we start with 1.

`E2` =IF(ROW()>C$2+D$2,"",1)
`E3:E500` =IF(ROW()>D$2+D$2,"",IF(F2>INDEX(A$2:A$200,E2),1+E2,E2))

The following is then the number of the column from which the second element of the tuple originates:

`F2` =IF(E2="","",1)   `F3:F500` =IF(E3="","",IF(E2=E3,1+F2,1))

Now we import the id of the context, which is the second element of the tuple.

`G2:G500` =IF(E2="","",INDEX(Contexts!I$4:T$200,E2,F2))

At this moment, consecutive rows in columns E and G contain the tuples of the *earlier-than* relation we should process. In column E they are represented by row numbers, in column G by real ids. They are grouped: all tuples that share the same value of the first coordinate form a contiguous block.

The next formula searches column with ids of the contexts in sheet Contexts to find the position of the context which is the second coordinate in the present tuple:

`H2:H500` =IF(OR(E2="",G2=0),-1,MATCH(G2,Contexts!A$4:A$200,0))

In case of nonexistent tuples (second coordinate "") or artificial ones (second coordinate 0) we produce -1 without performing the actual search, because IF is a lazy function, otherwise MATCH does the exact search (third parameter 0) for the value of G2 in the range Contexts!A$4:A$200 and returns the position of the match.

The last formula is the key one. Rows with -1 in column H get value 1 and are the beginning of the recursion. Otherwise a = INDEX(B$2:B$200,H2) gives the row number of the beginning of the block of tuples with the first coordinate equal to G2 (via the value in the previous column), and b = INDEX(A$2:A$200,H2) the size of that block. OFFSET then creates a range, which starts a rows below and 0 columns to the right of I1, and spans b rows and 1 column (default value, omitted in the formula). Now 1+MAX of that range does the recursion. It is well-founded if there are no cycles in the *earlier-than* relation, and results in a cyclic reference in case this relation contains a cycle.

`I2:I500` =IF(H2=-1,1,1+MAX(OFFSET(I1,INDEX(B$2:B$200,H2),0,INDEX(A$2:A$200,H2)+1)))

Therefore the correctness test is really the test if the above formulas produce a cyclic reference or not.

References

1. Bradgar: iPad 2 running Excel with VBA? post #13. http://www.mrexcel.com/forum/excel-questions/607337-ipad-2-running-excel-visual-basic-applications-2.html
2. Chintapalli, V.V., Tao, W., Meng, Z., Zhang, K., Kong, J., Ge, Y.: A comparative study of spreadsheet applications on mobile devices. Mobile Information Systems 2016 (2016). doi:10.1155/2016/9816152
3. CWBlack: apps that support Excel VBA. http://www.mrexcel.com/forum/general-excel-discussion-other-questions/830464-apps-support-excel-visual-basic-applications.html
4. Flood, D., Harrison, R., Iacob, C.: Lessons learned from evaluating the usability of mobile spreadsheet applications. In: Winckler, M., Forbrig, P., Bernhaupt, R. (eds.) HCSE 2012. LNCS, vol. 7623, pp. 315–322. Springer, Heidelberg (2012). doi:10.1007/978-3-642-34347-6_23
5. Flood, D., Harrison, R., Iacob, C., Duce, D.: Evaluating mobile applications: a spreadsheet case study. Int. J. Mob. Hum. Comput. Interact. (IJMHCI) 4(4), 37–65 (2012)
6. Herzog, I.: Group and conquer - a method for displaying large stratigraphic data sets. BAR Int. Ser. 1227, 423–426 (2004). http://www.stratify.org
7. kgkev: VBA & Mobile devices. http://www.mrexcel.com/forum/general-excel-discussion-other-questions/930944-visual-basic-applications-mobile-devices.html
8. QCMan: IPad and desktop. http://www.mrexcel.com/forum/excel-questions/923376-ipad-desktop.html
9. Sikora, J., Sroka, J., Tyszkiewicz, J.: Spreadsheet as a multi-platform mobile application. In: 2015 2nd ACM International Conference on Mobile Software Engineering and Systems (MOBILESoft), pp. 140–141. IEEE (2015). doi:10.1109/MobileSoft.2015.34
10. Sikora, J., Sroka, J., Tyszkiewicz, J.: Strati5 - open mobile software for Harris matrix. In: Campana, S., Scopigno, R., Carpentiero, G., Cirillo, M. (eds.) Proceedings of the 43rd Annual Conference on Computer Applications and Quantitative Methods in Archaeology, vol. 2, pp. 1005–1014. Archaeopress Publishing Ltd., CAA (2016)
11. Sroka, J., Panasiuk, A., Stencel, K., Tyszkiewicz, J.: Translating relational queries into spreadsheets. IEEE Trans. Knowl. Data Eng. 27(8), 2291–2303 (2015). doi:10.1109/TKDE.2015.2397440

Fragment-Based Diagnosis of Spreadsheets

Thomas Schmitz[1(✉)], Birgit Hofer[2], Dietmar Jannach[1], and Franz Wotawa[2]

[1] TU Dortmund, Dortmund, Germany
{thomas.schmitz,dietmar.jannach}@tu-dortmund.de
[2] Graz University of Technology, Graz, Austria
{bhofer,wotawa}@ist.tugraz.at

Abstract. Large spreadsheets are often difficult to understand and to test. Detecting the true cause of an observed wrong calculation outcome in a chain of calculations is even more challenging. In this work, we propose a novel approach that automatically decomposes large spreadsheets into smaller units called fragments. This decomposition serves two purposes. First, it allows us to apply fault localization procedures that can exploit such structural abstractions to find possible explanations for the wrong outcomes (called diagnoses). This results in a faster identification of the diagnoses. Second, it makes the testing process better manageable for the users, as they can provide simpler test cases to reduce the number of possible explanations of the fault. An empirical evaluation of our method shows that the required running times for computing the possible explanations can be measurably reduced when applying the proposed fragmentation approach and that fragment-based test cases help to significantly reduce the number of possible explanations.

Keywords: Fault localization · Spreadsheet fragmentation · Model-Based Diagnosis

1 Introduction

Spreadsheets are widely used in companies for a variety of purposes, e.g., budget planning, forecasting, price calculations, and investment decisions. One might think that spreadsheets which are used for decision-making are well-tested and free from faults, but the reality is disappointing as newspapers regularly report on financial losses because of faulty spreadsheets. A recent article in The Wall Street Journal [23] informs about a $ 100 million loss of the software company Tibco that was caused by a spreadsheet fault. In addition, the consulting company F1F9 lists twelve famous examples of faulty spreadsheets ("The Dirty Dozen") [6]. Furthermore, Schmitz and Jannach recently published a set of faults found in the spreadsheets of the Enron emails [21].

These examples demonstrate that faults in spreadsheets are a common problem and that many faults remain undetected even when domain experts inspect the spreadsheets. But even when a user detects a wrong calculation outcome in a spreadsheet, the process of visually tracing back the dependencies of calculations

© Springer International Publishing AG 2016
P. Milazzo et al. (Eds.): STAF 2016, LNCS 9946, pp. 372–387, 2016.
DOI: 10.1007/978-3-319-50230-4_28

to the faulty formula(s) can still be cumbersome for several reasons: (1) crossing dependency arrows are confusing, (2) the tracing has to be enabled cell-by-cell, which results in significant user effort for large spreadsheets, and (3) dependency tracking between worksheets is not possible [9]. Several automated or semi-automated approaches have been proposed to help the user to find the cause of an unexpected calculation outcome, see [18] for a recent overview.

One of these automated debugging approaches is based on the principles of Model-Based Diagnosis (MBD). MBD is applicable in situations where the user is able to specify the expected values for the output cells. Jannach and Schmitz [17] and Abreu et al. [1] have proposed MBD-based approaches for spreadsheet debugging which are capable of automatically identifying sets of formulas which can in principle be responsible for the observed faulty calculation outcomes. The sets of faulty formulas that can "explain" the wrong outcomes are called diagnoses. Unfortunately, "pure" MBD approaches have certain limitations when it comes to huge spreadsheets, as the number of diagnoses and the diagnosis time grows with the number of formula cells in the spreadsheet.

In this paper, we propose to use a hierarchical diagnosis process which allows us to apply MBD techniques to larger spreadsheets. The main rationale of our approach is that we first diagnose the problem at a coarse-grained level. To do so, we automatically partition the faulty spreadsheet into a set of smaller units, so-called fragments [16]. In the first phase of the hierarchical MBD process, these fragments represent the smallest "diagnosable units", i.e., there are fewer possible reasons for an unexpected outcome, namely the fragments, than when every single cell would be considered. The result of the high-level diagnosis process are those fragments that can be the cause of the problem. In the next phase, we present the fragments that explain the faulty outcome, i.e., the diagnoses, to the user. The user can then specify additional test cases for these small fragments to further isolate the true problem. Given these additional test cases, we apply the MBD technique on the more fine-grained level of the individual cells, which finally leads us to the true cause of the problem, i.e., the faulty formulas.

The main contributions of this paper are (i) a fragmentation approach to automatically partition a spreadsheet into smaller structurally connected parts (Sect. 4.1), (ii) an algorithm that applies hierarchical diagnosis techniques on the level of fragments (Sect. 4.2), and (iii) an empirical evaluation demonstrating the advantages of our approach in terms of computational efficiency (Sect. 5).

2   Motivating Example

The spreadsheet illustrated in Fig. 1 computes the velocity and the distance covered by an object within three phases (acceleration, constant velocity, and deceleration). The three formulas in row 5 are faulty. The spreadsheet creator has forgotten to divide the computed distance by two, which results in a triple fault comprising the cells B5, C5, and D5. In fact, the developer only made one mistake, but by copying the formulas the number of actually faulty formulas was tripled. At some stage, the user of the spreadsheet realizes that there is a

	A	B	C	D	E
1		Acceleration	Constant Velocity	Deceleration	Final state
2	Initial Velocity	0	6	6	0
3	Acceleration	2	0	-2	
4	Duration	3	4	3	
5	Distance	18	24	0	
6	Accum. Distance	18	42	42	

(a) Value view

	A	B	C	D	E	
2	Initial Velocity	0	=B2+B3*B4	=C2+C3*C4	=D2+D3*D4	Legend
3	Acceleration	2	0	-2		Input cell
4	Duration	3	4	3		Interim cell
5	Distance	=B2*B4+B3*B4*B4	=C2*C4+C3*C4*C4	=D2*D4+D3*D4*D4		Output cell
6	Accum. Distance	=B5	=B5+C5	=B5+C5+D5		

(b) Formula view

Fig. 1. Running example: velocity and distance calculation.

problem, because the accumulated distance remains constant from phase 2 (cell C6) to phase 3 (cell D6). When the user manually computes the values for the accumulated distance, he/she realizes that the values for the cells B6 and C6 are incorrect and the values for the cells D6 and E2 are correct.

When the user starts the traditional MBD process with the test data shown in Fig. 1 to locate the cause of this problem, eleven potential causes are computed: {B6, C6}, {B5, D6}, {B5, D5}, {B6, D6, C5}, {B6, D5, C5}, {B5, E2, D2}, {B5, C6, C5}, {B5, E2, C5, C2}, {B6, E2, B5, C2}, {B6, E2, C5, C2}, {B6, E2, C5, D2}. Given only one single test case, it can easily happen in MBD-based approaches that the system returns many combinations of formulas that could explain the faulty behavior. In our example, one of the reported diagnoses ({B5, D5}) is a subset of the true fault. This diagnosis does not comprise the cell C5, as the formulas of B5 and D5 could be changed in a way that would already result in the expected output values for the single test case provided by the user.

Overall, the example shows that basic MBD approaches have limitations in certain situations. Specifically, in our situation two improvements are desirable: (1) the number of diagnoses should be reduced so that the user has to inspect a smaller set of possible causes and (2) the diagnosis {B5, D5} should also contain the cell C5 to indicate that the user should change all of these formulas.

Besides being computationally more efficient, our proposed fragment-based decomposition approach helps us in both mentioned dimensions. Let us assume that the spreadsheet was automatically divided into the three fragments {C2, D2, E2}, {B5, C5, D5}, and {B6, C6, D6}. When using MBD on the fragment level instead of the cell level, only two fragments are reported as diagnoses, namely the fragment {B5, C5, D5} and the fragment {B6, C6, D6}. This in turn means that we can omit the fragment {C2, D2, E2} from further considerations. We can now ask the user to provide a simple test case containing only the cells {B5, C5, D5}. Given such an additional test case, applying the MBD procedure on the fine-grained level will immediately return the true cause {B5, C5, D5} as the only candidate. In this small example spreadsheet, all cells of the fragment are the true cause, but this is not necessarily the case for other spreadsheets.

3   Preliminaries

As Model-Based Diagnosis is a formal and logic-based approach, a logical framework for spreadsheets is required. In this section, we first describe the basic concepts of spreadsheets more formally before we explain the MBD process.

The smallest unit of a spreadsheet is a cell. A cell contains either a formula or a value. Formula cells use expressions and references to compute values. We refer the reader to [13] for more information about the structure of these expressions. For this section, it is sufficient to distinguish between formula and value cells.

Definition 1 (Formula Cells). *The function formulaCells(C) returns the set of formula cells contained in a set of cells C.*

Definition 2 (References). *The function ref(c) for a formula cell c returns all cells that are directly referenced in the formula of c [13].*

Cells are arranged in a matrix. Therefore, they have a unique position and they can be accessed by their coordinates.

Definition 3 (Coordinates). *The function $x(c)$ returns the column index of cell c. The function $y(c)$ returns the row index of cell c.*

There are two ways of referencing cells, A1 notation and R1C1 notation. In this paper, we use R1C1 notation for identifying cells with equivalent formulas.

Definition 4 (R1C1 Notation). *The relative position of a cell c with respect to another cell c' is indicated as '$R[y(c) - y(c')]C[x(c) - x(c')]$'. A formula expression with relative positions is called a formula in R1C1 notation. Absolute references to a cell c are indicated as '$Ry(c)Cx(c)$' in R1C1 notation.*

Definition 5 (Copy Equivalence). *Two cells c, c' are copy-equivalent if they have the same formula in R1C1 notation.*

When two cells are copy-equivalent it does not necessarily mean that their formulas have been copied, but it is a good heuristic to determine that these two cells are semantically equivalent.

Example 1. The formula of cell C2 of our running example from Fig. 1 is '=B2+B3* B4' in A1 notation and '=R[0]C[-1]+R[1]C[-1]*R[2]C[-1]' in R1C1 notation. The cells C2, D2, and E2 are copy-equivalent as well as B5, C5, and D5.

We distinguish between input, interim and output cells:

Definition 6 (Input, Interim and Output Cells). *The function input(C) for a set of formula cells C returns all cells that are referenced by formulas in C but that do not belong to C. A cell $c \in C$ is called an interim cell for a set of formula cells C if there exists at least one formula cell in C that references c. Otherwise c is called an output cell for C.*

$$input(C) = \bigcup_{c \in C} ref(c) \backslash C.$$

$$output(C) = \{c \in C | \nexists c' \in C \text{ where } c \in ref(c')\}.$$

A spreadsheet S consists of a set of formula cells $O = formulaCells(S)$ and a set of input cells $I = input(O)$. Labels and cells which are not referenced by others are not relevant in our approach.

Example 2. The spreadsheet in Fig. 1 comprises the following sets of cells: $O =$ {C2, D2, E2, B5, C5, D5, B6, C6, D6} and $I =$ {B2, B3, C3, D3, B4, C4, D4}. The output cells are a subset of the formula cells: $output(O) =$ {E2, B6, C6, D6}.

If a system under observation does not behave as expected, one can use Reiter's Hitting Set Tree algorithm [20] to determine the possible reasons for the differences between the expected and the observed behavior. We use Reiter's basic definitions and framework to describe the general ideas of MBD.

Definition 7 (Diagnosable System). *A diagnosable system is a pair* (SD, Comps) *where* SD *is a system description (a set of logical sentences) and* Comps *represents the system's components (a finite set of constants) [17, 20].*

In the context of spreadsheets, the set Comps comprises the spreadsheet's formula cells and SD describes the logic of the formulas. To model whether a formula is assumed to be correct or not, the abnormal behavior is represented in SD with a unary "abnormal" predicate AB(.).

Example 3. For our running example, we have SD = {AB(C2) $\lor$ C2 = B2 + B3 $*$ B4, AB(D2) $\lor$ D2 = C2 + C3 $*$ C4, ... , AB(D6) $\lor$ D6 = B5 + C5 + D5} and Comps = {C2, D2, E2, ... , D6}.

A diagnosis problem arises when a set of logical sentences Obs, which contains input values and expected output values of the spreadsheet, is inconsistent with the computed output of the system (SD, Comps).

Example 4. In our example, the set Obs contains the input values shown in Fig. 1(b) and the expected values for the output cells, i.e., Obs = {B2 = 0, ... , E2 = 0, B6 = 9, C6 = 33, D6 = 42}.

Definition 8 (Diagnosis). *Given a diagnosis problem* (SD, Comps, Obs), *a diagnosis is a minimal set* $\Delta \subseteq$ Comps *such that* SD $\cup$ Obs $\cup$ {AB$(c)|c \in \Delta$} $\cup$ {$\neg$AB$(c)|c \in$ Comps$\setminus\Delta$} *is consistent [17, 20].*

A diagnosis therefore corresponds to a minimal subset of the formula cells which, if assumed to be faulty, explains the system's faulty output, i.e., the system description without these formulas is consistent with the expected values in Obs. To calculate the diagnoses, Reiter proposes the Hitting Set Tree [20] algorithm. In our work, we translate the spreadsheet into a constraint satisfaction problem [17] and use Reiter's algorithm in combination with QuickXplain [19]. Details about our specific algorithm implementation can be found in [17].

4　Fragment-Based Diagnosis

In this section, we first describe an evolutionary fragmentation algorithm and then explain how MBD can be adapted to work on the fragment level.

4.1 Fragmentation Process

The fragmentation process proposed in this paper is based on the initial ideas presented in previous work [16]. While this previous work only introduced the basic idea, we now describe the fragmentation process itself. The main rationale is that we start with each cell forming its own fragment. These single-cell fragments are easy to understand. However, such a fragmentation does not reduce the complexity when searching for the possible causes of the problem, as too many fragments have to be considered. Therefore, we combine these small fragments to larger ones in an evolutionary process, which consists of two major parts: (1) collapsing copy-equivalent formulas and (2) merging fragments. When we collapse copy-equivalent formulas, all of them are represented by only one formula for which the user has to ensure the correctness. In contrast, merging fragments does not reduce the number of formulas to test but combines connected formulas into a group that can be tested together. While the process of collapsing the copy-equivalent formulas follows strict rules, we use a genetic approach for merging formulas into fragments. The goal of the genetic approach is not to merge as many fragments as possible, but to create fragments with a reasonable size and complexity. We will explain both the collapsing and the merging part below in detail, but first, we formally define fragments.

Definition 9 (Fragment and Fragmentation). *A fragment f is a set of formula cells $f \subseteq formulaCells(S)$. The set of formula cells of a spreadsheet S is partitioned into n disjunct fragments f_i, i.e., $formulaCells(S) = \bigcup_{i=1}^{n} f_i$ and $\forall i, j$ where $i \neq j : f_i \cap f_j = \emptyset$. We call $F = \{f_1, \ldots, f_n\}$ a complete fragmentation of a spreadsheet S.*

Example 5. A possible complete fragmentation for the spreadsheet in Fig. 1 is $F = \{\{C2, D2, E2\}, \{B5, C5, D5\}, \{B6, C6, D6\}\}$. Another complete fragmentation is $F' = \{\{B5, B6\}, \{C2, C5, C6\}, \{D2, D5, D6\}, \{E2\}\}$. Even a fragmentation containing only a single fragment ($F'' = \{\{C2, D2, E2, B5, C5, D5, B6, C6, D6\}\}$) is a complete and therefore valid fragmentation.

Collapsing. We start the fragmentation process by collapsing copy-equivalent cells which share the same column or row index. The idea behind this is that we want to avoid to collapse cells which appear somewhere else in the spreadsheet and have the same formula only by chance. To do so, we first define a fragment that is column-row-related, i.e., that only contains cells which share the same column or row with another cell of the fragment.

Definition 10 (Column-Row-Related). *A fragment f is column-row-related, if a graph can be spanned over all cells $c \in f$ with nodes f and edges e such that the graph connects all nodes in f and $\forall (c, c') \in e : x(c) = x(c') \lor y(c) = y(c')$.*

Example 6. In our running example, the fragment $f = \{D2, B5\}$ is not column-row-related, as the cells D2 and B5 do not share the same column or row. The fragment $f' = \{D2, B5, D5\}$, however, is colum-row-related, because cell D5 shares the same column with D2 and the same row with B5.

With this definition, we can now define base fragments that represent the collapsed formulas. They comprise either a single formula or a set of copy-equivalent formulas. The base fragments are later used in the merging step.

Definition 11 (Base Fragment). *We call a fragment a base fragment if all contained cells are copy-equivalent and if they share the same row or column with another cell. More formally, a fragment f is a base fragment if $\forall c, c' \in f :$ copy-equivalent$(c, c') \wedge$ column-row-related$(f) \wedge \nexists$ base fragment f' with $f \subset f'$. The left-most cell in the first row of a base fragment f is called the representative of f. The function representative(f) returns a cell $c \in f$ as the representative such that $\forall c' \in f : y(c) < y(c') \vee (y(c) = y(c') \wedge x(c) \leq x(c'))$.*

Collapsing copy-equivalent cells has the benefit that the complexity of test cases can be reduced. Instead of indicating input data for each individual input cell, the user has to indicate only the input data required for one cell (the representative) of a set of copy-equivalent cells.

Example 7. In our example, the copy-equivalent cells C2, D2, and E2 have the same column index and can, therefore, be collapsed. A test case for the fragment $\{C2, D2, E2\}$ only requires values for the input cells B2, B3, and B4 and the output cell C2. No values have to be specified for the cells referenced in D2 and E2 as well as for the cells D2 and E2 themselves. In total, our running example has five base fragments: $\{C2, D2, E2\}$, $\{B5, C5, D5\}$, $\{B6\}$, $\{C6\}$, and $\{D6\}$.

Merging. For the second part of the fragmentation process, i.e., merging the base fragments, the goal is to find the optimal fragmentation based on some complexity criteria. Because of the number of possible solutions, deterministically finding the optimal solution is not possible for larger spreadsheets. Therefore we use an evolutionary algorithm. Evolutionary algorithms follow two concepts from biology: evolution and selection, i.e., survival of the fittest. We implement the evolution process by randomly merging fragments. We use randomness to imitate biologic evolution; some of the newly created fragments are nearer to an optimal fragmentation, others are far away.

Definition 12 (Mergeable). *Two base fragments f, f' can be merged if $|f| = |f'| \wedge \forall c \in f\ \exists c' \in f' : (x(c) - x(r) = x(c') - x(r')) \wedge (y(c) - y(r) = y(c') - y(r'))$ where $r =$ representative(f) and $r' =$ representative(f').*

The result of merging two fragments is a fragment that contains the cells of both fragments. As the base fragments of a spreadsheet are defined in a unique way, a merged fragment can always be partitioned into its base fragments again. Therefore, we can generalize the merging process of arbitrary fragments as follows: two arbitrary fragments consisting of one or more base fragments can be merged if all the base fragments that they comprise can be merged.

Example 8. The base fragments {C2, D2, E2} and {B5, C5, D5} can be merged because the copy-equivalent cells of these fragments have the same distance to their representatives (C5/D5 is one/two column(s) left of B5; D2/E2 is one/two column(s) left of C2). {B6}, {C6}, and {D6} can be merged because they do not comprise any copy-equivalent cells. The result is the fragmentation {{C2, D2, E2, B5, C5, D5}, {B6, C6, D6}}. Both fragments are not base fragments as not all contained cells are copy-equivalent. Merging all combinations of base fragments is not possible, e.g., it would not be possible to merge the base fragments {C2, D2, E2} and {B6}, because the size of these two base fragments is different.

In the genetic process, we randomly test different fragmentations. These fragmentations are called mutants (or individuals). Several mutants build a population which evolves from generation to generation. Only the fittest mutants survive their generation. In each generation, the population is extended with newly generated mutants. The goal of this process is to find the fragmentation that leads to the most "useful" fragments, i.e., a well-structured and comprehensible partition of the spreadsheet. We measure the usefulness of a given fragmentation by means of the aggregated complexity of its fragments. To determine the complexity of each fragment, we use several heuristics: the number of input and output values, the spanned area of the fragment, and the complexity of the formulas. These heuristics are based on the ideas of code smells [11] and spreadsheet complexity measures [12]. Instead of considering all cells of the fragments in the heuristics, we consider only their representatives.

Definition 13 (Representatives). *The function representatives(f) for a fragment f which consists of n base fragments $(f_{b1}, \ldots, f_{bn})$ returns the set of representatives of the base fragments:*

$$representatives(f) = \bigcup_{f_{bi} \in f} representative(f_{bi}).$$

The heuristics are defined as follows.

$$H_{in}(f) = |input(r)| \qquad (1)$$

$$H_{out}(f) = |output(r)| \qquad (2)$$

$$H_{area}(f) = (max_x(r) - min_x(r) + 1) * (max_y(r) - min_y(r) + 1) \qquad (3)$$

$$H_{formulas}(f) = \sum_{c \in r} formulaComplexity(c) \qquad (4)$$

where $r = representatives(f)$, max_x returns the largest value for x for a set of cells, min_x returns the smallest value, and the *formulaComplexity* of a cell is measured by the number of conditionals and cell references in the formula.

Heuristic (1) aims to group cells which have the same input and the idea of (2) is to minimize the number of output cells. Heuristic (3) favors fragmentations that contain "physically" close cells over fragmentations that comprise distant cells. Heuristic (4) sums up the formula complexities of all representative cells to compute the formula complexity of a fragment.

Example 9. For the fragmentation $F = \{f_1 = \{C2, D2, E2\}, f_2 = \{B5, C5, D5\},$ $f_3 = \{B6, C6, D6\}\}$ of our running example, we have the following values:

Fragment	f_1	f_2	f_3
H_{in}	3	3	3
H_{out}	1	1	3
H_{area}	1	1	3
$H_{formulas}$	3	5	6

These four heuristics are used to determine the fitness of the individuals. Each heuristic results in a single number for each fragment. The heuristics vary in their importance for determining a good fragmentation. Therefore, we weight the different numbers before we sum them up for each fragment.

$$fragmentComplexity(f) = \sum_{i=0}^{|H|} H_i(f) * w_i \tag{5}$$

where H is the list of all implemented heuristics and w is a vector containing the weights of the individual heuristics. The weights can be set manually or with the help of some optimization technique. The fragment complexities are then used to determine the fitness of the fragmentation as a whole. To support a balanced fragmentation in which all fragments have roughly the same complexity, we also take the standard deviation of all fragment complexities into account.

$$fitness(F) = -\left(\sum_{f \in F} fragmentComplexity(f)\right) - \sigma(F) * w_\sigma \tag{6}$$

where $\sigma(F)$ is the standard deviation and w_σ is its weight:

$$\sigma(F) = \sqrt{\frac{\sum_{f \in F}\left(fragmentComplexity(f) - \frac{\sum_{f \in F} fragmentComplexity(f)}{|F|}\right)^2}{|F|}}.$$

The resulting number represents the fitness of the fragmentation, i.e., the inverse complexity. The higher the number, the less complex is the fragmentation. We aim to find the individual that has the lowest complexity.

Example 10. Assume we have the weighting vector $w = (2, 3, 4, 5)$ and $w_\sigma = 2$. The complexities for the fragments of Example 9 are $fragmentComplexity(f_1) = 3*2+1*3+1*4+3*5 = 28$, $fragmentComplexity(f_2) = 3*2+1*3+1*4+5*5 = 38$, $fragmentComplexity(f_3) = 3*2+3*3+3*4+6*5 = 57$. Then $fitness(F) = -(28 + 38 + 57) - \sqrt{\frac{(28-41)^2+(38-41)^2+(57-41)^2}{3}} * 2 = -147.1$.

Algorithm 1. Fragment Generation

```
 1: procedure GENERATEFRAGMENTS(S, p, g, s, w, w_σ)         ▷ S . . . set of cells
                              ▷ p . . . population       ▷ g . . . #generations
                              ▷ s . . . survival rate    ▷ w, w_σ . . . heuristic weights
 2:     B ← CollapseCopyEquivalentCells(S)
 3:     count ← 0
 4:     P ← createInitialPopulation(B, p)
 5:     while count < g do
 6:         P ← selectFittestIndividuals(P, s, w, w_σ)
 7:         P ← P ∪ getMutants(P, p − |P|)
 8:         count ← count + 1
 9:     end while
10:     F ← selectFittestIndividual(P, w, w_σ)
11:     return F
12: end procedure
```

Algorithm 1 illustrates the fragment generation process. As an input the algorithm takes the set S of formula cells of the spreadsheet that should be fragmented, the population size p, i.e., the number of individuals that can exist at any time, the number of generations g, the percentage s of mutants that should survive in the population in each generation, and the heuristic weights w and w_σ. The procedure *CollapseCopyEquivalentCells(S)* (Line 2) takes as input a set of cells and creates the base fragments according to Definition 11. The resulting fragmentation B is stored as the base fragmentation and is also used to create the initial population (Line 4).

In the evolution step, the fittest individuals are selected. The function *selectFittestIndividuals* takes as input the population P, the selection rate s, and the heuristic weights w and w_σ and computes the fitness value for each individual $F \in P$ according to (6). The $s * p$ individuals with the highest fitness are kept in the population. In Line 7 mutants are created until the number of individuals is equal to the population size p. The mutants are generated by randomly merging fragments or dividing them into their base fragments. All mergings are done with respect to Definition 12. In the next generations, evolution and selection repeat. In Line 10, the fittest mutant, i.e., the individual with the lowest complexity value and standard deviation, is returned.

4.2   Fragment-Based Diagnosis

The idea of fragment-based diagnosis is to efficiently locate the formulas that can be the cause of unexpected outcomes. To do so, we use the generated fragments as the smallest diagnosable components in the diagnosis process and reformulate the diagnosis problem accordingly. First, we set the diagnosable components COMPS as the generated fragments in F, i.e., COMPS $= F$. Then, we reformulate the system description SD so that the abnormal predicates use the fragment the corresponding formula cells belong to.

Example 11. In our example we reformulate the system description as $SD = \{AB(f_1) \vee C2 = B2+B3*B4, AB(f_1) \vee D2 = C2+C3*C4, \ldots, AB(f_3) \vee D6 = B5 + C5 + D5\}$ and $COMPS = \{f_1, f_2, f_3\}$.

The reformulation of SD ensures that once a fragment is considered to be incorrect in the MBD process, all the formulas of this fragment are also considered to be incorrect when searching for inconsistencies between the expected and observed calculation outcomes. With the help of this formulation, the complexity of the diagnosis process can be strongly reduced, as only entire fragments can be considered to be incorrect.

Overall, we can now automatically generate a fragmentation of a spreadsheet and then determine those fragments that can be the cause of the erroneous outcome. The user can then ignore all fragments (and their cells) that are not part of any diagnosis. For the remaining fragments, the user can inspect their formulas to manually find the fault or he/she can specify additional test cases for these fragments. To specify a test case for a fragment, the user can choose the values for the input cells of the fragment (regardless of whether these cells contained input values in the original spreadsheet or formulas) and then state the expected values for any of the output or interim cells of the fragment. These additional simple test cases help to reduce the number of diagnoses in the MBD process and therefore make it easier to find the true cause of the problem. If the user for example specifies complete test cases containing expected values for all interim and output cells for the fragments that contain the actually faulty formulas, the true cause of the problem will always be found as the only diagnosis.

5   Empirical Evaluation

In this section, we first describe the framework for evaluating our approach and the characteristics of the evaluated spreadsheets. Afterwards, we present and discuss the results of our initial empirical evaluation.

We integrated the proposed approach into the EXQUISITE Framework [15, 17]. The back-end used for calculating the fragmentation and the diagnoses was implemented in Java. We used JGAP to implement the genetic approach and Choco as the constraint solver for the MBD process. After preliminary tests we empirically set the weight vector for the fragmentation process to $w = (0.2, 1, 1, 1)$ and $w_\sigma = 0.2$ to obtain useful fragmentations. The experiments were run on a laptop computer with an Intel Core i7-4710MQ CPU running Windows 8.1.

We evaluated our approach on 5 different spreadsheets. The characteristics of these spreadsheets are shown in Table 1. The tested spreadsheets were quite diverse with regard to the number of formula cells, which range from 9 to 457. However, as it is common for most real-world spreadsheets [10], the number of unique formulas is much lower than the number of formulas itself. One spreadsheet contains a single faulty formula. The *Proteins* spreadsheet contains two unique faults. The other spreadsheets have a fault that was copied to other cells.

Table 1. Characteristics of the tested spreadsheets.

Spreadsheet	#Input cells	#Formula cells	#Unique formulas	#Faults
Wage planning	69	63	25	1
Proteins	14	98	14	2
Sales forecast	224	143	4	2
Course planning	126	457	10	2
Velocity calculation	7	9	5	3

Table 2. Results of the fragmentation process.

Spreadsheet	Time [ms]	#Fragments	#Collapsed cells	#Merged cells
Wage planning	151	13	38	12
Proteins	55	4	84	10
Sales forecast	26	4	139	0
Course planning	49	4	447	6
Velocity calculation	10	3	4	2

Table 2 shows the time needed for the fragmentation, the number of fragments that were generated, the number of cells that could be collapsed due to their copy-equivalence, and the number of merged cells to form larger fragments. The time needed for the fragmentation process mainly depends on the number of fragments that can be merged after the collapsing step. The fragmentation process was therefore faster for larger spreadsheets with many copy-equivalent cells (e.g. *Course planning*) than for smaller spreadsheets with many different formulas (e.g. *Wage planning*). Overall, most of the tested spreadsheets had many copy-equivalent cells that could be collapsed in the fragmentation process so that the merging step could be completed very fast. Regarding the number of generated fragments the second smallest spreadsheet (*Wage planning*) led to the largest number of fragments, as it had the highest number of unique formulas.

Table 3 shows the results of calculating the diagnoses with the different approaches. Calculating the diagnoses based on the fragments was faster for all tested spreadsheets than calculating the diagnoses based on the individual cells. Even for the most complex *Course planning* spreadsheet for which we needed almost 12 s to compute the cell-based diagnoses, we were able to compute the fragments that could be the cause of the error in about 14 ms. Regarding the number of diagnoses, the fragment-based diagnosis procedure determined about half of the fragments as possible diagnoses for the observed error. This is also promising, as the reduced number of fragments to inspect lets the user focus on those parts of the spreadsheet that can be the real cause of the error while the others can be ignored.

The columns "Cell-based using additional test cases" show the results of diagnosing the spreadsheets on the cell level, but with additional test cases for

Table 3. Results of the different diagnosis procedures. Times are given in milliseconds.

Spreadsheet	Cell-based		Fragment-based		Cell-based using additional test cases		Overall
	Time	#Diag	Time	#Diag	Time	#Diag	Time
Wage planning	14	24	3	6	15	1	169
Proteins	440	85	11	2	126	1	192
Sales forecast	102	144	3	2	48	1	77
Course planning	11,903	2,304	14	2	1,900	1	1,963
Velocity calculation	4	11	0	2	3	1	13

the generated fragments. For this measurement we simulated a user and manually created test cases by specifying values for all interim and output cells of those fragments that were part of a diagnosis. With this additional information, we were always able to exactly locate the true cause of the observed errors. For those spreadsheets for which the original cell-based diagnosis needed more than 100 ms, our approach was also much faster, even if we add up all calculation times in this process (last column of Table 3), i.e., the time to generate the fragments (see Table 2), the time to calculate the possibly faulty fragments, and the time to determine the true cause of the error with the additional test cases. In cases in which the fragmentation process requires more time than the cell-based diagnosis process, our fragment-based approach cannot help in terms of the overall computation time. However, our approach is still helpful to reduce the number of diagnosis candidates in these cases.

6 Related Work

Reiter has laid the groundwork for modern Model-Based Diagnosis (MBD) approaches with his theory about diagnosis reasoning from first principles [20]. In the last decades, researchers applied his concept to different areas of application, e.g., logic programs [4] and hardware design languages [8]. Due to the high computational complexity of "pure" MBD, various researchers have explored the consideration of abstractions in the process. There are two main types of abstraction: behavioral abstraction and structural abstraction. Behavioral abstraction simplifies the description of the model; structural abstraction aggregates components of the model. The approach presented in this paper belongs to the group of structural abstractions. Autio and Reiter were among the first proposing structural abstractions [2]. Other relevant works on structural abstraction include Chittaro and Ranon's work on hierarchical MBD in general [3], Stumptner and Wotawa's work on diagnosing tree-structured systems [22], and Felfernig *et al.*'s work on structural abstraction to debug configurator knowledge bases [7].

Our MBD approach directly builds upon the consistency-based approach presented in [17], in which diagnoses are computed indirectly via conflict sets. In contrast, the consistency-based approach presented in [1] computes the diagnoses directly by means of an SMT solver. To the best of our knowledge, structural abstractions have not yet been applied to MBD-based spreadsheet debugging techniques. However, Hofer and Wotawa have recently proposed dependency-based models for spreadsheets as behavioral abstractions [14].

Cunha *et al.* proposed a system to automatically infer a model from a spreadsheet [5]. Their approach is based on the values of the cells to decide on the structure of the spreadsheet, while ours uses the formulas. In general, spreadsheet debugging is a sub-field of spreadsheet quality assurance (QA), which also covers testing, static analysis, modeling, visualization, design, and maintenance support. An overview of QA techniques for spreadsheets can be found in [18].

7   Conclusion

Through our empirical evaluation we could demonstrate that partitioning spreadsheets into fragments can be a powerful means to improve MBD for spreadsheets. On the one hand, the number of diagnoses is decreased; on the other hand, the time required for computing the diagnoses is significantly reduced.

Furthermore, users can benefit from fragments when testing spreadsheets in additional ways. For large spreadsheets, it can be difficult to determine if the spreadsheet computes the correct output values for the given input values. Fragments are units that can be tested separately and a user can create several test cases for each fragment. Because of the small size of the fragments, a user can easily determine the correctness of computed values. In addition, it is easier for the user to manually specify values that cover special cases (e.g., conditionals, division by zero) for small fragments than for a whole spreadsheet. Testing on the fragment level can be compared to unit testing in software.

A number of research questions exist which we plan to answer in future work. First, we plan to evaluate our approach by means of a user study. This user study should settle the question of the usability of our approach for end users. Additionally, we plan to expand our approach to automatically create input values for test cases on the fragment level. These input values should help to test the "standard" behavior of the spreadsheet as well as the special cases. In a next step, we will evaluate whether users prefer to use these automatically generated fragments for testing over manually created ones.

The fragmentation process itself can be improved in several ways. Up to now, we have used fixed values for the population size and the weights of the heuristics. In our future research, we plan to examine whether or not we can obtain a better fragmentation when we change the values of these parameters. In addition, we plan to add additional heuristics to the fitness function. A further speed-up or a better quality of the fragment computation can be achieved when changing the algorithm termination criteria from a fixed number of generations to another criterion. For example, we could stop the evolutionary process when the fitness remains constant over several generations. Once these improvements are implemented, we will evaluate the approach on a larger set of spreadsheets.

Acknowledgment. The work described in this paper was funded by the Austrian Science Fund (FWF) under contract number I2144 and the German Research Foundation (DFG) under contract number JA 2095/4-1.

References

1. Abreu, R., Hofer, B., Perez, A., Wotawa, F.: Using constraints to diagnose faulty spreadsheets. Softw. Qual. J. **23**(2), 297–322 (2015)
2. Autio, K., Reiter, R.: Structural abstraction in model-based diagnosis. In: ECAI 1998, pp. 269–273 (1998)
3. Chittaro, L., Ranon, R.: Hierarchical model-based diagnosis based on structural abstraction. Artifi. Intell. **155**(1–2), 147–182 (2004)
4. Console, L., Friedrich, G., Dupré, D.T.: Model-based diagnosis meets error diagnosis in logic programs. In: Fritzson, P.A. (ed.) AADEBUG 1993. LNCS, vol. 749, pp. 85–87. Springer, Heidelberg (1993). doi:10.1007/BFb0019402
5. Cunha, J., Erwig, M., Saraiva, J.: Automatically inferring classsheet models from spreadsheets. In: VL/HCC 2010, pp. 93–100 (2010)
6. F1F9: The Dirty Dozen. http://blogs.mazars.com/the-model-auditor/files/2014/01/12-Modelling-Horror-Stories-and-Spreadsheet-Disasters-Mazars-UK.pdf. Accessed 7 Apr 2016
7. Felfernig, A., Friedrich, G.E., Zanker, M., Jannach, D., Stumptner, M.: Hierarchical diagnosis of large configurator knowledge bases. In: Baader, F., Brewka, G., Eiter, T. (eds.) KI 2001. LNCS (LNAI), vol. 2174, pp. 185–197. Springer, Heidelberg (2001). doi:10.1007/3-540-45422-5_14
8. Friedrich, G., Stumptner, M., Wotawa, F.: Model-based diagnosis of hardware designs. Artif. Intell. **111**(1–2), 3–39 (1999)
9. Hermans, F., Pinzger, M., van Deursen, A.: Supporting professional spreadsheet users by generating leveled dataflow diagrams. In: ICSE 2011, pp. 451–460 (2011)
10. Hermans, F., Murphy-Hill, E.R.: Enron's spreadsheets and related emails: a dataset and analysis. In: ICSE 2015, pp. 7–16 (2015)
11. Hermans, F., Pinzger, M., van Deursen, A.: Detecting code smells in spreadsheet formulas. In: ICSM 2012, pp. 409–418 (2012)
12. Hodnigg, K., Mittermeir, R.T.: Metrics-based spreadsheet visualization - support for focused maintenance. In: EuSpRIG 2008, pp. 79–94 (2008)
13. Hofer, B., Riboira, A., Wotawa, F., Abreu, R., Getzner, E.: On the empirical evaluation of fault localization techniques for spreadsheets. In: Cortellessa, V., Varró, D. (eds.) FASE 2013. LNCS, vol. 7793, pp. 68–82. Springer, Heidelberg (2013). doi:10.1007/978-3-642-37057-1_6
14. Hofer, B., Wotawa, F.: Why does my spreadsheet compute wrong values? In: ISSRE 2014, pp. 112–121 (2014)
15. Jannach, D., Baharloo, A., Williamson, D.: Toward an integrated framework for declarative and interactive spreadsheet debugging. In: ENASE 2013, pp. 117–124 (2013)
16. Jannach, D., Schmitz, T.: Using calculation fragments for spreadsheet testing and debugging. In: SEMS 2015, pp. 1–2 (2015)
17. Jannach, D., Schmitz, T.: Model-based diagnosis of spreadsheet programs: a constraint-based debugging approach. Autom. Softw. Eng. **23**(1), 105–144 (2016)
18. Jannach, D., Schmitz, T., Hofer, B., Wotawa, F.: Avoiding, finding and fixing spreadsheet errors - a survey of automated approaches for spreadsheet QA. J. Syst. Softw. **94**, 129–150 (2014)

19. Junker, U.: QUICKXPLAIN: preferred explanations and relaxations for over-constrained problems. In: AAAI 2004, pp. 167–172 (2004)

20. Reiter, R.: A theory of diagnosis from first principles. Artif. Intell. **32**(1), 57–95 (1987)

21. Schmitz, T., Jannach, D.: Finding errors in the enron spreadsheet corpus. In: VL/HCC 2016 (2016)

22. Stumptner, M., Wotawa, F.: Diagnosing tree-structured systems. Artif. Intell. **127**(1), 1–29 (2001)

23. Tan, G.: Spreadsheet mistake costs Tibco shareholders $100 million, 16 October 2014. http://on.wsj.com/1vjYdWE. Accessed 7 Apr 2016

TrueGrid: Code the Table, Tabulate the Data

Felienne Hermans[1,2]([⊠]) and Tijs van der Storm[1,2]

[1] TU Delft, Delft, The Netherlands
f.f.j.hermans@tudelft.nl
[2] CWI, Amsterdam, The Netherlands
storm@cwi.nl

Abstract. Spreadsheet systems are live programming environments. Both the data and the code are right in front you, and if you edit either of them, the effects are immediately visible. Unfortunately, spreadsheets lack mechanisms for abstraction, such as classes, function definitions etc. Programming languages excel at abstraction, but most mainstream languages or integrated development environments (IDEs) do not support the interactive, live feedback loop of spreadsheets. As a result, exploring and testing of code is cumbersome and indirect.

In this paper we propose a method to bring both worlds closer together, by juxtaposing ordinary code and spreadsheet-like grids in the IDE, called TrueGrid. Using TrueGrid spreadsheet cells can be programmed with a fully featured programming language. Spreadsheet users then may enjoy benefits of source code, including added abstractions, syntax highlighting, version control, etc. On the other hand, programmers may leverage the grid for interactive exploring and testing of code. We illustrate these benefits using a prototype implementation of True-Grid that runs in the browser and uses Javascript as a programming language.

1 Introduction

Spreadsheets are very popular tools for end-user programming. Their formula language is easy to learn and their grid interface is inviting. Apart from this, spreadsheets are *live*: the user interface reacts immediately to changes in input or code. Live programming helps bridging the gulf between code and behavior because the user receives immediate feedback on their actions [8]. More recently, live programming has found its way to a wider audience, for instance, by Bret Victor's influential talk *Inventing on Principle* [11]. Figure 1, taken from Victor's talk, illustrates the idea of live programming: on the right, we have source code and on the left, we have the result of that code, in this case, a tree drawing. Modifying the code will immediately affect the visual representation of the tree.

This liveness is one of the core features of most spreadsheet systems. When a users enters a formula and presses enter, they see the result, without a lengthy edit-compile-run cycle. This live characteristic of spreadsheets is often praised as their key success factor [3].

© Springer International Publishing AG 2016
P. Milazzo et al. (Eds.): STAF 2016, LNCS 9946, pp. 388–393, 2016.
DOI: 10.1007/978-3-319-50230-4_29

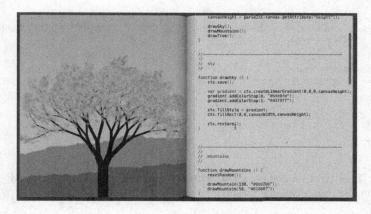

Fig. 1. Live programming: on the right the source code and on the left its instantiation of the code which changes immediately when the code is updated, screenshot from [11].

However, spreadsheets have a number of downsides too. For instance, the lack of abstraction mechanisms forces spreadsheet users to use copy-paste for reusing code. Although solutions to this problem have been researched [4,6], they do not provide the power of full programming languages to spreadsheet users. Secondly, the way formulas are edited in a spreadsheet system like Excel has important drawbacks from the programming perspective. For instance, Excel's formula editor lacks even the basic editor services, such as syntax highlighting and reference resolution. In general, the interface is not inviting to apply proper coding styles and practices. Another disadvantage of embedding the code within the sheet itself is that it prohibits versioning and sharing of the formulas separately from the data.

On the other hand, there is source code. All existing programming languages support abstraction, and modern editors help developers understand and structure their code. However, mainstream integrated development environments (IDE) lack the live and interactive style of interaction so coveted by spreadsheet users.

In this paper, we will describe *TrueGrid*, a light-weight approach to bridging the gap between programming and spreadsheets and describe ts implications in both worlds. The basic concept of TrueGrid is to allow a spreadsheet like grid to be programmed using a full featured programming language, in a consistent user interface. Figure 2 shows this idea as implemented in our prototype. The key charactertistic is that developers see the code and data at the same time. Furthermore, like a spreadsheet, TrueGrid is live, i.e. on a change of data or code, the grid is updated. In our example, we use JavaScript as a language, however, the idea itself is not limited to a single programming language.

In the next section we explore the implication of the TrueGrid user interface for spreadsheet users. Section 3 explores TrueGrid from the perspective of programmers. In particular we discuss conventions for relating code to the grid view.

```
1
2 ▾ function multiply(input1, input2) {
3        return input1 * input2;
4 }
5
6 ▾ function aBitMore(input1, multiply) {
7        return multiply+input1;
8 }
9
```

input1	input2	multiply
1	3	?
2	5	?
2	7	?

Fig. 2. A True Grid implementation, with the code editor on the left hand side and the grid on the righ, available via http://www.felienne.com/TrueGrid/

2   TrueGrid for Spreadsheet Users

As an implementation of TrueGrid for spreadsheet users, we hypothesize that existing spreadsheet system could be extended with a source code editor view, next to the grid-based view of the data. This allows users to use advanced features like PivotTables and charts on top of their TrueGrid, but also use professional IDE services for expressing computations. For spreadsheet users, using TrueGrid over spreadsheets presents several benefits. For example, the use of a professional editor supports the developer with editor services like syntax highlighting and error marking. Furthermore, the textual form of the code allows for easy diffing and merging, enabling more mature version control on spreadsheets. While learning a new programming language can be challenging, there are spreadsheet developers working with VBA now, which is a fully featured language. Unfortunately the integration between the code and a spreadsheet is low level and cumbersome. We envision TrueGrid having a less steep learning curve, because code and data are juxtaposed.

As an example consider the simple grade book sheet shown in Fig. 3. It shows the actual data (both provided and computed) in the grid. The average and class average are expressed using ordinary Javascript functions. The TrueGrid environment links functions or methods to the cells in the grid using a naming convention. For instance, a function starting with the `column_` prefix computes a

```
function column_avg(row) {
  return (row.lab + row.exam) / 2;
}

function cell_classAvg(col, row) {
  return sum(col) / col.length;
}
```

student	lab	exam	avg
Rich	7	8	7.5
Jacome	8	9	8.5
Birgit	9	9	9
			classAvg: 8.3

Fig. 3. Mockup of TrueGrid for spreadsheet use

complete column, given a particular row (an ordinary Javascript object). This is used in the computation of the avg column, where each cell contains the average of the lab and exam cells. The model also allows naming individual cells. This is illustrated in the function cell_classAvg. The function receives the current column (col, a Javascript array), and the current row. Based on the elements in the column the class average is computed.

One could imagine linking the code to the grid using row and column coordinates, just like ordinary spreadsheet formulas refer to (ranges of) rows and columns. However, this would lead to code that is not very intuitive if read separately. Furthermore, insertion of rows and columns in the grid would require updating the source code itself, similar to how spreadsheet systems realign cell coordinates.

3   TrueGrid for Developers

Like spreadsheet users, developers often work with (example) data when programming. For instance, developers use read-eval-print-loops (REPLs) to explore the behavior of a function. Another use case is developer testing which requires setting up test fixtures and inspecting the results. Both these use cases, however, suffer from a lack of immediacy. After a change to the code, the developer needs to reenter expressions in the REPL to observe expected changes in behavior. Similar for testing: reexecuting the test is an explicit step after every change to the code. TrueGrid eliminates these hickups and promises a more fluent, live experience.

In particular, TrueGrid can be seen as a persistent REPL, where expressions or method invocations are continuously evaluated, after every change to the code or input data. Consider the example shown in Fig. 4. On the left is a simple Javascript function for left-padding values with spaces or other padding characters. Using TrueGrid, the programmer can provide example data in the grid and explore the implementation. This can be especially valuable early in the development process when you have some data and only a vague idea of how certain functionality should be implemented.

```
function leftpad(str, len, ch) {
  str = String(str);
  var i = -1;
  if (!ch && ch !== 0) ch = ' ';
  len = len - str.length;
  while (++i < len) {
    str = ch + str;
  }
  return str;
}
```

function	0	1	2	Result
leftpad	"foo"	5		" foo"
leftpad	"foobar"	6		"foobar"
leftpad	1	2	0	"01"

Fig. 4. Exploring function behavior using TrueGrid

From the testing perspective, TrueGrid provides a kind of "FIT testing on steroids" [9], where the grid functions as a live dashboard of test success and failure. In this case, the grid shown in Fig. 4 could have an additional column indicating the success or failure of the function execution, or use green/red coloring of rows to the same effect. Again, the success indicators would be automatically updated upon changing the source code on left.

4   Related Work

This work is positioned at the intersection of end-user programming and professional software development [7]. The particular link between software engineering and spreadsheets has been explored before. For instance, Cunha et al. present model-based programming environments for spreadsheets [2]. The focus of this work is to improve reliability of spreadsheet engineering by applying model-driven techniques. In this work we primarily focus on improving programmer experience.

Integrating spreadsheet-based user interfaces with code editors leads to a simple form of a heterogeneous programming environment (e.g., [10]), originally pioneered in the work on structure editors, and recently popularized by the Jetbrains Meta Programming System [5]. Although this kind of work aims for a much more invasive integration, it is in line with the goal of having the best user interface for each aspect of the programming experience. A similar strand of research is explored in the context of DSLs by Adam and Schultz [1].

5   Conclusion and Outlook

Spreadsheets are live programming environments. However, their lack of abstraction mechanisms and editor support are impediments to professional spreadsheet development. Conversely, traditional programming environments lack the continuous feedback that makes spreadsheets so attractive. In this paper we have presented TrueGrid, a user interface design combining code editing and grid-based data view, with a live execution model.

TrueGrid presents a promising bridge between the domain of spreadsheets and software development. It has the potential to improve end-user programming experience from two perspectives:

- For spreadsheet users: computations are expressed using program code, instead of formulas in cells, so that end-users may enjoy both abstraction and liveness at the same time.
- For professional developers: spreadsheet-like grids support live exploration and testing of code, without explicitly invoking test scripts of entering expressions in a REPL.

We have implemented a prototype of TrueGrid which runs in the browser, using Javascript as the programming language. Further research is needed to empirically investigate the benefits of TrueGrid from both the programmer and spreadsheet user perspectives. We expect that TrueGrid provides a fruitful vehicle for exploring the middle ground between end-user programming on the one hand side, and professional software development on the other.

References

1. Adam, S., Schultz, U.P.: Towards tool support for spreadsheet-based domain-specific languages. In: Proceedings of the 2015 ACM SIGPLAN International Conference on Generative Programming: Concepts and Experiences, pp. 95–98. ACM (2015)
2. Cunha, J., Mendes, J., Saraiva, J., Visser, J.: Model-based programming environments for spreadsheets. Sci. Comput. Program. **96**, 254–275 (2014)
3. Hermans, F.: Analyzing and Visualizing Spreadsheets. Ph.D. thesis, Delft University of Technology (2013)
4. Hermans, F., van der Storm, T.: Copy-paste tracking: fixing spreadsheets without breaking them. In: Proceedings of the International Conference on Live Coding (2015)
5. Jetbrains: Meta programming system (2016). https://www.jetbrains.com/mps/
6. Jones, S.P., Blackwell, A., Burnett, M.: A user-centred approach to functions in excel. ACM SIGPLAN Not. **38**(9), 165–176 (2003)
7. Ko, A.J., Abraham, R., Beckwith, L., Blackwell, A.F., Burnett, M.M., Erwig, M., Scaffidi, C., Lawrance, J., Lieberman, H., Myers, B.A., Rosson, M.B., Rothermel, G., Shaw, M., Wiedenbeck, S.: The state of the art in end-user software engineering. ACM Comput. Surv. **43**(3), 21 (2011). http://doi.acm.org/10.1145/1922649.1922658
8. Lieberman, H., Fry, C.: Bridging the gulf between code and behavior in programming. In: Proceedings of the SIGCHI Conference on Human Factors in Computing Systems, CHI 1995, pp. 480–486. ACM Press/Addison-Wesley Publishing Co., New York (1995). http://dx.doi.org/10.1145/223904.223969
9. Mugridge, R., Cunningham, W.: Fit for Developing Software: Framework for Integrated Tests. Prentice Hall, Englewood Cliffs (2005)
10. Schrage, M.M., Swierstra, S.D.: Beyond ASCII - parsing programs with graphical presentations. J. UCS **14**(21), 3414–3430 (2008)
11. Victor, B.: Inventing on principle (2012). http://vimeo.com/36579366

Views on UML Interactions as Spreadsheet Queries

Martin Gogolla[1] and Antonio Vallecillo[2(✉)]

[1] University of Bremen, Bremen, Germany
`gogolla@informatik.uni-bremen.de`
[2] University of Malaga, Malaga, Spain
`av@lcc.uma.es`

Abstract. This paper explores the use of table-based representation for artifacts occurring in model-driven development as opposed to graph-based representation. As an example for table-based representation of models, we explain how views on object interaction that are traditionally represented as UML sequence or communication diagrams can be realized by spreadsheet queries.

1 Introduction

Models in Model-Based Engineering (MBE) are graph structures and as such they are typically expressed using graph-based representations; e.g., class and object diagrams are represented as nodes and edges in a graph. This sort of representation permits a natural, faithful and comprehensive description of the models and of their views, and its operation by theories and tools. However, graph-based descriptions of large systems can become cumbersome and difficult to understand, query and analyze by human users due to their size and complexity [4,8].

The modelling world has few connections to the spreadsheet world, despite the fact that spreadsheets provide a widely used description technique. Spreadsheets are able to represent complex information in a clearly structured way in tabular form. Together with relational databases, now they probably constitute the most used way of presenting and manipulating information.

This paper explores the use of table-based representation for artifacts occurring in MBE, as opposed to their traditional graph-based representation. As an example, we show how object interaction diagrams that are traditionally represented as UML sequence or communication diagrams [9,12], can be naturally expressed in tabular form; and how views on such models can be easily realized by spreadsheet queries. In principle, the table-based representation we show here can be used for all other UML-like models as well, hence facilitating the creation of views and their representation in a more appropriate manner for many purposes.

2 Preliminaries

The context of our work is the UML tool USE (Uml-based Specification Environment) [5] that allows the developer to describe (a) system structure with a

© Springer International Publishing AG 2016
P. Milazzo et al. (Eds.): STAF 2016, LNCS 9946, pp. 394–400, 2016.
DOI: 10.1007/978-3-319-50230-4_30

class diagram incorporating OCL (Object Constraint Language) invariants and (b) system behavior with OCL contracts, UML state machines and operation implementations in the language SOIL (Simple Ocl-like Imperative Language)

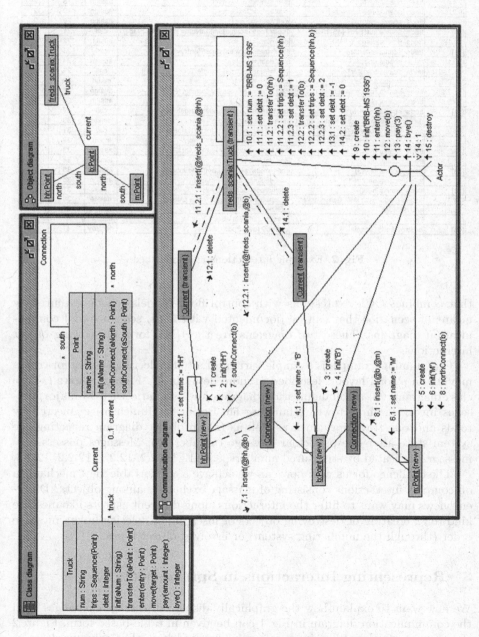

Fig. 1. Example interaction as UML communication diagram.

StrucNum	SpecificInteractionNotation	InstanciatedGenericInteractionNotation	Kind	FlatNum	Depth
•••	•••	•••	•••	•••	•••
[8]	m.northConnect(b)	[self=m].northConnect([aNorth=b])	call	15	1
[8.1]	insert(b,m) into Connection	insert(aNorth,self) into Connection	insert	16	2
[9]	create freds_scania:Truck	create [self=freds_scania]:Truck	create	17	1
[9.1]	freds_scania.num:="	self.num:="	assign	18	2
[9.2]	freds_scania.trips:=Sequence{}	self.trips:=Sequence{}	assign	19	2
[9.3]	freds_scania.debt:=0	self.debt:=0	assign	20	2
[10]	freds_scania.init('BRB-MS 1936')	[self=freds_scania].init([aNum='BRB-MS 1936'])	call	21	1
[10.1]	freds_scania.num:='BRB-MS 1936'	self.num:=aNum	assign	22	2
[11]	freds_scania.enter(hh)	[self=freds_scania].enter([entry=hh])	call	23	1
[11.1]	freds_scania.debt:=0	self.debt:=0	assign	24	2
[11.2]	freds_scania.transferTo(hh)	[self=freds_scania].transferTo([aPoint=hh])	call	25	2
[11.2.1]	insert (freds_scania,hh) into Current	insert (self,aPoint) into Current	insert	26	3
[11.2.2]	freds_scania.trips:=Sequence{hh}	self.trips:=self.trips->including(aPoint)	assign	27	3
[11.2.3]	freds_scania.debt:=1	self.debt:=self.debt+1	assign	28	3
[12]	freds_scania.move(b)	[self=freds_scania].move([target=b])	call	29	1
[12.1]	delete (freds_scania,hh) from Current	delete (self,self.current) from Current	delete	30	2
[12.2]	freds_scania.transferTo(b)	[self=freds_scania].transferTo([aPoint=b])	call	31	2
[12.2.1]	insert (freds_scania,b) into Current	insert (self,aPoint) into Current	insert	32	3
[12.2.2]	freds_scania.trips:=Sequence{hh,b}	self.trips:=self.trips->including(aPoint)	assign	33	3
[12.2.3]	freds_scania.debt:=2	self.debt:=self.debt+1	assign	34	3
[13]	freds_scania.pay(3)	[self=freds_scania].pay([amount=3])	call	35	1
[13.1]	freds_scania.debt:=-1	self.debt:=self.debt-amount	assign	36	2
[14]	freds_scania.bye()	[self=freds_scania].bye()	call	37	1
[14.1]	delete (freds_scania,b) from Current	delete (self,self.current) from Current	delete	38	2
[14.2]	self.debt:=0	self.debt:=0	assign	39	2
[14.3]	result:=1	result:=self.debt.abs()	assign	40	2
[15]	destroy freds_scania	destroy [self=freds_scania]	destroy	41	1

Fig. 2. Example interactions as spreadsheet.

that combines OCL expressions with control flow. Models can be executed by means of scenarios that can be documented with UML sequence and communication diagrams. These two diagrams are the UML form of showing object interactions.

Our running example is a simple variant of a toll collecting system for trucks moving on a road layout described in more detail in [5]. Figure 1 shows (a) the class diagram, (b) a communication diagram for a scenario with 15 major messages involving three towns (Hamburg hh, Berlin b, Munich m) connected by roads and one travelling truck as well as (c) an object diagram reflecting the system state after one particular message (number 12). Messages possess submessages indicated by structured numbers, e.g., 12.1, 12.2, 12.2.1, 12.2.2, 12.2.3.

The challenge for us was: how can we achieve a comfortable view mechanism on complex interactions consisting of message exchanges among objects? Different views may want to filter the interactions along different aspects like message kind (e.g., creating or destroying objects or inserting or deleting links), message order (through the numbering system) or involved object types.

3 Representing Interactions in Spreadsheets

We now want to explain how the graphically displayed message exchanges from the communication diagram in Fig. 1 can be given in table-based form. Figure 2 shows (part of) the object interactions in a spreadsheet. The columns describe

StrucNum	SpecificInteractionNotation	InstanciatedGenericInteractionNotation	Kind	FlatNum	Depth
			=create	<=16	
			=call	>=17	=1

StrucNum	SpecificInteractionNotation	InstanciatedGenericInteractionNotation	Kind	FlatNum	Depth
[1]	create hh:Point	create [self=hh]:Point	create	1	1
[3]	create b:Point	create [self=b]:Point	create	5	1
[5]	create m:Point	create [self=m]:Point	create	9	1
[10]	freds_scania.init('BRB-MS 1936')	[self=freds_scania].init([aNum='BRB-MS 1936'])	call	21	1
[11]	freds_scania.enter(hh)	[self=freds_scania].enter([entry=hh])	call	23	1
[12]	freds_scania.move(b)	[self=freds_scania].move([target=b])	call	29	1
[13]	freds_scania.pay(3)	[self=freds_scania].pay([amount=3])	call	35	1
[14]	freds_scania.bye()	[self=freds_scania].bye()	call	37	1

Fig. 3. Example query on interaction as spreadsheet query.

(1) the structured message number, (2) the message in instantiated form, (3) the message in generic form, (4) the message kind, (5) a flat message number, and (6) the message call depth. The distinction between columns (2) and (3) can be explained best by message 12.2.3 having flat number 34: the generic form shows the SOIL statement from the "move" implementation "self.debt := self.debt+1" whereas the instantiated form shows concrete, substituted values "self.debt := 2". The table-based representation contains even more details than Fig. 1, as attribute initializations and operation result values are shown. Every present information on messages is stated in the table. Apart from the depicted attributes, the table could contain further information, such as the sender and receiver of each message.

4   Views on Interactions as Spreadsheet Queries

Let us now turn to the question how complex interactions as present in Fig. 2 can be viewed and filtered for particular purposes. The developer will not be interested in all messages with all details, but will like to see only messages relevant in a particular context. For example, the developer might want to achieve a rough overview on the creation of the road layout and the operation calls in the later part of the scenario.

The spreadsheet query in the upper, grey-shaded part of Fig. 3 serves this purpose. The result of the query is stated in the lower part.

Thus, by expressing spreadsheet queries that can be formulated in the spreadsheet itself and that can use present constants and simple, but effective operators, the developer is able to interactively formulate requirements on the desired view and to satisfy the current information needs.

In order to compare this approach with similar queries on the UML metamodel, Fig. 4 shows the fragment on the UML metamodel that deals with Interactions. As we can see, every message requires the specification of several instances of class MessageEnd and of separate objects in case of arguments. For example, Fig. 5 shows how only one of the 41 messages in the Interaction is represented as an instance of the UML metamodel, namely the "enter(hh)" message. This illustrates the complexity required for navigating through these kinds of instances for expressing queries that can be easily specified in a spreadsheet.

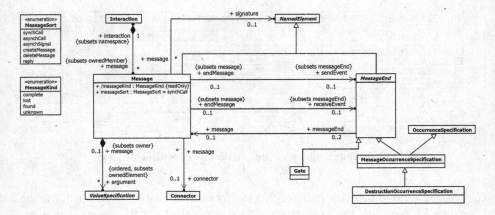

Fig. 4. UML interaction metamodel (from [9]).

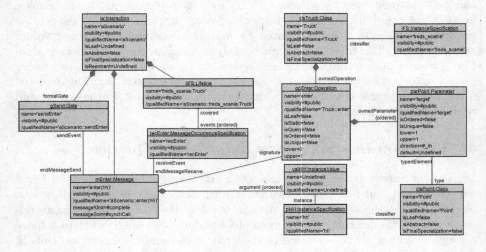

Fig. 5. Send message event as an instance of the UML metamodel (from [5]).

5   Conclusion

So far, most efforts for connecting the spreadsheet and Model-Based Engineering worlds have focused on representing spreadsheets as models [10] in order to make use of MBE concepts, mechanisms and tools to improve the specification, development, debugging, maintenance, and evolution of spreadsheets—see, e.g., [1,2] and many of the SEMS workshop series papers [6,7].

In this paper we have discussed an example that aims at showing the benefits of using a tabular representation of a model as opposed to its graph-based representation. In fact, models of non-trivial systems can become very complicated and their representation as spreadsheets can be quite simple and straightforward.

In this manner queries can be formulated in a natural and user-oriented way, too. Furthermore, we can use all the powerful operations provided by spreadsheets to implement some operations on the views, or even make use of advanced features for querying spreadsheets [3]. We could also keep them in sync, so that certain changes in the views (the spreadsheets) are propagated to the models, updating them accordingly.

Of course, each notation is more apt for particular goals, and probably the best approach consists of combining table- and graph-based representations, using one or the other depending on the kind of user querying the model [11], and on the operation we want to perform on the model. In the USE context we already count on graph- and table-based representations for object diagrams and interactions. Counting on spreadsheet-based representation of other aspects, such as complete object diagram evolution, would be desirable too.

Acknowledgements. This work is funded by Spanish Research Project TIN2014-52034-R and by Universidad de Málaga (Campus de Excelencia Internacional Andalucía Tech).

References

1. Bals, J., Christ, F., Engels, G., Erwig, M.: ClassSheets - model-based, object-oriented design of spreadsheet applications. J. Object Technol. **6**(9), 383–398 (2007)
2. Cunha, J., Fernandes, J., Mendes, J., Pereira, R., Saraiva, J.: MDSheet: model-driven spreadsheets. In: Proceedings of SEMS 2014, vol. 1209, pp. 31–33. CEUR (2014)
3. Cunha, J., Fernandes, J.P., Mendes, J., Pereira, R., Saraiva, J.: Embedding model-driven spreadsheet queries in spreadsheet systems. In: Proceedings of VL/HCC 2014, pp. 151–154. IEEE Computer Society (2014)
4. Gelman, A.: Why tables are really much better than graphs. J. Comput. Graph. Stat. **20**(1), 3–7 (2011)
5. Gogolla, M., Hamann, L., Hilken, F., Sedlmeier, M.: Modeling Behavior with interaction diagrams in a UML and OCL tool. In: Roubtsova, E., McNeile, A., Kindler, E., Gerth, C. (eds.) Behavior Modeling – Foundations and Applications. LNCS, vol. 6368, pp. 31–58. Springer, Heidelberg (2015). doi:10.1007/978-3-319-21912-7_2
6. Hermans, F., Paige, R.F., Sestof, P. (eds.): Proceedings of 1st International Workshop Software Engineering Methods in Spreadsheets (SEMS 2014). CEUR Proceedings, vol. 1209 (2014). http://ceur-ws.org/Vol-1209/
7. Hermans, F., Paige, R.F., Sestof, P. (eds.): Proceedings of 2nd International Workshop Software Engineering Methods in Spreadsheets (SEMS 2015). CEUR Proceedings, vol. 1355 (2015). http://ceur-ws.org/Vol-1355/
8. Kosslyn, S.M.: Understanding charts and graphs. Appl. Cogn. Psychol. **3**(3), 185–225 (2006)
9. Object Management Group: Unified Modeling Language (UML) Specification, version 2.5. OMG Document formal, 01 March 2015
10. Paige, R.F., Kolovos, D., Matragkas, N.: Spreadsheets are models too. In: Proceedings of SEMS 2014. CEUR, vol. 1209, pp. 9–10 (2014)

11. Sobreira, P., Tchounikine, P.: CSCL scripts: interoperating table and graph representations. In: Proceedings of CSCL 2013, pp. 165–168 (2013)
12. Wendland, M.-F., Schneider, M., Haugen, Ø.: Evolution of the UML interactions metamodel. In: Moreira, A., Schätz, B., Gray, J., Vallecillo, A., Clarke, P. (eds.) MODELS 2013. LNCS, vol. 8107, pp. 405–421. Springer, Heidelberg (2013). doi:10.1007/978-3-642-41533-3_25

Implementing Nested FOR Loops
as Spreadsheet Formulas

Paul Mireault[(⊠)]

SSMI International, Montréal, Canada
Paul.Mireault@SSMI.International

Abstract. A FOR loop is a computing structure that allows a set of calculations to be made repeatedly for each iteration of the loop where the number of iterations is known in advance. A nested loop happens when a loop is inside another loop. In a spreadsheet program like Microsoft Excel, one can program loops in VBA, its programming language. Spreadsheet developers who do not know how to program in VBA usually implement the equivalent of loops with static values (e.g. region codes and product types are typed as constants) or with formulas (e.g. the region code is the previous region code + 1). In this paper, we present similarities and differences between programming loops and spreadsheet formulas loops. We also present a set of formulas that implement nested loops for 1, 2 or 3 nested levels, along with a generalization for deeper nesting levels. We also provide model management formulas to help the spreadsheet developer ensure that his spreadsheet model covers all the iterations.

1 Introduction

Various research has reported important spreadsheet error rates. [1] surveyed studies showing a percentage of spreadsheet with errors as high as 86%. Spreadsheet errors have led to not only monetary losses [2] but have also caused career failures [3] and reputation losses [4].

Research has been done to help spreadsheet developers build complex spreadsheets by using Computer Science and Software Engineering concepts. For example, [5] studied the use of user-defined functions as a way to reduce formula complexity, [6] examines cell labels typed by the spreadsheet developer to infer a structure and provide type checking in formulas, and [7] proposes a model-driven approach. Finally, [8] developed a methodology based on the conceptual model of Information Systems.

2 Structure in Spreadsheets

Spreadsheet developers sometimes find themselves in a situation where they need to build a repetitive structure. For example, they may need to prepare a report or a model with multiple dimensions like years, products and regions, as illustrated in Fig. 1.

We have seen spreadsheet developers build such structures by typing values and repeatedly copying them to achieve the desired result. Some other developers type values and use reference formulas to produce the same result. While the latter approach

P. Milazzo et al. (Eds.): STAF 2016, LNCS 9946, pp. 401–414, 2016.
DOI: 10.1007/978-3-319-50230-4_31

	A	B	C	D	E	F	G	H	I	J	K	L	M	N	O	P	Q	R
1	Y-P-R Model																	
2																		
3	Year		2016	2016	2016	2016	2016	2016	2016	2016	2017	2017	2017	2017	2017	2017	2017	2017
4	Product		Cars	Cars	Cars	Cars	Trucks	Trucks	Trucks	Trucks	Cars	Cars	Cars	Cars	Trucks	Trucks	Trucks	Trucks
5	Region		North	South	East	West	North	South	East	West	North	South	East	West	North	South	East	West

Fig. 1. Example of a multi-dimensional structure

offers some flexibility by allowing the user to easily change a dimension's values, both approaches don't allow the user to easily add or remove values in the dimensions.

In a computer program, the same structure is normally implemented with nested loops. Any modification requires only that the user add or remove values and re-execute the program.

The objective of this paper is to devise a set of formulas to implement nested loops in a spreadsheet using nothing else but a plain version of Excel (i.e. not using external spreadsheet generator or add-ins.) We will start with a simple loop and proceed to a 1-level, 2-level and 3-level nested loop, explaining the how to implement each level's specific characteristics. Finally, we will illustrate how to adapt the general loop implementation to situations more suitable to general spreadsheet uses.

3 Loops in Computer Programming

Loops are a programming construct that cause the execution a series of instructions to be repeated a number of times. During the loop's execution, variables are assigned values and these values are overwritten in each execution.

Implementing a loop in a spreadsheet consists of setting up the iterations in columns or in rows. Since a spreadsheet is a static object, columns cannot be added programmatically during its utilization: the spreadsheet developer must create the appropriate number of columns.

A FOR loop is used when the number of iterations is known before its execution. It uses a loop counter which is initialized at the beginning of the loop. The loop instructions are then executed and the loop counter is then incremented by a specified value. If the loop counter does not exceed the maximum specified value, the loop is repeated. In its simplest case, the loop counter is initialized with the value 1 and it is incremented by 1 at the end of each iteration.

C	Java	BASIC
for (i = 1; i <= n; i++) {set of instructions}	for (i = 1; i <= n; i = i+1) {set of instructions}	FOR I = 1 TO N set of instructions NEXT I

A nested loop is a loop that occurs within another loop, as illustrated in the following code snippet:

```
BASIC
FOR I = 1 TO N
    FOR J = 1 TO M
        set of instructions
    NEXT J
NEXT I
```

The total number of iterations, i.e. the number of times the set of instructions will be executed, is N * M. As we nest more loops, the number of iterations can become quite large quickly. In a computer program this only affects the time it takes to execute the program. But in a spreadsheet, this has the effect of adding columns (or rows) to the spreadsheet.

4   Loops in a Spreadsheet

4.1   Simple Loop

We will use the SSMI (Structured Spreadsheet Modelling and Implementation) methodology described in [9] to illustrate the variables and the formulas that we will implement in the spreadsheet.

In a simple loop, the value of the loop counter is incremented in each column. The simple loop is illustrated in the Formula Diagram of Fig. 2 and the Formula List of Table 1.

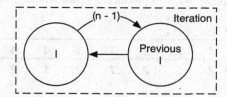

Fig. 2. Formula diagram of the simple loop

Table 1. Formula List of the simple loop

Variable	Formula
Previous I	I(n-1)
I	Previous I + 1, Initial value = 0

In the SSMI methodology, all formulas should refer to cells in the same column. When we need to use a value in the previous column, we create a variable whose sole purpose is to reference that value. This way, all references to other columns are well indicated. In this case, we create a variable, Previous I = I(n-1), to record the value variable I had in the previous column and use it to calculate the value of the loop index, I = Previous I + 1. Since we refer to one column on the left, we need to provide an initialization column to provide the initial values for the variables that are the object of a (n-1) reference. Figure 3 shows the SSMI implementation of the simple loop: column A contains the variable names, column B is the initialization column and columns C to G represent the loop iteration. Also, a variable is named in the row or column where it is defined, and a visual cue (bold italic) is used to show exactly where an Excel *name* has been created, such as Previous I and I in rows 6 and 9. 9.

	A	B	C	D	E	F	G		A	B	C
1	I Loop							1	=MID(CELL('		
2								2			
3	Iteration Counter		1	2	3	4	5	6	3	I Iteration C	=I_Iter	=I_Iteration_Counter
4								4			
5	I		0	1	2	3	4	5	5	I	=I	=I
6	*Previous I*			0	1	2	3	4	6	*Previous I*	=B5	
7								7			
8	Previous I			0	1	2	3	4	8	Previous I	=Previous_I	
9	*I*		0	1	2	3	4	5	9	*I*	0	=C8+1

Fig. 3. Implementation of the simple loop, normal view (left) and formula view (right)

Since we want the loop counter to start at 1, we explicitly initialize it to 0 in cell B9.

4.2 1-Level Nested Loop

In a 1-level nested loop, we want to produce a result similar to Fig. 4.

I	*1*	*1*	*2*	*2*	*3*	*3*	*4*	*4*	*5*	*5*
J	*1*	*2*	*1*	*2*	*1*	*2*	*1*	*2*	*1*	*2*

Fig. 4. Illustration of a 1-level nested loop

In this example, the inner loop index J has 2 values and the outer loop index I has 5 values. We can observe that whenever J reaches its final value it resets to 1, and when it resets, the value of I gets incremented, otherwise it remains unchanged.

To model that behavior, we introduce an indicator variable, Reset J Indicator, which takes the value 1 when the counter J needs to be reset and the value 0 otherwise. The condition for a reset is that the previous value of J has reached its final value. This is illustrated in the Formula Diagram of Fig. 5 and the Formula List of Table 2.

Since the loop counter I is initialized at 0 we need an initial condition to have the Reset J Indicator set to 1 immediately in the first iteration. To do so, we initialize J with its final value. Figure 6 shows the SSMI implementation of the 1-level nested loop.

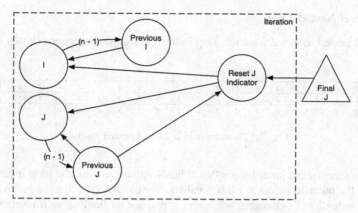

Fig. 5. Formula diagram of the 1-level nested loop

Table 2. Formula List of the 1-level nested loop

Variable	Formula
Previous I	I(n-1)
I	IF(Reset J Indicator = 1, Previous I + 1, Previous I), Initial value = 0
Previous J	J(n-1)
Reset J Indicator	IF(Previous J = Final J, 1, 0)
J	IF(Reset J Indicator = 1, 1, Previous J + 1), Initial value = Final J

	A	B	C	D	E	F	G	H	I	J	K	L
1	I-J Loop											
2												
3	Iteration Counter	1	2	3	4	5	6	7	8	9	10	11
4												
5	I	0	1	1	2	2	3	3	4	4	5	5
6	*Previous I*		0	1	1	2	2	3	3	4	4	5
7												
8	Reset J Indicator		1	0	1	0	1	0	1	0	1	0
9	Previous I		0	1	1	2	2	3	3	4	4	5
10	*I*	0	1	1	2	2	3	3	4	4	5	5
11												
12	J	2	1	2	1	2	1	2	1	2	1	2
13	*Previous J*		2	1	2	1	2	1	2	1	2	1
14												
15	Previous J		2	1	2	1	2	1	2	1	2	1
16	Final J		2	2	2	2	2	2	2	2	2	2
17	*Reset J Indicator*		1	0	1	0	1	0	1	0	1	0
18												
19	Reset J Indicator		1	0	1	0	1	0	1	0	1	0
20	Previous J		2	1	2	1	2	1	2	1	2	1
21	J	2	1	2	1	2	1	2	1	2	1	2

	A	B	C
1	=MID(CELL("filenai		
2			
3	I-J Iteration Count	=I_J_Itera	=I_J_Iteration_Counter
4			
5	I	=I	=I
6	*Previous I*		=B5
7			
8	Reset J Indicator		=Reset_J_Indicator
9	Previous I		=Previous_I
10	*I*	0	=IF(C8=1,C9+1,C9)
11			
12	J	=J	=J
13	*Previous J*		=B12
14			
15	Previous J		=Previous_J
16	Final J		=Final_J
17	*Reset J Indicator*		=IF(C15=C16,1,0)
18			
19	Reset J Indicator		=Reset_J_Indicator
20	Previous J		=Previous_J
21	J	=Final_J	=IF(C19=1,1,C20+1)

Fig. 6. Implementation of the 1-level nested loop, normal view (left) and formula view (right)

4.3 2-Level Nested Loop

In a 2-level nested loop we want the loop indices to follow the pattern shown in Fig. 7.

I	1	1	1	1	1	1	1	1	2	2	2	2	2	2	2	2	3	3	3	3	3	3
J	1	1	1	1	2	2	2	2	1	1	1	1	2	2	2	2	1	1	1	1	2	2
K	1	2	3	4	1	2	3	4	1	2	3	4	1	2	3	4	1	2	3	4	1	2

Fig. 7. Illustration of a 2-level nested loop

In this example, the inner loop index K has 4 values, the middle loop index J has 2 values and the outer loop index I has 5 values. We can observe that the behavior of the inner loop index hasn't changed: whenever it reaches its final value it resets to 1. The same can be said about the outer loop index: when the next loop index J resets, the value of I gets incremented, otherwise it remains unchanged. But now, the middle loop index J has 3 possibilities at each iteration: it remains unchanged, it is incremented or it is reset. We need two indicator variables to indicate when it should be incremented and when it should be reset. The condition for a reset is when K has been reset and Previous J has reached its final value. The condition for an increment is when K has been reset and Previous J has not reached its final value. This is illustrated in the Formula Diagram of Fig. 8 and the Formula List of Table 3.

Figure 9 shows the SSMI implementation of the 2-level nested loop.

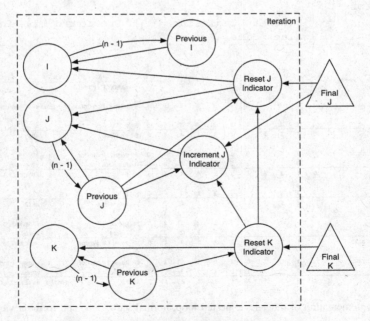

Fig. 8. Formula diagram of the 2-level nested loop

Table 3. Formula List of the 2-level nested loop

Variable	Formula
Previous I	I(n-1)
I	IF(Reset J Indicator = 1, Previous I + 1, Previous I), Initial value = 0
Previous J	J(n-1)
Reset J Indicator	IF(Reset K Indicator = 1 AND Previous J = Final J, 1, 0)
Increment J Indicator	IF(Reset K Indicator = 1 AND Previous J<>Final J, 1, 0)
J	IF(Reset J Indicator = 1, 1, IF(Increment J Indicator = 1, Previous J + 1, Previous J)), Initial value = Final J
Previous K	K(n-1)
Reset K Indicator	IF(Previous K = Final K, 1, 0)
K	IF(Reset K Indicator = 1, 1, Previous K + 1), Initial value = Final K

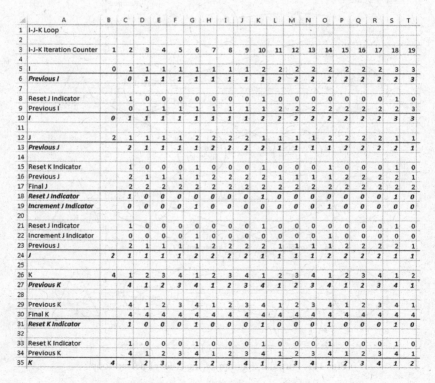

	A	B	C	D	E	F	G	H	I	J	K	L	M	N	O	P	Q	R	S	T
1	I-J-K Loop																			
2																				
3	I-J-K Iteration Counter	1	2	3	4	5	6	7	8	9	10	11	12	13	14	15	16	17	18	19
4																				
5	I	0	1	1	1	1	1	1	1	1	2	2	2	2	2	2	2	2	3	3
6	*Previous I*		0	1	1	1	1	1	1	1	1	2	2	2	2	2	2	2	2	3
7																				
8	Reset J Indicator		1	0	0	0	0	0	0	0	1	0	0	0	0	0	0	0	1	0
9	Previous I		0	1	1	1	1	1	1	1	1	2	2	2	2	2	2	2	2	3
10	*I*	0	1	1	1	1	1	1	1	1	2	2	2	2	2	2	2	2	3	3
11																				
12	J	2	1	1	1	1	2	2	2	2	1	1	1	1	2	2	2	2	1	1
13	*Previous J*		2	1	1	1	1	2	2	2	2	1	1	1	1	2	2	2	2	1
14																				
15	Reset K Indicator		1	0	0	0	1	0	0	0	1	0	0	0	1	0	0	0	1	0
16	Previous J		2	1	1	1	1	2	2	2	2	1	1	1	1	2	2	2	2	1
17	Final J		2	2	2	2	2	2	2	2	2	2	2	2	2	2	2	2	2	2
18	*Reset J Indicator*		1	0	0	0	0	0	0	0	1	0	0	0	0	0	0	0	1	0
19	*Increment J Indicator*		0	0	0	0	1	0	0	0	0	0	0	0	1	0	0	0	0	0
20																				
21	Reset J Indicator		1	0	0	0	0	0	0	0	1	0	0	0	0	0	0	0	1	0
22	Increment J Indicator		0	0	0	0	1	0	0	0	0	0	0	0	1	0	0	0	0	0
23	Previous J		2	1	1	1	1	2	2	2	2	1	1	1	1	2	2	2	2	1
24	*J*	2	1	1	1	1	2	2	2	2	1	1	1	1	2	2	2	2	1	1
25																				
26	K	4	1	2	3	4	1	2	3	4	1	2	3	4	1	2	3	4	1	2
27	*Previous K*		4	1	2	3	4	1	2	3	4	1	2	3	4	1	2	3	4	1
28																				
29	Previous K		4	1	2	3	4	1	2	3	4	1	2	3	4	1	2	3	4	1
30	Final K		4	4	4	4	4	4	4	4	4	4	4	4	4	4	4	4	4	4
31	*Reset K Indicator*		1	0	0	0	1	0	0	0	1	0	0	0	1	0	0	0	1	0
32																				
33	Reset K Indicator		1	0	0	0	1	0	0	0	1	0	0	0	1	0	0	0	1	0
34	Previous K		4	1	2	3	4	1	2	3	4	1	2	3	4	1	2	3	4	1
35	*K*	4	1	2	3	4	1	2	3	4	1	2	3	4	1	2	3	4	1	2

Fig. 9. Implementation of the 2-level nested loop

4.4 3-Level Nested Loop

In a 3-level nested loop, we want the loop indices to follow the pattern shown in Fig. 10.

I	1	1	1	1	1	1	1	1	1	1	1	1	1	1	1	1	1	1	1	1	1	1	1	1	2	2
J	1	1	1	1	1	1	1	1	1	1	1	1	2	2	2	2	2	2	2	2	2	2	2	2	1	1
K	1	1	1	2	2	2	3	3	3	4	4	4	1	1	1	2	2	2	3	3	3	4	4	4	1	1
L	1	2	3	1	2	3	1	2	3	1	2	3	1	2	3	1	2	3	1	2	3	1	2	3	1	2

Fig. 10. Illustration of a 3-level nested loop

In this example, the inner loop index L has 3 values and the other loops are as before. We can observe that the behavior of the middle loops J and K are the same: whenever their previous loop index reaches its final value they either reset to 1 or increment, otherwise they remain unchanged. This is illustrated in the Formula Diagram of Fig. 11 and the Formula List of Table 4.

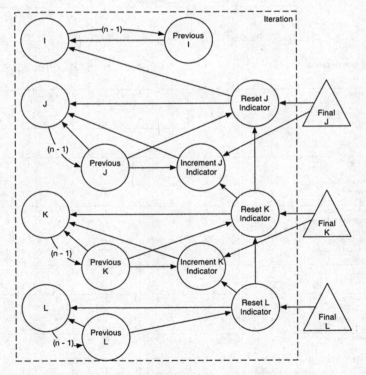

Fig. 11. Formula diagram of the 3-level nested loop

Table 4. Formula List of the 3-level nested loop

Variable	Value/Formula
Previous I	I(n-1)
I	IF(Reset J Indicator = 1, Previous I + 1, Previous I), Initial value = 0
Previous J	J(n-1)
Reset J Indicator	IF(Reset K Indicator = 1 AND Previous J = Final J, 1, 0)
Increment J Indicator	IF(Reset K Indicator = 1 AND Previous J<>Final J, 1, 0)
J	IF(Reset J Indicator = 1, 1, IF(Increment J Indicator = 1, Previous J + 1, Previous J)), Initial value = Final J
Previous K	K(n-1)
Reset K Indicator	IF(Reset L Indicator = 1 AND Previous K = Final K, 1, 0)
Increment K Indicator	IF(Reset L Indicator = 1 AND Previous K<>Final K, 1, 0)
K	IF(Reset K Indicator = 1, 1, IF(Increment K Indicator = 1, Previous K + 1, Previous K)), Initial value = Final K
Previous L	L(n-1)
Reset L Indicator	IF(Previous L = Final L, 1, 0)
L	IF(Reset L Indicator = 1, 1, Previous L + 1), Initial value = Final L

We see, in the Formula Diagram and in the Formula List, that the middle loops have the same set of 4 variables and similar formulas. Thus, this provides a generalization to adding nested loops.

Table 5 summarizes the actions that can be performed on the different loop indices and what their initial value must be.

Table 5. Actions that can be performed on a loop index depending on the loop's position

	Reset	Incremented	Unchanged	Initialization
Outer loop	-	X	X	0
Middle loop	X	X	X	Final
Inner loop	X	X	-	Final

5 Model Management Formulas

Unlike programming, where the total number of iterations is determined by each loop index's final value and can change from one program execution to another, the total number of iterations in a spreadsheet is determined by the number of columns in which the loop formulas have been copied. If the spreadsheet developer copied the formulas in 40 columns, that is good for loops with final values {2, 4, 5} and {5, 8} but not for {3, 2, 7} and {9, 5}, which require 42 and 45 columns respectively.

While it would be possible to program a VBA (Visual Basic for Applications) module to automatically adjust the number of columns according to the set of final values, this is beyond the scope of this paper. Many spreadsheet developers have never taken any programming course and would be incapable of programming such a VBA module.

The workaround we propose is to use model management formulas. We define a *model management formula* as a formula whose purpose is to inform the spreadsheet developer or user about errors or inconsistencies in the spreadsheet itself.

A simple model management formula will compare the expected number of columns with the actual number of columns in the different spreadsheets that use the loop. The expected number of columns is the product of the final values of the loops' indices plus the number of initialization columns. (That number is 1 most of the time, but a developer may need to adjust it to his needs.) The number of actual columns is the maximum value of the loop iteration counter. The difference between those two numbers should be zero, and it can inform the developer as to the number of columns to add or to remove from the spreadsheets that use the loop. Figure 12 shows a warning indicating that the loop formulas need to be copied in 31 more columns in two spreadsheets.

	A	B	C	D	E	F	G	H	I	J	K	L	M	N
20	Final I	5												
21	Final J	2												
22	Final K	4												
23	*I-J-K Iterations*	40	AP1											
24														
25														
26	*I-J-K Iteration Counter*	1	2	3	4	5	6	7	8	9	10			
27														
44	Initialization Columns	1												
45	I-J-K Iterations	40												
46	*Expected I-J-K Columns*	41												
47														
48	Expected I-J-K Columns	41												
49	Max Iteration Counter in Y-P-R Loop sheet	-10												
50	*Columns needed in Y-P-R Loop Sheet*	31												
51														
52	Expected I-J-K Columns	41												
53	Max Iteration Counter in Y-P-R Model sheet	-10												
54	*Columns needed in Y-P-R Model Sheet*	31												

Fig. 12. Model management formulas

6 Application to Different Contexts

In practice, spreadsheet developers use loops to represent objects that don't have the standard characteristics of the loops we used so far. Their first value may not always be a 1, and in some cases they may not even be quantitative. In this section we show two common examples: in the first case the loop models a set of years, and in the second case it models a set of qualitative variables.

Figure 13 shows the Year Loop parameters, where the user can enter the first and last years that the spreadsheet should consider. Mode management formulas calculate the Number of Years, which is used as `Final I`, and the `Base Year`, which will be explained shortly.

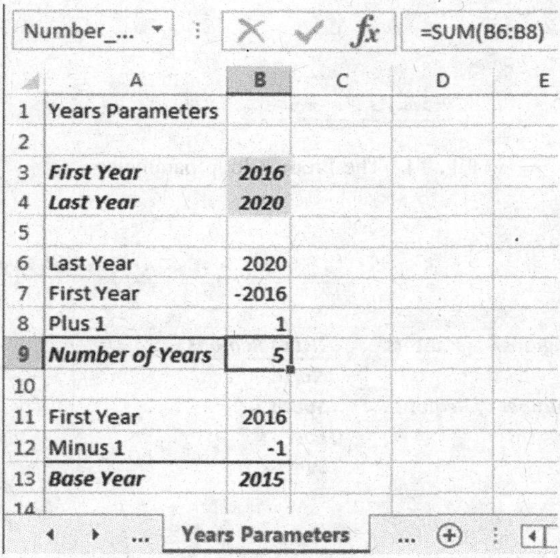

Fig. 13. The Year loop parameters

Figure 14 shows the Product Loop parameters. In this case, the user can enter product names in the `List of Products` and the `Number of Products` is calculated as the number of elements in the list and is used as `Final J`. Figure 15 shows the Region Loop parameters which behaves similarly and supplies the value of `Final K`.

After having prepared the different loop parameters, we can create the user's loops, as shown in Fig. 16. We can use Excel's `INDEX` function with the `J` and `K` loop indices because their starting value is always 1. The `Year` is calculated as `I + Base Year`.

Once the nested loops are set, the developer can use them in other worksheets. If the worksheet has the same column structure as the Y-P-R Loop worksheet, we can simply use the loop index's name as shown in Fig. 17.

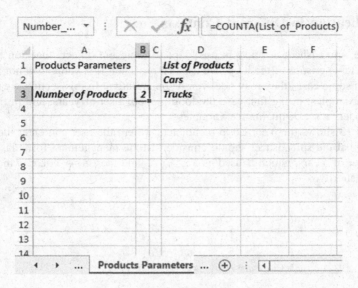

Fig. 14. The Product loop parameters

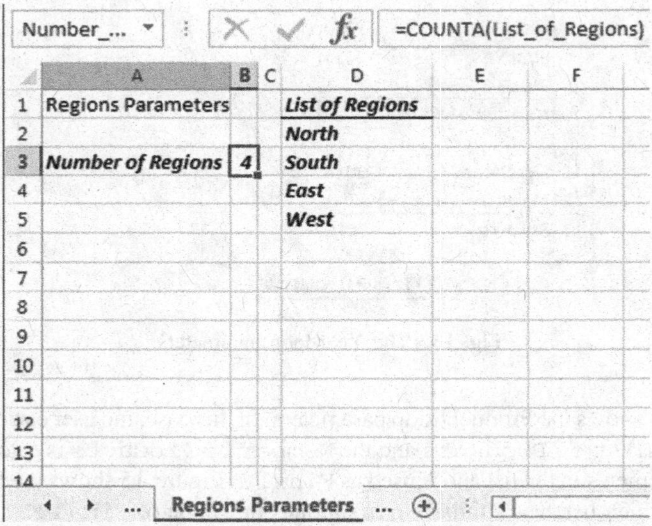

Fig. 15. The Region loop parameters

On the other hand, if the worksheet does not have the same column structure, the developer can create a row referring to Y-P-R Iteration Counter and use it with the INDEX function as shown in Fig. 18.

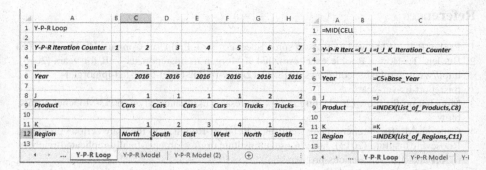

Fig. 16. Creating the actual loops

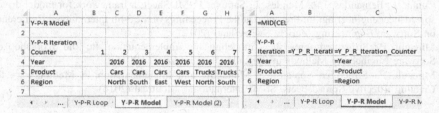

Fig. 17. Using the loop indices in a worksheet with the same column structure

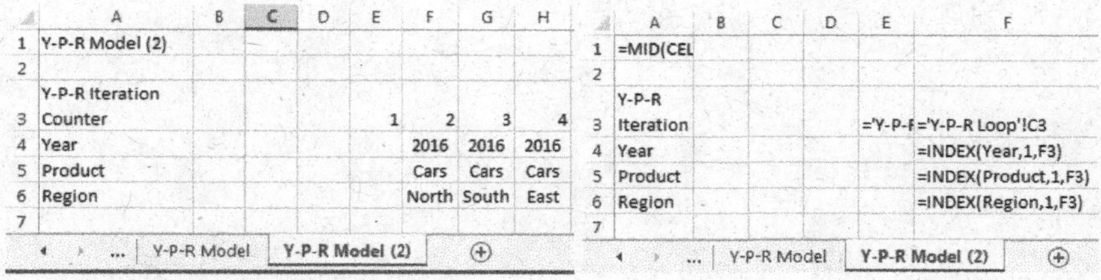

Fig. 18. Using the loop indices in a worksheet with a different column structure

7 Conclusion

The worksheets managing the loops are *behind the scene* activities. Once they have been implemented and tested, the developer can concentrate on the actual worksheet that needs to be built.

This paper shows that a well-known computer programming structure can be adapted to be used in the spreadsheet environment. The adaptation has its limitations, the most important one being that the spreadsheet's structure has to conform to the desired loops.

This paper contains all the formulas spreadsheet developers need to create their own worksheets to manage loop-like structures, whether they have programming training or not. They can be saved and re-used or distributed as templates.

References

1. Panko, R.R.: What we know about spreadsheet errors. J. End User Comput. **10**, 15–21 (2008)
2. Burden, T.: How a Rookie excel error led JPMorgan to misreport its VaR for years (2013). http://www.zerohedge.com/news/2013-02-12/how-rookie-excel-error-led-jpmorgan-misreport-its-var-years
3. Mouchel profits blow (2011). http://www.express.co.uk/finance/city/276053/Mouchel-profits-blow
4. Conczal, M.: Researchers finally replicated Reinhart-Rogoff, and there are serious problems. Roosevelt Institute (2013). http://rooseveltinstitute.org/researchers-finally-replicated-reinhart-rogoff-and-there-are-serious-problems/
5. Jones, S.P., Blackwell, A., Burnett, M.: A user-centred approach to functions in excel. ACM Sigplan Not. **38**, 165–176 (2003)
6. Erwig, M.: Software engineering for spreadsheets. IEEE Softw. **26**, 25–30 (2009)
7. Cunha, J., Fernandes, J.P., Mendes, J., Saraiva, J.: MDSheet: a framework for model-driven spreadsheet engineering. In: Presented at the Proceedings of the 34th International Conference on Software Engineering, Zurich, Switzerland (2012)
8. Mireault, P.: Structured spreadsheet modeling and implementation. In: 2nd Workshop on Software Engineering Methods in Spreadsheets, Firenze, IT (2015)
9. Mireault, P.: Structured Spreadsheet Modelling and Implementation: A Methodology for Creating Effective Spreadsheets. SSMI International, Montréal (2016)

SheetGit: A Tool for Collaborative Spreadsheet Development

Ricardo Moreira[✉]

NOVA LINCS, DI, FCT, Universidade NOVA de Lisboa, Lisbon, Portugal
rm.moreira@campus.fct.unl.pt

Abstract. Spreadsheets play a pivotal role in many organizations. They serve to store/manipulate data, and are often used to help in the decision process of organizations, thus having a direct impact on their success.

As the research community already realized, spreadsheets tend to have the same issues "professional" software has.

One of the most used mechanisms to manage software projects is version control. Thus, we present a version control system oriented for end-user programmers. It allows for seamless and risk-free collaboration between users, to graphically visualize the history of spreadsheet versions, to switch between different versions just by pointing and clicking, and to visualize the differences between two spreadsheets in an animated way.

Keywords: Spreadsheets · End-user software development · Microsoft excel · Version control · Excel add-in

1 Introduction

There have been multiple studies attempting to measure errors in spreadsheets, and they have always found them in abundance [8]. While spreadsheets are easy to share and modify, this actually makes it difficult to control and maintain their integrity [4]. The amount of user controls in spreadsheets do not approach the level of controls that professional programmers have found to be necessary for their development, so errors are more likely to happen and not be detected. Indeed it is common for spreadsheets to reach high levels of complexity and size, making them hard to comprehend and debug, ergo increasing the number of errors when they are used [2].

Essentially, spreadsheets are being used as cheaper, more agile replacements of professional programs that would normally cost large sums of money to create and maintain, but they have fewer controls and tools to prevent errors. If professional programmers are no longer making sure end users will not make mistakes, to prevent these from happening, end users must themselves start to adopt the disciplines and tools that professional programmers have long used when dealing with complex software [9]. One of these mechanisms is *version control*.

Version control is known to be extremely beneficial for experienced programmers [7], but it is also beneficial for end-user programmers, both for learning

P. Milazzo et al. (Eds.): STAF 2016, LNCS 9946, pp. 415–420, 2016.
DOI: 10.1007/978-3-319-50230-4_32

and debugging purposes [6]. Version control also helps in understanding spreadsheets as these reach high levels of complexity. With proper version control, one can see how the spreadsheet was built over time and, from its origin, gradually come to understand it. Moreover, this is the way professional programmers collaboratively work, and thus, it should also be used by end-user programmers.

Our goal is to bring version control to spreadsheet end-user developers, in an intuitive manner, to help modernize Excel's development tools, to help lower the risk of spreadsheet errors, to help end users create, manage, comprehend complex spreadsheets and to enable easy, risk-free collaboration and sharing of spreadsheets. For this purpose, we have created an add-in for Excel which automatically creates versions, branches, allows users to change between versions, and see the differences between them. Since end-user developers are the target demographic, the user interface is the prime focus of the application, and we intend to have it thoroughly validated to ensure it is easy to use.

2   SheetGit

In this section we introduce the tool termed SheetGit we have implemented as a version control solution for spreadsheet end-users. In this tool we have implemented a set of fundamental features: creating versions, switching between them, the option to see the differences between two versions, and sharing them through the Internet. In the next sections we describe each of these.

2.1   Showing Versions

Creating a proper user interface is challenging because the project's target audience consists of end users who most likely have never interacted with any type of version control. As a result, we designed the interface to be simple and intuitive, and for most of the features to be automated or easy to understand with a fast tutorial, though it still requires validation through an empirical study.

We chose to use a tree to display our versions, as seen in Fig. 1, because of its simplicity and adaptability, allowing for an intuitive graphical representation of many advanced version control functions such as branches and merges. Very popular version control services such as Github [5] or Bitbucket [1] also make use of a tree structure to display their version lists.

The versions are placed chronologically, the large white version being currently active, meaning it is the spreadsheet the user is seeing. In this case, the user restored his spreadsheet to a previous point in time, so it is not the most recent version of the spreadsheet.

2.2   Creating Versions

The default behavior for creating a version is to do so automatically, as to prevent any sort of data loss due to the user forgetting to save, and to not interrupt the user as he/she works. Since the number of versions may inflate greatly due to the

Fig. 1. A single branch tree displaying a set of commits

automated behavior, we have also implemented a method to combine or prune them where we believe the end result may be indifferent to the user, using metrics such as time since last edit and amount of data entered into the workbook. This only collapses those versions, but the user can always re-open them to a more detail view.

Branches are created automatically when users edit a version that is not at the last one. This will allow them to keep working seamlessly yet still providing a clear view of their current work parentage.

By default, all versions will have a summary of its changes stored in an additional text file, and also displayed on the version tree, as seen in Fig. 2. Users can then understand what actions occurred without having to open the version or write a version message beforehand. Nevertheless, the user has always the possibility of adding a version message.

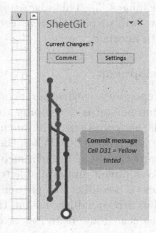

Fig. 2. Our mock up's version tree displaying a commit's details

2.3 Switching Between Versions

Another feature SheetGit supports is to switch from one version to another. To do so, the user has only to click in the desired version in the tree showing the versions. This will change the workbook so it is in the state of the particular version selected.

2.4 Showing Differences Between Versions

Showing differences between versions is one of the greater challenges of the project because, given the free-form factor of spreadsheets, the user is able to organize information in whatever way he feels best. Also because its authors may have never seen *diffs* in a version control system, so various concepts that seem normal to professional programmers can be difficult for some end users to understand.

Differences between versions are shown inside Excel itself. If the user selects a particular version, the mouse/cursor will recreate the actions required to turn one version into the other. If a user could not understand the list of changes in a version, he/she can visualize the animation to see all of them being performed one by one. There are options to speed up or skip the animations to not hinder the more experienced users. As a better illustration of this concept, we refer the reader to the tool's website, at http://spreadsheetsunl.github.io/sheetgit/, where a concept movie can be seen showing this mechanism.

Although the tool stores the changes performed between two consecutive versions, for versions more distant, we intend to use *SheetDiff* as our algorithm for detecting differences between versions as it has been proven to be very robust and efficient at discerning changes [3]. This algorithm will find the differences between two versions and we will display them as the set of changes necessary to switch from one version to another.

2.5 Collaborative Development

Users will have a shared repository with other people. To minimize possible conflicts when more than one person is developing the same spreadsheet, each user will be forced to use his/her own personal branches, created from the main branch or from his/her own other branches. When the user is satisfied with the changes, he/she can merge to the main branch such changes so they become incorporated in the main development and available to other users. When merging conflicts may arise. If there is a conflict in a particular cell, such cell can show the conflicting values and the corresponding version, through a list, allowing the user to select the intended choice. If an entire row or column is in conflict, then both can be shown and the user is guided to delete the wrong one.

Every version and branch is tinted with a unique color belonging to a specific user, with the master branch always being gray to show it can be used by multiple users, as seen back in Fig. 2.

This online portion of the application is optional but is fully automatic once the user grants SheetGit the appropriate permissions to their Bitbucket account.

2.6   Technological Choices

We have created our solution as an Excel add-in to keep it as closely knit to Excel as possible, as this potentially increases its acceptance among spreadsheet developers as opposed to being run as an external tool. This will also enable us to present information directly in the active spreadsheet, and grant us access to Excel's proprietary file formats.

The add-in functions as a self-contained task pane, that includes an embedded browser to allow us to make use of Javascript, while retaining the advantages of the more powerful C# add-ins. Our version tree is created using Gitgraph.js[1], a Javascript library.

The collaboration side of the application will be performed with the help of Bitbucket, using it as the online hosting service for the spreadsheets. This because Bitbucket offers free registration, a welcoming API, and private repositories, allowing users to maintain their privacy.

Availability. SheetGit is available as a Microsoft Excel open-source add-in at http://spreadsheetsunl.github.io/sheetgit/. Since this is an open-source project, we believe it will receive contributions from the community, and thus will be constantly improved.

3   Related Work

Many version control tools already exist to work with spreadsheets, such as Microsoft Sharepoint's *History*[2], Google Sheets[3], XLTools's Version Control[4] and Pathio[5], and while they all perform well, they generally have issues when it comes to perceiving changes in formatting and formulae.

They show their versions in the way of a chronological list, but this makes it difficult for users to perceive the parent of a version, which as been shown to be beneficial for end users [6]. Users tend to solve problems by searching for alternatives and then backtracking when required, which is easier when the parent is accessible [6]. With our tree and branch presentation, it is easy for users to keep track of the origin of all changes.

Also when it comes to presenting the differences, it is either done in a very simplistic manner, or in a more complete manner, but end users without version control experience might have a greater difficulty in understanding the presentation without a very rich tutorial.

In regards to collaboration, some tools exist with varying degrees of completeness in its implementation. Google Sheets, after each change, a new revision is automatically created. When viewing the version history, each user is assigned a

---

[1] http://github.com/nicoespeon/gitgraph.js.
[2] https://products.office.com/en-us/sharepoint/.
[3] https://www.google.com/sheets/.
[4] https://xltools.net/.
[5] https://www.pathio.com/.

unique color, and the altered cells are highlighted in the color of its author. This means, however, that what exactly changed is not explicitly shown. Moreover, in Google Sheets everything every user does is visible to every other user. Our approach allows to have private branches and merge only what is desired. Microsoft Sharepoint's revisions are created automatically just like Google Sheets but there is no method to view the differences between versions.

4   Conclusion

A version control system is a very helpful tool for professional software development as it allows for both collaboration and controlled development. Such features are also desired when developing spreadsheets by end-user developers. It is however necessary to adapt such systems to the necessities and restrictions of this kind of developers.

Although more features can be added, we believe that the next important step is to validate our proposal with spreadsheet end-user developers. Such an evaluation is complex and should be done in a long term study where the potential benefits would be assessed in the usage of the tool in a considerable period of time ideally in a collaborative development environment.

Acknowledgements. This work has been partially supported by NOVA LINCS through the FCT project with reference UID/CEC/04516/2013.

References

1. Atlassian: Bitbucket. https://bitbucket.org/. Accessed 03 Mar 2016
2. Bradley, L., McDaid, K.: Using Bayesian statistical methods to determine the level of error in large spreadsheets. In: 31st International Conference on Software Engineering-Companion, ICSE-Companion 2009, vol. 2009, pp. 351–354. IEEE (2009)
3. Chambers, C., Erwig, M., Luckey, M.: SheetDiff: a tool for identifying changes in spreadsheets. In: 2010 IEEE Symposium on Visual Languages and Human-Centric Computing (VL/HCC), pp. 85–92, September 2010
4. Deloitte: spreadsheet management: not what you figured (2009). http://www2.deloitte.com/us/en/pages/audit/articles/spreadsheet-management.html. Accessed 18 Jan 2016
5. GitHub, Inc.: Github. https://github.com/. Accessed 03 Mar 2016
6. Kuttal, S.K., Sarma, A., Rothermel, G.: On the benefits of providing versioning support for end users: an empirical study. ACM Trans. Comput. Hum. Interact. **21**(2), 901–943 (2014). http://doi.acm.org/10.1145/2560016
7. Mitchell, L.: You're not using source control? Read this! (2014). http://www.lornajane.net/wp-content/uploads/2013/01/source-control-whitepaper-v1.1.pdf. Accessed 11 Jan 2016
8. Panko, R.R.: What we know about spreadsheet errors. J. Organ. End User Comput. (JOEUC) **10**(2), 15–21 (1998)
9. Panko, R., Halverson, R.P.: Spreadsheets on trial: a survey of research on spreadsheet risks. In: Proceedings of HICSS-29, 29th Hawaii International Conference on System Sciences, vol. 2, pp. 326–335 (1996)

VeryComp

Context-Aware Design of Reflective Middleware in the Internet of Everything

Marina Mongiello$^{(\boxtimes)}$, Tommaso di Noia, Francesco Nocera,
Eugenio di Sciascio, and Angelo Parchitelli

Politecnico di Bari, Via Orabona, 4, 70125 Bari, Italy
{marina.mongiello,tommaso.dinoia,francesco.nocera,
eugenio.disciascio,angelo.parchitelli}@poliba.it

Abstract. We daily experience the interaction with physical objects which are becoming smarter and smarter with the ability to communicate with each other as well as with different information systems. While, on the one hand, we are assisting to the rise of a pervasive Internet of Things (IoT) or an Internet of Everything (IoE), on the other hand we face the need of a new generation of objects able to adapt to external inputs coming from the environment they are dipped in.

New modeling techniques, pattern and paradigm for composing and developing software and services able to deal with changing context and requirements are necessary.

Self-adaptive systems are modern applications whose running part should be able to react on its own, by dynamically adapting its behavior, in order to sustain a required set of qualities of service, and dynamic changes in the context or in the user requirements. Here, we propose a solution allowing a IoT Middleware to conform to Reflective programming paradigm thus giving more flexibility and adaptability to the network behavior.

1 Introduction

The Internet of Things (IoT) and its extension Internet of Everything (IoE) is for sure one of the most influential technological shift we are facing in the last years. Thanks to the spreading of sensors and to the diffusion of low-cost miniaturized computational resources, we are able to make objects that produce data and interact with each other thus producing a network of interconnected things, data, processes. IoE makes possible to distribute data sources and data consumers in the real world to produce, collect, exchange and consume information usually with a high rate. Elements of the IoT are quite evolved piece of hardware that may be programmed and covered by a software layer implementing complex functionalities.

One of the challenges in building Internet of Services and Things is the way software will be developed and composed on the top of flexible infrastructures and integration architectures. Despite the great interest in software composition and verification methods, when developing service- and thing-based software

© Springer International Publishing AG 2016
P. Milazzo et al. (Eds.): STAF 2016, LNCS 9946, pp. 423–435, 2016.
DOI: 10.1007/978-3-319-50230-4_33

systems, strong challenges still regards the way a smart IoT-based architecture is designed in order to make it robust with reference to the contextual changes it continually undergoes. Therefore, new software composition paradigms and patterns that deal with heterogeneity, dynamicity, adaptation are needed.

We all known that the physical world is not a static environment and it changes accordingly to sometimes unpredictable events. Then, informative objects which are dipped in the physical world should be able to adapt and change their behavior accordingly to the surrounding context. This means that the software they have on board should be able to react in order to change and modify its functions to comply with the new environmental variables. From the point of view of a software architecture, IoT poses many interesting challenges due to its unpredictable yet adaptive requirements. In order to be as effective as possible, in IoT solutions the intelligent objects are usually coordinated by a middleware that acts as a facilitator towards a smoother and homogeneous communication among the various components. A huge work is available in the literature about IoT middleware. Interesting and structured surveys are in [2,7,10,15]. IoT middleware is also facing multiple challenges [1,6] that are mainly induced by IoT features. In this paper we propose a reflective extension of an IoT middleware. The approach aims to show a possible solution to make a IoT middleware conforming to the pattern of reflective programming, which allows a software system to dynamically change its logic without internal changes to the code.

The remainder of the paper is structured as follows: in the next section we describe the a formal model of the approach we propose. Section 3 describe a practical example of a use case scenario. In Sect. 4 the formal model is instantiated in the use case scenario. The details of the reflective implementation are provided in Sect. 4.

Conclusion and future work close the paper.

2   Modeling Reflective Middleware

While designing a IoT solution, the use of traditional methods may lead to excessive complexity of the code that may become slow and/or little maintainable. Among the different patterns available to design a software system, *Reflection* allows the developer to produce an extensible architecture from the beginning. A IoT middleware can surely benefit from the use of a reflective approach. As an example, we have the possibility of designing a completely configurable system and adaptable to different operating environments.

The main concept in *Reflection* pattern is the distinction between *base-level* and *meta-level*. A base level includes the core application logic. Its runtime behavior is observed by a meta level that maintains information about selected system properties to make the software self-aware. Changes to information kept in the meta level thus affect subsequent base-level behavior. [4] The adaptation of the meta level is performed indirectly with help of a specific Interface, *Meta-Object Protocol* (*MOP*). This allows users to specify a change, checks its correctness, and automatically integrates the change into the meta level. [5]

MOP also makes possible the change of connections between the *base-level* and *meta-objects*. A *meta-object* is an object that manipulates, creates, describes, or implements other objects (including itself). Thus, a proper configuration of the base-level and meta-objects defines the behavior of an application. [11] In addition, using a programming language that supports reflection, it is possible to change the structure of the objects themselves at run-time and then make the software system more flexible.

In this Section, we define a formal model of a reflective middleware for Internet of Things. Let S be the set of sensors $S = \{s_1, s_2, ..., s_n\}$ where each s_i is the stimulus, i.e. the physical, biological, chemical etc., quantity that the sensor detects and $D = \{d_1, d_2, ..., d_n\}$ the Domain of sensor's output for each sensor in S.

Definition 1 *(Condition). Given S and D, a Condition C is a relation R between s and d where $s \in S$ and $d \in D$ or a boolean combination of relations between s and d.*

For example, suppose sensor s_i detects changes in concentration of pm_{10} in the air, a condition may be: IF pm_{10} GREATER THAN 35 or IF HUMIDITY MINOR THAN 15 AND pm_{10} GREATER THAN 35.

Let $AR = \{arg_1, arg_2, ..arg_n\}$ a set of arguments that can applied to given operations:

Definition 2 *(Action). Given a set $A = \{a_1, a_2, ..a_n\}$, an Action a_i is the operation to be performed when a Condition occurs, applied to the argument arg_j, $a_i(arg_j)$.*

For example: if an increase in the fine dust emission is detached, an *action* necessary for managing the problem resolution may be sending an e-mail to an office responsible for safeguarding, the *action* is notification, the *argument* is sending e-mail.

Definition 3 *(Rule). A Rule is defined as a function associating Condition to an Action $R : C- > A(arg)$.*

Let B be the MESSAGE BROKER component that models the Publish/Subscribe mechanism for defining the relationships between physical sensors and actions:

Definition 4 *(Message). A message m_i is defined as $m_i =< s_i, d_i, a_i, arg_i >$ where s_i is the sensor, d_i the sensor's output, a_i the given action and arg_i the argument passed to the action a_i.*

Definition 5 *(Message bus). The Message Bus is the channel where the MESSAGE BROKER publishes messages from sensors and receivers subscribe to receive notifications of a relevant message.*

The proposed model maps an Iot middleware on the three levels of a classical reflection pattern according to the following matching: the *Condition* to the *Meta level*, the *Action* to the *Base level* and the *Rule* to the *Meta-Object Protocol*. RULES are modeled and stored in a RULE-BASED SYSTEM. A RULE ENGINE models the reasoning algorithm that automates the rules R. Figure 1 shows a graphical schema of the proposed approach using an abstract architecture. The architecture models the main elements of our approach that are represented as components. The abstract architecture can be instantiated in several contexts and scenarios. Conditions are represented at the condition level where conditions are defined, Actions at several action levels, the rule engine that implements the reasoning algorihtm on the rules. The ADAPTOR component works as a driver and translates the received command in a real action. It is possible to use place more Adaptor, one for each desired application.

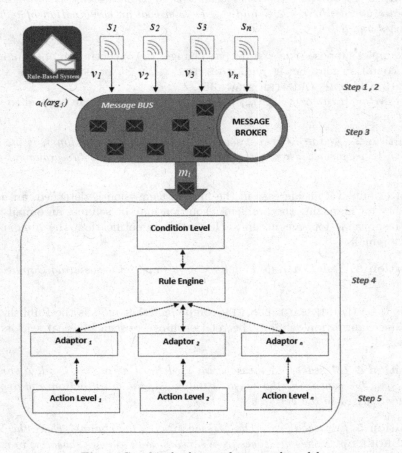

Fig. 1. Graphical schema of proposed model.

Steps for performing the reflective mechanism:

- Step 1: Sender publishes messages on the *Message Bus*.
- Step 2: Receivers subscribe to the *Message Bus*.
- Step 3: The MESSAGE BROKER passes the message m_i through the *Message Bus* to the *Condition level*.
- Step 4: The RULE ENGINE executes the rule.
- Step 5: An *Action level* is activated.

The reflection mechanism is activated precisely in the last one step. Especially the Reflection is implemented through rules triggered by the messages.

3   Use Case Scenario

To explain the formal model let us consider its instantiation in a use case scenario, i.e. consider a smart environment, specifically in a Smart city domain. Particularly, in this domain management of energy, environmental protection and mobility are some interesting applications of Internet of Everything. The devices can be spread over the whole area of urban land to monitor, through appropriate sensors, meteorological and environmental variables as depicted in Fig. 2.

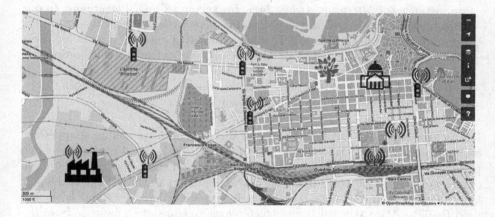

Fig. 2. Smart environment scenario.

Typically variables to be monitored are air, temperature, humidity, fine dust emissions.

Other variables to be monitored are related to the use of municipal services such as the position of city buses at their respective sections, the residual capacity of the car parks, the urban lighting control. Suppose now that a network of sensors monitors the city traffic and at the same time the fine dust emissions.

A slowdown occurs in an area of the town, the data is sent from the controller to the middleware that analyzes the data and compares it with a set of pre-established rules. The controller will trigger a series of procedures to solve the slowdown (special signals indicating for alternative routes are lighted on). Suppose now that there is an increase in the fine dust emissions: the constant monitoring unit sends the data to the middleware which will activate the necessary actions for the resolution of the problem. The two main action to solve the critical events maybe: sending an email to the municipal section for safeguard of environment and of the land or to the section for land and infrastructure and mobility.

4   Instantiation of the Model

In this section we instantiate the model defined in Sect. 2 in the use case scenario described in Sect. 3.

The DeviceHive middleware. We choose DeviceHive as IoT middleware for several reasons.

Ease of installation, the rich documentation and the high integration with a wide range of programming languages and IoT protocols. By using DeviceHive, the set up of a IoT system is made by the following three steps:

- Create: the user must create an instance of the *Cloud by DeviceHive*. There are instances of *Microsoft Azure, Juju, Docker* and *Cloud Playground*. In our implementation, we used the shell instance *Cloud Playground*.
- Connect: using the specific IoT Toolkit, a dedicated gateway is installed. This is the link between the devices and the cloud of DeviceHive. The gateway is written in Go, and in our case communicates with a Python script that is responsible for receiving the data from the sensors within the network.
- Visualize: sent data can be displayed via a Web page.

Redis as a Message Broker. In our instantiation of the model we adapt Redis as MESSAGE BROKER. Redis[1] is a NoSQL DBMS. It is based on the key-value paradigm but has some characteristics that make it different from other database of its own category: it works in RAM, provides support to the storage of the pair key-value, it offers four data structures: lists, sets, ordered sets and hash. We used Redis as MESSAGE BROKER, which allows to translate a message from the messaging protocol of the sender to the recipient's messaging protocol. Through appropriate Publish/Subscribe directives Redis implements the mechanism of Publish/Subscribe, whereby senders do not send messages directly to recipients; rather the messages are published and sorted into channels, without knowing who is really writing to the channel. Interested parties express their intention to subscribe to notifications of one or more channels of interest. This decoupling between publishers and subscribers allows for greater scalability and a dynamic network topology.

---

[1] http://redis.io/.

Observer. An OBSERVER component observes rules extracted from the Rule based-systems. In our implementation, the rule based systems is a config file.

The OBSERVER (of the data flow) notifies the MESSAGE BROKER about the arrival of new data and the active rule.

Event-driven Component. We use Node JS as Event-driven component. It receives data about the sensor and the variable of the sensor through a REST interface.

Message Bus. Instantiation of the *Message Bus* of our model is obtained using the Redis Message channel. To implement the Publish/Subscribe mechanism, publishers publish messages on the Redis channel, recipients subscribe on the channel and read information about the available services.

Condition Level. The meta-level of the reflective mechanism is the *Condition Level* of our model. In the instantiation of the model it contains a simple call to a generic function, with the string identifying the function and the class of the function. In is instantiated in a separate component of our reflective component connected to the RULE ENGINE.

According to this mechanism, the logic of the program can be dynamically changed depending on the data got from the sensors and changes are transparent to the internal structure of the software.

The *Condition Level* can be extended with the meta-objects to develop considerably more advanced functionality external to the server. In fact, it is sufficient to connect the component to the Redis server for listening to the messages coming from the server. The *Condition Level* has access to basic levels via the object DBCLASS containing instances of basic objects identified by a particular name which is specified in the configuration file of the *Action Level*, that will be eventually analyzed. In the message received by Redis the class name and the name of the function to call are specified in special strings. The data to be written is contained in a separate object, which will be the argument of the function.

Rule Engine. A RULE ENGINE component implements the algorithm for the extraction of the action from the rule, given a condition.

Adaptors and Action Level. In order to determine which are the *Action Levels* available at runtime, a system for loading dynamic components within the same *Condition Level* has been implemented. Two files for each *Action Levels* are available: a JSON file containing configuration data and a JS file containing the class itself. Objects instantiated with the data in the JSON file will then be stored in an array, and referenced by the name of the same class, specified within each rule.

5 Reflective Implementation of the Middleware Architecture

In this Section we analyze the flow of control in the implementation of the use case scenario. In our implementation, the system will automatically perform actions according to the values received by the sensors of devices by matching the set of formal rules.

The hardware used to provide a source of data is based on the *Arduino* platform, a small electronics board equipped with a microcontroller, which is used to quickly achieve hardware prototypes. In addition to the *Arduino* board we have used the *RaspberryPi B+* board to send and receive data from/to the local server which then makes a transition of data to *Cloud DeviceHive* servers.

In Fig. 3 the architectural scheme of the proposed solution is depicted. Within the component, a configuration file will contain the definition of the rules on the data and the actions to take if the rule is checked. The OBSERVER (of the data flow) notifies the NODE JS that forward to the MESSAGE BROKER about the extracted active rule. The active rule together with the information about sensors and variables, (the predicate of our Condition) is published on the *Message Bus*. On the message channel is published information about the arrival of new data. The MESSAGE BROKER works as a through for data flow and the active rule that are forwarded to the Reflective part of our component.

We can analyze the exchange of information between the various components involved in which the environmental monitoring unit sends a message to the middleware with the following form:

```
{"device":"Arduino_Raspberry_PM10_sensor",
 "value":40,
 "sensor":"pm10_sensor",
 "timestamp":"1452357172"}
```

The message reaches the middleware where it is published on the *Message Bus*; now it has the following form:

```
{"id":"EJH8rmcDl",
 "rule":"notification",
 "rule_where":"send_email",
 "data":{"device":"Arduino_Raspberry_PM10_sensor","value":40,
         "sensor":"pm10_sensor",
          "timestamp":"1452357172"}
}
```

Receivers subscribe to the MESSAGE BROKER and are notified of the message. The MESSAGE BROKER forwards the whole message made up of sensor, variable, (the predicate of the condition) and the rule, (extracted from the config file) to the Rule Engine that executes it. Reflection is applied thanks to the signing of the receiver component of the Redis channel. This component will read the published messages that contain specific information on the function to be called, the class of which the function is a member and topics. The *Condition Level* and the RULE ENGINE contains enable the action level of the reflective component. The RULE ENGINE contains among other specifications a simple call to the generic function to notify to execute the email application to communicate the proper recipient the exceeding the threshold with respect to the value contained in the catalog of rules.

Implementation of the *rule* is:

```
{
    "id" : "Arduino_Raspberry_PM10_sensor",
    "sensors" : ["pm_10_sensor",
    "temperature_sensor"],
    "rules" : [
        {
            "sensor": ["pm10_sensor"],
            "action": "notification",
            "argument": "send_email",
            "variable_action" : {
                "condition" : "moreThan",
                "value": "35
            }
        }
    ]
}
```

In this case the PM10 value greater than admitted threshold value of 35. The level of detail in the rules of the system is of the single sensor and can group

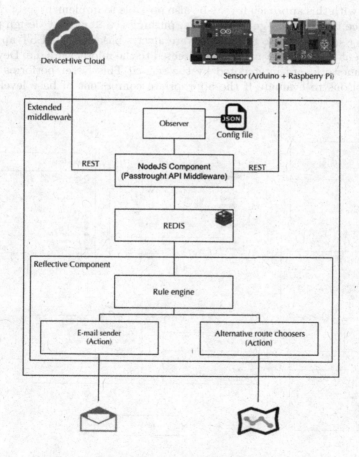

Fig. 3. Architectural schema of proposed scenario.

multiple sensors in logic "AND" between them. The activations are managed via a plugin system. Each plugin is self-consistent and controls an appropriate device in Plug & Play mode.

In Fig. 4 we show the class diagram of our architecture. Our component is placed between the devices and the *Cloud DeviceHive*.

The wrapper replaces the middleware for passing the requests delivered from devices that will connect to our component, instead of connecting directly to the middleware. This part of the server, implemented by classes `GenericServer` and `Server`, contains a simple HTTP server. Performed steps are:

1. receives the HTTP request from the gateway and analyzes the content;
2. composes a new HTTP request to the server DeviceHive, creating all the headers required by the function `getDHHeaders`;
3. as soon as the server has received the answer from DeviceHive, forwards it to the gateway of the device.

Note that with this approach it may be also possible to implement a set of classes that replace the function `getDHHeaders`, pushing the `Strategy` design pattern, to process requests sent to the middleware always based on a REST approach.

Data sent by the gateway initially directed to the middleware, i.e. DeviceHive in our framework, are intercepted by the server. This latter performs a series of comparisons to evaluate if the appropriate component of base level will be

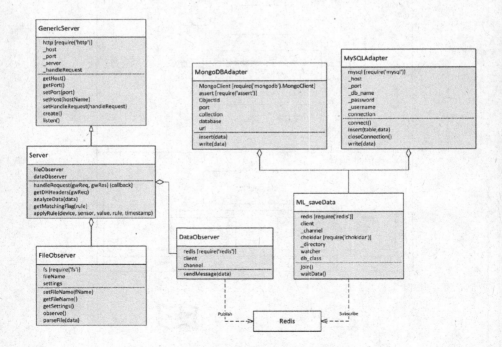

Fig. 4. Class diagram of the proposed architecture.

activated. Comparisons are based on checking the rules in the Configuration File, each one related to one or more sensors present on a given device.

The class delegated to parsing the configuration file (FileObserver) scans the file and analyzes the rules. In fact, a single rule could be related to several sensors.

In this way, given a NOTIFICATION message received by the gateway, it only needs to check if the condition specified in `variable_action` is verified. In case it is verified, the wrapper publishes a message on the Redis Publish/Subscribe server via a DATAOBSERVER class object. FILEOBSERVER parses the configuration file in case of modification while the server is running.

6   Related Work

In this section we present a state of the art of existing approaches for reflective middleware. A survey of reflective middleware for Iot is in [13]. The survey addresses a broad range of techniques, methods, models, functionalities, systems, applications, and middleware solutions related to context awareness and IoT. The paper analyzes, compares and consolidates past research work. One of the first approaches is in [3] that presents an architecture for reflective middleware based on a multi-model approach. Through a number of working examples, they demonstrate that the approach can support introspection, and fine- and coarse-grained adaptation of the resource management framework. More recent relevant approaches of reflective middlewares are in SOAR (SOA with Reflection) [8].

[9] presents a chemical reaction-inspired computational model using the concepts of graphs and reflection, which attempts to address the complexities associated with the visualization, modelling, interaction, analysis and abstraction of information in the IoT. [12] presents Internetware which consists of a set of autonomous software entities distributed over the Internet, together with a set of connectors to enable collaborations among these entities in various ways. To support on-demand collaboration, Internetware middleware employs an RSA and reflection mechanisms on its own application server. [14] extends the Multinetwork INformation Architecture (MINA), a reflective (self-observing and adapting via an embodied Observe-Analyze-Adapt loop) middleware with a layered IoT SDN controller.

7   Conclusion and Future Work

In the recent years, there has been a huge effort to provide an immediate access to information about the physical world through Internet technologies. IoT vision aims to integrate the virtual world of information to the real world of things. The role of a IoT middleware is to provide the connectivity between the virtual world and physical world and an interface between heterogeneous physical devices and applications. We present a reflective extension of an IoT middleware which makes possible the design of a software resulting completely configurable and adaptable to different operating environments. The proposed framework enables to automatically perform actions according to the values received by the sensors by triggering a set of rules. Our current implementation relies on the commercial DeviceHive middleware and wraps it with an adaptable layer thus transforming the whole middleware in a reflective architecture. The approach is general enough and can be extended to deal with diverse functionalities other than the ones currently implemented. We are working to extend the proposed framework with the addition of new Plug and Play actions. Also we are working to extend the framework and enable it for the integration of several middlewares. The idea is to build an "adaptive wrapper" of middlewares able to adapt the reflective middleware to the different clouds.

Acknowledgment. The authors acknowledge partial support of PON03PE_00136_1 Digital Services Ecosystem: DSE. Furthermore, the author Francesco Nocera acknowledges support of Exprivia S.p.A Ph.D grant 2016.

References

1. Bandyopadhyay, S., Sengupta, M., Maiti, S., Dutta, S.: Role of middleware for internet of things: a study. Int. J. Comput. Sci. Eng. Surv. (IJCSES) **2**(3), 94–105 (2011)
2. Bandyopadhyay, S., Sengupta, M., Maiti, S., Dutta, S.: A survey of middleware for internet of things. In: Özcan, A., Zizka, J., Nagamalai, D. (eds.) Recent Trends in Wireless and Mobile Networks. CCIS, vol. 162, pp. 288–296. Springer, Heidelberg (2011)
3. Blair, G.S., Costa, F., Coulson, G., Delpiano, F., Duran, H., Dumant, B., Horn, F., Parlavantzas, N., Stefani, J.B.: The design of a resource-aware reflective middleware architecture. In: Cointe, P. (ed.) Meta-Level Architectures and Reflection. LNCS, vol. 1616, pp. 115–134. Springer, Heidelberg (1999)
4. Buschmann, F., Henney, K., Schmidt, D.C.: Pattern-Oriented Software Architecture. Wiley, New York (2007). A Pattern Language for Distributed Computing
5. Buschmann, F., Meunier, R., Rohnert, H., Sommerlad, P., Stal, M.: Pattern-Oriented Software Architecture: a System of Patterns. Wiley, New York (1996)
6. Chaqfeh, M.A., Mohamed, N. et al.: Challenges in middleware solutions for the internet of things. In: 2012 International Conference on Collaboration Technologies and Systems (CTS), pp. 21–26. IEEE (2012)
7. Fersi, G.: Middleware for internet of things: a study. In: 2015 International Conference on Distributed Computing in Sensor Systems (DCOSS), pp. 230–235. IEEE (2015)
8. Huang, G., Liu, X., Mei, H.: SOAR: towards dependable service-oriented architecture via reflective middleware. Int. J. Simul. Process Model. **3**(1–2), 55–65 (2007)
9. Ikram, A., Anjum, A., Hill, R., Antonopoulos, N., Liu, L., Sotiriadis, S.: Approaching the internet of things (IoT): a modelling, analysis and abstraction framework. Pract. Experience Concurrency Comput. **27**, 1966–1984 (2013)
10. Issarny, V., Georgantas, N., Hachem, S., Zarras, A., Vassiliadist, P., Autili, M., Gerosa, M.A., Hamida, A.B.: Service-oriented middleware for the future internet: state of the art and research directions. J. Internet Serv. Appl. **2**(1), 23–45 (2011)
11. Maes, P.: Concepts and experiments in computational reflection. In: ACM Sigplan Notices, vol. 22, pp. 147–155. ACM (1987)

12. Mei, H., Huang, G., Xie, T.: Internetware: a software paradigm for internet computing. Computer **12**(6), 26–31 (2012)
13. Perera, C., Zaslavsky, A., Christen, P., Georgakopoulos, D.: Context aware computing for the internet of things: a survey. IEEE Commun. Surv. Tutorials **16**(1), 414–454 (2014)
14. Qin, Z., Denker, G., Giannelli, C., Bellavista, P., Venkatasubramanian, N.: A software defined networking architecture for the internet-of-things. In: 2014 IEEE Network Operations and Management Symposium (NOMS), pp. 1–9. IEEE (2014)
15. Razzaque, M., Milojevic-Jevric, M., Palade, A., Clarke, S.: Middleware for internet of things: a survey. IEEE Internet Things J. **PP**(99), 1–21 (2015)

Composition of Advanced (μ)Services for the Next Generation of the Internet of Things

Amleto Di Salle, Francesco Gallo$^{(\boxtimes)}$, and Claudio Pompilio

Department of Information Engineering, Computer Science and Mathematics,
University of L'Aquila, 67100 L'Aquila, Italy
{amleto.disalle,francesco.gallo}@univaq.it,
claudio.pompilio@graduate.univaq.it

Abstract. In recent years, technologies such as Machine to Machine (M2M) and the Internet of Things (IoT) have become core technologies of tomorrow's world that probably we will go to inhabit. Potentially, everything that belongs to the environment around us is or will be connected, and it will produce data or provide services of some kind. The big penetration of technologies such as sensors, electronic tags, micro-controllers, etc., and the inexorable growth of the Internet, improve the understanding of the physical environment, from industrial buildings or the workplace, up to the farmland. The proliferation of all these devices, often able to host in a very small footprint, an entire TCP/IP stack, has meant that the M2M world was incorporated into the world IoT establishing an environment where things and people are able to communicate, share information and generate knowledge.

It is now clear that to support the growth and development of a global network of devices connected in an autonomous way to the Internet and with the ability to communicate and exchange information between them, two key actors are need: first, the adoption of a technological standard that can "disconnect" the Things from a specific application, in order to shift towards application independent Things; and second, to transform Things into systems able to make decisions or support decisions.

In our visionary paper, we will describe a high level software architecture based on features from *embedded SIM* (eSIM) technology and (μ)services technology, in order to develop IoT systems of new generation, able to leverage on LTE or 3G cellular networks to combine services provided not only from the Cloud, but also by Things themselves, and from of them networks.

Keywords: IoT · Service composition · Embedded SIM

1 Introduction

In the longer term, a new IoT [2] and M2M [6] ecosystem will enable intelligent creatures exchanging information, interacting with people, supporting business processes of enterprises, and creating knowledge. Thanks to wireless and cellular

© Springer International Publishing AG 2016
P. Milazzo et al. (Eds.): STAF 2016, LNCS 9946, pp. 436–444, 2016.
DOI: 10.1007/978-3-319-50230-4_34

technologies and rapid deployment of cellular 3G and 4G or Long Term Evolution (LTE) systems on global scale, the instant access to the Internet is available virtually everywhere today. Furthermore, the IoT technologies will play a central role in the optimization for citizens and enterprises within the urban realm, and it is evident that now it is absolutely necessary to increase significantly the levels of **system integration** and **standards development**. The bold requirements are relevant for the following considerations:

1. IoT solutions bring together devices, networks, applications, software platforms, cloud computing platforms, business processing systems, knowledge management, visualization, and advanced data analysis techniques.
2. Embedded processing is evolving, and this enable very constrained devices with a very low power consumption, to be capable of hosting an entire TCP/IP stack including a small web server or web container.
3. Decision support or even decision-making systems will therefore become very important in different application domains for IoT, as well the set of tools required to process data, aggregate information, and create knowledge. Knowledge representation across domains and heterogeneous systems are also important, as are semantics and linked-data.

Since the considerations above, we will introduce a new software architecture in order to address the challenges posed by these systems, and provide preliminary guidelines to build next-generation of IoT systems.

2   Motivation

In the first part of this section, we will give a brief description of the "implementation" of current IoT systems. However, in the second part, we give you a different view of an IoT system in order to address the bold points introduced in the Sect. 1.

Figure 1 shows the way in which currently is possible to implement an IoT system: the integration of device in several processes merely implies the acquisition of data from device layer, its transportation (Network layer) to the Enterprise systems (in general, the Cloud), its assessment, and once a decision is made, potentially the control (management) of the device, which adjust its behaviour. However, in the future, such implementation could be not viable due to:

- the large scale of IoT, as well as the huge data that the devices will generate, the heterogeneity of the data type and the continuous stream of data;
- access and use of enterprise systems is often characterised by free accounts, that are often strongly limited in the number of allowed accesses, quantity of data, assigned resources, etc.;
- data transport from the place where the data originates or collected to the backend system where evaluate their usefulness, will not be practical for communication reasons, as well as due to the processing load that it will incur at the enterprise side, thus resulting in an highly centralised approach;

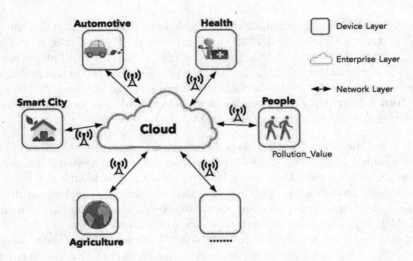

Fig. 1. Simplified description of actual IoT System

- often, the data is strongly linked to the application, despite by its nature can also be used in other contexts. For example, considering the Fig. 1, a *Pollution_Value* generated by *People* application, might also be used in *Automotive* or *Agriculture* application, etc.

Since the considerations above, it is clear that current solutions for the design and implementation of new generation IoT systems not meet those requirements of integration, scalability and standardisation desired. A new approach should:

- minimise communication with enterprise systems. With the increase on devices (more memory, multi-core CPUs, etc.), it makes sense not to host the intelligence and the computation required for it only on the enterprise side, but even on the device themselves;
- partially outsource functionality within the real devices, in order to realise distributed business processes whose sub-processes may execute outside the enterprise system;
- model businesses processes focusing on the functionality provided and that can be discovered dynamically during runtime, and not on concrete implementation of it; we care about what is provided but not how, indeed
- allow devices, as they are capable of computing, to realise the task of processing and evaluating business relevant information they generate by themselves or in clusters;
- allow heterogeneous devices to exploit the network to communicate between them, although physically distant. The goal is to make it "visible" on the net, without the need to pair it with other master devices. For example, many wearable smart devices on the market must be connected to a smart-phone, tablet or pc to share data collected.

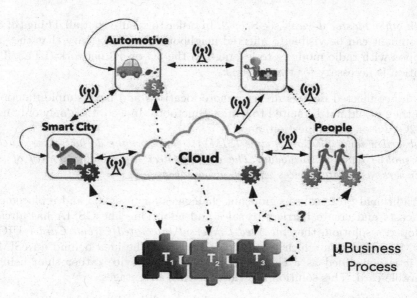

Fig. 2. Simplified new IoT system

In order to meet the challenges identified above, we offer a different view of IoT system, where the enterprise component (i.e. Cloud) is only one of several actors that can constitute the system but not the main one, Fig. 2.

These requirements are driving the need to scale to approaches that are capable of enabling intelligence directly on device, in order to improve the distribution of services and functionality between devices themselves. We need to develop a new generation of devices and services capable of aggregating information and generate knowledge, in order to shift from device-centric approaches to application-centric approaches, i.e. the (heterogeneous)devices must be able to offer services or change their behaviour in order to meet the (μ)business process.

3   ESIM Technology as Host for the Next Generation of (μ)Things

In this section, we will introduce the main concepts behind to Embedded Sim technology (eSIM) [4]. After a brief summary on benefits of the new technology, we will see as we can use and extend specific characteristic of it to build a new generation of IoT systems.

Embedded Sim Overview

One of the main challenges for the new generation of IoT is: *heterogeneous devices must be able to exploit the network to communicate between them, although physically distant. The goal is to make it visible on the net, without the need to pair it with other master devices*, see Sect. 2. In order to ensure that all Things of our environment can be visible to affected neighbours, it is necessary that they are equipped with radio modules to leverage on the 3G or 4G network (LTE). This condition is necessary for two reasons:

1. many connected devices are in remote locations and have simple functions, so they would not be suited to wifi or Bluetooth. Indeed, they may only need a 2G, 3G or 4G connection, and
2. *subscriber identification module (SIM)* [1] *cards are the de facto trust anchor of mobile devices worldwide. The cards protect the mobile identity of subscribers, associate devices with phone numbers,* etc.

Traditional SIMs cause significant challenges for insertion and replacement, raise costs and create barriers to sales and adoption. The GSMA has already developed a solution, the *embedded Universal Integrated Circuit Card* (eUICC) [5] SIM specification which lowers these barriers. The idea behind an eSIM is that it is embedded as a chip into the hardware device rather than being a removable card. This solution has the following advantages:

– the possibility to miniaturise radio modules, and the elimination of traditional sim slot, will allow to extend in a consistent way the type of heterogeneous device that can be equipped with this technology;
– the eSIM card will contain security information, such as private key information, which could be used in authenticating user equipment in a cellular network, and will make it easier to locate lost or stolen devices through *Data Loss Prevention* [13] and *Mobile Device Management* [8] solutions;
– embedded SIMs are generally more hardy than regular SIMs. They can be hermetically sealed (especially where devices are placed in wet or hot environments - like smart meters), which means the card can not be swapped.

Another important capability introduced with the new standard is the *Remote Provisioning*, i.e. the ability to remotely change the SIM profile on a deployed SIM without having to physically change the SIM itself. In order to achieve this, the SIM has extra memory and is therefore capable of holding more than one operator profile (rather than only one on the traditional SIM).

4   (μ)Services for (μ)Things

In the previous section, we illustrated a new technology that could be a good choice for next-generation of Internet of Things, satisfying the requirement related to access to radio networks in an autonomous way. These new features will create a source of data that will consist of a myriad of new "occasionally connected" devices, presenting associated challenges.

In a hypothetical scenario, where heterogenous and distributed devices populate the network, we may ask whether it is possible to take another step forward, in order to build systems that meet the vision represented in Fig. 2. In particular, as the device are capable of computing, they can either realize the task of processing, or provide information on resources able to satisfy that particular task. We want devices announcing themselves and reacting to the actions of other devices, people or vehicle. We believe that such a role can be played by micro services ((μ)Services) [3]. *Microservices are small, autonomous services that work together* [11].

How can the new generation of devices for the IoT exploit (μ)services? To answer this question, we can list some of the most important characteristics of micro services [11]:

- **autonomous**, each (μ)service is a isolated entity, and in order to enforce separation between services, all communication between the services themselves are via network calls, and they must be able to change independently of each other;
- **heterogeneity**, by their nature, the new IoT systems are heterogeneous, i.e. composed from many different devices with different computational capabilities. Consequently, any (μ)services may have features linked to the type of technology that hosts them;
- **scalability**, small and well confined services can run on other parts of a system on a smaller and less powerful hardware;
- **composability**, we allow for our functionality to be consumed in different ways for different purposes.

Therefore, the decision support or decision-making systems will become very important in different application domains of IoT, as well as the set of tools required to process data, aggregate information, and create knowledge across domains and heterogeneous systems.

Given this not exhaustive list of characteristics, it is evident how the use of micro services for the implementation of a system composed of Thing with appropriate capacity, it will enable us to address many of the challenges enumerated in the previous sections.

5   (μ)Thing Architecure

In this section, we will introduce a new architecture in order to set some fundamental roles in a new generation of IoT system, based on previous sections. The goal is not to reinvent the wheel, but just to propose guidelines for the design and implementation of these new systems.

The concepts and technologies identified in the previous sections are relevant to Layer 3(**L3**), depicted in Fig. 3.

In **L3**, there are all Things that define our system. Through the use of eSIM, each of them can play an "active" role in the network, commensurate with the resources and services offered.

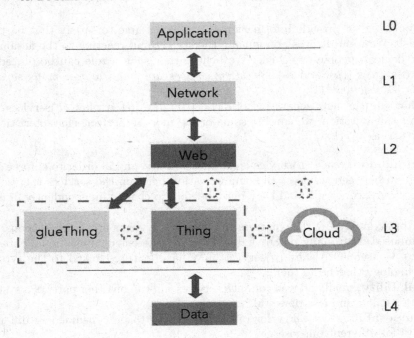

Fig. 3. (μ)Thing services architecture

In particular, we have identified two types of Thing:

- **glueThing.** These elements have high computational capability, such as to allow them to be interposed between the upper and lower layers, or between the Things of the same Layer (**L3**), in order to play a role of glue or an intermediary between the parties. The purpose is to allow the composition of services or functionality exposed by heterogeneous Things of the network.
- **Thing.** This network elements do not provide services or functionalities, but generate or collect data to be shared with the other layers of the stack. We can not say in advance whether they have capacity or computational resources reduced.

Obviously the two roles can be interpreted by the same Thing. From our point view, the Remote Provisioning capability, see Sect. 3, is quite interesting. The idea is to use the Remote Provisioning in order to inject profiles that can enable use, in *glueThing/Thing* mode, the functionalities provided/required by the device. The profile can be changed dynamically, allowing different behaviours according to the (μ)business process defined, Sect. 2.

6   Considerations and Future Works

In our visionary paper, we introduced a new informal service-based architecture with the aim of supporting the development and implementation of a new generation of Things, and service oriented system. In the previous sections, we have highlighted how every aspect of our environment will soon be an active component with which we will relate and collaborate.

One of the major problems that so huge and heterogeneous number of devices will present, is linked to the unambiguous identification in the network. Indeed, in the perspective in which even a "road user" will be able to expose data and offer services through a (smart)device, it will be essential to introduce or maintain a high level of security and reliability in the network. In our view, the adoption of *eSim* technology allows the respect of the safety and traceability required, delegating the security management to the telephone network operators and phone operators, and not to the developer or users of the services offered.

Particularly interesting are the potential capabilities offered to *Remote Provisioning* uses. Actually, the new standard allows to user to change "freely" the SIM profile: i.e., add a data or voice profile, or combining one or two of them, depending on the country where he/she/it is located, without replacing the SIM. A more sophisticated way of using this feature would be to change the role of a Thing within **L3**, so as to enable dynamically services or functionality, or inject a "new behavior" if the host allows it.

Given the great interest is generating the IoT world, there are tools [12], approaches [10], and protocols [7,9] that enable the design and development of IoT systems. The protocols implement *a messaging protocol* model that consists of a number of publishers and subscribers connected to a broker. Publishers send (publish) messages to the broker on a specific "topic". Subscribers register (subscribe) their interest in certain topics with the broker. The broker manages the connections to the publishers and subscribers and distributes the messages it receives from the publishers to the subscribers according to their subscribed topics. The [12] and [10] provides infrastructure for the design and development of IoT systems cloud based.

Our approach, presented in preliminary form, encourages the use of technologies that can relax the close relationship between devices and the cloud of the current framework, promoting the development of applications that leverage the full potential of new devices and benefits from applications based on the (μ)services composition. Based on these considerations, the next steps will be to test and evaluate new devices with eSim technology embedded and create profiles compliant with the new standards, allowing safely modify the behavior Things.

Acknowledgment. The work described in this paper has been supported by the European Union's H2020 Programme under grant agreement number 644178 (project CHOReVOLUTION - Automated Synthesis of Dynamic and Secured Choreographies for the Future Internet), and by the Ministry of Economy and Finance, Cipe resolution n. 135/2012 (project INCIPICT - INnovating CIty Planning through Information and Communication Technologies).

References

1. 3rd Generation Partnership Project (3GPP). 3gpp home (2016). http://www.3gpp. org
2. Chen, S., Xu, H., Liu, D., Hu, B., Wang, H.: A vision of IoT: applications, challenges, and opportunities with china perspective. IEEE Internet Things J. **1**(4), 349–359 (2014)
3. Fowler, M., Lewis, J.: Microservices (2014). http://www.martinfowler.com/ articles/microservices.html
4. GSMA documents (2016). www.gsma.com
5. GSMA: Remote provisioning architecture for embedded UICC technical specification (2016). http://www.gsma.com/connectedliving/wp-content/uploads/ 2014/01/2.-GSMA-Remote-Provisioning- Architecture-for-Embedded-UICC-Technical-Specification-Version-1.0.pdf
6. Hller, J., Tsiatsis, V., Mulligan, C., Karnouskos, S., Avesand, S., Boyle, D.: M2M and IoT technology fundamentals. In: Hller, J., Tsiatsis, V., Mulligan, C., Karnouskos, S., Avesand, S., Boyle, D. (eds.) From Machine-To-Machine to the Internet of Things, chap. 5, pp. 81–143. Academic Press, Oxford (2014)
7. Hunkeler, U., Truong, H.L., Stanford-Clark, A.: A publish/subscribe protocol for wireless sensor networks. In: 3rd International Conference on Communication Systems Software and Middleware and Workshops, COMSWARE 2008, pp. 791–798, January 2008
8. Jensen, C.S., Xie, X., Zadorozhny, V., Madria, S., Pitoura, E., Zheng, B., Chow, C. (eds.): 16th IEEE International Conference on Mobile Data Management, MDM 2015, Pittsburgh, PA, USA, 15–18 June 2015, vol. 1. IEEE (2015)
9. Kovatsch, M.: Coap for the web of things: from tiny resource-constrained devices to the web browser. In: Proceedings of the 4th International Workshop on the Web of Things (WoT 2013), Zurich, Switzerland, September 2013. (Best paper)
10. Microsoft: Microsoft's azure in IoT (2016). www.microsoft.com/en-us/ server-cloud/internet-of-things/
11. Newman, S.: Building microservices: designing fine-grained systems (2015)
12. Samsung: Artik cloud (2016). https://artik.cloud
13. Shabtai, A., Elovici, Y., Rokach, L.: A Survey of Data Leakage Detection and Prevention Solutions. Springer Publishing Company Incorporated, New York (2012)

A Formal Approach to Error Localization and Correction in Service Compositions

Julia Krämer and Heike Wehrheim[✉]

Paderborn University – Computer Science, Paderborn, Germany
juliadk@mail.upb.de, wehrheim@uni-pardeborn.de

Abstract. Error detection, localization and correction are time-intensive tasks in software development, but crucial to deliver functionally correct products. Thus, automated approaches to these tasks have been intensively studied for standard software systems. For model-based software systems, the situation is different. While error detection is still well-studied, error localization and correction is a less-studied domain. In this paper, we examine error localization and correction for *models of service compositions*. Based on formal definitions of *error* and *correction* in this context, we show that the classical approach of error localization and correction, i.e. first determining a set of suspicious statements and then proposing changes to these statements, is ineffective in our context. In fact, it lessens the chance to succeed in finding a correction at all.

In this paper, we introduce *correction proposal* as a novel approach on error correction in service compositions integrating error localization and correction in one combined step. In addition, we provide an algorithm to compute such correction proposals automatically.

1 Introduction

In modern software development, *Service-Oriented Architectures (SOA)* emphasize the construction of software out of existing services to facilitate the construction of large software system. Such software systems then consist of service calls, which are assembled to contribute to a specific task, using standard operators from workflow construction like sequential composition, decisions and repetitions. A very important assumption in the SOA setting is that all information, which is available about a single service, is its interface, i.e. its input and output variables and its pre- and postcondition. SOA favor a model-based development because at design time, only a *model* of the service composition under construction is developed.

Debugging, i.e. the *detection, localization* and *correction* of faults, is one of the most important tasks to deliver functionally correct products. While these tasks are well-studied for standard software systems (and especially imperative programs), the situation is different for models of service compositions.

This work was partially supported by the German Research Foundation (DFG) within the Collaborative Research Centre "On-The-Fly Computing" (SFB 901).

© Springer International Publishing AG 2016
P. Milazzo et al. (Eds.): STAF 2016, LNCS 9946, pp. 445–457, 2016.
DOI: 10.1007/978-3-319-50230-4_35

Models of software in general typically abstract from details of the final systems, which facilitates error detection in terms of verification, leading to the existence of a broad range of verification approaches for models of software (and of services), e.g. [10,11,22].

In contrast, error *localization* becomes more difficult for models of service compositions, because most standard approaches for standard software systems cannot be applied to models of software. The reason is that almost all error localization techniques for standard software rely on the availability of a larger number of test cases or the ability to executed the system under consideration at will. Techniques like *Delta Debugging* [5,25–27], *Tarantula* [13], Pinpoint [3] and *AMPLE* [7] inspect test cases and compare, for instance, how often a statement is executed in a failing and how often in a successful test cases. Slicing [17,24,28] and trace formula approaches to error localization [4,9,14–16,19], which encode single executions of the programs, examine dependence information between single statements to find errors. Unfortunately, models of software usually fail to provide a larger number of test cases and – being models and not software – cannot be executed arbitrarily. For a detailed discussion, see [18].

Similarly, for standard software, several effective *error correction* approaches exist (see [20] for a detailed survey). However, most of them make assumption about their domain of application not valid for models of software, and service compositions in particular (cf. Section 2).

Providing effective error localization and correction methods for models of service composition remains an open challenge. In this paper, we provide a novel and formally rigorous approach that combines the computation of error localization and correction in one step. As we will argue, the standard approach to error localization and correction, i.e. the computation of suspicious statements, followed by attempts to correct the errors within these statements, appears to be unrewarding for models of service composition in general.

Organization of the Paper. We present our definition of service compositions in 2. In 3, we formally define error localization and correction. Our automated approach to the computation of corrections is presented in Sect. 4. Section 5 discusses why both error localization and correction need to be combined into a single step for service compositions. We conclude the paper with discussion and future work in Sect. 6.

2   Services and Service Compositions

In this section, we introduce service compositions and their formal semantics. Service compositions consist of single services assembled together to finally assure a given postcondition for the outputs. While we still use standard concepts of workflow modeling like sequential composition, decisions and repetitions, we use a textual representation inspired by service effect specifications (SEFFs) [2] to denote service compositions. Various other graphical and structural notations, for instance, WS-BPEL [21], exist.

In the following, we associate each service and service composition with a *domain* $D = (\mathcal{T}_D, \mathcal{P}_D, \mathcal{R}_D)$, which consists of a set $\mathcal{T}_D$ of types, a set $\mathcal{P}_D$ of predicates and a set $\mathcal{R}_D$ of rules to reason within the domain. In our context, predicates are functions $p\colon \bigotimes_{i \in I} T_i \to \mathbb{B}$ where $\mathbb{B} = \{true, false\}$, I is a finite index set and T_i denotes a type for all $i \in I$. The set $\mathcal{P}_D$ of a domain must always satisfy $\bigcup_{p \in \mathcal{P}_D} use_\mathcal{T}(p) \subseteq \mathcal{T}_D$, where $use_\mathcal{T}(p)$ denotes the set $\{T_i \mid i \in I\}$ of all types occurring in the specification of predicate p.

Service providers offer services in a *service market*. A *service market* $\mathsf{SM}(D)$ on a domain D is a set of services, which operate in D.

Definition 1 (Service Composition). *Let $D = (\mathcal{T}_D, \mathcal{P}_D, \mathcal{R}_D)$ be an abstract domain. The set of all service compositions $\mathcal{SC}$ is given by the following grammar in Backus-Naur-form:*

$$\mathcal{SC} \ni \mathsf{S}_1, \mathsf{S}_2 ::= [Skip]^\ell \mid \mathsf{S}_1; \mathsf{S}_2 \qquad \mid [(T_1\ u_1, \dots, T_n\ u_n) := \mathsf{S}(v_1, \dots, v_m)]^\ell$$
$$\mid \mathbf{while}\ [B]^\ell\ \mathbf{do}\ \mathsf{S}_1\ \mathbf{od} \mid \mathbf{if}\ [B]^\ell\ \mathbf{then}\ \mathsf{S}_1\ \mathbf{else}\ \mathsf{S}_2\ \mathbf{fi};$$

where $m, n \in \mathbb{N}$, $B \in \mathcal{P}_D$, ℓ is a label, $T_1, \dots, T_n \in \mathcal{T}_D$ and S has m input and n output variables.

In the following, $\mathsf{def}(\mathsf{SC})$ denotes the set of variables assigned to in a service composition SC. Each statement st of a service composition has a special label ℓ in order to identify the statement. As in Definition 1, we write $[st]^\ell$ if ℓ is the label of st. We assume that different statements have different labels and use natural numbers as labels in the following. If a service composition SC is not in this form, we can rename all occurring statements by traversing the control-flow graph s.t. SC complies to this criterion.

Figure 1 shows a simple service composition example. The input to the service composition is the painter *painter* and a painting *painting*. The aim of the composition is to frame the painting and then, to sell the resulting image at the highest price possible. As advertising is costly, we assume that the highest price with an unknown artist is achieved only if the image is not advertised at all. In contrast, if the artist is famous, the highest price is achieved if the image is advertised before. The output of the service composition is the money gained (M).

A service composition calls a service according to its specification, i.e. its name, its input and output variables as well as its pre- and postconditions (also called effects).[1] While this information is not part of our syntax, we annotated Fig. 1 accordingly for the convenience of the reader.

Formally, the domain of our example comprises the types *Painting*, *Image*, *Money*, *Gain* and the predicates *unknown*, *isGainOf* and *highest*. In addition, we assume the following rules to be known:

$\neg unknown(painter) \wedge isGainOf(I, painter, G)) \wedge price(M, I, G, painter) \Rightarrow highest(M, painter, I)$
$unknown(painter) \wedge \neg isGainOf(I, painter, G)) \wedge price(M, I, G, painter) \Rightarrow highest(M, painter, I)$

---

[1] In WSDL (https://www.w3.org/TR/wsdl), all four components together are called *IOPE*.

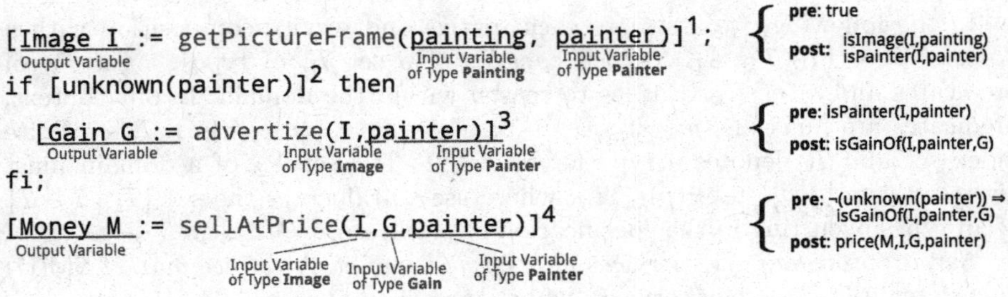

```
[Image I := getPictureFrame(painting, painter)]¹;
 Output Variable              Input Variable   Input Variable
                             of Type Painting  of Type Painter
if [unknown(painter)]² then

   [Gain G := advertize(I,painter)]³
    Output Variable      Input Variable   Input Variable
                        of Type Image    of Type Painter
fi;

[Money M := sellAtPrice(I,G,painter)]⁴
 Output Variable
                    Input Variable  Input Variable   Input Variable
                    of Type Image   of Type Gain     of Type Painter
```

{ pre: true
  post: isImage(I,painting)
        isPainter(I,painter)

{ pre: isPainter(I,painter)
  post: isGainOf(I,painter,G)

{ pre: ¬(unknown(painter)) ⇒
        isGainOf(I,painter,G)
  post: price(M,I,G,painter)

Fig. 1. A Simple Service Composition

In its current state, however, the service composition is faulty. The condition in the if-statement leads to a call of service advertise when the painter is not well-known and not – as intended – when the painter is famous.

Definition 2 (Service). *Let* $D = (T_D, P_D, R_D)$ *be a domain. A* service specification *(or short,* service*) consists of a* name *together with an* interface. *An* interface I *over the domain* D *is a tuple* $I = (In, Out, pre, post)$ *such that*

- In, Out *are sets of* typed input *and* output variables *such that* $In \cap Out = \emptyset$, $use_T(In) \subseteq T_D$ *and* $use_T(Out) \subseteq T_D$,
- *and* pre *and* post *are logical formulas build over the predicates in* D *using* $\neg, \vee, \wedge$ *and are called the* pre- *and* postcondition *of the service, respectively. We have* $var(pre) \subseteq In$ *and* $var(post) \subseteq In \cup Out$.

In addition, we assume that services do not modify their input variables, *i.e. if the precondition holds before a service call, then it also holds afterwards.*

If a service S changes its inputs, we replace every call $T\ x := S(x^I{}_1, \ldots, x^I{}_m)$ with two assignments service $x'_1, \ldots, x'_m := x^I{}_1, \ldots, x^I{}_m; T\ x := S'(x'_1, \ldots, x'_m)$ such that the actual input variables are not changed.

We write $Out_S, In_S, pre_S, post_S$ for the components of a service S. In the following, we say that a service with interface $I_1 = (In_1, Out_1, pre_1, post_1)$ *refines* a service with interface $I_2 = (In_2, Out_2, pre_2, post_2)$, denoted by $I_1 \sqsubseteq I_2$, if $In_1 \subseteq In_2$, $Out_1 \supseteq Out_2$ and additionally, $pre_2 \Rightarrow pre_1$ and $post_1 \Rightarrow post_2$.

Remark 1. From a logical perspective, services are implications because they do not modify their input variables, i.e. services guarantee that whenever the precondition holds, the postcondition can be established for the output variables.

Remark 2. Note that Definition 2 can be generalized to service *compositions* immediately, as from an abstract perspective, service compositions can be considered services themselves. For instance, the service composition in Fig. 1 has the input variables *painter* and *painting*, the output variables M, the precondition *true* and the postcondition *highest(M,painter,I)*.

$$\mathsf{sp}(Skip, \varphi) = \varphi$$
$$\mathsf{sp}(S_1; S_2, \varphi) = \mathsf{sp}(S_2, \mathsf{sp}(S_1, \varphi))$$
$$\mathsf{sp}(\text{if } [B]^\ell \text{ then } S_1 \text{ else } S_2 \text{ fi}, \varphi) = \mathsf{sp}(S_1, B \wedge \varphi) \vee \mathsf{sp}(S_2, \neg B \wedge \varphi)$$
$$\mathsf{sp}(\text{while } [B]^\ell \text{ do } S_1 \text{ od}, \varphi) = \varphi \wedge Inv[\bar{x}/\bar{\hat{x}}] \wedge \neg B[\bar{x}/\bar{\hat{x}}]$$

Fig. 2. Strongest Postcondition Semantics for Service Compositions

Strongest Postcondition Semantics. In this section, we define a partial-correctness *strongest postcondition semantics* for service compositions [1,8]. Partial correctness here refers to that we do not consider termination as correctness criterion. W.l.o.g., we assume all service compositions to be in *single static assignment form* (SSA)[2].

In addition, we assume loops to be annotated with invariants. We consider this assumption practically feasible. Even if not every loop is annotated with an invariant by its developer in practice, various existing automated invariant generation methods can be applied to overcome this (e.g. [12]).

Strongest postconditions for service compositions and for programs mainly differ in the treatment of service calls. The postcondition of a service does not uniquely determine the values of outputs. Due to SSA form, services never change values of variables (especially not the inputs of the service), but only make assignments to previously unused, *fresh* variables. Therefore, *all properties, which hold before a certain statement, also hold afterwards*. Note that in a service call $(u_1, \ldots, u_n) := S(v_1, \ldots, v_m)$, the inputs and outputs are thus disjoint, i.e., $\{u_1, \ldots, u_n\} \cap \{v_1, \ldots, v_m\} = \emptyset$. In the following, we write $\bar{x} = (x_1, \ldots, x_n)$ for a tuple of variables. The sp-semantics of service calls is

$$\mathsf{sp}(\bar{u} := \mathsf{S}(\bar{v}), \varphi) = \varphi \wedge \mathsf{post}_\mathsf{S}(\bar{v}, \bar{u}).$$

Strongest postcondition definitions for the remaining cases can be found in Fig. 2. Please note that we abstract the loop by its invariant and therefore, only know that the invariant holds at the end of the loop and the loop predicate does not. Due to variable renaming in SSA form, we need to rename the variables occurring in the invariant and in the predicate of the loop to the variable names introduced by the transformation to SSA form (variable names of join-nodes). For branches, it suffices to treat join-nodes as special service calls, which assign the correct value to variables occurring in both branches.

3   Errors and Corrections

In this section, we discuss all three steps of debugging of service compositions. First, we shortly present how to detect errors in service compositions using verification. Second, we formally define the types of errors, which we consider here. Finally, we define corrections for service compositions.

---

[2] Using [6], SSA form can be established for all service compositions.

Please note that we still *only* consider services compositions in SSA form. Services are in general well-tested pieces of code, thus, we assume that single services are correct, i.e. services used in a service compositions always correctly implement their interface. Moreover, we assume that all loops are annotated with loop invariants capturing the complete loop behavior. In Sect. 4, we shortly discuss how to correct faulty loops.

Correct Service Compositions. Service compositions are specified using interfaces (cf. Definition 2), where pre- and postconditions describe the expected behavior in terms of predicates over input and output variables. Intuitively, a service composition is correct if the output satisfies the postcondition whenever the input meets the precondition. Formally, we say that a service composition is *correct*, if it can be proven (for instance, using the approach in [23]), that the service compositions complies to its interface. Otherwise, we call the service composition *faulty*. If we apply [23] to our example (Fig. 1), we see that the service composition fails to establish the precondition of the service sellAtPrice.

Error and Correction. We restrict ourselves to the localization and correction of errors, which can be detected as follows:

1. the correctness requirement is not met, i.e., when started in a state satisfying pre_{SC} we might reach a state outside $post_{SC}$,
2. the execution of a service composition blocks at some service call because the precondition of the service is not satisfied, and
3. during an execution a loop is reached but the loop invariant does not hold.

In Definiton 3, the first case corresponds to a global error, whereas the second and the third case are subsumed by local errors. The first type of error mainly occurs if the service composition does not make enough progress towards the postcondition, whereas the second type of error is mainly caused by calling the wrong service, which invalidates the precondition of the next service or the invariant of a succeeding loop.

Definition 3 (Error). *Let* SC *be a service composition,* ℓ *one of its labels, and* (pre, post) *the requirement on* SC. *An* error *in* SC *occurs at* ℓ *if one of the following conditions hold:*

1. $\ell = \ell_\perp$ *and* $sp(SC, pre) \not\Rightarrow post$ *(a global error),*
2. $\ell \notin \{\ell_\perp, \ell_\top\}$ *and* ℓ *is not inside an if or while statement, and* $sp(SC_{\rightarrow\ell}, pre) \not\Rightarrow$ pre_ℓ *(a local error).*

Please note that pre_ℓ denotes the precondition of a statement ℓ. If the statement is a service call S, it holds $pre_\ell = pre_S$. We use the invariant of a loop as its precondition and for all remaining cases, the precondition is *true*.

Our example has a local error as it fails to establish the precondition of the service at label 4.

A *correction* serves as a replacement of a part of the service composition. Therefore, a correction consists of two labels, which specify the part the correction might eventually replace and an interface, which specifies the service, which should be inserted between the two labels.

Definition 4 (Correction). *Let* SC *be a service composition. A correction* cor *for* SC *is a triple* $(\ell, \bar{u} := S(\bar{v}), \ell')$ *such that* SC *can be divided into* $SC_{\to \ell}; SC'; SC_{\ell'}$. *Applying* cor *to* SC *(by replacing* SC'*) yields* cor(SC) = $SC_{\to \ell}; \bar{u} := S(\bar{v}); SC_{\ell'}$.

The key difference between imperative programs and service compositions w.r.t. error correction is now the fact that not all services we like to use in a correction are available in the service market. It is essential to note that markets *cannot* and *do not* offer every possible service operating in the domain. Hence, we call a correction *realizable in a service market* SM(D) if every service S occurring in the correction, is contained in SM(D). Error localization for service compositions can thus only *propose* corrections, which afterwards needs to be checked for their realizability.

4   Correction Proposals

In this section, we present an automatic approach to compute corrections for service compositions. The aim is to provide *small* correction proposals first. Small here refers to the number of statements, which are replaced by the correction. Nonetheless, the easiest correction of a faulty service composition with requirement (pre, post) is to replace the entire composition by a single service call of a service S with $pre_S = pre$ and $post_S = post$. Quite likely this is not a realizable correction (since otherwise one would not have bothered to construct the service composition at first hand).

Corrections for Global Errors. We assume service compositions to be in SSA form. Thus, we have at most one assignment to every output variable of the service composition. Most likely, this output is determined at the end of the service composition (otherwise, the statements behind that can be discarded because they do not affect the output anymore). Hence, we start the correction of global errors, i.e. when the service composition in its entirety has failed to establish the postcondition, at the end of the service composition.

The key to the correction of global errors is to determine the functionally missing in the current service composition. We specify the missing part in terms of so-called *bridges*.

Definition 5 (Bridge). *A* bridge *between two logic formulas* φ *and* ψ *is a formula* ρ *such that* $\varphi \wedge \rho \Rightarrow \psi$ *holds. The set of bridges between* φ *and* ψ *is defined as* $\psi \setminus \varphi := \{\rho \mid \rho \text{ is a bridge between } \varphi \text{ and } \psi\}$.

As an example: $\varphi := p(x)$, $\psi := p(x) \wedge q(z)$. Then $\psi \setminus \varphi$ contains for instance *false*, $q(z)$ and ψ. We use the notation $\setminus$ here since a bridge can easily be computed as set difference when both φ and ψ are given as conjunctions (sets) of literals – as for our strongest postconditions. As the sp-semantics does not introduce quantifiers, it is sufficient to consider propositional logic formulae φ and ψ.

Proposition 1. *For arbitrary formulae φ and ψ, it holds that $\psi \setminus \varphi$ is infinite.*

Proof. The set always contains *false* as $\varphi \wedge$ *false* $\equiv$ *false* and *false* implies everything. The set is non-finite as *false* can be expressed with infinitely many formulae.

While there always exists a bridge, there does not necessarily exist a service, which has the bridge as postcondition. Thus, the corrections which we propose below, might not be realizable.

Computing Corrections for Global Errors. Corrections for global errors need to range from some label ℓ of the service composition (not contained in a branch or a loop) to the end of the service composition denoted by $\ell_\perp$. Thus, we need to construct a bridge between the strongest postcondition, which can be guaranteed at ℓ and the postcondition post.

The correction from ℓ to $\ell_\perp$ thus proposed to add a service call using the service $\mathsf{S}_{\mathsf{cor}}$ of the following form $(o_1, \ldots, o_l) := \mathsf{S}_{\mathsf{cor}}(x_1, \ldots, x_k)$ where

- $\{o_1, \ldots, o_l\} = \mathsf{Out} \setminus (\mathsf{def}(\mathsf{SC}_{\to \ell}) \cup \mathsf{In}_{\mathsf{SC}})$,
- $\{x_1, \ldots, x_k\} = \mathsf{def}(\mathsf{SC}_{\to \ell}) \cup \mathsf{In}_{\mathsf{SC}}$,
- $\mathsf{pre}_{S_{\mathsf{cor}}} := \mathsf{sp}(\mathsf{SC}_{\to \ell}, \mathsf{pre})$ and
- $\mathsf{post}_{S_{\mathsf{cor}}} := \rho$

and $\rho \in \mathsf{post} \setminus \mathsf{sp}(\mathsf{SC}_{\to \ell}, \mathsf{pre})$. The bridge, which we take here, needs to be chosen such that $\mathsf{var}(\rho) \subseteq \{o_1, \ldots, o_l, x_1, \ldots, x_k\}$. One candidate is post itself. It is, however, preferable to use smaller (in terms of variables used) ρ's since this increases the chances of proposing a realizable correction. We do not need to rename the variables of the service calls as the service $\mathsf{S}_{\mathsf{cor}}$ takes the variables defined so far as inputs and must provide all output variables of the service composition.

Theorem 1. *Let* SC *be a service composition with requirement* (pre, post) *and let* SC *have a global error (and no local errors). Let $\ell \neq \ell_\perp$ be a label of* SC. *Then, the correction $(\ell, \bar{u} := \mathsf{S}(\bar{v}), \ell_\perp)$, where $\mathsf{S} \sqsubseteq \mathsf{S}_{\mathsf{cor}}$, is a refinement of $\bar{o} := \mathsf{S}_{\mathsf{cor}}(\bar{x})$ as given above, corrects the error.*

Proof. We have to prove that $(\ell, \bar{u} := S(\bar{v}), \ell_\perp)$ is a correction, i.e. we have to prove that the service composition

$$\mathsf{SC}_{\to \ell}; \bar{u} := S(\bar{v}); \mathsf{SC}_{\ell_\perp}$$

satisfies the postcondition $\mathsf{post}_{\mathsf{SC}}$ for every input, which satisfies the precondition.

Formally, we thus need to show the following:

$$\mathsf{sp}(\mathsf{SC}_{\to\ell}; \bar{u} := S(\bar{v}); \mathsf{SC}_{\ell_\perp}, \mathsf{pre}_{\mathsf{SC}}) \Rightarrow \mathsf{post}_{\mathsf{SC}}.$$

(A) First, we show that there does not exist a local error in the corrected service composition:
- $\mathsf{SC}_{\to\ell}$ does not contain a local error by assumption.
- The following holds:

$$\begin{aligned}
&\mathsf{sp}(\mathsf{SC}_{\to\ell}; \bar{u} := S(\bar{v}); \mathsf{SC}_{\ell_\perp}, \mathsf{pre}_{\mathsf{SC}}) \\
&= \mathsf{sp}(\bar{u} := S(\bar{v}); \mathsf{SC}_{\ell_\perp}, \mathsf{sp}(\mathsf{SC}_{\to\ell}, \mathsf{pre}_{\mathsf{SC}})) \\
&= \mathsf{sp}(\mathsf{SC}_{\ell_\perp}, \mathsf{sp}(\bar{u} := S(\bar{v}), \mathsf{sp}(\mathsf{SC}_{\to\ell}, \mathsf{pre}_{\mathsf{SC}})))
\end{aligned}$$

By definition, $\mathsf{pre}_{\mathsf{S}_{\mathsf{cor}}} := \mathsf{sp}(\mathsf{SC}_{\to\ell})$ and the service S refines $\mathsf{S}_{\mathsf{cor}}$, i.e. $\mathsf{pre}_{\mathsf{S}_{\mathsf{cor}}} \Rightarrow \mathsf{pre}_{\mathsf{S}}$. Thus, it holds that $\mathsf{sp}(\mathsf{SC}_{\to\ell}) \Rightarrow \mathsf{pre}_{\mathsf{S}}$, and S is applicable and does not block.
- $\mathsf{SC}_{\ell_\perp}$ is the empty program and therefore, cannot contain a local error.

(B) Second, we prove that there does not exist a global error. The strongest postcondition of the service call is given by

$$\mathsf{sp}(\bar{u} := S(\bar{v}), \mathsf{sp}(\mathsf{SC}_{\to\ell}, \mathsf{pre}_{\mathsf{SC}})) = \mathsf{pre}_{\mathsf{S}}(\bar{x}) \wedge \mathsf{post}_{\mathsf{S}}(\bar{x}, \bar{o}) \wedge \mathsf{sp}(\mathsf{SC}_{\to\ell}, \mathsf{pre}_{\mathsf{SC}}).$$

By definition, it holds that $\mathsf{sp}(\mathsf{SC}, \mathsf{pre}_{\mathsf{SC}}) \wedge \mathsf{post}_{\mathsf{S}_{\mathsf{cor}}} \Rightarrow \mathsf{post}_{\mathsf{SC}}$ as the postcondition of the service $\mathsf{S}_{\mathsf{cor}}$ is defined as a bridge between $\mathsf{sp}(\mathsf{SC}, \mathsf{pre}_{\mathsf{SC}})$ and $\mathsf{post}_{\mathsf{SC}}$. As $\mathsf{S} \sqsubseteq \mathsf{S}_{\mathsf{cor}}$, it holds that $\mathsf{post}_{\mathsf{S}} \Rightarrow \mathsf{post}_{\mathsf{S}_{\mathsf{cor}}}$.

The service composition $\mathsf{SC}_{\ell_\perp}$ denotes the empty program as $\ell_\perp$ does not correspond to any program label. Therefore, the following holds:

$$\mathsf{pre}_{\mathsf{S}}(\bar{x}) \wedge \mathsf{post}_{\mathsf{S}}(\bar{x}, \bar{o}) \wedge \mathsf{sp}(\mathsf{SC}_{\to\ell}, \mathsf{pre}_{\mathsf{SC}}) \Rightarrow \mathsf{sp}(\mathsf{SC}_{\to\ell}, \mathsf{pre}_{\mathsf{SC}}) \wedge \mathsf{post}_{\mathsf{S}_{\mathsf{cor}}}(\bar{x}, \bar{o}) \Rightarrow \mathsf{post}_{\mathsf{SC}}.$$

Thus, the service composition $\mathsf{SC}_{\to\ell}; \bar{u} := S(\bar{v}); \mathsf{SC}_{\ell_\perp}$ is correct wrt. the sp-semantics and $(\ell, \bar{u} := S(\bar{v}), \ell_\perp))$ is indeed a correction.   □

The theorem does not consider *realizability* of the proposed correction. If the pre- and postcondition of a service composition are incompatible or even *false*, or the proposed service cannot be found in the market, the proposed correction cannot be applied. Then, another proposal has to be computed and checked for realizability.

Correction of Local Errors. A local error occurs when the precondition of a service (or the invariant of a loop) is not established upon the call of the service (start of the loop). Every local error can be rephrased as a global error in the following way. If ℓ is the location of the local error, we only consider the service composition up to ℓ, and use the precondition of ℓ as postcondition of the subcomposition.

Proposition 2. *Let SC be a service composition with a local error at ℓ and requirement $(\mathsf{pre}, \mathsf{post})$. Then the following holds: SC has a local error at ℓ iff $\mathsf{SC}_{\to\ell}$ has a global error with respect to $(\mathsf{pre}, \mathsf{pre}_\ell)$.*

Hence, we can reuse the algorithm to compute correction proposals for global errors also for local errors by simply modifying the considered service composition and pre- and postconditions. An alternative correction proposal for local errors is $(\ell, \bar{u} := \mathsf{S}(\bar{v}), \ell_\perp)$, where the precondition of S is the strongest postcondition of $\mathsf{SC}_{\rightarrow \ell}$ and the postcondition of S is the postcondition of SC.

We have already seen that our service composition has a local error at label 4. As one correction, we propose to replace the block before 4 (the if-statement) by a new service call. As input, it gets all the variables used so far, i.e., *painter*, *painting* and I. As output variable, it gets G. Its precondition is *isImage(I,painting)* and the postcondition is $\neg unknown(painter) \Rightarrow isGainOf(I,painter,G)$. Thus, We need to check whether this service is available in the service market and if yes, can use it at the place of the if-statement. This correction also leads to an error-free service composition as the strongest postcondition of cor(SC) wrt. pre together with the rules of the ontology now imply the overall postcondition post.

Correction of Loops and Branches. We treat loops and branches as a single block in the above approach and do not allow to correct errors, which occur inside of loops and branches. Nevertheless, we can also correct errors in loops and branches using the same approach as above.

Let **while** B **do** S_1 **od** be a loop and *Inv* its invariant. We say that the loop has a *while-global error* if $\mathsf{sp}(S_1, Inv \wedge B) \not\Rightarrow Inv$. We then consider S_1 as a complete service composition with precondition $Inv \wedge B$ and postcondition *Inv* and apply the correction proposal algorithm for global errors.

Similarly, we can correct local errors in loops and branches. We say a loop **while** $[B]^\ell$ **do** S_1 **od** has a *local error* at label ℓ' if $\ell' \in \mathcal{L}(\mathsf{S}_1)$ and

$$\mathsf{sp}(\mathsf{S}_{1 \rightarrow \ell'}, \mathsf{sp}(\mathsf{SC}_{\rightarrow \ell}, \mathsf{pre}_{\mathsf{SC}}) \wedge Inv \wedge B) \not\Rightarrow \mathsf{pre}_{\ell'}.$$

Analogously, we say that a branch **if** $[B]^\ell$ **then** S_1 **else** S_2 **fi;** has a *local error* at label ℓ' if either $\ell' \in \mathcal{L}(\mathsf{S}_1)$ and $\mathsf{sp}(S_{1 \rightarrow \ell'}, \mathsf{sp}(\mathsf{SC}_{\rightarrow \ell}, \mathsf{pre}_{\mathsf{SC}}) \wedge B) \not\Rightarrow \mathsf{pre}_{\ell'}$ or $\ell' \in \mathcal{L}(\mathsf{S}_2)$ and $\mathsf{sp}(S_{2 \rightarrow \ell'}, \mathsf{sp}(\mathsf{SC}_{\rightarrow \ell}, \mathsf{pre}_{\mathsf{SC}}) \wedge \neg B) \not\Rightarrow \mathsf{pre}_{\ell'}$. Also for local errors in branches or loops, we first propose corrections in S_1 and S_2, respectively, by considering both of them as single service composition and then, applying the algorithm given above. Afterwards, we again treat loops and branches as single blocks and try to replace them with new services.

5   Discussion

In this section, we discuss why existing error localization methods are not helpful w.r.t. to error correction in service compositions. We start with the following artificial service compositions, which illustrates that considering only a subset of statements (i.e. only a set of suspicious statements) of the service composition in fact lessens the chance to find a realizable correction.

$$B \ b := \mathsf{makeA}(a); \ C \ c := \mathsf{makeB}(b); \ D \ d := \mathsf{makeD}(c)$$

The requirement on this service composition is $(\mathsf{pre}, \mathsf{post}) = (isA(a), isD(d))$ using the services makeA, which has precondition $isA(a)$ and postcondition $isB(b)$, makeB, which has precondition $isB(B)$ and postcondition $isC(c)$ and makeD, which has precondition $\neg isC(c)$ and postcondition $isD(d)$.

The local error (precondition of service makeD not met) can be corrected in various ways, for example,

- it can be considered as a missing code problem – the service with precondition $isC(c)$ and postcondition $\neg isC(c')$ (whereas both the input and the output variable have type C) needs to be inserted or
- it can be solved by exchanging the service makeB with a service with the same precondition, but the postcondition $\neg isC(c)$ or
- it is also possible to replace both the service calls makeA and makeB by, for example, services with precondition $isA(a)$ and postcondition $\neg isB(b)$ and precondition $\neg isB(b)$ and postcondition $\neg isC(c)$, respectively.

This construction can be repeated arbitrarily often and we do not know, which correction to prefer unless we know the available service markets, and thus, which alternative services exist.

The previous example shows why errors in service compositions can be at any places. The next example shows why reducing the set of statements does not help with error localization. Assume that the requirement on the service composition given below is $(\mathsf{pre}, \mathsf{post}) = (isA(a), isD(d) \wedge isE(e))$.

$$B \ b := \mathsf{makeA}(a); F \ f := \mathsf{makeF}(a);$$
$$C \ c := \mathsf{makeB}(b); D \ d := \mathsf{makeNotC}(c); E \ e := \mathsf{makeE}(f)$$

The service makeE has the precondition $isF(f)$ and the postcondition $isE(e)$, the service makeF has the precondition $isA(a)$ and the postcondition $isF(f)$ and the service makeNotC has precondition $isC(c)$ and the postcondition $\neg isD(d)$. The pre- and postcondition of all other services remain unchanged. For any input, the service composition already guarantees $isE(e)$, but not $isD(d)$. Thus, we could apply slicing to only correct the part of the service composition, which is responsible for the error $isD(d)$, i.e. we only correct the service composition $B \ b := \mathsf{makeA}(a); C \ c := \mathsf{makeB}(b); D \ d := \mathsf{makeNotC}(c)$. Nevertheless, this may obliterate the only existing correction. For example, the service composition can be fixed with a service $D \ d := \mathsf{makeNotC}(f, c)$, which has the precondition $isF(f) \wedge isC(c)$ and the desired postcondition $isD(d)$. As the variable f is not in the slice, slicing cannot propose this correction.

6 Conclusion

In this paper, we addressed the problem of automated error localization and correction for models of service compositions. We therefore needed to find a way to overcome the lack of executability of single services, which makes most error localization and correction methods for standard software inapplicable. Thus, we proposed correction proposals, which state where and how to modify existing service compositions in terms of alternative services. Correction proposals can be statically computed based on the strongest postcondition semantics of our service compositions and thus, are completely independent from test cases or executability. Hence, the computation of correction proposals is a good way to the localization and correction of errors in model-driven design approaches in general. Moreover, the computation of correction proposals can easily be generalized to every setting, which has a formal semantics in terms of strongest postconditions. Hence, even automated correction of imperative programs might benefit from our approach.

As future work, we want to practically evaluate the effectiveness of correction proposals for existing service markets w.r.t. to the existence of alternative markets. Moreover, we want to examine whether existing approaches to error localization and correction might be reused for more specific classes of errors (for instance, errors caused by a missing negation in conditions of loops or branches). Finally, we want to study the generalization of our approach to software systems.

References

1. Apt, K.R., Olderog, E.-R.: Verification of Sequential and Concurrent Programs: Graduate Texts in Computer Science, 2nd edn. Springer, Heidelberg (1997)
2. Becker, S., Koziolek, H., Reussner, R.: The palladio component model for model-driven performance prediction. J. Syst. Softw. **82**, 3–22 (2009). Special Issue: Software Performance - Modeling and Analysis
3. Chen, M.Y., Kiciman, E., Fratkin, E., Fox, A., Brewer, E., Pinpoint: problem determination in large, dynamic internet services. In: International Conference on Dependable Systems and Networks (2002)
4. Christ, J., Ermis, E., Schäf, M., Wies, T.: Flow-sensitive fault localization. In: Giacobazzi, R., Berdine, J., Mastroeni, I. (eds.) VMCAI 2013. LNCS, vol. 7737, pp. 189–208. Springer, Heidelberg (2013). doi:10.1007/978-3-642-35873-9_13
5. Cleve, H., Zeller, A.: Locating causes of program failures. In: Proceedings of 27th International Conference on Software Engineering, ICSE 2005. ACM (2005)
6. Cytron, R., Ferrante, J., Rosen, B.K., Wegman, M.N., Zadeck, F.K.: Efficiently computing static single assignment form and the control dependence graph. ACM Trans. Program. Lang. Syst. **13**(4), 451–490 (1991)
7. Dallmeier, V., Lindig, C., Zeller, A.: Lightweight defect localization for java. In: Black, A.P. (ed.) ECOOP 2005. LNCS, vol. 3586, pp. 528–550. Springer, Heidelberg (2005). doi:10.1007/11531142_23
8. Dijkstra, E.W., Scholten, C.S.: Predicate Calculus and Program Semantics: Texts and Monographs in Computer Science. Springer, New York (1990)
9. Ermis, E., Schäf, M., Wies, T.: Error invariants. In: Giannakopoulou, D., Méry, D. (eds.) FM 2012. LNCS, vol. 7436, pp. 187–201. Springer, Heidelberg (2012). doi:10.1007/978-3-642-32759-9_17
10. Fahrenberg, U., Larsen, K.G., Legay, A.: Model-based verification, optimization, synthesis and performance evaluation of real-time systems. In: Liu, Z., Woodcock, J., Zhu, H. (eds.) Unifying Theories of Programming and Formal Engineering Methods. LNCS, vol. 8050, pp. 67–108. Springer, Heidelberg (2013). doi:10.1007/978-3-642-39721-9_2

11. Güdemann, M., Poizat, P., Salaün, G., Dumont, A.: VerChor: a framework for verifying choreographies. In: Cortellessa, V., Varró, D. (eds.) FASE 2013. LNCS, vol. 7793, pp. 226–230. Springer, Heidelberg (2013). doi:10.1007/978-3-642-37057-1_16

12. Gupta, A., Rybalchenko, A.: InvGen: an efficient invariant generator. In: Bouajjani, A., Maler, O. (eds.) CAV 2009. LNCS, vol. 5643, pp. 634–640. Springer, Heidelberg (2009). doi:10.1007/978-3-642-02658-4_48

13. Jones, J.A., Harrold, M.J.: Empirical evaluation of the tarantula automatic fault-localization technique. In: Proceedings of 20th IEEE/ACM International Conference on Automated Software Engineering, ASE 2005. ACM (2005)

14. Jose, M., Majumdar, R.: Cause clue clauses: error localization using maximum satisfiability. ACM SIGPLAN Not. 46(6), 437–446 (2011)

15. Jose, M., Majumdar, R.: Cause clue clauses: error localization using maximum satisfiability. In: Proceedings of 32nd ACM SIGPLAN Conference on Programming Language Design and Implementation, PLDI 2011. ACM (2011)

16. önighofer, R.K., Bloem, R.: Automated error localization and correction for imperative programs, FMCAD 2011. FMCAD Inc. (2011)

17. Korel, B., Laski, J.: Dynamic program slicing. Inf. Process. Lett. 29(3), 155–163 (1988)

18. Krämer, J., Wehrheim, H.: A short survey on using software error localization for service compositions. In: Aiello, M., Johnsen, E.B., Georgievski, I., Dustdar, S. (eds.) Service Oriented and Cloud Computing, ESOCC 2016 (2016). (to appear)

19. Lamraoui, S.-M., Nakajima, S.: A formula-based approach for automatic fault localization of imperative programs. In: Merz, S., Pang, J. (eds.) ICFEM 2014. LNCS, vol. 8829, pp. 251–266. Springer, Heidelberg (2014). doi:10.1007/978-3-319-11737-9_17

20. Monperrus, M., Automatic software repair: a bibliography. Technical report hal-01206501, University of Lille (2015)

21. OASIS. Web Services Business Process Execution Language v2.0. http://docs.oasis-open.org/wsbpel/2.0/OS/wsbpel-v2.0-OS.pdf

22. Schäfer, W.: Model driven development with mechatronic UML. In: Stapleton, G., Howse, J., Lee, J. (eds.) Diagrams 2008. LNCS (LNAI), vol. 5223, p. 4. Springer, Heidelberg (2008). doi:10.1007/978-3-540-87730-1_3

23. Walther, S., Wehrheim, H.: Knowledge-based verification of service compositions - an SMT approach. In: Engineering of Complex Computer Systems (ICECCS) (2013)

24. Weiser, M.: Program slicing. In: Proceedings of 5th International Conference on Software Engineering, ICSE 1981. IEEE Press, Piscataway (1981)

25. Zeller, A.: Yesterday, my program worked. today, it does not. why? In: Nierstrasz, O., Lemoine, M. (eds.) ESEC/SIGSOFT FSE -1999. LNCS, vol. 1687, pp. 253–267. Springer, Heidelberg (1999). doi:10.1007/3-540-48166-4_16

26. Zeller, A.: Isolating cause-effect chains from computer programs. In: Proceedings of 10th ACM SIGSOFT Symposium on Foundations of Software Engineering, SIGSOFT 2002/FSE-10. ACM (2002)

27. Zeller, A., Hildebrandt, R.: Simplifying and isolating failure-inducing input. IEEE Trans. Softw. Eng. 28(2), 183–200 (2002)

28. Zhang, X., He, H., Gupta, N., Gupta, R.: Experimental evaluation of using dynamic slices for fault location. In: Proceedings of Sixth International Symposium on Automated Analysis-driven Debugging, AADEBUG 2005. ACM (2005)

Pure Edge Computing Platform
for the Future Internet

Mirko D'Angelo$^{(\boxtimes)}$ and Mauro Caporuscio

Linnaeus University, Växjö, Sweden
{mirko.dangelo,mauro.caporuscio}@lnu.se

Abstract. Future Internet builds upon three key pillars – namely, Internet of Things, Internet of Services, and Internet of Contents – and is considered as a worldwide execution environment that interconnects myriad heterogeneous entities over time, supports information dissemination, enables the emergence of promising application domains, and stimulate new business and research opportunities. In this paper we analyse the challenges towards the actualisation of the Future Internet. We argue that the mobile nature inherent to modern communications and interactions requires a radical shift towards new computing paradigms that fully reflect the network-based perspective of the emerging environment. Indeed, we position the adoption of a Pure Edge Computing platform that offers designing and programming abstractions to specify, implement and operate Future Internet applications.

1 Introduction

The evolution of the Internet has radically changed our life: while initially simply used to exchange data between selected hosts, today the Internet is essential for the provision of daily-life software resources (e.g., data, and services) distributed all over the world. Future Internet (FI) builds upon three key pillars – namely, *Internet of Things*, *Internet of Services*, and *Internet of Contents* – and is formed by real world things connecting to one another, which are all around us, everywhere and anytime, and can be discovered, composed and consumed as needed [20]. Indeed, FI can be considered as a worldwide execution environment, where a large open-ended collection of heterogeneous resources dynamically interact with each other, to provide users with rich functionalities, e.g., real *thing* consumption, *service* provisioning, and *content* sharing [10].

FI enables the emergence of appealing and promising application domains, stimulating new business and research opportunities. In these settings, software vendors are no longer considered as independent units, where all software is built in-house. Rather, they will be networked and depend on each other services. Indeed, vendors will be part of a software ecosystem: "A set of actors functioning as a unit and interacting with a shared market for software and services, together with the relationships among them" [17]. These characteristics should be underpinned by a common technological platform, which facilitates the development of FI applications through the provision of proper designing

© Springer International Publishing AG 2016
P. Milazzo et al. (Eds.): STAF 2016, LNCS 9946, pp. 458–469, 2016.
DOI: 10.1007/978-3-319-50230-4_36

and programming abstractions for (i) uniformly representing *things*, *services* and *contents*, and (ii) deploying, discovering, composing, and consuming them at run time [16]. To this end, nowadays technological platforms leverage on computing paradigms that employ the so called *everything-as-a-service* (XaaS) abstraction – i.e., cloud and fog computing. Cloud computing [1] platforms heavily rely on distributed processing and available bandwidth from the peripheral devices to the (centralised) backend server: most data is sent to the cloud to be processed, leaving edge devices as simple portals into the cloud. Even though this architecture works well today, it fails when considering FI, where myriads of mobile devices interact each other by exchanging micro-data. To this end, fog computing [6] promotes a decentralised approach, where the edge devices play a key role to achieve geographical distribution, location awareness, real-time interactions and data streaming. However, device mobility is not fully supported and edge devices are still considered to be simple portals to reach the real infrastructure.

The high mobile nature inherent to modern communications and interactions requires a radical shift towards architectures that fully reflect the network-based perspective of the FI. Specifically, network-based systems rely on the explicit distribution of resources, which interact by means of (asynchronous) message passing. Indeed, network-based systems differ from distributed systems in the fact that the involved networked resources are independent and autonomous, rather than considered as integral part of a conceptually monolithic system [25]. To this end, we position in this paper the adoption of a Pure Edge Computing platform that offers designing and programming abstractions to specify, implement and operate FI applications. Moreover, we discuss a set of key challenges towards its actualisation, namely: *discovery*, *composition* and *communities*.

This paper is organised as follows. Section 2 introduces a motivating scenario. Section 3 discusses the requirements for a FI technological platform, and analyses existing solutions. Section 4 illustrates the Pure Edge Computing platform and discusses key challenges, and Sect. 5 sketches our perspectives for future work.

2 Motivating Scenario

This section introduces *Lost Child*, a Future Internet scenario that serves as running example to illustrate the proposed approach. *Lost Child* extends the scenario presented in [22] and points out a number of concepts that are central to elicit the requirements of the Future Internet platform:

A five year old child who is attending a parade in Manhattan with his parents goes missing among all the people, and his parents only notice he is missing after some time. A police officer, once advised, sends out an alert to all entities within a two kilometre radius, requesting them to share all photographs they have taken in the parade during the past hour containing people with a red shirt. After the request a community of entities participating to the search emerge. Many smartphones are able to filter and send the images that match the officer description to a final endpoint, while others despite having relevant informations may be incapable to execute the task due to some missing functionality (e.g.

computer vision capabilities to process, analyse, and understand images) or to a low battery level. However, these devices are able to participate to the search by offloading the computation to near devices able to carry out the service on their behalf. Given the importance of the task, also the smart traffic cameras in the area collaborate to the search sending relevant informations, while personal computer in the surrounding houses grant their infrastructure as an offloading point for other devices to carry out complex computations. With John's parents, the police officer searches through the relevant photographs received on his phone. After looking through some pictures, they are able to spot John in one of the images, which they identify to be taken at a nearby location. Soon, the parents are reunited with their child.

Functional requirements for *Lost Child* are specified as follows:

R0: Devices may enter/leave the network dynamically, since a key aspect is the prominent role of mobile devices as rich sensors and service providers.

R1: Devices self-organise into emerging communities with a common goal.

R2: Devices within the community opportunistically make transient use of the shared infrastructure (e.g., storage, network, memory, processing power).

R3: Devices within the community opportunistically interact each other by providing/consuming services of interest.

R4: Devices within the community opportunistically interact each other by sharing data of interest enriched with contextual information.

R5: Devices within the community opportunistically interact each other by providing/consuming things of interest (e.g., camera, gps, sensors, etc.).

3   XaaS Platforms for the Future Internet

Best practices suggest to develop complex applications by exploiting the abstractions offered by an underling platform. A platform is an extensible software system that provides a set of core functionalities shared by applications that interoperate with it, and the interfaces through which they interoperate [3].

Choosing the platform is quite critical, because it affects the resulting application architecture and behaviour. In fact, each specific platform imposes architectural/behavioural constraints, and has architectural/behavioural properties that might be well-suited for some situations and ill-suited for others [13]. Indeed, a platform that induces a wrong architecture/behaviour might prevent the application from achieving certain properties of interest.

To this extent, a platform for the FI should provide designing and programming abstractions for (*i*) uniformly representing *things*, *services* and *contents*, and (*ii*) deploying, discovering, composing, and consuming them at run time. Further, the platform should be confronted with the following set of properties:

Scalability: to accommodate a high number of networked services/devices; it is a key property to satisfy **R0** and **R1**.

Interoperability: to enable the composition of services that are heterogeneous in many dimensions, e.g., location, functionalities and data; it is a key property to satisfy **R3–R5**.

Mobility: to natively support service location and relocation; it is a key property to satisfy **R0–R5**.

Adaptability: to react to the changing environment and keep requirements fulfilled; it is a key property to satisfy **R0** and **R1**.

Dependability: to support sensitive cross-domain requirements, e.g., performance, and security; it is a key property to satisfy **R2–R5**.

Nowadays platforms promote the adoption of computing paradigms that employ the so called *everything-as-a-service* (XaaS) abstraction to uniformly represent heterogeneous resources irrespectively of their specific nature (i.e., thing, service, and content). Although these platforms leverage on the same abstraction, they differ with respect to the architectural decomposition of internal functionalities, namely: *presentation logic*, *application logic*, *data access logic* and *data storage*. The position of these four elements identifies the specific architectural style employed by the different computing platforms. Table 1 classifies them with reference to the set of properties analysed within next sections.

Table 1. Cloud, Fog and Pure Edge Computing properties

Properties	Cloud Computing	Fog Computing	Pure Edge Computing
Architectural Style	Client-server	Client-server	P2P
Latency	High	Low	Very Low
Location of Service	Within the Internet	At the edge of the network	In the network
Physical Model	Centralised	Distributed	Network-based
Logical Model	Centralised	Centralised	Network-based
Support for Client Mobility	Limited	Supported	Supported
Support for Server Mobility	Not supported	Not supported	Supported
Number of Server Nodes	Few	Large	Very Large

3.1   Cloud Computing

Cloud Computing (CC) [1] rapidly changed the landscape of information technology. CC platforms heavily rely on distributed processing and available bandwidth from the peripheral devices to the central backed server. As showed in Fig. 1(a), all functional elements reside on the server side and most of the data is sent to the central server to be processed, leaving peripheral devices as simple portals into the cloud.

Referring to Table 1, platforms based on a CC architecture are not good candidates for dealing with the FI, as the architectural style employed by CC is client-server, and both physical and logical models are centralised. *Scalability* is one of the key property of CC, and is usually managed by increasing/decreasing at run time the number of servers. Client-side *Mobility* is partially supported and latency between client and server is generally very high. On the other hand, server-side mobility is not supported. *Interoperability* is often not supported, since two different CC platforms usually adopt different technologies (e.g. languages, and protocols). *Dependability* attributes like performance and reliability are often guaranteed. *Adaptability* is usually provided by the platform developer; however, the constraints imposed by this architectural pattern (e.g., mobility) could limit the application of some feasible strategies. Finally, CC architectures fail when considering myriads of devices that interact each other by exchanging micro-data, which is incredibly latency sensitive. Referring to the *Lost Child*, CC fails to provide the application with the required properties, and thus it prevents the fulfilment of requirements **R1**, **R3** and **R5**.

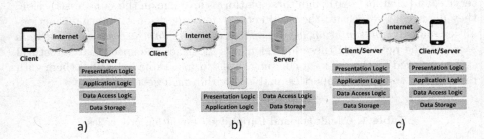

Fig. 1. Cloud vs. Fog vs. Pure Edge Computing

3.2   Fog Computing

Fog Computing (FC) [6] recently emerged as a platform that makes use of near-user peripheral servers to provide storage and processing power where they are needed. The FC platform employs a distributed computing infrastructure where services can be handled either at the periphery of the network (e.g., by smart routers) or at the central server. As showed in Fig. 1(b), the functional elements are subdivided between the near-user fog servers and the central server.

Still referring to Table 1, FC platforms are also not good candidates for dealing with the FI. In fact, the FC architecture is based on client-server style and, while the physical model is distributed, the logical one is still centralised. *Scalability* is partially supported by FC, since new peripheral-servers can be dynamically added when new entities join the network. Client-side *Mobility* is supported and latencies between client and server are usually very low. Also in this case, server-side mobility is not supported, since FC nodes are fixed entities. *Interoperability* is often not supported, for the same reason of CC and, also here, *Adaptability* strategies are limited. *Dependability* attributes like performance and reliability are often guaranteed. Even though FC well addresses latencies issue, it is not the appropriate architectural candidate for the FI platform. In fact, server-side mobility is not supported and devices are still considered to be simple portals to reach the real infrastructure. Indeed, FC paradigm still suffers the client-server nature of the approach. Referring to the *Lost Child*, CC fails to provide the application with the required properties, and thus it prevents the fulfilment of requirements **R1**, **R3**, and **R5**.

4 Pure Edge Computing Platform: Vision and Challenges

Edge Computing (EC) [24] pushes the frontier of computing applications, data, and services away from centralised nodes to the logical extremes of the network. EC is envisioned as a further extension of CC and FC, and aims at moving the control and trust decision to the edges of the network, in order to allow for novel human-centred applications [18].

Our vision is that FI must embrace the edge computing philosophy with the adoption of a distributed computing platform unifying things, services, and contents into XaaS. To this end, we position the design and development of a *Pure Edge Computing* (PEC) platform to break the monolith and enable a self-scaling mobile environment. PEC will employ a peer-to-peer (P2P) architecture, where all functional elements reside on the edge devices, and no central server exists (see Fig. 1(c)). Specifically, to improve dependability, PEC platform will adopt a hierarchical and hybrid P2P architecture, which exploits CC/FC nodes to play the role of super-peers and provide PEC nodes with supporting functionalities.

According to the P2P architecture employed by PEC, both the physical and the logical model are network-based (see Table 1). Therefore, *Scalability* is natively supported, as adding new clients to the network simultaneously adds new computational resources to the computing environment. Both client-side and server-side *Mobility* is supported and latencies between nodes are very low. *Interoperability* is natively supported by the P2P architecture. *Dependability* attributes (e.g., performance and reliability) and *Adaptability* are addressed, although satisfying these requirements is challenging. Further, still referring to *Lost Child*, PEC provides the application with the set of properties needed to fulfil the functional requirements.

PEC platform seems to be promising, as it provides the set of key characteristics required to deal with FI. Next sections discuss a set of key challenges towards its actualisation, namely: *discovery*, *composition* and *communities*.

4.1 XaaS Discovery

FI applications should dynamically aggregate services of interest, and be able to adapt to the evolving situation in which they operate, such as the physical environment and the computational entities populating it or the device on which the service runs. The challenges related to *XaaS Discovery* concern the ability of *discovering*, *understanding*, *selecting*, and *correlating* services of interest.

Discovering XaaS of interest in an open-ended world asks for mechanisms to semantically describe both functional and extra-functional properties of the services, and to reason about them and their actual context. The adoption of Semantic Web (SW) technologies enhances the discoverability of devices by enriching their descriptions with machine-interpretable semantics [5]. However, having semantic models and ontologies alone is not sufficient to achieve interoperability. In fact, ontologies developed by different parties are not guaranteed to be compatible with each other. Indeed, due to the inherent high degree of dynamism characterising FI, having a well established a-priori semantics is not

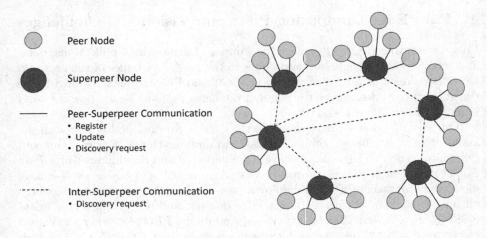

Fig. 2. Peer-to-peer XaaS discovery

possible in practice. Rather semantics should "emerge" from online negotiations among involved parties [9]. However, accuracy of the matching is frequently not satisfying and significant amount of human effort is still needed. Someone advocates to adopt the Linked Data principle [23]. Linking to existing knowledge rather than creating repetitive one helps to facilitate navigation, discovery and more importantly, interoperability.

Considering the high dynamic nature of the FI and the large number of entities participating into the system, developing an efficient and scalable discovery mechanism is challenging. To this end, the platform should employ fully decentralised techniques to discover and select XaaS of interest [11,14]. On the one hand, fully decentralised service discovery mechanisms on unstructured networks provides for scalability and self healing proprieties, at the expenses of a large communication overhead. On the other hand, discovery mechanisms based on structured networks have low communication overhead over the network, but they fail when dealing with dynamic systems.

The CAP theorem [15] states that it is impossible for a distributed computer system to simultaneously provide all three of the following guarantees: Consistency, Availability and network Partitions. Since obtaining strong consistency guarantees in extremely distributed and dynamic systems is not only difficult but often unnecessary, we envision a discovery mechanism based on *eventual consistency model* [26], which guarantees availability and network partitions. Our idea is to build a service discovery tool relying on distributed AP-based P2P technologies that use techniques like epidemic gossip. Referring to Fig. 2, to avoid large communication overhead a distributed service registry could be managed by the superpeer nodes of the system (see dark nodes in Fig. 2). Superpeer nodes would provide registration and lookup functionalities to the nodes they manage while, interacting with other superpeer nodes, they would carry out the distributed lookup task. In fact, instead of attempting to coordinate a large amount of components to enable service discovery, the problem can be reduced to coordinating superpeer nodes. This semi-structured approach unites the benefit of both the structured and unstructured approach since scalability and self-healing properties would be fully accommodated with a low communication overhead over the network.

4.2   XaaS Composition

Service composition allows for dynamically building complex applications by aggregating a large number of simple, distributed and heterogeneous services. Composing XaaS requires a paradigm shift from software services to real world services, and from application-centred services to user-centred services that demands for situation-aware composition techniques [12]. The composition process in the FI must deal with the uncertainty and complexity of the environment, as well as with other important factors, such as device mobility, battery management and context informations. Because of the high number of dimensions to consider simultaneously, the service composition is challenging, and finding the optimal solution is often computationally infeasible.

The PEC platform should exploit enhanced algorithms able to learn from the dynamic environment and determine optimal service compositions accordingly. Indeed, machine-learning based selection algorithms should be able to understand the context and self-adapt their behaviour according to both the user needs and the execution environment [8].

Once the composition process ends, the composite services are coordinated either by means of choreography or orchestration. Even though choreographies always provide a global view, and allow for parallel execution of services, resource-constrained devices might not support choreography engines [12]. On the other hand, orchestrations significantly reduce network traffic and

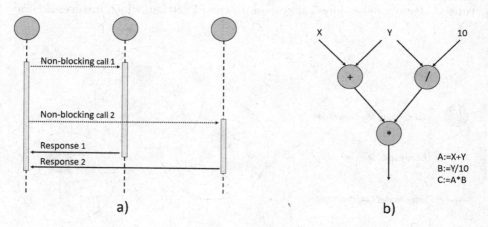

Fig. 3. Asyncronous message passing and data-flow model example

communication complexity between nodes. The platform should employ an integrated and automated run-time support for both orchestrations and choreographies [2].

Network-based systems rely on the explicit distribution of resources, which interact by means of (asynchronous) message passing. Employing asynchronous interaction model between the participating nodes (see Fig. 3(a)) would decouple them, and their communication flow, in both time – allowing concurrency – and space – allowing distribution and mobility. To this extent, we position to build the PEC platform on the asynchronous message-passing paradigm to provide support for both orchestrations and choreographies. Indeed, a key requirement for the PEC platform is the adoption of a coordination languages able to deal with the asynchronous nature of FI [9]. As shown in Fig. 3(b), data-flow languages [19] structure applications as a directed graph of autonomous software components that exchange data by asynchronous message passing. In the data-flow paradigm the components do not "call" each other, rather they are activated by the run-time system, and react according to the provided input (received message). Once the output is available, the run-time system is in charge of moving data towards the proper destination. Data-flow applications are inherently parallel. Exploiting the data-flow paradigm introduces a set of advantages in the PEC platform: (1) concurrency and parallelism are natural and components can be easily distributed across the network, (2) asynchronous message passing is natural for coordinating independent and autonomous components, and (3) applications are flexible and extensible since components can be hierarchically composed to create more complex functionalities.

4.3 XaaS Communities

FI devices should be able self-organize into emerging communities with a common goal. The combination of devices with their XaaS "representatives" constitutes de-facto a cyber-physical system. In the FI setting, which involves a large

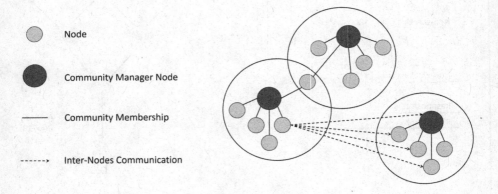

Fig. 4. Dynamic management of XaaS communities

number of entities, flat organizational structures are not appropriate. Therefore some "structural thinking" is necessary, leading to the organization of such entities in "communities" or "societies" ("ecosystems") of cyberphysical artifacts [7].

A large complex network is said to have community structures if nodes can be grouped into (potentially overlapping) sets such that each set is densely connected internally [21]. These connections can represent different type of associations such as: social relations, physical proximity or groups of interest. The vision is that FI devices will have integrated models of their knowledge (i.e., content), functionality (i.e., service) and infrastructure (i.e., things) available, which can then be linked and exchanged in a peer-to-peer fashion to create online social networks of collaborating devices. PEC platform for FI should provide proper mechanisms for allowing XaaS to self-organize into communities of interest. Specifically, the platform should provide support for detecting, managing and reconfiguring service communities.

Referring to Fig. 4, our idea is to manage communities structures through dynamic groups management. Communities can be build statically by the participating applications but the platform must be able to adopt mechanisms of communities identification. For example, similarly to techniques also used in the social networks, an high number of interactions between nodes (see the dashed arrows in Fig. 4) could imply the membership in a common group. To this end we are investigating on the possibility to extend the A3 middleware [4] to deal with community organizations through dynamic group management.

5   Future Work

FI can be considered as a worldwide execution environment, where a large openended collection of heterogeneous resources dynamically interact with each other.

The high dynamic nature inherent to FI requires a radical shift towards new computing paradigms able to fully reflect the network-based perspective of the emerging environment.

To this end, we position the adoption of a PEC platform that offers proper abstractions to specify, implement and operate FI applications. Specifically, the PEC platform should provide (i) a XaaS abstraction for uniformly representing things, services and contents, and (ii) a set of mechanisms for deploying, discovering, composing, aggregating and consuming XaaS at run time.

As consequence, a set of groundbreaking challenges make the development of the PEC platform ambitious. To this extent, future work is towards the exploitation of a rigorous and systematic model driven development process that, starting from the deep investigation of the FI domain, will incrementally produce a set of intermediate artifacts, which will be finalised into the actual implementation of the PEC platform. This development process will exploit a logical two-phases methodology: the first phase ($P1$) aims at producing a PEC platform able to homogenise the underlying FI heterogeneity. Concurrently, as well as complementary, the second phase ($P2$) aims at providing software engineers with a set of development tools enabling for the design, analysis, implementation and validation of applications exploiting the PEC platform.

References

1. Armbrust, M., Fox, A., Griffith, R., Joseph, A.D., Katz, R., Konwinski, A., Lee, G., Patterson, D., Rabkin, A., Stoica, I., Zaharia, M.: A view of cloud computing. Commun. ACM **53**(4), 50–58 (2010)
2. Autili, M., Inverardi, P., Tivoli, M.: Choreos: large scale choreographies for the future internet. In: Proceedings of Conference on Software Maintenance, Reengineering and Reverse Engineering (2014)
3. Baldwin, C.Y., Woodard, C.J.: The architecture of platforms: a unified view. In: Platforms, Markets and Innovation, chap. 2 (2009)
4. Baresi, L., Guinea, S., Saeedi, P.: Achieving self-adaptation through dynamic group management. In: Assurances for Self-adaptive Systems - Principles, Models, and Techniques, pp. 214–239 (2013)
5. Berners-Lee, T., Hendler, J., Lassila, O.: The semantic web. Sci. Am. **284**, 34–43 (2001)
6. Bonomi, F., Milito, R., Zhu, J., Addepalli, S.: Fog computing and its role in the internet of things. In: Proceedings of Workshop on Mobile Cloud Computing (2012)
7. Camarinha-Matos, L.M., Goes, J., Gomes, L., Martins, J.A.: Contributing to the internet of things. In: Proceedings of Technological Innovation for the Internet of Things (2013)
8. Caporuscio, M., D'Angelo, M., Grassi, V., Mirandola, R.: Reinforcement learning techniques for decentralized self-adaptive service assembly. In: 5th European Conference on Service-Oriented and Cloud Computing (2016)
9. Caporuscio, M., Funaro, M., Ghezzi, C.: PaCE: a data-flow coordination language for asynchronous network-based applications. In: Gschwind, T., De Paoli, F., Gruhn, V., Book, M. (eds.) Software Composition, pp. 51–67. Springer, Heidelberg (2012)
10. Caporuscio, M., Ghezzi, C.: Engineering future internet applications: the prime approach. J. Syst. Softw. **106**, 9–27 (2015)
11. Cardellini, V., D'Angelo, M., Grassi, V., Marzolla, M., Mirandola, R.: A decentralized approach to network-aware service composition. In: Dustdar, S., Leymann, F., Villari, M. (eds.) ESOCC 2015. LNCS, vol. 9306, pp. 34–48. Springer, Heidelberg (2015). doi:10.1007/978-3-319-24072-5_3
12. Dar, K., Taherkordi, A., Rouvoy, R., Eliassen, F.: Adaptable service composition for very-large-scale Internet of Things systems. In: Proceedings of Middleware Doctoral Symposium (2011)
13. Di Nitto, E., Rosenblum, D.: Exploiting ADLs to specify architectural styles induced by middleware infrastructures. In: Proceedings of International Conference on Software Engineering (1999)
14. Fredj, S.B., Boussard, M., Kofman, D., Noirie, L.: Efficient semantic-based IoT service discovery mechanism for dynamic environments. In: Proceedings of International Symposium on Personal, Indoor, and Mobile Radio Communication (2014)
15. Gilbert, S., Lynch, N.: Brewer's conjecture and the feasibility of consistent, available, partition-tolerant web services. SIGACT News **33**(2), 51–59 (2002)
16. Issarny, V., Caporuscio, M., Georgantas, N.: A perspective on the future of middleware-based software engineering. In: Briand, L., Wolf, A. (eds.) Future of Software Engineering. IEEE-CS Press (2007)
17. Jansen, S., Finkelstein, A., Brinkkemper, S.: A sense of community: a research agenda for software ecosystems. In: Proceedings of International Conference on Software Engineering - Companion (2009)

18. Lpez, P.G., Montresor, A., Epema, D.H.J., Datta, A., Higashino, T., Iamnitchi, A., Barcellos, M.P., Felber, P., Rivire, E.: Edge-centric computing: vision and challenges. Comput. Commun. Rev. **45**(5), 37–42 (2015)
19. Morrison, J.P.: Flow-Based Programming: A New Approach to Application Development, 2nd edn. CreateSpace, Paramount (2010)
20. Papadimitriou, D.: Future internet - the cross-ETP vision document. Technical report, European Future Internet Portal (2009)
21. Porter, M., Onnela, J., Mucha, P.: Communities in networks. Not. Am. Math. Soc. **56**(9), 1082–1097 (2009)
22. Satyanarayanan, M.: Mobile computing: the next decade. In: Proceedings of the Workshop on Mobile Cloud Computing (2010)
23. Serrano, M., Nguyen-Mau, H.Q., Hauswirth, M., Wang, W., Barnaghi, P.M., Cousin, P.: Open services for IoT cloud applications in the future internet. In: Proceedings of International Symposium on a World of Wireless, Mobile and Multimedia Networks (2013)
24. Skala, K., Davidovic, D., Afgan, E., Sovic, I., Sojat, Z.: Scalable distributed computing hierarchy: cloud, fog and dew computing. Open J. Cloud Comput. **2**(1), 16–24 (2015)
25. Tanenbaum, A.S., Van Renesse, R.: Distributed operating systems. ACM Comput. Surv. **17**, 419–470 (1985)
26. Vogels, W.: Eventually consistent. Commun. ACM **52**(1), 40–44 (2009)

Author Index